Protected Places

PROVINCIAL PARKS
1893-1993
CENTENNIAL
CENTENAIRE
PARCS PROVINCIAUX

Protected Places

A History of Ontario's Provincial Parks System

GERALD KILLAN

Published by Dundurn Press Limited
in association with the
Ontario Ministry of Natural Resources

Cette publication sera également
disponible en français

Ministry of Natural Resources Book Number 4763

Editing: Kathleen Harris
Design and Production: GSN
Printing and Binding: Gagné Printing Ltd., Louiseville, Quebec, Canada

In addition to the generous assistance received from the Ontario Ministry of Natural Resources, the publisher wishes to acknowledge the ongoing support of **The Canada Council, The Book Publishing Industry Development Program of the Department of Communications, The Ontario Arts Council,** and **The Ontario Publishing Centre of the Ministry of Culture, Tourism and Recreation.**

Care has been taken to trace the ownership of copyright material used in the text (including the illustrations). The author and publisher welcome any information enabling them to rectify any reference or credit in subsequent editions

J. Kirk Howard, Publisher

Canadian Cataloguing in Publication Data

Killan, Gerald, 1945–
Protected places : a history of Ontario's provincial parks system

Includes bibliographical references and index.
ISBN 1-55002-180-X

1. Provincial parks and reserves – Ontario – History. I. Title.

FC3063.K54 1993 333.78'09713'09 C92-095297-6
SB484.C2K55 1993

Dundurn Press Limited
2181 Queen Street East
Suite 301
Toronto, Canada
M4E 1E5

Dundurn Distribution
73 Lime Walk
Headington, Oxford
England
OX3 7AD

Dundurn Press Limited
736 Cayuga Street
Lewiston, N.Y.
14092-1797
U.S.A.

Contents

Maps

Foreword

While the one-hundred-year history of Ontario's provincial parks system reflects many themes, the great value the people of Ontario place on parks and the landscapes they protect is foremost.

It is with pride and a sense of awe that generations have worked to ensure that our unparalleled natural heritage will remain to be discovered by those who follow.

From a notable beginning with Algonquin in 1893, Ontario's provincial parks have been a safe haven for plants, animals, geological features, and remnants of our past. Our parks system protects both rare and representative features of our natural heritage, while providing opportunities for outdoor recreation, interpretation, and tourism.

Ontario's parks have each been created for many reasons. Common links throughout the past one hundred years have been the foresight of interested individuals and groups, and the dedication of public servants and government leaders, in creating a parks system for present and future generations to enjoy.

To ensure the permanence of these areas for present and future generations, the province announced in 1992 the Endangered Spaces Action Plan. Through this plan Ontario hopes to complete its network of provincial parks and protected areas by the year 2000.

Protected Places is an important part of the province's Parks Centennial. The book celebrates our past by reminding us why parks exist and why they are important. *Protected Places* will also inform future generations of the continuing need to safeguard these special places we know as our provincial parks.

Howard Hampton
Minister of Natural Resources

For my mother and father

Preface and Acknowledgments

In 1954, Premier Leslie M. Frost created the Division of Parks within the Department of Lands and Forests and set in motion an era of parkland expansion that lasted for over three decades. That expansion came to a halt in 1989, following the provincewide Strategic Land Use Planning program, which identified over 150 new parks required to flesh out the provincial parks "system." In 1954, there were only 8 provincial parks; by 1989, there were 261. They embrace some of the most scenic and historically and recreationally valuable land in the province, a total of over 6 million hectares, or about 6 percent of the land and water base of Ontario, an area larger than the province of Nova Scotia. Within the system of 8 Wilderness, 29 Waterway, 63 Natural Environment, 83 Nature Reserve, 74 Recreation, and 4 Historical parks a representation of Ontario's great diversity of land forms, plant and animal life, and outstanding recreational landscapes can be found.

What follows in this volume is an analysis of how Ontario's provincial parks system, considered to be one of the world's best, came into being. The focus is directed toward those groups and individuals whose opinions and attitudes, actions and decisions, shaped the course of events: the provincial bureaucracy, mandated to plan, develop, and manage the system; the conservationist groups, which influenced acquisition and management policies; park users, whose often conflicting activities had to be accommodated and harmonized; and the politicians, who made the ultimate decisions on policy matters.

The first two chapters deal with the original eight parks that predate 1954. All were created in a policy and planning vacuum, on an ad hoc basis, in response to different combinations of social and political pressures. Prior to 1954, no one thought in terms of a "system" of provincial parks made up of different classes and zones, and selected to fit into sophisticated policy frameworks. When it came to managing the early parks, considerations of "use and profit" were paramount. Timber, fish and wildlife resources, and even recreation, were all viewed in revenue-producing terms. Not until the appearance of the Quetico-Superior Council in 1928 and the Federation of Ontario Naturalists in 1931 did any groups question the paramountcy of utilitarian thinking and demand that scenic and natural areas protection be given priority in the management equation. Frank A. MacDougall, the superintendent of Algonquin Park from 1931 to 1941, and later deputy minister of lands and forests (1941–66), first responded to the protectionist impulse. He introduced a policy of multiple use as a conflict-resolution formula to strike a balance between commercial timber extraction, recreation, and preservation in Algonquin and Quetico parks.

MacDougall's initiatives provided only a temporary solution to the problem of harmonizing the various purposes served by the provincial parks. Regrettably, his policy rested on the notion that all large parks could be all things to all users. As chapters 3 and 4 reveal, that assumption was rendered invalid during the 1950s and 1960s by the postwar outdoor recreation boom, changing forest industry technology, and the emergence of the environmental and wilderness preservation movements. By the late 1960s, the outdoor recreation explosion had created an imbalance between recreation and preservation in many parks and an almost overwhelming set of management problems – overcrowded campgrounds, environmental degradation, rowdyism, crowded canoe routes, and heightened tensions between user groups such as hunters and naturalists, motorboat fishermen and wilderness trippers, loggers and preservationists. It became obvious that no single park, no matter how large, could accommodate all of these interests and activities. Accordingly, in 1967 the Parks Division embraced a new policy framework – a classification and zoning system – to sort out the confusion and conflicts in the parks.

Chapters 5 through 7 trace the metamorphosis of the rudimentary classification and zoning policy of 1967 into a comprehensive system plan. This process was greatly accelerated and encouraged, by environmentalists, calling for the establishment of a network of Wilderness and Nature Reserve parks to represent the province's natural diversity, by recreationists in southern Ontario, demanding more parkland and day-use recreational opportunities, especially in near-urban locations, and by the professionalization of the Parks Division planning staff. During the 1970s, the division responded to the compelling demands of the preservationists and recreationists by undertaking a system planning effort of world-class quality. In 1978, the planning process resulted in the production of two landmark documents, the cabinet-approved *Ontario Provincial Parks Policy* and the companion manual, *Ontario Provincial Parks Planning and Management Policies,* the so-called "Blue Book," often referred to as "the gospel relating to parks." These documents provided definitive answers to the questions that had long perplexed bureaucrats, conservationists, and politicians alike. What were the goals and objectives of the parks system? How many of each type of park did Ontarians require and why? Where should parks be located and why? What activities should be permitted or prohibited in each class of park and zone? The answers provided have formed the blueprint for the parks system of the future.

The economic climate of the late 1970s and early 1980s did not bode well for the swift implementation of the parks system plan. Constraints, inflation, and the recession of 1981–82 wreaked havoc with established programming. Nonetheless, as explained in chapter 8, parks personnel met the challenge posed by the constraints. They pursued new tourism and marketing strategies, and in a partnership with the Ontario Heritage Foundation and the Natural Heritage League began to develop alternative, "private stewardship" approaches to the protection of natural areas. Finally, chapter 9 deals with the momentous developments of the 1980s, when the parks system plan was largely implemented; by the end of 1989, some 150 new parks had been created.

Such expansion required an extraordinary concatenation of character and circumstance, including the dovetailing of parks system planning with the provincewide Strategic Land Use Planning program (SLUP), an infusion of strong political leadership, and a coordinated campaign by provincial and regional park and environmental advocacy groups. In 1988, the Liberal administration of Premier David Peterson provided a fitting climax to the parks system building effort by reversing a controversial policy decision, made in 1983 by the Davis Conservatives, to scrap many of the protectionist elements of the "Blue Book" and to permit a variety of nonconforming activities in the new parks.

Over the ten years it took to research and write this book, I have incurred many debts. For financial support, I am grateful to the Provincial Parks and Natural Heritage Policy Branch of the Ontario Ministry of Natural Resources (MNR) and the research grants committee and administration of King's College, affiliated with the University of Western Ontario, where I have taught since 1973.

Research was expedited by the generous cooperation of the staffs of the MNR Library, the Land Records Branch at the Whitney Block, Queen's Park, John Mezaks (now retired) and his crew at the Ontario Archives, and Dallas Lindgren at the Minnesota Historical Society Archives in St. Paul. In Minnesota, Charles S. Kelly and Charles A. Kelly kindly granted me permission to use the Quetico-Superior Council records. Daryl Smith at the MNR district office in Chatham graciously opened his extensive historical file and archives on Rondeau Provincial Park to me, as did Dan Strickland and Ron Tozer in Algonquin, and Shirley Peruniak and the late Shan Walshe in Quetico. George Warecki, a former student of mine, did yeoman service as my research assistant during the summer of 1982. Subsequently, he wrote a master's thesis on Quetico-Superior under my supervision, before moving on to McMaster University, where he completed a doctoral dissertation on wilderness preservation in Ontario. On several occasions, George kindly gave me access to his research notes. During the summer of 1988, Scott Poser diligently collected most of the illustrative material for this volume.

My professional connection to Ontario's provincial parks began in 1972 when Robert Bowes, then supervisor of research and planning in the Historical Sites Branch of the MNR, invited me to serve as an historical parks system planner in the preparation of *A Topical Organization of Ontario History* (MNR, 1974). Subsequently, my understanding of parks issues deepened while serving as a member of the original Provincial Parks Advisory Council (PPAC) (1974–80). It was a rare privilege and a remarkable learning experience to have been associated with George Priddle and the other seventeen knowledgeable members of the council as we crisscrossed the province, seeking to advance the cause of harmony and balance within the parks system.

Originally, Tom Lee, the philosophical guru of the Parks Division planning team in the early 1970s, agreed to co-author this book. After infecting me with his enthusiasm, however, he disappeared without a word into the bureaucratic wilds of British Columbia. I have long since forgiven him for abandoning me to this project and now appreciate how much I owe him for introducing me to the mysteries of parks policy and system planning. In 1981, Parks and Recreational Areas Branch Director Ron Vrancart commissioned me to write this history; then he, too, abruptly left the branch for a position with the Niagara Escarpment Commission. Like it or not, his unsuspecting successor, Norm Richards, inherited me and the parks history project. For Norm's patience, support, and encouragement, I will be forever grateful. Gary Forma served as my contact person in the ministry over the years. Let it be known that he met my every request for information and assistance with exceeding good cheer.

A host of busy individuals made themselves available to answer my questions. It is impossible to mention them all, but I must give special thanks to Tom Beechey, Bob Davidson, the late William Foster, Don Hallman, Alan R.K. MacDonald, Ken McCleary, George Moroz, Rick Phillips, William Sargant, and Russ Tilt. I have also benefited enormously from the constructive comments provided by the MNR's editorial team, who read the entire manuscript, thereby weeding out many errors of detail and interpretation: Dave Boggs, John Featherston, Jim Keenan, John Sloan, Dan Strickland, and Grant Tayler. Other readers have examined all, or sections of, the manuscript: Bob Bowes, Gary Forma, Arlin Hackman, Patrick Hardy, Alan Helmsley, Gavin Henderson, Bruce Litteljohn, Bob Mitton, Ron Tozer, and Ron Vrancart. The volume would be far poorer had it not been for their contributions.

At King's College, my colleague Jacques Goutor read and reread the entire manuscript; his extensive and incisive commentary improved the final product immeasurably. Dr. Goutor represents my ideal of the senior scholar, ever willing to assist his younger colleagues in every possible professional and personal way. I cannot thank him sufficiently for all he has done on my behalf over the years. From the beginning, Cathy Mendler has provided exemplary word-processing and proofreading services. Finally, the keen eye and sound judgment of Kathleen Harris saved this manuscript from many an awkward sentence and confusing passage.

The most important persons in this effort have been the members of my family. Without the personal equilibrium provided by the devotion, sacrifice, and love of my wife, Linda, this book could not have been written. "The three Js" – Jeremy, Jared, and Jessica – also provided a much needed balance in my life by drawing me away from the writing desk. Finally, this book is dedicated to my mother and father for reasons too many to recount here.

Parts of this book pertaining to Quetico Provincial Park have appeared in "The Battle for Wilderness in Ontario: Saving Quetico-Superior, 1927 to 1960," co-authored with George Warecki, and published in *Patterns of the Past: Interpreting Ontario's History* (Toronto and Oxford: Dundurn Press, 1988), a collection of historical articles published on the occasion of the centenary of the Ontario Historical Society. Sections of chapter nine were included in "The Development of a Wilderness Park System in Ontario, 1967–1990: Temagami in Context," in Matt Bray and Ashley Thomson (eds.), *Temagami: a Debate on Wilderness* (Toronto and Oxford: Dundurn Press, 1990). I wish to thank both the Ontario Historical Society and the Institute for Northern Ontario Research and Development, Laurentian University, for permission to reprint portions of these essays.

Finally, a word to the general reader. The Ontario provincial parks story has many dimensions, not all of which will excite any one person. This volume has been written thematically, in such a way that all but the most avid student might skip over sections within chapters (and, I dare say, over entire chapters) without losing sight of the organizational structure and essential story line. Enjoy and savour what interests you. Ignore the rest.

Chapter 1

The First Parks, 1893–1953

A mere generation ago, in 1954, Ontario possessed only eight provincial parks. They had been created in an ad hoc fashion since the late nineteenth century. Algonquin appeared first in 1893, followed by Rondeau (1894), Quetico (1913), Long Point (1921), Presqu'ile (1922), Ipperwash (1938), Sibley (1944), and Lake Superior (1944). No sophisticated system plan detailing goals and objectives, classification and zoning policies, and acquisition frameworks lay behind the founding of these parks. Instead, each had been set aside to solve specific problems, in response to unique combinations of social, economic, and political pressures.

The Mowat Era

The establishment of the first publicly owned parks in Ontario can be attributed to the impact of the late-nineteenth-century conservation movement.[1] The early conservation impulse spread widely in reaction to the intensive urban and industrial growth of the period, and the resulting destruction and exploitation of Ontario's natural, scenic, and recreational resources. Late-nineteenth-century conservationism contained two main currents of thought, the so-called "gospel of efficiency" and the "doctrine of unselfishness." Proponents of the "gospel of efficiency" or wise-use conservation emphasized matters of utility and profit, together with the judicious and scientific management of natural resources to prevent depletion and destruction. Those who subscribed to "the doctrine of unselfishness" tended to be more idealistic and less mindful of questions of utility and economics. Conservationists of this persuasion sought to protect scenic and wildlife resources for aesthetic reasons and deemed it a moral responsibility to preserve natural values for future generations. The two elements of the early conservation movement should not be viewed as being mutually exclusive "realist" and "purist" streams of thought, flowing in opposite philosophical directions. They are best understood as currents in a single conservationist stream, sometimes converging to their mutual benefit, at other times flowing at cross purposes. Both impulses contrasted sharply with the prevailing mentality toward nature as an unlimited storehouse, to be exploited at will.

In the beginning, public support for the first provincial parks comprised a loose grouping of interests that represented a remarkable and, for the most part, harmonious blend of the idealistic and the practical-minded, the public-spirited and the self-interested. Within the ranks of the conservation coalition, scenic preservationists, concerned primarily with the aesthetic, found unlikely allies in businessmen, attracted by the potential for tourist revenues. Sport anglers and hunters, interested in restocking a province depleted of fish and game, lobbied with naturalists, desirous of preserving flora and fauna. Ottawa timber barons, anxious to perpetuate their industrial empires, found common cause with Toronto bureaucrats, professionals, and intellectuals attracted by modern forestry's claim to efficiency and scientific management. Recreationists united with commercial interests whose concern was harbour protection. Notwithstanding their different motives, mutual interests animated these groups, since they all focussed on the same thing – the need for publicly owned parkland.

The complexity of the conservation movement is well illustrated in the effort to establish Ontario's first publicly owned park at Niagara Falls. The idea of a park originated in the mid-1870s, in a growing conviction of the need to preserve what remained of the natural state of the Niagara gorge for aesthetic and moral reasons. As early as the 1820s, when an enterprising innkeeper named William Forsyth had attempted to control the tourist trade at Niagara Falls by fencing off some of the best viewing sites, the commercialization of the world-famous natural wonder had become something of a public embarrassment for provincial officials. As the decades slipped by and Niagara Falls became the greatest single natural attraction in North America, tourists frequently complained about the excesses of unprincipled innkeepers and the hordes of hack drivers, photographers, and pedlars. By the 1860s, organized criminal elements had also become entrenched at the falls. Eventually, a provincial royal commission, appointed to investigate the situation in 1873, made recommendations that led to the more effective policing of the area. The royal commission also proposed that a small, provincially operated park be established at Niagara, but Premier Oliver Mowat turned down the idea. All he sought to accomplish at this time was to protect tourists and salvage the province's reputation by maintaining the rule of law.[2]

The royal commission of 1873 did not address the issue of scenic and natural preservation. That question only became a matter for political consideration five years later, in September 1878, when the Governor General, Lord Dufferin, proposed that "the Governments of New York and of Ontario, or Canada" establish "a small public international park," in order to restore the area around the falls to a state of nature. Dufferin had been prompted to take up this cause by a small group of prominent New Yorkers which included:

William Dorsheimer, a New York State district attorney; Frederick Law Olmsted, a landscape architect, and his partner, Calvert Vaux; Henry Hobson Richardson, one of the era's most influential architects; and Frederick E. Church, a popular landscape artist. Their goal at Niagara was "to protect landscape aesthetics in a total sense, to preserve woods and wildflowers, vines and bushes, as well as a spectacular waterfall."[3]

Oliver Mowat soon found himself swept along on a tide of preservationist sentiment when New York Governor Lucius Robinson endorsed the international park idea in January 1879. Prodded by Dufferin and his successor, the Marquis of Lorne, on the one side, and by the Americans on the other, Ontario's premier had little choice but to cooperate. On 27 September 1879, Mowat met with New York officials to discuss the issue. In his subsequent report to the cabinet in December 1879, Mowat affirmed that action in "the direction of acquisition and regulation" at Niagara Falls was imperative, given the proliferation of commercial and industrial enterprises in the area. All the same, the premier added, his government would not undertake this costly project. That responsibility, he insisted, belonged to the federal authorities. Accordingly, in March 1880, Mowat rushed through the provincial legislature "An Act Respecting Niagara Falls and the Adjacent Territory," giving Ottawa the right to acquire any private or Crown lands required for the park.

Legislated into the limelight by Mowat, and with petitions descending upon him signed by hundreds of Canadian, American, and British citizens, Sir John A. Macdonald soon found himself in a delicate political situation. His ministers from the Maritimes, supported by some Quebec members, argued that if New York State contemplated underwriting the park project without federal assistance, then Ontario should do likewise. The Maritimers also contended that since few of their constituents would ever see Niagara Falls, the general revenues of the dominion should not be expended on what seemed to be a distinctly "Ontario" project. Despite this opposition, Prime Minister Macdonald still attempted to advance the park idea by approaching Mowat about joint, federal-provincial funding. The Ontario premier ignored these overtures, and a five-year standoff resulted.

With the park proposal stalled between Toronto and Ottawa in late 1880, the Niagara Falls preservation movement entered a second and quite different phase. Until this time, the influential people behind the conservation effort had been motivated by the "doctrine of unselfishness"; they were convinced of the uplifting effects of nature's beauty, and of their moral responsibility to preserve that beauty for future generations. Now their influence waned, at least on the Canadian side, and the leadership of the movement was assumed by business interests, who wished to protect Niagara from destruction because they saw it as a resource to be conserved and exploited for their personal gain.

Local resident William Oliver Buchanan, the quintessence of the nineteenth-century speculator, whose career had run the gamut from engineer and bridge builder to real-estate promoter, quickly assumed the pivotal role in the park story. In the autumn of 1880, his thoughts fixed on the idea of forming a private syndicate to develop the Niagara park. His plans included a toll road (and later a miniature railway) from the falls to the whirlpool, along the water's edge under the bank of the gorge, staircases to the top of the cliff, landscaped picnic and recreational grounds, hotels, and refreshment kiosks. William Buchanan's definition of conservation was clearly of the wise-use, profit-motive variety.

For the next four years, Buchanan strove to find the necessary financial backing for a private park. Premier Mowat encouraged his efforts and promised to incorporate a private company if satisfactory investors could be found. In time, prominent businessmen did take interest in Buchanan's scheme, particularly after the American park movement gained impetus. With the support of Governor Grover Cleveland, the state of New York began to survey in 1883, and in 1884 to appraise the lands required for a public park reservation. Canadian businessmen now saw the potential for an expanded tourist industry at the falls and rushed to take advantage of the situation. Before long, Premier Mowat found himself in the awkward position of having two rival park syndicates – Buchanan's Niagara Falls Restoration and Improvement Company and the Niagara Falls Railway Company – both with close ties to the Liberal party, seeking his blessing to operate private parks at Niagara.

To complicate the situation further, powerful public pressure suddenly made its presence felt in early 1885. Ratepayers in Stamford and Niagara Falls, aware that New York State intended to create a publicly operated park, and hostile to any private monopoly, denounced the plans of both syndicates. "We consider the Park should belong to the Government," one petition read, "and held by them in trust for visitors from every part of the world." Pressure mounted as the opposition press across the province voiced similar sentiments.

Despite this strong antimonopoly opinion, Mowat was still determined to push ahead with the private park concept. In 1885 his government introduced "An Act for the Preservation of the Natural Scenery about Niagara Falls." This legislation rescinded the Niagara Falls Act of 1880, which had provided for federal involvement in the project, and established the Niagara Falls Park Commission. Chaired by Casimir Gzowski, the noted Polish-Canadian engineer, the commission was directed to select, survey, and appraise the land required for a park, and to determine which private company should operate the park under government guidelines.

In spite of the premier's expectations, the private park concept was not to be realized. The Gzowski commission, impressed by the New York State Reservation at Niagara, recommended in September 1885 that the government establish a free public park under direct provincial control. The commission also linked itself to Dufferin's scenic conservation ideal by recommending that the area "be laid out and planted, not as a showy garden or fancy grounds, but as nearly as possible as they would be in their natural condition." This call for total, aesthetic conservation represented a dramatic shift away from Buchanan's plans for an intensively developed park, previously endorsed by the premier.

Mowat needed time to consider these recommendations. He accepted the commission's proposal for the park boundaries and permitted the valuation and arbitration processes to commence, but it took him eighteen months to abandon the concept of a private park. George Pattullo, the politically appointed secretary to the commission, prepared several memoranda on the issue, which helped the premier reach a decision. As editor of the *Woodstock Sentinel-Review* and a key Liberal party organizer in Oxford County, Pattullo enjoyed the premier's confidence. In his memoranda, Pattullo emphasized that Ontarians would welcome a publicly owned park at Niagara. The drift of editorial opinion in both the Liberal and opposition press generally endorsed the idea. Philosophically, he argued, it was now "a recognized duty of Governments" to protect natural wonders like the falls. He cited the precedents set by the American Congress, which had designated California's Yosemite Valley for public use in 1864, and in 1872 had established Yellowstone National Park to conserve a spectacular landscape containing geysers and hot springs. Pattullo concluded his arguments on an imperial note by suggesting that the creation of a public park at Niagara would be a fitting way for Ontario to commemorate Queen Victoria's Golden Jubilee. There can be no doubt that Pattullo's memoranda were taken seriously, for Mowat cited them extensively when at last he introduced the Queen Victoria Niagara Falls Park Bill in March 1887. This legislation, which received royal assent on 23 April, turned over to the Niagara Parks Commission the lands already selected for the public park. The commissioners were empowered to raise $525,000 through a special bond issue for land acquisition and development purposes.

With the passage of the Niagara Falls Park Act, Ontario gained its first publicly owned park. In ushering in its creation, Premier Mowat had taken one of the most important steps in the history of scenic conservation in North America. Indeed, the establishment of the Niagara Falls Park stands as a unique episode in the story of Ontario's parks. As one of the world's greatest natural wonders, Niagara commanded the attention of influential people from across North America and Europe. Aware that the good name of his province was at stake, the premier of Ontario himself had assumed a central role in all dealings pertaining to the question.

In contrast to the Niagara story, the problems, the circumstances, and the cast of characters associated with the creation of Algonquin Park, situated on the Ottawa-Huron tract of the District of Nipissing, were of quite a different sort. No governors general, prime ministers, or premiers were to be found at the forefront of this indigenous movement. Instead, the park story involves a host of minor civil servants, anglers and hunters, naturalists, loggers, urban intellectuals, and politicians.

At midcentury, the notion of reserving a million acres of Crown land for the purposes of protecting wildlife, forests, and watersheds would have seemed preposterous. In 1850, as the expansive pioneer phase of settlement in southern Ontario (then Canada West) drew to a close, the early settlers' attitudes toward forests and wildlife still prevailed, and would do so for several decades to come. In the myth structure of the pioneers, nature, particularly the "forest primeval," was perceived as a malevolent force that threatened survival. Settlers looked upon the forest as "their natural enemy, to be got rid of at any cost, hacked down, burnt out of the way."[4] The myth of unlimited abundance also remained a fundamental feature of the prevailing mentality at midcentury.

Before anyone could seriously entertain the idea of a large game and forest reserve, attitudes toward nature and its resources would have to change. The pioneer notion of abundance would have to give way to the realization that Ontario's natural riches were limited. The official view of the forest as a nonrenewable resource, to be cut once by the loggers before the land was passed on to the agriculturalist, would have to be replaced by the modern concept of the forest as a permanent, renewable resource which, if managed properly, could be harvested in perpetuity. And finally, the view of nature as a malevolent force would have to make way for the positive concept of nature as a place for urban residents to restore themselves psychologically, physically, and spiritually.

In Ontario, wildlife conservation emerged as an issue of public debate before the demand for forest protection. Accelerating urban and industrial development, the advent of the railway era after 1850, and the intensive settlement of Canada West all put enormous pressures on fish and wildlife stocks. The actual and impending scarcity of certain species of game and fish belied the myth of unlimited natural resources. The alarm generated by the demise of some species, the deepening anxiety among sport anglers and hunters over the obvious depletion of wildlife in general, and a concomitant welling up of anger over the ineffectiveness of fish and game legislation culminated in the 1880s in a provincewide protest in favour of conservation. The primary motive force behind the wildlife conservation lobby was the sportsmen's practical, wise-use philosophy. To ensure their recreation in the future, anglers and hunters turned to the ideal of harvesting rather than senselessly slaughtering wildlife. In support of this dominant impulse came a much less powerful, but equally earnest, call from naturalists and nature lovers for the establishment of wildlife sanctuaries.

As a consequence of the linkages developed between the many hunting, angling, and conservation associations across southern Ontario, sportsmen enjoyed considerable political clout. Their ranks embraced all social and economic classes, both urban and rural. Club delegates met in convention, hammered out recommendations, and circulated petitions among their memberships. For instance, on 26 March 1884, the clubs lobbied strenuously, following their convention in Toronto, for a major revision of the game laws. Within two years they succeeded in obtaining legislation to end the spring shooting of ducks and other game birds, and shortly afterward they won a two-year suspension of the quail hunt. Other influential voices joined the sportsmen's chorus in favour of more stringent game laws. A few trappers, furriers, and dealers in fur, alarmed over declining sources of supply, also demanded longer close seasons.[5]

Converging with the utilitarian arguments of the sportsmen and trappers were the protests of urban-based naturalists, particularly the powerful, opinion-making scientific, educational, and professional elites based at the Canadian Institute in Toronto. The institute began to take a keen interest in conservation matters following its amalgamation in 1885 with the Natural History Society of Toronto. The latter group became the biological section of the Canadian Institute, and also served as a branch of the international Audubon Society. Alarmed by the depletion of animal species everywhere, the Canadian Institute petitioned the government in 1886 to establish "a National Park for the preservation of our Nature Animals."[6]

The wildlife conservationists made a major breakthrough on 13 November 1890, when the Mowat government appointed the Royal Commission on Game and Fish, headed by Dr. G.A. MacCallum, a physician in Dunnville, Haldimand County. "The establishment of our Fish and Game Commission," admitted A.D. Stewart, the secretary, "was forced upon the Government by reason of public opinion, and the representations made by sportsmen in Ontario to the effect that if something was not done very quickly, the Fish and Game in our Province would be totally destroyed and eliminated." After touring the province to hold public hearings, circulating questionnaires, and studying the laws of several American states, the commission, on 1 February 1892, submitted a devastating critique of existing fish and game management in Ontario. The MacCallum commission's report confirmed what sportsmen had been arguing for years. "On all sides, from every quarter," MacCallum wrote, "has been heard the same sickening tale of merciless, ruthless, and remorseless slaughter." The commission found that the province did not have an "organized service for game and fish protection"; in this respect, Ontario had fallen behind "several Canadian Provinces" and "all the immediately adjacent States of the Union." This was deplorable, and was to be regretted from an economic perspective, the commission explained. If the slaughter of game and fish continued, sportsmen would be denied their recreation, and the supply industries for tourism and outdoor recreation would be undermined.

The commission submitted an enormous number of recommendations to cope with the problems it had documented, and many were immediately implemented.[7] One in particular had considerable significance for the future of parks in Ontario. The commissioners "very strongly" recommended "the formation of a Provincial Game Park" to serve as a wildlife sanctuary, to restock Ontario's depleted stocks of "Game and fur-bearing animals."[8] Precisely one week after MacCallum tabled his report in February 1892, the Mowat government appointed the Royal Commission on Forest Reservation and National Park in preparation for establishing Algonquin Park.

The MacCallum commission did not bring about this development alone. As we shall see, a forest conservation movement had also emerged during the 1880s and, along with the Canadian Institute, had pressured the Crown Lands Department for some eight years to establish a forest reserve in the Nipissing District. Prior to the advent of the forestry movement, few people concerned themselves with the way timberlands were being ravaged by settlers, lumbermen, and fire. Not until the late 1870s, when the alarming spread of sand dunes and erosion problems in some southern counties forced progressive agriculturalists to face the need to conserve trees, did the forestry movement emerge. The first influential group in the province to support forestry principles was the United Fruit Growers Association of Ontario, which advocated tree planting as the solution to the spread of sand dunes and the more general environmental problems of drought, erosion, extremes in climate, and the maintenance of water levels in the Great Lakes. Their views were echoed in the *Report of the Ontario Agricultural Commission* (1881).[9]

In 1882, at the behest of the United Fruit Growers Association, the Ontario government sent a small delegation to the American Forestry Congress in Cincinnati (25–29 April) and Montreal (21–23 August). Here influential politicians, civil servants, forestry and agricultural experts, timber men, and concerned citizens from across North America met to discuss all dimensions of the forest problem. Dozens of speakers warned that the certain consequence of indiscriminately laying waste to the forests would be the destruction of the harmony and balance of nature, and would invite a host of natural disasters, ranging from massive soil erosion and flooding to unwanted climatic alterations, serious declines in river levels, and the depletion of wildlife. Parallelling this message ran a second sobering theme: the forests of North America were not limitless. In fact, the supply of marketable timber in many areas was now scarce.

"It is evident," the Ontario delegation to the congress reported, that "the first step to be taken … is to create an enlightened and healthy sentiment on the whole subject of forestry."[10] On the basis of this recommendation, the Mowat government in 1883 appointed Robert W. Phipps, a one-time printer and journalist, as clerk of forestry in the Department of Agriculture and the Arts. In this post, he would emerge as a significant figure in Ontario conservationist history, as one of the founders of Algonquin Park. Phipps's educational work as clerk of forestry (1883–92) was principally intended to warn southern Ontario farmers of the dangers of denuding their properties of trees and to promote replanting and the farm woodlot idea. Yet his briskly written and widely distributed reports also emphasized that the future of forestry in the province depended on the maintenance of and, ultimately, the scientific management of the great northern forests. He made this point forcefully in his *Forestry Report* for 1884, after touring what he called "the watershed of eastern Ontario," the crescent-shaped height of land from Kingston to Lake Nipissing. For this highland area, he proposed a radical revision of Crown lands policy, which had hitherto emphasized settlement. "There is no part of the science of forestry more beneficial," he explained, "than that which teaches to keep covered with forest the principal heights of land." Such watersheds, "when covered with extensive woods, form reservoirs which supply the sources of numerous rivers, give moisture to the numerous small lakes and water-courses ... below them, and preserve throughout the whole country a fertility, invariably much impaired when the forests above are destroyed." With the support of the major timber licensees in the area, and the advice of A. Russell, the crown timber agent in Pembroke, Phipps recommended that a twenty-to-thirty-township block of unpatented land south of Lake Nipissing be reserved exclusively for forest purposes and thereby removed from the threat of settlement. This was the heart of the area destined to become Algonquin Park. "It is time we understood," he wrote in 1886, "that the cry, 'Clear the forest; make the woodland into farms,' has no application to the great, stony, granitic, pine-covered belt which hems our more fertile region. That is for forest, in forest for ever it should remain."[11]

Phipps stressed that other jurisdictions had already acted to protect heights of land through forest reserves. In northern Quebec, the powerful timber interests in the Quebec Limitholders' Association had persuaded the province in 1883 to set aside a large reserve solely for timber production. The federal government had recently amended the Dominion Lands Act to provide for forest reserves on the slopes of the Rocky Mountains. To the south, New York State had in 1883 frozen the sale of public lands around the headwaters of the Hudson River in a bid to protect water levels on that important commercial and industrial artery, and was moving to establish Adirondack Park. The American Congress was also in the process of reserving 3,238 hectares of forested high ground in Montana.

Almost immediately, various individuals and groups came out in support of Phipps's proposal. Henry Small, a well-known sportsman and naturalist, enthusiastically endorsed the forest reserve recommendation in his book, *Canadian Forest: Forest Trees, Timber and Forest Products* (1884), and quoted Phipps at length. But more importantly, Alexander Kirkwood, chief clerk in the land sales section of the Department of Crown Lands, stepped forward to champion Phipps's idea. It was Kirkwood, in fact, who succeeded in broadening the discussion far beyond Phipps's narrow focus on watershed conservation, by adding game protection and recreation as reasons for setting aside a reserve. An Irish immigrant, Kirkwood had been associated with the public service since the mid-1850s. In 1878 he had published, with fellow civil servant J.J. Murphy, *The Undeveloped Lands in Northern and Western Ontario*, a volume written to promote agricultural settlement in the northern districts of the province. By 1885, however, experience had dampened Kirkwood's enthusiasm for the agricultural future of the north; he now shared with Phipps the belief that certain lands were not suited for settlement purposes.

In a letter to Crown Lands Commissioner Timothy Pardee, dated 21 December 1885, Kirkwood proposed that most of the ten townships in Nipissing that contained the headwaters of the Muskoka, Petawawa, Bonnechère, and Madawaska rivers (about 133,550 hectares) be set aside and called "Algonkin Forest and Park," a name he chose to honour "one of the greatest Indian nations that has inhabited the North American continent."[12] Echoing the arguments of Phipps and the earlier American Forestry Congress, Kirkwood explained that the primary purpose of the park would be to preserve the forest of the headwaters region in order to promote rainfall and to maintain the water levels of rivers, a matter "of great importance ... to the manufacturer." Yet, while Kirkwood urged the primacy of watershed protection over logging, he did not view the situation simply as a choice between wood and water. Logging, too, would have a place. "The timber need not be permitted to rot down," he argued. "The mature trees can be cut in due season to allow the next in size a chance for growth." In this way, "utility and profit will be combined: the forest will be of great benefit as a producer of timber, and will add to the provincial revenue."

While forestry objectives were of primary consideration to Kirkwood, he also raised other important themes. Obviously aware of the wildlife crisis, he recommended that the proposed park be managed as a provincial game sanctuary, with a ban on hunting and trapping. Finally, he added recreation to the list of reasons for his park. "Seekers for health and pleasure in the summer season," he wrote, "may be allowed to lease locations for cottages or tents on the shores of the Great Opeongo Lake, and a site on that lake for a hotel and farm can be offered to public competition at an annual rental." In recommending cottage leases and a lodge concession, Kirkwood was not responding to any specific demand for such facilities in the area; rather, he was sensitive to an emerging "back to nature" trend in an increasingly urban southern Ontario. Among the upper and middle classes, at least, nature was now being conceived as a place of health and refuge, a sanctuary from urban pressures and ennui. Moreover, as Darwinism and science challenged traditional religious teaching, spiritual uncertainty was prompting some Ontarians to seek in nature religious meaning and evidence of the hand of God.[13]

Commissioner Pardee's response to Kirkwood's letter seems to have been one of cautious approval, but he was too much the politician to endorse the scheme without further investigation into its political implications, especially in an election year. Questions had to be answered, not the least of which was the amount of support the forest reserve and park idea would receive from local economic interests and the public at large. As a means of stimulating discussion and testing the political waters, Kirkwood, almost certainly with Pardee's permission, published his letter in pamphlet form in August 1886.

One of the first positive reactions came from James Dickson, a provincial lands surveyor who worked out of Fenelon Falls, and knew the proposed park area as well as anyone. That very year Dickson published *Camping in the Muskoka Region* (1886), an account of a canoe trip to the headwaters of the Muskoka, Petawawa, and Madawaska rivers. The book's objective was to promote wilderness recreation in an area whose scenic beauty he deemed "equal" to, "if not greater" than that of any other part of Canada. "Here ... the overworked and confined city clerk can spend his brief summer holiday, and recruit his shattered nerves, inhaling the pure air of forest and lake," and return to his labours "invigorated and strengthened, both in mind and body."[14] Robert Phipps also endorsed the forest reserve and park idea, although he recommended a reservation of about 404,670 hectares, much larger than the one proposed by Kirkwood. Stimulated by Kirkwood's thinking, Phipps also expanded his own conception of a forest reserve to include such uses as recreation and wildlife protection, silvicultural research, and supervised commercial logging.[15]

Early in 1887, influential elements outside the civil service finally entered the public discussion initiated by Kirkwood and Phipps. The Canadian Institute recognized that by combining the battle for wildlife with the cause of forestry, both movements would be mutually advanced. In March 1887, a delegation from the institute met with Commissioner Pardee and urged "the establishment of a large park reserve in the district of Nipissing, for the protection of wild animals and of timber."[16] Pardee indicated that he sympathized with the proposal and promised his support. So, too, did the lumber interests in the city of Ottawa, particularly J.R. Bronson, Member of the Legislative Assembly (MLA) for Ottawa, who controlled extensive territory on the Nipissing watershed and endorsed the concept of a forest reserve. Faced with instability in the forest industry, depressed market conditions, and declines in both the quality and quantity of timber, the Ottawa lumber interests were looking seriously, albeit belatedly, toward conservation and scientific forestry to perpetuate their business empires.[17]

With evidence of growing public and industry support for the forest reserve and park concept, Pardee chose to pursue the matter by despatching James Dickson, in mid-1887, to report on the area, especially on the yet unsurveyed townships in the heart of the watershed. This close examination was warranted, considering that Kirkwood had never set foot in the headwaters region, and Phipps had toured it only once. When Dickson reported back in January 1888, he too waxed poetic about the potential of the area to serve forestry, wildlife conservation, and recreational purposes. "The preservation from destruction of moose, deer and beaver would ... alone warrant the Government in making this a reservation," he concluded. Dickson saw at once that, combined with enforced provincewide close seasons on fur-bearing animals, a carefully supervised game refuge would help restock the province and assuage the wildlife crisis.[18]

Within days of reading Dickson's report in January 1888, Commissioner Pardee received another delegation from the Canadian Institute. They presented him with a petition, reiterating the demand for "a tract of land" to be set aside "for the preservation of the forests and wild animals in this Province." After a further series of meetings, the institute, at Pardee's request, prepared still another memorial on the subject with a map showing the townships they had in mind.[19]

That the Crown Lands Department was taking the park and forest reserve idea seriously became evident in March 1888, during a legislative debate on timber policy. Conservative Opposition Leader William R. Meredith severely criticized the department for emphasizing timber revenues at the expense of forest conservation. The evidence existed, he argued, that Ontario did not possess "an inexhaustible supply of pine." The situation was serious enough, he added, to warrant the appointment of a select committee of the legislature to conduct an inventory of the province's timber resources and the best means of conserving them. Citing a variety of expert sources, and noting

Alexander Kirkwood (left), chief clerk in the Lands Branch of the Ontario Crown Lands Department, presented the case for establishing Algonquin Park in his celebrated letter "Algonkin Forest and Park" to Crown Lands Commissioner Timothy Pardee in 1885. James Dickson (right), a provincial lands surveyor based in Fenelon Falls, figured prominently in the effort to set aside Algonquin Park by extolling the area's wilderness recreation and wildlife conservation potential.
Courtesy: Ministry of Natural Resources.

that Quebec and various states to the south had already created forest reserves, Meredith made a powerful presentation in favour of designating similar areas in Ontario. In a spirited response for the government, Acting Crown Lands Commissioner Christopher Fraser spoke on behalf of the ailing Timothy Pardee. Given existing consumption of pine timber, he insisted, "Ontario had a supply equal to meet the demands for the next 100 years." As for forest reserves, "The time might come when it would be necessary to consider that question, but that time had not yet come." And yet, following this unequivocally negative statement of policy on forest reserves, Fraser conceded that an area "might be set aside for a national park" in the Nipissing District.[20] Thus, while the government denied the existence of a tree shortage in the province as a whole, it appeared receptive to the idea of watershed and game protection in the Nipissing uplands. Indeed, that very year the park movement seemed close to realizing its objective, when Alexander Kirkwood prepared for Commissioner Pardee a draft "Algonkin Forest and Park Act, 1888."[21]

Regrettably, after reaching the advanced stage of drafting legislation for the future Algonquin Park, the government's commitment to the scheme faltered. On 19 January 1889, a terminally ill Timothy Pardee was replaced as commissioner of Crown lands by Arthur S. Hardy, member for South Brant. Although Hardy insisted in the legislature that the subject of "a national or provincial park ... was an important one," he obviously did not consider the Algonquin program a priority item. Speaking in May 1891, he claimed that he had intended to take action on the matter the year before, but "the House had hardly risen when the [June 1890] elections were on the country." Then, between the election and the new session in the spring of 1891, his attention had been given to more urgent matters connected with the Royal Commission on the Mineral Resources of Ontario. Since the Algonquin Park proposal "involved the absorption of timber lands" that could generate some one million dollars in bonuses, "it was impossible to fully consider this subject during the recess."[22]

Notwithstanding his excuses and professed support of the park scheme, Hardy failed to advance the project in the second half of 1891, despite prodding from the conservationists. The historical section of the Canadian Institute reminded the commissioner of his responsibilities and appealed to his patriotism. "The establishment of natural parks," the institute now argued, "will conduce to the fostering of a patriotic spirit and be a means of increasing interest in Canada abroad."[23] Edward W. Harris, a prominent London lawyer and businessman, active in fish and game protection efforts, also tweaked the government's conscience with his pamphlet *Is Game of Any Value to the Farmer?* (1891). In this short work, Harris detailed the deplorable wildlife situation and urged the province's farmers to demand effective conservation legislation including the creation of "a National Park." Such appeals seemed to have little effect. Something extraordinary and shocking was required to jolt the government out of its lethargy. The event that served the purpose of creating a "crisis mood that acted as a catalyst" was the MacCallum Commission Report on Game and Fish.[24] On 8 February 1892, one week after MacCallum submitted his findings, an obviously embarrassed and worried Mowat government appointed the Royal Commission on Forest Reservation and National Park.

The royal commission was made up entirely of civil servants: Alexander Kirkwood, James Dickson, Robert Phipps, Director of Mines Archibald Blue, Assistant Commissioner of Crown Lands Aubrey White, with Thomas Gibson as secretary. This group met only twice – on 4 November 1892 and 3 January 1893 – before submitting its report in March 1893. They recommended that eighteen designated townships be set aside as "The Algonquin National Park." Historians have tended to place considerable importance on this commission, in the belief that the decision to create the park hinged on its recommendations.[25] Interestingly, the evidence does not support such an interpretation. Crown Lands Commissioner Hardy revealed in the provincial legislature in March 1892 that the government had, in fact, already decided to establish the park even before the commission was selected. All that was required of the royal commission was "to investigate the character of the townships and ascertain those best adapted for the purpose" and to determine "the mode, system and cost of maintaining such reservations as the Adirondack and the Yellowstone Parks."[26] Following their appointment, the commissioners, doubtless under instructions, waited nine months before convening, so that the government could auction off the remaining pine limits in the area of the proposed park.[27] Immediately after the timber sale in October 1892, the Algonquin Park commission met hurriedly, without public hearings, and served up an essentially precooked report.

The royal commission's report was largely a synthesis of the various ideas discussed over the years by Phipps, Kirkwood, Dickson, and the wildlife conservation forces. The commissioners argued that the most important reason for creating the park was maintenance of the water supply, by preserving the forest cover on the headwaters area. In importance and utility, game preservation ran a close second to watershed management as a reason for the park. As a wildlife sanctuary, it would serve as a breeding ground to restock large portions of the province, to the everlasting delight of sport hunters and tourist interests. Compared to watershed and game protection, the remaining objectives – recreation and silvicultural research – were of secondary importance, mere byproducts of conservation.[28]

There is great irony in the fact that while the Kirkwood commission accommodated the concerns of the various elements in the conservation coalition, no thought was given to protecting the interests of the aboriginal peoples, after whom Algonquin Park was being named. Indeed, throughout the years of lobbying for the park, no one seems to have considered the hunting, fishing, and trapping rights of the native peoples of the region. Crown Lands

Commissioner Hardy frankly acknowledged the oversight, shortly after creating Algonquin: "It will be a ticklish business to prevent Indians killing wild animals in the Park where they have been in the habit of hunting, and their ancestors before them. I am free to say this Indian hunting did not occur to me at the time the whole matter was under discussion. Now I see nothing for it but to exclude the Indians as well as the white men. But great care and tact will be required to handle these people so as not to embitter them or leave them feeling they have a substantial grievance."[29] This proved to be a vain hope. The failure to recognize aboriginal rights contributed to a sense of injustice that would smoulder for decades. That pent-up resentment eventually burst forth in 1983, when the Golden Lake First Nation petitioned the governments of Canada and Ontario, claiming ownership of "all lands in the Province of Ontario which form part of the watershed of the Ottawa River below the Mattawa River." The Golden Lake band argued that this area, which included Algonquin Park, had been "occupied and enjoyed" by the Algonquin Nation "since time immemorial" and had not been ceded by any treaty entered into by the Algonquin Nation.[30]

The Mowat government, unable to foresee the challenge that aboriginal rights would pose to its successors almost a century in the future, moved swiftly during May 1893 to pass "An Act to Establish the Algonquin National Park of Ontario." Those who drafted the act copied the basic structure and some of the wording of the 1887 federal legislation that had created the Rocky Mountains Park at Banff, Canada's first national park. Algonquin National Park was set apart "as a public park and forest reservation, fish and game preserve, health resort and pleasure ground for the benefit, advantage and enjoyment of the people of the Province" under the control and management of the Department of Crown Lands. As recommended by the royal commission, title to the land remained with the Crown, settlement was prohibited, hunting and trapping were banned, angling was limited to rod and line under permit, a short-term lease policy was established for hotels and summer residences, and lumbering was restricted to mature pine trees.

Considering the pressure of the conservation lobby, the many benefits promised by the park program, and the minimal costs involved, it is not surprising that the Algonquin National Park Act sailed through the Ontario legislature without serious opposition. Only one Conservative MLA, James Clancy of West Kent, took a hard line and spoke against the continuation of logging in Algonquin. "It would be a great pity," he argued, "if the forests were not maintained in their natural state in the park." The existence of logging would mean that "the park would exist wholly on paper." Clancy's opinions were not endorsed by his fellow MLAs. Most shared Crown Lands Commissioner Hardy's newfound enthusiasm for the park and considered it a daring leap forward "to preserve for all time one of the most valuable heritages of the people." The bill, according to James Dickson, met with universal approval, both in the house and within the province at large. "No scheme ever conceived by any government in any part of the Dominion has met with such general approval. All shades of politicians seemed to unite for once in its favor."[31]

Why was Algonquin called a "national" park? In 1893, when there was only one federally operated park at Banff, the idea that national parks would be a separate administrative entity, entirely under federal control, with a mandate distinct from that of provincial parks, had not yet crystallized. It seemed perfectly appropriate to Ontario's public servants and politicians that if they wished to create a park with similar management goals and objectives, and on a scale comparable to the prototype of a federal park in the Rockies, they too might use the word "national." Function and size, not political jurisdiction, seem to have been the determining factors in designating Algonquin a national park. The province of Quebec took the same view, creating Mont Tremblant Park in 1894 and Laurentides Park the following year, and classifying both as "national."

Predictably, within a few months of the creation of Algonquin, the Mowat government faced demands for a second provincially owned park to be located in southwestern Ontario. In January and February 1894, a flurry of petitions from Chatham and Kent County was submitted to legislators in both Toronto and Ottawa, requesting that the renowned Pointe aux Pins, a beautifully wooded peninsula on the north shore of Lake Erie at Rondeau Harbour, be turned into a "public and national park."[32] Pressures on the provincial government to preserve the peninsula for harbour protection and recreation purposes had been mounting for years, but now the Algonquin Park initiative prompted local interests in Kent to demand that the province protect the forest at Rondeau and manage more effectively what was already a booming tourist resort.

Pointe aux Pins had actually been a management problem for the Crown Lands Department since Confederation. Settlers had chosen to bypass the Rondeau peninsula because of the infertility of the sandy soil; in 1872, only one of seventeen lots surveyed eight years before had been granted. That left some 1,800 hectares of land and marsh under the province's care, with another 200-hectare block of ordnance land (set aside in 1795 by Governor John Graves Simcoe for its pine timber) and a small lighthouse site in the hands of the dominion government. While settlers may have turned their back on the available land at Rondeau, the valuable forested areas of the point did not go unused. As early as 1867, heavy logging of the area alarmed Kent County officials, who complained that the province had permitted an excessive amount of timber extraction around Rondeau Bay. Pointe aux Pins, for instance, was the source of all the lumber required in 1844 for the major harbour improvements at Erieau, situated at the entrance to the bay. Logging should be controlled, the county demanded, "to preserve the Harbour."[33]

By this time, as well, Pointe aux Pins had become a magnet for hunters.

The renowned Colonel John Prince, magistrate and politician from the Windsor area, leased exclusive hunting privileges on the peninsula from 1848 to 1853.[34] After his tenure expired, access to sport hunters was unrestricted and uncontrolled, with the result that the deer herd and other game species on the peninsula were decimated. Holidayers also discovered the pleasure of Rondeau Bay and picturesque Pointe aux Pins. Despite the difficulties of reaching the peninsula by boat from Shrewsbury Landing, picnickers and bathers in large numbers frequented the area by the late 1860s.

Eventually, user pressure warranted the appointment of a provincial caretaker to protect the timber. Isaac Swarthout, the lone resident on the peninsula, became the first person to assume the post in 1876. In return for his services, he was permitted to use any fallen timber. The new resident caretaker brought a welcome measure of control to Pointe aux Pins and, during the remainder of the 1870s, his efforts sufficed to protect the peninsula.[35] However, that situation changed dramatically during the following decade, when Rondeau Bay felt the effects of Ontario's first recreational boom.

With the arrival at Shrewsbury Landing of the Erie and Huron Railroad in 1883, Rondeau Bay came into its own as a tourist resort, for both rural and urban residents of Kent County and beyond. Luxury hotels, cottages, and modestly priced boarding houses appeared at the resort village of Erieau and around the shoreline. Rondeau's reputation spread south, and after 1880 steamers brought American vacationers from Erie and Cleveland. On summer Sundays, the launch *Jubilee* ferried large group picnics and reunions across the bay to Pointe aux Pins. In the autumn, with the arrival of the duck-hunting season, excursionists were replaced by hundreds of sportsmen. Thus, by the mid-1880s, Rondeau had become the Lake Erie equivalent of such resorts as Burlington, Grimsby, and Scarborough beaches along Lake Ontario, and of Belle Ewart and Jackson's Point on Lake Simcoe. Because of its central location, in one of the richest and most populous agricultural regions in the province, its close proximity to Chatham, and the availability of cheap transportation, middle- and lower-income people were attracted to Rondeau. Although the area had its share of "society" hotels and cottages for people of means, its predominantly lower middle- and working-class clientele set it apart from more exclusive resorts.[36]

As could be expected, the tourist explosion at Rondeau brought with it demands on the Crown Lands Department to permit the development of Pointe aux Pins. With the coming of the railroad, two local businessmen, George and William Weldon, were granted permission to construct a small guest-house on a leased lot at the neck of the peninsula.[37] Regrettably, the caretaker system, because it lacked official regulations to guide the management of the area, proved insufficient to prevent the gradual commercial exploitation of Pointe aux Pins. By the mid-1880s, a large fishery had been located on the lake side of the peninsula. Two Indian families lived on the point and made a living by selling souvenirs to vacationers. Swarthout and his successor in 1888, Mark Soper, allowed nearby farmers to pasture cattle and swine on the point; visitors commonly encountered up to 700 head of cattle grazing in Rondeau's fields and marshes. On various occasions, commercial interests exploited the forest resources for their own profit. One individual took out red cedar for the manufacture of pencils; others tapped the pine resin for the production of turpentine. "Mr. Swarthout," confessed Crown Lands Commissioner Hardy, "cut down timber without authority," and Mark Soper was believed to have permitted a local farmer to rebuild his barn with timber from the peninsula. In short, concluded James Clancy, the Tory MLA who had opposed logging in Algonquin Park, "it had been generally discussed in the locality that a system of vandalism had been permitted to go on in the park, and that a large number of trees had been cut down under the eye of the caretaker."[38] Many others shared Clancy's belief that all was not well at Pointe aux Pins. Within this context, then, when the Algonquin Park movement reached a happy conclusion in 1893, the various elected councils of Harwich and Howard townships, Kent County, and Chatham launched their campaign for the establishment of a park at Rondeau.

Two reasons – recreation and conservation – formed the basis of the argument for preserving Pointe aux Pins "in a state of primeval forest," by declaring the area a park. In contrast to the Algonquin situation, recreation was the paramount concern at Rondeau and not merely an adjunct to the conservation impulse. The beaches and the Carolinian forest, explained the petitions, had made the area "a popular and favorite resort for picnic and pleasure parties" numbering in the thousands. In a classic expression of the doctrine of usefulness, the petitioners also argued that besides recreation, a park would serve to protect the timber stands so necessary for maintaining Rondeau Bay as "the largest, safest and most commodious" harbor of refuge on the north shore of Lake Erie. "The present and future commerce of the St. Lawrence and Great Lakes are vitally interested in the preservation of the pines and other forests, they being not only a great protection to the shipping, but absolutely necessary to the existence of the point itself." Interestingly, the naturalist's point of view was muted in the Rondeau park movement. Those promoting a national park made no mention of setting aside Pointe aux Pins as a wildlife sanctuary. Waterfowl hunting traditions were too entrenched for local politicians to tamper with them. Nor were the naturalists vocal in demanding the preservation of the so-called "forest primeval." The arguments presented in the petitions were based entirely on conservation for wise use.[39]

The Mowat government reacted to the Kent petitions with uncharacteristic speed. The Rondeau Provincial Park bill, setting aside Pointe aux Pins as "a public park, reservation and health resort" was introduced in March 1894 and received royal assent on 5 May. The rapidity with which Mowat and his friends moved to establish the park was probably related to the fact that an election was pending in June. That the new park would require little in the way of operating or development funds facilitated matters, as well. Crown Lands Commissioner Hardy, under whose department the control of the new park would lie, explained that he did not propose to develop Rondeau as a manicured park. One ranger – "a small expense" – would suffice to "protect the timber and prevent shooting and fishing during the close season."[40] "It was not proposed to make [Rondeau] a fish or game preserve," stressed Hardy, his eye fixed firmly on the local sportsmen's vote.[41]

With only one ranger to supervise the park, there was, on the face of things, little practical difference between the new administration and the old caretaker system. But, at least, now the park overseer and his superiors in the Department of Crown Lands had a legislative mandate and, by September 1894, a set of regulations to guide the management of the park. The Rondeau Provincial Park Act banned settlement, prohibited the sale of alcoholic beverages, and established a logging policy that prohibited timber extraction, save for "dead or down wood, or in clearing for roads or other park purposes ... and then only under the direction of the park ranger." The regulations respecting Rondeau Provincial Park, established by order-in-council on 8 September 1894, laid down a twenty-one-year, renewable-lease policy for summer cottages, and restricted the number of concessions (initially two) that could sell refreshments or rent "boats and other conveyances" to park users. Other regulations provided for camping under permit and placed a ban on grazing.[42]

Because of its modest size and primarily recreational objective, Rondeau was not considered worthy of "national" park status. All the same, it warranted the designation "provincial" – the first park to be so classified in Canada – since, as A.S. Hardy explained, "the park would be a delightful summer resort not only for people living in the vicinity, but throughout the province."[43] Most MLAs agreed and gave the bill easy passage through the legislature. James Clancy found much to his liking in this bill, although he hoped that in future the sale of fallen timber would not be part of the park ranger's remuneration, and that "the regulations for the preservation of the timber would be very stringent." The only serious opposition came from Solomon White, the Tory member for North Essex, who had acquired notoriety during the Commercial Union debates of the late 1880s by declaring himself in favour of Canadian annexation to the United States. "The province was reaching a stage at which it would have too many parks," White claimed. Moreover, he objected to "the fact that another ranger would be foisted on the province," adding yet another link to Oliver Mowat's patronage chain. Few others shared White's point of view. "Nothing in the western section of the Province," retorted one MLA, "could have been more popular than the present proposal."[44]

The creation of Rondeau Provincial Park in 1894 brought to a conclusion the formative phase of Ontario's provincial park development. As we have seen, no simple explanation will suffice to account for the origins of the first three parks. They would not have been established without the convergence of various compelling conservationist pressures – the need to protect a world-famous cataract and tourist attraction, a fish and wildlife crisis, a forestry movement, and an outdoor recreation boom. These pressures arose from the concerns of a wide spectrum of social and special interest groups, including scenic preservationists, speculators, ratepayers, sportsmen, operators of tourist resorts, naturalists, urban intellectuals, timber men, and recreationists, as well as enlightened civil servants and politicians. Whatever the explanation, in the final analysis, the Mowat government addressed in a positive way the concerns of most of these groups by creating Niagara, Algonquin, and Rondeau parks. It would be a long time before another administration surpassed Mowat's record.

The Whitney Era, 1905–14

Subsequent administrations made few attempts to follow suit. In the twenty years before World War I, the Ontario government established only two more parks – Burlington Beach (1907) located at the western end of Lake Ontario, and Quetico (1913) located on the Rainy River watershed to the west of Thunder Bay, on the Minnesota border. One may well ask why the vigorous conservation lobby, galvanized into action by the wildlife crisis and the influence of forestry ideas in the late 1880s and early 1890s, did not continue to demand large northern parks in addition to Algonquin. Why did the late-nineteenth-century outdoor recreation boom not generate more Rondeaus?

Part of the answer to these questions lies in the fact that the establishment of Algonquin Park and the changes to the fish and game laws, following the MacCallum commission report, defused the wildlife crisis and dissipated much of the emotion that had fuelled the conservation lobby. Forestry ideas continued to influence government policy, but in a way that obviated the need for large northern provincial parks. With the passage of the Forest Reserves Act (1898), extensive tracts of Crown land were set aside, ostensibly to provide lumbermen with a perpetual source of pine timber and the government with a permanent source of revenue. In 1901, some 570,000 hectares were reserved in the Temagami region of northeastern Ontario (expanded to 1.5 million hectares in 1903), followed in 1904 by the 777,000-hectare Mississagi Reserve in Algoma, and the massive 1.9-million-hectare Nipigon Forest in the Thunder Bay District. At the outset, Crown Lands Department officials expected timber harvesting to be the dominant activity in the provincial forests; however, the reserves, particularly those accessible by rail, became popular recreation areas, perceived by many as parklands in all but name. By 1914, the Temagami Forest had evolved into a multiple-use area that accommodated tourism, fishing and trapping, native hunting, and even mining.[45] Furthermore, some of the reserves also served another park function – wildlife conservation. In short, then, the several provincial parks and the new provincial forests sufficed to meet the demands of both conservationists and urban middle-class recreationists before 1920.

Any explanation for the slow growth of provincial parks in this period must also take into account the lack of interest shown in the subject by the majority of Ontarians. For the great mass of urban labourers and artisans, the notion of outdoor recreation at distant resorts and parks was quite irrelevant, considering the long hours of work they had to endure and the limited financial resources at their disposal. In 1900, most male blue-collar workers faced a grinding sixty-hour, six-day work week. And even then, most families required two wage earners to survive. During the first two decades of the twentieth century, decades characterized by rapid and sustained urban and industrial growth, most urban working-class families continued to face a life of enduring poverty.[46] Rather than wishing for distant provincial parks, working-class Ontarians in this period demanded recreational space that was local and accessible; in short, neighbourhood parks with play areas and facilities for athletic activities.

The factors that influenced the slow growth of provincial parks also determined the low rank of the few operating parks on the scale of values of the Crown Lands Department. This became apparent in the way the various parks were unceremoniously shuffled from one ministry to another. In 1896, for example, Algonquin and Rondeau became the responsibility of the attorney general, before being moved back to Crown Lands in 1899. Later, in 1913, Rondeau Park was transferred to Public Works, along with Queen Victoria Park, previously overseen by the Attorney General's Office. Rondeau remained under the aegis of the Department of Public Works until 1920, when it was reunited with Algonquin and Quetico under Lands and Forests. This fluidity of administrative responsibility for the provincially owned parks prior to 1920 underscores the fact that there existed no overall general plan of park development. No prominent politician or civil servant thought in terms of an interrelated "system" of parks. In fact, Crown Lands officials, who regarded their department as a revenue-generating agency, had never entertained the notion of creating a large park network, whose operating costs would greatly exceed revenues. This meant that parks were created and services expanded largely in response to local political pressures.

Such was the case in 1907 with the establishment of Burlington Beach, located on the sandspit that divides Lake Ontario from Burlington Bay, "as a park and place of public resort." Before it became a provincially operated park, managed by a commission, the beach area had been leased by the city of Hamilton. From 1878 to 1907, the city had subdivided the area and leased lots to cottagers and commercial interests. By the mid-1890s, at least ten hotels operated on the beach, as well as the Royal Hamilton Yacht Club. Dozens of impressive summer homes, erected by wealthy Hamiltonians, also gave parts of the area the appearance of a small town. Although in many respects a "society" resort, the less developed shorelines of the beach also attracted the lower-middle and working classes of the vicinity.[47]

The difficulty of managing such a heavily used and intensively developed recreation area soon plagued the city. As early as 1893, the summer residents, disgruntled at the lack of municipal services, petitioned the Ontario legislature for legal status as an incorporated village.[48] The Crown Lands Department, however, chose not to transform into a municipality an area it considered to have been "reserved principally for park purposes." The issue festered for another fourteen years, until the cottagers persuaded the administration of Premier James Pliny Whitney to revoke the city's lease and to create the Burlington Beach Commission as an alternative to village incorporation. Given the success of the commission park concept at Niagara Falls, the government looked to the new commission to provide the necessary services, without sacrificing the status and future improvement of the beach "as a park and place of public resort."[49] Moreover, the idea of a commission park meant that the Department of Lands, Forests and Mines could avoid the expense of being involved in the day-to-day operation of the beach and the financing of developments desired by the residents. In short, in 1907 a major recreational land-use problem had been taken out of the department's hands; it was a solution in perfect harmony with its "use and profit" outlook.

The Whitney administration's reluctance to engage in potentially costly provincial park initiatives surfaced again in its initial response to conservationist suggestions that the Quetico-Superior region of both Minnesota and Ontario be set aside as an international park, forest, and game reserve. The region remained wilderness, largely untouched by the logging, mining, and railroad developments in the surrounding portions of the Rainy River watershed. The idea of setting this area aside had first been proposed by Minnesota's forestry commissioner, Christopher C. Andrews, after he canoed the boundary waters route from Basswood to Crane Lake in 1905. Andrews began by persuading the Minnesota legislature to reserve from sale as "a pleasure resort for the people" some 57,060 hectares of timbered land along Crooked Lake and Lac la Croix. Meanwhile, he urged Ontario to follow Minnesota's example in order to create "an international forest reserve and park of very great beauty and interest." While declaring that their department would do "all in its power to preserve natural beauty spots and the value of woodlands," officials at the Ontario Department of Lands, Forests and Mines did nothing to advance Andrews's proposal.[50] The government had little incentive to do so, since there existed no indigenous pressure for such action.

Three years later, however, prominent individuals began to concern themselves with Quetico, when it became evident that the big game in the region was under threat of annihilation. The moose, in particular, could not for long withstand the depredations, both of organized parties of professional hunters, hired to provide meat for lumbering camps in the Rainy River watershed, and of the mindless trophy hunters who slaughtered the animals for the sake of their antlers. Spearheading the protest in Ontario against such activities was the influential gold-mine operator and MLA for Rainy River, William A. Preston of Fort Frances. Preston, who sought to establish a game sanctuary in the Quetico, a part of his constituency, found an ally in the offices of the Canadian Northern Railway. The superintendent of publicity for the railway, Arthur Hawkes, believed that his company might benefit by promoting the scheme to safeguard and enhance the tourist and sporting potential of the Canadian Northern's hinterland. Accordingly, the company supported the efforts of the internationally based North American Fish and Game Protection Association to lobby for a joint Ontario-Minnesota game reserve in the Quetico-Superior country. Following the annual meeting of the association in Toronto in early February 1909, Preston and Hawkes informed Lands and Forests Minister Frank Cochrane (1905–11) that President Theodore Roosevelt, prompted by conservationists such as C.C. Andrews, was about to establish Superior National Forest in northeastern Minnesota, and that the state of Minnesota was preparing to declare the area a game preserve. Evidently impressed, Cochrane indicated that Ontario might also reserve a large tract of land in the Hunter's Island portion of the Quetico (the section bounded by the international border, Lakes Saganaga and Kawnipi, and the Maligne River).[51]

Arthur Hawkes and other members of the North American Fish and Game Protection Association followed up these discussions by lobbying in Minnesota. Hawkes himself contacted prominent civil servants and politicians, "spoke to the [Minnesota] Editorial Association, which passed a suitable resolution, presented the resolution to a joint committee of the State House and Senate; and addressed the Commercial Club of Duluth."[52] These efforts produced results beginning on 13 February 1909, when President Roosevelt created the Superior National Forest. On cue, Aubrey White, deputy minister of lands, forests and mines, presented Frank Cochrane, on 29 March, with a memorandum in support of the conservationist position. White recommended that about 405,000 hectares of "the celebrated Quetico region, which contains one of the largest bodies of pine timber in the Province" should be withdrawn from sale and settlement under the Forest Reserves Act. The establishment of a forest reserve, he stressed, required minimal commitment from the government, since the region was Crown land and possessed no agricultural value and little mineral potential. Although there were two Indian reserves in the territory, "the Indians would not be interfered with." The province would benefit from the protection and eventual harvesting of the enormous pine and pulpwood stands in the proposed reserve.[53]

But what of the main concerns raised by the North American Fish and Game Protection Association? What special protection would wildlife be given in the reserve? According to Aubrey White, under the terms of the Forest Reserves Act (1898), the proposed Quetico forest would possess the same status as a game reserve since the legislation prohibited fishing and hunting. What he did not mention, however, was that an amendment to the act in 1900 had removed the prohibition to allow fishing and hunting subject to regulations. As soon as the government chose to issue regulations (and it would do so in October 1911), forest reserves would lose their status as game reserves. All the same, on the basis of White's memorandum and the support it received from Frank Cochrane, the Whitney cabinet issued an order-in-council on 1 April 1909, creating the Quetico Forest Reserve.

Unfortunately, over the next several years, the reserve provided little protection for the big-game and fur-bearing animals of the region. Game and Fisheries Commissioner Kelly Evans, who had been charged in 1909 to investigate the management of all the public parks and forests from the dual perspective of wildlife protection and tourist development, deplored the fact that Quetico "itself has not been declared a game reserve." He discovered that for seven months of the year, from October to May, "no protection [was] afforded" the wildlife, because no rangers patrolled the reserve. Even during the spring and summer, when ten men, working in pairs, oversaw the forest, the protection of game was inadequate, with "the great bulk of the reserve left practically uncared for." Hunters and trappers were accordingly free to exploit the area "to their heart's content."[54]

The Evans commission report (1911), with its revelations about the destruction of game in Quetico, evidently impressed government officials, for early in 1912, the Department of Game and Fisheries despatched D.D. Young to serve as game warden in the reserve. He established a headquarters at French Lake, began the work of "cutting trails, building landing and camping grounds for tourists," and made the first serious effort to enforce the game laws. Still, poaching continued on a massive scale. Young reported that employees of the Canadian Northern Railway "kill game for food at all times." The smaller lumber camps were "the greatest law breakers," since "they actually hire men at $40 to $50 a month to keep them supplied with moose, deer and fish all winter ... If reports can be believed, some camps have actually used from fifty to a hundred moose during the winter."[55] Such information apparently jolted Lands and Forests officials into further action; on 7 November 1913, the Whitney cabinet issued an order-in-council, creating Quetico Provincial Park.

Quetico had the distinction of being the first park to be created under the new Provincial Parks Act, passed just six months earlier, in May 1913. According to Lands, Forests and Mines Minister William Hearst (1911–14), the legislation was significant, in that it allowed the government to create a provincial park by order-in-council and to dispense with the previous practice, which required special legislation.[56] It is not unlikely that events in the Quetico Forest Reserve influenced the timing of this legislation. After the revelation of the Evans report, Lands and Forests officials realized that Quetico would have to be given park status as a measure to protect game. Furthermore, considering the problems in Temagami and elsewhere, they probably anticipated that other wildlife issues or recreational land-use problems would require the creation of additional provincial parks in the years ahead. The 1913 act provided officials with a simplified procedure to create such new parks and common policy guidelines for their management. A "provincial park" was now defined as an area of Crown land, "not suitable for settlement or agricultural purposes," set apart "as a public park and forest reserve, fish and game preserve, health resort and pleasure ground, for the benefit, advantage and enjoyment of the people of Ontario, and for the protection of the fish, birds, game and fur-bearing animals therein." Both Algonquin and Rondeau became subject to the provisions of the new act; this meant that Algonquin now officially became a provincial park, and the designation "national" disappeared from its name.

As a postscript to the story of Quetico park's origins, it is noteworthy that Aubrey White's statement of 29 March 1909 that "the Indians would not be interfered with," proved to be tragically wrong. The small Sturgeon Lake Ojibway band of Reserve 24C, located within the forest reserve, was affected quickly, and negatively. In the late autumn of 1910, necessity obliged band members to leave their reserve in search of a winter supply of game. They established a seasonal encampment in the Hunter's Island section of the Quetico forest. Although the band members had surrendered the area in question under Treaty No. 3 (1873), they had been assured that the lands would not be wanted for a long time, and that they would be able to exercise their hunting, fishing and trapping rights in the region. It is unclear whether this isolated band even realized that the forest reserve had been established.

All the same, provincial officials forced the band to break camp in December 1910. Leo Chosa, the operator of a trading post on Basswood Lake, considered the decision to be cruel and callous. "What are to become of those Indians?" he asked. "You cannot annihilate them ... their reservation at present cannot support them ... I doubt very much that there exist today a civilized people under the sun that would uphold and compel its officers to enforce a law that would deprive a man of his home and throw his wife and little ones on the mercies of a northern winter to endure the tortures that the Indians in question will have to undergo if they are compelled to move from Hunter's Island this winter."[57] The enforced removal resulted in the dispersal of the Sturgeon Lake people. Lacking a sufficient food supply to survive the winter, they sought refuge with other Ojibway communities, particularly with the Lac la Croix band, whose reserve was located at the southwest corner of the forest reserve on the Minnesota border.

Following the creation of Quetico Provincial Park in 1913, the Ojibways' litany of woe continued. They were arrested for trapping, hunting and fishing in the park, and their access to sacred ceremonial sites was restricted. In 1915, without consultation with the survivors of the Sturgeon Lake band, the federal and Ontario governments declared Reserve 24C abandoned.

The memory of these events would come back to torment the government of Ontario. In 1991, the members of the Lac la Croix First Nation, who consider themselves to be related to and descendants of the Sturgeon Lake Ojibway, pressed two long-standing grievances against the province – the cancellation of Reserve 24C, and the effective extinction of the Treaty Rights of Lac la Croix Ojibway, due to the creation of Quetico Provincial Park on their traditional lands.[58]

The Interwar Years

The strains and dislocations produced by World War I within the Ontario body politic dampened any inclination within the Conservative administration of William Hearst (1914–19) to take more initiatives under the new Provincial Parks Act. Only after the termination of hostilities and the surprise election of Ernest C. Drury's Farmer-Labour government in October 1919 was the stage set for new developments. "I am favourably disposed toward the policy of setting aside suitable areas in the Province for the creation of further Provincial parks along lines similar to Algonquin Park and Rondeau Park," reflected Drury's minister of lands and forests, Beniah Bowman.[59] The premier himself, a Simcoe County farmer, took pride in his own conservationist record. Before the war, he had been an active member of the Ontario Agricultural College's Experimental Union and a strong proponent of Edmund J. Zavitz's program of wasteland reclamation.[60] Once in office, Drury set Zavitz to work, establishing new reforestation centres in Simcoe County, and authorized the establishment of two new provincial nurseries at Orono and Midhurst. In 1958, the latter would become Springwater Provincial Park.

What distinguished the Drury administration in the development of provincial parks was its responsiveness to a variety of demands for parkland, especially to pressures brought to bear by individuals and groups with linkages to the United Farmers movement. Drury's decision to create Long Point Park on Lake Erie illustrates this tendency. The call for the park arose during the summer of 1920, when the Department of Lands and Forests began to survey a 186-hectare parcel of unpatented land, located at the neck of Long Point. The main portion of the peninsula itself was owned by the Long Point Company, made up of wealthy Americans and Canadians, who had served an important function since 1866 by conserving the flora and fauna of their 4,737-hectare property. Because the company prohibited public access to its lands, local residents harboured considerable ill-will toward those who owned the point. This resentment manifested itself when the rumour spread that the Long Point Company might acquire the new lots under survey in 1920 and prohibit access to what had traditionally been a public waterfowl-hunting area. Joseph Cridland, United Farmers of Ontario member for South Norfolk, railed at the prospect of his constituents losing their main "shooting and hunting grounds."[61] Another prominent regional politician, John L. Buck, reeve of Port Rowan, also urged Premier Drury and his officials to set aside the area being surveyed as parkland. Asked whether the property might be "put into the hands of the Municipal Council of Port Rowan," Buck rejected the idea and recommended instead a commission form of administration, to prevent the park from becoming "a football in municipal politics."[62] The park commission idea appealed to Drury. It had been successful at Burlington Beach and Niagara Falls; moreover, it blended nicely with the United Farmers' position in favour of decentralizing power away from the seat of government at Queen's Park. Indeed, the commission idea appealed to politicians of all stripes, most of whom still extolled the traditional nineteenth-century notion of local control over local affairs, and resisted the expansion of provincial initiatives in social and economic matters. Thus, with the premier's blessing, the Long Point Park Act (1921) vested the 187 hectares of unpatented land at the point in a three-person board of commissioners and designated the area "a park, forest reservation and health resort." In the time-honoured fashion of patronage politics, Joseph Cridland, MLA, named the persons to sit on the commission. Since these worthies had little idea of how to proceed, they turned to the Burlington Beach Commission for a quick lesson in park management.

Not everyone was pleased with this outcome. The lawyer for the Long Point Company voiced strong personal opposition to the commission park idea. "I think the scheme is an unwise one," he wrote, for the area would soon be overrun with summer cottages to the detriment of the "wild nature" of the place. He doubted, too, that waterfowl shooting by the public could survive residential development.[63] In the decades ahead, his predictions would be largely borne out, but in 1921 his warnings went unheeded.

The Drury government also responded to the importunities of the residents of Brighton and vicinity in Northumberland County, who lobbied during 1921–22 for the establishment of a park on nearby Presqu'ile Point. Since 1871, the 445-hectare peninsula jutting into Lake Ontario had been under federal jurisdiction in order to protect the harbour and to operate a lighthouse. To protect the standing timber as well, federal authorities resisted local pressures for resort development on the point until 1904, at which time recreational demands forced Ottawa to survey and lease cottage lots. In 1905, the impressive Presqu'ile Hotel appeared and quickly became the entertainment centre of the region with its big-band concerts, dance contests, and social events. Recreation boomed at the Point until, by 1920, thousands of people flocked to its beaches and attractions. Meanwhile, the Lake Ontario schooner industry had gone into eclipse and with it the reason for federal control over Presqu'ile. Ottawa returned the bulk of the peninsula to provincial jurisdiction in November 1920. Subsequently, a clamour arose in the Brighton area for a park at Presqu'ile.

On 7 June 1921, a delegation of businessmen and politicians from the village and township of Brighton, all alert to the benefits to be derived from a burgeoning motor-tourist trade, presented its case to the Drury government for a provincial park. The delegates hoped that the province would assume the costs of developing Presqu'ile. Neither the government nor Lands and Forests officials were enthusiastic about this proposal, and may have suggested as an alternative the concept of a local commission to assume the responsibility for developing and managing the recreational area. Regardless of who injected the idea into the discussions, a spate of petitions favouring the commission form of park administration subsequently reached government officials in Toronto. All the major interested local groups – the municipalities of Brighton village and township, the board of trade, and the leaseholders on the peninsula – saw it in their best interests to vest the control over Presqu'ile Point in a small five-person park commission, appointed from among themselves. Thus, with consensus attained, the Presqu'ile Park Act, a virtual copy of the Long Point Park Act, slipped quietly through all three readings in the provincial legislature on 17 March 1922.[64]

While the Drury government favoured self-sustaining commission parks to operate southern recreation areas where cottage communities existed, it also took advantage of the Provincial Parks Act when political pressure emerged for recreational parkland elsewhere. Such was the case in January 1920, when the government received a petition bearing 378 signatures, circulated by the Severn River Improvement Association, requesting that a small acreage of Crown land be reserved for public use near the Canadian Pacific Railway (CPR) station at Severn Falls. Premier Drury, his political antennae sensitive to rumblings in his home county, gave the go-ahead to the proposal, with the result that, on 17 May 1922, a three hectare tract in Matchedash Township was set apart by order-in-council as Severn River Provincial Park. Two years later, the Department of Lands and Forests joined with the Severn River Improvement Association to construct a community hall on the property. Thereafter, this tiny provincial park served as an access point to the Severn River and as a recreation centre for cottagers and tourists.[65]

As the Department of Lands and Forests moved to establish Severn River Provincial Park, the Georgian Bay Association, representing cottage owners from Midland to Pointe au Baril, urged the Drury government to declare as parkland the 877-hectare Franklin Island, located offshore from Carling Township, on the boat channel between Parry Sound and Pointe au Baril. Aware that private interests were rapidly buying up most of the available island and shore properties on Georgian Bay, the association hoped to set aside Crown land for the preservation of natural areas and for recreational use. Franklin Island seemed most appropriate because of its size and accessibility to boaters, its mature stands of pine, and its potential value as a wildlife sanctuary and fish spawning grounds. Citing all of these reasons, and not unmindful of the fact that no significant development or maintenance costs would be involved, the Drury cabinet issued an order-in-council, on 9 May 1923, establishing Franklin and forty-two smaller islands as a provincial park.[66]

No planning lay behind the decision to create this park. The problem of accessibility had not been addressed by a well-meaning government, anxious to respond positively to the call of the conservationists and recreationists. Predictably, once the Conservatives, led by G. Howard Ferguson, returned to power in 1923, the park languished for want of both public access and official interest. The primary users for many years were the clients of Camp Franklin, a commercial tourist operation. Interestingly, during the late 1930s and early 1940s the Federation of Ontario Naturalists (FON) used this lodge for their first summer nature camps. Still, the Department of Lands and Forests (DLF) chose not to appoint a superintendent or to develop the island. Apart from harvesting the mature timber in the late 1930s, management of the area was minimal. Such was the lack of commitment to Franklin Island that DLF officials actually neglected to register the order-in-council establishing the park with the registrar of regulations; as a result, the order became invalid in 1944, and the island lost its park status.

E.C. Drury's Farmer-Labour government went down to defeat in June 1923 at the hands of George Howard Ferguson's Conservatives. The new administration, determined to end the string of annual deficits that went back to 1918, sought to improve provincial finances by emphasizing retrenchment and economic development. As part of the effort to stimulate the economy, the Ferguson government began to view provincial parks within the framework of a tourist development strategy. The government sought to reap the economic benefits of the automobile revolution that was rapidly altering the social and economic life of North America. Registering a mere 100,000 passenger vehicles in 1918, the province could count nearly half a million automobiles by the mid-1920s. The official austerity program notwithstanding, highway construction continued unabated at an annual rate of 320 kilometres. With the help of their new mobility and an expanding highway system, middle-class Ontarians set in motion the resort boom of the 1920s. Automobile owners who could not afford the luxury of a resort or cottage soon discovered the delights of sleeping under canvas. Ontario's splendid highway network also attracted out-of-province tourists. It was estimated that 2 million tourist-driven cars entered Ontario for a day trip in 1927, with another 400,000 vehicles and their passengers staying in the province for periods of up to two months.[67]

As their numbers increased, automobile owners organized and made political demands. In 1923, the Canadian Automobile Association–Ontario Motor League lobbied for the reservation along highways of "natural scenic attractions" for the benefit of the motoring public, and recommended to Premier Ferguson "that the publicity work already started be conducted on a larger scale." The province's efforts to date, the league commented, were "a mere bagatelle" compared to the publicity campaigns of other jurisdictions in Canada and the United States.[68] Businessmen such as Canadian Investors Ltd. and the Western Ontario United Boards of Trade also urged the province to advertise widely in American newspapers and magazines. The Ferguson government responded favorably to their arguments. "The educational campaign conducted last year [1924] by various means caused an unprecedented influx of tourists," reported Lands and Forests Minister James Lyons. Furthermore, "the wild life of the parks ... their scenic beauty, preserved in its natural state, and varied allurements are being given steady publicity through the press and radio by those who have come and have seen and have been conquered."[69]

Premier Ferguson's efforts to promote tourism took on a new dimension in 1926 when he personally instructed the recently created Department of Northern Development to clear two small campground and picnic areas about fifty kilometres apart along the new Highway 11 between North Bay and Latchford. "My idea is to start this at a minimum cost to see whether there is any demand," the premier explained.[70] As it happened, these roadside parks were extremely popular from the beginning, and became a standard feature on all new provincial highways subsequently constructed across the northern districts. Many of them would eventually become provincial parks.

In October 1926, Premier Ferguson appointed William Finlayson to the Lands and Forests portfolio, bringing to political prominence a first-rate administrator, forestry proponent, and provincial parks enthusiast. Even before entering the cabinet, Finlayson had been actively promoting a plan to set aside as a provincial park some 10,500 hectares of Crown land in Matchedash Township, located within his own riding of North Simcoe. Apart from the personal political benefits to be derived from this scheme, he argued that the area bounded by the Gloucester Pool, the Severn River, and Sparrow Lake would be ideal for a game and timber reserve, bird sanctuary, and recreation area, to serve the densely populated region of south-central Ontario. Premier Ferguson himself approved of the proposal in principle and, in 1926, authorized a stop to land sales in the area.[71] During 1931, Finlayson brought the Matchedash proposal before cabinet, only to learn that his colleagues deemed expenditures on new parks to be frivolous in view of the worldwide economic crisis. As an alternative, he was authorized to approach Ottawa with the suggestion that the Matchedash site be incorporated into Georgian Bay Islands National Park. That proposal was also rejected by the financially strapped federal authorities. "It is going to be difficult or impossible to get any money for the proposed park ... this year either from the Dominion, or the Provincial Government," lamented a dejected Finlayson in April 1932. "I think we will have to let the matter stand."[72]

Despite the obstacles to formal provincial park expansion, Finlayson advanced a few park-related projects. Several areas of Crown land were reserved from sale, so that "the question of [their] use as a park ... [may be]

carefully considered before any disposition ... is made."[73] Similarly, the device of establishing shoreline reservations to preserve scenic areas was used effectively. For instance, in 1932, the lakeshore of Trout (today OSA) Lake in the Killarney area was protected by an exchange of timber limits with the Spanish River Company, following pleas made by prominent artists and members of the newly organized Federation of Ontario Naturalists (1931). In 1964, OSA Lake, its spectacular beauty still intact, would become part of the new Killarney Provincial Park.[74] Finlayson also took advantage of favourable circumstances in 1931 to establish a large campground on a 26-hectare peninsula on Lake Temagami, along Highway 11. Set aside by order-in-council on 16 December 1931, the campground was appropriately named Finlayson Point. Conveniently located, both for the motoring public and those seeking access to the Temagami waterways, Finlayson Point quickly became a popular recreational area. In the mid-1950s, it, too, would be incorporated into the provincial parks system.[75]

William Finlayson was perhaps the first influential politician to acknowledge and to respond to the "rapidly increasing demand for Public Parks ... in the older part of the Province, within reasonable distance from Toronto and the border cities."[76] Even during the Depression, this recreational pressure grew relentlessly. In the 1930s, municipalities around Lake Simcoe first complained of the lack of public beaches to serve the growing crowds of vacationers and day-trippers, who were motoring north from the urban centres of south-central Ontario. Moreover, as early as 1935, the Liberal government of Mitchell F. Hepburn "observed with regret that so little shore-line along the Great Lakes is free and open to the common folk," and promised to acquire "choice park locations" close to "populated centres and readily accessible to the millions of tourists from the South." The politicians only began to address this problem when owners of shoreline properties claimed possession of the Great Lakes beaches between the high-water mark and the low-water mark, and initiated lawsuits to reserve the area for their exclusive use. The concern expressed by the public elicited the sympathy of politicians like Lands and Forests Minister Peter Heenan, who pledged to ensure "free and untrammeled access to and from the beaches."[77]

In the midst of this general controversy, Ipperwash Beach on Lake Huron, at the north end of Lambton County, became a focus of debate in southwestern Ontario. Owned by the Chippewa people of the Stony Point Reserve, the heavily used beach was an ideal location for a park, located as it was along the Blue Water Highway between Sarnia and Goderich. Beyond the need to ensure future access for the general public, the area urgently required proper management to check the deterioration of the natural features and to provide adequate sanitation, roads, parking, and other facilities. In 1935, the Hepburn administration acted upon a petition signed by some 1,600 residents of Lambton, Middlesex, and Huron counties, and endorsed by many municipalities, urging that Ipperwash Beach be acquired for parkland. Following successful negotiations with the Stony Point band, the province purchased forty-four hectares of land, including over a kilometre of lake frontage and a well-timbered back area, suitable for picnicking and automobile camping. Ipperwash Provincial Park was subsequently created by order-in-council in 1938. It was the DLF's hope that the new park would not only serve the residents of southwestern Ontario, but would also attract American tourists.[78]

Ipperwash was the only area acquired for provincial park purposes during the 1930s. The Hepburn administration, elected in 1934 on a platform of fiscal restraint, refused to purchase additional costly, privately owned frontage property on the southern Great Lakes. Besides, the slow economic recovery that began after 1933 was interrupted by the sharp recession of 1937–38. Understandably then, the province, burdened first by a depressed economy and later by the wartime emergency in 1939, gave the acquisition of more parkland a low priority. Still, the Hepburn administration did endeavour to solve the problem of access to the beaches by legislative means. In 1940, an amendment to the Beds of Navigable Waters Act declared that the strip of beach along Great Lakes shorelines between the high- and low-water marks was part of the beds of navigable waters and thus presumed not to have been granted in any previous "patent, conveyance or deed." Regrettably, this legislation did not provide a permanent solution to the problem. In 1951, the amendment was repealed on the grounds that it had been "confiscatory in nature,"[79] and the public was again denied access to the shorelines.

After 1941, other factors continued to work against the expenditure of funds by the province on recreational parklands in southern Ontario. The new deputy minister of lands and forests, Frank MacDougall, tended to view matters from the perspective of a forester and a northerner and initially, at least, showed scant appreciation of southern Ontario's outdoor recreational scene. As superintendent of Algonquin Park in the 1930s, he had reached the dubious conclusion that "Ontario has plenty of park area compared with the country south of us."[80] It would take time and experience to sensitize MacDougall to the dimensions of the outdoor recreational needs of southern Ontarians. The politicians also lost interest in the issue of access to the Great Lakes, an understandable development considering the more urgent problems of war and reconstruction. Major political changes and uncertainty further complicated matters. During 1942–43, the Hepburn Liberal Party disintegrated, paving the way for the "Tory dynasty" that was destined to dominate the politics of Ontario for over four decades.

Shortly after assuming power in June 1943, the Conservative government of George Drew completed two initiatives launched by its predecessor and, on 13 January 1944, created Sibley and Lake Superior provincial parks by orders-in-council. In sharp contrast to the objectives of conservation and recreation that lay behind the establishment of earlier parks, the primary reason for setting aside Sibley and Lake Superior was to promote tourism along the projected routes of the Trans-Canada Highway – Highway 11, then under construction across northern Ontario, and Highway 17, north of Sault Ste. Marie.

Political pressure for a park on the magnificently rugged Sibley Peninsula – a provincial forest reserve since 1900 – had emerged in 1936, a consequence of several speeches made by Prime Minister William Lyon Mackenzie King in favour of "establishing National Parks throughout the Dominion of Canada" to help reduce unemployment and to promote tourism. In Port Arthur, the city council and chamber of commerce, supported by the local Liberal association, pounced upon the prime minister's suggestion and requested that the 20,700-hectare Sibley Forest Reserve be transformed into a national park. Besides containing a rich variety of flora and fauna and outstanding scenery, the peninsula was ideally located on the "best-surfaced portion of the Trans-Canada Highway," accessible to tourists from Minnesota, and less than fifty kilometres from the twin cities of Port Arthur and Fort William. The scheme seemed within reach, considering that the federal representative for Port Arthur, Minister of Transport C.D. Howe, approved of it and raised the possibility of providing dominion relief funds for park development.[81]

However, the national park proposal foundered on a combination of local opposition and attitudes toward provincial rights. In 1938, sport hunters in the Thunder Bay area came out against the project, because they feared that under the National Parks Act the Sibley peninsula would be closed to hunting. That same year, the Fort William Chamber of Commerce suddenly declared itself in favour of a provincial as opposed to a national park, a politically astute move, given the traditional hostility of most Ontario governments to suggestions that Crown lands be turned over to the dominion for park purposes. Indeed, prior to 1938, no provincial government had deigned to transfer any territory to Ottawa for this reason. In the entire province of Ontario, there existed but three tiny national parks, comprising a paltry 3,035 hectares – St. Lawrence Islands (1914), Point Pelee (1918), and Georgian Bay Islands (1929). Each of these had been created on property already under dominion control.[82]

Ontario politicians and bureaucrats clung to the belief that the province would itself continue to satisfy any demand for large natural parks. Dominion interference was deemed unnecessary and undesirable. Under these circumstances, federal Transport Minister C.D. Howe bowed to the province's determination to retain the Sibley peninsula. All the same, in August 1938, he notified the DLF through informal channels that he might still provide relief funds for provincial park development. Nothing came of this suggestion. The two governments never discussed it formally, a consequence perhaps of the unhappy state of dominion-provincial relations during the years of the Hepburn-King feud.[83]

Fortunately, the Sibley provincial park idea survived, even if the national park proposal did not. The Ontario Department of Northern Affairs endorsed the suggestion from the point of view of tourism, and local boosters continued to make representations to the province. Following its victory in 1943, the Drew government saw little to lose by declaring the forest reserve a provincial park in January 1944, since few costs were anticipated. Indeed, beyond tightening timber regulations and undertaking biological surveys prior to restocking the park lakes, Sibley Provincial Park received minimal attention for many years. Until the Superior route of the Trans-Canada Highway (17) was completed in 1960, the DLF wisely resisted local demands to develop the park, or to open it to leaseholders and other recreational resort schemes.[84]

The story of Lake Superior Provincial Park followed a similar pattern. When N.O. Hipel became minister of lands and forests in 1941, he "received considerable correspondence and ... several delegations" from municipal politicians and businessmen in Sault Ste. Marie, requesting that a large provincial park be created north of the Montreal River, along the proposed route of Highway 17, which at the time ended at Agawa Bay. In January 1943, Hipel wrote to all members of cabinet, proposing the establishment of a park to embrace a 220,000-hectare area "of great scenic beauty," situated between the Superior shoreline on the west and the Algoma Central Railway on the east, and between the Michipicoten River to the north and the Montreal River to the south. The project would cost little, Hipel emphasized, for the region was nonagricultural Crown land and already cut over by the timber men. "No immediate development requiring an expenditure of funds is planned," he added, but this area should be immediately designated a provincial park, "so that following the War we will be in a position to ... develop this Park into a recreational area which will attract many tourists." Hipel's cabinet colleagues unanimously endorsed the project. They failed to establish the park prior to the Liberal government's demise in June 1943, but the Drew Conservatives acted decisively and set aside the park the following January.[85]

For the next sixteen years, Lake Superior Provincial Park existed in name only. The first investigative survey of the area was made in 1946 by H.N. Middleton, a forester in the Sault Ste. Marie district, who recommended that until Highway 17 was completed, around the hump of Lake Superior, the park should remain in a "static" or "deferred" condition. The budget-conscious DLF eagerly accepted his recommendation. Significantly, Middleton's survey revealed that the province had unwittingly set aside an area of more than local interest. In January 1948, C.H.D. Clarke, then a biologist with the Fish and Wildlife Division of the DLF, wrote to his chief, W.J.K. Harkness: "It is evident that this park more nearly approaches the scenic and biological standards generally associated with [major nature preserves] in various parts of the world," and that it should in time be managed according to international protectionist standards.[86]

Not all northern communities located along the Trans-Canada Highway experienced the same measure of success upon lobbying for a provincial park during this period. The small communities of White River and Schreiber, situated along the proposed route of the Trans-Canada Highway on the north shore of Lake Superior, managed to have highway park reserves set aside in 1938. However, it took over twenty years before these sites became the nucleus of new provincial parks – White Lake (1961) and Rainbow Falls (1963).[87]

The residents of Kakabeka Falls, located west of Fort William, had no luck whatsoever during the late 1930s and early 1940s in persuading the province to create a park at the famous cataract on the Kaministiquia River, known regionally as the "Niagara of the North." In 1937, the DLF dismissed as economically impracticable the requests made by residents, civic authorities, and the chambers of commerce of both Kakabeka Falls and Fort William that the government purchase patented land for a provincial park. Instead, then-Deputy Minister Walter Cain dampened local ardour for the project by suggesting that if "any public body undertake to secure the privately-owned lands" for park purposes, "the Department of Lands and Forests will undertake its administration." The agitation for a provincial park reemerged in 1943, this time led by the Thunder Bay Historical Society, which emphasized reasons related to both history and tourism for creating a park at Kakabeka Falls. Local historians explained how the site, located as it was on the great Kaministiquia voyageur route, was evocative of the province's fur-trading past. They suggested that a small fur-trading post that had once existed on the site might be reconstructed as a tourist attraction. Such ideas fell on deaf ears. "This perpetuation of historical sites is not a function of the Department of Lands and Forests at the present time," replied H.W. Crosbie, chief of the Division of Land and Recreational Areas. A provincial park would eventually be located at Kakabeka Falls, but not until 1955, by which time departmental officials were beginning to acknowledge the potential for mixing parks, history, and tourism.[88]

As one examines the story behind the origins of Ontario's first provincial parks, several themes stand out prominently. The total absence of planning is especially noticeable. Each new park was established without reference to the others, because no one had yet conceived of a system of interconnected parks. When a government created a new park, it was invariably on an ad hoc basis in response to specific social and political pressures. Moreover, those pressures for parks largely reflected utilitarian, conservationist thinking. Few voices demanded that natural areas be set aside to preserve scenery, flora and fauna, or the wilderness for its own sake. The so-called preservationists possessed minimal political force; it was mainly their wise-use counterparts who shaped public policy. Not that it mattered; both conservationist groups were of one mind in their desire to set aside the first parklands. For almost four decades, a harmony of interest existed between the two currents of thought in the conservationist stream. Not until the 1930s did their courses cease to be parallel, thus creating turbulent crosscurrents. At that point, the conservationists inclined toward protection began to challenge the primacy of the gospel of efficiency and utility in the management of the province's parks.

Chapter 2

Managing the First Parks
The Ascendancy of Use and Profit, 1894–1945

During the first half century of provincial park development in Ontario, utilitarian, conservationist attitudes conditioned most aspects of management policy. Administrators and politicians accepted the proposition that parks should be managed for "use and profit," as Alexander Kirkwood put it. Over the decades, such management policies resulted in the exploitation of timber and wildlife, creeping commercialization, the proliferation of leaseholders and of the facilities to service them. Eventually, after 1927, the protectionist impulse quickened in response to various logging, road, and hydro-electric developments that threatened the natural areas and recreational landscapes of both Algonquin and Quetico parks. The Quetico-Superior Council, a wilderness lobby based in Minnesota, appeared in 1928, followed in 1931 by the Federation of Ontario Naturalists (FON). Both groups challenged the dominance of the gospel of efficiency in park management policy by arguing that wild lands should be treasured for recreational and aesthetic reasons, and valued even for scientific and educational considerations. Frank A. MacDougall, the legendary "flying superintendent" of Algonquin Park (1931–41), and later deputy minister of lands and forests (1941–66), emerged as the first field administrator to acknowledge the legitimacy of the policies espoused by these new groups and to implement a multiple-use philosophy that embraced both utilitarian and protectionist positions.

Logging the Parks for Use and Profit

> No effort ... should be spared to obtain the greatest possible income from these natural resources of scenery, fish and game.
>
> (Ontario Game and Fisheries Report 1911)

Game and Fisheries Commissioner Kelly Evans need not have exhorted the overseers of Ontario's parks to pursue a strategy of "use and profit." Administrators in all the provincially owned parks were already pursuing revenue-production policies. Out of necessity, the Niagara Park Commission set early precedents in this respect. The commissioners were bound by legislation to provide free entry into the park grounds, yet were expected to finance the original land acquisition debt and to operate on a self-supporting basis. In these circumstances, they turned to a variety of stratagems to generate revenues. They granted concessions, sold a franchise for the Queenston-Chippawa Railway (1891), and in 1892 even exploited the falls through the rental of hydro-electrical production privileges. Hydro-electricity enabled the commissioners to achieve their goal of self-sufficiency. Subsequently, the concept of a small "natural" park, envisioned by Governor General Dufferin and the Mowat government in the late 1870s and 1880s, had to be sacrificed under the combined impact of hundreds of thousands of tourists, enormous hydro-electric development schemes, and major expansions of the commission's property. From its modest beginnings in the 98-hectare Queen Victoria Park, the commission gradually extended its holdings to create an extraordinary system of scenic, recreational, and historic parklands along the Niagara frontier between Lakes Erie and Ontario.

The tendency "to obtain the greatest possible income from ... natural resources" took a different turn in the other provincially owned parks. In creating Algonquin, for example, the provincial government never intended to sacrifice its timber revenues by preserving the forest. The timber operators had been extracting pine from the area for over fifty years, and the government had no plans to terminate their licences. "If the establishment of the Park had depended upon the preservation of the pine," reflected Thomas W. Gibson in 1896, "the scheme would have had to be abandoned."[1] Not only did the province want the revenues, but the survival of many communities depended upon ongoing logging operations in the park. It occurred to some officials that the loggers might one day voluntarily abandon Algonquin, since the park act restricted timber extraction to pine (then the only commercially valuable timber), and since it was commonly believed that pine, once removed, would not regenerate itself.[2] However, the assumption that the days of the timber operators in Algonquin were numbered proved to be erroneous. Pine, it was learned during the late 1890s, could be regenerated. At the same time, market conditions appreciably increased the demand for hardwoods, spruce pulpwood, and hemlock bark. With the completion of J.R. Booth's Ottawa, Arnprior, and Parry Sound Railway through the park in 1897, it became feasible to extract hardwoods otherwise impossible to remove by river drive. As economic circumstances changed, those timber operators who had held licences in the park prior to 1892 complained that the Algonquin Park Act had stripped them of their "property" by removing from their licences the right to cut species other than pine. The provincial government accepted their argument and amended the act in 1900 to permit the old licensees to cut spruce, hemlock, birch, cedar, black ash, and tamarack for a thirty-year period.[3]

Controlling the licence holders proved to be no easy task. Loggers ruined

Superintendent Peter Thomson's plans for park headquarters on Canoe Lake. Thomson reported that while he and his rangers were on patrol in October 1893, employees of the Gilmour Company "built a lumber camp ... within ten or twelve feet of our head-quarters. They also entered the grove and took out the pine, at the same time cutting down a great number of other trees, and marring the beauty of the place, which I had hoped to preserve."[4] The same camp angered the second superintendent, John Simpson, by locating a garbage dump within sight and smell of park headquarters.[5] The Gilmour Company created another major clean-up problem on Canoe Lake, the location of its saw- and planing mills. Following the opening of the mills in 1896, the site developed into the lumbering village of Mowat, its peak population reaching some 700 residents. When a depressed timber market in 1900 drove the mills into bankruptcy, the site fell into a dismal state of neglect, in violation of the lease, which required the area to be kept in a clean and sanitary condition.

None of these incidents generated much public indignation. It required more sustained and widespread scenic destruction by the logging companies to accomplish that result. Without regard for scenic values, some companies regularly logged the shorelines of canoe routes and left unsightly slash for all to see. In the spring, they dammed outlets of lakes to facilitate log driving, and sometimes maintained the high-water level into summer to permit their steam "alligators" to ply the park waterways. The result was an ugly fringe of dead and fallen trees along miles of shoreline. Initially, the superintendents could do little about this state of affairs; they did not obtain authority to regulate the operators' dams until 1914.

Eventually, the scenic and natural degradation of parts of Algonquin became a matter of public concern.[6] The issue exploded in 1910, when the Munn Lumber Company perpetrated the most flagrant instance of timber buccaneering in the history of the park. On 5 May of that year, Superintendent George Bartlett reported that the company had commenced logging the hills around Cache Lake. "They have only been cutting half a day," he wrote, "but already from this office window you can see the peeled trees all along the hill. They bark all the timber taking out the hemlock bark and leaving the rest in the woods." Several days later, he reported that "trees are falling fast in front of the house [at park headquarters] this morning ... It would not be so bad if only the matured timber was carefully taken out but they are cutting the hemlock down to the size of a stove pipe and it certainly is making a fearful slash."

The Munn plunder of Algonquin climaxed toward the end of May. A desperate George Bartlett urged Queen's Park to stop the company's operations. "The Munn Lumber Co. have started on the birch right here at headquarters. Five trees have fallen since I sat down to write you ... The people are sitting on the hotel veranda watching the trees fall and some very angry things are being said."[7] The resulting public outcry prompted the Department of Lands, Forests and Mines to halt the cutting by opening negotiations to purchase the Munn

George W. Bartlett (standing) and family at the superintendent's house at Cache Lake, Algonquin Park, in 1913. *Courtesy: Algonquin Park Museum.*

The Barnet Lumber Company's "alligator," a steam-warping tug, with its pointer boats, towing a log boom on Burntroot Lake, 1908. *Courtesy: Algonquin Park Museum.*

licence. In February 1911, the province reached a settlement with the company and paid $290,000 for the surrender of the title to the 90,650-hectare area.[8] Removing the Munn Lumber Company from Algonquin did not imply that logging would be terminated in the limit. "In the future," explained Deputy Minister Aubrey White, "under government management, the thinning out of the [mature] timber ... will bring in a considerable revenue."[9]

Two years after the acquisition of the Munn licence, the increasing demand for all species of timber in Algonquin Park alarmed Deputy Minister White. He considered the situation serious enough to recommend that the government control logging activities by purchasing as many of the long-term licences as possible. The investment would be recovered in due course, argued White, "for in another generation not only will the timber so preserved have increased enormously in quantity, but also in value, and with proper protection and regulations as to cutting, a large revenue ... will be available. It would be an act of vandalism to allow this magnificent Park to become a total waste, as it infallibly would if all the timbers were permitted to be cut for even the next fifteen years."[10] Lands and Forests Minister Hearst accepted this assessment and in 1913 announced the new policy in the legislature. As it happened, the outbreak of World War I prevented the government from purchasing timber licences. Wartime dislocations also brought commercial logging in Algonquin to a virtual standstill because of labour shortages and a depressed building industry, with the result that the logging pressures which had worried Aubrey White were alleviated. Depressed timber prices continued to curtail the extent of timber operations in the park through the mid-1920s.

As for managing the old Munn limit, the Department of Lands, Forests and Mines followed the advice of park superintendent George Bartlett and encouraged a limited amount of logging of downed and mature timber. In 1917, for example, Bartlett pointed out that considerable burnt timber could be removed for "the relief of the poor in our cities" and urged that "something be done to derive a revenue from the vast quantity of matured hardwood on the limits acquired."[11] The following year, in the midst of a drastic wartime coal shortage, contracts were let for the removal of 35,000 cords of fuel wood, an action requiring the construction of two new rail sidings and the extension of a third. Furthermore, the municipalities of Hamilton, Guelph, Kitchener, Barrie, and Mimico accepted a government offer to extract fuel wood from the park.[12]

Immediately after the war ended, Bartlett again recommended that the "many million feet of the choicest hardwood" on the old Munn limit be "judiciously taken out and the Province get the benefit of the revenue."[13] Depressed market conditions prevented action on Bartlett's proposal until 1923, when the John S.L. McRae Lumber Company applied for permission to cut the mature timber in the unlicenced portions of Nightingale and Lawrence townships, located to the south of the main recreational areas of the park. Walter C. Cain, deputy minister of lands and forests (1921–41), responded sympathetically, knowing that 400 people in the village of Whitney, located on the southeastern boundary of the park, and the sawmill hamlet of Bellwood depended on the McRae Lumber Company for their livelihood. All involved parties would benefit, explained Cain: "the government from the timber revenues; the company and the communities which depended upon logging; and the forest itself, which would be healthier if the dying trees were removed. Moreover, few tourists would come into contact with the bush operations." In any event, remarked Cain, "it happens that a too frequent emphasizing of the health, wildlife and recreative factors submerges the importance of the commercial factor." Thus, in July 1925, the government offered the timber in Nightingale Township for sale by public competition. The successful bidder, as expected, was John McRae. To ensure strict supervision over the company, Deputy Minister Cain instructed his district forester in Pembroke to reach "a thorough and distinct understanding" with McRae as to the trees to be cut and to conduct a close supervision of the operations, selecting, if necessary, the trees to be extracted.[14] Cain's policy for Algonquin sought to balance a utilitarian, conservationist ethic with a philosophy of economic development. It was a policy in keeping with the thinking of the Tory administration of G. Howard Ferguson.[15]

As the DLF opened part of the old Munn limit to supervised logging, the unsolved problem of tightening the reins on the eighteen other licence holders, who still held cutting rights to some 68 percent of the park, seemed to be moving closer to solution with the passage of time. In 1930, the thirty-year term that permitted many of them to remove species other than pine was scheduled to lapse. The impending deadline greatly worried the financially strapped licence holders, because they had been able to clear only about ten percent of the marketable (non-pine) timber from their limits. Because many of the operators had obtained credit from the banks by pledging their licences as collateral, they faced serious financial difficulties if these lapsed before the timber was extracted. Not surprisingly, they petitioned the Department of Lands and Forests in December 1926 for an extension of the cutting deadline. The department responded favourably to their request but, at the same time, seized the opportunity to establish cutting regulations in the park area then under licence. The timber companies had little choice but to accept the terms, laid down in top-level meetings with Lands and Forests Minister William Finlayson (1926–34) and Premier Ferguson himself.[16]

In return for having the Provincial Parks Act amended to extend the cutting of pine for another thirty years, that is, until 1960, and other woods for fifteen years, until 1945, the licence holders agreed that henceforth, logging operations in the park would be under the direct control of provincial forestry officials. They would have "power to direct the extent and sequence of yearly operations ... to control the cutting and impose a diameter rule where this may be considered necessary or appropriate, and ... to order that any stands of timber be left for the beautification of the Park, protection of game or for re-seeding purposes."[17] Lands and Forests Minister Finlayson, when introducing these changes to the parks act, claimed that the licence holders had now submitted to "complete control of their operations by the Government." He was deluding himself. The timber operators had a much more limited understanding of how the new regulations would be applied in practice than did Finlayson.[18]

Compared to the complexities of the Algonquin situation, timber management in Rondeau Provincial Park should have posed few problems. By statute, timber extraction in Rondeau was limited to dead or fallen wood, the removal of timber in clearing for roads and buildings, and taking out underbrush for maintenance purposes. Despite these straightforward restrictions, timber policy in Rondeau caused heated discussion. Invariably, debate stemmed from a too liberal interpretation of the cutting regulations by officials interested in generating revenues from the park. For instance, Isaac Gardiner, first superintendent of Rondeau (1894–1913), proposed in his initial report that timber management be extended to include the harvesting of "dying timber." Eleven years later, his position on this question remained unaltered. "[If] the Government could place a saw-mill in the park and cut ... all the standing trees that have come to maturity," he wrote, "the bush would not only be left in a better state of preservation, but we would have all the ... timber that will be required [for] ... improvements, and could sell more than enough to pay for them."[19] This proposed harvesting policy went far beyond the intentions of the Rondeau Park Act. Nevertheless, Gardiner's logic appealed to his superiors in Toronto who, in 1908, despatched forestry expert Edmund J. Zavitz to survey and mark the mature trees before calling tenders for their removal. There emerged such a storm of protest in the regional press that the project was suspended. Zavitz returned to Rondeau in 1910 and attempted to resume the work, only to be thwarted a second time by an outraged public. The logging issue refused to go away. Two decades later, Superintendent Ralph Carman, a forester, still found most park users opposed to the introduction of an intensive management policy for the Rondeau timber stand and in favour of leaving the park forest in a natural state. Suspicion ran high when Carman located a small sawmill in the park to extract downed timber for park needs and provide custom lumber for the market and fuel wood for cottagers. With a vigilant public on the alert, he prudently kept his bush operations on a modest scale.[20]

Managing the timber of Quetico Provincial Park in 1913 should also have been a relatively uncomplicated matter, given the absence of entrenched licence holders within the park boundaries and the small number of recreationists who used the park. Unfortunately, unsavoury political dealings greatly complicated matters, just four years after Quetico was established. In 1917, for instance, Howard Ferguson, then lands and forests minister, abused his discretionary power to dispense with statutory regulations regarding tender and public competition and sold a timber limit in the park to the Shevlin-Clarke Lumber Company of Fort Frances. The licence set dues well below the prevailing rate. James A. Mathieu, Conservative MLA for Rainy River, happened to be general manager of the company. Other improprieties came to light during the sensational Timber Commission hearings of 1920–22. Two months prior to the provincial election of 30 October 1919, Ferguson had granted, without public competition, a licence to the Shevlin-Clarke Company to cut in timber berths 45 and 49 in Quetico Provincial Park, an area of about 5,400 hectares. James A. Mathieu himself admitted that he had set the dues of $9.50 per thousand board feet when the going rate was closer to $20.[21]

Ostensibly, the licence to berths 45 and 49, and the generous terms obtained by the company, were granted on the grounds that Shevlin-Clarke would conduct special brush-burning and reforestation experiments on behalf of the Department of Lands and Forests. The Timber Commission, however, dismissed the experimentation arguments as a ruse to circumvent the Crown Timber Act regulations. In subsequent litigation against Shevlin-Clarke, the courts upheld the findings of the Timber Commission. The 1919 licence to berths 45 and 49 was declared null and void, although the company later succeeded in obtaining a licence and continued to log the berths. From that time on, the rules of tender were rigorously applied in the Quetico, under the watchful eye of Deputy Minister Cain.[22]

With Cain at the helm, the logging companies in Quetico found it more difficult to ignore park regulations. Shevlin-Clarke discovered this in 1925, after altering water levels in the park and causing damage to shorelines and government property. The deputy minister required the company to rebuild a bridge and dock at park headquarters on French Lake, both of which had been destroyed by flooding caused by the company dam at the outlet of Pickerel Lake. Although this episode cost Shevlin-Clarke about $1,000, it did not deter a repeat performance the following year. Again the company had to make restitution for flooding park headquarters, damaging portages, and destroying some thirty trees at the celebrated "Pines" camping ground on Pickerel Lake. When the problem recurred a third time, Cain finally declared that the department would henceforth assume control of the dam, with expenses to be charged to the company.[23] It may have been Cain's resolve to monitor the logging companies that prompted J.A. Mathieu to declare that he was "very much opposed to the placing of any more lands in the District into parks."[24]

Conditioned as it was by the philosophy of use and profit, timber management in Ontario's provincial parks had very little time for silvicultural experimentation and research during this period. Reforestation or extensive silvicultural programs were out of the question, given the costs involved, the lack of professional foresters in a patronage-ridden department, and inadequate, overworked ranging staffs. Peter Thomson, the first superintendent of

Algonquin Park (1893–94), appears now to have been extraordinarily naïve in hoping that "a systematic attempt might be begun to reforest some of the areas of the Park which have been denuded of their pine trees."[25] Instead of a system, what emerged were occasional attempts, by individual superintendents with no forestry or biological training, to conduct forestry experiments on a hit-or-miss basis. Their efforts to promote reforestation now seem pathetically inadequate. Witness the unsuccessful efforts of both Peter Thomson and his successor, John Simpson, to extract seed from pine-cones in the park, or to introduce fruit trees into the harsh Algonquin environment.

On rare occasions, the forests in the provincial parks were used for educational purposes. In 1908, E.B. Fernow, dean of the University of Toronto's Faculty of Forestry, and his colleague, Dr. J.H. White, conducted a field camp for three students in Algonquin and studied lumbering methods around Burnt Lake. This same group, under the direction of Edmund J. Zavitz, planted about 7,000 nursery trees (five varieties of pine and some black locust) on a 1.6-hectare site in Rondeau Park. "This work," explained Superintendent Gardiner, "is to demonstrate to the farmers ... that reforestation can be carried on by them profitably."[26] As for the University of Toronto's field camp, it did not return to Algonquin until 1924.

Recreation, Wildlife, and the Gospel of Efficiency

Recreation and wildlife management also came to be viewed by park administrators in terms of revenue production. Although no government officially adopted a policy of economic self-sufficiency for provincial parks – in contrast to the commission parks – the Department of Lands and Forests held to the policy that a substantial portion of park expenditures should be recovered through various fees, leases and licences, and for a time, the harvesting of wildlife.

Superintendent Isaac Gardiner of Rondeau Provincial Park pioneered ways of tapping the revenue potential of the parks. Sixty-three years old when he assumed the superintendency in 1894, this stubborn, practical-minded ex-farmer set out to establish Rondeau as an elaborate resort with tidy, shaded picnic grounds, stately forested areas, tame wildlife, attractive cottages, and various polite amusements. In part, his plans for Rondeau seem to have been a pragmatic response to existing recreational pressures; the park teemed with visitors from the outset. As early as 1896, a single school picnic brought 2,500 children to Rondeau, with thousands of other fun seekers flocking there on peak summer weekends, this in striking contrast to Algonquin Park, which recorded a mere thirty-eight users in 1895.[27] To accommodate his visitors and to attract others, Isaac Gardiner disregarded the original intention of the Mowat government to minimize development at Rondeau and leave it in a natural state.

During Gardiner's tenure, the grassy picnic areas expanded inexorably, much of the forest underbrush disappeared, and picnic tables and old church pews were conveniently located throughout the grounds. A pavilion appeared in 1896, playground swings in 1905, and a baseball diamond two years later. Impressive docking facilities served boaters, fishermen, and swimmers.[28] Road development became another of Gardiner's priorities. In 1911, construction started on a circular scenic parkway, "to run through about the centre and best timbered portion" of Rondeau. "This would make one of the most beautiful and popular driveways in this western peninsula," explained Gardiner, and "it has been strongly urged, especially by people who visit the Park in autos and those who take an interest in the Park forest."[29]

Superintendent Gardiner believed that his chances of obtaining permission to introduce the facilities and services he desired would be enhanced if he could increase revenues. Consequently, he invited commercial fishing companies to locate their undertakings within the park. Visitors in the early spring were sometimes treated to the sight of freshly tarred nets drying in the fields and picnic grounds. In 1903, for the same reason, the superintendent encouraged exploratory drilling for gas and oil in Rondeau. Had sufficient quantities of either resource been discovered, mining operations would probably have been permitted. The Provincial Parks Act of 1913, in fact, allowed for mining in all provincial parks, as long as the operation did not "in any way impair the usefulness of the Park for the purposes for which it is designed."[30]

Although the gas and oil discoveries in Rondeau were not commercially viable, the inventive Gardiner thought up still other ways to attract users and generate income. Over time, various concessions found their way into the park: a refreshment booth, a restaurant and store, a boat livery, and change houses. Cottage leases also became a source of park income and tourist dollars. Gardiner surveyed forty lots in 1894 and made them available to the public through twenty-one-year renewable leases. By 1905, thirty individuals, mainly the professional and mercantile elite of nearby Ridgetown, had built cottages in Rondeau. In only one major respect did Isaac Gardiner fail to convert his overseers in Toronto to his point of view. Despite his incessant pleas, the department refused to permit the construction of a hotel to accommodate several hundred guests.[31] Queen's Park opposed the building of a major commercial establishment that would compete with the resort hotels that existed at nearby Erieau.

Wildlife management also assumed a central place in Superintendent Gardiner's concept of a resort park. As early as 1896, he had constructed an aviary and begun a program of raising native and exotic game birds. Eggs of prairie chickens, capercaillies, and various species of pheasant were imported from locations in North America and Europe and hatched at Rondeau. The reasons for such an initiative are not clear. The program may have been part of the larger official response to the wildlife crisis revealed by the MacCallum commission in 1893; Rondeau seems to have been perceived as a potential breeding ground to restock parts of southwestern Ontario with game birds. Gardiner may also have hoped, vainly as it turned out, that his bird management efforts might turn a profit. This would explain why he rapidly became involved in the business of purchasing, selling, and bartering eggs, and in selling adult birds. The priority given to the aviary conditioned his attitude toward other aspects of wildlife management. With departmental blessing, a serious effort was made to eliminate game bird predators – hawks, owls, weasels, skunks, and foxes – by poisoning and trapping.[32]

Another aspect of Gardiner's wildlife policy that would generate controversy in the future was his decision, in 1898, to acquire for public display several white-tailed deer and two moose from Algonquin Park. The moose did not last long, but the deer escaped their enclosure and reproduced at a rapid rate. By 1909, some 150 animals roamed unmolested in the park; three years later the deer herd numbered close to 400. With so many of the animals browsing in the area, the young growth in the Rondeau forest suffered badly. Consequently, an effort was made in 1912 to thin the herd by some ninety animals, and the superintendent delighted in the fact that the venison from the kill produced a revenue of some $800.[33]

Although a ban existed on the public hunting of game in Rondeau, the fall duck shoot provided people in the area with another recreational activity, and

Superintendent Isaac Gardiner (right) of Rondeau Provincial Park with his son Herb at the aviary built in 1896, when they commenced a program of raising native and exotic game birds. *Courtesy: Daryl Smith.*

generated revenue. After 1900, Gardiner encouraged gun clubs to locate their premises in the park, since only small parties had hunted there in previous years. Several groups built stone clubhouses for their members' convenience. The superintendent even laid down bird food in strategically located ponds to help hunters bag their limit. These courtesies attracted dozens of sportsmen to Rondeau from across southwestern Ontario, Michigan, and Ohio.[34]

In the first thirty years of provincial park history, only George W. Bartlett, superintendent of Algonquin Park from 1898 to 1922, rivalled Rondeau's Isaac Gardiner when it came to influencing provincial park policy. Forty-seven years old when he assumed the superintendency, Bartlett possessed years of experience as a foreman in road, bridge, and railway construction, and in lumber camps. He viewed the problem of park management and development from the same utilitarian and conservationist perspective as did the park's founders. As we have seen, Bartlett promoted the policy of harvesting timber for revenues and forest improvement but modified that approach with a determination to protect the watershed cover and park aesthetics from the likes of the Munn Lumber Company. Not unnaturally, his wildlife management policy reflected the same balance of conservation and utilitarianism.

In the matter of protecting wildlife and enhancing the value of Algonquin as a game sanctuary, Bartlett played a key role, by expanding the size of the park. Encouraged by his reports, the government added a string of four half townships to the eastern boundary in 1904, and ten years later incorporated eight more townships on the eastern side. Bartlett could well take pride in the size of his domain, which by 1914 encompassed nearly thirty-three townships.

Poaching proved to be his most difficult and persistent wildlife management problem. The reason for this was obvious: "It is vain," explained Game and Fisheries Commissioner Kelly Evans in 1912, "to expect such a small staff [of fifteen rangers] to provide proper and sufficient protection."[35] The fact that local residents did not perceive poaching to be a serious crime compounded the problem. Trappers who had worked the area prior to 1893 continued to practise their trade. With insufficient personnel to rid Algonquin of these poachers, Bartlett resigned himself to the reality of the situation and seemed content to control only the most flagrant examples of illicit trapping.

Although Bartlett may have grown lax in his battle with the poachers, the same cannot be said of his war of extermination against another kind of predator, the wolf. His ideas on wolf control were in keeping with contemporary North American opinion. "Every effort," he declared, "should be made to rid the woods of this pest that annually destroys more deer than the sportsman's rifle."[36] The rangers took up this cause with enthusiasm, especially since they could supplement their income with the wolf bounty. By 1915 park rangers were using poisoned bait to kill some sixty to a hundred wolves annually.[37] Unfortunately, the deadly bait also doomed uncounted numbers of other mammals and birds until the rangers switched to wire snares in the 1920s.

In spite of the poachers and the wolves, Algonquin Park did live up to the expectations of its founders to reverse the depletion of wildlife in the Nipissing District. All of the early superintendents marvelled at the increase in beaver, otter, martin, mink, fish, deer, and moose. "Of course," Bartlett wrote in 1908, "all these overflow into the surrounding country, and ... beaver are fast filling up townships adjoining the Park, where they have been unknown for many years. The deer also keep the surrounding country well stocked, and splendid hunting in the season can now be had on all sides of the park."[38]

That year, the ever utilitarian Bartlett first proposed the idea that surplus beaver might well be harvested, should the department "desire a large and lasting revenue." The Department of Lands, Forests and Mines, intrigued by the possibility of a self-supporting park operation, permitted Bartlett to trap several hundred beaver in 1910. The following year, pelts taken from Algonquin raised $3,340 at the government fur auction in Toronto. Nine live beaver were also trapped and sold, the beginning of another profitable sideline for the park operation. In 1913, the rangers removed some $5,424 worth of pelts from a variety of species, as well as live beaver and mink, which sold for $605 to fur farmers in Ontario, Prince Edward Island, and the United States.[39] Significantly, the Provincial Parks Act of 1913 entrenched Bartlett's philosophy, by permitting the harvest of "any species of fur-bearing or game animal or bird" deemed surplus to the park, the proceeds of which would be "applied towards defraying the expenses" of park administration.

During World War I, Bartlett discovered other ways to derive revenues from the commercial exploitation of fish and wildlife. Using the wartime meat shortage as a justification, the superintendent sought permission for a Whitney butcher to net lake trout and whitefish in Lake Opeongo from 1916 to 1918. Similarly, in 1917–18, Bartlett arranged a lucrative controlled kill of surplus deer for the meat markets of Toronto and Hamilton. In 1918 alone, the venison derived from 650 deer generated a revenue of $5,000.[40] After the war, however, Bartlett concentrated again on the harvesting of fur-bearing animals. The trapping program reached its zenith in 1920 by producing "the nice sum of $14,179.00."[41]

And then, abruptly, the Drury government terminated supervised trapping in Algonquin Park. The program had not been trouble free. Poaching had increased to embarrassing levels. Even a few park rangers had lined their pockets with the profits of pelts taken illegally as they undertook the fur harvest. More seriously, trappers in the regions surrounding Algonquin, angered by the competition posed by the trapping program in what was supposed to be a wildlife sanctuary, engaged increasingly in illicit operations. Under the circumstances, Lands and Forests officials decided that supervised trapping in the park was simply not worth the trouble, or the criticism it brought down upon their heads.[42]

George Bartlett's "use and profit" philosophy extended beyond timber and wildlife management to encompass recreation and tourism. Beginning in

Deer killed in Algonquin Park in 1917 to alleviate the wartime meat shortage.
Courtesy: Ministry of Natural Resources.

1905, he encouraged Lands and Forests officials to develop Algonquin as a tourist resort for an affluent middle-class clientele. The park possessed ample natural attractions to draw visitors and became easy to reach after the completion of the Ottawa to Parry Sound railway (which ran through the park) in 1897, but it lacked two other ingredients necessary to the development of tourism – hotel accommodation and advertising. The superintendent was keenly aware of the economic benefits to be derived from increased tourism. Park visitors, he emphasized, "leave a lot of ready money with our merchants ... They also employ a large number of guides to whom they pay a good wage."[43] Relying heavily on Bartlett's advice, the department opened Algonquin Park to cottagers in 1905 and, soon after, to hotels and youth camps.

To Bartlett's credit, he strove to balance this recreational activity with the protection of Algonquin's wildness. Cottages, he insisted, should be kept out of the park interior and restricted to lakes near the railway line and close to park headquarters.[44] This policy decision was perhaps Bartlett's single most important contribution to the protection of the park's natural values. Cottage development grew slowly, but surely, over the years; by 1931, some 213 leaseholders were generating a substantial $5,011 in annual revenues.

Privately operated hotels entered Algonquin Park on a leasehold basis in 1908. The Grand Trunk Railway Company, which had taken over the southern park line in 1903, dominated the accommodation business. It built the Highland Inn, near park headquarters and overlooking Cache Lake, and located the new Algonquin Park Station directly in front of the hotel. In 1912–13, the company also constructed two wilderness lodges – Nominigan on Smoke Lake and Minnesing on Burnt Island Lake – modelled on similar establishments in New York's Adirondack Forest. Here guests enjoyed all the comforts of home

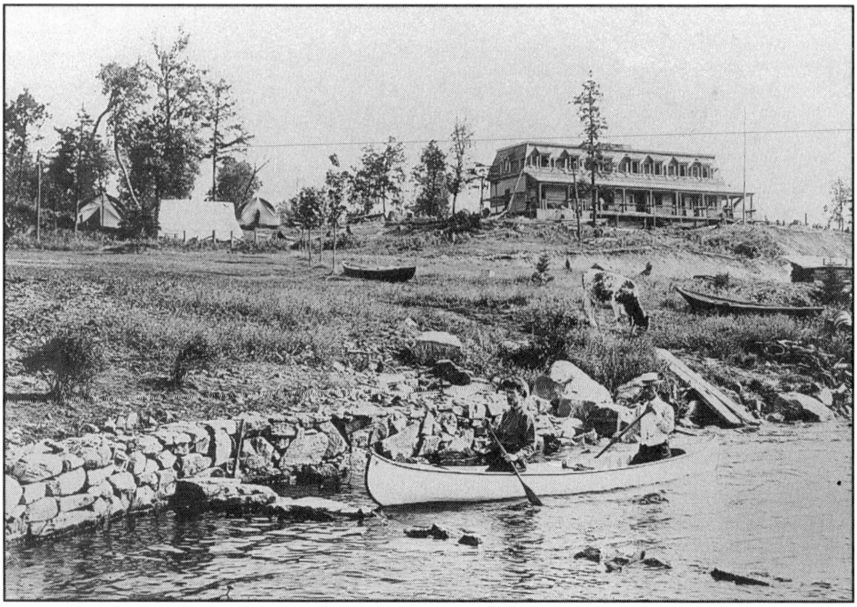

The first and only winterized section of the Highland Inn, Cache Lake, Algonquin Park, constructed in 1908 by the Grand Trunk Railway. *Courtesy: Algonquin Park Museum.*

Guests on the verandah of the Highland Inn, about 1910. Typically, women amused themselves around the lodges while their menfolk fished. *Courtesy: Algonquin Park Museum.*

behind a facade of log cabin rusticity. Few of the hotel and lodge guests of the Grand Trunk establishments or their competitors – Hotel Algonquin (1908) and Mowat Lodge (1913), on Joe and Cache Lakes respectively – came to experience the true wildness of the Algonquin interior. Typically, the men were content to paddle short distances to fish, while the women amused themselves around the lodges. Each evening, guests would end their day suitably attired for formal dining. This pleasant amalgam of nature and civilization proved to be extremely popular, since all the hotels and lodges were operating to capacity by 1913. The Highland Inn even operated year-round and initiated the first winter use of Algonquin Park by recreationists.

George Bartlett basked in the success of his park's recreation boom. He reported that, in contrast to the several dozen American tourists who had struggled into the park each year prior to the coming of the railway, now "hundreds of visitors from Canada, the United States, Great Britain, and other countries" annually visited Algonquin.[45] The extensive advertising campaign undertaken by the Grand Trunk Railway played no small part in drawing tourists, as did the publication of Joseph Adams's widely read *Ten Thousand Miles Through Canada* (1912), a chapter of which described the author's sojourn in the park in 1910. Outdoor magazines drew considerable attention to the superb angling to be found there. In 1914, Superintendent Bartlett boasted that "nearly all the prizes offered by sporting journals won this year were taken by fish from Algonquin Park."[46] Ironically, by this time some of the lakes near the hotels were already being overfished. "The lakes most frequented by the tourist are kept stocked annually," Bartlett reported in 1919. "This year we put in here something like one hundred thousand salmon trout fry, and as many small-mouthed bass ... also a car of mature bass."[47] Revenues from fishing licences had reached $1,782 by 1913 and doubled over the next decade,[48] furnishing striking testimony to the growth of park usage in the last years of Bartlett's rule. The war temporarily set back tourism, but once hostilities had ceased, the lodges were soon turning away guests again.

No less successful than the early hotels and lodges in drawing tourists to Algonquin were the private youth camps. Fanny L. Case, an educator from Rochester, New York, established the first one – Northway Lodge camp for girls, in 1908, on Cache Lake. By 1915, four boys camps, associated with various schools or military academies in the United States, had also moved to the park. Eventually, Taylor Statten founded the first Canadian youth camps in Algonquin; Ahmek for boys in 1921 and Wapomeo for girls in 1924. Both achieved international renown for being in the van of camping theory and practice.

In contrast to the resort development taking place in both Rondeau and Algonquin, Quetico Provincial Park remained the wilderness preserve of a few hundred American sport fishermen and canoe trippers. "There were two Canadian travellers only in the Park this year," reported Superintendent A.J. McDonald in 1915.[49] Tourist access from the Canadian side, complained

Hugh McDonald, superintendent from 1917 to 1925, was virtually impossible, "principally because the Canadian National Railway [CNR] through trains were not scheduled to stop at Kawene, the chief point of entrance on this side. The result is that the moneys spent by ... tourists is spent with American merchants instead of Canadians, as we would desire."[50] This complaint would become a recurring one in the decades ahead. Recreational development was further curtailed by the decision not to permit leaseholders into Quetico, since department officials feared that cottages would increase the fire danger and complicate their efforts to establish efficient game protection.[51] Thus, with recreation relegated to secondary importance at Quetico, timber and game conservation remained the primary park objectives.

The 1920s and 1930s: Utilitarianism and Austerity Combined

In February 1924, Ontario Provincial Treasurer W.H. Price shocked Ontarians by announcing that the province faced a staggering and unprecedented deficit of over $15 million. The government of Howard Ferguson denied responsibility, of course, and blamed the financial mess on E.C. Drury's recently defeated Farmer-Labour government. There had in fact been deficits since 1918, and they would continue until 1927, when the province finally achieved its first surplus in a decade, as new liquor revenues flooded in following the end of prohibition. In the mid-1920s, then, austerity was the order of the day. Within this context, Deputy Minister Walter Cain sought to tighten his control over provincial park expenditures and development. His efforts were also part of a trend toward centralization, as Queen's Park entered the era of the efficiency expert and the application of business methods to government.[52] Under these conditions, park superintendents lost a considerable measure of independence. They were now ordered to shelve capital projects and to conjure up new revenue-production schemes, so as to reduce their operating deficits. "The department's position," Cain informed George Goldworthy, superintendent of Rondeau from 1913 to 1927, "is to administer the affairs of the Park with the strictest economy possible ... [It] is of primary importance at the present time that ways and means should be devised whereby the revenue from the various sources in the Park may be adequately increased."[53]

Goldworthy offered few proposals, beyond resurrecting the stale idea of constructing "a modern summer hotel" in Rondeau. His colleague in Algonquin, John Millar, on the other hand, bubbled over with recommendations to open his park to a wide array of commercial endeavours. In 1922, he had already initiated the practice of having his rangers produce maple syrup for sale to tourists. Now he proposed to sell licences to those wishing to graze livestock in the park, to operate canoe liveries and riding stables, and to extract gravel and sphagnum moss. Millar also wanted to license pedlars, egg collectors, and taxidermists, and to establish "retail stores of every description," including a pool hall and bowling alley.[54] Even the revenue-hungry Department of Lands and Forests found many of these recommendations unpalatable. Rather than take up Millar's proposals, the department cut costs by reducing staff and froze the level of expenditures in the park. Capital projects were severely curtailed, until by 1927–28 the department was spending a paltry $89.50 on capital development in Algonquin.[55]

The main thrust of the department's search for revenues involved promoting recreation and tourism in the parks, with the emphasis on attracting leaseholders to Rondeau and Algonquin. To this end, the department placed impressive exhibits at the Canadian National Exhibition in Toronto and at other regional fairs. The campaign to attract leaseholders bore fruit. From 1923 to 1928, two new lodges, four more youth camps, and dozens of cottages appeared in Algonquin. At Rondeau, the number of cottages grew from 60 in 1921 to 268 in 1931, with Americans holding about 45 percent of the leases by the end of the decade. Automobile tenting also became popular; by the late 1920s, an average of 65 camping groups could be found in Rondeau each day during the summer. A census of automobile traffic over a ten-day period in July 1929 revealed that some 10,087 cars entered the park, some 25 percent of which carried out-of-province licence plates. During July and August, about 3,000 people could be found in the park on weekdays and 10,000 per day on weekends. Special events, such as the Howard Councillors–United Farmers of Ontario picnic in late August each year, attracted as many as 30,000 people to the Rondeau peninsula.[56]

The park policy of the mid-1920s, which combined retrenchment with the promotion of dollar-producing recreation activities, may have succeeded from the provincial treasurer's point of view, but it also gave rise to unanticipated and not altogether desirable results. The policy was little short of a disaster for Rondeau. By 1927, complaints about deteriorating conditions in the park prompted Lands and Forests Minister William Finlayson to assign Ralph Carman, a professional forester, to investigate the problem. Carman's report gave Finlayson a shock. Virtually every government building and facility required repairs. Benches, tables, wastebaskets, and signs were few and far between. An inadequate road system and badly located services and buildings created unnecessary traffic flow and parking problems. Vandalism, motor vehicle and liquor violations went largely unchecked. Even the waterfowl hunting regulations had not been strictly enforced for years, and game poaching was common. Carman's report laid bare the fact that Rondeau's problems were rooted in a long tradition of ad hoc decision making, a paucity of planning, and insufficient funding. Beyond the exposé of past sins, Carman's report included a detailed five-year development plan for the park, which took into consideration such critical interrelationships as the location of buildings and services, cottage areas, camping and picnic grounds, roads, and parking lots.[57]

Impressed by Carman's proposals and determined to restore order at Rondeau, Finlayson appointed him superintendent in 1928. With a mandate for reform and an increased budget, Carman reversed the administrative rot, albeit only temporarily. He expanded the park staff and hired a motorcycle-patrol officer to enforce the regulations. As unsightly old frame buildings came down, the superintendent constructed a new two-storey workshop, expanded the pavilion, and renovated the wharf, restaurant, aviary, and wildlife enclosures. The campgrounds were expanded and provided with toilets, water, and picnic benches. Carman also implemented a road-maintenance schedule, laid out two new parking areas, and launched a five-year road building program. Had he been given full rein, Carman would have introduced a variety of new concessions, including a publicly owned hotel, a golf course, tennis and lawn bowling, and an automobile service station. As it happened, his superiors vetoed all these proposals, although he did succeed in getting a miniature golf course and shuffleboard operation.[58]

Ralph Carman's star declined as quickly as it had risen. In August 1933, disgruntled leaseholders met and voted nonconfidence in the superintendent. This unprecedented cottagers' revolt had various causes. Some leaseholders with memories of the lax administration of the mid-1920s resented Carman's no-nonsense regime, especially the rigorous enforcement of sanitation and building regulations, and the crackdown on speeding, parking, and liquor violations. Others bristled at the superintendent's talk of seeking a ban on waterfowl hunting. Much of the discontent was not of Carman's making, but rather the consequence of reductions in services, following new budget cutbacks determined in Toronto. When dusty roads went unoiled and streets unlighted, some leaseholders had no qualms about venting their anger on the superintendent. Carman's fate was sealed by the cottagers' actions.[59] Early in 1934, the department removed him from the park.

Carman's loss did not augur well for Rondeau, which once again started on a downhill course. The Liberal government of Mitch Hepburn, which assumed power in 1934, stiffened the Conservatives' austerity program and demanded that the new superintendent, Lloyd McLaren, emphasize revenue production above all else. The new government laid off park personnel, vetoed all capital expenditure, and slashed ordinary expenditures by two-thirds. All the regular maintenance schedules and improvement programs introduced by Carman were abandoned. Under these conditions, Rondeau Park actually turned a profit in 1935 for the first and only time in its history. This was "use and profit" with a vengeance.[60]

Arguably, the most insidious consequence of the park policy of the 1920s and 1930s was the tendency to manage and develop the parks to suit the interests of the leaseholders. Cottagers organized quickly and requested services and facilities. In 1922, for instance, the leaseholders at Rondeau succeeded in obtaining major street improvements in their subdivisions, the introduction of hydro-electricity, a modern icehouse, and a gas station operated by one of their own on the right of way in front of his cottage.[61] The leaseholders in the parks proved to be a tenacious lot and expected full value for their annual rental fees, a consideration that was not fully appreciated by the Lands and Forests officials who had invited them into the park in the first place.

Nowhere was the temptation to operate and develop parks as the private preserves of the leaseholders more powerful than in the several commission parks which, denied provincial subsidies, perforce had to balance their books. At Burlington Beach, in particular, the cottagers dominated events so completely that the park became an urban municipality in virtually every respect. Officials like Howard Ferguson and Walter Cain declared the intensive development of the beach to be "wonderful work," since the one-time "unsightly, barren waste" had been transformed into a beautiful "summer rendezvous," and all without cost to the province.[62] Colonel J.J. Grafton, the public-spirited Hamilton merchant who served as the unpaid chairman of the commission from 1910 to 1928, took enormous pride in his accomplishments. With the revenues raised through rentals, taxes, and land sales (leaseholders were permitted to purchase their properties after 1910), he had provided the residents with every urban service, including a water system, fire and police protection, electric lighting, paved boulevards and sidewalks, a pavilion, a restaurant, an esplanade, and even a school with two teachers for seventy-five children. By 1917, there were 540 cottages on the beach, about one-fifth of them serving as permanent homes for 800 people. During the summer months, the resort population exploded to over 6,000 residents and 10-20,000 day users.

Over the course of the 1920s, the social structure of the beach community changed dramatically. Affluent Hamiltonians abandoned the resort, when it became increasingly congested and prone to water, air, and noise pollution. As early as 1918, the beach road had become a main thoroughfare between Toronto and the Niagara peninsula; 4,000 cars and trucks passed through the resort daily or sat idling in line-ups caused by the operation of the swing bridge over the Burlington Canal. As the wealthy departed, Hamiltonians of lesser means took over the area, and more and more of them purchased the aging cottages as permanent homes. By the end of the decade, the beach had taken on a seedy appearance. The year-round population by then consisted of 2,600 people, "the large majority of whom," one official noted, "are workingmen and their families, who are dependent on work they receive from the industrial plants of Hamilton and vicinity, and others of small or no means whatever."[63] When the Depression struck, the beach commission found itself in dire financial straits, unable to cope with demands for relief by the unemployed and their families. Finally, in November 1935, to help to solve the problems of the area, the cabinet transferred control of the beach from Lands and Forests to the Department of Municipal Affairs. As a public park and tourist resort, the once-renowned Burlington Beach no longer counted.

Regrettably, both Long Point and Presqu'ile Parks headed down the same path from their very beginning. The first major decision taken by the Long

Point Commission, for instance, was to subdivide the park for cottages; only the lack of road access delayed growth until the end of the 1920s. In 1926, Premier Ferguson announced that in order "to throw this Park open not only to the local people, but to ... thousands of tourists," the province would absorb the cost of constructing an access road.[64] In the decades following, various commissioners pursued cottage development with a single-mindedness that defied the conservationist intent of the original legislation. After the Second World War, so little land remained for public use that the original Long Point Park had to be abandoned and a new provincial park created on adjacent property.

Only the great size of Presqu'ile Point Provincial Park saved it from a similar fate; but here, too, the commissioners developed and managed the area largely to suit the leaseholders, who voiced strong opposition to spending money derived from property taxes on facilities for the general public. When the commissioners constructed a golf course and club house during 1922–23, they did so "as an advertising scheme," which they expected would "do a lot in bringing settlers to Presqu'ile."[65] Private individuals leased and operated the course for the park commission. Similarly, local sportsmen erected a clubhouse and administered the fall duck shoot. Inexorably, the summer community took on all the features of an urban centre with small stores, a school, and a church. The luxury Presqu'ile Summer Hotel continued to serve as the social centre for park residents. A close-knit sense of community naturally developed among those fortunate enough to be a part of this exclusive recreational scene.

The social composition of the cottage communities in the commission parks very clearly reflected the growth of restrictions on access to these ostensibly public areas. During the 1920s, the cottagers began to control access on the basis of race, colour, and creed. "It has been the steady policy of the Park Commission ever since its organization," the secretary of the Long Point Commission reminded the cottagers in October 1941, "to prevent any infiltration of Jewish lease holders, or for that matter any others, who for any reason, either political or religious, would be unable to unite in the general idea of a congenial gathering for the summer months." Similarly, at Rondeau, with its high number of American leaseholders, the cottage association forbade its members to lease to non-whites and non-Christians. Black residents of Kent County rarely used Rondeau's beaches and congregated instead across the bay at Shrewsbury.[66] Discrimination and bigotry, of course, were not new phenomena in Canada or in Ontario; they were deep-rooted tendencies that had simply become more pronounced following the arrival of hundreds of thousands of immigrants from central and southern Europe between 1896 and 1929.

Challenging the Primacy of Utility and Profit in "The Quetico"

Over three decades of unplanned growth and development, shaped primarily by considerations of utility and profit, unleashed many enduring conflicts and problems in Ontario's provincial parks. For one thing, the harvesting of timber and wildlife, and the promotion of resource-consumptive recreational uses had been undertaken with few questions asked as to their long-term effects on natural areas and scenic landscapes. Beginning in the late 1920s, recreational and preservationist interests within the conservationist movement emerged to ask such questions and to jostle the "utilitarian" old guard, demanding a more important role in the shaping of management policies for Algonquin and Quetico parks.

The first conservation group to object to the extreme utilitarian emphasis in park management policy appeared in 1928 in Minnesota. This was the Quetico-Superior Council (QSC), an organization dedicated to the protection of recreational and wilderness values in the area of the Rainy Lake watershed, a vast region embracing some 3.8 million hectares of lake-spangled and forested land, lying on both sides of the Ontario-Minnesota border. It stretches from Rainy Lake on the west to Lake Superior on the east, and includes both Quetico Provincial Park and Superior National Forest. Edward W. Backus, the imperious Minnesota timber baron, who controlled much of the forest products industries on the watershed, provoked the conservationists into action by unveiling a huge industrial scheme to construct a series of dams in the boundary waters from Fort Frances to the eastern side of Quetico Park. If completed, the dams would raise water levels in the border lakes by at least 4.6 metres and as much as 24 metres, with incalculable damage to the scenic and recreational qualities of the area.[67]

Backus's industrial vision for Quetico-Superior raised the ire of conservationists in the United States, where wilderness protection had already emerged as a national political issue. To wild-country enthusiasts in the American Midwest, Quetico-Superior had great symbolic value as "the last of the North Woods," the only nationally owned lake country of its kind, and a place unrivalled for canoeing in primitive surroundings.[68] Those who appreciated the significance of the region resolved to block Backus at every turn and to argue their case before the International Joint Commission, which opened public hearings on the Backus plan – the Rainy Lake Reference – in 1925. Confidence surged in conservationist ranks in 1926 when, after a bitter struggle against other development interests, three roadless areas, encompassing some 260,000 hectares of exceptional canoe country were set aside in the Superior National Forest, with logging prohibited in shoreline reserves along all waterways and portages.

The conservationists realized that in order to defeat Backus, they would have to fashion an alternative plan for the Rainy Lake watershed. This task fell largely upon Ernest C. Oberholtzer, a Harvard-trained landscape architect, self-educated naturalist, and woodsman, who lived on an island in Rainy Lake. He received advice and encouragement from a small group of wildland enthusiasts, including Sewell T. Tyng, an influential Wall Street lawyer; officials of the Izaac Walton League in Chicago; and a dozen young Minneapolis professionals, mainly lawyers such as Frank Hubachek, Charles S. Kelly, and Fred Winston. In June 1927, one Ontarian joined the group – Arthur Hawkes of Toronto, the one-time publicity agent for the Canadian Northern Railway who, in 1909, had been instrumental in the establishment of the Quetico Forest Reserve.

In November 1927, Oberholtzer completed his plan for the Rainy Lake watershed. He proposed a multiple-use program with the primary emphasis on wilderness recreation and scenic preservation. "The key note of the plan [was] a treaty between the Dominion of Canada and the United States" that would secure four main objectives throughout the watershed: (1) that all shorelines be reserved from logging, flooding, or other form of exploitation; (2) "that all the hinterlands" beyond the shoreline reserves "be devoted to practical forestry for economic purposes"; (3) "that all fish and game be regulated for maximum productivity"; and (4) that the watershed be administered by an international commission, made up of Canadian and American forestry, park, and wildlife officials. Oberholtzer considered that these four objectives should be entrenched in a treaty in order to ensure permanent protection.[69]

Oberholtzer and his associates had to be taken seriously; their remarkable plan could not be dismissed as the product of unrealistic, preservationist thinking. On the contrary, these conservationists accepted the fact that the "main economic destiny" of the region would be timber production. Still, they were calling for a reworking of the wise-use equation; they demanded that, along the waterways of Quetico-Superior, primacy be given to recreation and scenic protection rather than to timber extraction.

Having completed the conceptual stage of their campaign to stop Backus, the conservationists moved into the second, organizational phase of their work. On 27 January 1928, they founded the Quetico-Superior Council, "an international organization associated with the Izaac Walton League of America for the sole purpose of obtaining, with the consent of the Province of Ontario, a treaty ... to protect ... the Rainy Lake watershed."[70] In the United States, the QSC received an enthusiastic public reception, which climaxed with the passage through Congress of the Shipstead-Nolan Act in 1930. This legislation placed huge obstacles before the Backus scheme by establishing a 122-metre shoreline reserve policy on all federally owned property in the boundary waters area and by requiring congressional approval for each dam project.

When first presented with the QSC plan in November 1927, the Ontario minister of lands and forests, William Finlayson, promised to cooperate with American federal and state authorities to harmonize management policies in the watershed. Although he saw much merit in the QSC proposals, there were two features of the program that he found unacceptable. He rejected both the treaty aspect of the Oberholtzer scheme and the idea of an international commission to administer the region. No provincial government, whether Conservative or Liberal, would agree to a treaty that carried with it the prospect of federal control over a vast, resource-rich expanse of provincially owned Crown land. Unfamiliar with dominion-provincial relations in Canada and influenced by American centralist biases, the QSC leaders failed to plumb the depths of the Ontario government's hostility to the idea of a treaty. As a result, Oberholtzer naïvely proceeded in February 1928 to invite the province to commence negotiations with the American and dominion governments for a watershed agreement. The invitation was brusquely declined.[71]

The American conservationists had difficulty in understanding why their cause generated so little public interest in Ontario. Few newspapers covered the QSC program, a situation that Oberholtzer attributed to "a conspiracy of silence."[72] Actually, Ontario's apathy was due, not to a Backus-inspired conspiracy, but rather to a general lack of knowledge about the Rainy Lake watershed. Few southern Ontarians visited distant Quetico Provincial Park, since there were no cottages, camps, or resorts to attract them and access remained difficult. Most visitors to Quetico were Americans, who entered the park from Minnesota. Of the 1,234 recorded visitors in 1930, a mere half dozen identified themselves as Canadians. The journalist and outdoorsman, Gregory Clark, of the *Toronto Daily Star*, added another reason for the public's indifference to the QSC program: "You cannot expect from the Canadian public," he wrote to Oberholtzer, "anything like the response ... in the United States because ... you have suffered and lost so much of your wilderness and we are merely in the process of losing it."[73] Given the absence of indigenous political pressure in Ontario, no matter how hard they tried during the 1930s, the American conservationists could not budge either the Henry Conservatives or the Hepburn Liberals on the treaty question.

Meanwhile, Edward Backus had fallen on hard times, and in November 1931 his Minnesota and Ontario Paper Company went into receivership. Much to the chagrin of the conservationists, the receivers continued to pursue a modified version of Backus's original design for the watershed. Only in 1934 was the issue resolved when, after nine years of hearings and engineering studies, the International Joint Commission ruled against the plan to dam the lakes along the boundary waters between Quetico Provincial Park and the Superior National Forest.[74]

Striking a Balance between Utility and Protection in Algonquin: Frank A. MacDougall, the "Flying Superintendent"

As the QSC carried on its campaign after 1927, conservationists and recreationists in southern Ontario also began to demand that considerations other than the purely utilitarian be weighed more heavily in management decisions affecting Algonquin Park. Recreationists first flexed their collective muscles in 1929, upon learning that the McCrae Lumber Company had received authorization to log in Canisbay Township, the tourist centre of the park. Members of the Cache Lake Leaseholders Association, haunted by the spectre of woodsmen laying waste to the scenery near their cottages, orchestrated an effective public protest in the Toronto press. Lands and Forests Minister Finlayson defused the controversy in 1930 by withdrawing from the McCrae limit a 30.5-metre scenic reservation around the shoreline of Cache Lake.[75]

Finlayson inadvertently created another lively controversy in 1930 when he announced, without any public consultation, that a highway would be constructed as a relief project from Huntsville to Whitney through the southern sector of Algonquin. Cottagers denounced the project, claiming that an army of motorists would destroy the beauty and tranquility of the park. Naturalist clubs and sportsmen's associations, led by the Ontario Federation of Anglers, added to the uproar by arguing that the road and its users would have a detrimental impact on fish and game stocks. Startled by the intensity of the opposition, Finlayson dropped the highway proposal. Some of his cabinet colleagues, irritated by the fact that Algonquin was becoming "the problem child of government," half seriously mooted the question of abolishing the park altogether.[76]

Under the circumstances, Finlayson concluded that the traditionally ill-trained, politically appointed superintendent of bygone years could not provide the quality of leadership required in these complicated times. He decided, therefore, to appoint to the superintendency a university-trained professional forester with experience in resource planning and management. Finlayson first selected J.H. McDonald, the district forester in Pembroke, but he died prematurely on New Year's Day 1931, after a mere four months in the post. Again Finlayson scanned the ranks of his department and eventually settled on the thirty-five-year-old district forester at Sault Ste. Marie, a craggy-faced, steely-eyed bush pilot named Frank A. MacDougall.

Born in Toronto in 1896 and raised in Carleton Place, MacDougall served in the artillery in France during World War I. He entered the University of Toronto's Forestry School in 1919, graduated in 1923, and embarked upon a career in the Department of Lands and Forests. As district forester in Sault Ste. Marie after 1924, he distinguished himself as a first-rate field administrator. He impressed his superiors by promoting reforestation on a major scale near Thessalon, in what became the Kirkwood Forest Management Unit. It was in the Sault, the home base of the Ontario Provincial Air Service, that MacDougall acquired his pilot's licence. Frank MacDougall could not be described as an ordinary individual. He possessed an astonishing variety of skills and interests. Respected as an expert woodsman, angler, and hunter, he was also something of a scholar and blessed with a photographic memory. His intellectual interests ranged from history to natural resource management. His choice of hobbies was no less eclectic; among other things he was noted as a maker and player of violins, a photographer, carpenter, gardener, and cook. Most importantly, MacDougall was admired for his exceptional administrative and leadership qualities; few doubted his integrity, judgement, or fairness, and his staff regarded him with an esteem that sometimes bordered on awe.[77]

MacDougall's impact on Algonquin was instantaneous. Before he accepted the post, he insisted on changes in the administrative structure of the park. Prior to his arrival, two distinct ranging staffs worked in Algonquin, the park rangers reporting to the superintendent, and the fire rangers to the district forester in Pembroke. MacDougall insisted that he be given "one-man control," with both groups of rangers falling under his authority. He immediately put an end to the distinction between fire and park rangers and made each man responsible for all facets of park work. The reorganization resulted in the staff being pared by some thirty men, with a substantial $6,000 reduction in operating expenditures. The fact that MacDougall accomplished these economies without a corresponding loss in the effectiveness of the park administration only served to ingratiate him with his superiors in Toronto. Many of the men released from duty were actually elderly political hangers-on, ripe for superannuation. "These old men are constantly sick," he had reported, "and unable to do their share."[78]

When he accepted the superintendency, MacDougall also insisted that he be provided with an aircraft. With responsibility for such a vast, roadless area, he deemed air transportation to be essential for fire and game protection, routine inspections, and emergencies. Convinced by such arguments, Finlayson and Cain provided MacDougall with a three-seat Fairchild KR-34 biplane in July 1931. The airplane soon became a fundamental tool of park management. For the first time, the superintendent could regularly inspect his widely scattered rangers; he covered distances in a few hours that had taken his predecessors days or weeks to travel by canoe. The Fairchild, in combination with the construction of a new steel fire tower system, also vastly improved the fire protection service in the park. Soon nicknamed the "Flying Superintendent," MacDougall also became the scourge of poachers, especially in the winter, when their activities were easily detected in the snow.

Once these preliminary administrative matters had been resolved, MacDougall turned to the task of preparing a long-term plan for the park. For eight months he familiarized himself with his domain; then, in the autumn of 1931, he drafted his development program for Algonquin, which laid out the policies he would pursue in the years ahead.[79] The most critical element in MacDougall's plans was his reconfirmation of a policy first introduced by George Bartlett at the turn of the century: to maintain the interior of Algonquin "for all time in a state of wilderness." In practice, this meant no public roads and no cottage or lodge development in the park interior. Leaseholders were to be restricted to lakes near railway lines or a highway, if such a project came to fruition. MacDougall was very annoyed when he learned that a few cottage leases on Opeongo Lake, near the centre of the park, had recently been granted.

The second element of his program involved placing more emphasis on the recreational potential of Algonquin; MacDougall envisioned the park as a year-round tourist mecca. Tourists generated revenues, and that remained the priority in the Department of Lands and Forests, especially as the Depression deepened. To attract tourists, however, the park required improved hotel and lodge accommodations and better transportation facilities than the inadequate train service then being provided by the Canadian National Railway. In MacDougall's estimation, the public would be best served by the construction of a road across the southern fringe of Algonquin. Those who persisted "in the idea that a highway will spoil the Park," he wrote, were looking at matters from "a selfish view-point."

Aware of the potential for conflict between loggers and recreationists, particularly if the new highway were constructed, the superintendent proposed policies similar both to those being advocated for the Rainy Lake watershed by the Quetico-Superior Council and to those already in place in the Shipstead-Nolan area of the Superior National Forest. MacDougall recommended that as timber licences came up for renewal, clauses be inserted to establish scenic no-cut reserves along shorelines and portages of major canoe routes and along transportation corridors. Such a policy would give priority to recreationists, not to the timber operators. The licence holders, added the superintendent, should be reimbursed for the areas withdrawn from logging.

When it came to managing the forest, fish, and wildlife in Algonquin Park, Frank MacDougall promised a major shift of direction toward administering the park on a more scientific basis. He was the first superintendent to understand that the sound management and conservation of natural resources had to be based on systematic and scientific research. To accomplish the necessary field work, he recommended that foresters and biologists be added to the park staff. Concerned that many lakes were being overfished, MacDougall believed that first priority should be given to the initiation of an annual creel census and the preparation of a fish management program. In fact, the superintendent had already made tentative arrangements with the Department of Game and Fisheries to undertake fish studies across Algonquin during 1932, as a preliminary step to shaping a restocking policy. Similarly, he asked the University of Toronto Forestry School field camp, located in Achray, to help in the preparation of a forest management program by requiring the students to develop a silvicultural research plan as part of their curriculum.

Such, then, was MacDougall's master plan for Algonquin Park. It reflected some of the most advanced thinking in North American land-use planning. In only one major respect did he later modify his scheme, by adding what might be called a "preservationist" element. If policy must be changed, he asserted in

1934, "it would seem wise to give consideration to the viewpoint of the National Parks of the United States," which emphasized scenic and wildlife protection, recreation and visitor education, rather than the exploitation of natural resources.[80] Accordingly, MacDougall proposed a radical idea for the times; that nature sanctuaries be set up in the park to function as ecological benchmarks. He had borrowed the idea from the first publication of the newly formed Federation of Ontario Naturalists, a pamphlet entitled *Sanctuaries and the Preservation of Wildlife in Ontario* (1934). In all probability, it was Professor J.R. Dymond, a biologist at the University of Toronto, a frequent visitor to the park, and a founder of the Federation of Ontario Naturalists, who brought the pamphlet to MacDougall's attention and convinced him of its merits.

By championing a nature reserve policy for Algonquin Park, MacDougall revealed that he had advanced well beyond utilitarian, conservationist thinking. "In most civilized countries today," explained the FON booklet, "sanctuaries are being set aside for the preservation of representative samples of the natural conditions, including the plants and animals, characteristic of those countries. This movement for the preservation of nature as a whole has important points of difference from the 'conservation movement' as ordinarily understood." Since the nineteenth century, that movement had been "frankly based on utilitarian motives." The wise-use conservation impulse was still "deserving of support," argued the FON, "but there is real danger that over-emphasis upon the conservation of a particular form may prove detrimental to the preservation of nature as a whole ... The need for nature preservation does not depend only on the economic value of the natural life usually considered worthy of consideration."[81]

Superintendent MacDougall did not find the going easy as he endeavoured to implement his policies. The Depression conditioned his every activity. Government-wide austerity forced the postponement of the fish studies scheduled for 1932 by the Department of Game and Fisheries. Three years later, financial exigency required the University of Toronto to terminate its field camp at Achray before the students had completed a silvicultural plan for the park. By October 1933, budget cutbacks drove the usually imperturbable Frank MacDougall to protest that he had been unable to provide an adequate "degree of protection and supervision" with the funds available.[82]

As MacDougall gingerly steered his way through the financial straits, political uncertainty further complicated his life. In June 1934, the Conservative administration of George Henry went down to defeat at the hands of the Liberals led by the flamboyant Mitchell F. Hepburn. Heads soon rolled throughout the Ontario public service. In the Department of Lands and Forests, the pioneer forester Edmund Zavitz was replaced as deputy minister by Frederick Noad, a one-time Toronto journalist with no particular qualifications for the job. Described as a "small insignificant-looking man with a bitter tongue," Noad himself would be sacked in 1935; but before he went, he unleashed a veritable reign of terror upon the DLF. He fired fourteen of forty-one district and assistant district foresters and reassigned all but eight senior officers.[83] Frank MacDougall survived the Liberal purge – in spite of the fact that he made no attempt to pander to his new political masters. On the contrary, he defended his programs and stoutly resisted those who thought of replacing his park staff with political appointments. Evidently, Noad and others in the Liberal regime were impressed by MacDougall's forthright style and his carefully considered policy proposals.

Notwithstanding economic and political difficulties, MacDougall succeeded in implementing many aspects of his master plan for Algonquin. He kept the park interior free of leaseholders by seeing to it that the province issued no more leases on Opeongo or other lakes outside the zones he designated for cottages and resorts. With the construction of Highway 60 through the southern fringe of the park, MacDougall also realized his objective of making Algonquin a major tourist destination. The road development easily stands as the single most important event of his superintendency, if not of the park's history. While MacDougall had been an outspoken proponent of the highway from the beginning, the decision to begin construction in 1933 was primarily shaped by the news that the Canadian National Railway (CNR) was going to abandon its southern park line. That same year – the worst tourist season of the 1930s – the CNR even closed the once-renowned Highland Inn. Threatened with the loss of their only means of access to Algonquin, the leaseholders, previously in the forefront of the antiroad movement, reversed their position on the highway issue. They petitioned William Finlayson, whom they had reviled in 1930 for proposing to build the highway, and requested him to resurrect the project. He acted swiftly. Road surveys were under way by July, with actual construction beginning in October, as a relief project. Although there was no alternative to a highway, once the CNR closed its line, the Ontario Federation of Anglers, boasting some fifty affiliated local associations with a combined membership of about 10,000 people, continued to oppose road development. Since "the primary reason for setting up the park was to provide a fish and game sanctuary," the anglers argued, they did not favour "widening the park's purpose as a playground."[84] On this occasion, however, the antiroad forces did not prevail.

In July 1935, considerable numbers of automobiles were able to enter Algonquin from Huntsville on the partially completed highway. By summer's end, a total of 1,600 vehicles had made an excursion into the park. Even in 1935, the still incomplete road had already "changed the character of the Park," according to MacDougall. Until then, park users had been relatively few in number and had come to Algonquin for extended visits at a cottage, lodge, or children's camp. Now these traditional visitors were being outnumbered by a new breed of user, the middle-class motorist and his family, who entered the park to view the scenery and wildlife, to picnic and to swim, or to tent overnight

Frank A. MacDougall (right), the legendary "flying superintendent" of Algonquin Park (1931–41), seen here with P.O. Rhynas at Lake of Two Rivers, Algonquin Park. *Courtesy: Ministry of Natural Resources.*

The unpaved Highway 60 reached Algonquin Park headquarters at Cache Lake in 1936. Construction began in 1933 after the CNR abandoned its southern park line. Here, one automobile pulls another out of the mud. *Courtesy: Algonquin Park Museum.*

at a roadside lake. The number of tourists more than doubled in 1936, when the highway reached park headquarters at Cache Lake, and doubled again within two years. The children's camps soon boasted of record enrolments – over 700 youngsters in 1935. Lodges were also filled to capacity, in spite of the depression conditions. To meet growing demand for accommodation, the construction of Killarney Lodge began at the Lake of Two Rivers in 1935, and the following year, new leases were issued for a boys camp and tourist lodge on Tea Lake. Essentially, the highway dictated that henceforth, recreation would no longer be a mere by-product of conservation in Algonquin Provincial Park.[85]

While Frank MacDougall enthusiastically promoted the idea of Algonquin Park as "a people's playground," he harbored no illusions about the serious road-related difficulties that loomed ahead. He knew the road had the potential for creating congestion, user conflicts, and scenic degradation, unless he took strong action. Subsequently, as he had indicated in 1931, MacDougall moved swiftly to protect aesthetic values along the highway corridor by establishing a scenic, no-logging reserve along its length. To minimize congestion and conflict between cottagers and automobile campers, he constructed the first large 14-hectare campground on the Lake of Two Rivers, well away from the main leasehold lakes. The campground was in full operation by 1938.[86]

MacDougall anticipated correctly that one of the most serious repercussions of the new highway would be heightened tensions between loggers and recreationists. The potential for a clash increased dramatically as the number of motorists, campers, and canoe trippers grew at the same time as the wood products industry emerged from the economic doldrums of 1932–33, when only one company had operated in Algonquin. By 1934–35, fourteen licence holders, employing some 1,500 men were again active in the bush.[87]

In keeping with his 1931 plan, MacDougall endeavoured to prevent a clash between loggers and tourists by gradually amending timber licences, but in a way that would not have a negative economic impact on the region's forest products industries. "It is a difficult question to reconcile logging operations to fishing and recreation," he observed. "It will take decades of adjustment and will be a process of evolution to be carried out as the old licences lapse."[88] The first licence modifications were completed in 1934, in order to establish scenic reserves along Highway 60 and several popular canoe routes. By 1938 shoreline reserves had been placed on some thirty-nine lakes, as well as their connecting rivers and portages.[89]

As it turned out, MacDougall's gradualist approach proved insufficient to prevent the emergence of an antilogging protest. Canoe trippers who ventured away from the well-travelled routes to explore the interior of the park frequently came into contact with unrestricted bush operations. There were also instances when the timber operators deliberately encroached upon the no-cut reserves. MacDougall burned with anger when these infractions occurred. "There are very few accidental trespasses," he reported. "It is quite discouraging and wasted effort to work for such reservations and then ... have a 100-year setback to the scenic attractions of a Park."[90] Evidently, many others agreed and, in the late summer of 1938, the Federation of Ontario Naturalists lashed out at the Department of Lands and Forests, charging that Algonquin Park "was being ruined for all time by present lumbering activities." Suddenly, for the first time, influential voices began to ask why any commercial logging at all should be permitted in the park.[91]

The idea of a logging ban was anathema to a forester like Frank MacDougall. From his study of the multiple-use policies applied by the United States Forest Service, he believed that logging, recreation, and nature conservation could coexist in an area the size of Algonquin. Multiple-use doctrine held that "where two or more ... main uses can be served at the same time on the same area they are carried forward side by side ... Whenever two of these uses come into conflict, some authority determines which is likely to render the greater public service ... On principle [sic] areas of the national forests recreation is an incidental use; on some it is a paramount use; on a few it becomes the exclusive use."[92]

In the face of the public outcry against logging in Algonquin, MacDougall recognized that he must make explicit the philosophy that had been shaping his park policies since 1931. "Multiple land use is a new desire for conservationists," he explained. "In Algonquin Park there is one of the few areas in North America where land is being so used. The solution of the problems here will be of benefit to the rest of Ontario."[93] Based on MacDougall's recommendations, all timber licensees were informed, in June 1939, of a new standard shoreline protection policy, designed "to establish a just and fair balance between the interests of the lumberman and the tourist." Henceforth, scenic preservation would be given priority over timber extraction as the first principle of multiple use in Algonquin. Park regulations now decreed that no timber could be cut "within three hundred feet of any lake or highway or within one hundred and fifty feet of any river or portage" unless special dispensation was obtained from the superintendent. Significantly, the new regulation had teeth. "In future," declared Deputy Minister Cain, "any trespass on a reserved area shall be subject to a minimum charge of five times the regular price" of the timber illegally extracted.[94] Frank MacDougall was well pleased with these developments. "Progress has been made," he believed, "toward [the] ideal conception of Algonquin Park as a multiple land use area."[95]

The following year, in May 1940, MacDougall set another precedent by creating the first nature reserve in Algonquin Park. He withdrew two small areas of virgin pine forest for both educational and scientific reasons from the licences of the J.R. Booth Co. and Gillies Bros. Ltd. Although a mere 100 mature trees were involved in this action, the two companies complained that they had not been consulted. The exasperated superintendent reminded both companies that he had, indeed, raised with them the issue of scenic reserves, "but they were loathe to do anything voluntarily."[96]

All in all, Frank MacDougall's efforts succeeded in striking an acceptable balance between the demands of loggers and recreationists. Not until the 1960s, when wilderness enthusiasts, environmentalists, and recreationists confronted what had become a year-round, heavily mechanized logging industry, dependent on diesel trucks and elaborate road systems, skidders and chain saws, did MacDougall's compromise break down and the search for a new modus vivendi begin again in earnest. Ironically, the winds of technological change were already being felt in the late 1930s, as timber companies began to use trucks to haul logs out of the park, presaging the end of the teamster era.

The opening of the highway intensified other long-standing problems in Algonquin Park. For example, in view of the additional angling pressures on already overfished waters, it heightened the need for a fish management policy. The realities of Depression politics had soon taught MacDougall that his initial proposal of 1931 for systematic fish studies in all sections of the park was too ambitious. Still, in spite of budgetary restrictions, he had struggled with some success to avoid a purely ad hoc approach to fish management. He had consulted biologists in the Department of Game and Fisheries for technical information and advice. Such assistance contributed to the decision, in 1932, to prohibit winter fishing in Algonquin. Furthermore, to avoid the "indiscriminate and unplanned restocking" of years past, MacDougall issued questionnaires to anglers, in order to gain a rough knowledge of fishing conditions across the park. Then, with the help of Game and Fisheries biologists, he worked out a restocking program. By 1935, two lakes, Costello and Brewer, had been cleaned out, closed to the public, and stocked with adult brown and rainbow trout to establish natural rearing ponds.[97]

As a "more economical and practical" alternative to a parkwide fish study, MacDougall turned to the idea of establishing a field laboratory in Algonquin. "After 40 years of waiting," he remarked in 1935, "it seems right that the park should commence to fulfil its function as a research area on natural life problems." A year later, Professor William J.K. Harkness of the University of Toronto accepted MacDougall's invitation to set up what would become the renowned Ontario Fisheries Research Laboratory on Lake Opeongo. As a beginning, Harkness instituted an annual creel census, by asking all anglers to provide information on their catches. Over time, the census produced data on the size, numbers, and rates of growth of game fish in Algonquin, information which the park administration used to determine policy on the restocking and closing of lakes.[98]

Within a few years of establishing the Fisheries Research Laboratory, Harkness and other specialists such as Dr. F.P. Ide and Dr. R.R. Langford were engaged in studies on the food supply of trout, parasites, stream insects, and plankton. Harkness later reflected on the importance of these projects in shaping management decisions. "In the first years ... it was learned that some ... lakes gave much better return than others to the anglers"; consequently, a "definite programme for maintaining and improving the fishing was undertaken. These conservation measures consisted in stocking certain lakes and streams with speckled trout fry and fingerlings, transferring lake trout from in-Park lakes to those more heavily fished, closing certain lakes in alternate years, and introducing food fish such as perch and lake herring for bass and trout into those lakes where ... the food supply was sparse."[99]

Only in the area of wildlife management did MacDougall experience something close to failure. Repeated calls for a full-time park forester-biologist fell on deaf ears in a department that had only two biologists on staff as late as 1942. An alternative proposal for a jointly funded cross-appointment with the Royal Ontario Museum (ROM) of Zoology also came to naught, as did his recommendation for the establishment of a wildlife research centre on Cache Lake. Apart from the work of a few biologists like C.H.D. Clarke on ruffed grouse and Duncan McLulich on bird species, few advances were made in wildlife research. Thus, the park administrators continued to lack the most basic information on wildlife populations and possessed little understanding of the factors affecting the population of most species. Without such knowledge, scientific wildlife management was impossible.[100]

Understandably, then, wildlife conservation efforts in these years focussed on the traditional problems of law enforcement and wolf control. MacDougall refused to turn a blind eye to poaching, as had some of his predecessors, and relentlessly pursued illegal trappers. With the combined use of dog teams, air patrols, and tighter supervision, winter poaching was virtually eliminated, although illegal trapping during the spring and autumn proved more difficult to control. MacDougall ignored his critics in the local communities, people who romanticized the poacher's life. Discreet investigations enabled him to identify most of the suspected fur thieves active in Algonquin, as well as the chief buyers who grubstaked them. "There are about 11 crack gangs of poachers, figuring two men to a gang," he recorded in 1940. They confined their efforts to one month in the spring and another in the fall, with each gang taking out about $2,000 annually in illegal fur. In the autumn of 1940, the careful investigation reached a climax with what MacDougall called "the big clean-up" of the main poaching rings.[101] By the time he left Algonquin in 1941, the combination of his effective enforcement of the regulations and the lifting of depression conditions reduced the incidence of poaching to minor proportions.

MacDougall also found new ways to address the so-called wolf problem. Initially, he followed traditional park policy, which had as its objective the extermination of all wolves. Before long, he discarded this policy. Extermination proved to be an impossible task in so large an area, and besides, he had learned from biologists like J.R. Dymond that wolves played an important role in the park ecology. Among other things, the partially eaten carcasses of large mammals killed by wolves provided winter food for small mammals and birds. Wolves were also useful in reducing and dispersing deer populations.

Consequently, by 1935, policy had evolved from one of extermination to a more enlightened approach of wolf control. "Our policy in this respect," explained MacDougall, "agrees with the thought of the American Game Association and the Canadian Federation of Naturalists who condemn exterminating predators over large areas."[102]

In May 1941, Frank MacDougall left Algonquin to fill the position of deputy minister vacated by Walter Cain. MacDougall took pride in the fact that during his superintendency, Algonquin Park had become "the first large scale example [in Ontario] of multiple use of the forest under a technical forester."[103] Now, as the first professional forester to reach the rank of deputy minister, he had the opportunity to apply his creative ideas on a wider scale. From his new position of influence, MacDougall also took every opportunity in the years that followed to advance the policies and projects he himself had pursued as superintendent of Algonquin Park.

In 1944, for instance, at the request of the Federation of Ontario Naturalists, he saw to it that a 7,770-hectare wilderness area in Canisbay and McLaughlin townships was set aside by order-in-council for wildlife and silvicultural research. The accommodation and laboratory facilities subsequently erected for these biologists became known as the Algonquin Park Wildlife Research Station, an institution that would bring the park and the Ontario government international renown in scientific circles.[104]

MacDougall was also able to rectify a deficiency in Algonquin Park, about which he had complained in every report as superintendent – the lack of published material describing the park, its natural features, facilities, and canoe routes. By 1944, he saw to it that funds were made available to produce an information booklet, as well as a canoe route map. While at the park, MacDougall had also regretted the lack of any kind of interpretive programs to help users appreciate the natural history of Algonquin. He had looked with envy at the naturalist programs found in American state and national parks. As deputy minister he vowed to address this problem, and once again, he turned for assistance to Professor J.R. Dymond. This indefatigable scientist, a leaseholder on Smoke Lake, had of his own volition already started to conduct nature hikes for cottagers and their guests. Impressed by this initiative, MacDougall invited Dymond to establish a nature education program in Algonquin. During the summer of 1944, Dymond laid out a self-guiding, labelled nature trail, conducted nature tours for tourists, and lectured at the children's camps. "The first season's work," reported Dymond, "indicates that there is real interest on the part of many visitors in becoming acquainted with the natural history of the Park. It is desirable that the work be continued and expanded." MacDougall ensured that it was.[105]

Finally, Deputy Minister MacDougall sought to make Algonquin Park more familiar to the public by highlighting its fascinating human history. While superintendent of the park, MacDougall, a history buff himself, had interviewed old-timers and often written about historical matters in his park *News Letter*, published several times a year since 1932. In 1939, he had permitted ROM archaeologist Kenneth Kidd, under the direction of T.F. McIlwraith, to excavate an old Indian site on Tea Lake – the first official archaeological research in the park. Once ensconced in Toronto, MacDougall determined to publish a full-scale park history. In 1944, after discussions with various University of Toronto historians, MacDougall hired a young teacher and recent M.A. history graduate named Audrey Saunders to write the book. The result of her research was a pioneering work in Canadian oral history, the popular *Algonquin Story* (1946).[106]

Frank MacDougall's promotion to the deputy minister's post also meant positive policy changes for Quetico Provincial Park. Anxious to apply his multiple-use philosophy, whenever the occasion arose, he soon found an opportunity "to have the logging in the Quetico managed in the same manner as in the Algonquin Park."[107] This development occurred in October 1941, after the Izaak Walton League petitioned against the plans of the J.A. Mathieu Lumber Company to cut in the vicinity of Crooked Lake along the international boundary. The Waltonians urged the DLF to withdraw from timber harvesting a 400-foot (122-metre) shoreline reserve around the lake, as had been done in similar zones across the border in the Shipstead-Nolan area.[108] Instead, MacDougall stunned everyone concerned by abruptly ending the ad hoc creation of shoreline reserves and instituting a uniform 300-foot (91-metre) reserve policy along all canoe routes in Quetico, just as he had done earlier in Algonquin.[109]

Aging timber baron J.A. Mathieu found these new restrictions hard to swallow and denounced the 300-foot (91-metre) reserves as "a 100% waste and an unsound forestry policy in a large portion of the shoreline in question." Regional Forester W.D. Cram begged to differ. After inspecting several canoe routes himself, he found the earlier narrow reserves to be inadequate. "From 200 yards out on Sturgeon Lake," he had discovered, "you could see the brown pine tops through [the] reservation."[110] Small wonder, he admitted, that the recreationists were up in arms. A year later, the results of MacDougall's dramatic policy were evident. Ernest Oberholtzer paddled Crooked Lake and complimented the Ontarians "on the improvement over previous operations anywhere in Quetico Park. I saw no logging dams or flooded shores. I saw no islands that had been logged ... There was a real effort to protect shore-line timber and usually with much success."[111]

Not surprisingly, the Quetico-Superior Council thought it had found a kindred spirit in Frank MacDougall. Perhaps, here was the Ontario official who would support their campaign to protect the recreational and scenic qualities of the Rainy Lake watershed under international treaty. But meetings with MacDougall and the new lands and forests minister, N.O. Hipel, in late 1941, disabused the American conservationists of this notion. MacDougall and Hipel were no more interested in negotiating a treaty than their predecessors had been. Still, the Americans were encouraged by the "friendly and co-operative" reception they received in Toronto. Kenneth Reid of the Izaak Walton League found that the QSC and the Ontario officials agreed "in all essentials of management policies ... for both sides of the border." Lands and Forests Minister Hipel concluded the discussions with the Americans in January 1942 by instructing the regional forester, W.D. Cram, to meet twice a year with his counterpart in the U.S. Forest Service, Jay H. Price, in order to coordinate the management policies in Quetico Park and the Superior National Forest.[112]

Regrettably, not everyone concurred with the policy decisions being shaped by Frank MacDougall in Toronto. Opposition was stiff in the Fort Frances office of the Department of Lands and Forests. Acting District Forester J.M. Whalen resented the QSC's successes. In April 1942, for instance, he angrily objected to the deputy minister's decision to prohibit logging on two large points of land on Basswood Lake. MacDougall had based his decision to reserve these areas, said to contain "the last conspicuous stand of pine in the Park," on the advice of renowned ecologist Aldo Leopold and Ernest Oberholtzer. Whalen dismissed the scientific and recreational rationale for setting aside these timber stands as nature reserves, on the grounds that the decision was detrimental to the local economy.[113]

By 1944, Whalen's resentment had hardened to the point that he recommended that Quetico be stripped of its park status. "My opinion," he wrote, "is that Quetico Park is of no value whatever as a recreational area for Canadians." All but a handful of those who used the park were Americans. The province received no economic benefits from the American tourists, since they outfitted themselves in Ely, Minnesota. Moreover, park operating expenditures greatly exceeded revenues. Whalen's solution to all of this was to convert the park into a forest reserve and to replace it with small highway campgrounds throughout northwestern Ontario.[114]

Whalen was correct in one respect. There would be a need for parks on all the northern highways in postwar Ontario. What he failed to foresee was the vital role that Quetico would play in the decades ahead as a wilderness area. Fortunately, his viewpoint proved to be a minority opinion, and his recommendations were questioned, in Toronto, by MacDougall and, in the district, by Quetico Park Superintendent Lloyd Rawn. "In Canada today," argued Rawn in 1942, "every person, business or organization that derives any benefit [sic] from the tourist trade are striving to their utmost to build and prepare for the greatest tourist influx in our history, yet some in our organization are trying to tear down what little progress we have made ... We should be building for this expected rush rather than trying to dispose of our only outstanding asset."[115]

The sharp exchange of views between the administrators of Quetico Provincial Park during the early 1940s reflected the wider debate then rippling through the ranks of conservationists in Ontario. No longer did the utilitarians go unchallenged, as they had earlier in the century. Now, recreationists concerned with scenic protection, and naturalists dedicated to the preservation of natural areas, jostled their "use and profit" rivals for greater input in the management of parks like Algonquin and Quetico. Buffeted by the turbulent crosscurrents in the stream of conservationist thinking, park officials struggled to reconcile the conflicting interests. They eventually found the answer to their problems south of the border, in the multiple-use doctrine of the United States Forest Service. As applied in Algonquin and Quetico, multiple use meant that whenever a clash occurred between recreationist and logger, scenic protection became a variable in management policy. Increasingly, too, nature preservation became a factor, as Frank MacDougall created the first nature reserves in the two parks and set aside the wilderness research area in Algonquin. How long MacDougall's multiple-use balance would last remained to be seen. Looming ahead was an unprecedented boom in outdoor recreation that would create a considerable imbalance and call forth powerful responses from both utilitarian and protectionist elements.

Chapter 3

Outdoor Recreation Boom

Parks for the People, 1945–1967

During the two decades following World War II, dramatic social and economic changes in Ontario generated unprecedented demand for parklands. A larger, more affluent, highly mobile urban population with newly acquired leisure time took to the highways in search of outdoor recreational opportunities. So great were their numbers that they saturated the few available parks and created a crisis in outdoor recreation. Initially, officials in the Department of Lands and Forests underestimated these changes in behaviour and, instead of expanding their efforts to satisfy the demand, sought to restrict their mandate, hoping to rid themselves of increasingly bothersome management problems in the southern recreational parks. Accordingly, in the late 1940s and early 1950s, the DLF attempted to thrust responsibility for Ipperwash, Long Point, Presqu'ile, and Rondeau into the hands of the Department of Municipal Affairs.

As it happened, the social and political realities of the early 1950s scotched this reductionist line of thinking within the DLF. The presence of a broad base of public support for more parks with beaches, picnic and camping facilities, all within a few hours' motoring distance of the major southern urban centres, could not be denied. That pressure, coupled with a new appreciation of both the developments in parks systems in the United States and the failure of the commission parks in Ontario to provide public recreational facilities, compelled politicians and bureaucrats alike to review provincial park policy. The outcome was a reversal of previous decisions. In 1954, the government passed a new Provincial Parks Act, created a Division of Parks within the Department of Lands and Forests, and launched an era of provincial park expansion in which the number of provincial parks grew rapidly, from 8 to 94 in 1967.

Outdoor Recreation Crisis and the Question of Responsibility

After World War II, rapid social and economic changes enabled much greater numbers of people to take part in outdoor recreational activities. In the first place, Ontario's population grew steadily from 3.8 million in 1946 to 4.6

million in 1951, 5.4 million in 1956, and 6.2 million in 1961. This phenomenal growth was due in large part to a natural increase, the "postwar baby boom." Ten years later, the population of Ontario had jumped by another 24 percent to 7.7 million. Waves of new immigrants also added to the population, producing a dramatic turnaround from the 1930s, when depression and restrictive policies had reduced immigration to a trickle. Between 1946 and 1955, Ontario received 636,033 newcomers, over half the total of new entrants to Canada in those years. During the following decade, another 900,664 immigrants entered the province, about half of them listing Toronto as their destination.[1]

Not only did the population expand rapidly, but it became more urbanized, industrialized, and concentrated in the south-central region of the province. The urban-industrial growth of the great postwar expansion was heavily concentrated in the six counties of Hamilton-Wentworth, Halton, Peel, York, Durham, and Metropolitan Toronto. Here could be found approximately half of Ontario's total population in the 1940s and over two-thirds by the 1960s. Not surprisingly, these demographic trends put enormous pressures on existing parklands and outdoor recreation facilities in southern Ontario.

Looking back, it is easy to see that the living standards of most Canadians rose everywhere after World War II, especially in Ontario. People were spared a return to the Depression conditions of the 1930s and, indeed, enjoyed a remarkably smooth transition from a wartime to a peacetime economy. During the late 1940s, enormous consumer demand, pent-up by the decade of the Depression and six years of enforced wartime saving, fueled impressive growth in the Canadian economy, as did the reconstruction demands of war-ravaged Europe. This economic boom proved to be the beginning of three decades of "a steady upward progress in output, employment and prosperity," during which time "the average Canadian's living standard doubled."[2] Real per capita income in Ontario grew steadily, from $1,641 in 1941, to $2,557 in 1960, and $3,792 in 1970. A large proportion of blue-collar workers now possessed the means to acquire substantial material goods. The average annual unemployment rate in Ontario between 1945 and 1970 remained low (under 4 percent) with the exception of the recession of 1957–61. And as levels of personal income rose sharply after 1945, providing Ontarians with greater disposable income, most workers also had more free time at their disposal. The forty-hour, five-day work week became standard by the mid-1950s, as did the two-week paid vacation. The buoyant, expanding economy, and larger, more affluent population, in turn provided governments with the revenues to launch social security programs, to create more cultural institutions, and to expand outdoor recreational facilities and parklands.

During this period, Ontarians also experienced the full impact of the automobile revolution. They formed the first generation whose lifestyle was fundamentally affected by the car. The number of passenger vehicles registered in Ontario grew from 585,604 in 1946 to 1,292,133 in 1955. By 1960,

1.7 million Ontarians, or 76 percent of the province's households, owned at least one automobile. Sixteen years later, registrations had more than doubled again to 3.9 million, and on average every 2.6 persons owned an automobile. To accommodate the increasing traffic, successive provincial governments undertook massive programs to build new highways and upgrade older ones. Ontario's total road and highway mileage expanded from 116,734 kilometres in 1949 to 152,000 kilometres by the early 1970s. The improved highway network further stimulated the development of tourism, especially from the United States. "Recreation was given as the purpose for coming to Ontario by 72% of the respondents" to surveys of American tourists taken from 1955 to 1958.[3] Many of them came to enjoy Ontario's provincial parks.

Finally, the age structure and education level of the province's population affected rates of participation in outdoor recreation. In 1961, the percentage of the population in Ontario four years of age and younger reached a peak; a decade later, five- to twenty-four-year-olds, taken as a percentage of the population, reached a maximum for the period ending in 1975. According to the congressionally appointed Outdoor Recreation Resources Review Commission (ORRRC) in the United States (1958–62), a dynamic was at work here. "The children of today do more kinds of things outdoors and acquire experience and skills in things like swimming and camping that their parents never had. This new generation, as it grows up, will spend a great deal more leisure time outdoors than the parents of today and so will their children and their children after them."[4] Higher education levels also played an important part in boosting outdoor recreation demand. The ORRRC discovered through its nationwide surveys that the more education young people acquired, the more active they were likely to be as adults. In Ontario, too, as elsewhere in North America, young people were spending more time in school and postponing their entry into the labour force. Between 1956 and 1971, the rate of participation in Ontario's labour force for males in the fourteen- to twenty-four-year-old age bracket fell from 70.3 percent to 60 percent. Full-time enrolment in the province's universities expanded from 12,410 in 1940 to 159,701 in 1975; at the same time, enrolment in community colleges and other post-secondary institutions rose from roughly 11,000 in 1955 to 60,000 in 1975.[5]

Together, then, all these variables – population growth, urbanization, higher standards of living, increased levels of leisure time, more personal mobility, American tourism, and a younger and more educated population – combined to bring about the crisis in outdoor recreation that hit Ontario, beginning in the late 1940s. More and more Ontarians had the means, the time, the mobility, and given their urban residential environments, the psychological need, to seek recreation in natural settings. They quickly strained the few existing parklands beyond acceptable limits and caused park administrators no end of headaches.

In Algonquin Park, for example, Superintendent George Phillips reported as early as 1946 that the campgrounds, children's camps, and resorts were "filled to capacity during July and August ... There are too many [visitors] sleeping in chairs, canoes, etc., around the Park Hotels on weekends."[6] The Lake of Two Rivers campground, opened in 1938, had already begun to suffer the effects of overuse. "The toilet facilities are unsanitary ... The water supply is inadequate ... The tables are not cared for," complained one disgruntled American scoutmaster in 1945. "We do a great deal of camping in the State Parks through Pennsylvania, New York, and Virginia. But this is the worst spot we've hit."[7] In October 1947, Professor J.R. Dymond wrote to Frank MacDougall to express his concern about the litter problem that was spreading throughout the park and the damage that was being inflicted upon natural features by recreationists insensitive to the environment and lacking basic woodcraft skills. MacDougall himself investigated the park, which he had left in such exemplary condition just six years earlier, and was most displeased by his findings. "We now seem to be in a period of deterioration," he admitted sadly, "and forthright steps will have to be taken ... to stabilize the situation."[8]

Stabilizing a situation in constant flux because of the intensifying user pressures proved difficult. The number of motor vehicles entering Algonquin Park increased annually, from 28,662 in 1950 to 47,200 in 1953. Cottage leases doubled from 1950 to 1954. The garbage dumps required to service these users created a new problem in the early 1950s, when dozens of foraging black bears began to terrorize cottagers and damage property. Incinerators temporarily alleviated the difficulty, but by October 1953, the problem had reached the point where over 100 animals had to be shot by the rangers. Not surprisingly, the resulting publicity damaged the park's reputation as the province's leading game reserve.[9] Worse still, park administrators were stunned to learn, in June 1952, that the once-pristine waters of Cache Lake were polluted and unfit for drinking. W.D. Cram urgently requested the Department of Health to inspect all "the sanitary conveniences of the various cottages" to determine the source of the pollution. "You will appreciate the fact," he wrote in a classic example of understatement, "that if a typhoid epidemic should occur it would have a very detrimental effect on Algonquin Park."[10]

Record numbers of fly-in anglers also began to put inordinate pressures on the Algonquin interior. In 1950, for instance, some 1,000 float planes flew 1,137 anglers into isolated areas of the park. Lodge owners, guides, and tourist outfitters, organized into the Algonquin Park Tourist Association, demanded that tighter controls be placed on the float planes which, since 1943, had been restricted to landing on twenty-two interior lakes. The association members knew well enough that their livelihood depended on the maintenance of both the wilderness atmosphere of the park and the superb angling. They believed that these features could not survive the impact of the commercial airplane operations, which provided a shuttle service into the park and cached boats and equipment on interior lakes for their clients' use. Park administrators shared the association's concern and, in 1949, ordered the removal of all boats and equipment stored in the interior. Ironically, the guides and outfitters protested loudly upon learning that they, too, would be prevented from caching boats in the park, with the result that the policy was not enforced. In 1950, the Department of Lands and Forests again tried to restrict air traffic to the interior lakes, by requiring all planes to check in and out of one of the three administrative centres at Achray, Brent, and Smoke Lake. This allowed the staff to monitor the numbers of fly-in anglers, but the additional red tape failed utterly to discourage them.[11]

Farther south, the outdoor recreation problem was no less severe. Ipperwash Provincial Park attracted even larger numbers of day users during the summer months than did Algonquin. On hot summer weekends, crowds of between thirty-five and fifty thousand people could be found at the beach. "What struck me most forcibly," reported the regional forester, F.S. Newman, in 1949, "was the fact that [the] Park grounds, approaches and buildings are absolutely inadequate."[12]

The severe shortage of public access to beaches and shorelines extended beyond the Great Lakes to Lake Simcoe, the Muskoka Lakes, and the Kawarthas. In February 1949, District Forester J.F. Simmons, of the Lake Simcoe District, deplored the lack of parkland within his jurisdiction. "With the exception of a few small Municipal Parks, there is no place on the entire [Lake Simcoe] shoreline of approximately three hundred miles where the public has access to the water ... For this reason," he concluded, "I would recommend strongly that this matter be treated as an urgent necessity for the health and recreation of the people." Eighteen months later, Simmons again warned that "present overcrowding of available picnic and bathing grounds is becoming intolerable. I ... have seen on a summer week day (not a public holiday) over 300 people ... crowded on the shoreline at the end of a concession road – 66 feet wide ... I know that each concession road had similar conditions prevailing particularly on the west shore."[13]

In the late 1940s, neither the minister nor the senior managers in the Department of Lands and Forests were prepared to acknowledge that they should assume responsibility for providing recreational parkland in southern Ontario, instead remaining wedded to the older tradition of limited state and local initiative. Park and recreational facilities, they reasoned, could still be handled at the community level, and many local politicians shared this belief. In December 1949, for instance, instead of asking the province to take action on Lake Simcoe, the Toronto and York Planning Board placed the onus upon York County to acquire thirteen desirable properties – 330 hectares in total – along the lake shore as public parkland.[14]

Such attitudes were so prevalent that the provincial government permitted opportunities to acquire exceptional parkland to slip through its fingers. In 1951, the DLF declined to purchase the 200-hectare Sibbald Point property, located on the southern shore of Lake Simcoe, and left it to the county of York to obtain the site as parkland. Within five years, the county discovered that it had assumed more cost and trouble than it had bargained for, and was forced to seek provincial assistance. Fortunately, by that time, the DLF was willing to act, and acquired the area to establish its first provincial park on Lake Simcoe.[15]

A similar story unfolded with respect to the area on Lake Huron between Ipperwash and Grand Bend, known as the Pinery. The location contained one of the largest remaining oak savannah and red pine forests in southwestern Ontario, expanses of undulating sand dunes, and a magnificent beach some ten kilometres in length. In 1947, the Canada Company, which owned most of the Pinery, sought to liquidate the last of its holdings in the old Huron Tract, and offered its 1,862-hectare property to the province for $250,000. Lands and Forests Minister Harold R. Scott declined the offer as too expensive, and the burden of acquiring and managing all or part of the Pinery fell by default to the township of Bosanquet and the Ausable River Conservation Authority. Scott again refused to act in 1951, when urged by a delegation representing municipalities in southwestern Ontario to create a provincial park at the Pinery.[16] Rather than creating more new provincial parks in southern Ontario, the minister was, in fact, attempting to get rid of the ones his department already administered – adopting a policy that had been promoted for several years by many of the professional foresters in the department, including Deputy Minister MacDougall. Trained to manage vast timbered areas of Crown land, these officials were out of their element when faced with administering small, crowded, and problem-ridden southern recreational areas and beaches. Moreover, they thought the responsibility for providing recreation parks in heavily populated districts was too far removed from the basic DLF mandate. When they pondered the department's role in the parks, they thought in terms of large multiple-use areas like Algonquin and Quetico, Sibley, and Lake Superior. Accordingly, in 1949, Frank MacDougall began to disentangle his department from the southern recreational areas by transferring the commission parks at Long Point and Presqu'ile to the Department of Municipal Affairs (DMA).

MacDougall planned the same fate for Ipperwash and even for the venerable Rondeau Provincial Park. For over a decade, Rondeau had apparently been heading toward the same end as the ill-fated Burlington Beach area; by the late 1940s, the number of cottages in Rondeau had grown to 450. Outdoor recreation in a natural setting took a poor second place to the various resort and amusement facilities. When capital projects had been authorized in 1939, priority had gone to the construction of a new dance pavilion, with the result that Rondeau's popularity in subsequent years depended to a considerable extent on its big-band dances, held four nights a week. New concessions, such as lawn bowling, box ball, and a shooting gallery, when added to the miniature golf, shuffleboard, tennis, pony ride, and bicycle operations, gave the place a carnival-like atmosphere.[17]

Rondeau also attracted enormous crowds that overtaxed existing facilities. By 1948, the public store and restaurant (eventually declared unsanitary by local health officers), the bathing houses, picnic shelters, park office, and superintendent's house all needed replacing. From the point of view of those concerned with natural values, the future looked glum, indeed. Then, in the mid-1940s, the leaseholders and local politicians began to demand that a small plaza be located in the park, containing a "Super Market, Drug Store, Dining Room and kitchen, soda bar, post office and rest rooms."[18] In the face of these demands, officials in the DLF sought to rid themselves of Rondeau altogether. Eventually, in 1952, an amendment to the Provincial Parks Act placed both Rondeau and Ipperwash under the aegis of the Department of Municipal Affairs. It seemed as if the foresters had succeeded in liberating themselves from the task of supplying recreational parklands south of Algonquin Park.

The relief experienced within the DLF at having escaped from the difficult park and outdoor recreation problem in the south was short-lived. Within two years, the exclusive northern parks policy lay discarded, a casualty of political and social realities. In fact, the DLF never succeeded in freeing itself of the responsibility for southern parks, since the legislation transferring Rondeau and Ipperwash to the Department of Municipal Affairs could not be proclaimed. During May 1952, as Municipal Affairs personnel prepared to assume control of these parks, they ran into several unanticipated obstacles, particularly with regard to Rondeau's future, which prevented the transfer taking place. Their plans for the park included the establishment of a commission to administer the recreational and natural zones of the peninsula, while the cottage subdivisions would be designated a municipal improvement district, administered by a board of trustees. Existing provincial statutes, however, did not provide for the protection of the civil servants, who were to be retained by the commission. Furthermore, the Department of Municipal Affairs discovered that it had no legislative authority to transfer funds budgeted for provincial park purposes to the trustees of an improvement district. And finally, before Rondeau could be divided into both a commission park and an improvement district, land surveys of the entire peninsula would be required. Because of these difficulties, Rondeau and Ipperwash remained under the aegis of the DLF.[19]

As news spread of the proposal to remove Rondeau's designation as a provincial park, considerable opposition emerged. The township of Aldborough demanded assurances that the Rondeau forest would be preserved and commercialism resisted, in the event that Municipal Affairs ever should take over the park. So, too, did the new Conservation Council of Ontario, an umbrella group, which spoke for seventeen member organizations representing agriculture, forestry, fish and wildlife, naturalists, and sportsmen. The council had been created in 1952, through the efforts of Francis H. Kortwright, the founder of the Canadian National Sportsman's Show. Taking a more aggressive posture, the Ontario Federation of Anglers and Hunters (OFAH) went directly to Premier Frost and demanded "that Rondeau Park be left under the Department of Lands and Forests, and that under no consideration, should any Committee appointed under Municipal Affairs have any jurisdiction over the Forests, Fish and Wildlife of this Park."[20]

In response to these pressures, Deputy Minister Frank MacDougall instructed his staff to review their plans for Rondeau. Accordingly, they recommended in November 1952 that only the developed sections of the park – the neck of the peninsula and the cottage subdivisions along the Lake Ontario shoreline – be handed over to Municipal Affairs and administered by a commission. The remainder of the peninsula, including the forest and marshland, should be retained by the DLF as parkland. These recommendations were not well received in political circles. By this time, local members of the Legislative Assembly (MLAs) were voicing opposition to any proposal of a park commission, because they anticipated a public backlash if fees were levied for the use of recreational facilities.[21]

Some politicians and civil servants had other reasons for questioning the proposal to appoint commissions to administer southern parks. Apart from the admirable achievements of the Niagara Parks operation, the experience

Cottages at Rondeau Provincial Park, 1954. *Courtesy: Ministry of Natural Resources.*

with commission parks elsewhere had been unhappy. All too frequently, people appointed as commissioners at Presqu'ile and Long Point had been local political worthies, often leaseholders or businessmen with vested interests in the parks they were expected to administer for the benefit of the public. And although the Presqu'ile and Long Point park commissions had been charged with the duty of managing the areas under their control as parkland, forest reserves, and health resorts for the general public, neither group had succeeded in doing so. Instead, both commissions had deliberately worked in the interests of the cottagers, whose annual rents provided the bulk of operating revenues. In 1946, the Presqu'ile commission, lacking both the will and the funds to cope with the many recreationists using the undeveloped areas of the park, gave up all pretence of serving the public, and asked the DLF to operate a separate provincial park on those parts of the Presqu'ile peninsula frequented by the unwanted visitors. Rather than pursuing this line of action, however, the DLF passed the problem on to the Department of Municipal Affairs.[22]

Upon assuming responsibility for supervising the Presqu'ile and Long Point park commissions in 1949, Municipal Affairs officials discovered to their dismay how badly these parks had been managed. At Presqu'ile, "about 40 per cent" of the peninsula was privately controlled, either by leaseholders or by individuals, holding squatter's titles dating back to the nineteenth century. "[The] only real development of the Park," noted one report, "has been almost entirely towards the goal of a summer resort peopled by families who occupy their own cottages erected on [leased] Crown or privately owned lands."[23] The same situation held true for Long Point, where most of the park had been subdivided into cottage lots, about 550 in all. A trifling six hectares of the original park remained undeveloped for public use. "Generally speaking," concluded a DMA investigator, "the development which has taken place [at Long Point] has tended away from the conception that the Park was to be an area for general use of the public ... towards the creation of a colony of summer cottage occupants, whose desires and interests clash with the avowed purposes for which the Park was set aside."[24]

Notwithstanding the administrative problems they had uncovered at both Long Point and Presqu'ile, and the obstacles to the transfer of Rondeau and Ipperwash to their control, Municipal Affairs planners forged ahead to draft a parklands policy for southern Ontario. In January 1953, they circulated a proposal that special legislation be introduced to create a new class of parks called "Provincial Recreational Areas." The four existing southern parks would be designated the first of such areas, and each managed by an appointed commission.[25] DMA personnel anticipated that henceforth they would establish and administer "provincial recreational areas" in the south, while the Department of Lands and Forests would manage "provincial parks" in the north. The proposal, however, was too simple a solution for such a complex problem. It ignored the substantial opposition to the commission park concept at Rondeau and neglected to explain why appointed commissions, which had failed at Long Point and Presqu'ile, were the preferred method of administration. Moreover, district foresters in the southwestern region of the Department of Lands and Forests, hoping to create more provincial parks of their own, opposed the DMA plan.

Finally, the Municipal Affairs plan had nothing to say about the role of conservation authorities in providing near-urban recreational space. Since 1946, fifteen authorities, with more soon to follow, had been set up by various municipalities under the supervision of the Conservation Branch of the Department of Planning and Development. Although the Conservation Authorities Act (1946) had not included recreation as part of the mandate of the regional conservation authorities – flood control was the primary concern – the subject had been raised in virtually all of the reports prepared by the Conservation Branch since 1945. In fact, the Upper Thames River Conservation Authority had decided of its own volition to engage in recreation in a major way at the Fanshawe Dam, near London. When William K. Warrender assumed the Department of Planning and Development portfolio in January 1953, he enthusiastically embraced the idea of expanding the mandate of the conservation authorities to include outdoor recreation. To that end, he amended the Conservation Authorities Act in order to empower the various authorities "to use lands acquired in connection with a [conservation] scheme, for recreational purposes." Recreation, however, would remain ancillary to the conservation objectives of the river authorities. Lands could not be acquired by a local authority solely for the purpose of creating a recreational area.[26] In short, then, the conservation authorities would play a limited regional role in providing near-urban, outdoor recreational space in southern Ontario. This still left unresolved the question of which other department would play a provincial, or at least interregional, role in providing parklands south of Algonquin Park.

With at least three ministers jostling for a share of the limelight in early 1953, the parklands question moved up on the cabinet's agenda. The Pinery controversy of 1951 had already alerted Premier Frost to the fact that a broad base of public support for more parks was being laid down across the province. Support for the expansion of the parks was also growing on the back benches of the legislature and in many municipal councils. Even northern politicians had an opportunity to grapple with the outdoor recreation question, when Deputy Minister MacDougall launched a recreational land-use planning program in February 1953. In each of the DLF's sixteen northern districts, the district forester was instructed to chair a committee made up of the regional forester, a local MLA, the senior conservation officer, a biologist, and a representative of each of the following: the Northern Ontario Outfitters Association, the Ontario Federation of Anglers and Hunters, the forestry industry, and the Department of Highways, to prepare a district recreational land-use plan by September of that year. Using the latest data from the inventory of forest resources, each committee set out to identify Crown lands best suited for specific kinds of use, including recreation, and to zone them according to standard criteria. In October, MacDougall asked each of his regional foresters to synthesize the district information into a regional plan. These documents were to form the basis of discussion at the annual meeting of the regional and district foresters, in January 1954, whose theme would be "Land Planning for Recreational Use."[27]

By this time, Deputy Minister Frank MacDougall had also begun to have second thoughts about his department's bias in favour of northern parks. Some district foresters, especially those in the southwestern region, insisted that the policy was misguided. Experience had taught them that the massive public demand for outdoor recreational space should not be entirely thrust upon other agencies. These administrators also knew that natural resource agencies in the United States had assumed responsibility for providing all kinds of parks. Why then, they asked, should not their department attempt to do likewise? Typically, MacDougall decided to research the matter thoroughly. In the fall of 1953, he despatched his seven regional foresters to study the policies and practices of national, state, and municipal park systems in the U.S., to prepare for the foresters' conference in January.

The Park Policy of 1954

For most of September and early October 1953, the regional foresters fanned out across the eastern half of the United States. A.S. Bray embarked on a tour of park systems in five states in the deep South, while Peter Addison set a grueling itinerary for himself through eight central states, from Minnesota and Wisconsin to Mississippi and Arkansas. Others made a more intensive analysis of one or two jurisdictions. Ben Greenwood, for instance, focussed on forty state parks and forests in New York and New Jersey, and E.L. Ward concentrated his efforts entirely in Pennsylvania. All returned home greatly influenced by what they had seen. They discovered that Ontario now lagged behind many American states in providing recreational parkland. In contrast to the Ontario and Canadian experience, state park systems had expanded during the Depression years, thanks to the availability of federal funding through U.S. President Franklin D. Roosevelt's New Deal programs, particularly that establishing the Civilian Conservation Corps.[28]

The seven foresters made special note of those aspects of the American park systems that, they thought, had relevance for Ontario. Ben Greenwood admired the "numbers of recreational areas both large and small, many within very short distances of densely populated areas." Peter Addison highlighted the American visitor service programs, especially the nature museums, which he described as "a most important and most popular medium for the teaching of conservation." American recreation planners, the foresters discovered, placed primary emphasis on providing opportunities for water-based activities, but picnicking and camping were close behind.

The most significant feature of the regional foresters' reports, however, was their new appreciation of the southern Ontario outdoor recreation crisis. They seemed genuinely shocked at discovering how badly the province had fallen behind the American state park systems. Our parks are "hopelessly overcrowded," wrote F.S. Newman. "There is a problem and the problem will increase year by year unless we take a definite stand now," added E.L. Ward. The Department of Lands and Forests was best suited to solve it, he went on to argue. In northern Ontario, "sufficient areas" should be set aside immediately, "so that there will not have to be an expensive purchasing programme later on." In southern Ontario, "a policy of land purchases should be started now." For Ward, the sojourn in Pennsylvania had been a revelation. "I believe that the most important thing I learned on the trip was the part that publicly owned lands played in the life of the ordinary individual ... It has been proved by heads of labour and industry that the working man or average citizen, who spends his free time in the out-of-doors, is a much better citizen for it."

Of all the regional foresters, F.S. Newman of the southwestern region was most keen to emulate the American example. His study of Ohio and New York had only confirmed what he and his staff had known for years. Accordingly, immediately after his return, he conferred with his three district foresters to hammer out a set of proposals for inclusion in his report. Rondeau Park, they decided, should be retained by the DLF. In the park, the spread of the cottage subdivisions should be halted, amusement concessions removed, and a back-to-nature policy introduced. Every district in his region, Newman explained, required new provincial parks of between 200 to 400 hectares in size. In each case, he went on, "we are thinking in terms of a public park, preserved in its natural state as much as possible, and available for casual picnic groups, juvenile and adult camping trips, afternoon hikes or a week's camping."

The regional foresters' surveys of the American park scene indicated that a profound change in attitude was occurring within the Department of Lands and Forests, where senior management had previously paid little attention to the parklands problem in southern Ontario. At the annual foresters' conference held in Toronto from 11–13 January 1954, the new pro-park sentiment surfaced. Out of this landmark conference emerged a strongly worded policy recommendation for Premier Frost and his cabinet. "Our Provincial Parks are too few and too small," the document boldly declared. "Lack of a recreational plan in the past is now evident. With the industrial progress of the Province and the great influx of people since the last war, a situation is created that was unforeseen. But the situation is here, and we must rise to meet it."[29]

The document asserted that the need for a crash program of park development was indisputable. Land in southern Ontario should be acquired immediately by purchase or donation, and Crown land should be set aside in the northern districts. But, "after the land is acquired the work really begins," the foresters hastened to add. American officials had stressed that "too much emphasis cannot be placed on sound planning." The ad hoc responses to local political pressures, which had accounted for the founding of parks in the past, would no longer suffice. The services of professional park planners would be required to draft land acquisition policy, to set standards, and to create master development plans for each park. Moreover, in the acquisition and planning stages, previously "under-rated" considerations such as "historical sites preservation and promotion, extraordinary natural phenomena, and nature museums" should be given emphasis.

The foresters acknowledged that the proposed parks expansion would be expensive. "Nothing can be done without the expenditure of money ... If the government accepts the recommendations of the conference, then there must be a willingness to spend." Land acquisition and capital costs would have to be "written off," and only "40 to 60% of current running expenses" could be recovered from fees charged for the use of park facilities. The foresters further recommended that a new parks section be created within the Land and Recreational Areas Division of the DLF to advise the district staffs; a final proposal to create a separate division of parks received "no support ... at all."

While able to reach a consensus on most matters, the district foresters could not agree on two potentially explosive issues and left them to the politicians. No conclusion was reached on the question of the place of leaseholders in provincial parks, nor could they recommend how responsibility for parks and recreational areas in southern Ontario should be divided. They recognized that the DLF must assume part of the task in the south, but expected that the Department of Highways, as well as the Conservation Branch of the Department of Planning and Development, would figure prominently in the provision of recreational space. Evidently, by omitting any reference to the Department of Municipal Affairs, the foresters perceived no place for that agency in the future of the parks system.

On 22 January 1954, just one week after the district foresters' conference, the government took its first initiative. Acting Minister G.A. Welsh ordered an end to "further disposition of lands within any Provincial Park until further notice."[30] This proved to be the first step in a long process of phasing out the leaseholders. Six weeks later, George Challies presented both a new Provincial Parks Act and a policy statement in the legislature.[31] The objectives of the new policy were twofold. Ontario's provincial parks would serve the "dual function" of "protecting and conserving natural advantages and providing recreation for all our citizens." Beyond these immediate objectives, the act embodied certain basic principles. "Recreational areas must be developed without discrimination and according to needs," Challies explained. Racial and religious discrimination would not be tolerated in the parks system, as they had been during the 1920s and 1930s at Long Point, Presqu'ile, and Rondeau. Since

World War II, racist and anti-Semitic attitudes had fallen into general disrepute, after Hitler's Germany had demonstrated to a horrified world where such beliefs could ultimately lead. To Ontario's credit, Premier George Drew's government had already struck a blow at overt racism by introducing the first human rights statute in Canada – the Racial Discrimination Act of 1944 – which prohibited the publication, display, and broadcast of anything suggesting an intent to discriminate on the basis of race or creed. The legislation was designed to get rid of the "Whites Only" signs commonly found in resorts, beaches, shops, and other public places. In 1945, the statute was used by Justice Keiller Mackay of the Ontario High Court to strike down a restrictive covenant, by which the parties had agreed to prohibit the sale of land to "Jews or persons of objectionable nationality." Thereafter, racial barriers began to crumble in the resort areas and cottage communities of the southern recreational parks, although discriminatory practices and attitudes lingered on for many years.

The new parks policy also called for equality of opportunity in outdoor recreation, and an end to the de facto discrimination based on wealth and class. "The average citizen must not be prevented from enjoying the natural benefits of the province," explained Challies. "Summer cottage colonies must be controlled ... Picturesque sites and easy access to beach areas are not the prerogatives of the few." Furthermore, to ensure that the majority of Ontarians enjoyed adequate outdoor recreational opportunities, "the development of smaller parklands close to urban centres where population pressures are greatest is most desirable." These new parks would be of sufficient size to accommodate seasonal fluctuations of population. Provincial parks would also be located and developed with tourism in mind. "With foresight and planning recreation areas for the people of Ontario can develop with the tourist industry." And finally, historical interpretation would play a larger part in the new parks. "Ontario has a fascinating and varied history," Challies emphasized. "[The] memories of our pioneer forefathers can be preserved in park museums, reminding us of their trials and hardships and encouraging us in our own advancement."

Although the principles embedded in the new Parks Act would stand the test of time, the legislation fell short of the mark in one major respect. It failed to resolve the controversy over departmental responsibility for parkland. Indeed, instead of clarifying the situation, the act generated confusion by not naming the ministers who would be responsible for two of the three new classes of provincial parks created by the legislation. Class 1 provincial parks, Challies explained, would "remain under the jurisdiction of the Department of Lands and Forests," although some parks currently managed by the DLF "may be transferred to another department." Challies expected that the large northern parks would remain under DLF jurisdiction, but that Rondeau, and presumably Ipperwash, would lose their Class 1 status and be designated Class 2 provincial parks, along with Presqu'ile and Long Point. Each Class 2 park would be administered by commissions appointed "under the authority of a designated Minister," as yet undetermined. This section of the act clearly bore the imprint of the Department of Municipal Affairs's policy proposal of January 1953. Smaller recreational areas, such as the Department of Highways roadside picnic spots, were designated Class 3 provincial parks, also to be administered by an unnamed minister.

Liberal Opposition Leader Farquhar Oliver and others found all this very perplexing and enquired whether the decision not to designate a minister responsible for Class 2 and 3 provincial parks meant that a new parks portfolio was in the offing. "Oh no, there is no suggestion of a new department," retorted Premier Frost. "To that, I would say emphatically 'no.'"[32] One can only speculate as to why Frost did not sort out the jurisdictional question on southern parklands before rushing through the Provincial Parks Act in March 1954. It can be reasonably assumed that the government was confused by conflicting advice from rival departments. Like any canny politician with no obvious solution in sight, Premier Frost chose to temporize. Apparently, as late as March 1954, no one had yet championed the idea of consolidating all classes of provincial parks and placing them under the control of the Department of Lands and Forests.

Notwithstanding its indecision on this question, the government dealt promptly with the "problem" of Algonquin Park. On 17 June 1954, the cabinet approved a new policy and a long-term plan to restore the park to a more natural state. In future, there would be no new leases, licences of occupation, or permits granted for private, public, or commercial purposes. "Were land to be made available in the park to satisfy the ever-growing demand of recent years for cottage sites," the government argued, "it is apparent that in a few years there would be little left ... for ... the public at large." As for the 454 leaseholders in the park, they would be phased out over the next four decades, as their twenty-one-year renewable leases expired. "There will be nothing arbitrary in the gradual acquisition of leases," the government promised, but that was small consolation to many aggrieved cottagers, who had been encouraged to locate in Algonquin in the first place. While the new policy anticipated the withdrawal of the cottage leases, the government did not intend to remove all youth camps and lodges. It was expected that as the camp and lodge leases expired, some of the facilities might be acquired by the province and operated on a "money-making concession" basis.[33]

One park-related announcement followed another during the summer of 1954. In July, Premier Frost unveiled exciting plans for the surplus property that would become available, following the completion of the massive hydro-electrical development along the International Rapids section of the St. Lawrence River. According to the terms of the Canada-Ontario Agreement of 23 December 1951, the province had promised to establish a commission (today the St. Lawrence Parks Commission) to administer these lands "to safeguard and enhance the scenic beauty and historical nature of the area." Thus, the premier announced that a system of parks would be developed and managed along the St. Lawrence River, following "the pattern established at Niagara Falls." He declared that "ample funds" would be made available. Time would prove him true to his word.[34]

The Quetico Question

On 14 August 1954, the new minister of lands and forests, Clare E. Mapledoram, chose the occasion of the official opening of the Fort William–Atikokan highway to reveal the government's policy for Quetico Provincial Park.[35] In keeping with the back-to-nature philosophy being emphasized elsewhere, the minister confirmed that cottages and resort leases would continue to be banned in the park. Provision for cottage and resort development would be made on lakes contiguous to the new highway. Access roads from the new highway would not be permitted to penetrate to the interior of the park. A public campground would be constructed at the end of the first access road to French Lake. Shoreline reserve clauses, to protect "all lakes and streams, islands and portages," would be inserted in future timber licences, a statement of policy that seemed academic at the time, since the timber men had all left the park in 1946 and would not resume bush operations until 1961.

In two major respects, the 1954 policy for Quetico fell short of the objectives of the program originally introduced in 1927 by Ernest Oberholtzer and the Quetico-Superior Council. Like all his predecessors, Mapledoram rejected the idea that the Rainy Lake watershed, which included Quetico Provincial Park, should be protected by a Canadian-American treaty and administered by a joint commission. "This great natural park will be controlled and operated by the province of Ontario," he declared. "It will not be an international proposition."[36] The Quetico park policy also deviated from the QSC program in one other respect; its protectionist features were restricted to the park and did not apply to the rest of the Ontario portion of the Rainy Lake watershed. None of this came as a surprise to the QSC leaders who had been active in the policy making. Theoretically, they were still committed to the treaty concept, and would raise it again in the future, but for the time being, political realities had led the QSC to adopt an incremental strategy.

In fact, as early as 1945, the QSC's original program had been recast into a less grandiose form, one acceptable to politicians, local economic interests, and conservationists alike. One individual above all others had acted as the catalyst in the revision of the Oberholtzer plan – Chester S. Wilson, appointed Minnesota's Commissioner of Conservation in 1943. Minnesota officials, no less than their Ontario counterparts, rejected the centralist-federalist bias of the QSC program. Taking a firm position in favour of states' rights, Wilson refused to accept the idea that Minnesota should hand over title to the extensive state forest lands in the Shipstead-Nolan area and other parts of the watershed. And, for the same reasons as those Ontario was citing, he opposed the notion of a Canadian-American treaty to protect the watershed, since such a treaty would require undue federal interference in state-owned lands. The very idea of setting apart the entire Rainy Lake region, Wilson explained to the Ontario Department of Lands and Forests, seemed impracticable.[37]

By challenging the QSC objectives, Chester Wilson angered Ernest Oberholtzer, who denounced him in 1944 as a tool of the hydro and timber interests. The charge was unfounded. Wilson himself sought to create an international wilderness zone in the border lakes region, a place that would be free of "roads, tourist resorts, commercial airplane traffic, or other developments inconsistent with preservation of wilderness values."[38] But he believed that this wilderness zone should be restricted to a tract of land about one-fifth the size of the Rainy Lake watershed. It would only encompass the federally owned roadless areas of the Superior National Forest, and the Hunter's Island portion of Quetico Provincial Park (the section bounded by the international border, Lakes Saganaga and Kawnipi, and the Maligne River).

At the end of the war, Wilson argued that conservationists and government agencies should give urgent priority to the acquisition of the 55,465 hectares of private lands scattered throughout the Superior roadless areas. Resorts on these lands were growing in popularity, and posed an enormous threat to the solitude of the wilderness canoe country. By 1945, some two dozen aircraft regularly crisscrossed Quetico-Superior, carrying passengers and supplies to forty interior resorts, some nineteen of which were located in the roadless areas. Since Minnesota had determined to prevent the federal government from taking over the state forest lands and adding them to the Superior National Forest in keeping with the QSC scheme, conservationist groups and the U.S. Forest Service had little choice but to concentrate on purging the roadless areas of the resorts. Blinded by his resentment of Wilson, Ernest Oberholtzer resisted this change in strategy. All the same, during 1945, the Minnesota Conservation Department, the U.S. Forest Service, and the conservationist groups finally reached a consensus; the federal government must attempt both to acquire the private holdings in the roadless areas of the Superior National Forest and to seek a ban on aircraft for the border lakes. Subsequently they combined to draft a federal acquisition bill to enable the American Secretary of Agriculture to purchase the resorts within the roadless areas.

Wilson eventually received Ontario's support for his modified version of the QSC program, but not without having to overcome serious opposition. In Fort Frances, Acting District Forester J.M. Whalen proved to be a formidable opponent. He was of the opinion that Quetico Park should be abandoned, because it ran annual operating deficits and few Ontarians used it. Then in 1944, just as the Americans were beginning to consolidate the roadless areas, Whalen approved the applications of two established American fly-in resort operators to lease land in the Hunter's Island portion of the park.[39]

H.W. Crosbie, chief of the Division of Land and Recreational Areas, agreed that the commercial leases should be granted and advised Deputy Minister MacDougall that "no advantages [would] be gained by Ontario" in acceding to the American proposal for cooperation in creating an international wilderness region, even on the limited scale proposed by Chester Wilson. The sole beneficiaries of such a scheme, Crosbie believed, would be the tourist operators in Minnesota. He thought that the Americans only wanted Ontario to maintain Quetico Park in a wilderness state for the benefit of the resort owners in the Superior National Forest. Since the Forest Service proposed only to remove the nineteen resorts in the roadless areas, the remaining operators in the national forest would be ideally located to exploit Quetico Park. After studying the matter, Premier George Drew also concluded that the American joint wilderness scheme smacked of a conspiracy. "It seemed to me," Drew recalled in 1948, "that under the guise of an appeal to preserve and protect the [Quetico] Park area, this actually was an attempt to continue an exclusive resort playground" for a group of Chicago millionaires.[40]

As luck would have it, local business interests in Fort Frances entered the debate and tipped the scales in favour of leaving the Quetico interior free of resorts, at least for the time being. Both the chamber of commerce and the Canadian Legion vigorously opposed the prospect of American businessmen gaining a foothold in Quetico Provincial Park. The Fort Frances interests demanded a moratorium on resort leases until after the war, when a highway would probably be built from Port Arthur; at that time, the future of the park could be carefully planned and developed by and for Ontario residents! The chamber of commerce also requested that the decision on the international wilderness zones be deferred until the question of highway access had been resolved. Acting District Forester Whalen yielded to this intense local pressure and in September 1944 withdrew his recommendation to grant leases to the American resort operators.[41]

With this threat neutralized, Chester Wilson set out to promote his wilderness concept in Ontario. In March 1946, he led a delegation to Toronto, which included Superior National Forest Supervisor Galen W. Pike and Kenneth Reid, executive director of the Izaak Walton League, to confer with officials of the DLF. The Americans outlined their plan to set up a revolving fund to acquire private lands in the Superior roadless areas.[42] In June, Wilson and Pike addressed the Port Arthur Convention of the Northwestern Ontario Associated Chambers of Commerce, before moving on to Kenora and Fort Frances for talks with local business and political interests. "We made it clear," Wilson explained, "that we were not fronting for any program of federal or international control of the whole Rainy Lake watershed, and that our aim was simply to get the existing authorities ... to co-operate in protecting ... the wilderness canoe country along the boundary on both sides." As Wilson and Pike undertook their public-relations tour, distrust of American intentions began to dissipate. Northwestern Ontario businessmen responded warmly to Wilson's statement that he fully endorsed the construction of a Fort Frances–Port Arthur highway to the north of Quetico Park. That road, he hoped, would stimulate a local tourist industry, an activity that would chiefly benefit Ontario merchants, tourist outfitters, and resort owners. "Our plan is not to isolate this territory," he insisted, "but to protect wilderness zones of reasonable size and make them accessible to the public by encouraging construction of roads, resorts, and summer homes around the margin."[43]

Following these productive meetings, Governor Edward J. Thye of Minnesota, in conjunction with the Izaak Walton League, asked the Ontario government to declare a temporary suspension of land disposition in Quetico Park, while the American conservationists moved their bill to acquire and thereby eliminate the private holdings in the Superior roadless areas through Congress. "Naturally, our whole purchase program would be futile, and would have to be dropped if those we bought out on the American side merely hopped across on your side," explained Kenneth Reid of the Izaak Walton League.[44] After conferring with the chamber of commerce and the Conservative association in Fort Frances, the Ontario government agreed to the request. Clearly, Chester Wilson's work had paid dividends; his public relations efforts had been the critical element in winning over both the economic and political power brokers in northwestern Ontario and ultimately the Drew cabinet. A year later, in May 1948, Lands and Recreational Areas chief Wilson Cram confided to Sigurd Olson of the Quetico-Superior Council that the suspension on leases "would be extended indefinitely." Olson wrote excitedly to his colleagues: "It is a set policy, and will be continued [until] such time as we give up the fight on our side."[45] However, there was little chance of the American conservationists "giving up the fight"; indeed, the assault on commercialism in the Superior roadless areas intensified in December 1949, when President Harry S. Truman signed a precedent-setting executive order, establishing an airspace reservation above these areas. The order also specified that, beginning on 1 January 1952, the owners of private land in the roadless areas would be forbidden to use aircraft to reach their properties.

In the postwar era, as Chester Wilson and others modified the original Quetico-Superior Council scheme, the QSC did not abandon its goal of protecting the entire Rainy Lake watershed by formal treaty between Canada and the United States. With the help of several influential Canadians – Clifford Sifton, who controlled a string of newspapers and radio stations; Harold C. Walker, a prominent Toronto lawyer; and Vincent Massey, formerly Canada's first ambassador in Washington – the American conservationists finally succeeded in establishing a Canadian Quetico-Superior Committee, the first wilderness society to be formed in Ontario. In March 1949, no less a patron than General Dwight D. Eisenhower had written, in his capacity as president of Columbia University, to University of Toronto Chancellor Vincent Massey, endorsing Ernest Oberholtzer's 1927 scheme for Quetico-Superior. With Eisenhower's letter in hand, Massey organized a luncheon for a group of eminent Ontarians who had shown an interest in the QSC cause. Evidently Eisenhower's endorsement, combined with Massey's personal suasion, did the trick; all the luncheon guests agreed to form the Canadian Quetico-Superior Committee. Thirty-one individuals, mainly businessmen and intellectuals, eventually joined the group. Vincent Massey agreed to serve as chairman, with Harold Walker as vice-chairman. Other members included former Lands and Forests Minister William Finlayson, Abitibi Pulp and Paper Company President D.W. Ambridge, Toronto public relations executive James A. Cowan, General H.D.G. Crerar, *Globe and Mail* editor Oakley Dalgleish, Massey-Harris Chairman James S. Duncan, Professor J.R. Dymond, Steep Rock Mine President Donald M. Hogarth, and his successor M.S. "Pop" Fotheringham, conservationists John C. Irwin and C. Aubrey Walkinshaw, *Saturday Night* editor B.K. Sandwell, Clifford Sifton, and industrialist-financier E.P. Taylor.

Encouraged by the momentum building in Ontario, the American conservationists rushed hastily into action in late 1949 and prepared a draft "Treaty for the Establishment of an International Forest in the Quetico-Superior Area."[46] Written largely by Ernest Oberholtzer and reworked by the American State Department, the document reached the Ontario government in January 1950. It called for the joint management of the Rainy Lake and Pigeon River watersheds, "to protect the rare natural values" of the area, and "to perpetuate the wilderness character of the region in the form of an international memorial forest." Its many virtues notwithstanding, the draft treaty had no chance of being accepted by Ontario. Article 11 sealed its fate by proposing to oblige the Canadian and American governments to establish an international advisory committee as the mechanism for implementing joint management of the region. Unfortunately, the QSC's proposal specified that the dominion cabinet would appoint the three Canadian representatives, something certain to anger the provincial government. Harold Walker tried gamely to argue that the treaty would "not involve the surrender of sovereignty, management or jurisdiction," but Ontario officials found his logic confusing and unconvincing.[47]

The draft treaty also came under scathing attack by the Northwestern Ontario Associated Chambers of Commerce, whose members petitioned both the federal and provincial governments "not to surrender Quetico Park to an International authority." So, too, did the Northern Ontario Outfitters Association.[48] Both groups feared that international control under a treaty would jeopardize the construction of a highway from the head of Lake Superior to Fort Frances. Their opposition was not a case of businessmen versus wilderness, for the associated chambers of commerce had already approved Chester Wilson's zoning proposals, which blended wilderness protection for the canoe country with resort development along a Fort Frances–Port Arthur highway. Moreover, the business organizations were not far off the mark in harbouring suspicions of the intentions of the more inflexible proponents of the wilderness. Ernest Oberholtzer, for one, did not relish the thought of a development road cutting through the centre of the Rainy Lake region.

With the treaty proposal in tatters, the Canadian Quetico-Superior Committee had, perforce, to review its plans. Donald P. O'Hearn, hired as executive secretary of the committee in August 1950, was assigned to assess the status of the group. A highly regarded member of the parliamentary press gallery, O'Hearn enjoyed open-door privileges in the office of Premier Leslie Frost. Through his ties with the premier, O'Hearn obtained access, in September 1950, to the DLF file on Quetico Park. As O'Hearn perused the documents, he realized that "the project had been very badly handled from the start" by his American colleagues. "The initial suggestion ... that the Dominion should take over the land," he reported, seemed "in the light of practical politics ... absolutely fantastic ... The initial impression these first overtures made still remains." O'Hearn was also struck by the weight given to the opinions of the business and political interests

Map 1: Quetico-Superior Area

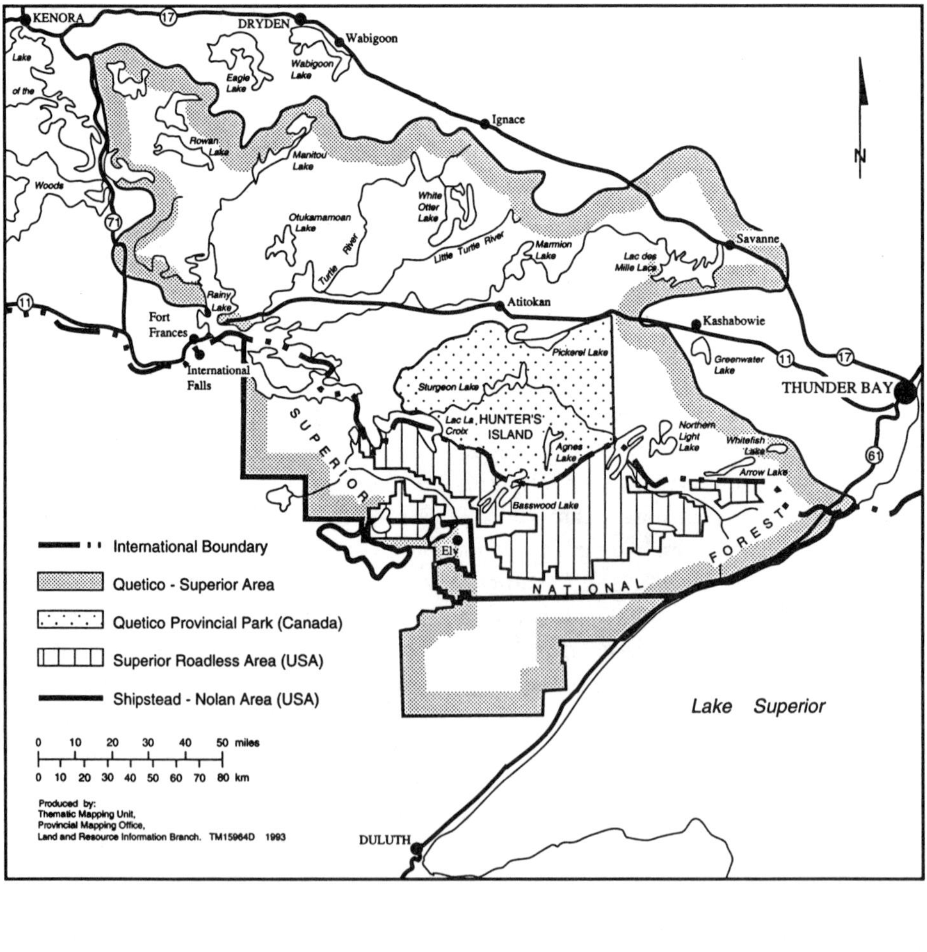

in Fort Frances. Unless the local people could be won over, he concluded, the QSC did not stand a chance of realizing its objectives.[49] Nowhere in the Ontario government could O'Hearn find sympathy for the concept of a Canadian-American treaty. Later, in private discussions with the premier, he discovered that Frost had "made up his mind that the [QSC] project, particularly the treaty aspect, wasn't feasible." On more than one occasion, Frost told O'Hearn that "the province would do 'acre for acre' what the U.S. did," but "that 'Old Man Ontario would not give away control of his land.'"

Subsequently, O'Hearn recommended a "practical politics" strategy for the Canadian Quetico-Superior Committee, one that placed him closer to Minnesota's Chester Wilson than to Ernest Oberholtzer. "If the prime purpose of the committee is early implementation of the treaty," he wrote, "I would recommend its discontinuance." Retain the treaty idea simply "as an ultimate objective without any real expectation of seeing it for many years," urged O'Hearn. The first priority of the committee must be the cultivation of "sympathetic opinion in the Rainy River and Lakehead districts," and to accomplish that the Committee "should heartily endorse [the Fort Frances–Port Arthur] road" to be built to the north of Quetico Park. Every effort must be made to promote tourist resorts and outfitters along this transportation corridor, in order to match the long-established American tourist industry based on the recreational use of the wilderness canoe country. Then, perhaps, the province might "look on the treaty in an entirely different light."

O'Hearn's report fueled an intense debate within the QSC movement. Eventually, in the light of the certainty that a highway would be built between Atikokan and Fort William, the voices of moderation sided with O'Hearn over the opposition of Ernest Oberholtzer. In 1952, the Canadian QSC declared in favour of the highway and called for a cooperative effort among all interest groups and the government to fashion a management plan for the highway corridor. On cue, the Northwestern Ontario Associated Chambers of Commerce resolved to assume this planning challenge and, in September 1952, struck the Quetico Committee of Northwestern Ontario, with M.S. "Pop" Fotheringham as chairman. The establishment of this committee had been engineered in part by the conservationists, particularly through the influence of Fotheringham, president of Steep Rock Mine in Atikokan and a founding member of the Canadian QSC. In the spring of 1954, Fotheringham's planning group completed its task and submitted a report to the Department of Lands and Forests. The committee's recommendations became the basis of the government's policy for Quetico, announced, as we have seen, by the minister of lands and forests, Clare Mapledoram, in August of that year.

Parks for the People, 1954–67

Having dealt with the Quetico question, Mapledoram proceeded to make other important decisions pertaining to provincial parks. On 1 October, he surprised many senior personnel within his department by creating an entirely new Division of Parks, not a mere section of the Division of Lands and Recreational Areas as the foresters had advised the previous January. To head the new division, he selected a top-ranking field man, the regional forester in the Eastern Region, W. Ben Greenwood. A graduate of the University of Toronto School of Forestry in 1925, Greenwood had begun his career with the DLF but resigned in 1935 during the Hepburn purge. For twelve years he engaged in various logging operations, worked with the timber controller during the war, and later supervised the tie operations of the Algoma Central Railway. He returned to the DLF in 1947 to join the Land and Recreational Areas Division, where Deputy Minister MacDougall placed him "in charge of parks and the development of recreational areas in the Province, for which no one [had] been trained." That experience made Greenwood the ideal choice as chief of the new Division of Parks.[50]

Greenwood was a spark plug of an administrator, who delighted in the thought of being the advance man for a parks system that was soon to explode. Routine and detail did not appeal to him; he revelled in the major policy issues and the challenge of adapting to constantly changing situations. A diminutive man, his white hair closely cropped, he exuded self-confidence. Vibrant and intense, yet engaging and charming, he enjoyed a good joke, slipped easily into the vernacular of the lumberman, and was noted for his gift of the gab. In the grey, dowdy world of the civil service, Ben Greenwood stood out; whether at Queen's Park or in the field, he dressed impeccably, looking as if he had stepped off a page of the latest fashion magazine.

With the proclamation of the Provincial Parks Act on 1 December 1954, Premier Frost ended months of speculation by assigning to the minister of lands and forests the responsibility for managing all eight Class 1 and 2 parks, a decision which stripped the Department of Municipal Affairs of any responsibility for provincially operated parklands like Long Point and Presqu'ile. Within a few weeks, Greenwood rushed to rationalize the management of his eight parks by calling for the abolition of the Long Point and Presqu'ile park commissions. He recommended that both areas, then designated as Class 2 parks, be reclassified as Class 1 provincial parks under the control of a district forester or superintendent. His recommendations reached cabinet in February 1955 and came into effect on 1 July 1956.[51]

In late 1954, Greenwood also addressed the issue of an aircraft ban for the interior of both Quetico and Algonquin. The question could no longer be easily postponed, considering the promises made by DLF officials to their counterparts in the U.S. Forest Service: Ontario would prohibit the landing of aircraft in the boundary waters area of Quetico-Superior if the Americans succeeded in doing so on their side. By this time, President Truman's executive order of 1949, prohibiting the use by resort owners in the Superior roadless area of float planes to enable them to reach their properties, had come into effect and successfully withstood challenges in the courts. Greenwood accordingly began negotiations with the

Ben Greenwood, Ontario's first chief of the Division of Parks, serving from 1954 to 1960.
Courtesy: Quetico Park Archives.

Two men who shaped provincial parks policy in Ontario – Leslie M. Frost (left), premier of Ontario 1949–61, and Frank A. MacDougall – chatting in Lindsay, Ontario, in 1969.
Courtesy: Archives of Ontario.

federal Department of Transport and the Air Transport Board for permission to establish a ban on aircraft landings in the interior of both Algonquin and Quetico. On 25 April 1955, landings by private and commercial aircraft were restricted to a half-dozen locations, just inside the boundaries of each park.[52] With that last element of the back-to-nature policy in place, Ben Greenwood steeled himself to tackle the outdoor recreational crisis, and to provide the urgently needed "parks for the people."

The Division of Parks began on a small scale. Initially, Ben Greenwood recruited only one casual and three permanent employees to staff the main office in Toronto. The division's operating budget that first year amounted to a modest $16,000. Since the parks program was to be dovetailed with the Department of Lands and Forests' district administrative system, the division could rely on the twenty-two district foresters and their resource experts to assume much of the responsibility for the planning, development, and management of individual parks. All that would be required in the way of new field personnel, then, would be a park supervisor in each district office and some labour, mainly seasonal, to operate the parks. In 1956, Greenwood began to appoint the district park supervisors who were destined to serve as the backbone of the division's field organization. These people were mainly recruited from the ranks of the fish and wildlife, lands, and timber management divisions. Most had no background in the parks, but what they lacked in experience, they quickly made up for in dedication, creativity, and common sense.

Greenwood intended the main office staff to serve as the driving force of the expansion program by devising policies on fee schedules and concessions, determining land acquisition and development priorities, providing assistance to the districts in the master planning and management of the larger parks, and setting standards for the construction of buildings, roads, signs, and the like. As his planning supervisor, the parks chief selected Alan R.K. MacDonald, a young forester, who had worked previously as a recreational planner in the old Lands and Recreational Areas Division. Tom Van Deusen served as office manager and George Delahey as parks inspector. The latter possessed many years of experience in Quetico and as a district forester in northwestern Ontario. Once expansion got underway in 1955, new personnel joined the head office team. Alf B. Wheatley became assistant chief and construction supervisor in charge of the increasingly complex operations side of the provincial parks system, while Art Chappelle, a draftsman, assisted with various tasks, such as designing park development plans, buildings, entrances, and even furniture. Alan F. Helmsley, who had been in charge of the Algonquin Park nature program, arrived in September 1955 to expand interpretive services across the system. By the end of the Greenwood era (1954–60), division headquarters had grown to thirteen permanent staff and four limited-term employees, a department with an operating budget of $1.3 million and separate development and land acquisition budgets of $2.5 million and $285,632 respectively.[53]

The division launched the provincial parks expansion program, determined that sound planning would precede any development. Indeed, no development funds were budgeted for 1954–55. During the first year, top priority went to the basic task of identifying and rating potential park sites across the province. In the heavily populated southern districts with extremely limited public access to shorelines around the Great Lakes and other major lakes and waterways, the district foresters received instructions to survey their domains for beach properties. Even in the northern districts, beaches were a primary criterion in the selection process. The question of the size of provincial parks was not initially clarified, although by 1957 the idea had taken root that new parks should normally be no smaller than 200 hectares, so that provision could be made for a variety of recreational activities, particularly camping, picnicking, and hiking. District staff were also asked to identify sites with unusual topography, scenic or historical features, or unique flora and fauna. Beyond these general considerations, the new parks in the south were to be located within a two-hour drive of large urban centres and, in northern Ontario, situated approximately 160 to 240 kilometres apart, along Highways 11 and 17 and their connecting routes. As for the question of administrative jurisdiction, the division attempted to apply the principle that small park sites, situated near population centres, should be the responsibility of local conservation authorities or municipalities. Evidently, these general criteria sufficed to guide the district foresters and park supervisors in the initial half-dozen years of the ongoing site identification process. As soon as the district reports reached his desk, Greenwood himself inspected most locations, in order to set priorities for land acquisition in southern Ontario and for the reservation of Crown land in the north. Once new parkland had been selected, it fell to the district personnel to initiate the site planning phase and to submit a draft development plan to the main office for review and approval, before any construction began.[54]

By April 1956, the district surveys had resulted in the acquisition or reservation of 112 properties for provincial park purposes, including forty-five roadside picnic areas or campgrounds, formerly administered by the Department of Highways. Greenwood did not welcome the acquisition of the highway properties, because so many were "too small to fit into the Provincial Parks system." In his opinion, they had been "dumped" on the division by order of the premier and the Treasury Board. Greenwood's opinion notwithstanding, the politicians were seeking to rectify a situation, in which "the public were being accommodated free in the Department of Highways' parks where overnight camping was permitted," while the DLF charged entrance and campground fees in provincial parks.[55] The roadside recreational areas, the Treasury Board decided, should also be made to generate revenues. As it happened, Greenwood's vigorous objections to the highway properties had some effect. When the formal transfer of the roadside areas took place by orders-in-council in 1957, the number involved had been reduced to thirty.

Ben Greenwood still considered this number excessive, and within a few years six sites were returned to the Department of Highways and several others abandoned altogether. As for the remaining roadside areas, he took consolation in the fact that they had been selected in the first instance for their scenic qualities; some possessed beaches, shaded picnic grounds, and a limited number of campsites on well-travelled auto routes. A few locations of substantial size – Rushing River, in the Lake of the Woods vicinity, for example, and Pancake Bay, with its superb beach on Lake Superior, north of the Sault – could even be developed into first-class recreational areas.

Apart from the Department of Highways' properties, the Division of Parks also succeeded by 1960 in locating, reserving, or acquiring some seventy-six other provincial park locations. In northern Ontario, many of the sites selected for the parks system had been set aside earlier as "Deferred Development Zones" by the District Land Use Planning Committees. This designation had saved many prime recreational areas from alienation and development.

Four new parks in southern Ontario were obtained in part or in whole through donations: Mark S. Burnham Provincial Park near Peterborough, a 44-hectare tract of land, containing one of the few remnants of virgin timber in the region, given to the Crown by the Burnham family; John E. Pearce Provincial Park (named in honour of its donor), a 12-hectare wooded tract on

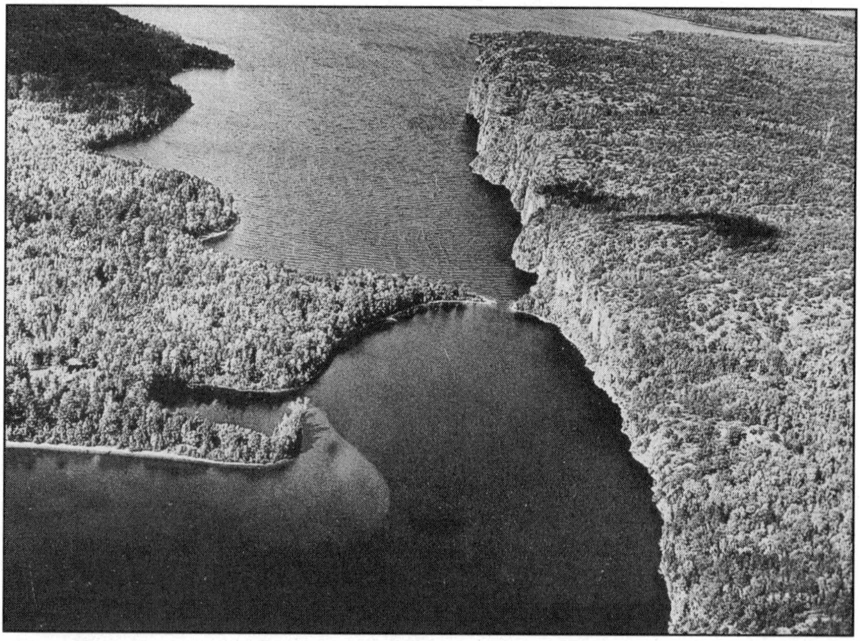

Bon Echo Provincial Park: the narrows at Mazinaw Lake, looking north.
Courtesy: Ministry of Natural Resources.

Lake Erie near Wallacetown; Emily Provincial Park on the Pigeon River in the Kawarthas, a gift of the township of Emily in Victoria County; and Earl Rowe Provincial Park (named after the donor, a former lieutenant governor of Ontario), along the Boyne River, west of Alliston. The outstanding Bon Echo Provincial Park, the largest in eastern Ontario, also owed its establishment in part to the generosity of a private citizen. In 1959, Canadian playwright and author Merrill Denison sold to the Crown his highly desirable 480-hectare property on both sides of the narrows on Lake Mazinaw for the modest sum of $12,000. Denison had been attempting to arrange such a sale since the 1930s, but it took Greenwood to bring the matter to fruition. With the addition of other private and public lands, Bon Echo became a substantial 6,644-hectare park, one which combined ideal recreational facilities and scenery of a truly magnificent quality with a fascinating human history. Along the imposing cliffs on Lake Mazinaw are to be found over one hundred aboriginal rock paintings, attributable to an Algonkian people, probably Ojibway. No other pictograph site in Ontario rivals this one in terms of the quantity of the rock symbols to be found there.[56]

Other southern Ontario provincial parks had to be acquired by purchasing expensive private property. Much to his credit, Greenwood acted decisively during 1955–56 to obtain both the magnificent Pinery on Lake Huron and the Sibbald Point property on Lake Simcoe. With rapid development – some 900 tent and trailer sites were constructed by 1961 – the Pinery became second only to Algonquin Park as a camping destination in Ontario. Likewise, Sibbald Point, with its 600-metre beach, space for hundreds of campsites (428 in 1960), boat-launching facilities, extensive picnic grounds, and parking for 3,000 cars, emerged quickly as one of south-central Ontario's most popular summer recreational parks.[57]

Greenwood also moved with alacrity to obtain the Serpent Mounds property on the north shore of Rice Lake, a beautiful recreation spot, with enormous significance from an archaeological point of view. Some archaeologists believe that the elongated burial mound on the site was deliberately shaped in the form of a serpent effigy. The mounds date back to ca. 100–300 AD and were constructed by a Middle Point Peninsula people indigenous to the Trent waterway, who were apparently influenced by the distant Ohio Hopewell culture. When notified in the spring of 1955 by Royal Ontario Museum archaeologist Kenneth Kidd and Provincial Archivist George Spragge that the Rice Lake band, who owned the site, intended to subdivide the shoreline for cottage lots, Greenwood and the district officials took immediate action. Happily, the band agreed to terminate their cottage development and lease the Serpent Mounds property as a provincial park.[58]

On the south shore of Georgian Bay, the division also assumed control of some eleven kilometres of the extraordinary Wasaga Beach, which swept in a huge crescent around Nottawasaga Bay. Until 1959, the sections of the beach that became the provincial park had been maintained under licences of occupation by the village of Wasaga Beach and the township of Sunnidale. In the mid-1950s, however, the municipalities realized that the sanitation and traffic problems associated with servicing some 30,000 to 50,000 visitors on a summer weekend far exceeded their capability to handle them. Consequently, local officials invited the province to step in and manage the Crown beach as a provincial park. Ben Greenwood and Deputy Minister Frank MacDougall initially recoiled from the proposal, viewing it as a dangerous precedent, one likely to encourage other municipalities to foist upon the province the costs of developing recreational facilities.[59]

All the same, civil servants and politicians alike came around to the view that conditions on the beach demanded a provincial, rather than a municipal response. The great natural resource that had attracted people to Wasaga in the first place had been sadly abused over the years. No off-beach parking had been provided, so that on summer weekends, the shoreline between the dunes and the water resembled a gigantic parking lot. Traffic control was nonexistent. Pollution had become a serious issue, since the busiest stretch of beach – eight kilometres long – contained only one washroom facility. Reluctantly, then, in 1959, the Division of Parks assumed control of the three kilometres of beach near the village as a provincial park, and added the section previously administered by Sunnidale Township the following year.[60]

Following the policy that provincial parks in southern Ontario, below the French–Mattawa Rivers line, be located on the Great Lakes or other major bodies of water, Greenwood managed to obtain some of the best parkland sites available within the recreational hinterlands of Ontario's largest cities. The Pinery, Sibbald Point, Serpent Mounds, and Wasaga Beach represent only a small portion of his legacy. On Lake Erie, three new provincial parks – Holiday Beach, Rock Point, and Turkey Point – all suitable for high-density, recreational use, were opened to the public by the 1960 season. Sauble Falls Provincial Park, adjacent to the popular Sauble Beach, and Inverhuron Park, noteworthy both for its beaches and its archaeological resources, were established on Lake Huron. On surplus farmland, originally obtained by the government for the construction of Highway 401, the Parks Division created Darlington Provincial Park, to the east of the city of Oshawa on the shoreline of Lake Ontario. At the eastern extremity of the lake, in Prince Edward County, the division acquired two contiguous park locations, areas long frequented by Picton residents for swimming and picnicking – Outlet and Sandbanks. The latter, previously part of a forestry station established in 1921, held special significance. The giant dunes to be found there, some of them rising to a height of nearly thirty metres, were a unique geographical feature, possibly the best landform of its kind in Canada. The 486-hectare sand peninsula also contained an eight-kilometre-long beach which, after development in 1966, became the finest public beach on the Canadian shore of Lake

Ontario. In the eastern part of the province, other valuable properties were added to the system and most of them rapidly opened to public use – Rideau River, Fitzroy and Driftwood on the Ottawa River, and Samuel de Champlain Provincial Park on the Mattawa River, the historic route of the voyageurs.

In the highly developed resort areas of Lake Simcoe and the Muskoka Lakes, the division ran into insurmountable obstacles when trying to find parklands. "We have ... made a very intensive survey of ... the Muskoka Lakes," Greenwood reported in 1960, but "it is almost impossible to find any sizeable, suitable area, which is not highly developed; furthermore, land values are tremendously high."[61] The identical situation existed on Lake Simcoe. Not to be denied, Greenwood looked to adjacent areas. In Simcoe County, three new parks were established – Springwater, Six Mile Lake, and Bass Lake. With the Muskoka Lakes closed to them, division staff focussed the search for parkland in the Parry Sound District, along Highway 11, immediately north of Huntsville, and along Highway 69, from Parry Sound to the French River. Mikisew Provincial Park, near South River on Highway 11, about halfway between Huntsville and North Bay, opened in 1958. Along the Highway 69 corridor, which follows the Georgian Bay shoreline, two large parks were in operation by 1960 – Grundy Lake and Killbear – each an exceptional site from the point of view both of recreational and natural facilities. Killbear Provincial Park, located on Georgian Bay north of Parry Sound, lay in the popular Thirty Thousand Islands zone. It contains broad sandy beaches, smooth, sloping rocks, an extraordinarily scenic combination of glacier- and wave-smoothed pink granites, violently twisted gneisses, and gnarled pine trees. Not surprisingly, Killbear soon became the third most popular camping park in Ontario after Algonquin and the Pinery.

With the relative abundance of Crown land in northern Ontario, the Parks Division had little difficulty in implementing the policy of locating provincial parks at convenient intervals along the highways crossing the north. Many of these northern parks were large enough to serve more than recreational objectives; they often contained representative units of northern forest types, typical and sometimes unique geological and biological features, outstanding scenery, and occasionally, significant cultural resources. Greenwood especially concentrated his attention on the northeast, along the Highway 11 corridor, between North Bay and Kapuskasing, an area devoid of provincial parks in 1954. Within six years, a chain of parks had been created, each lying close to the region's major population centres: Marten River, near North Bay; Kap-Kig-Iwan, near Englehart; Esker Lakes, close to Kirkland Lake; Kettle Lakes, over 1,261 hectares in size, technically located within the boundaries of the city of Timmins; Greenwater, near Cochrane; and Remi Lake, just east of Kapuskasing.

While the northeast sector of Highway 11 benefited greatly in the first six years of expansion, the other northern regions were not overlooked. For instance, two new parks were developed at roughly 160-kilometre intervals along Highway 101, between Timmins on the east and Wawa on the west – Ivanhoe, near Foleyet, and Five Mile Lake, near Chapleau. Farther north, below the junction of Highways 11 and 631 between Hearst and Longlac, a huge area, eventually expanded to over 8,100 hectares, became Nagagamisis Provincial Park. On the south shore of Lake Nipigon, the largest lake contained entirely in the province of Ontario, the division found an ideal park location and opened it in 1960. Originally known as Blacksand, but renamed Lake Nipigon, this site offered visitors grand scenery from towering cliff tops, unusual black sand beaches, canoe routes, legendary fishing, and historical features in the form of an old Hudson's Bay Company post and Indian settlement. In northwestern Ontario, beyond Thunder Bay, parks were also created at intervals along the Trans-Canada Highway corridor at Kakabeka Falls,

Kakabeka Falls Provincial Park, 1959. *Courtesy: Ministry of Natural Resources.*

Upsala (Inwood Provincial Park), and Dryden (Aaron Park). Blue Lake Provincial Park was established eight kilometres north of Vermilion Bay. And finally, four new parks were located in the vicinity of Lake of the Woods, a resort mecca for thousands of Ontarians, Manitobans, and Americans – these were named Rushing River, Sioux Narrows, Caliper Lake, and Lake of the Woods. The last named, a choice property, rich both in natural and archaeological features, was acquired from the Little Grassy River Indian band.

All in all, Ben Greenwood had made a remarkable contribution during his six years as parks chief. Having started with the original eight parks, the division had twenty-three in operation in 1956, fifty-five in 1957, and seventy-seven in 1961. Year after year, Ontarians flocked into them in numbers beyond all expectations. An estimated 2.1 million visitors arrived in 1957, 5.1 million in 1959, and 6.2 million in 1961 – an almost 300 percent growth in numbers over five years. Even more impressive were the figures for campers, which revealed an astounding 995 percent increase, from 86,641 in 1956 to 862,559 in 1961. Many camping enthusiasts graduated from organized campgrounds to the wilderness in the interior of Algonquin and Quetico. Park staff in Algonquin, for example, were staggered by the threefold jump in the numbers of interior visitors, from 10,633 in 1958 to 32,802 in 1961.[62]

Clearly, Ontarians had enthusiastically embraced the camping craze that was sweeping North America. In 1958, when the number of campers using American state parks increased by a noteworthy 24 percent over the 1957 season, the increase in Ontario was an amazing 68 percent. Only six American state park systems that year recorded a larger total number of camper days than Ontario's provincial parks.[63] Residents of the province made up 71 percent of all campers in 1956, with 6 percent coming from other parts of Canada and 23 percent from the United States. The availability of new parkland and facilities contributed greatly to the camping phenomenon. Technological advances in outdoor recreation equipment enticed a larger proportion of the population to go camping. The Coleman company led all its competitors by marketing portable ice chests, pressure-fed gas stoves, and lanterns. For those who combined camping with boating and fishing, the 1950s witnessed a boom in the production and use of small aluminum and fibreglass boats, canoes, and outboard motors. By the 1960s, wilderness trippers were enjoying a previously unimagined mobility, self-sufficiency, and comfort, with a full range of new, lightweight equipment and dehydrated foods. At the other end of the spectrum, those who preferred the comforts of home while they communed with nature were able to purchase mass-produced tent trailers, house trailers, and more and more recreational vehicles.[64]

The Division of Parks, renamed the Parks Branch in 1959, could scarcely keep up with the camping explosion. Ben Greenwood noted in his first statistical report (1957) that "practically all campground facilities were overcrowded" during the summer months. "We should be prepared to increase all camper

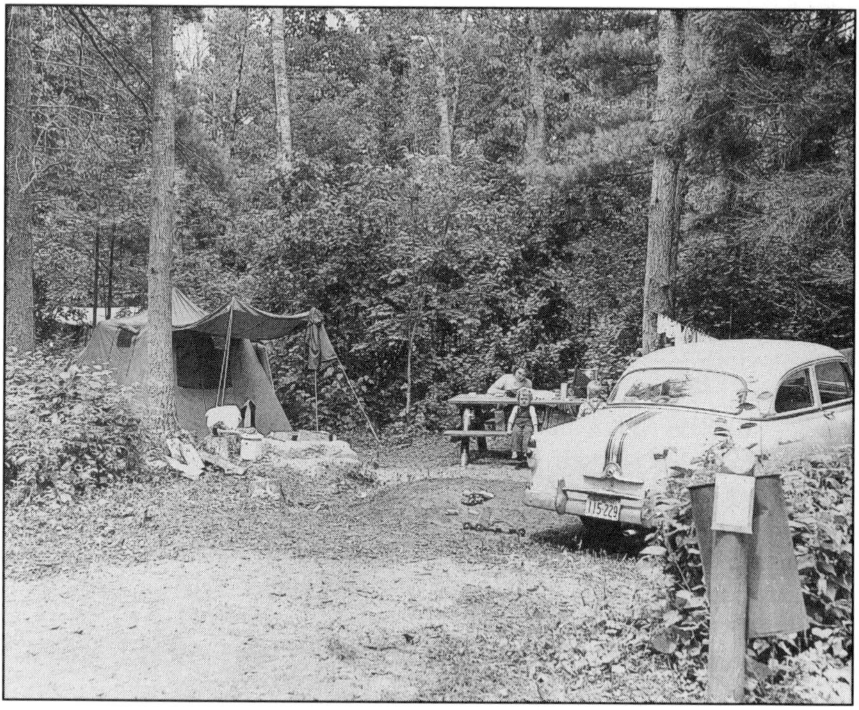

Car camping exploded in popularity during the 1950s and early 1960s. Seen here is a typical campsite at Grundy Lake Provincial Park, 1960. *Courtesy: Ministry of Natural Resources.*

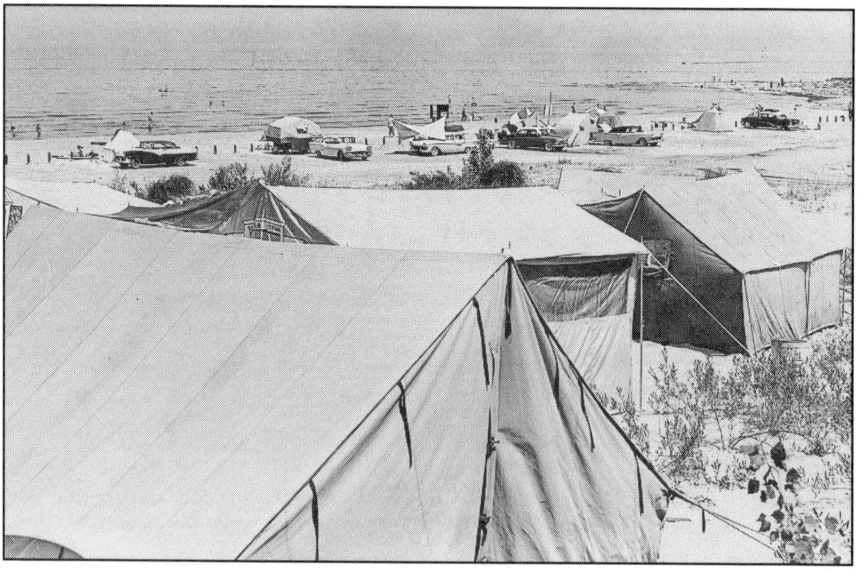

Camping on the beach at Ipperwash Provincial Park, 1958. *Courtesy: Ministry of Natural Resources.*

facilities by a very minimum of 50%." In fact, by the summer of 1958, the number of campsites doubled from 1,849 to 3,687. Nevertheless, demand for sites still ran ahead of the supply. More campgrounds had to be rushed to completion, raising the number of available tent and trailer sites to 10,591 by 1961. The Parks Division development budget jumped from $455,000 in 1956 to $3.3 million in 1959 and $2.5 million in 1960. Operating costs climbed from $500,000 in 1957 to $1.3 million three years later. These were impressive statistics. In 1959, only three American states expended more on park expansion, development, and operation than did Ontario.[65]

Fortuitously, beginning in the winter of 1958–59, the federal government of Prime Minister John G. Diefenbaker launched the federal-provincial winter works program to alleviate unemployment during the recession of 1957-61. This resulted in an infusion of funds ($1.4 million in 1958–59, $862,415 in 1959–60, and $1.2 million in 1960–61) for a great many undertakings – roads, parking lots, boat-launching ramps, comfort stations, picnic shelters, and reforestation projects. In 1960, the federal and provincial governments also agreed to share equally in the cost of establishing campgrounds in parks along the Trans-Canada Highway.[66]

In spite of the many accomplishments of the Parks Division during the Greenwood years, the applause in some quarters was muted. Premier Leslie Frost, for one, shuddered at the escalating costs of the several, provincially funded park agencies, the apparently open-ended nature of their programs, and the potential for the duplication of effort among them. In addition to the growth of the provincial parks system, conservation authorities were rapidly expanding their recreational areas, with 50 percent of the capital costs being assumed by the government of Ontario. By the summer of 1958, twenty-five conservation authorities were operating seventy-two separate recreation areas across southern Ontario. Meanwhile, between 1955 and 1961, the Ontario–St. Lawrence Development Commission opened fifteen recreation and historical parks along the St. Lawrence River, between the Quebec border and Adolphustown, west of Kingston. The St. Lawrence parks system included two special historical tourist attractions, Kingston's Old Fort Henry and Morrisburg's Upper Canada Village. As these park agencies expanded their work in outdoor recreation, Premier Frost frowned upon the modest role being assumed by local municipalities. "I do not want this [government]," Frost declared emphatically on several occasions, "to be saddled with the entire park development for the whole Province." Local governments, he insisted in 1955, should carry a share of the expenses.[67]

The premier expected Greenwood and the heads of the other park authorities to be more helpful. He was frustrated when they could not answer his questions as to how many and what kinds of parks were required across Ontario. When would supply equal demand? Where should each agency locate its parks and why? At what cost? Over how long a time would the costs be spread? How did the park agencies propose to avoid duplication of effort? What role should the municipalities be expected to play? Whether he realized it or not, Frost wanted nothing less than an overall parks and outdoor recreation plan for the province. He was not alone, for across North America, politicians and civil servants were pondering the same questions. In 1958, the American Congress created the Outdoor Recreation Resources Review Commission (ORRRC) to determine the nation's outdoor recreation needs, first currently, then for the years 1976 and 2000, and to recommend policies and programs to meet those needs. At the state level, the California legislature acted in 1957 to fashion a public outdoor-recreation plan for the next twenty years, a task completed in 1960. Maine and New York were also among the first states to conduct studies of recreational demands and, on the basis of those surveys, to publish long-range outdoor recreation plans. By the end of 1961, some twenty of the fifty states had made surveys of future needs, although only a few had produced long-range plans that specified objectives.[68]

Only vaguely aware of what such surveys and long-range planning entailed, yet astute enough to sense the direction in which his government must proceed, Frost called a joint meeting of the Treasury Board and the cabinet budget committee on 26 October 1955 and invited the senior administrators of all the key park agencies to attend. After voicing his concerns, the premier struck a special "parks committee" of cabinet ministers and senior civil servants, chaired by Charles Daley, minister of labour and chairman of the Niagara Parks Commission. The committee's mandate was to bring forward recommendations on the type of central administrative organization that was required to prevent costly duplication, "the underlying principles which should govern the establishment of provincial parks and the acquisition of land therefor," and the idea of financing all the park agencies by pooling in a special fund the water-rental revenues collected by the Niagara and St. Lawrence park commissions. Three months later, on 23 January 1956, the committee submitted its report to cabinet and, on the basis of the recommendations it contained, the Frost government established the Ontario Parks Integration Board (OPIB) in March of that year.[69]

The primary tasks of the new OPIB were to supervise, control, and integrate all policies involving the acquisition, development, and management of parks operated by the Ontario Department of Lands and Forests, the Niagara Parks Commission, and the St. Lawrence Development Commission, and to fashion "an overall policy on parks" for the province. The original board was composed of the chairmen of the Niagara Parks Commission and the St. Lawrence Development Commission, the treasurer of Ontario, and the ministers of lands and forests and of planning and development. Since most members were ministers of the Crown, the board enjoyed the de facto status and influence of a committee of cabinet. According to the OPIB act, the government intended to allocate to the board "all or any part of the moneys accruing to the Crown ... from water rentals" derived from the Niagara and St. Lawrence commissions. "To be frank with you," Premier Frost told the Legislative Assembly, "the motivating idea came from the great success of the Niagara Parks Commission." He wished to extend to the OPIB "the same policy ... followed by the Mowat government of 75 years ago, in giving the board revenues which would be independent of the consolidated revenue fund, and ... assure them always of a basic revenue upon which to operate." "Our idea," he announced, "is to develop the parks system from border to border."[70] As it turned out, Frost and his successors made good on the promise of creating a parks "system," but the idea of funding it through revenue from water power rentals never came to pass.

The OPIB's members soon discovered that the premier had assigned them an unenviable task. They had little idea how to proceed. "We are trying to find out what this board is supposed to do," blurted the slightly bewildered chairman, Charles Daley, during the second meeting of the group in September 1956.[71] As ministers of the Crown, weighed down by the many responsibilities of their departments, the board members could meet only briefly, once or twice a month, to deal with park issues. They had to rely on the civil service for background reports and recommendations on most questions, and for a context within which to make political decisions. For these reasons, the OPIB created an advisory committee of senior civil servants, drawn from relevant government departments and chaired by Ben Greenwood from 1956 to 1960. Much of the routine administrative activity of the board eventually fell to the OPIB's secretary, C. Russell Tilt of the Parks Division. A graduate of McMaster University (1949) in conservation and recreational planning, with a special certificate in horticulture from the Royal Botanical Gardens, Tilt joined the Parks Division in July 1957 as a landscape planner, the post of OPIB secretary being added to his job description in February 1958. It was a position of some influence, particularly after the OPIB dispensed with the advisory committee, following Greenwood's death in December 1960. Subsequently, the board members relied on Tilt to brief them on all agenda items and to explain the implications of the various options awaiting their decision. Given his training, personality, and proclivities, there were few people better suited for the sensitive position. Not surprisingly, Tilt retained the post until the board's demise in 1972.

Under the guidance of its advisory committee, the OPIB immediately began in 1956 to function as a clearing house for the three agencies under its mandate. No longer did each agency work in ignorance of the operations and plans of the others. The board reviewed and approved development budgets, parkland acquisitions, and proposals for new parks, and set fee and concession policies. The OPIB also allayed some of the premier's concerns about duplication and competition for parkland, especially in eastern Ontario, where the Division of Parks and the Ontario–St. Lawrence Development Commission had designs on some of the same properties. The board ruled that the development commission would restrict its park system to the waterfront of the St. Lawrence River and the Bay of Quinte, and saw to it that Ben Greenwood's division did not impinge upon the area.[72] Furthermore, the board acted as a buffer between the cabinet and the myriad public groups and local interests that sought to shape park development and policy decisions. In this capacity, the OPIB entertained briefs and delegations, deliberated over the various requests, and offered political advice to the premier.

Yet, no matter how useful the OPIB may have been, it did not fulfil the task of drafting a general policy statement, outlining the underlying principles governing the acquisition, development, and management of parkland by the agencies under its jurisdiction. The board functioned on an ad hoc basis; instead of approving the acquisition of parkland on "a planned basis, area-wise and policy-wise," one member frankly admitted, it selected sites on a "hit-and-miss [basis] which comes about when this property and that property are proposed by sundry individuals or authorities throughout the province."[73] To be fair, given the lack both of research data on outdoor recreation and of experts in system planning, the OPIB could scarcely have operated differently. For the board to solve such questions as how many parks the province needed and where they should be located to satisfy current and future demand, reams of statistical data, gathered from ongoing annual user surveys, were required, data the division had only begun to collect in 1957. Still, the OPIB's failure to grapple with general policy questions worried Premier Frost so much that he discarded the idea of turning over to the board the water-rental revenues promised in 1956. The budget-conscious premier was not inclined to release substantial funding to the OPIB until he had a clear idea of the scope of the parks system it projected and of the development and management principles that would apply at the provincial, regional, and local levels.

Much though the Frost government worried about the ultimate scope and cost of park expansion, the politicians recognized that public demand for parkland and outdoor recreation opportunities was showing no sign of slackening, especially in southern Ontario. In fact, the number of visitors entering provincial parks would jump from 6.2 million people in 1961 to 10.2 million in 1967, while the numbers of campers in the same period increased from 862,559 to 1.2 million. Elected officials could deny that demand only at their peril. In the early 1960s, the shortage of parkland in southern Ontario had reached a point where thousands of disgruntled campers were being turned away from parks already filled to overflowing on summer weekends. On the July and August holiday weekends in 1963, for instance, some 7,500 camping groups, or about 30,000 people, were denied access to provincial parks, mainly in southern Ontario. Parks Branch officials estimated in 1964 that simply to meet the existing demand for camping and recreation space in southwestern and south-central Ontario, they required over 3,600 hectares of additional parkland in order to add another 3,600 campsites to the 4,500 then available in these regions.[74]

The new administration of Premier John P. Robarts (1961–71) did not ignore the southern parkland issue. In May 1962, the premier ordered all government departments to prepare five-year program and expenditure forecasts for the Treasury Board, in what was his government's first effort "to develop a long-range timetable for Government policies and programmes."[75] As a consequence of this general priority-setting exercise, the concerns of the Parks Branch received special attention. In the throne speech of 27 November 1962, the government announced a $200-million, 20-year parkland acquisition program for recreational land along the Great Lakes shorelines and other priority areas.

Just before the throne speech, a new minister, A. Kelso Roberts, was given the charge of the Department of Lands and Forests. Formerly the attorney general of Ontario (1955–62), Roberts had been runner-up to John Robarts in the 1961 campaign to succeed Leslie Frost as premier and provincial Conservative Party leader. Kelso Roberts's appointment to Lands and Forests was viewed as a sign that his political star was on the wane; all the same, this tough-minded, energetic politician soon demonstrated that he was not yet ready to fade from public view. Before long, he gained the reputation among Parks Branch staff as being the most effective minister they had served to date.[76]

Kelso Roberts was also a keen Tory partisan, who immediately gave a political hue to the parkland selection and acquisition process. He inaugurated the "$200 million over 20 years" program by communicating with Conservative MLAs, seeking their recommendations on potential park locations in their ridings, and soliciting patronage lists of local realtors to assist in the purchase of desirable properties. Throughout his tenure at Lands and Forests (1962–66), he also heeded the advice of his caucus colleagues on acquisition matters and on decisions involving expropriation. Some Conservative MLAs even called the tune when it came to naming provincial parks. So solicitous was Roberts to the concerns of his fellow party members that some opposition critics claimed that unless a riding voted Tory, its chances of being selected for a new provincial park were slim to zero. Such charges were exaggerated, for in almost all cases when a new park appeared, the selection reflected Parks Branch priorities.[77]

Notwithstanding his partisan nature, Roberts moved with alacrity to implement the new land acquisition program. In 1963, all remaining publicly owned shorelines on the Ontario side of the Great Lakes were withdrawn from disposition. Within the next four years, 73 kilometres of privately owned shoreline, fronting some 1,077 hectares of property, were accumulated for recreational use at a cost of $3.54 million. Seventy-five percent (54.7 kilometres) of this newly obtained shoreline became part of the provincial parks system. Of the total Great Lakes park acquisition budget for 1962–67,

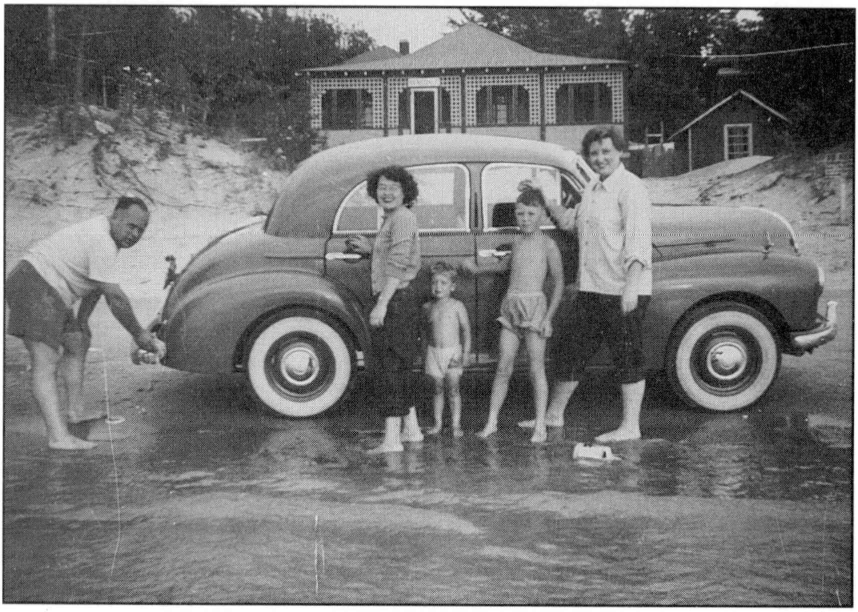

In the fifties, families thought nothing of washing cars in the shallow waters of Wasaga Beach.
Courtesy: Gerald Killan.

The automobile problem at Wasaga Beach Provincial Park in the early sixties.
Courtesy: Ministry of Natural Resources.

$3.29 million or 98 percent was spent to obtain 7.14 kilometres of shoreline on Lake Erie and 11.16 kilometres on Lake Huron.[78]

These dry statistics represented major gains toward meeting the outdoor recreational needs of the densely populated south. Two small new provincial parks – Wheatley (1965) and Selkirk (1966) – were rapidly developed on Lake Erie. Point Farms Provincial Park opened in 1965 on Lake Huron, near Goderich. Farther north, the Parks Branch amassed large portions of the land base for several future parks. At the top of the Bruce Peninsula, near Tobermory, the government had by mid-1967 purchased some 328 hectares, including 3.2 kilometres of spectacular Georgian Bay shoreline, for what would become Cyprus Lake Park. Similarly, by August 1967, some 1,215 hectares of property, embracing a variety of significant archaeological and geological features and over six kilometres of lake shore, had been accumulated for the future Awenda Provincial Park, at Methodist Point, in the historic Huronia tourist region.

From the perspective of providing high-quality day-use opportunities for a maximum number of people in south-central Ontario, the most important and expensive provincial park project on the Great Lakes involved the development of Wasaga Beach. During the 1960s, this park became one of the most important recreational resources in the provincial parks system. Over 1 million visitors used the beach in 1967, about 10 percent of the visitors that year to all provincial parks in Ontario. By January 1967, the government had already expended $1.6 million on 132 small properties, and this was but the beginning of what would be a massive acquisition program to provide off-beach parking space and remove automobile traffic from the beach.[79]

Planning Supervisor Alan MacDonald was one of the first to glimpse the recreational potential of Wasaga. He envisioned the park being massively used, on a scale akin to that of metropolitan recreational areas like Jones Beach, Long Island, or of the tourist resorts in the heavily urbanized areas of southern Europe. Potentially, he argued, Wasaga Beach could dominate the recreational land-use pattern of south-central Ontario, since it contained one of the finest, pollution-free freshwater beaches on the continent, within a two-hour drive of half the population of the province. After conducting studies of Wasaga's potential in 1962, he concluded that the beach area, free of vehicles, could accommodate twice the number of users and still provide a high-quality recreational experience. The same studies indicated that unless automobiles were removed, the number of people able to use the beach would reach capacity by 1970. With these considerations in mind, MacDonald completed in 1963 a first master plan for the park, which called for the acquisition of a 122-metre-wide strip of shoreline along most of the beach, embracing some 1,200 properties.[80]

Considering the complexities and estimated costs of this single project ($8.5 million in 1965), and the future impact of an expanded provincial park on local municipalities, the Parks Branch hired a consulting firm to appraise

MacDonald's master plan. In their highly acclaimed first report, the consultants approved of the idea of purchasing property for off-beach parking, but deemed the linear development scheme to be "much too narrow in concept." The consultants recommended instead a design concept that took into consideration the physiography of the entire Wasaga area, including the Nottawasaga River and the dune areas away from the bay.[81] The second phase of their work (1966–67) detailed an impressive and radical plan for the park and the adjacent communities, but the staggering estimate of costs ($88 million) and the political difficulties that would be involved soured all levels of government on their proposal. Nonetheless, despite the negative reaction, the planning process had not been entirely in vain. Broad agreement had been reached among a number of government departments on the concept of a multipurpose provincial park, integrated within a recreation community. Even municipal authorities, fearful of excessive provincial involvement in their local affairs, agreed to proposals to push ahead with land acquisition for five thousand off-beach parking spaces and other road, bridge, and sewer projects. Making a virtue of a necessity, the Ontario Parks Integration Board and the cabinet accepted this level of agreement as the basis for future planning.[82]

As the Department of Lands and Forests responded to pressures for southern outdoor recreation facilities by purchasing substantial beach and park properties on Lakes Erie and Huron, it also took innovative action in recreational land and resources management along the last remaining accessible shoreline on north Georgian Bay. Attention turned to this semi-isolated region with the completion in 1961 of Highway 637, linking Killarney Village to Highway 69, the main transportation corridor between Sudbury and southern Ontario. The land in question, selected in part because it did not possess high mineral potential, lay south of Highway 17, within a roughly triangular area, its southern corner located twelve miles north of Parry Sound, the northwest corner just east of Blind River, and the northeast corner near the middle of Lake Nipissing. This one-million-hectare territory contained an extraordinary combination of recreational resources: the renowned boating waters of the Thirty Thousand Islands and the North Channel between Manitoulin Island and the mainland; the sparkling indigo-blue lakes and magnificent quartzite ridges of the La Cloche Mountains; the historic French River, the route of the voyageurs; and the marvellous shorelines of both Georgian Bay and Lake Nipissing. Anticipating that this still largely Crown-owned region would soon be intensively used, the province introduced legislation to create the Killarney Recreational Reserve, renamed the North Georgian Bay Recreational Reserve in 1964, to avoid confusion with the new Killarney Provincial Park.[83]

The legislation placed the reserve under the control and management of the minister of lands and forests, and called for the formulation and implementation of "a land-use plan for the development of the public lands in the ... Reserve that have a potential for recreational use." The government intended the reserve to be a multiple-use area, open to many public and private activities, although year-round recreation would be the dominant land use. Ideally, if the area was managed according to the guidelines, development could be coordinated rather than haphazard, the environment protected, and optimum recreational use achieved. The Killarney Recreational Reserve was not conceived as parkland, although the government assumed that provincial parks would be created within its boundaries. In fact, Killarney Provincial Park, located near the end of Highway 637, opened for business in 1964.

To begin the planning process for the recreational reserve, the DLF terminated all land sales in the area and, in April 1963, appointed a committee of influential citizens under the chairmanship of Assistant Deputy Minister G.H.U. Bayly. His committee received instructions to give special attention to the development of a world-class ski resort in the Silver Peak vicinity, part of the new Killarney Park.[84] The government's scheme never came to pass. The consultants commissioned to undertake a feasibility study discovered that Silver Peak could not accommodate a ski facility of international calibre. Meteorological analysis revealed that the annual snowfall in the park was inadequate, and geological studies showed that the extremely rough terrain provided insufficient soil cover to allow for the grading of ski runs. With the collapse of the Silver Peak project, the story of Killarney Provincial Park took a dramatically different turn. As the various inventories and feasibility studies proceeded, a transformation in thinking occurred; planners and politicians alike began to appreciate the natural qualities of this wilderness area. Canoe route studies, for instance, revealed that Killarney was possibly superior to Algonquin Park as a destination for wilderness seekers. The public soon discovered the area, especially after 1966, following the distribution of 35,000 copies of the DLF brochure "Canoe Routes – North Georgian Bay Recreational Reserve." Five years later, Killarney would be classified as one of Ontario's first Wilderness parks, a decision that represented a complete reversal of the original scheme for the area.

In order to plan the larger North Georgian Bay Recreational Reserve, the DLF engaged the services of one of Canada's foremost regional planning specialists, Professor Norman Pearson of the University of Waterloo. In 1966, he submitted his study, entitled *Planning for the North Georgian Bay Recreational Reserve*, a painstaking examination of virtually all aspects of the area – its history, cultural and natural resources, and current levels of urban and industrial development. His recommendations on planning policy and zoning became guidelines for those who subsequently prepared the land-use plan for the reserve. In the context of the history of Ontario's parks, Pearson's report evokes memories of the Quetico-Superior Council's land-use plan of 1927, which aimed to perpetuate the recreational and scenic values of the Rainy Lake watershed.[85]

While the Great Lakes received top priority after 1962 in the effort to meet public pressures for recreational facilities, the interior districts of the province were not neglected. Between 1962 and 1967, Balsam Lake and Ferris provincial parks (the latter donated by the Ferris family) were opened on the Trent waterway, and two small recreation parks, Mara and McCrae Point, on the northeast shore of Lake Simcoe. Regrettably, repeated attempts to find properties on the Muskoka Lakes came to naught, but the Parks Branch selected Arrowhead Lake in 1964 as the site of a provincial park in the Huntsville area. Farther north, Restoule Park, opened in 1962, lies just below Lake Nipissing and the French River. In the Lower Ottawa Valley, five years of protracted negotiations with the Ontario Hydro-Electric Power Commission, local politicians, and the ratepayers of East Hawkesbury Township, eventually resulted in the acquisition of the land for Carillon Provincial Park in 1966. Opened two years later, this park was situated on the reservoir created by the Carillon power project. It filled a serious need in that section of Ontario, where the only other provincial park was South Nation, a tiny five-hectare site, obtained from the Department of Highways in the mid-1950s.

The completion of the Trans-Canada Highway (Route 17) around the hump of Lake Superior in 1961 resulted in the creation of more parks along its length: Chutes, between Sudbury and Sault Ste. Marie; Obatanga, White Lake, and Neys, between Wawa and Terrace Bay; and west of Thunder Bay, Ojibway and Sandbar Lake, the last-mentioned located at the junction of Highway 599. Elsewhere along the expanding northern highway network, the Parks Branch continued to acquire substantial parcels of Crown land in the mid-1960s. Among the most significant were those for The Shoals (10,600 hectares), midway along the new Highway 101 between Wawa and Chapleau, and for the wild, Missinaibi Lake Park (44,000 hectares), north of Chapleau.

Of all the new northern parks created in these years, Tidewater, opened in 1967 near Moosonee, claimed to be unique. No highway access existed to this remote area; visitors arrived either by watercraft or the Ontario Northland Railway's "Polar Bear Express." Previously, islands had been rejected as sites for provincial parks but, in the case of Tidewater, there was no alternative to locating the park on four islands in the Moose River, about nineteen kilometres upstream from James Bay. The absence of sufficient high ground on the mainland, the landscape being predominantly muskeg, made it necessary to bend policy, so that the small but growing numbers of tourists and sportsmen to Moosonee might be provided with camping facilities. Haysey Island, part of Tidewater Park, also possessed historical significance as the site of the original Moose Fort, built in 1673.[86]

Had not the Ontario government created the expectation of a $200-million parkland acquisition program over a twenty-year period, the expansion of the parks system from 1962 to 1967 might have been applauded as a commendable record of achievement. Ten new provincial parks began operating in southern Ontario alone, and the number of park reserves across the province increased from nine to sixty-one. From 1963 to 1967, the Robarts government expended $5.8 million to purchase 13,233 hectares of parkland, and negotiations were underway for the acquisition during 1968 of another 4,070 hectares at a cost of over $3 milion.[87] Over $7 million had been poured into development projects in provincial parks across the province. Unfortunately for the government, many people had been led to expect a great deal more. Under the pledge of $200 million over 20 years, land acquisition expenditures alone should have averaged about $10 million a year. As time passed however, the land purchase promise of 1962 became a matter of considerable political embarrassment for the government. Predictably, members of the opposition seized the chance to denounce the Robarts administration for failing to resolve the crisis in outdoor recreation.[88]

Serious overcrowding in the southern parks gave credence to the opposition's charges. Notwithstanding the acceleration of acquisition and development programs since 1962, demand for outdoor recreation opportunities in the parks had continued to outstrip supply. "All parks in the south are operating above capacity," admitted Parks Chief Donald Wilson in August 1966.[89] Worse still, the facilities in many parks were not up to standard. "We have had to open new parks sooner than [desirable]," Wilson added. "The result is that we have 92 partially developed parks with facilities which are primitive ... in comparison with those of many other park jurisdictions."[90] Visitors complained frequently about the lack of flush toilets, washroom facilities, trailer hook-ups, and dumping stations.

Nowhere was the park shortage more critical than in the heavily populated Niagara Peninsula counties of Lincoln, Welland, Brant, and Wentworth. The combined public and private parklands in these counties amounted to 1.9 hectares per 1,000 persons, less than half the recommended minimum of 4 hectares per 1,000. It was a deplorable situation, considering that within sixty miles of major American cities like Boston, Detroit, San Francisco, and New York, there existed 6.9 hectares of public recreation land for every thousand people. Although sites along the shorelines of Lakes Ontario and Erie had been identified as suitable for provincial parks, the Parks Integration Board resisted meeting the prices demanded by the owners.[91]

The Robarts government came under enormous pressure from Niagara-area residents, especially those in Welland County, who lacked both a provincial park and adequate public beach facilities. Since the late 1950s, "almost every organization in the county" – municipal authorities, chambers of commerce, home and school associations, women's institutes, sportsmen, and naturalist clubs – had petitioned at one time or another for the establishment of a provincial park in the county on the shore of Lake Erie. Throughout the 1960s, the indefatigable Conservative MLA for Welland, Ellis Morningstar, assumed the leadership of this park movement and missed no opportunity to assist Parks Branch officials and the OPIB in locating a suitable site. The Toronto *Globe and Mail* acknowledged the plight of Welland residents in

July 1963. "On hot summer weekends the 66-foot beach strips [at the end of access roads] are crowded with bathers while on each side stretching for miles, beaches fronting private homes have only a few persons using them." At the commercially operated beach parks, "fences topped with barbed wire enclose private beaches operated for profit." By 1966, frustrated over the unwillingness of the government to act, Welland residents organized a protest organization, APEEL (Association for the Preservation of East Erie Lakefront), and literally took to the streets. "Men, women and children carrying signs such as 'Fences are for cattle, not people'" demonstrated outside the private Crystal Beach park, reported the *Globe and Mail*, an action symbolic of "the anger felt by many residents of Ontario who have found that public beaches are either overcrowded, polluted or virtually inaccessible because of distance."[92]

Spiralling real estate prices along the shorelines of Lakes Erie and Ontario eventually forced all the participants concerned to look inland for provincial park sites. The most promising location, one that local conservationists had brought to the attention of Ben Greenwood as early as 1956, lay along the Niagara Escarpment in the Effingham–St. John vicinity. Until the mid-1960s, however, the Ontario government refused to act. "Our department is geared to take care of the large parks that are away from the settled portions of communities," declared Lands and Forests Minister Wilfrid Spooner in 1961, reflecting the thinking of then-Premier Leslie Frost, "so I would ... suggest ... that the Niagara escarpment ... should be in the hands of the conservation authority or a group of municipalities."[93] Such views came under scrutiny during the 1960s, as more Ontarians began to appreciate the beauty and uniqueness of the escarpment and its enormous recreational potential. No organization did more to educate the public to the benefits of the area than the Bruce Trail Association, established in 1963, which completed a walking trail along the length of the escarpment, from Queenston to Tobermory, by 1967. The Federation of Ontario Naturalists, the Nature Conservancy of Canada, and residents in the region also expressed concern over the threats to the escarpment posed by intensive development, particularly by residential subdivisions and quarry operations.

Alive to all these currents of opinion, Ellis Morningstar intensified his efforts to see a provincial park located in the Effingham area of his riding. In April 1965, his work came to a successful conclusion, when the OPIB instructed the Department of Public Works to begin purchasing parkland in Thorold and Pelham townships. The initiative came none too soon, as government realtors found themselves in keen competition with private developers, eager to secure options on the same properties. Although members of the OPIB had second thoughts, when they learned of the hefty prices demanded for the Effingham properties, they deferred to the recreation imperative and continued to accumulate land, for what would eventually become Short Hills Provincial Park.[94]

During 1967, the Robarts government at last made an about-face on the question of the Niagara Escarpment. "There is at present a significant shortage of parklands in Southwestern Ontario," Lands and Forests Minister René Brunelle informed the premier, "[and] it will never be possible to purchase sufficient lakeshore lands to meet the growing demand. I believe that the Niagara escarpment up to and including the Bruce Peninsula offers a tremendous opportunity for public outdoor recreation use, and would strongly recommend to you that the land acquisition program in this area be accelerated."[95] As a first step in this direction, Premier Robarts announced in March 1967 that he intended to launch "a wide-ranging study of the Niagara escarpment with a view to preserving its entire length from Queenston to Tobermory and Manitoulin Island as a recreation area for the people of Ontario."[96] Subsequently, the government commissioned Leonard O. Gertler, director of the School of Urban and Regional Planning at the University of Waterloo, to conduct a study of the escarpment, to delineate areas worthy of protection for their recreational and environmental values and to recommend how they might be preserved.

In the three decades since the end of World War II, the thinking of Lands and Forests officials and politicians alike on the question of providing provincial "parks for the people" had evolved considerably. Prior to 1953, they were reluctant custodians of all but the few large northern parks like Algonquin and Quetico, Lake Superior and Sibley, and looked for ways to shed the responsibility for managing parkland in the southern districts. After 1953, these attitudes rapidly eroded, under a relentlessly expanding and compelling demand for more provincial parks. Ontarians wanted access to beaches, campgrounds, day-use areas, and natural environments, for any number of recreational activities, all within a few hours' drive of the major cities. Although the Division of Parks, and after 1959, the Parks Branch, was unable to meet this demand, especially in the south-central and southwestern portions of Ontario, much had been accomplished by 1968 in terms of the numbers of new parks acquired and developed. Around the southern Great Lakes and waterways and throughout the northern highway network, the basis of an impressive system of provincial parks had taken shape in a remarkably short period of time. Of course, the Parks Branch's mandate included far more than the acquisition and development of parkland. Managing the growing system provided no less a challenge, as a myriad of conflicting groups, each pursuing a different set of recreational, preservationist, or commercial priorities, jostled each other for a place in the sun.

Chapter 4

The Problems of Expansion, 1954–1967
Lack of Harmony, Lack of Balance

The rapid evolution of the provincial parks program from 1954 to 1967, driven as it was by the recreation imperative, unavoidably raised problems. As early as 1958, the Federation of Ontario Naturalists and other conservation organizations questioned the primacy of recreation in park planning and management decisions, and complained that insufficient consideration was being given to the protection of natural areas. The FON called for policies to maintain the ecological integrity of parkland and to establish a system of nature reserves. Sensitive to the criticisms of the naturalists, the Frost government issued in 1959 a parks policy that attempted to address many of the FON's concerns, and passed the Wilderness Areas Act, thereby providing for the setting aside of areas of natural, historic, and scenic importance.

Circumstances combined in the 1960s to render these initiatives ineffective. By mid-decade, the provincial parks system was suffering from a lack of harmony among its users and a lack of balance between its component parts. In southern Ontario, problems of overcrowded campgrounds, rowdyism, and a deteriorating natural environment plagued park officials. Discordant notes also rang through the northern districts, as crowded canoe routes, excessive litter, and conflict between canoeists and motorboat users became facts of life in the interior, both of Algonquin and of Quetico. At the same time, mining and timber interests, worried about their economic future on a shrinking Crown land base, were resisting the priority that was being given to recreationists in the larger parks and reserves, and fighting the efforts to establish new provincial parks.

Within this whirlpool of tension and confrontation, the politics of provincial park planning, development, and management grew enormously complex. At first, Parks Branch personnel were overwhelmed by the issues; they lacked the expertise for long-range planning and did not possess the management tools that would have helped them to resolve conflicts. Eventually, in 1965 the branch was reorganized and expanded until it had acquired the personnel necessary to restructure the parks system. The new staff quickly reached the conclusion that the most promising means of achieving balance and harmony in the system lay in the development of management policy, specifically in the form of a classification and zoning policy, which was introduced in 1967.

The FON Addresses the Recreation-Preservation Imbalance

During the period of expansion between 1954 and 1967, the balance between the dual objectives of the parks system – recreation and preservation – tipped heavily in favour of the former. Understandably, as the staff of the Division of Parks struggled through the 1950s, with the herculean task of satisfying the seemingly insatiable public appetite for beaches, campgrounds, and picnic areas, their first priority was to open as many new parks as rapidly as possible. Under these hothouse growth conditions – eight parks were operating in 1954, seventy-seven in 1961 - division planners could do little more than respond on a crisis management basis when it came to establishing protectionist policies. For instance, because timber extraction from provincial parks did not emerge as an issue in the 1950s, general policy guidelines regulating timber licences in the province's parks did not appear until 1961.

In contrast, the question of leaseholders in provincial parks was more pressing, required immediate attention, and became one of Ben Greenwood's priorities. Even before the establishment of the Division of Parks, the government had decided, in June 1954, that no new leases or licences of occupation were to be granted in any park. In Algonquin, cottagers were to be phased out by 1996, as their twenty-one-year renewable leases expired. Upon becoming parks chief, Greenwood accelerated the removal process in Algonquin by persuading the government to authorize negotiations for the acquisition of unexpired leasehold agreements offered for sale. In this way, by September 1956, some sixty-nine cottage and commercial leases had been returned to the Crown. That same year, the Frost cabinet also announced that it would begin to purchase pockets of patented land within provincial parks, either through negotiation or expropriation.[1]

During 1956, Greenwood also moved to solve the problem of the cottage communities in the old commission parks at Long Point and Presqu'ile. The government accepted his recommendations that the existing Long Point Provincial Park be closed and that the leaseholders be offered the opportunity to purchase their lots. As replacement parkland, the division acquired an adjacent, undeveloped property, which provided access to several kilometres of beach. At Presqu'ile, the problem was more easily resolved, simply by altering the park boundaries to carve out the cottage subdivisions. Finally, in 1959, the axe fell on the Rondeau leaseholders. Aylmer District Forester J. Keith Reynolds explained why the cottagers had to be removed: "The almost unbelievable increase in demand for public recreational facilities that has marked this immediate post–World War II era clearly indicates that we need every available square foot of ... public parks space, especially here in southwestern Ontario." The 459 cottages in Rondeau, built under twenty-one-year renewable leases, were "so situated that they effectively obstructed public use of the much-needed and better use beach areas." Another 109 "decidedly inferior and objectionable" wood-frame cottages, which had been erected under annually issued land-use permits, collectively resembled "shacktowns" that drew "a great deal of adverse public criticism." For these reasons, then, in August 1960, the government extended to Rondeau the lease phase-out policy being applied in Algonquin Park.[2]

In the mid-1950s, mining in the provincial parks emerged as another policy issue that could not be deferred. During World War II, in view of the national emergency and the need for strategic minerals, mining exploration and prospecting in Algonquin and Quetico parks had been approved by order-in-council (1942); in 1945, the government extended the same policy to Lake Superior and Sibley provincial parks. Over the next ten years, many claims were staked, particularly in Quetico and Lake Superior, although none resulted in the establishment of an actual mining operation. Then, in March 1956, the status quo changed abruptly when Ben Greenwood received an alarming communication from District Forester William T. Foster in Fort Frances. "With the current rash of prospecting interest in Quetico Park ... I feel that mining exploitation is a real threat to the existence of Quetico." Consequently, he urged a ban on mining to preserve the "wilderness values" of the irreplaceable canoe country.[3] Within a month of receiving this recommendation, Greenwood had extended Foster's arguments to all provincial parks. "Unless a regulation to this effect is instituted," he argued, "the future of Ontario's Provincial Parks as recreational areas is in jeopardy."[4]

Fortunately, Premier Leslie Frost shared the assumption that mining and parks did not mix. In fact, just as the question of mineral extraction in the Quetico arose, Frost was pondering how to keep the miners out of his favourite fly-fishing haunts in Clyde and Bruton townships, located directly to the south of Algonquin Park. With mining activity quickening on the eastern side of Haliburton County in 1956, the premier, in his inimitable way, simply ordered that Clyde and Bruton be added to Algonquin Park. The two townships, embracing 41,958 hectares of territory, were immediately reserved from mining and officially became part of the park in 1961.[5]

The premier accordingly moved with remarkable speed when approached by the Division of Parks for a policy decision on mineral extraction in the parks. On 22 August 1956, the cabinet issued an order-in-council, banning prospecting, staking, and mining in the four parks previously open to the mining industry. "The ban is aimed at implementing a new parks policy of keeping ... the major parks wholly for recreation," reported the Quetico Foundation. In reality, the matter was not that simple. The prohibition did not apply to mining rights and interests acquired prior to the new regulation. Moreover, Minister of Mines Philip T. Kelly announced that his own geologists would conduct mineral surveys in the provincial parks. "Should a valuable mineral deposit be discovered," he asserted, "the Cabinet would review its decision and, if circumstances demanded it, release that area of a park for mining development." If a discovery did lead to park boundary revisions, however, Kelly expected that "the Province would set aside an equivalent area of park land to replace it." It was clear that the mining issue would not easily go away.[6]

While the Parks Division, of necessity, followed a crisis management approach in drafting general policies for the parks, naturalist programs were implemented carefully. Through interpretive services, division personnel found the means to satisfy both the recreationists' desire to learn about the parks in which they chose to spend their leisure time, and the division's need to inform visitors about the proper use and protection of the parks. Greenwood and his staff understood park interpretation to be something different from general education about nature. Special programs had to be designed for specific parks, for the purpose of providing visitors with an understanding and appreciation of the unique environment and the inspirational values of each park, its geology, glaciation, topography, soils, flora and fauna, and human history. Ben Greenwood had one person specifically in mind for the position of naturalist supervisor at head office: Alan Helmsley, a veteran of the Royal Canadian Air Force (RCAF) and a geographer, who had worked each summer during his undergraduate years as a naturalist in both Algonquin and Rondeau. Since graduating from the University of Toronto in 1949, he had taught the fish and wildlife courses at the Dorset Forest Ranger School and supervised the summer naturalist program in Algonquin Park.

When Helmsley joined head office in 1955, full naturalist programs had been introduced at only two parks, Algonquin and Rondeau. Thanks to J.R. Dymond's pioneering efforts and Helmsley's own later contributions, Algonquin Park provided a model service, including a new museum and visitor centre (opened in 1953), four labelled nature trails, conducted trips, evening slide shows and lectures, and special events for the children's camps. By every measure it was the premier interpretive program in Canada. In devising ways to expand beyond these traditional offerings, Alan Helmsley had to rely on his own wits or look for ideas to the United States national parks system, which had inaugurated interpretive programs in the 1920s, and to the various state parks systems, many of which had already recognized the importance of such visitor services. No other Canadian provincial park system had yet embraced interpretation. British Columbia would begin to do so only in 1957, under the direction of R. Yorke Edwards, and in 1958, under that of the Canadian National Parks Service.[7] By the time Alan Helmsley resigned from the Ontario civil service to become chief park naturalist and head of interpretation for

Tourists feeding a white-tailed deer along Highway 60 in Algonquin Park, 1951. This activity became a major park attraction and pastime for day visitors.
Courtesy: Ministry of Natural Resources.

Canada's national parks in 1965, he had established interpretation as an essential feature of the provincial parks system. Complete naturalist programs on the Algonquin model were operating in Rondeau, Sibley, Quetico, and Presqu'ile, and partial programs in the Pinery and Inverhuron in southwestern Ontario, and Lake Superior, Kap-Kig-Iwan, Kettle Lakes, and Remi Lake in the north.

Helmsley also widened the focus of interpretation by including the human history of the parks. Following a number of archaeological excavations in Algonquin, for instance, the museum was expanded in 1956 to include exhibits on the park's prehistory. Archaeology also became a focal point of interpretation at Serpent Mounds and Inverhuron. Meanwhile, during the summers of 1957 and 1958, the Quetico Foundation and the ROM funded expeditions to record the Indian pictographs of Quetico. Initiated by Kenneth E. Kidd, curator of the Department of Ethnology, ROM, and conducted in the field by London artist and author Selwyn Dewdney, their findings were published in *Indian Rock Paintings of the Great Lakes* (1962). Purely historical interpretation also came into its own, with the opening in 1959 of the Eildon Hall Museum at Sibbald Point, where interpreters used the history of the Sibbald family to set the park in the context of wider provincial and international

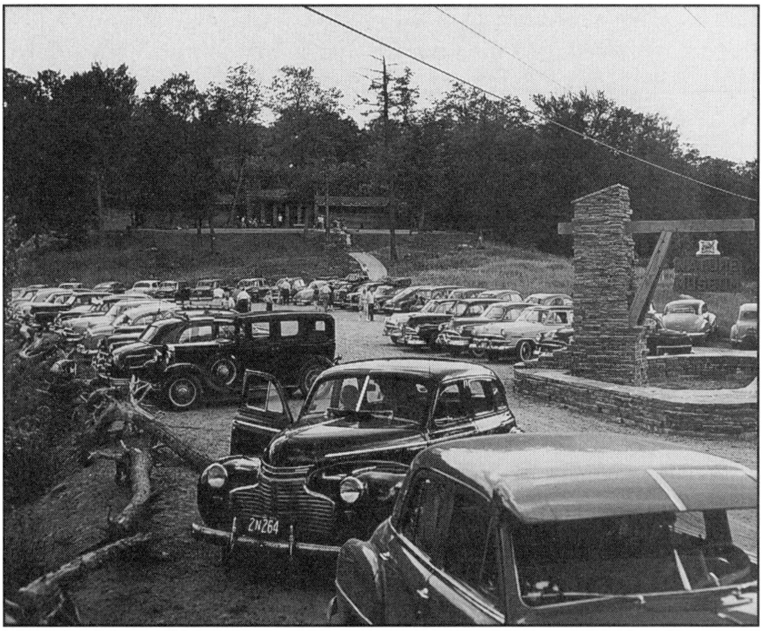

When it opened in 1953, the Algonquin Park Nature Musem was the centrepiece of what was considered the premier park interpretive program in Canada. *Courtesy: Ministry of Natural Resources.*

Algonquin Park naturalist Alan Helmsley conducting a nature hike with the girls of Camp Tanamakoon in 1951. *Courtesy: Ministry of Natural Resources.*

themes. That year also, with the establishment of Wasaga Beach Provincial Park, the DLF acquired the Nancy Island Museum, which housed the salvaged hull of the schooner HMS *Nancy*, a vessel burned to the waterline in the Nottawasaga River during the War of 1812.

Helmsley and his field staff, with the assistance of Bruce Harding, the first permanent artist and exhibit designer hired by the division in 1955, brought in further new features by using outdoor exhibits to interpret special features of particular parks. At Serpent Mounds, one of the first outdoor displays invited visitors to peruse artifacts, photographs, and sketches pertaining to the archaeological excavations being undertaken by the Royal Ontario Museum over a five-year period. The exhibit at Craigleith, erected in 1958, focussed on the geology and palaeontology of the area. In Algonquin, the Pioneer Logging Exhibit, located near the East Gate on Highway 60, opened in 1959. Designed to portray the saga of the park's white-pine logging era, it featured a full-sized replica of a camboose shanty, a saddle-back locomotive, a steam "alligator," and various display cases. "It is the first exhibit of its kind in Canada," reported a justifiably proud Alan Helmsley.[8] In the late 1950s, the naturalists in Algonquin and Rondeau also introduced the first of a series of specialized publications on park flora and fauna, designed to assist visitors to understand and enjoy the ecology of each park.[9]

Interpretation required the services of a knowledgeable and dedicated staff, capable of infecting their listeners with enthusiasm for the natural wonders and cultural features to be found in the provincial parks. In 1960, there were only two permanent park naturalists, Grant Tayler in Algonquin and Dick Ussher in Rondeau. The division relied on seasonal personnel to mount the interpretive programs each summer, a total of seventeen people by 1960. "Trained naturalists or interpreters are difficult to find," Helmsley admitted in 1959.[10] By all accounts, those he did engage were a remarkable group of people, acclaimed by park visitors for their ability to inform, guide, educate, entertain, and inspire those with whom they made contact. Some of the seasonal interpreters, hired and trained in the 1950s and early 1960s, including Dan Strickland, Ron Tozer, and Shan Walshe, later became permanent employees in the Ontario parks system.

Notwithstanding the dedication of the seasonal employees, Helmsley came to recognize that a number of them suffered from a serious morale problem. The "general feeling among naturalists," he complained, "is that they are working alone and the job does not warrant the interest of superiors." Too many district officials viewed naturalist programs as "a non-essential service which could be regarded as a luxury."[11] To be sure, the fact that the interpretive services in the various parks annually attracted thousands of visitors, bringing no little credit to the park system, helped to whittle away resistance at the district level. The number of people using interpretive services across the system increased from 127,099 in 1956 to 531,300 in 1964, a growth of over 400 percent. By 1960,

Campers enjoying an evening presentation at the Lake of Two Rivers amphitheatre, Algonquin Park, July 1963. *Courtesy: Ministry of Natural Resources.*

Archaeology became the focal point of interpretation at Serpent Mounds Provincial Park on Rice Lake in 1957. *Courtesy: Ministry of Natural Resources.*

approximately half of the visitors to Algonquin were using one or more of the interpretive facilities. Ironically, the success of the program in Algonquin bred new problems. The conducted hikes attracted more people than the guides could reasonably handle; in 1960, an average of eighty-three. The four labelled trails were heavily used; indeed, the Lookout Trail had to be closed in August 1959 and an alternative found, due to overuse. Helmsley worried that Algonquin might be going the way of some American national parks, where programs had to be discontinued during peak visitor seasons because of the enormous demand. It was, therefore, fortunate that not all visitors to the provincial parks made use of the naturalist and historical programs, especially in places like Rondeau and Presqu'ile, where the main interests of day users remained the beach and picnic areas. "Such numbers," noted Helmsley, "could not be accommodated by the present interpretive facilities and staff, which, even now, are being pushed to the limit and, in some cases beyond."[12]

Just as general policy development fell short of the mark as recreational pressures were leading to an increase in the number of parks, master planning for individual sites also left a great deal to be desired. Ben Greenwood tried to encourage sound planning by ordering that new parkland not be developed until master plans, prepared at the district level, had received approval at head office.[13] After attending a conference on state parks, held in Grand Teton National Park, Wyoming, in 1956, Greenwood reported that Ontario's approach to planning provincial parks was "comparable to anything ... south of the border."[14] In theory, he may have been correct, but in view of the massive expansion of the system that was to follow, the master planning and development of Ontario's parks often failed to meet expectations. As late as 1967, no approved master plans existed for Algonquin and Quetico, and those prepared for new parks were crude documents that merely detailed natural features and topography, proposed building and road locations, and use zones. The districts did not possess the field staff, either to compile wildlife inventories in the parks or to assess the significance of life and earth science features and cultural resources, in order to recommend appropriate guidelines for their proper management. Without such data, however, the impact of various development projects upon natural values could not be ascertained. To make matters worse, once the development of a park actually got under way, local officials frequently deviated from the master plans approved by head office. As the years passed, Planning Supervisor Alan MacDonald began to fret about the uneven quality of park planning and development from one district to the next. After inspecting northwestern Ontario in July 1961, he deplored the unacceptable "quality of work done and standards kept" across the region. "Personally," he reported to Parks Chief Alf Wheatley, "I feel much of the fault is ours since the field staff receive too little supervision from Head Office and too little planning assistance."[15]

The absence of general policies, management guidelines and master plans eventually aroused the ire of conservationist groups interested in enhancing the protectionist objective of the Ontario parks system. In 1957, two controversies erupted in Algonquin Park – the questions of deer hunting and access roads – which showed that without an official policy statement and related management guidelines embedded in a master plan, park administrators and politicians could manage any park to suit themselves. This point was first driven home in August 1957, when the Department of Lands and Forests announced that public deer hunting would be permitted, in season, in the eastern and southern sections of the park. The pressure for this decision had arisen from the powerful Timber Management Division of the DLF. Foresters were alarmed at the extensive damage, caused by the browsing of the abnormally large deer population, to young stands of pine and yellow birch seedlings in the Bonnechère and Petawawa valleys. Unless the deer population was reduced through a public hunt, the foresters argued, the timber industry in the region would be jeopardized.[16] Since there was no official policy on hunting in parks, the timber managers had free rein to move ahead with their proposal. Conservationists, including both naturalists' and sportsmen's clubs, exploded in anger upon learning of the scheme. They believed it would betray one of the original reasons for establishing Algonquin Park – to provide a sanctuary for wildlife. The reaction of public and press proved, indeed, sufficient to force the timber managers to reverse their decision.[17]

A second controversy further awakened conservationists to the realization that without an official policy statement and without master plans, administrators and politicians could change long-standing management policies with the stroke of a pen. In May 1958, Lands and Forests Minister Clare Mapledoram succumbed to political pressure during a by-election in North Renfrew and opened four logging roads, to provide automobile access for recreational fishermen to the northern and eastern sections of Algonquin.[18] The public outcry was predictable. The Conservation Council of Ontario charged that the access roads announcement amounted to "a complete reversal of the Government's previously announced decision to restore Algonquin Park to as near natural conditions as possible." Harold Walker, chairman of the Quetico Foundation, fearing that similar political decisions could just as easily threaten the future of Quetico as a roadless area, urged voters "to write to Mr. Frost in protest ... let us show him that real woodsmen and fishermen in Ontario like their wilderness on the raw side – just as natural as it can be."[19]

Some influential public groups were more ambivalent. They did not object in principle to these access roads to the northern and eastern perimeters of the park, since most of the interior would remain free of automobiles. They took the same position as the Parks Division, that the congestion along the Highway 60 corridor might be lessened by providing more access points to the park perimeter. Gavin Henderson, chairman of the Federation of Ontario Naturalists' parks committee, explained that while members of the FON were "not unduly concerned about granting public use of these particular roads," they were "greatly disturbed by the fact that decisions with respect to our Provincial Parks do not apparently follow a rigidly defined policy." He explained to Premier Frost that "it is going to be increasingly difficult as time goes on to preserve our wilderness parks from those who would seek to exploit them for one purpose or another. It will only be possible to do so, in fact, by sticking, without compromise, to a clearly established policy. We sincerely hope that your Government will announce such a policy in the near future."[20]

Embarrassed by this controversy, Deputy Minister Frank MacDougall instructed his district personnel, on 9 July 1958, to provide him with a preliminary master plan for the park, with special emphasis on the future of logging operations, road access, preservation of wilderness areas, and recreational facilities. This difficult task fell to the Pembroke district forester, D.M. Omand, and his staff. As ordered, they rushed together a draft master plan within four weeks and submitted it to head office for approval. It was not well received.[21] "The report by the District is a start, but I do believe it was done on a hurry-up basis, without too much thought given to planning as a whole," bluntly commented Planning Supervisor Alan MacDonald. "Since Algonquin is ... 'Queen' of our parks system, it surely deserves special attention and thought, rather than our going off half cocked in the development." MacDonald identified the fundamental weakness in the plan: no attempt had been made to specify what sections of the park should be zoned as roadless areas or as no-logging zones. Only after such boundaries had been determined, he wrote, would anyone be "in a position to study the areas available ... for development and to submit a proposal."[22] Under such withering criticism, the district plan collapsed and was filed away and forgotten. Over the next decade, various combinations of district and head office staff struggled with the planning of Algonquin, but to no avail. They produced several draft master plans, all of which foundered on the rocks of conflict between logging, recreational, and preservationist interests, an extraordinary struggle that developed during the 1960s.

Shocked by the implications of the lack of an official policy statement in favour of setting aside and managing provincial parks, two leading conservationist groups sought to remedy the situation. In October 1958, the Quetico Foundation petitioned the government for the development of a general policy on parks and the reservation of some 1,335,492 hectares of additional parkland in northern Ontario.[23] The following December, the Federation of Ontario Naturalists went a step further and submitted an "Outline of a Basis for a Parks Policy for Ontario" (December 1958), the first attempt to define "the principles which should govern the establishment and management of public parks" and nature reserves from an ecological perspective. It was a statement that anticipated the revolution in environmental thought which lay ahead.

The FON document would not have been possible without the many advances made by professional ecologists in North America and Britain during the previous quarter-century, the period when ecology – the branch of biology concerned with the normal, but extremely complex, interrelationships among all forms of plant and animal life in time and space – came of age. At the heart of the ecologists' creed, popularized in North America by Aldo Leopold's *A Sand County Almanac* (1949), lay a genuine respect for all forms of life, based on an understanding that every living thing was part of an intricate, interdependent, dynamic biotic community, that every living thing filled a special niche, and played a unique role in maintaining the character and stability of the shared environment. The removal of, or damage to, one element in the system inevitably undermined the healthy operation of the whole, sometimes imperceptibly, at other times drastically. In this view of the natural order, man was perceived merely as one, dependent member of the biotic community, to which he belonged but could make no claim to possess.

Based on this understanding of the natural world, Aldo Leopold exhorted his readers to develop an "ecological conscience" and "land ethic," a philosophy of what was right and wrong in the man-land relationship. He urged his readers to "quit thinking about decent land-use as solely an economic problem. Examine each question in terms of what is ethically and esthetically right, as well as what is economically expedient. A thing is right when it tends to preserve the integrity, stability, and beauty of the biotic community. It is wrong when it tends otherwise."[24] Such an anti-utilitarian philosophy, used in 1958 as the bedrock of a parks policy by the Federation of Ontario Naturalists, led to the conclusion that parks should be set aside and managed primarily to preserve natural areas.

The function of any park, asserted the FON, was "to enable the public to come into contact with the world of nature."[25] By bringing people into contact with nature, parks served five purposes – recreational, aesthetic, educational, historical, and scientific. It was the provincial government's responsibility to establish parks to fulfil these needs, and to manage parkland so as to harmonize recreation and ecology, and to minimize commercial influences such as logging. Provincial parks, the federation argued, provided educational opportunities for visitors to obtain an understanding of nature "through observation of plants and animals living under undisturbed natural conditions ... through observing how plants and animals are associated in communities in which each plays its part," and "by observation of the relations of communities to the character of the country." Such understanding "above all ... leads to a realization that there is a pattern in nature into which man, if he is to survive, must fit." In addition to educational purposes, parks gave biologists the chance to pursue intensive and prolonged scientific research into the interrelationships of plant-animal communities. Even the historical function of parks, involving the protection and interpretation of cultural resources, was couched in essentially ecological terms. "Parks may be looked upon as outdoor, informal museums ... preserving, among other things, such works of man as have developed in close contact with and under the direct influence of living nature."

To reduce the tension between recreational and ecological interests, the federation stressed that parks had to be large enough to be effectively zoned, with "each zone managed so as to preserve its values for the specific purpose for which it is best adapted." Recreational activities which "interfere with the preservation of natural conditions" should be restricted to appropriately zoned areas. The federation also hoped to minimize the impact of recreationists on all park environments by recommending that activities dependent on "the use of mechanical power" be discouraged.

The ecological point of view placed the FON in sharp opposition to those who would log, hunt, or trap in Ontario's provincial parks. "Since the function of parks should be recreational, aesthetic, educational, historical, and scientific," the federation asserted, "harvesting of wood products or animals should be strictly limited to areas where it will not interfere with primary park purposes." And even then, "cutting of trees or control of animal numbers ... should be carried out by park authorities," not by logging companies, trappers, or sport hunters.

In addition to discussing the traditional types of provincial parks, the naturalists' policy document returned to a theme its members had assiduously pursued since the 1930s, that legal provision be made for setting aside nature reserves "for purely scientific purposes." Two classes of reserves – sanctuaries and research areas – would be required, both within provincial parks and as separate units on Crown land. The FON recommended not only that unique geological and physical features and endangered plant or animal species be included in sanctuaries, but also that "samples of each type of natural environment primitively found in Ontario should be preserved in different parts of the Province." Some nature reserves would be used purely for research, as outdoor laboratories for both observation and ecological experimentation under controlled environmental conditions. In proposing management policies for the reserves, the FON advised the government to look for inspiration to the National Parks and Access to the Countryside Act (1949) of Great Britain. Since being set up in 1948, the British Nature Conservancy had created some 140 nature reserves, ranging from 1.6 to 15,783 hectares in size. Given the functions of nature reserves, the federation warned, access would have to be limited to qualified persons, and management would best be monitored by advisory committees of experts.

The "Outline of a Basis for a Parks Policy for Ontario" was arguably the most sophisticated statement on the subject yet produced. Greenwood and his staff recognized its importance and welcomed the ideas put forth. It would take many years of sometimes quite heated public debate, but by the early 1970s, many of the policies recommended by the FON would have been adopted by the government. Premier Frost, too, found the statement impressive, although his enthusiasm was tempered by the knowledge that the Ontario Parks Integration Board had for two years done nothing to draft such a policy document. The stage had been reached, however, where Frost would brook no more dallying.

As early as 22 October 1958, in the aftermath of the Algonquin roads controversy, the premier despatched his executive assistant, T.C. Clarke, to instruct the OPIB to complete a parks policy for all agencies "as soon as convenient." A month later, on 19 November, Frost himself descended upon an OPIB meeting and asked for a policy statement by Christmas. Again on 17 December, an agitated Frost, having just received the FON policy outline, cornered OPIB members in his council chamber to reiterate his concerns.[26]

When the new year came and went and the OPIB had still not presented him with a policy document, the determined premier appeared at yet another board meeting, on 17 February 1959. The board members gaped when he produced a draft copy of the speech from the throne, to be read a few days later, and quoted sections of the document that referred to the future of parks, promising a statement on parks policy during the session. The premier ordered the OPIB to "take into consideration briefs presented by the Naturalists and other organizations and formulate a policy for dealing with all the parks across the Province." After this extraordinary example of involvement, the board had no choice but to comply. A month later, on 24 March, OPIB Chairman Charles Daley tabled a parks policy in the legislature.[27]

The policy declaration of March 1959 reaffirmed previous statements that recreation and preservation were the primary objectives of all provincial parks. The challenge at hand was to redress the balance between these objectives, a balance that had leaned too heavily in a recreational direction as expansion took place. Nine distinct classes of parks were created, ostensibly to serve as the basis of site selection and management by all agencies. Five of the classes – Overnight Camping and Picnic Grounds, Hunting Grounds, Picnic Grounds, Roadside Parks, and Beaches – would be operated essentially as recreational areas. The province still required more of these parks, explained Daley, especially "in areas close to large population centres." Echoing the oft-repeated statement of Premier Frost, Daley indicated that municipal governments would also be expected to provide parks of the recreational type to serve local or regional needs and to relieve pressure on the provincial parks. To encourage local initiative, he promised the municipalities financial support, and invited them to "make application through the Ontario Parks Integration Board for assistance in the establishment of parks." The government later made good on this promise with the passage of the Parks Assistance Act (1960), which provided for a grant of 50 percent of the cost of acquiring land and a similar proportion of development costs, up to a maximum of $50,000 per municipality. At the same time, the mandate of the OPIB was widened, to include parks established under both the Parks Assistance Act and the Conservation Authorities Act, thereby giving the board supervisory control over all parks funded by the province.[28]

The most significant aspect of the 1959 policy was the emphasis given to the protection objective of the parks system, as formulated by the conservationists.

Three new classes of parks – Nature Reserves, Wilderness Areas, and Historic Sites – were created to protect significant natural and cultural resources. In theory, at least, Daley committed the government to select as Nature Reserves and Wilderness Areas "only the most satisfactory" and "only the best" samples of Ontario's natural heritage. Finally, the government suggested that large parks like Algonquin, Rondeau, Sibley, and Lake Superior, now to be classified as Multiple Use parks, would be able to offer recreational opportunities, while preserving natural and wilderness values. Application of the zoning mechanism would make this possible.

On 26 March 1959, two days after Daley's policy announcement, the legislature gave third reading to the Wilderness Areas Act, legislation which stemmed directly from the FON campaign for the protection of natural areas. The act represented a turning point for the preservationist cause, insofar as it recognized the concept of nature reserves, although the misleading term "Wilderness Area" would be used to designate such tracts of land. Under the legislation, the DLF could "set apart any public lands as a wilderness area for the preservation of the area as nearly as may be in its natural state in which research and educational activities may be carried on, for the protection of the flora and fauna, for the improvement of the area, having regard to its historical, aesthetic, scientific or recreational value, or for such other purposes as may be prescribed." Lands and Forests Minister J.W. Spooner candidly described the legislation as an attempt to remedy the mistakes of his predecessors, who had neglected to preserve "examples of our finest primitive conditions" in southern Ontario. Fortunately, he continued, "there are many examples left in the north country particularly." Spooner hastened to add, for the benefit of the mining industry, which objected strongly to the withdrawal of large tracts of land from industrial exploitation, that there would be rigid limits to the protection afforded by the act. "There is no intention that there will be any interference with mining development," Spooner insisted. "Quite the contrary, if there should be a discovery of minerals, its development would be encouraged in every way possible." Any fears the miners may have entertained were dissipated when they learned that the act would only provide intensive protection to wilderness areas under 640 acres (259 hectares) in size; the natural resources contained in Wilderness Areas over that limit would be subject to "development and utilization."[29]

Although not a point of contention in 1959, the 640-acre clause would come under critical scrutiny in the mid-1960s by preservationists, who argued that it provided an obstacle to the creation of both nature reserves and large wilderness parks, free of all resource exploitation and dedicated solely to recreational and ecological purposes. In 1959, however, conservationist groups opted to accentuate the positive. The Conservation Council of Ontario only regretted the use of the word "wilderness" in the title of the act. "It gives the impression that the areas which should be preserved ... are to be found only in the north, far from civilization. This ... is not the case." The FON concurred that the critical region for the preservation of nature lay in southern Ontario. Both groups also expressed concern that the act failed to distinguish sufficiently between nature reserves and parks: "the preservation of an area in its natural state is, generally speaking, incompatible with recreational use."[30] All the same, the conservationists were mollified, when informed that the DLF intended to place the administration of the act in the hands of the Lands and Surveys Branch, rather than the Parks Branch with its recreational bias. Despite their misgivings, the conservationist groups commended the Frost government for introducing the legislation. It was undeniably progressive, the first of its kind in Canada. Lands and Forests officials knew of only one other jurisdiction in North America that had comparable legislation in place, the state of Wisconsin.

By July 1961, the DLF, with the assistance of the Federation of Ontario Naturalists, had set apart thirty-five Wilderness Areas, all but ten of which had been selected as nature reserves.[31] Seven of these reserves were located in provincial parks: the Rondeau forest, with its extraordinary number of Carolinian species; a similar forest remnant within Turkey Point Provincial Park; and four sections of the Pinery, embracing scientifically valuable samples of the oak savannah forest, shoreline, and flood plain. Another Wilderness Area, the "Sleeping Giant," overlooking Thunder Bay, was eventually added to Sibley (today Sleeping Giant) Provincial Park. Furthermore, five of the original Wilderness Areas were destined to become fullfledged parks in their own right. This would occur after 1967, when the opportunity arose to preserve Wilderness Areas more effectively as components of a system of Nature Reserves, to be created under provisions of the the Provincial Parks Act. These included the Matawatchan Wilderness Area, set apart as a sample of the transitional, deciduous-evergreen forest, typical of the Madawaska Valley; Porphyry Island, located off the Black Bay Peninsula on the north shore of Lake Superior, a site featuring unique flora and significant geological features (the bedrock dates from the Late Precambrian age, consisting of some 300 volcanic lava flows, collectively known as the Osler group); the Montreal River Wilderness Area, situated just south of Lake Superior Park, designated for its remarkable, raised cobble beaches; and Bat Cave Wilderness Area (today Cavern Lake Park), established to protect what is considered the longest cave to be found in the Precambrian rocks of Ontario, the summer roosting site and wintering den of four species of bats.[32]

All but one of the original thirty-five Wilderness Areas created by July 1961 were small in size and fell within the 640-acre nonutilization limit. The exception was the 580,000-hectare Cape Henrietta-Maria, located at the extreme northeastern tip of Ontario, separating Hudson and James bays.[33] This area contained some of the world's most southerly Arctic tundra. The province's only polar bears, at least eleven species of birds that bred nowhere else in Ontario, and one of the largest breeding colonies of snow geese in the world all inhabited the cape. The area also supported bearded seals, walruses, arctic foxes, tundra wolves, a herd of some 300 caribou, and an abundance of tundra flowers. In 1968, the Cape Henrietta-Maria Wilderness Area would become the nucleus of the 1.8-million-hectare Polar Bear Provincial Park, one of the world's great parks.

Significantly, too, the first large national park to be established in Ontario – Pukaskwa, on the north shore of Lake Superior – was first set aside under the Wilderness Areas Act. In June 1960, E.L. Ward, land-use planning supervisor in the Lands Branch, began discussions with officials in the White River District to preserve for recreational use a 259,000-hectare tract of Crown land as "a true wilderness area … in which no exploitation of the natural resources takes place." The location Ward selected was inaccessible, rugged, scenic, and bordered on Lake Superior, a region containing many narrow valleys, rushing rivers, rapids, and waterfalls. Apart from its many natural and scenic qualities, Ward was attracted to Pukaskwa in 1960 because it was "not contributing to any great extent to the economy."[34] The area possessed little mining potential and was largely free of timber licences. After four years of study, Pukaskwa became a Wilderness Area in 1964. Fourteen years later, the government of Ontario would transfer Pukaskwa to the federal authorities to provide the basis for a national park.

Following the introduction of the 1959 policy statement and the passage of the Wilderness Areas Act, the Frost government tidied up two loose ends in park policy. In March 1960, Lands and Forests Minister Spooner unveiled the government's position on hunting in the provincial parks. Here the naturalists' influence was limited, since Spooner rejected the ban on hunting called for by the FON. He declared that hunting was a legitimate recreational pursuit that would be encouraged in some provincial parks. Subsequently, in December, the Provincial Parks Act was amended to permit the use of the parks as "managed hunting areas during the season when this will not interfere with other forms of recreation … In the many new parks which are being established," explained Spooner, "the principle of multiple use is being applied, and in accordance with this, hunting, as recreation, should not be abolished unless its prohibition meets with some special needs."[35]

Interestingly, Parks Branch staff disagreed with this new hunting policy. It had been forced upon them by the combined efforts of the Lands and Surveys Branch and Fish and Wildlife personnel, who had been under growing pressure to provide more opportunities for public hunting. When first approached about opening southern parks for small-game hunting, Ben Greenwood had strongly objected to the suggestion, foreseeing all kinds of user conflicts and administrative expenses. "Hunting is not in keeping with the park theme," he insisted. "Visitors expect to see and enjoy wildlife without the association of hunting." Philosophically, he did not even endorse the existence of the traditional autumn waterfowl shoot, which had been allowed for decades in several parks. "Perhaps, if we consider all the ducks taken in ... [these] parks, and all the hunters, satisfied and unsatisfied, we could argue that the three areas would be more useful as sanctuaries where more people could be encamped to observe waterfowl."[36]

On the hunting issue, the Parks Branch found little support from other segments of the Department of Lands and Forests, and after 1960, hunting of various kinds expanded throughout the provincial parks system. The policy was flexible and applied judiciously, on a park-by-park basis, when public pressure and need indicated a demand for this type of recreational experience, and where areas of natural significance would not be adversely affected. In 1961, pheasant shooting of stocked birds for a five-week season was introduced on an experimental basis in Sibbald Point Park, and extended the following year to Presqu'ile and Darlington. Waterfowl shooting in season was also permitted in Darlington and Long Point. The department opened Lake Superior Park to the moose hunters in 1961, when aerial surveys indicated a high population of moose in the area. After the addition of Clyde and Bruton townships to Algonquin Park in 1961, the DLF also permitted the hunting of moose and deer in the townships, on a controlled basis. Despite the gnashing of teeth among some ecologically inclined groups, the flexible hunting policy proved to be workable, and few user conflicts were reported.

Commercial trapping was also permitted to continue in Ontario's provincial parks, the rationale being that it did not "conflict with recreation and [did] not have a significant effect upon the number of animals seen by summer visitors."[37] This decision was largely shaped by the employment needs of the aboriginal peoples. The Lac la Croix band worked twenty-one registered traplines in the northwest sector of Quetico Park, a privilege granted in 1948, after the Indian Affairs Branch of the Department of Mines and Resources in Ottawa appealed to the province for trapping rights for the band, on the grounds that the native people had had no other source of income since the termination of logging in Quetico in 1946. Similarly, in Algonquin, the Golden Lake band worked nineteen registered traplines on the east side of the park in 1958.

Apart from the hunting issue, the second of the loose ends in parks policy tied up by the Frost government in 1960 concerned Quetico-Superior. In April 1960, the premier announced a formal diplomatic exchange of letters between the Ontario and United States governments, wherein each side promised to cooperate with the other and to give reasonable notice of any change in management policies relating to the protection of the wilderness character of Quetico Provincial Park and the Boundary Waters Canoe Area (the name given to the roadless areas of the Superior National Forest in 1958). The exchange of letters could not have occurred, had the Quetico Foundation and the American president's Quetico-Superior Committee not established a close rapport with the premier and officials in the DLF. Since its establishment in

1954, the Quetico Foundation had earned the respect of politicians and civil servants alike by temporarily putting aside the demand for an international treaty to protect the Rainy Lake watershed. Instead, the foundation chose to advance the cause of the wilderness by funding research projects on the archaeology and geology of Quetico, and by instituting a program of publicity and education that included the publication of books, magazine articles, the Quetico *Newsletter*, and the production and distribution of Christopher Chapman's award-winning film *Quetico* in 1958. Impressed by the foundation's accomplishments, Clare Mapledoram invited the group in 1956 to expand its mandate to include a watchdog role over Ontario's other large northern parks like Algonquin and Lake Superior.[38]

Even the foundation's American ally, the president's Quetico-Superior Committee, convinced provincial officials of its good intentions. Beginning with a meeting at Basswood Lake in 1955, Charles Kelly, chairman of the president's committee, greatly influenced Ben Greenwood and other DLF personnel by mapping out the progress made by the American government in reclaiming the alienated lands within the roadless areas of the Superior National Forest. Private holdings had been reduced from 141,650 to 26,260 hectares since the late 1940s. After the meeting, Greenwood reported that he saw "no reason why this U.S. Committee should be looked upon with suspicion."[39] By 1957, the middle of the Eisenhower administration (1952–60), all but 2 percent (12,140 hectares) of the roadless areas lay in the public domain. So impressed were Ontario officials with the progress of the acquisition program that they willingly cooperated with the Americans when problems arose. In 1957, for instance, the province suspended Crown land sales on the Canadian side of the international border, on Saganaga Lake to the east of Quetico Park, and on Lac la Croix to the west, when it was learned that American resort owners were attempting to relocate on the Ontario shore of these lakes, waters that stretched along the northern boundaries of the roadless areas.[40]

Basking in the glow of the close relationship with Ontario officials, the leaders of the Quetico-Superior movement decided it was an opportune time to resurrect the proposal for a Canadian-American treaty to perpetuate the Quetico-Superior wilderness as an international forest and peace memorial. The leading activists – Harold Walker and Donald P. O'Hearn of the Quetico Foundation, and Charles Kelly and Sigurd Olson for the president's Quetico-Superior Committee – pinned their hopes on obtaining the support of major interest groups in northwestern Ontario. Accordingly, they placed before various regional organizations a harmless-sounding resolution that called for an "international agreement" to protect "for all time the finest canoe country in the world." The word "treaty" was studiously avoided. Their campaign collapsed at the annual meeting of the Northwest Ontario Municipal Association in Port Arthur, when Lands and Forests Minister Clare Mapledoram, together with W.G. Noden, MLA for Rainy River, sharply criticized the resolution and forced its withdrawal without a vote. Mapledoram had seen through the QSC's strategy. The term "international agreement" was simply a euphemism for "treaty," and a treaty of any kind threatened to compromise provincial sovereignty over the Rainy Lake watershed, something no Ontario politician could condone.

It was in the wake of this defeat in late 1957 that the moderate elements within the Quetico-Superior movement proposed an alternative – a diplomatic exchange of letters between the Ontario and American governments, committing each jurisdiction to cooperate in working out informally, through biannual meetings of a joint advisory committee, common management policies for the wilderness reserves on both sides of the border. Here was a pragmatic suggestion that found instant favour among all concerned. Subsequently, negotiations for the exchange of letters with the American State Department were conducted though the office of Howard C. Green, Canada's secretary of state for external affairs. The announcement of the exchange took place simultaneously in Washington and at Queen's Park, Toronto on 12 April 1960.

"Now our sole obligation is this," emphasized Frost, "that if we change policy at any time, we give notification of that to the American committee, so that we are not doing things which are running counter to what they are attempting to do on their side. Likewise, they would give us notice of any changes that would apply on their side." Through "friendly co-operation – without binding either side to any policy," he concluded, "we can work out policies which will be of benefit to both sides of the line."[41] His optimism was shared by Charles Kelly, who believed that Frost had committed his government to the protection of wilderness "almost as fully as if we had obtained the treaty." This was an exaggeration; Frost had simply confirmed the longstanding policy of previous Ontario administrations to cooperate with the Americans in managing the Quetico region. Nevertheless, Kelly instinctively admired and trusted Ontario's premier. "I regarded Leslie Frost ... as the finest public servant with whom I have ever had any contact," he recollected many years later – a noteworthy testimonial from a seasoned Chicago lawyer who had hobnobbed with presidents and many of America's leading political and business figures.[42]

The Southern Parks in the 1960s: Overuse and Rowdies

At first glance, the flurry of park-related policy initiatives in 1959 and 1960 seems remarkable. Yet it would be begging the question to claim that those actions were effective in solving the kinds of problems that had prompted a government response in the first place. Had the recreation-protection imbalance in provincial parks been sufficiently addressed? Was the 1959 classification scheme of lasting value? Was it supported by a framework of general management policy guidelines that was sufficiently useful to park administrators? Regrettably, time would soon tell; none of these questions could be answered in the affirmative. The classification scheme of 1959 was a failure from its inception. Hastily drafted under intense pressure from Premier Frost, it proved to be hollow, a shell lacking essentials such as objectives and management guidelines. The Parks Branch found it of no value as a tool for use in the selection or management of parkland, and it fell by the wayside; indeed, when a new generation of Parks Branch planners drafted a more sophisticated classification system in 1966, they did so in blissful ignorance of the 1959 text.[43]

The 1959 policy statement also failed to establish a framework of guidelines broad enough to prevent major decisions being made at the whim of politicians or civil servants. For example, conservationists discovered in November 1959 that the government, eight months earlier, had set apart a 2,222-hectare section of Algonquin Park, near Lake Traverse, for the construction of a radio observatory by the National Research Council of Canada. The council had applied for a location in Algonquin because research in radio astronomy had to be conducted in isolated areas, free of man-made electrical noise. The facility would contain laboratory buildings and residences, several large antennae, and a series of dishes (some over thirty metres in diameter) extending in a line over several kilometres.[44]

When they learned of this fait accompli, groups like the FON, the Conservation Council of Ontario, the Canadian Audubon Society, and the Quetico Foundation all registered their displeasure at yet another assault on the natural environment of the Algonquin interior. "It is inconceivable to me," wrote Patrick Hardy, managing director of the Canadian Audubon Society, "that there is not another spot in the whole of Ontario which is sufficiently isolated and interference-free for the location of the radio telescope." What was needed, he argued, was "legislation which would prevent incursions of any kind on our provincial parks without first having the matter thoroughly aired in debate."[45]

The work of the American Outdoor Recreation Resources Review Commission opened the eyes of Ontario conservationists and park officials to what was required in the way of planning and policy for parks and outdoor recreation. In 1962, the ORRRC concluded an intensive nationwide investigation of the present and future outdoor recreation needs of the American people to the year 2000. During its tenure, it published twenty-seven volumes of special studies and summarized its findings and recommendations in the landmark report *Outdoor Recreation for America* (1962).[46] Stewart Udall, Secretary of the Interior in the Kennedy administration, immediately implemented the two chief recommendations of the commission: first, that funds be made available for acquisition and development programs by both federal and state agencies; and second, that a bureau of outdoor recreation be created, to coordinate the activities of federal agencies and to serve as a conduit for federal grants. To promote broad recreation resource planning, the grants were made conditional upon the existence of state outdoor recreation plans which, ideally, would take into account long-term recreational factors like supply and demand, and which would specify objectives, targets, and time frames.

Aware of all these developments, conservationists in Ontario resolved to hound the provincial government into undertaking comprehensive outdoor recreation planning, based on the American model. Given the overcrowded conditions and related problems in southern provincial parks, and the emerging user conflicts in northern parklands, such action could not be deferred for long. In May 1961, the Conservation Council of Ontario and the Quetico Foundation petitioned the Cabinet Committee on Conservation and Land Use to express "concern over the explosive demand for outdoor recreation opportunities in Ontario and the lack of an over-all long-term plan to meet this demand, especially as it relates to parks easily accessible for day use to the large urban population of southern Ontario." The conservationists suggested that an independent recreation consultant be contracted immediately to undertake a provincial recreation survey and to make recommendations for action to meet the outdoor recreation needs of Ontarians over the next twenty-five years.[47]

A month later, in June, the conservationists descended upon the select committee of the legislature appointed to study the administrative and executive problems of the Ontario government. The FON sharply criticized the Ontario Parks Integration Board, both for its lack of "a clear understanding of the parks and recreational problems of this Province" and its tendency to "stress the transformation of natural areas into recreational areas exclusively."[48] Gavin Henderson, the executive director of the Conservation Council of Ontario, created a stir when he stated: "Ontario may boast that it has one of the finest parks systems on the continent if one considers only the type of parks provided by the Department of Lands and Forests ... in the north, but with respect to day use facilities in southern Ontario, the situation is deplorable and getting worse all the time ... It is to our everlasting shame that the long stretch of Lake Ontario shoreline between Oshawa and St. Catharines ... is now virtually inaccessible for public recreation purposes. Other vital areas are going the same way for the same reason: lack of imagination, lack of planning, and lack of decisive action."[49]

Lands and Forests Minister Spooner attempted to counter Henderson's argument by noting that together the American national and state parks systems provided only one-eighth of an acre (724 square metres) of recreational land per capita, compared to Ontario's provincial park system, which offered half of an acre (2,895 square metres) of land for each of its citizens. Henderson countered with the argument that the minister's statistics were misleading, since the half-acre per capita figure applied to the entire province and not to southern Ontario, and especially not to the park-starved "Golden Horseshoe" region, which contained nearly 75 percent of the province's population. Citing planning standards then being used in the United States, Henderson asserted that the Oshawa-to-Niagara area required some 42,000 acres (17,000 hectares) of non-urban parkland to service the existing population. At the time, the citizens of the region had access to a mere 3,000 acres (1,214 hectares). By the year 2000, they would require an estimated 96,000 acres (38,850 hectares) of outdoor recreation space. The Toronto *Globe and Mail* gave full coverage to this incident and subsequently endorsed Henderson's position.[50] To its credit, the Conservation Council of Ontario persisted in its campaign to convince the government of the urgent need for a comprehensive survey of outdoor recreation. In April 1963, the council aimed a lengthy brief specifically at Premier John Robarts and appealed to his interest in upgrading the administrative capacity of the government.[51]

The increase in user pressure on parklands in southern Ontario during the 1960s gave credence to the conservationists' arguments. Overcrowding in the southern provincial parks was generating all kinds of problems, a flood of complaints, and unprecedented negative publicity. The crush of people was straining existing water and sanitation facilities, and greatly increasing wear and tear on the buildings and equipment. More seriously, in the many campgrounds where use exceeded the optimum 60 percent occupancy rate over a season, campsite deterioration became a major concern. Excessive numbers of recreation-seekers in the parks also took a toll on the natural environment. Nowhere was this more evident than at the Pinery, where 1,075 campsites had been developed by 1963. "The load of camping ... is presently destroying the Pinery Provincial Park," reported Regional Forester Peter Addison in February 1964.[52] University professors who taught ecology classes in the Pinery shared Addison's concern. "At the present rate of use," one botanist calculated in 1967, the park "will be valueless [for educational and scientific purposes] in less than ten years."[53]

To compound the problems of recreational overuse and the deteriorating natural value of the parks, there emerged in the mid-1960s a new and unwelcome social phenomenon – rowdyism – a term that covered all kinds of deviant behaviour. Those responsible for the problem were mainly pleasure-seeking young people in their teens and twenties, eager to escape parental restraints and to enjoy for themselves the hedonistic, beach-party lifestyle so frequently glamorized in the media. In August 1963, following the civic holiday weekend, Parks Chief Wheatley informed Deputy Minister Frank MacDougall that the Parks Branch had received a flood of complaints from distressed family campers who had come into contact with the raucous younger crowd in the campgrounds of some of the southern parks.[54] Such complaints would occur more frequently in the years ahead, as unsuspecting families with young children were subjected to the obnoxious, irresponsible, and sometimes threatening behaviour of bands of inebriated youths. The costs of vandalism jumped dramatically in many parks and, with the advent of the motorcycle boom, some bikers wreaked havoc in fragile natural zones. "They are travelling over trails in Presqu'ile, and running up and down the beaches at Outlet and Pinery," complained one despondent park official in 1965.[55]

By mid-decade, the problem had grown to such proportions that in most southern parks, regular patrols by local detachments of the Ontario Provincial Police (OPP) were required. At Holiday Beach, Long Point, Outlet, Pinery, Rondeau, Sibbald Point, and Wasaga Beach, OPP officers had to be stationed in the parks throughout the summer months.[56] Regrettably, these measures seemed to have little effect. In June 1967, Peter Addison recognized that since the phenomenon of rowdyism had appeared, park personnel had been "unable to cope with the situation."[57] His pessimistic assessment came shortly after he had received news from the Pinery that a state of anarchy had existed in the park during a portion of the Victoria Day weekend. "On May 19th," reported the superintendent, "the teenagers were in control of the park." Over half of the 391 occupied campsites had been registered to London residents under the age of twenty. "It was impossible to keep up to gangs leaving for Grand Bend and gangs coming back, all of which were drunk, speeding, racing and screaming." When he appealed for assistance to the Grand Bend detachment of the OPP, he found to his dismay that all available officers had been called to deal with a near riot in that resort town. In fact, authorities did not regain control of the Pinery until the following day.[58] This was only the beginning of what was to become a chronic problem for park managers and, within the next decade, would require drastic measures, including a ban on the use of alcohol in some parks and the prohibition of motorcycles in the Pinery.

Mining and the Northern Parklands

Across northern Ontario, the explosion of outdoor recreation in the affluent 1960s gave rise to issues of a different sort. The outcome was, however, similar – imbalance and disharmony in the provincial parks system. While the concern in southern Ontario focussed on the lack of opportunities for outdoor recreation along the Great Lakes shorelines, the debate in the north centred on the need for more large parks of the wilderness type. While southern administrators fretted over problems of rowdyism, overuse, and environmental deterioration, their northern counterparts grappled with the issues of mining, logging, conflicting uses in Quetico and Algonquin, and the carrying capacity of wilderness zones.

In addressing these northern issues, the Parks Branch attempted to work within the framework of multiple-land-use policy. As defined by the DLF in the mid-1960s, multiple use was "the deliberate and carefully planned integration of various uses so as to interfere with each other as little as possible and to complement each other as much as possible with due regard for their order of importance in the public interest." The term did not simply imply "an assemblage of single uses"; rather, the "conscious, co-ordinated management of the various renewable resources" in any given area, for five major purposes – wood production, fish and wildlife habitat, outdoor recreation, watershed protection, and other resource developments, such as agriculture and mining. When it came to applying multiple use to provincial parks, recreation was to be given primary consideration. The difficulty with the multiple-use philosophy was that it was open to different interpretations. Park managers tended to interpret the policy from a recreational and preservationist point of view. Other multiple-use proponents, on the other hand, urged that all units of land, including parks, be managed for their "highest sustained productivity," an emphasis that gave industrial interests a foundation upon which to argue that mineral and timber extraction should be permitted in the province's parks.[59]

During the 1960s, the Parks Branch and its various conservationist client groups engaged the Department of Mines, various northern chambers of commerce, and the Ontario Mining Association in a debate over the question of mineral extraction. This issue, thought by some to have been settled in 1956, when Premier Frost prohibited prospecting and staking in the parks, was reopened in 1960, when the Conservation Council of Ontario, the Quetico Foundation, and the FON jointly argued for the creation of more parks of the Algonquin and Quetico type, to embrace up to 4.5 percent of the province's forested areas, which amounted to a threefold increase in territory then devoted to parkland. As the government committed more and more Crown land to industrial expansion, the conservationists sought to ensure that "recreational, scenic and historic values" be considered "on an equal basis with purely economic developments."[60]

The call for a tripling of parkland acreage in northern Ontario alarmed mining interests and those in related economic areas. The president of the Northern Ontario Associated Chambers of Commerce opposed the creation of more large parks because, under existing policy, mining would be prohibited in them, and "no one can determine without extensive exploration ... that any area has a minimum mining potential."[61] He was essentially correct in arguing that most park reserves and established parks had been set aside without sufficient geological investigation. With the support of the Department of Mines, mining interests worked diligently behind the scenes to counter the conservationists. Success came in April 1961, when the Public Lands Investigation Committee came down on the side of the mining industry. "We must continue to progress economically or perish," the committee wrote. "If there are valuable mineral resources to be found in provincial parks, from the standpoint of economics, provision should be made to permit their development ... there is no good reason why there should not be multiple use of the lands in parks."[62]

Such statements sent shudders through the Parks Branch. In the staff's opinion, mining and the preservation of recreational and natural values were incompatible. "Mining readily falls into the category of destructive operations," A.B. Wheatley argued, "which, in a provincial park, could hardly be received with favour by the public."[63] His thinking on the subject hardened in November 1961, when the Head of the Lakes Iron Company Ltd. declared that it wished to develop its claims in Quetico, which contained deposits of high-grade hematite. Since these claims had been surveyed during World War II, the company's mineral rights had been maintained under the policy laid down in 1956. If the politicians authorized the company to begin operations, the result would be open-pit mining, a railway, road, and pipeline, and a townsite of some 5,000 people being located in what Wheatley considered "the best part of the Park from the viewpoint of rugged scenery, virgin timber and wilderness."[64]

The Robarts government denied the company permission to mine the Quetico, since the iron ore in the park was not required by the provincial or national economies. The cabinet had doubtless also heeded the warnings of a political storm on both sides of the border if Quetico was opened to mining. The knowledge that many residents of northern Ontario opposed mining in provincial parks probably also coloured the government's thinking. New Democratic Party (NDP) leader, Donald C. MacDonald, noted that this was one of the few issues on which "southern and northern Ontario found common ground."[65] For all these reasons, then, Premier John Robarts announced in the legislature on 4 April 1962 "that the Government contemplates no changes in the present situation relating to ... the prohibition against prospecting and staking in Provincial Parks." "Our parklands are a priceless heritage," declared the premier, "and it is our aim to develop them for the use of all the people."

There the matter might have ended, had it not been for the persistence of the mining interests. Part of their tenacity sprang from the knowledge that other provinces, such as British Columbia, Manitoba, and Saskatchewan, permitted mining activities in their parks. Alberta generally prohibited mining operations, but authorized oil exploration in remote parks. British Columbia permitted mining in its Class B parks, and the government reclassified parkland when valuable mineral deposits were known to exist. In 1965, the Social Credit administration of W.A.C. Bennett issued an order-in-council, allowing mining exploration and development in all parks in British Columbia larger than 2,025 hectares, regardless of classification. Quebec's Liberal administration under Jean Lesage also decided, in September 1963, to modify traditional no-mining policy, and to permit mineral exploration in Gaspésie Park. Such events only served to fuel the determination of the mining lobby in Ontario to fight the ban on prospecting and staking in their own provincial parks.

As the mining operators maintained the pressure on government, the Department of Mines took another line of action. It began to deny all requests by the Parks Branch to withdraw Crown land from staking, either for park reserves or for additions to existing parks. The expansion of parks in the northern districts came to a grinding halt, a result that the Parks Branch had partly brought upon itself. An anonymous head-office staff member acknowledged that "we are not wholly blameless ... [because] some districts have reserved areas which will not be required in the forseeable future."[66] Under these conditions, relations between the Parks Branch and the Department of Mines went from bad to worse, and the Lands and Surveys Branch had to act "in a 'go-between' capacity."[67]

Mutual self-interest eventually forced the two agencies to reestablish more amicable relations. The occasion that brought them back to speaking terms involved the discovery of rich mineral deposits in the area surrounding the Mississagi park reserve, near the uranium town of Elliot Lake. The Mississagi reserve had a unique history. In 1960, following the collapse of the uranium market, Premier Leslie Frost had instructed the DLF to establish a new provincial park near the economically depressed town in order to create jobs and to stimulate a tourist industry. On the basis of Frost's directive, the Parks Branch set aside Mississagi Provincial Park Reserve, an area covering 38,445 hectares. Because the new reserve was located in a zone known for occurrences of copper, lead, zinc, and uranium, the minister of lands and forests acceded to a Department of Mines stipulation that when the park was put under regulation, special provision would be made to allow staking in Mississagi.[68]

In February 1964, the Parks Branch learned that copper had been discovered in a township adjacent to the reserve. At the request of the Department of Mines, the branch agreed that a 5,060-hectare parcel of land, contiguous to the copper strike, be withdrawn from the park reserve. Over the next two years, prospectors combed the townships around the site and staked over 2,000 claims. Predictably, when significant copper discoveries were made and the uranium market began to recover in 1966, the Department of Mines sought to have Mississagi opened to prospectors.[69]

Parks Branch officials recognized a golden opportunity. The Mississagi issue gave them leverage to advance other projects. In ensuing discussions with the Department of Mines, the branch agreed to reduce the Mississagi park reserve to a mere 2,023 hectares, thereby freeing some 31,566 hectares for mining exploration and development, but warned that unless the Department of Mines gave up something substantial in return, it could expect a strident reaction from the conservationists. Mines officials accordingly agreed to withdraw from staking the 242,400-hectare Pukaskwa Wilderness Area for a period of one year, during which time they would undertake an intensive geological survey. If no significant mineral discoveries were made, the area could be designated as parkland. The Department of Mines also grudgingly agreed to cooperate with the Parks Branch in creating two new classes of parks – Wild River and Primitive – in which no resource exploitation would be permitted.[70] Deputy Minister of Mines D.P. Douglass insisted that these new parks must be located "in areas where the mineral potential appears to be very poor, and where it can be proved that there is a need for a Primitive Park." His department still found this procedure to be "dangerous and unsatisfactory … because it is impossible to forecast with certainty that any area is completely devoid of mineral possibilities." The Department of Mines would abide by the agreement worked out with the Parks Branch over the Mississagi deletion, but both sides recognized that the issue of mining in Ontario's provincial parks would continue to generate interdepartmental conflict in the foreseeable future.[71]

Logging in the 1960s: Algonquin and Quetico

Commercial logging in provincial parks emerged as another serious issue, destined to generate an intense political storm in the late 1960s and early 1970s. Prior to 1966, timber operations in the largest northern parks had caused minimal concern outside the ranks of the DLF. This period of public quiescence soon ended, as several elements combined to create a highly volatile situation in the forests of Algonquin and Quetico. Since World War II, technological and market changes in the forest industries had brought about a transformation in logging practices. Gone were the days of the teamster, winter camp, and spring drive. Now the timber men sought a highly mechanized and automated, year-round operation. Furthermore, in the booming economy of the postwar period, market demand had expanded to include timber of lower quality, while new manufacturing techniques made it possible to produce lumber, small-dimension stock, pulpwood, and chips out of trees once deemed inferior by the loggers. Technological advances in equipment, particularly in the form of chain saws, wheeled tractors, and skidders also allowed the harvesting of trees previously considered uneconomic. Logging sites came to reverberate with the scream of chain saws and the roar of engines. Timber operators also required permanent, wide, and ballasted gravel roads through formerly inaccessible areas to accommodate the massive trucks that were needed to haul the logs to the mills.[72] As this technological revolution occurred in the forests of Algonquin, Quetico, and other parks, the ranks of wilderness enthusiasts swelled to hitherto unanticipated numbers, setting the stage for another clash between loggers and recreationists. With the appearance of a militant preservation movement in the mid-1960s, the final ingredient was added to the political mix, making it potentially explosive.

As early as March 1960, Parks Branch officials anticipated the difficulties ahead and recommended that "the time has come ... [to] prepare a definite ... policy on the utilization of timber resources in Provincial Parks." Subsequently, discussions were initiated with the Timber Management Branch, the most powerful unit of the DLF. For a year, draft policy statements bounced back and forth. "When parks are established," insisted the Parks Branch, "all other uses become secondary. It is not the intention to prohibit timber operations and harvesting within any park area or park reserve, but it is imperative that such procedures are not given precedence over park interests."[73] In March 1961, with the distribution of a circular to the district offices, outlining policy guidelines permitting timber licences in provincial parks and reserves, negotiations reached what seemed to be a satisfactory conclusion.[74] In many ways, the circular represented a general and more stringent application of the kind of timber management policies Frank MacDougall had pursued thirty years earlier in Algonquin Park. The circular directed field staff to prohibit cutting in Nature Reserves and public-use areas, designated in park master plans. Any cutting near a public-use area was to be controlled by "a selective marking of trees." The circular required all logging roads constructed by a timber operator to be temporary, as "unobtrusive as possible," and to be posted and gated, if necessary, to prevent public access. Any logging within 400 feet (122 metres) of lake shores, or 200 feet (61 metres) of portages and rivers on canoe routes, and within "scenic vistas of aesthetic value" was to be rigidly supervised and, if allowed at all, restricted to selectively marked trees.

The success of the guidelines depended on the cooperation of the timber operators holding licences in provincial parks, and on the vigilance of district officials. Sadly, in Quetico during the early 1960s, either one or both of these vital conditions were usually lacking. In 1961, after a fifteen-year period when no commercial logging had taken place in the park, the Jim Mathieu Lumber Company of Sapawe resumed operations in the northeast portion of Quetico. From the outset, subcontractors ran afoul of the guidelines by occasionally disregarding the clauses in their work permits that forbade logging in the shoreline reserves or near public-use areas. During Mathieu's first year of operation, the DLF fined the company for operating too close to the Dawson Trail campgrounds and, the following year, for cutting over a portion of the Cascades Hiking Trail. Eventually, such infractions came to the attention of NDP leader Donald MacDonald, who in February 1963 flailed the Robarts government for failing to control Jim Mathieu, the so-called "sawdust Caesar of Sapawe" and a leading figure in local Conservative Party circles.

"The most serious violation of all," MacDonald argued, "is the cutting along the navigable portions of the French River and Baptism Creek. This cutting is not confined to a few isolated patches ... but is on both sides of the river, and extends for at least a quarter of a mile." Mathieu had located a logging camp at the confluence of the two streams. "It is a cleared area larger than a football field, and has in it an enormous two-storeyed bunk house ... a large cookhouse, and numerous stables and shops ... The site of this camp along a canoe route clashes garishly with the popular image of Quetico as the world's finest wilderness canoe country ... It would have been no trouble at all to have Mathieu build out of sight from the water."[75] Even before MacDonald's revelations in the provincial legislature, the DLF had fined the company for the Baptism Creek trespass and assigned an employee to supervise the company's bush operation, the cost to be charged to Mathieu.[76] With such tighter supervision, and the NDP on the alert, blatant cutting violations in Quetico came to an end.

Apart from the difficulty of controlling the Mathieu Lumber Company and its subcontractors, the resumption of logging in Quetico forced park officials to determine which areas of the park should be designated no-cut zones. This question became urgent in 1965 after the American government, in the wake of the new Wilderness Act (1964), announced that it intended to manage the Boundary Waters Canoe Area (BWCA) as a primitive-type recreation area and to double the no-logging zone. In addition to the American stimulus, the anticipation of an influx of canoeists in the northern segments of Quetico, following the completion that spring of the Atikokan–Fort Frances Highway, prompted district officials to ponder where the no-cut reserves should be located. Accordingly, they recommended that the province should continue to maintain the Hunter's Island area contiguous to the BWCA as a no-logging zone, and implement a skyline-reservation policy along all water routes in logging areas, rather than the standard shoreline reserves.[77]

In Toronto, Alan Helmsley worried that the Parks Branch might be unable to resist the counterpressure brought by the timber interests to penetrate Hunter's Island. Already, the Mathieu Lumber Company was constructing an all-weather logging road in the direction of the proposed no-cut zone, and had enquired about the granting of a long-term licence, an increase in its allowable cut, and the possibility of extending its operations into areas closer to Hunter's Island. Before making any decisions on these matters, Helmsley urged, a master plan for the park had to be established. To create such a plan, he admitted, would require that systematic inventories be undertaken of the earth and life science, cultural, recreational, and scenic resources of the park. After half a century of managing the Quetico, the DLF still knew little about the place. Only after undertaking such inventories, Helmsley concluded, would park administrators be able to defend their decisions as to "where cutting can be undertaken under the present restrictions, where it can be undertaken on a highly selective basis and where, for ecological and/or historical reasons, it should not be undertaken at all."[78] Whether a master plan could be fashioned in time to prevent a clash between loggers, recreationists and preservationists remained an open question.

In contrast to Quetico, where timbering had been discontinued from 1946 to 1961, the loggers had never abandoned Algonquin Provincial Park. The forests there had remained an important source of hardwood timber for the veneer furniture and other wood-using industries of southern Ontario. Foresters estimated that in 1966–67, Algonquin provided roughly 10 percent of the white pine, 15 percent of the red pine, 14 percent of the yellow birch, and 30 percent of the maple cut from Crown lands in the Great Lakes–St. Lawrence forest region. In 1965, some twenty-five companies held timber licences, embracing roughly 65 percent of the park. Given the economic importance of Algonquin, timber officials wanted to have the deciding voice in the way the park forests were managed, a proposition the Parks Branch could not accept.[79]

The struggle for the control of Algonquin came into the open in October 1962 when W.L. Plonski, a forester in the Timber Management Branch, submitted a controversial report entitled "Opinion on the Forest Management of Algonquin Provincial Park." Plonski jolted the Parks Branch by recommending that logging, not recreation, should be recognized as the primary use in Algonquin. Among other things, he extolled the benefits of constructing a permanent logging-road system which, in the century or two ahead, would provide recreationists with "a complete access network throughout the park." His report also questioned the need for the Wilderness Research Area, set aside in 1944, in which logging was prohibited. He argued that wildlife management and research would be better served in a managed forest. The responsibility for harmonizing the interests of all DLF branches in Algonquin and for preparing necessary management and operating plans, he ended, "will be the task of Timber Branch."[80]

From the Parks Branch perspective, Plonski's report was anathema, an attempt to treat Algonquin Park like any other unit of Crown land where timber management was the primary factor in the multiple-use equation. Parks officials cringed at the report's potential for negative effects if it were adopted as policy. Plonski did not appreciate the fact that Algonquin's appeal as a place where canoeists could experience solitude, quiet, and a sense of personal achievement, in an area which at least appeared to be virgin forest, depended upon keeping the interior free of public roads. Parks Branch personnel also deplored the forester's lack of appreciation of the scientific and aesthetic value of wilderness areas and biotic reserves, "set aside to change as they will," without active management. Fortunately, leading professionals in the DLF's Research Branch and at the University of Toronto in the areas of fish, wildlife, and even forestry joined parks personnel in effectively challenging Plonski's assumptions.[81]

For all its deficiencies, his report had one positive consequence. It reminded park administrators that they had yet to define their goals for the long-term management of Algonquin. "Unless we get off the pot," wrote T.W. Hueston, development supervisor at Parks Branch from 1961 to 1965, "the proponents of other conflicting uses will eventually snow us under."[82] Hueston himself was given the responsibility for drafting a master plan for Algonquin, when he assumed the superintendency of the park in 1965. For several years, as he grappled with this task, park and timber branch officials attempted to resolve a myriad of issues: the optimum size of the no-cut zones; control of access to the park on the twenty-four logging roads that crossed the park boundary; the merits of an annual volume allotment for timber operators, rather than the traditional licences based on areas; the need for sawmills in the park; and the desirability of curtailing cutting operations in July and August.

As Hueston and others looked more closely at the timber operations that were going on in Algonquin Park, they were surprised by what they discovered. "The quality of control on logging operations has not been of the standard expected in a Provincial Park," noted Hueston. "Not only are some companies cutting outside the areas shown on the cutting authority, but also in a few instances outside the licence and in reserve areas. The worst aspect ... is that these infractions have not been recognized by our own field men." Donald Wilson, shortly after becoming regional director in southern Ontario, bluntly concluded that it was scandalous that timber operations in Algonquin were carried on no differently inside the park than on Crown lands elsewhere. "In fact, as far as shoreline reservations are concerned, we completely reserve the first 100 feet and mark timber in the next 400 feet inside the park, while outside we completely reserve the first 400 feet if there is any likelihood of cottage development in the future." Wilson warned his superiors in April 1967 that unless timber operations were more strictly controlled, public opinion could swing against the continuation of "the multiple use concept of provincial park operations."[83]

Canoeists, Motorboat Fishermen, and Perceptions of Wilderness

Ironically, as the intradepartmental debate over timber management in provincial parks raged on, most visitors to Algonquin and Quetico did not consider logging to be a pressing concern. Surveys of interior users conducted in the early 1960s in Quetico-Superior by Professor Robert C. Lucas of the University of Minnesota, and in Algonquin by George Priddle, then a graduate student at Clark University, indicated that neither canoeists nor motorboat fishermen saw logging as a major problem. "At the present time," Priddle demonstrated statistically in 1964, "logging operations are not conflicting with interior recreationists."[84] From 1963 to 1967, the district office in Pembroke received an average of only six written complaints annually on the subject of timber practices in Algonquin. A marketing survey of visitor attitudes toward Quetico carried out in 1967 revealed that a mere 8 percent of interior users were even aware of logging activity, and only one-third of these people thought that timber harvesting detracted from their enjoyment.[85]

Rather than commercial logging, the main causes of user dissatisfaction and disharmony in Quetico and Algonquin were crowding and motorboats. By the early 1960s, the number of canoeists and boaters visiting the two parks had reached a point where they threatened to destroy the wilderness, the environment that had attracted most of them in the first place. Popular canoe routes in both Algonquin and Quetico had become badly refuse strewn, beaten down, and stripped of vegetation. In 1966, the garbage problem reached such proportions that the Parks Branch had to initiate a "pack out your own litter project," involving a variety of publicity techniques to raise the consciousness of visitors toward the issue. Special yellow plastic litter bags were designed and distributed to interior users in the hope that they would pack out their refuse.[86] In Algonquin, the litter bags were numbered, recorded, and distributed to interior users at new registration centres.

The crowding problem in Algonquin and Quetico involved several factors. At its simplest level, it meant congestion on some lakes and streams, especially near major access points. The excessively used route leading out of Canoe Lake in Algonquin was derisively called "Main Street" by park personnel. Similarly, severe congestion existed in the northeast section of Quetico, partly because, as late as 1965, all wilderness trippers entering the park from the north were funnelled through a single access point at the Dawson Trail Campground. To ardent wilderness canoeists, however, the perception of "being crowded" did not necessarily mean being in the company of large numbers of people. Wilderness enthusiasts, who came to Quetico for solitude, quiet, and to look at wildlife in a primitive setting, complained of "crowding" upon encountering more than two camping parties on a single lake, or whenever they came within sight or sound of a motorboat. So serious had the matter become that by 1967, one-third of all canoeists using Quetico indicated that they had felt crowded at some point during their visit.[87]

Closely related to the issue of crowding, and a serious problem in its own right, was the irreconcilable conflict of interests between canoeists and motorboat users. These recreationists could not coexist in the same areas of the large parks. Social scientists like Robert Lucas and George Priddle explained this conflict in terms of the vastly different ways in which the two groups saw the wilderness. "Man's 'wilderness' perception varies with time, space, his

Piles of garbage await removal from the interior of Algonquin Park in 1965. The garbage problem resulted in a mandatory "pack out your own litter" policy the following year.
Courtesy: Ministry of Natural Resources.

place in society, and his unique personal characteristics," Priddle explained.[88] According to survey data, paddlers were generally younger, better educated, and from a relatively higher socioeconomic background than the motorboating group. Canoeists were attracted to Algonquin, and most especially to Quetico, by the primitive qualities of each park, while the motorboat users came primarily for the fishing. Paddlers complained of being "crowded" long before the motorboat group cried out that the saturation point had been reached on a waterway. Above all else, canoeists objected to motorboats and deemed them to be inappropriate to a wilderness setting. In Quetico, the boating problem was further complicated by the presence of houseboats on the lakes, along the international border between the park and the Boundary Waters Canoe Area.

The findings of the social scientists had enormous practical significance for park managers, whose goal in both Algonquin and Quetico had long been to maintain the wilderness qualities of the interior. Lucas recommended to the United States Forest Service that since boating and canoeing were incompatible activities, they should be separated. The most logical approach to separation seemed to be zoning, a mechanism that would certainly alleviate the "crowding" problem for canoeists. Lucas estimated that a motorboat ban in the interior of Quetico-Superior would enhance the carrying capacity (the number of paddlers that could be accommodated, while maintaining optimum satisfaction levels), since "canoeists seemed willing to accept roughly three times as much canoe use as mixed boat and canoe use." Beyond eliminating motorboats from interior lakes, he recommended that efforts be made to reduce crowding by moving canoeists from heavily used routes to lightly used areas. If these policies failed, then park managers would have to consider adopting a quota system to limit the number of users allowed at any one time on the canoe routes.[89]

The idea of managing the interior of Quetico and Algonquin for canoeing under primitive conditions was not received kindly by the motorboat users. To these recreationists, such a policy smacked of elitism and was tantamount to pandering to an affluent minority. Nevertheless, there was a strong argument for a motorboat ban in certain zones. In the first place, the areas set aside for wilderness canoeing comprised only a small part of the Crown land base in Ontario. Secondly, because the canoeists held that motorboats and wilderness did not mix, "without priority the opportunity to choose wilderness canoeing would be reduced or lost."[90] Giving priority to canoeists in Algonquin and Quetico could also be justified in part because the user surveys had revealed that the wilderness qualities of both parks were much more important to the canoe tripper than to the motorboat user. The "degree of wilderness appreciated by most motor-boat enthusiasts might easily be satisfied in many places outside, or on the periphery of, the Quetico," wrote Bruce Litteljohn, a former park ranger and DLF historian, then a teacher at Upper Canada College.[91] Finally, the justification for prohibiting motorboats in the interior of Algonquin and Quetico rested on the fact that canoeists, seeking a wilderness experience, had fewer and fewer alternative locations at their disposal.

Since the "back to nature" thrust of the mid-1950s, Parks Branch officials had been predisposed to regulate motorboats in the interior of the two largest provincial parks. They recognized motorboating as a legitimate form of recreation in provincial parks and sought to provide a place for it, but not at the expense of wilderness values. "The continual use of motors, by increasing numbers of people, can only lead to the rapid deterioration of a park interior, and the discouragement of a growing number of people who seek canoe country," branch personnel concluded.[92]

The first regulation designed to control the use of boats in provincial parks was issued in 1961 to prohibit the leaving of boats unattended in any park. Angry outfitters and lodge operators, who had traditionally cached motorboats in the interiors of Algonquin and Quetico for the benefit of their customers, lobbied furiously for a revision of the regulation. Evidently, the politicians considered the grievance legitimate and modified the regulation in 1962, to allow for the caching of boats in Algonquin during the spring fishing season from 1 April to 20 June each year. This satisfied the anglers, who frequented the trout lakes in the eastern and northern parts of the park, at a time when few paddlers visited Algonquin. During the remainder of the year, boats could only be left unattended at designated places on some twenty-five lakes. Similarly, in Quetico, the caching of boats was permitted at designated places in the Dawson Trail area, the ranger station at Beaverhouse Lake, Cache Bay, Lac la Croix, Prairie Portage, and Ottawa Island.[93]

As technological changes in the production of outboard motors and fibreglass watercraft contributed to the popularity of water-skiing and powerboating through the 1950s and 1960s, regulations had to be issued for the first time to control these activities in the interior of the large parks. Consequently, in 1965, the government banned the use of water skis, surfboards, water sleds, and the like in Algonquin Park, with the exception of sixteen leasehold lakes, and lakes with organized campgrounds.[94] That same year, Lands and Forests Minister Kelso Roberts, attempting to preserve the wilderness of the interior lakes in Algonquin and Killarney provincial parks, received cabinet approval to prohibit the use of powerboats on most lakes in both parks. Powerboats of any size would only be permitted on thirty-four lakes in Algonquin and on three lakes in Killarney, all of which were readily accessible by boat or by land. The new regulation created a political uproar. Tory MLAs from ridings around Algonquin demanded that outboard motors of three horsepower or less be allowed anywhere in the park. The cabinet buckled under the pressure and revised the regulation, to permit the use of boats with motors of ten horsepower or less on all the interior lakes of Algonquin and Killarney.[95] On the more accessible lakes, no restriction was placed on the size of outboard motors. It was a setback for Parks Branch officials, who had been seeking to protect recreational opportunities in the wilderness and to end the clash of canoeists and boaters in the two parks.

The Preservationist Movement

Conflicts between users, timber and mining pressures in the large, resource-rich parks, and overuse by recreation seekers all worked to erode the protectionist objective of the provincial parks system. Conservationists soon realized that both the policy initiatives and the Wilderness Area Act of 1959 were ineffective in the attempt to resolve the conflict between preservation, recreation, and resource extraction. It was, accordingly, only a matter of time before the conservationists reacted to the expanding array of threats to the natural areas of Ontario's provincial parks. One of the controversies that snapped them back into fighting form involved the proposed development plan for Sandbanks Provincial Park, announced in February 1964. To the horror of many naturalists, the Parks Branch sought to satisfy recreational needs at the expense of natural values, by proposing to build a paved road through the sand dunes of the park, an area deemed to be of considerable geological significance. Opponents of the road sprang into action, arguing that the fragile dunes would suffer irreparable damage if construction went forward. Surprised by the protest, the Parks Branch jettisoned the road scheme and pledged to protect the dunes area.[96]

The Sandbanks episode made a profound impression on Douglas H. Pimlott, chairman of the Canadian Audubon Society's park policy committee, and a person destined to become a guiding force in the militant preservationist movement of the decade ahead. Trained as a forester before becoming a biology professor at the University of Toronto, he already enjoyed an international reputation for his research on the ecology of the timber wolf in Algonquin Park.[97] For Pimlott, Sandbanks confirmed what he had observed in Algonquin; those responsible for planning and managing Ontario's parks were operating without the benefit of an adequate framework of preservationist policy and legislation. In short, they were suffering from a "'no philosophy' disease."[98]

Pimlott believed that in Algonquin Park, the no-philosophy disease had had the effect of shifting the balance in favour of logging in park management decisions. During his wolf research, he had flown over every section of Algonquin and travelled most of the park logging roads, where he had witnessed timber operations first-hand. It appalled him to see that so little consideration was being given to the protection of a significant natural environment. Part of the problem, he knew, stemmed from the fact that most senior positions within the DLF were held by foresters, who had been taught to think in utilitarian, conservationist terms. "It took me years to shake the idea that a piece of wood left to decompose on the ground was being wasted; to shake the idea that it was sinful to let even an occasional overmature stand disintegrate and change naturally."[99] Forestry education, Pimlott knew from his own experience, failed "to emphasize basic ecological relationships." With such training, foresters did not always make ideal managers of parks and natural areas. If anyone required proof of this assertion, they needed only to investigate management practices in any of the large multiple-use parks, where "the number one priority is not the use of it by people but the use of it by the forest industries."[100] In Pimlott's opinion, the once-effective multiple-use policies of shoreline reserves and regulated logging, the formula for conflict resolution successfully introduced in Algonquin by Frank MacDougall in the 1930s, would no longer suffice.

Pimlott's observations of planning and management practices within Ontario's parks system left him in a state of righteous indignation. "In years to come," he informed Parks Chief D.R. Wilson in May 1965, "it seems likely that I will work fairly hard, both as an individual and as a member of private organizations, to stir up interest" in the need to preserve Ontario's natural areas.[101] His crusade took him in two different but related directions. He responded first as an academic and offered annually a postgraduate course in multiple-resource-use management at the Faculty of Forestry in the University of Toronto, designed especially for middle and senior management foresters and biologists within the DLF. By the mid-1970s, most senior Lands and Forests staff had taken the course and come under Pimlott's influence.

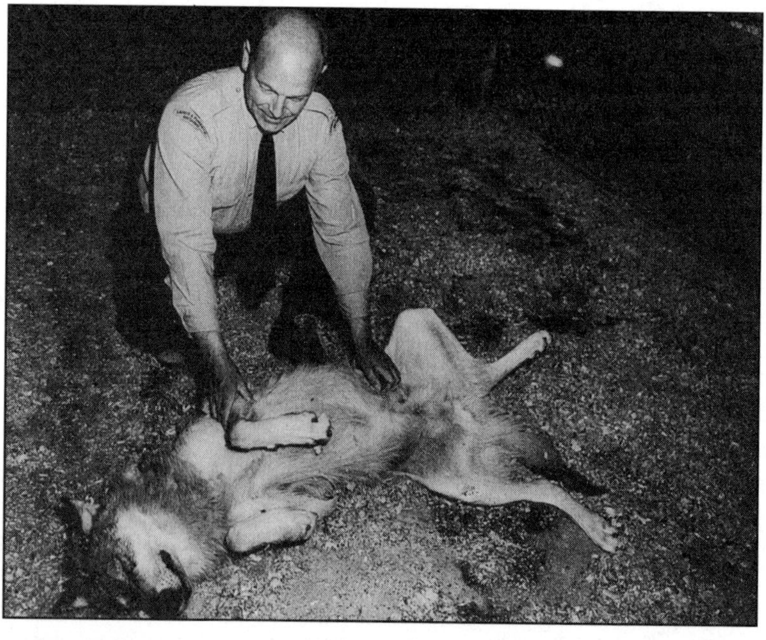

Douglas H. Pimlott, renowned for his research on the timber wolf in Algonquin Park, became a central figure in the emergence of Ontario's wilderness preservation movement in the mid-1960s. *Courtesy: Mark Pimlott.*

Beyond the academic approach, Pimlott began to organize public and media support for the preservationist concept of parks. In this regard, he drew upon the public relations techniques he had learned as an advocate of wolf protection. For years he had been endeavouring to dispel the deeply ingrained public and professional attitudes and misconceptions about wolves, an effort that was eventually rewarded by the termination of the provincial wolf bounty in 1972. Pimlott's crusade to influence public and political attitudes toward the protection of natural areas was no less successful. Beginning in 1965, he lobbied politicians, rebuked the Federation of Ontario Naturalists for neglecting "to develop and organize public support for the preservation of fauna and flora,"[102] and systematically distributed information to daily newspapers, a public-relations device which generated considerable investigative reporting and editorial comment. In lectures and articles in journals, Pimlott dispelled all illusions about the efficacy of the Wilderness Areas Act and existing park policy. He demonstrated that the clause in the act that allowed resource utilization in any wilderness area over 640 acres (259 hectares) in size, destroyed the legislation's value as a means of setting aside natural environments, either as Nature Reserves or as Primitive-class parks. That the DLF had failed even to apply the Wilderness Areas Act in an imaginative way particularly irritated Pimlott. No Wilderness Areas, he pointed out, had been designated in either Algonquin or Quetico.

During his study of the province's record in the preservation of natural areas, Pimlott also unearthed the startling fact that the Wildlife Research Area in Algonquin Park, set aside in 1944 as the Wilderness Area, no longer had official status, because the relevant order-in-council had lapsed, thanks to a bureaucratic oversight. Worse still, Pimlott discovered that a wedge of land covering over a hundred hectares had been placed under timber licence. The land affected contained a mature stand of red spruce, "one of the rarest forest associations in Algonquin Park." All of these examples, Pimlott wrote, led to the conclusion that the government of Ontario had shown "little regard, or appreciation, for the preservation of natural environments."[103]

By the end of 1965, Pimlott had laid out the preservationist agenda for the decade ahead. He emphasized the need for a revision of the Provincial Parks Act, so that it included a detailed statement of the basic elements of park policy. In this regard, he expected the province to follow the lead of the federal government, which had made public, in September 1964, a statement of national parks policy that emphasized preservation. To resolve conflicts between recreation, preservation, and logging, and to ensure that preservation be accorded equal status with recreation in park planning and management, Pimlott believed that any new policy must embrace a workable classification of parks. No single park could be expected to satisfy all kinds of users; different classes had to be designated and managed for different groups of recreationists, as well as for the preservation of natural areas. Only through a sophisticated classification and zoning scheme, Pimlott explained, could an area like Darlington Provincial Park, a "mundane campground," located on "poor farmland," be separated "in name, in policies and in programs" from a Sandbanks or an Algonquin, which contained outstanding natural features. As things stood, he observed, "there is little evidence that the parks policy of the Department of Lands and Forests recognizes the difference between a piece of coal and a diamond."[104]

Beyond policy reform, Pimlott called for the expansion of the parks system along certain lines. The province required large, Primitive-type parks of no less than 100,000 acres (40,470 hectares) in size, the standard established by the American Wilderness Act of 1964. In addition, he hoped that conservationists would be able to create sufficient public pressure to move the government of Ontario to facilitate the establishment of several large national parks in the province. Pimlott insisted that the Wilderness Areas Act, which limited the size of nature reserves to 640 acres (259 hectares) should be scrapped, and new legislation introduced to create a system of natural areas, with a 5,000-acre (2,023-hectare) size limit for each reserve. In the area of administration, he recommended that the proposed nature reserve system be overseen by a new, natural environment section of the Parks Branch, to be staffed by ecologists and geologists. For every park and nature reserve in the system, he expected a master plan to be fashioned, which would identify recreational, natural and cultural features, state the primary purpose for which the area was set aside, and specify mandatory management guidelines. Only in this way would "a reasonable balance between preservation and other uses" be attained.[105]

Pimlott's call to action proved to be one of the catalysts of a preservationist upsurge, and others soon spoke out in support of the themes he had raised. Within the Federation of Ontario Naturalists, for instance, Fred Bodsworth, a noted author and journalist, devoted his presidential address in April 1966 to an exploration of the parks question and began to write in support of wilderness preservation.[106] Likewise, in 1965, J. Bruce Falls, a biologist at the University of Toronto and chairman of the FON's Parks and Reserve Committee, breathed new life into the flagging effort to establish a system of nature reserves in Ontario, and began ongoing and ultimately successful discussions toward that end with Lands and Forests officials.[107] The FON devoted the December 1967 issue of the *Ontario Naturalist* to the themes of wilderness, nature reserves, and parks. Outside the naturalists' ranks, other individuals and organizations rallied to the preservationist cause. For instance, Bruce Litteljohn published "Quetico-Superior Country – Wilderness Highway to Wilderness Recreation" in the *Canadian Geographical Journal* (1965), later reissued as a booklet by the Quetico Foundation. The essay documented the recreational and commercial pressures endangering the wilderness canoe country. Like Pimlott, he deplored the deficiencies of policy and legislation in Ontario that aimed to preserve large primitive areas, especially in view of the recent activities in the United States since the proclamation of the Wilderness Act of 1964. "There is not one area in the Province of Ontario," he wrote, "protected by legislation for the sole use of those who wish to experience the wilderness under primitive conditions."

In 1965, a new organization – the National and Provincial Parks Association of Canada (NPPAC) – stepped into the limelight as a champion of "the preservation concept of parks." The idea of such a body, to serve as an informed, nongovernmental watchdog over all Canadian park agencies, was first given serious consideration during the dominion-provincial "Resources for Tomorrow" conference of 1961. Delegates from the Toronto area to that conference founded the NPPAC in 1963, giving it a national board of directors. The association became a force to be reckoned with in November 1964, when Gavin Henderson, renowned for his years of dedicated work for the Conservation Council of Ontario and the Federation of Ontario Naturalists, assumed the position of executive director. The NPPAC "wants the people of Canada to know about their parks," declared Henderson, "to take pride in them, to understand their purposes – and to get angry and militant whenever they are threatened."[108] Shortly after Henderson's appointment, Douglas Pimlott began to agitate for a new organization – the Algonquin Park Association was the name he originally suggested in September 1965 – to work at the provincial level alongside the NPPAC. Although the proposed organization would focus its interest around Algonquin Park, Pimlott explained, it would also express the opinions of its members on all park-related issues in Ontario. That month, nine private individuals and representatives of the Canadian Audubon Society, the Conservation Council of Ontario, the Federation of Ontario Naturalists, and the Ontario Federation of Anglers and Hunters met in Algonquin and agreed on the need for a special organization to sort out the "complex facts – ecological, sociological, economic and political – surrounding the management of Ontario's wilderness." A steering committee subsequently drew up a constitution and applied for letters patent for what would be known as the Algonquin Wildlands League. It is noteworthy that the idea of creating the league came in part from the ranks of Algonquin Park staff themselves, especially those who were frustrated, both by the dominance of the Timber Management Branch on park policy, and by the Fish and Wildlife Branch professionals who promoted policies that favoured hunting and trapping.[109]

The quickening preservationist impulse in Ontario during the mid-1960s was part of a larger, growing phenomenon, the North American environmental movement. Modern environmentalism, according to Samuel P. Hays in *Beauty, Health, and Permanence* (1987), emerged from the social and economic transformations following World War II and the concomitant general rise in living standards. Many North Americans reached a level of affluence that enabled them to look beyond the acquisition of necessities and conveniences and to give priority to considerations affecting the quality of life. For instance, the newly affluent came to value outdoor recreation space, undefiled natural areas, and clean air and water as essential aspects of a better standard of living.

During the 1950s, the postwar outdoor recreation boom helped to shape, and in turn was sustained by, new attitudes toward the environment. Those who took part in the great rush to get outdoors began to view natural areas differently from their utilitarian forebears. Public conceptions of forests and rivers changed. In contrast to earlier conservationists, who had viewed forests primarily as tree farms, to be managed on a sustained-yield basis, or who valued rivers primarily for navigational, irrigation and hydro-electrical purposes, the environmentally inclined population conceived of forested areas and waterways both as environments with biological merit and as "aesthetic resources that provided amenities and enhanced daily life."[110] Accordingly, the first phase of environmental politics in the United States largely involved "the amenity values of wild lands." Under pressure from rapidly growing, preservationist organizations like the Sierra Club, the Wilderness Society, the National Parks Association and the National Wildlife Federation, the administrations of presidents John F. Kennedy and Lyndon Baines Johnson responded with long lists of legislation, dedicated to the protection of "the aesthetic qualities of nature and wildlands" – the Wilderness Act (1964), the Land and Water Conservation Fund (1965), the National and Scenic Rivers Act (1968), and the National Trails Act (1968).

The new environmental way of thinking also included ecological conceptions of nature and humans' place there. For example, this was evident in the growing appreciation of the importance of wetlands. Whereas previous generations had viewed wetland environments as unhealthy swamps, valuable only if drained for agricultural purposes, the environmentally sensitive public came to appreciate wetlands as essential wildlife habitat, areas of lush vegetation of enormous diversity, providing food and shelter for myriad insects, molluscs, fish, amphibians, reptiles, birds and mammals. The importance of wetlands in slowing down shoreline erosion or in contributing to the natural water purification process was also being gradually understood.

Ecological awareness also lay behind the public's fear that pollution was having an enormous deleterious impact on natural environments and the realization that this posed a threat to their health and well-being. Concern about air and water pollution, indeed, became the hallmark of the second phase of environmental activism, which began in the mid-1960s. Public anxiety grew during the radioactive-fallout scares of the late 1950s and early 1960s, and peaked with the pesticide scare stimulated by the publication of Rachel Carson's *Silent Spring* (Boston: Houghton Mifflin Co., 1962). Carson wrote about ecology – "the web of life – or death" she called it – in terms average people could understand, and explained to her shocked readers how humankind was poisoning itself by introducing dichloro-diphenyl-trichloroethane (DDT) into the food chain. *Silent Spring* opened the floodgates of discussion to environmental issues of all kinds. It became apparent that no one could avoid the effects of air, land, and water pollution. This realization did not sit well with the generation of North Americans that had grown affluent during the postwar economic expansion, and who now placed increasing importance on matters of lifestyle and family, home, and leisure. With pollution and economic and urban expansion threatening the areas in which they lived and played, more and more people began to heed the environmentalists' message. Moreover, as the baby boomers flooded into universities across North America, environmentalism became one more element of campus protest and dissent over the Vietnam War, civil rights, nuclear disarmament, student rights, and feminism.

During the 1960s, Ontarians imbibed a steady stream of information and commentary on environmental questions and realized that their province was not immune to the problems plaguing many other parts of the world. When they read of killer smog in London or Los Angeles, their thoughts went to the 1962 Grey Cup football game, rudely interrupted when a thick blanket of fog, partly caused by dirt and sulphur fumes, settled over the Canadian National Exhibition Stadium in Toronto. Five years later, they were shocked by a Canadian Broadcasting Corporation (CBC) television documentary, "Air of Death," which claimed that toxic air threatened the lives of the residents of Port Maitland. Ontarians also had to face the fact that a water pollution crisis of immense proportions threatened the Great Lakes. In the middle of the decade, scientists declared Lake Erie "near death," due to eutrophication. A massive algae bloom, thick mats of green, decomposing slime, created by pollutants – chemical fertilizer runoff, phosphate detergent, industrial effluent and raw sewage – covered some 207,200 hectares of the lake.[111] Revelations of new environmental threats appeared regularly in newspaper articles and popular magazines. Scientific papers delivered to the conferences on "Pollution and Our Environment" in Montreal in 1966, and on "Ontario Pollution Control" in Toronto, the following year, added to the public's fears.

For those interested in the protection of natural areas, these were worrisome times. R. Yorke Edwards lamented in the *Canadian Audubon* that "Our generation is witnessing a world-wide disaster to overtake the thin film of life that paints our planet green." In previously remote areas, "exploitation of the landscape by man has already destroyed much of their wildness, and from all of them come warnings of wildlife about to be literally pushed off the earth."[112] In such a world, concluded the environmentalists, the preservation of natural areas was urgently required. In view of their own, steadily deteriorating environment, many informed southern Ontarians came to believe that the quality of their lives, and perhaps even their survival, depended on their shrinking natural inheritance. Gavin Henderson put it bluntly: "In all nature, environment is the key to success of every organism. If the habitat is favourable a species will thrive. If it is unfavourable it will die out."[113] In "The Importance of Wilderness to Science," *Ontario Naturalist* (December 1967), Bruce Falls focussed on the same urgent theme. "If man is to survive, he must learn to manage his environment more wisely," Falls wrote. "The way things are going, he may do irreversible damage to the natural world which will lead ... to a severe restriction in the choices open to future generations."

This powerful context of environmental awareness explains the intensity, both of the emotions behind the fight in Ontario for more nature reserves, wilderness and national parks, and of the upcoming political battles to ensure that recreational and commercial activities did not negate natural values in established parks. The preservationists understood the importance of their cause, and it steeled them against charges that they were "dreamy-eyed visionaries" or "dicky birders," "selfish naturalists" or "pseudo-scientists." Furthermore, they drew inspiration and confidence from their counterparts in the United States. Ontario's environmentalists avidly perused American literature like the reports of the Outdoor Recreation Resources Review Commission, and books such as Stewart Udall's *The Quiet Crisis* (1963), William O. Douglas's *A Wilderness Bill of Rights* (1965), and reprints of Aldo Leopold's classic *A Sand County Almanac* (1949). When the American preservationist movement succeeded in having Congress pass the Wilderness Act in 1964, legislation designed to create a system of wilderness areas on federal lands, Ontarians rejoiced and aspired to follow suit.

The Parks Branch Reorganized

Confronted with a bewildering array of issues, and increasingly caught in the crossfire between conflicting parkland users and interest groups, Ontario's Parks Branch personnel stewed in frustration in the early 1960s, unable to meet the challenge before them. Much of that frustration stemmed from the fact that a new era of professionalism and expertise in park planning and management had descended upon them, and it took time to adjust. More than any other single influence, the American Outdoor Recreation Resources Review Commission had clarified what was expected of park agencies across North America. If they wished to meet the needs of their populations for outdoor recreation, state and provincial governments could not avoid taking inventories of outdoor recreation resources, undertaking systematic marketing surveys and social science analyses, cost-benefit studies, and long-term planning.

Ontario's park administrators were ill-prepared to assume such a weighty mandate. "Here in Ontario," Parks Chief A.B. Wheatley candidly admitted in 1961, "our parks are planned and decisions made on a day to day basis ... Literally speaking, we have no long-range plans and ... no qualified staff available to prepare research programs."[114] Three years later, the situation remained unchanged. "The Parks Branch is slowly but surely stagnating," wrote a disgruntled Alan MacDonald in June 1964. "This has been brought about because of the tremendous growth in the system and a lack of parallel growth in professional and technical staff, both in the field and head office." He found it "next to impossible to keep abreast of current affairs, to study new techniques or to spend time on problems which should be given serious consideration."[115] The backlog of unfinished park master plans was an embarrassment to the branch. "To prepare a plan for Algonquin," commented Russell Tilt, "the staff of Parks Branch should be at least tripled."[116]

One ray of light shone through this otherwise gloomy picture. During these years, branch staff met annually with their counterparts from across Canada in the so-called Federal-Provincial Parks Conferences. The idea for this regular forum had arisen during the recreation workshops of the "Resources for Tomorrow" conference in 1961. Park administrators in attendance resolved to continue meeting with their peers from across the country to discuss mutual problems of recreation resource management and to coordinate their work. At the first conference, held in Ottawa in November 1962, the themes and issues raised in the ORRRC's *Outdoor Recreation for America* understandably commanded the delegates' attention. Most realized that priority should be given to laying the foundation for intergovernmental cooperation, especially in the area of recreation research. The ORRRC had set an impressive precedent by completing an inventory of all public outdoor recreation areas in the continental United States, and by conducting a national recreation survey to discover the outdoor recreation habits and preferences of the American public. As a start in that direction, the Canadian National Parks Branch agreed to serve as an interim clearing house for data on recreation research compiled by the provinces. The delegates were also intrigued by the ORRC's proposal for a standard framework for the classification of parks. Again the National Parks Branch offered to take the lead by compiling, with each province's assistance, an inventory of existing parklands across the country, and using that information to draft a common classification format appropriate to the Canadian situation. From this promising beginning, the Federal-Provincial Parks Conferences went on to generate and to sustain intergovernmental cooperation throughout the 1960s and 1970s.[117]

When Ontario's conservationists intensified their demands that the provincial government engage in outdoor recreation inventories, planning, and surveys, as recommended by the ORRRC, and as politically sensitive problems sprang up across the provincial park system, the need to reorganize and expand the Parks Branch became compelling. Fortunately, the government of Premier John Robarts proved receptive to arguments for administrative reform. Robarts had already begun the long process of breaking out of the mould of the Frost regime, with its personal, rural dominated style of government, short, eight-week legislative sessions, and simple, departmentalized structures of government and civil service. On the horizon loomed a modern style of government, "an administratively centralized, management-oriented governing system capable of processing the volume of work and conflicting demands generated by modern, technologically based urban society."[118]

An appropriate occasion for major changes in the branch came with the retirement of A.B. Wheatley after a lengthy illness, on 31 December 1964. Wheatley's replacement, Donald R. Wilson, was a shrewd young individual, well versed in both the technical and environmental aspects of park management. Before his appointment as branch chief in May 1965, he had served as district forester in Lindsay, where he had become a protégé of former Premier Leslie Frost. Wilson remained with the Parks Branch for a mere twenty months, before moving on to the position of director of the southern region, and a year after that, to the post of general manager of the Niagara Parks Commission. Peter Addison took over as parks chief in January 1967. No stranger to provincial parks, Addison had been one of the regional foresters who had toured the United States in 1953. A hardworking, no-nonsense perfectionist, with a wealth of experience in integrated resource management, he would lead the Parks Branch through one of its most trying periods.

The reorganization and expansion of the branch in 1965 involved the creation of three sections, with new hands at the helm of each. William G. Cleaveley was appointed head of the Park Management Section, with responsibility for the operations side of parks, including interpretive services. Grant Tayler became his interpretive supervisor, replacing Alan Helmsley, who joined the National Parks Service. The responsibility for park master planning and the actual development of new parks fell to the Parks Planning and Development Section, headed briefly by D.M. Peacock, and then for many years by Robert H. Hambly, formerly a regional forester. Alan MacDonald continued as planning supervisor in this section until August 1966, when he joined the Indian Affairs Branch of the Department of Northern Affairs and Natural Resources in Ottawa. George A. Ashenden became development supervisor under Hambly.

The most important feature of the reorganization involved the creation of the new Recreational Land Use Planning Section headed by James W. Keenan, a forester by training and a bright young administrator, destined to leave an indelible mark on the provincial parks system. His primary task involved forecasting the quantity, location, and types of provincial park facilities that would be required in the future. To this end, Keenan rapidly expanded the research activities of the branch. In 1966, he collaborated with Roy Wolfe, a geographer and recreation research professional in the Department of Highways, to conduct the most sophisticated survey of day-use visitors and campers in provincial parks ever attempted in Ontario. Using the latest techniques of data processing, the survey information was tabulated by computer and analyzed by experts, both in the Electronic Computer and Research Branches of the Department of Highways (DHO), and sociologists at the University of

Waterloo. This research enabled planners to begin to understand why various socioeconomic groups used which parks and to predict their future needs and patterns of behaviour.[119]

The joint DLF-DHO park-user survey represented only the first of a stream of marketing studies to determine the recreational habits, preferences, attitudes, and motives of the various segments of the public who frequented provincial parks. Much of the new research allowed for problem solving of a specific sort. For instance, some 311 residents of Metropolitan Toronto who camped in provincial parks were targeted for a special attitude survey by telephone in the fall of 1966; a similar provincewide telephone survey took place the following year. Trailer owners were also singled out for special study in 1967, as were the visitors to Quetico. From these projects, the Parks Branch discovered the major grievances of its clientele, and subsequently took steps to address complaints about inadequate washroom and toilet facilities in organized campgrounds, insufficient electrical and water hookups for the trailer fraternity, crowding and rowdyism, and the clash of canoeists and motorboat users in Quetico and Algonquin.[120]

Fortuitously, as the Parks Branch underwent reorganization and built up its research and planning expertise, the ongoing work of the Federal-Provincial Parks Conferences began to pay dividends. In 1965, the participants reached agreement on a framework for the classification of parks, a scheme based to a considerable extent on the format recommended in the ORRRC's *Outdoor Recreation for America*, supplemented by the proposals of the International Commission on National Parks. For Ontario's Parks Branch, this development came at an opportune time. A consensus was building among the organizations and individuals watching over the provincial parks that a classification and zoning policy, as a framework for the administration of the system, offered the best hope for resolving the conflict between recreation and preservation, for controlling commercial interests, and for facilitating the rational planning of a balanced parks system. Experience in Ontario and elsewhere had shown that governments must provide a spectrum of parks, ranging from intensively developed sites, offering a variety of recreational opportunities for high-density use, to unspoiled Nature Reserves and extensive, Primitive parks, for use by limited numbers of people. Each type of park would serve a different primary purpose and be managed accordingly. During the mid-1960s, organizations as diverse as the Ontario Federation of Anglers and Hunters and the National and Provincial Parks Association of Canada subscribed to this line of thinking. As the environmental movement grew stronger, the Progressive Conservative Association of Ontario took notice and, at its annual meeting in 1966, passed a resolution, endorsing the classification of provincial parks.[121] Acting quickly to exploit this momentum, James Keenan consulted with district personnel and several conservation groups, and drafted the landmark document entitled *Classification of Provincial Parks 1967*. Lands and

Forests Minister René Brunelle outlined the new policy in a statement to the provincial legislature on 16 March 1967.

Classification of Provincial Parks, 1967

"It is the primary purpose of this new programme," Brunelle declared, "to achieve a complete and balanced park system and to establish a policy framework for its positive and effective development and management."[122] Henceforth, all established and new provincial parks would be classified under one of five types – Primitive, Wild River, Natural Environment, Recreation, and Nature Reserve. The main aim of Primitive parks was "to set aside representative areas of natural landscapes for posterity and to provide for ... wilderness recreation activities and for educational and scientific use." Interestingly, Keenan also included in the classification document an acknowledgment that this new type of park recognized "the psychological need, of many people, to know that unspoiled wilderness areas exist."[123] This idea was inserted at the behest of Gavin Henderson, who had reviewed a draft of the statement. The management guidelines for Primitive parks prohibited timber harvesting, as well as the recreational use of mechanized equipment like motorboats and snowmobiles. Anticipating criticism of these restrictions, the government veered away from preservationist thinking that Wilderness-type parks should be a minimum 100,000 acres (40,470 hectares) in size, and set instead a less impressive, 20,000-acre (8,100-hectare) minimum standard.

A second new type of provincial park, the Wild River class, was created "to preserve the natural, aesthetic and historic quality and the natural flow of significant rivers and sections of rivers for present recreational use and enjoyment for posterity." Given the enormous role that river transportation had played in the history of both the province and the nation, this initiative was of signal importance to the evolving movement concerned with the preservation of Ontario's heritage. The concept of wild-river legislation came from the United States; the ORRRC had endorsed the idea in *Outdoor Recreation for America* and, by 1967, a Wild and Scenic Rivers Bill was being guided through the American Congress.[124] Significantly, in his preliminary draft of the classification scheme, circulated in the summer of 1966, James Keenan had not included the Wild River class of parks. It was the district foresters and park supervisors who urged him to do so. As in the proposed American bill, which became law in 1968, timber harvesting would be permitted in these linear parks beyond a 400-foot (122-metre) shoreline reservation, but development facilities would be minimal, limited to essentials such as portages, access points, and primitive campsites.

Large parks like Algonquin and Quetico, Killbear and the Pinery, Brunelle added, would be classified as Natural Environment parks. The primary aim of this class was "to set aside for the ... purpose of recreation and education, areas of outstanding scenic, natural or historic significance." The DLF intended to manage these parks "under the multiple-use principle" and permit commercial logging to continue, although recreation would be recognized as "the dominant use in all areas." Interpretive services would be essential features of Natural Environment parks. The fourth class of parks – "Recreation" – would be "dominantly user-oriented and while every attempt [would be] made to retain the natural environment, the environment may be substantially modified to accommodate intensive campground and day visitor recreational use." Timber extraction would be prohibited in Recreation parks, but hunting in season, where feasible, would be encouraged. Some two-thirds (sixty-four) of the operating parks in the system would be placed in this category. At the opposite end of the classification spectrum, a system of Nature Reserves would be established, "to preserve unique natural areas for scientific and educational uses." Tracts of Crown land so designated would serve as living museums of aspects of Ontario's flora, fauna, and geological features. Again, the government took a conservative stance by declaring that the 640-acre (259-hectare) size limit, the bane of the Wilderness Areas Act, would normally apply when setting aside Nature Reserves under the Provincial Parks Act.

Under the new policy, each park in all classes would be zoned for planning, development, and management purposes according to a system of five zones – Primitive, Natural (possessing the status of a Nature Reserve), Historic, Multiple-Use (where timber extraction would take place), and Recreation. Finally, Brunelle concluded by promising that long-range master plans, based on the classification and zoning policies, would be prepared for each of the parks, old and new, so that its development and management would be in harmony with the purpose of the park class to which it belonged.

Following the policy statement of March 1967, the Robarts government received much praise from conservationists. "Our Association is greatly impressed by the outstanding parks program of your Government," wrote NPPAC President A.P. Frame to the premier.[125] Likewise, the Federation of Ontario Naturalists judged the classification policy "to be among the most enlightened legislation in this field in the western hemisphere."[126] When the government announced, in April 1968, that Polar Bear would be the first Primitive-class park, further plaudits came from the preservationist camp. Polar Bear was an impressive achievement, a 1.8-million-hectare goliath around Cape Henrietta-Maria, bordering both James and Hudson bays. In Canada at that time, only Wood Buffalo National Park could claim to be larger. "The importance of this action," FON Executive Director James Woodford said enthusiastically to Premier Robarts, "will become abundantly clear in future years, when it [Polar Bear Park] has become one of the great parks of the world. You have rendered a great service, to the people of Ontario, by ensuring that this unique region, which contains some of the southernmost tundra in the world, is preserved for all time."[127] The NPPAC president paid further tribute to the Robarts administration by describing the establishment of the park as "a major landmark

Tidal flats, Polar Bear Provincial Park.
Courtesy: Ministry of Natural Resources.

Successive beach ridges, Hudson Bay lowlands, Polar Bear Provincial Park.
Courtesy: Ministry of Natural Resources.

Lake Algonquin erosional shoreline, Waubaushene Beaches Provincial Nature Reserve.
Courtesy: Ministry of Natural Resources.

in the already outstanding parks program of your Government," an action to "be applauded by all Canadians of present and future generations."[128]

The Parks Branch also acted quickly to identify areas suitable for designation as Nature Reserves and Wild River parks. Early in 1968, the Ontario Parks Integration Board authorized the conversion of five sites, previously designated under the Wilderness Areas Act, to Nature Reserve status under the Provincial Parks Act – Bat Cave, Gibson River, Matawatchan, Montreal River, and Porphyry Island. At the same time, the OPIB endorsed the designation of two new sites as Nature Reserves – Trillium Woods and Waubaushene Beaches – both of which had been purchased by the government in the spring of 1967 at the behest of the naturalists.[129] By year's end, Lands and Forests Minister René Brunelle had decided to establish a special advisory committee of experts to advise his department on the planning and development of a system of Nature Reserves.

Meanwhile, during 1967, inventories of rivers in the northern districts began, and by the end of the year, sections of two waterways – the Mattawa and the Winisk – emerged as the first areas to be slated for Wild River designation. The forty-eight-kilometre section of the Mattawa in question, located between Trout Lake in the west and Samuel de Champlain Provincial Park in the east, possessed great historic significance and outstanding scenic attributes. Still primitive in character, it contained most of the original portages used over the centuries by the aboriginal peoples, explorers, Montreal-based fur traders, and settlers until 1845. The 360-kilometre segment of the Winisk River between Winisk Lake and Hudson Bay was selected for its wilderness canoeing potential. The fledgling Wild River park program, the first of its kind in Canada, was the envy of other provincial agencies.

The lavish praise heaped upon the Ontario government and the Parks Branch of the Department of Lands and Forests, both for the policy statement of 1967 and the Nature Reserve, Primitive, and Wild River parks initiatives that followed, gave the impression, one destined to be proved false, that suddenly all was roses in the "garden" of Ontario's provincial parks. The new policy framework was not a quick fix to cure all the ills of a parks program that had been suffering from want of harmony and balance throughout the 1960s, but only a means to an end. Some of the people who gushed enthusiastically over the classification scheme ignored the fact that the tough decisions would have to be taken in the future, when the policy was applied, especially as the Parks Branch endeavoured to classify the parks and create master plans for them accordingly. The euphoria over the 1967 policy statement was short-lived; political storms lay ahead, in mid-1968. One of the liveliest episodes in the history of Ontario's provincial parks was about to unfold.

Chapter 5

The Politics of Preservation, 1968–1974

The release of the Provisional Master Plan for Algonquin Provincial Park in October 1968 dashed expectations that had been raised the year before by the introduction of the classification policy for provincial parks. The provisional plan, a first attempt to apply the principles of classification and zoning, satisfied no one. Subsequently, the leaders of the preservationist movement resolved to take their stand at the master-planning level, where the crucial management policy decisions would be made. Year after year, fighting for park after park – Algonquin, Killarney, Quetico, Lake Superior – preservationists stormed into political combat, led by the newly formed Algonquin Wildlands League, and succeeded in making the disposition of the major provincial parks a litmus test of governmental sensitivity toward matters concerning the environment. When the smoke of battle cleared, their accomplishments were manifest. Logging practices in the province's parks had been reformed. Public participation had been entrenched as an essential part of the planning process. Quetico and Killarney had been reclassified as Primitive parks, three new Wild River parks had been regulated, the province had signed an agreement with Ottawa to permit the establishment of Ontario's first large national park at Pukaskwa, and systems planning for Nature Reserve and Wilderness parks was well launched.

The Algonquin Wildlands League and the Preservationist Onslaught

On 13 March 1968, Abbott Conway, a mild-mannered tannery executive from Guelph, appeared before the annual meeting of the Standing Committee of the Ontario Legislature on Tourism and Natural Resources to express his concerns about the management of Algonquin Park. "The timber assets of Algonquin Park, so far as a saw log economy is concerned, are nearing an end," he argued. "The demand for recreation and the experience of life in natural surroundings is increasing every year ... We must plan how Algonquin Park can cope with the tide of outdoorsmen and their families that is already upon it. Commercial interests must be phased out. Lumbering ... is not compatible with its future."[1] Aware that district officials were drafting a master development and management plan, Conway recommended that approximately 50 percent of Algonquin, including the western uplands section, be zoned as a primitive area, and that logging be restricted to a multiple-use zone on the eastern side of the park. Unfortunately, the politicians who listened to Conway did not appreciate the fact that his comments reflected the collective thinking of some of Ontario's most ardent conservationists, nor did they realize that Conway and those he represented were poised, ready to do battle for the wilderness. The existing park planning process was about to be thrown into disarray.

Four months later, on 1 June 1968, eight people gathered in Huntsville, Ontario, for the inaugural meeting of the Algonquin Wildlands League. The officers and directors of the league included Abbott Conway (president), Douglas Pimlott (first vice-president), Patrick Hardy (secretary), Fred Bodsworth, Walter Gray, a Toronto public relations professional, and Kingston's Jack O'Dette, a stalwart of the Ontario Federation of Anglers and Hunters. From a handful of charter members, the league would boast a paid-up membership of 1,200 within

Map 2: "A Recommendation for the Zoning of Algonquin Provincial Park," Prepared by the Algonquin Wildlands League, March 1968

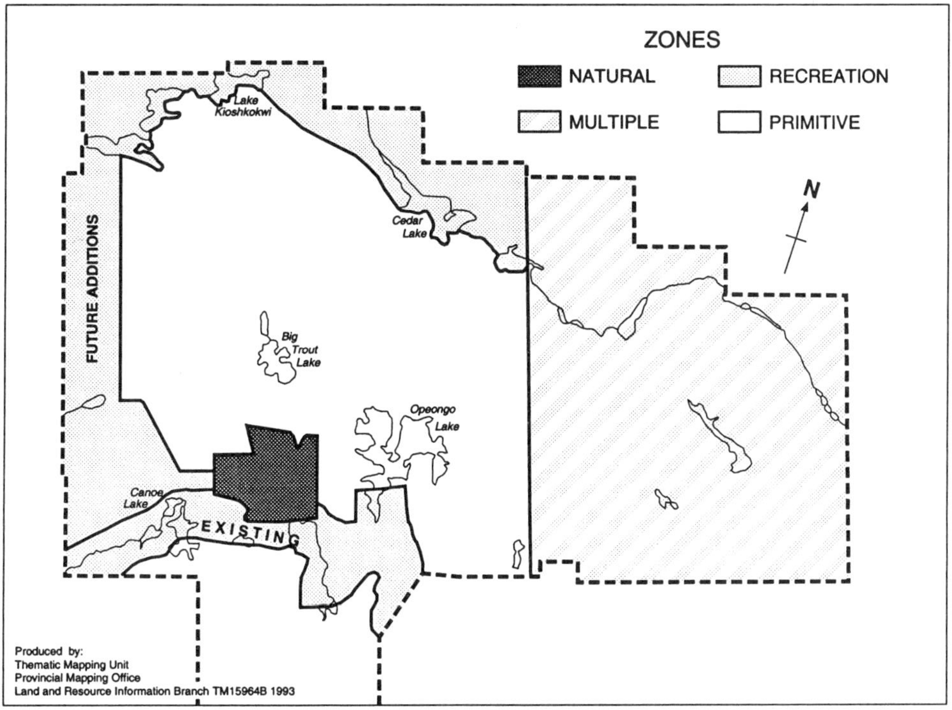

eighteen months. At a press conference on 10 July, held appropriately in the Algonquin Room of the Royal York Hotel in Toronto, Abbott Conway introduced the league as a special organization, created with the blessing of most provincial conservation groups. Its purpose, he explained, was "to protect the wilderness values of Ontario's parks from destruction by commercial or other uncontrolled interests ... We insist the people of Ontario have a right to reasonably accessible areas that are set aside for wilderness recreation, and that the government must provide clear policies to protect these areas."[2] Initially, the AWL would expend its energies on a campaign to save Algonquin Park "from the many intrusions into its wilderness areas." League members objected to the expansion of logging activities and the spread of lumber roads, the "rapid increase" of water, air, and noise pollution, the presence of various forms of mechanized transportation in the interior of the wilderness, and the intrusion of permanent construction into the centre of the park. Conway announced the beginning of an "Algonquin Alert" and invited the public to report any activity which it thought violated the park's wilderness values.

On this occasion, Abbott Conway and the league did not fail to attract the attention of the media, thanks largely to the advice and organizational talents of communications consultant Walter Gray. A former journalist – he had served as Ottawa bureau chief for both the Toronto *Globe and Mail* (1960–63) and the *Toronto Star* (1967–68) – he had been recruited to handle public relations and publicity strategies. Gray's insider knowledge of how the media operated and his many contacts in the industry proved to be invaluable. For example, prior to the press conference announcing the formation of the league, Gray alerted CBC news, which despatched a film crew to the park and carried the story on the national network. Later, CFRB radio talk-show hosts Betty Kennedy and John Bradshaw both provided air time for the amiable Conway; so, too, did Joe Forster, the open-line host on Toronto radio station CHIN. The Algonquin issue also received extensive press coverage across the province, especially in Toronto, where all three dailies published editorials sympathetic to the league. Meanwhile, Liberal MLA Eddie Sargent (Grey-Bruce), voiced the preservationist position in the provincial legislature.[3]

Lands and Forests officials expressed mixed feelings about the upstart new pressure groups. "This organization will undoubtedly make waves," Peter Addison wrote, but in "many cases such groups assist rather than hinder governmental action."[4] Deputy Minister G.H.U. Bayly thought that the Wildlands League might "have a balancing effect"; it could offset the powerful commercial interests and improve "the Department's position for planning between the two extremes."[5] Time confirmed both predictions, but neither official anticipated the powerful influence that the AWL would exert. With the assistance of investigative journalists and citizens responding to the "Algonquin Alert," the league kept the park issue before the public throughout the summer of 1968. In July, for instance, many Ontarians were shocked to read about the construction of a new logging road (complete with stop sign) across one of the busiest portages in Algonquin, between Big Trout and Otterslide Lakes.[6] Such disclosures prompted Liberal Opposition Leader Robert Nixon to enter the fray and criticize the Robarts government for permitting excessive commercial exploitation in Algonquin and for disregarding "the principles of conservation."

On 7 August, the League denounced the nine-year renewal of a timber licence to Weyerhaeuser Canada Ltd. for an area that included over three townships in the park. Such decisions, the preservationists claimed, should not be made until after the matter of the zoning of Algonquin had been settled. The following week, on 12 August, the *Toronto Telegram* reported that a fishing party had been discovered using motorboats hauled illegally over logging roads to Booth Lake, four miles inside the park boundary. Two days later, the *Telegram* disclosed that four vacationing members of the American Federal Bureau of Investigation had left the same area of the park in disgust, vowing never to return, after suffering the sight and sound of motorboats and the noise of trucks hauling logs late into the night.[7]

By summer's end, these incidents had aroused the public's interest in the future of Algonquin Park. Aware now that many people were primed to scrutinize the provisional master plan due that fall, the government sought to harness that interest by promising to hold public hearings on the document and incorporating "useful suggestions" into the final draft.[8] Surprisingly, in view of the climate of concern surrounding the plan, the Ontario Parks Integration Board released it for public consumption in early November, despite negative reviews of the document from Parks Branch staff in Toronto. "I believe the plan to be lacking in the imagination and initiative required to chart a new course for this important area," wrote Recreational Planning Supervisor James Keenan in September. The zoning scheme seemed "totally inadequate," since 90 percent of Algonquin would remain under timber licence in multiple-use zones. "Surely our economy can afford to preserve a more meaningful proportion of Algonquin Park than has been recommended," he wrote. Timber management policies suggested "only a long term continuation of the status quo," something preservationists had already deemed inappropriate. The proposed policy on outboard motors also raised Keenan's ire: "Surely they can be prohibited on at least some lakes outside of the Primitive Zone," an area which included less than 5 percent of the park.[9] Interpretation Supervisor Grant Tayler shared these concerns and added that "there appears to be little thought given to the need for preservation of large ecosystems."[10]

Predictably, the preservationists excoriated the provisional master plan at the public hearings, held between 26 and 28 November in Huntsville, Pembroke, and Toronto.[11] That only 5 percent of the area of the park had been zoned primitive caused the biggest controversy. Conservationist groups insisted that the number of multiple-use areas be reduced and the primitive zone expanded. It is interesting to note that all the conservationist groups accepted the application of the multiple-use principle in Algonquin Park; even the Wildlands League did not call for the abolition of lumbering. At issue were the extent and the intensity of logging in Algonquin. The league took the position that the commercial use of the park must always be secondary to the preservation of the natural and recreational environment. If a road threatened to damage the wild surroundings of a canoe route, then the road should not be built. If timber operations in certain areas interfered with the recreation of those seeking solitude, then logging should not be allowed. For ecological reasons, logging should be prohibited in large primitive zones.

While the preservationists conceded that they could live with some logging in Algonquin, they indicated that they no longer subscribed to the notion that the wilderness could be protected, largely by means of a policy of shoreline reservations along canoe routes. Such a mechanism to resolve conflict had sufficed for over three decades, but the modern concept of wilderness rendered it unacceptable now. As the National and Provincial Parks Association of Canada briefly explained, shoreline reserves within timber limits simply created a "false front," a sham wilderness. For aesthetic, recreational, and ecological reasons, the modern wilderness concept was based on the notion of vastness, and as George Priddle noted in his submission, that notion had been sadly neglected in the provisional master plan.

The ill-fated planning document also came under virulent attack from forest industry spokesmen, who, ironically, viewed it as a victory for the preservationists, because of the new timber management restrictions it contained. The plan proposed that bush operations and road construction would be prohibited during July and August. Shoreline reservations would be expanded to 1,500 feet (457 metres) of waterways and portages. Existing timber licences would be terminated, as of 31 March 1979, and replaced by a system of timber allocation by volume. Finally, park officials would assume control over the planning, construction, and location of logging roads. Such regulations, claimed R.B. Loughlan of the Ontario Forest Industries Association, would "kill the industry" and destroy the livelihood of hundreds of workers. "The way it looks from this side of the table," he argued, "the Department has put in those restrictions as a major concession to the Wildlands League ... We call on the Department ... to disregard the Wildlands League as dreamers in canoes who don't realize what they can do to the lives of innocent people." The International Woodworkers of America joined industry spokesmen in branding the proposed restrictions as extremist and a dire threat to the economic health of communities like Huntsville, Pembroke, Barry's Bay, Madawaska, and Whitney.

During the hearings, preservationists and industry representatives alike hotly debated forestry questions and laid out arguments that would be repeated many times in the years ahead. Forestry spokespersons advanced the proposition that the ideas of the preservationists endangered the public good. "Emotional groups demanding more parks and wilderness areas," suggested K.A. Armson of the University of Toronto Forestry School, who was also president of the Ontario Professional Foresters Association, "may be more damaging to Ontario forests than the timber barons of a century ago."[12] Basic to this thesis was the idea that healthy forests required scientific timber management, which meant road networks to control fire, disease, and insect outbreaks. "When timber stands age, they mature ... and eventually die," explained the brief of the Ontario Forest Industries Association. "When they become overmature, they become prime targets for fire and breeding grounds for insects and disease." Blow-downs would inevitably occur in overmature stands, resulting in "wilderness slums," of little use to recreationists and a source of frustration to the loggers required to clean up the mess.

Preservationists scoffed at such arguments. Rather than describing Algonquin's mature forests as "slums," they spoke of awe-inspiring cathedral-like stands of pine and ancient hardwoods, areas that should be left undisturbed as outdoor museums and scientific benchmarks, to be studied and enjoyed by future generations of Canadians. Since Algonquin Park contained the last remaining accessible stands of quality hardwood and red pine in southern Ontario, the preservationists urged that these areas not be sacrificed for the sake of a few years' short-run profits by the forest industry that had created the timber shortage in the first place. Ontarians were now paying the price of a century of poor silvicultural practices over the Great Lakes–St. Lawrence Forest region; government and industry had failed to manage wisely the publicly owned timberlands. Instead of encroaching on Algonquin Park and sacrificing the last remnants of accessible and still protected semiwilderness, argued the preservationists, the public and private sectors should immediately initiate vigorous silvicultural programs outside the park to rehabilitate the red and white pine areas and to improve the quality of the hardwood forests.

The industry's arguments about the necessity of scientific forest management were countered, point by point, by the preservationists. Dead and dying trees in mature stands, they explained, were part of a natural process and formed an essential part of the habitat of a variety of animal and bird species. Preservationists also dismissed as specious the hypothesis that when trees died and fell to the ground in a primitive zone, they became a severe fire menace and a breeding ground for insects and harmful bacteria. Normal blow-downs were nothing compared to the mountain of slash left on the forest floor after a typical bush operation. Besides, Algonquin Park, with its great diversity of tree species, was not as prone to disease as a forested area covered predominantly by one type of tree. In a restrained and professional brief, Douglas Pimlott added that the timber operators in Algonquin Park could never be accused of having practised sustained-yield forestry. High grading, the removal of only the best quality trees, had always been the modus operandi of the timber men. Even Conservative MLAs representing the Ottawa Valley, who for political reasons sided with the pro-logging forces, acknowledged as much in private briefing meetings with the minister of lands and forests.[13]

The profusion of argument and counterargument put forth during and after the public hearings in November 1968 served to clarify one thing: the Algonquin Park Provisional Master Plan was premature and inadequate. All the players in the verbal fist-shaking, as well as the academics and professional planners who submitted briefs, showed that the plan rested on shaky foundations and was not supported by sufficient interdisciplinary research and analysis. Comprehensive inventories of the earth and life science features of the park had not been made; consequently, the zoning had been based on incomplete ecological data. No economic impact studies had been conducted to establish the cost-benefit ratios of various zoning options. Without such research and analysis, no one could possibly assess the accuracy of the contradictory claims in the logging versus wilderness controversy. Only with such data could park officials and politicians make rational decisions about the size of the primitive zone and the future of logging. The provisional master plan also suffered from serious gaps in basic information about visitors to the park. Further, it contained no estimates of user demand in the future. No carrying capacity studies had been undertaken to sort out the problem of distributing canoe trippers to reduce overcrowded conditions in the park interior and to minimize conflicts between canoeists and motorboat fishermen. Unless the DLF addressed these matters, concluded James Keenan, park planners did not stand a chance of establishing a politically acceptable rationale as to the regional and provincial significance of Algonquin, from which would evolve clear statements of purpose, objectives, and policies, and a zoning plan for the park.[14]

The public hearings, held in November 1968, generated unprecedented interest. A total of 103 individuals and groups submitted briefs, while some 1,000 people attended in person. A wider audience followed the controversy through the media. In Toronto, the three daily newspapers continued to support the Wildlands League. "Save Algonquin Park for the People," urged a *Star* editorial after the hearings.[15] The *Globe and Mail* ran an editorial entitled "Don't Wreck the Heritage," and described the league's brief as "perhaps the most sensible yet to be heard on the subject."[16] The Sunday night CBC television series "The Way It Is," hosted by John Saywell and Patrick Watson, explored the Algonquin question on 1 December and assailed logging practices in the park. For its part, the league operated booths at sportsmen's shows, distributed "Parks Are for People" buttons, and bought space in Toronto newspapers, urging readers to contact their MLAs. By early January 1969, the government had received over four hundred letters, the majority of which sided with the preservationists.[17] The logging industry began to marshal its considerable sources of support. Petitions were circulated throughout the Ottawa Valley, one of which contained 6,673 names. Meanwhile, the Ontario Forest Industries Association placed advertisements in various newspapers, with clip-out sections, which 473 people elected to mail in to the government.[18]

The Robarts administration and the Department of Lands and Forests were smarting under the negative publicity the Algonquin Park Provisional Master Plan was receiving. Such publicity raised the question of the government's competence to manage Crown lands. The situation called for a creative response before the preservationists' campaign evolved into a major issue and became another source of government unpopularity. The Robarts cabinet had difficulties enough with the controversies already brewing over regional government, tax reform, and mandatory school board reorganization. Accordingly, in December 1968, Lands and Forests officials created a special Algonquin Park Task Force (APATAF), made up of senior administrators from every branch of the department, to establish interim management policies for the park and to produce a final master plan by January 1975.[19] In the months following, the task force launched the most extensive and sophisticated battery of research studies ever undertaken for planning purposes by a Canadian parks agency. By 1970, some thirty-seven different study papers and reports had been completed or were under way, and another thirty-four research projects were being contemplated. The studies touched every aspect of the park, its ecology, fish and wildlife management, geology, forest conditions, recreational patterns, archaeology, and history. Specialists from other government departments, the universities, and the private sector were also engaged for specific assignments. For instance, Kaplan Consulting Associates Ltd. of Montreal was commissioned to undertake an Algonquin Park Economic Impact Study,[20] while Professor George Priddle initiated a study of interior users and of their perceptions of the wilderness.[21] For the first time, also with provincial and industry support, the Canadian Forestry Service began forest acoustics research on the noise levels created by timber operations.[22]

In April 1969, acting on the advice of the task force, Lands and Forests Minister René Brunelle announced a series of new restrictions to be placed on logging operations in Algonquin Park as an interim measure. "Basically," Brunelle explained to the legislature, "it is the evidences of logging such as noise of trucks, bulldozers, and power saws, as well as roads and bridges in certain areas, which have proven to be most offensive to the recreationist."[23] Through the new restrictions, the minister hoped to minimize "these irritations to the canoeists." Along 1,175 kilometres of designated canoe routes, a 1,500-foot (457-metre) reservation was established, in which only marked trees could be cut. No logging was to be allowed within 100 feet (30 metres) of shorelines or within 200 feet (60 metres) of portages. The department also created a two-mile-wide "sound buffer zone," within which no cutting would be permitted. Road construction was prohibited in all reservations, and all road locations and construction specifications required the approval of the superintendent. The only concession made to the twenty-three companies

Lands and Forests Minister René Brunelle (front), a strong defender of the multiple-use policy in parks, seen here on a canoe trip in Killarney Provincial Park, July 1969.
Courtesy: Ministry of Natural Resources.

operating in the park was the permission to cut during the summer months; however, the hauling of logs would be permitted only from 8:00 a.m. to 5:00 p.m., Monday through Friday. No hauling would be allowed on weekends or holidays, and no mechanized equipment was to be used at night. "We thought the mountain had actually moved an inch," reflected Abbott Conway.[24]

The DLF hoped the restrictions on logging and the extraordinary planning initiatives being undertaken by the task force would defuse the Algonquin controversy until the master plan was completed. What the government did not anticipate was the unwillingness of any of the participants to call a truce. Journalists derided the Robarts government for its procrastination. That a master plan would not be forthcoming until 1975, suggested the *Globe and Mail*, "leaves Algonquin Park to the mercies of the logging industry."[25] Columnist Bruce West, of the *Toronto Telegram*, also judged the planning schedule to be excessively long and a deliberate stratagem to reduce public interest in the issue.[26]

Buoyed by this kind of media support, and unwilling to lose the momentum it had so assiduously cultivated, the Algonquin Wildlands League intensified its efforts. In March, it established a twenty-three-member committee in Ottawa, headed by a retired brigadier-general, Paul Smith. League members also maintained the "Algonquin Alert," and in August raised the issue of a serious water pollution problem at Lake of Two Rivers, caused by raw sewage flowing from ten campground privies and a nearby lodge. Water samples taken by the DLF revealed a coliform count 150 times greater than the level considered safe for bathing. These findings resulted in the closing of the beach at Algonquin Park's biggest and most popular campground before the Labour Day weekend. Park personnel quickly eliminated the sources of pollution, but the episode stood out as a public-relations nightmare and lent support to the preservationists' claims of mismanagement at Algonquin.[27]

In the meantime, the government came under pressure from a worried forest-products industry and officials from communities economically dependent on logging in the park. The mayor of Pembroke, for instance, wrote to municipal and provincial politicians across Ontario and appealed, with no little success, for expressions of support for the continuation of commercial logging in Algonquin.[28] For its part, in August 1969, the Ontario Forest Industries Association (OFIA) organized a press tour of logging operations in the park, and subsequently published a glossy pictorial pamphlet containing excerpts from columns favourable to their cause.[29] The Canadian pulp and paper industry lent its assistance by publishing another pamphlet, entitled *Algonquin Park Will Be a Better Place Because Loggers Have Been There* (Toronto: Maclean Hunter, 1969).

Caught in this tightening vise, the Robarts government resorted to a practice it had frequently used during the 1960s – establishing a special study, inquiry, or royal commission. According to Robarts' biographer, such inquiries served to produce "an understanding of a situation as it really existed, not as politicians and/or the media thought it existed."[30] The premier believed that a study by experts, perhaps even several studies, would establish the "real" nature of the problem and provide options as to what should be done about it. Consequently, when the Algonquin controversy refused to go away, he appointed the Algonquin Park Advisory Committee to examine park policy and management and make recommendations on all aspects. The committee had fifteen members, representing all three parties in the provincial legislature, the mayors of Huntsville and Pembroke, conservationist groups, the logging industry, park leaseholders, and the Ontario Camping Association. The mix of interests was a volatile one but, to maintain some control, the government appointed a forceful and respected personality to the chair – former premier Leslie M. Frost. At the first meeting of the advisory committee in September, the members agreed to conduct their work in camera and to divulge no information to the press until their task had been completed. With these procedures in place, Frost succeeded in putting a lid on the Algonquin controversy.

Much to the chagrin of government officials, the appointment of the committee did not result in a moratorium on the broader issue of logging in all parks. With evangelical fervour, the AWL turned its attention to other parks, where decisions on logging and the preservation of the wilderness had yet to be made. On 24 June 1969, the Robarts government reeled in surprise when Abbott Conway held another press conference, to announce the "totally disheartening" news that while the debate over Algonquin was at its peak, the DLF had approved the extension of commercial logging into Killarney Provincial Park, considered by many experts to be the "crown jewel" of Ontario's parks system. Ground and air reconnaissance by the league had led to the discovery of a new logging road, wide enough to accommodate two-way traffic, constructed twelve miles into the heart of the park to reach a stand of yellow birch. "If ever a park were suitable for classification as a primitive park," Conway insisted, "Killarney is it." Compared to Algonquin, Killarney was "almost virginal in its wilderness environment." It encompassed 36,260 hectares, and offered the visitor strikingly beautiful vistas of white quartzite mountains, crystal-clear blue lakes, meadows, and streams. The league demanded that timber licences in Killarney be withdrawn and that the park be reclassified as Primitive.[31]

Lands and Forests Minister Brunelle justified his department's decision to authorize logging in the affected area by claiming that the road was located in a multiple-use zone, as prescribed in a recently completed preliminary zoning plan. Killarney would remain a Natural Environment park, he went on, but 53 percent of the park would be zoned primitive and closed to logging. When the Wildlands League asked to see the document, it was informed by park officials that the zoning plan had not yet been completed. "It seems clear," the preservationists charged, "that the logging company concerned was given permission to construct the logging road before any plan was formulated." "Mr. Brunelle has bowed to the logging operators," opined the Toronto *Globe and Mail* on 26 June 1969.[32] The question was also raised as to why the conservationists had not yet been consulted in the planning of Killarney.

After involving the public in the master planning of Algonquin Park, through hearings and the appointment of a special advisory committee, government officials now discovered that they could not avoid public participation in the planning of all the other major parks. The rules of the game had been fundamentally changed. In October 1969, Chief of Parks Peter Addison, acting on this realization, informed his superiors that henceforth his branch would develop a standard procedure in master-planning large parks like Killarney, Lake Superior, and Quetico. Public submissions would be invited at the outset. A task force of experts from all branches of the DLF would be appointed to coordinate research and analysis and to prepare a preliminary planning document. Before final authorization of the plan, the public would once again be consulted.[33] The mountain, it seemed, had moved another inch.

The Battles for Quetico and Lake Superior

In March 1969, Ferguson Wilson, the district naturalist in Fort Frances, observed the Algonquin Park controversy with trepidation. Having just completed a draft preliminary master plan for Quetico Park, he appreciated perhaps more than anyone the potential turmoil ahead, when the Algonquin Wildlands League turned its attention his way. Two timber companies held cutting rights in Quetico. Domtar Pulp and Paper Products Ltd. had acquired a controlling interest in the Jim Mathieu Lumber Company and, with it, the licence to cut in the northeast quadrant of the park. A second corporation, the Ontario-Minnesota Pulp and Paper Company, a subsidiary of the Boise-Cascade Corporation of Idaho, possessed a volume agreement in the northwest section, although it had not yet sought a licence to begin logging. Wilson predicted that the Domtar licence would "create severe conflicts with recreation" on all the interior canoe routes originating from the main access on French Lake. Likewise, when the Ontario-Minnesota Company began cutting and building logging roads across major waterways, the conflicts would prove "insurmountable for any timber operations."[34]

Subsequent discussions of these problems within the DLF did nothing to ease Wilson's anxiety. The Timber Branch advised the minister, René Brunelle, that if logging was banned on the Domtar limit, the mill at Sapawe would close.[35] For Brunelle, that eventuality was unthinkable. He was determined to expand the forest industries in the region. As the MLA for Cochrane North and a resort owner at Remi Lake, near the pulp and paper town of Kapuskasing,

Map 3: Quetico Provincial Park: Timber Licence Areas, 1969

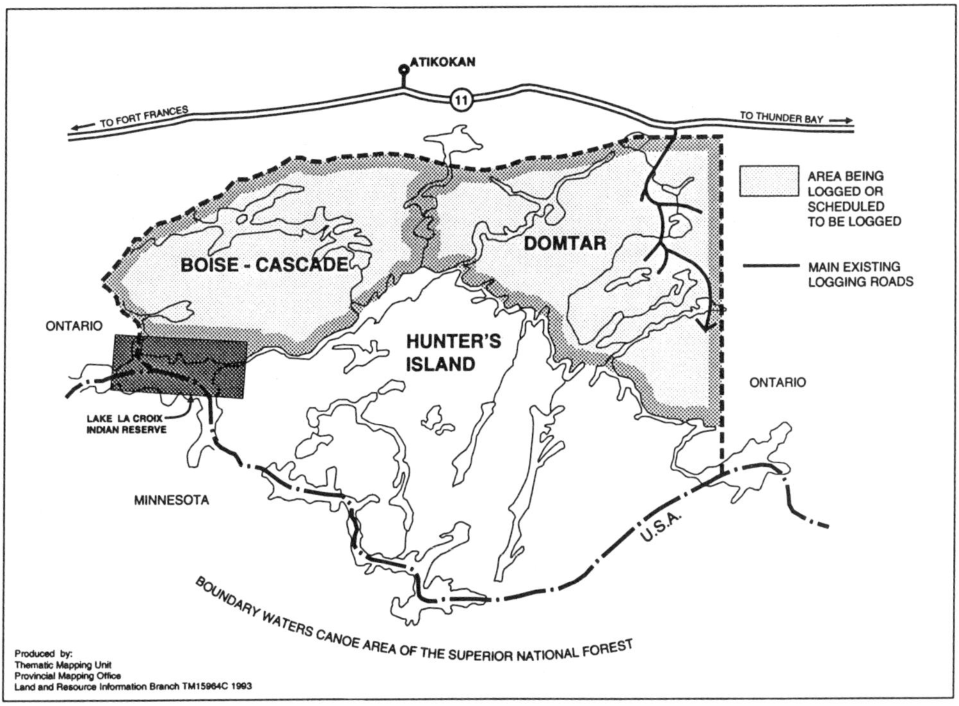

Brunelle had considerable knowledge of the problems besetting Ontario's forest industries. He worried about their eroding general competitiveness because of rising costs for wood, hydro and transportation, and plant obsolescence. Forest industries accounted for 69 percent of all manufacturing employment in the northwestern region of Ontario. In Brunelle's estimation, these jobs had to be protected. "For these reasons," he wrote in October 1969 to Stanley J. Randall, Ontario's minister of trade and development, "it is highly desirable that we create a suitable economic environment to stimulate forest industry growth." Brunelle hoped to see the American-owned Ontario-Minnesota Company establish a new pulp mill in the Fort Frances area, and was prepared to offer concessions, in the form of lower stumpage charges and shared road construction programs, if the company agreed to expand its manufacturing capacity in Ontario and to limit exports of pulpwood and veneer logs.[36]

When Brunelle and his officials weighed the pros and cons of logging in Quetico Park, their thinking was shaped by the knowledge that if the timber operators were properly regulated, the government could count on the support of the Quetico Foundation, Ontario's original "watchdog over wilderness." The foundation, a long-time supporter of the principle of multiple use, did not object either to the classification of Quetico as a Natural Environment park or to the continuation of commercial timber operations, as long as the Hunter's Island area was designated a primitive zone and strict controls were placed on logging along canoe routes elsewhere in the park.[37] In the foundation's estimation, such policies would be in keeping with zoning practices across the border, where no-cut primitive zones respectively amounted to 20 and 60 percent of the Superior National Forest and the Boundary Waters Canoe Area.[38]

Brunelle also knew that the foundation had spurned an invitation by the Algonquin Wildlands League to coordinate a campaign for the reclassification of Quetico as a Primitive park.[39] The two organizations had little in common. The foundation's members were generally older men who were approaching or had reached retirement age; they were also a more affluent group, often corporate leaders or successful professionals who gave generously of their time, means, and experience to worthwhile causes. Possessing a keen sense of dignity and occasion, these people had for many years successfully used their influence behind the scenes, after having struck amicable relationships with high-ranking civil servants and cabinet ministers. In contrast, the leading members of the AWL were younger people, professionals and businessmen of lesser influence, writers, teachers, and university professors. They had no qualms about using the confrontation tactics so common in the rebellious sixties. To the staid Quetico Foundation, the Wildlands League's approach seemed excessive and dependent on staging media events, simplifying the issues, and confronting politicians and DLF personnel in an unseemly manner. What the foundation did not fully appreciate was the fact that the AWL's leaders were serious students of conservation issues, people with impressive scientific credentials and considerable on-the-ground knowledge of Algonquin and Quetico parks. They might have been guilty of hyperbole, but had never had to withdraw a statement. Conservationists in this period, then, suffered from the generation gap, a gap that the minister of lands and forests thought worked to his advantage, insofar as logging in Quetico Provincial Park was concerned.

Although their proposal for an alliance with the Quetico Foundation was rejected, the leaders of the AWL pressed forward with their plan to battle for the reclassification of Quetico. In October 1969, they circulated a statement to MLAs and the press, criticizing the expansion of commercial logging in major northern parks like Killarney and Quetico, and recommending that such areas be classified as Primitive rather than Natural Environment parks, in order to create the first accessible, protected wilderness areas under the provisions of the 1967 classification document. Brunelle responded by rising in the legislature to castigate the league for its attack on his department's multiple-use policies.[40] His statement evoked a spirited retort from the Liberal opposition, in the person of Patrick Reid, the young MLA for Rainy River, who insisted that it was "absolutely vital" that Quetico "be maintained in an unspoiled state" as a Primitive-class park. "The Minister misses the point when he says that logging and recreation can go hand in hand. Of course they can. But what cannot go hand in hand is logging, recreation and preservation of a unique ecosystem." Logging could be removed from Quetico without throwing people out of work and without harming the industry, Reid claimed, because alternative timber limits were available outside the park.[41]

Elements of the public became involved in the issue, when the Algonquin Wildlands League held an open meeting in Toronto on 10 November, an event which attracted an audience of 200. Atikokan's Charlie Erickson, an imposing, red-haired and bearded giant who ran a wilderness tripping operation for young people, caused a minor sensation with his presentation. He screened slide after slide to prove that the Domtar timber operations were marring the recreational and aesthetic features of canoe routes, and that motorboat fishermen were routinely gaining access to interior waterways on restricted logging roads. An alarmed Timber Branch chief, A.J. Herridge, reported to Deputy Minister G.H.U. Bayly that the AWL had "staged the meeting in such a way that if Domtar's offices ... had been within a mile, a large group would have been prepared for a confrontation."[42] The meeting had ended with the passage of three resolutions, demanding that the Domtar licence be terminated, that Quetico be classified a Primitive park, and that the responsibility for provincial parks be transferred to another government department, less dedicated to resource extraction.

"One cannot but feel that their [the Wildlands League's] cause is one to be treated most seriously," Herridge warned the deputy minister. Parks Chief Peter Addison agreed. If Charlie Erickson or others made similar presentations "at various points in the province," he argued, it would result in "a very great criticism of the government and the department."[43] These warnings did not go unheeded, especially after press, radio, and television coverage of the November meeting resulted in a heavy mail-in protest.[44] Once again, the preservationists got results. The Parks Branch invited Erickson to address a meeting of regional and district foresters and park superintendents. In April 1970, the Timber Branch issued new and tighter logging regulations for Quetico,[45] and the following month, the Ontario Parks Integration Board placed the first restrictions on powered watercraft in the park.[46] And finally, in June, the government announced the appointment of a Quetico Advisory Committee, as it had previously done for Algonquin, to examine the issues concerning Quetico Park and to make recommendations for their resolution.[47] The committee was instructed to conduct public hearings, deliberate on the information provided, and report periodically to the minister so that the public might be kept informed of the progress achieved.

No sooner had the Robarts government temporarily neutralized the Quetico controversy than the Wildlands League created another uproar, this time over Lake Superior Provincial Park. The preservationists had sounded the first alarm the previous April by informing the media that extensive commercial forestry operations were taking place in what appeared to be sensitive natural areas. Further inquiries revealed that two American subsidiaries, Weyerhaeuser Canada and Weldwood of Canada, held timber licences covering approximately 95 percent of Lake Superior Park. Abbott Conway was aghast and claimed that the extent of timber operations in provincial parklands was far greater than even he and his colleagues had imagined.[48] He took his concerns to the Frost Advisory Committee on Algonquin Park, of which he was a member, and moved a resolution that the committee be reconstituted to conduct a special inquiry into parks policy pertaining to wilderness and logging matters. After this initiative failed, the preservationists prepared for a fight. In June 1970, the Wildlands League despatched an investigative team – Dr. C.B. Cragg, professor of chemistry and natural science at York University, Bruce Litteljohn, Douglas Pimlott, and Dennis Voigt, a graduate forester – to conduct a five-day, on-site study of management and logging practices in Lake Superior Provincial Park.[49]

Government personnel found themselves again on the defensive. Upon arriving back in Toronto on 27 June, the investigative team requested an audience with Lands and Forests Minister Brunelle to discuss a matter of great urgency. Evidently, an area of "striking ecological significance," just north of the Agawa River, was being logged by Weldwood of Canada. The tract in question contained a remarkable variety of tree species, representative of the transition zone between boreal and southern forests, and a fascinating diversity of physical and biological features. In a meeting with the minister on 30 June, Litteljohn and Pimlott presented the case for an immediate moratorium on the Weldwood cut and the designation of the area as a Nature Reserve.[50] Given its proximity to the Agawa Bay campground, they argued, the proposed reserve was ideally situated for interpretive programs and a nature trail. The following week, the DLF moved the company out of the disputed area and assigned Quetico Park naturalist Shan Walshe to evaluate the site. He confirmed that it was indeed worthy of designation as a natural zone. "The League may be justified in criticism of our lack of foresight in the location of Natural Zones within the Park," admitted J.R. Oatway, the district forester in White River.[51]

Meanwhile, on 6 July, AWL President Abbott Conway, with "a reaction of both sadness and extreme frustration," presented the preliminary report of the investigative team to the government. According to Conway, the report confirmed "that the destructiveness of the multiple-use policy as evidenced in Algonquin, Killarney and Quetico ... is of equal or greater consequence in Lake Superior Provincial Park." Current timber operations and the potential threat posed by long-standing mining claims "combine to suggest the eventual destruction of yet another of Ontario's unique ecological areas."[52] An impressive document, the report reflected the technical and scientific expertise of the investigators and could not easily be ignored by park and forestry officials. District personnel had been candid with the preservationists in explaining that earth and life science inventories in Lake Superior Park had only just commenced, and that the basic substructure of research data for the "intelligent zoning of the park" did not yet exist. Not one Nature Reserve had been established or identified in the twenty-six years of the park's existence.

Forestry practices in the park particularly concerned the investigators. From their brief analysis of forest conditions and economic factors, they concluded that there was "virtually no possibility that the liquidation cut ... being undertaken" by Weldwood and Weyerhaeuser would "be a prelude to sustained yield management of the forest." Within thirty-five years, they predicted, all the marketable timber would be removed and commercial logging operations would probably end. "If, as our investigation indicates, logging operations cannot be supported beyond the limit of the present liquidation cut, then the wisdom of invading large areas of the park is especially open to question." Beyond this problem, the report described, in site-specific detail, the deleterious aesthetic and ecological impact of the timber company skidders, bulldozers, and road construction practices. The team observed no evidence that environmental and recreational considerations influenced the daily operations of the loggers. All in all, the league concluded, "the end result of commercial logging operations in Lake Superior Park is either a degraded forest from which the superior trees have been removed and in which the diversity of species had been reduced," or a second-growth cultured forest, producing timber of commercial quality, but short on aesthetic appeal.

The preliminary report concluded by recommending that the government of Ontario critically reassess its multiple-use policy in the major provincial parks. In the interim, all logging in provincial parks should take place under the control of Crown Management Units, in which responsibility for forest management and road construction would fall to department officials, not the timber companies. As for Lake Superior Park, the league recommended that a moratorium be placed on the extension of logging and road construction until ecological inventories had been completed and zoning decisions entrenched in a master plan.[53] On the subject of the eight mining patents and thirty-eight claims in the park,[54] all of which predated the 1956 ban on mining, the report called for their expropriation. As long as the patents and claims remained, the threat of mining hung over the park like a "Sword of Damocles." Finally, the league urged that moose hunting and the killing of wolves be terminated on a trial basis, and that the system of registered traplines be phased out.

Although some regional officials of the DLF dismissed the report as unsubstantiated, James Keenan and other park planners in Toronto were impressed. They informed Peter Addison that "with the exception of a few minor points, we are in agreement with the comments made in the brief. We feel that the League has pinpointed some areas which should have been recognized and dealt with by the Branch if indeed Lake Superior is worthy of provincial park status."[55] In the light of this kind of assessment, the government began to address several of the AWL's concerns. In August 1970, Lands and Forests Minister René Brunelle informed Abbott Conway that the area north of the Agawa River had been reserved as a natural zone, and that staff specialists were busy "identifying additional areas which should be similarly protected." A survey of forest communities in the park was also scheduled for the following summer, to identify representative and unique areas of ecological significance for designation as natural zones in a future master plan. Logging operations would be monitored closely. "Some of your comments on logging roads are valid," Brunelle acknowledged.[56] Not satisfied with these concessions, and determined to have an impact while the inventories and zoning studies were being undertaken, the league approached the Eaton Foundation for a grant to publish its findings on the park. The resulting book, *Why Wilderness: A Report on Mismanagement in Lake Superior Provincial Park* (Toronto: New Press, 1971), appeared the following year. Edited by Litteljohn and Pimlott, it contained the detailed story of the investigative team's work, the final report, and a collection of previously published articles on the importance of wilderness preservation.

At this point, September 1970, the Quetico controversy was reignited when the AWL learned that the Ontario-Minnesota Pulp and Paper Company was seeking to obtain the logging rights in the northwest quarter of the park by acquiring Domtar's controlling interest in the Jim Mathieu Company. If consummated, the deal would provide the Ontario-Minnesota Company with cutting rights across the entire northern half of Quetico. If Domtar no longer required the licence, argued the preservationists, the DLF should "seize this opportunity to reclaim the area as part of the Primitive section of the Park."[57] The AWL issued its press release on this issue two days before the appearance of a feature article on logging in Quetico, entitled "This Beauty Must Be Preserved," in the *Toronto Star's Canadian Magazine*.[58]

As they planned strategy for the Quetico battle, AWL leaders grappled with a thorny question: how should they handle the nationalist implications of the issue of wilderness versus logging? In both Quetico and Lake Superior parks, subsidiaries of American multinational corporations dominated logging. Should the preservationists focus their arguments on the need to prevent the sale of Canadian natural resources to foreign interests? The temptation to do so was strong in 1970, when nationalist and anti-American sentiment ran high in urban Ontario. Many people were becoming protective of the traditions of their so-called "peaceable kingdom," after watching with shock and sadness the excesses of American political culture during the sixties, including the assassinations of John and Robert Kennedy and Martin Luther King, race riots, and the social turmoil over the war in Vietnam. Intellectuals, businessmen, journalists, and politicians of all shades were warning Canadians about the many threats to their economic and cultural sovereignty posed by influences from the south. These concerns would lead to the formation of the Committee for an Independent Canada in 1971. Meanwhile, the Ontario NDP had targeted the multinationals as a menace to the Canadian quality of life and seized every opportunity to blame these alleged agents of American economic imperialism for plant shutdowns, unemployment, and pollution. Cultural nationalists also claimed that the Canadian publishing industry, broadcasting, and university faculties had fallen under American influence.

For philosophical reasons, and because they had many allies in Minnesota, the Wildlands League's leaders decided to use the nationalist issue with great care and to base their fight for the Quetico wilderness on its own merits. They would leave the multinational issue in Quetico to the Ontario NDP and its new leader, Stephen Lewis, elected on 4 October 1970. The league chose instead to evoke positive elements of Canadian nationalist sentiment by stressing the integral relationship between the wilderness and the Canadian identity. The best expression of this theme appeared in Bruce Litteljohn's "Wilderness: Canadian Cultural Heritage," first published in the *Bulletin* of the Conservation Council of Ontario (October 1970) and reprinted in *Why Wilderness* (1971). "Our history, our painting, and our literature are all fundamental elements of Canadian culture and the Canadian identity," wrote Litteljohn. "All have been deeply influenced and distinguished by the wilderness. Without even considering the vital scientific and enormous recreational values of natural preserves, this, surely, stands as reason enough to safeguard, perpetuate, and expand our wilderness park area in Ontario."

Once rekindled, the Quetico controversy grew into the most intense struggle of the wilderness preservation campaign and became a symbol of the new environmental awareness in Ontario society. To publicize the latest issue, the Wildlands League organized a "summit meeting" in the park, on 3 October 1970. About a hundred people, including representatives of the conservationist groups, woods industry spokesmen, DLF officials, and a contingent of television and newspaper reporters, were bussed into Quetico to attend this carefully staged media event, the brainchild of Walter Gray. During the inspection of the Mathieu logging operation, those in attendance listened to statements from Abbott Conway, Domtar Vice-President Andrew Fleming, and an impromptu speech by the legendary Sigurd Olson, delivered from the Domtar bridge over the French Creek canoe route. The "summit" concluded with the endorsement of a resolution demanding that Quetico be classified a Primitive park and that a moratorium on logging be imposed until the reclassification took place.

The "summit" had a profound impact on Gavin Henderson, executive director of the National and Provincial Parks Association of Canada. Angered by what he had observed, he resigned in protest from the advisory committee to the minister of lands and forests. He refused to remain associated with a government committed to applying multiple-use policies in Quetico and other parks which, in his view, placed natural and recreational values second to the production of wood for industrial use. The news of Henderson's resignation caught the attention of a Toronto resident, Ethel Teitelbaum, who thought his arguments were so important that she decided to help establish the Prevent Destruction of Quetico group in Toronto and to organize a "Town Hall Meeting" in November. She also arranged an interview for Henderson with Barbara Frum, on CBC Television's "Weekday" on 15 October.[59]

Meanwhile, Henderson penned an article entitled "Will Quetico Pay the Price of Progress?" for the 26 October 1970 issue of the Toronto *Globe and Mail*, a seminal piece that transformed the Quetico controversy into a symbolic battle and "a test of the sincerity of [the government's] environmental policies" in general. "The issue is simple," he explained. "On the one hand there are those, including the Government of Ontario, who still believe passionately in economic growth at almost any cost; on the other hand are the swelling numbers of people ... who ... are angry ... because they know that the extent of pollution and mindless destruction of nature that has accompanied this growth, is an unnecessary and intolerable price to have to pay ... Some are parents and grandparents, others are children at school. All are concerned about the kind of environment and the quality of life that we and our children are going to inherit. Quetico is a symbol of this concern."

Once the preservationists began to present the Quetico battle to the public in these terms, the political stakes involved rose considerably. The government's credibility was now at issue because the throne speech of February 1970 had emphasized environmental protection and the future quality of life for Ontarians. As with earlier preservationist flare-ups, the Robarts administration was surprised by the wave of protest that developed over Quetico during October and early November 1970. The media coverage devoted to the issue was noteworthy, considering that the country's attention was riveted on the dramatic "October Crisis," which was unfolding in Ottawa and Montreal – the terrorist kidnappings of James Cross and Pierre Laporte, and the Trudeau government's controversial peacetime invocation of the War Measures Act. In the midst of this national emergency, the preservationists picked up invaluable regional support when the *Thunder Bay News Chronicle* called for an end to logging in Quetico.[60] Meanwhile, both opposition parties repeatedly raised the Quetico issue in the legislature. The Liberals even assigned Patrick Reid to use their time on CBC Television's "Provincial Affairs" program to call for Primitive park status for Quetico and the removal of the loggers.[61]

In late October, cracks appeared in the government's defence of multiple use when the minister of lands and forests accepted the recommendation of the Quetico Advisory Committee. No more licences would be issued to cut timber in Quetico Park under the Ontario-Minnesota volume agreement until the committee had submitted its final report. This development alarmed Timber Branch personnel and even some Parks Branch officials. Chief of Parks Peter Addison, for one, remained unshaken in the belief that multiple use could be made to work in Quetico, and he continued to advise René Brunelle to resist "the classification of the entire park as primitive."[62]

As government officials dug in their heels, "Save Quetico" organizations began to appear across the province, in Fort Frances, Atikokan, Thunder Bay, Dundas, Hamilton, and Toronto. In Toronto, Ethel Teitelbaum's Prevent Destruction of Quetico (PDQ) group organized the "Town Hall Meeting" at the St. Lawrence Centre for the Arts, on 3 November. The event attracted some 1,200 people, nearly half of whom had to be turned away at the door. Those who obtained entry sat enthralled as broadcaster Charles Templeton chaired a panel discussion and question period involving such personalities as the cinematographer Christopher Chapman, Bruce Litteljohn, Douglas Pimlott, Gavin Henderson, Deputy Minister G.H.U. Bayly, Domtar Vice-President Andrew Fleming, MLAs Pat Reid (Liberal, Rainy River), Jack Stokes (NDP, Thunder Bay), and Jim Jessiman (Conservative, Fort William). Half of the people in the audience indicated that they had never been to Quetico, and that they were content to experience the park wilderness vicariously. "For these people," commented Henderson, "to know such places exist is what counts, and there is a very real psychological need." Ethel Teitelbaum expressed a sentiment shared by many urban Ontarians: "I want everyone to know that no one is going to get me into a canoe, sleeping in tents and listening to wolf calls." All the same, she went on, "we have a responsibility to our grandchildren to preserve this park. I probably would never use it, but my grandson may very well want to."[63]

In the middle of the discussions, Deputy Minister Bayly made a startling revelation. He admitted publicly that if the government declared Quetico a

Primitive park and banned logging, sufficient alternative timber areas were available outside the park to keep the Sapawe mill open and the loggers employed. Why then, the audience wondered, was it necessary to harvest timber in Quetico? The debate angered Charlie Erickson. "The time has come for the rational to cease and all hell breaks loose," he bellowed. "I say let's break it loose, it's long past due! I've got an idea that the boys who pull the strings and tear down the trees in Quetico can take calm and rationality in large doses." In the days following the meeting at the St. Lawrence Centre, the Quetico debate raged on in the media and the provincial legislature. On 8 November, radio station CKEY staged an on-air discussion, pitting Litteljohn, Pimlott, and Erickson against Domtar's Andrew Fleming. The following day, on the same station, Charles Templeton and Pierre Berton castigated both the logging companies in Quetico and René Brunelle's park policy during their show, "Dialogue." By mid-November, the Parks Branch had been bombarded with some three hundred protest letters pertaining to Quetico and the premier's office with four hundred more.[64]

On 12 November 1970, Lands and Forests Minister Brunelle attempted to defend himself against his critics. In a statement to the legislature, he applauded his department's management record in Quetico: "the park is not now being desecrated or destroyed as has been charged ... and the possibility of conflict between recreation and commercial cutting in the park today is slight." Quetico, he declared, would remain a Natural Environment park subject to the policy of multiple use. As for the sale of the Jim Mathieu Lumber Company to Ontario-Minnesota, the issue which had triggered all the fuss in the first place, Brunelle refused to intervene. "Ontario-Minnesota is a good corporate citizen of long standing ... in ... Fort Frances, employing more than 1,000 persons," the minister claimed. "It will need the pulpwood and chips from the Jim Mathieu licence and sawmill at Sapawe for its $53-million expansion at Fort Frances ... This government has earnestly sought expansion of the woods industry ... in northwestern Ontario ... we have a responsibility to Ontario-Minnesota to meet the wood requirements of their expanded facilities." What Brunelle failed to address was his deputy minister's admission that this commitment could be met in areas outside the park. Paradoxically, on the same day, the minister instructed the Quetico Advisory Committee to ensure "that the ecological point of view be considered" in their deliberations. "Our management practices in all parts of the park must be ecologically sound, or deterioration will ensue," he wrote.[65] Preservationists would have replied that an ecologically sound policy required the removal of commercial logging from Quetico.

In any event, Brunelle's statement in the legislature served only to anger those seeking to have Quetico reclassified as a Primitive park. The opposition parties moved in for the attack. "Quetico is the test bed of our future ability to survive in the ecological climate which will follow this age of mechanization and dominance [of nature] by man," railed Liberal MLA Leonard Braithwaite.[66] In early December, the Ontario Federation of Labour (OFL) joined the fray and included the preservation of Quetico Park as a natural wilderness in its eleven-point program on environment, conservation, and pollution control.[67] On a half-dozen university campuses, students and professors embraced the wilderness cause and denounced logging in Quetico. Parks Branch officials, despatched to campus debates to defend government policy, found the experience a trying one. Upon his return from a forum at Brock University in late November, James Keenan wrote directly to the deputy minister to voice his concerns. "These are personal, and not necessarily branch views," he explained, but "if we are to span the credibility gap, we should be establishing additional primitive areas (parks or zones) as soon as we can."[68] Keenan had, indeed, found it impossible to explain to the public why no reasonably accessible Primitive parks had been created since his classification policy had been introduced in 1967.

Premier William G. Davis and the Preservationist Breakthrough

On 8 December 1970, Premier John P. Robarts announced his retirement from politics. For the next three months, routine political activity in Ontario was suspended as the Conservative Party chose a new leader. On 12 February 1971, Brampton's William G. Davis, formerly minister of education, emerged as the party's choice, and he assumed office on 1 March. Many political pundits predicted, correctly, an election before the year's end.

During the first months of 1971, the Algonquin Wildlands League took advantage of the period of political transition. Since the uproar over logging in Quetico, the league had been swamped with requests for background information. To meet the demand, and to prepare its supporters for the public hearings that were to be conducted by the Quetico Advisory Committee in the spring, the league obtained grants from both the White Owl Conservation Committee and the Wilderness Society in Washington to produce 1,000 copies of an information kit. Labelled "Quetico: Let It Be," the kit contained numerous "fact sheets" in a detailed question-and-answer format, along with reprints of nineteen articles on Quetico and other general or more technical matters related to parks. The fact that this information package had been widely disseminated and effectively used became apparent in the quality of the many letters and briefs presented to the Quetico Advisory Committee during the five public hearings held in Fort Frances, Atikokan, Thunder Bay, and Toronto in the first two weeks of April.[69]

The number of groups and individuals who took an active part in the hearings process was extraordinary; the committee received 262 written and 144 oral presentations, as well as some 4,500 letters. "The committee ... can report without hesitation," wrote the chairman, S.G. Hancock, "that the vast majority of them stressed the wilderness aspect of the Park's future and in particular the elimination of commercial logging."[70] The hearings, of great importance from a political point of view, revealed that the wilderness movement was drawing strength from northwestern Ontario as well as from the southern regions, and from all age and social groups, including businessmen and organized labour, teachers and students, professionals, and homemakers. The charge that the preservationists only represented affluent, Toronto-based canoe enthusiasts, insensitive to local economic needs and determined to ram their views down the throats of northerners, could no longer be taken seriously. Interestingly, prominent among those residents of northwestern Ontario who submitted briefs to the advisory committee calling for an end to logging in Quetico was high school teacher William D. Addison of Thunder Bay, a forester and ecologist by training, and the son of Peter Addison, the chief of the Parks Branch.

Following the completion of the public hearings, the Quetico Advisory Committee had less than six weeks to submit a recommendation on logging to the minister. Premier Davis himself had told René Brunelle that he wanted a policy on timber harvesting established by June.[71] The committee met in early May, with tension high as five conservation groups – the Algonquin Wildlands League, Canadian Audubon Society, Federation of Ontario Naturalists, National Campers and Hikers Association, and Pollution Probe – publicly expressed nonconfidence in the committee's capacity to reach an unbiased decision, ostensibly because it was "loaded with members favoring logging," and contained no women or young people.[72] These critics soon were forced to eat their words. On 11 May 1971, the advisory committee unanimously recommended that commercial logging inside Quetico Provincial Park be eliminated, subject to the provision that the government provide alternative timber areas outside the park for the Jim Mathieu Lumber Company.[73] "From this point onwards," the premier announced in the legislature on 13 May, "there will be no further commercial logging in Quetico Provincial Park." The preservationists congratulated the premier for the "great step forward in government thinking," but warned that the battle for wilderness would not end until Quetico was designated a Primitive-class park.[74]

The cheering in preservationist ranks was short-lived. Less than twenty-four hours after Premier Davis's Quetico announcement, René Brunelle released the report of the Frost Advisory Committee on Algonquin Park. For social and economic reasons, the report indicated, commercial logging could not be removed from the park. "Recognizing the strategic importance of forest resources in the economy of the region and the Province," the committee wrote in its proposed policy statement, "the forests of the park will be managed to ensure a continuing supply of wood products while safeguarding the recreational values involved."[75] The committee further recommended that the timber operators form a consortium for the management of all lumbering in Algonquin. Failing that, the government should create a Crown corporation to oversee lumbering operations. Surprisingly, the committee was silent on zoning, a deliberate omission, which outraged the Wildlands League. Richard Howard, the principal of the Upper Canada College Preparatory School, who had replaced Abbott Conway as the league's representative on the committee, and Dr. Martin Edwards, a former president of the FON, had failed to convince the other members that they should specify in the report the location and size of the primitive zone in Algonquin. "We wanted the heartland of the park at least preserved from the loggers," Howard informed the press. "But the pro-lumbering committee members wouldn't agree."[76]

When the advisory committee addressed the recreational problems in Algonquin, they accepted Leslie Frost's conception of the park as "the average man's wilderness," a place for urbanites to experience "the feeling of a back-to-earth interlude." To realize that objective, the committee recommended that motorboats be phased out, that snowmobiles be prohibited, and that the 1954 policy on leaseholders be maintained. All of these proposals pleased the preservationists. To relieve congestion along the Highway 60 corridor, the committee also recommended the development of a system of ring roads, complete with satellite parks connected by access roads to interpretation centres on the perimeter of Algonquin, where the canoe routes originated. These proposals also impressed the preservationists, but they were less pleased with the suggestion that one or more low-speed scenic-loop roads be built within the park, starting and ending at the interpretation centres.

In the estimation of the Wildlands League directors, who had been demanding that the western half of the park be designated a primitive zone, the advisory committee report rang "the death knell for Algonquin." Abbott Conway described it as "the most arrogant sell-out of the people and their heritage we've come across yet."[77] On this occasion, however, not all preservationist organizations agreed with the AWL's assessment, nor were they inclined to create another environmental cause célèbre over the report. Speaking for the NPPAC, Gavin Henderson declared that the advisory committee had "produced a generally satisfactory series of recommendations." He acknowledged, reluctantly, that it was "too late" to save the park as a primitive area. "We have to recognize the fact that the forest operations in Algonquin are important to the livelihood of many people both in the park area and in those industries in southern Ontario and elsewhere that rely on the hardwoods of Algonquin for their supplies."[78]

The Davis cabinet accepted most of the recommendations contained in the Algonquin Park Advisory Committee's report and issued instructions for the next phase of policy development. Since the committee's statement could be implemented by a wide range of management strategies, each depending on the location and amount of land to be removed from logging in primitive, natural and recreational zones, and shoreline reserves, the cabinet wanted to examine a variety of feasible alternatives, with detailed cost-benefit data and analyses attached to each.[79] Once the government had made a political decision on a specific policy and management framework option (a decision it reached only in mid-1973), the master plan for Algonquin Park could then be completed.

With the twinning of the Quetico and Algonquin announcements in May 1971, the Davis regime had sent mixed signals to environmentally concerned Ontarians. If, as his advisers were recommending, the premier intended to build an image of himself as "a decisive, modern ecology-minded leader," he still had work to do.[80] During the spring and summer prior to the provincial election of 21 October, Premier Davis did succeed in fashioning such an image of himself as a competent and trustworthy leader. These months were, indeed, full of legislative activity and dramatic announcements designed to illustrate his concern for the quality of life. On 3 June, for instance, Davis made the historic decision to stop Metro Toronto's Spadina Expressway project, arguing that the effect of such an inner-city highway would devastate local communities. Three weeks later, to the further surprise and delight of environmentalists, the premier announced in the legislature that Killarney would be reclassified as a Primitive-class park.

The premier's dramatic pre-election initiatives on parks climaxed on 13 July with the signing of the agreement between the Ontario and federal governments to create a national park at Pukaskwa. To its credit, the Davis administration thereby brought to an end a decade of resistance to conservationists' demands for a large national park in the province.

The complex chain of events that led to the creation of Pukaskwa National Park can be traced back to 1962, when the Canadian Audubon Society launched a campaign to persuade each province to set aside an extensive tract of unspoiled, natural landscape as a national park to commemorate the centennial of Confederation in 1967. Kelso Roberts, Ontario's minister of lands and forests at the time, did not favour the idea, since the province would be required to purchase any patented property on a national park site before handing over the land to federal authorities, free of encumbrances. He also objected to the fact that national park policy, particularly after 1964, restricted resource development (logging, mining, and hunting) on these lands.[81] For these reasons, both Kelso Roberts and his successor René Brunelle argued that when Ontario required more parkland, it would establish provincial parks and manage them according to multiple-use policies.

Notwithstanding his strong objections to turning over large tracts of Crown land to federal authorities, Lands and Forests Minister Roberts grudgingly entered discussions with Ottawa on the issue of a national park at the request of his fellow Tories in the Diefenbaker government. For over a year, provincial and dominion parks officials conducted site reconnaissance studies before concluding that the area of the Bruce Peninsula between Cabot Head and Tobermory would make an ideal location for a national park. Unfortunately, this proposal ran into insurmountable opposition from both provincial wildlife officials and sportsmen, who wished to retain the area for public hunting, and from politicians, who objected to the land purchase costs that would be involved. Consequently, in March 1964, the Robarts government informed the new Liberal regime in Ottawa that Ontario, rather than agreeing to a national park, would continue to develop its own provincial park, Cyprus Lake, at the tip of the Bruce Peninsula.

At this stage, purely political considerations became the primary concern in the selection process. As an alternative to the Bruce Peninsula, Ottawa favoured the Pukaskwa area, an outstanding example of wilderness landscape on the north shore of Lake Superior. Since Pukaskwa was already reserved under Ontario's Wilderness Areas Act, and remained of little interest to loggers and miners, it seemed the logical choice for a national park. The wily Kelso Roberts had other plans, however, and insisted that the national park should be located near Elliot Lake, in the area that embraced the Mississagi Provincial Park Reserve. His choice was dictated by the economic gains to be made in this severely depressed region hard hit by the collapse of world uranium prices in the late 1950s. Since the Elliot Lake site happened to be in Prime Minister Pearson's riding, provincial officials calculated that Ottawa would pour more development money into this location than it would into any other site.[82] The federal government was accordingly informed that if it wanted a national park site in Ontario, it would have to be in the Elliot Lake area.

Ironically, the Elliot Lake proposal was withdrawn in 1966, when valuable mineral deposits were discovered near the Mississagi Provincial Park Reserve. But with preservationist sentiment mounting, and public expectations high that a national park would soon be established in the province, the Robarts government could not easily suspend negotiations with Ottawa. Instead, provincial officials continued to go through the motions of exploring the possibilities for a national park, but neither Kelso Roberts nor René Brunelle was interested in bringing the matter to a speedy conclusion.[83] Only after the preservationist movement had peaked (in 1970), and William Davis had become premier, did the province drop its obstructionist stance and conclude an agreement to create Pukaskwa National Park. "I must admit that we have been talking about this park for a long time," remarked Minister of Northern Affairs Jean Chrétien at the signing ceremony, "but now ... we have not only a new national park but the largest national park in Eastern Canada. I find this rather typical of this Province of Ontario – when they do something, they do it big."[84]

Had James Keenan and his staff prevailed in the months following the Pukaskwa agreement, Ontario would not have waited another sixteen years, until July 1987, before the two governments again collaborated to establish a second large national park in the province, this time at the tip of the Bruce Peninsula. Keenan recognized that national parks relieved his staff of some of the pressure to provide recreational space in the wilderness and to protect natural areas. He also admitted that the job of providing for the recreational needs of Ontarians was beyond the capacity of his division, given the retrenchment policies of the early 1970s. Acting accordingly, Keenan distributed in 1972 a proposed policy on national parks for internal discussion within the new Ministry of Natural Resources. It was rejected by "upper management," which took "a traditional resource loss attitude" and failed "to see the rationality" of tapping into federal revenues to expand opportunities for outdoor recreation in Ontario.[85]

William Davis and his Conservative Party handily won the general election of 21 October 1971. Since Davis had assumed the premiership in March of that year, his government had shown itself more responsive than its predecessors to public attitudes toward environmental problems, especially as they affected parks and outdoor recreation. The Quetico logging decision, the reclassification of Killarney as a Primitive-class park, and the agreement to establish Pukaskwa National Park, all played only a minor role in the Davis victory, but when combined with issues like the Spadina Expressway, a commitment to protect the Niagara Escarpment, and the announcement of a $25-million lawsuit against Dow Chemical for mercury pollution, Premier Davis established his credibility among that segment of the electorate concerned with "quality of life" and environmental issues.[86]

By late 1971, the hitherto frenetic pace of the preservationist campaign was beginning to lag. As they awaited the policy decisions on Quetico and Algonquin, Wildlands League directors had time to reflect upon the "what, where and how much" questions of wilderness protection and to draft a comprehensive statement on the subject. In the spring of 1972, they published *Wilderness Now*, a booklet which set out the league's wilderness philosophy, together with recommendations as to how it might be implemented. It was a noteworthy first attempt to define a policy on wilderness preservation for Ontario, and would stimulate park planners to follow suit. There was little more that the Wildlands League could do, since the advisory committees on Quetico and Algonquin remained behind closed doors to complete their assignments, and the various master planning task forces were synthesizing mountains of background research data.

It was now being appreciated that the task of producing a master plan involved an enormous amount of work over an extended period of time. The Quetico Advisory Committee, for example, required a year after the public hearings, held in April 1971, before submitting a final report, on 26 May 1972. The report was then subjected to further public scrutiny and government analysis before being accepted almost in its entirety by the new minister of natural resources, Leo Bernier, in June 1973. The process may have seemed excruciatingly slow to the Algonquin Wildlands League, but in the end, the wilderness movement won the battle for Quetico. The advisory committee reached the same conclusion as the preservationists. "Quetico has been promoted as a wilderness area, classified as a natural environment park, and managed as any other piece of Crown Land," concluded the committee. Bernier agreed that the "ad hockery" must end and, in his statement of June 1973, declared that Quetico would be reclassified and managed as a Primitive park.[87]

The minister also outlined the policies that would eventually be entrenched in the master plan for Quetico. Logging, mining, and hunting would be prohibited. Boundaries would be adjusted to conform with natural water limits, and buffer zones would be created around the park. Additional access points from the north would be developed, both as a means of stimulating tourism in the northwestern region and of relieving user pressure on congested canoe routes near the international border. Daily visitor quota systems at each access point would also reduce interior user pressures on the crowded waterways and encourage the use of the northern entry points. A can and bottle ban, a policy introduced in the Boundary Waters Canoe Area of the Superior National Forest in May 1971, would also be instituted in Quetico to control the mounting litter problem. Eventually, Bernier promised, outboard motors would also be prohibited, but the policy would be phased in, to reduce the impact it would have on the livelihoods of the Lac la Croix Indian band, who served as guides in the park. Although the motorboat ban would not apply on certain lakes for an interim period, motors would immediately be restricted to ten horsepower. Trapping rights would also be granted only to aboriginal peoples; however, all other owners of registered traplines would be allowed to work their lines until they chose to abandon them. "These new policies," Bernier predicted, "will do much to reduce user conflicts and will establish long-term protection for this important natural resource in northern Ontario."

On 17 July 1973, a month after the minister unveiled his plans for Quetico, he announced the government's decisions on Algonquin Park. Not until March of that year had Parks Division officials been able to present the Davis cabinet with analyses of the economic impact of five options on zoning and logging.[88] Appearing to defer to the political clout of the preservationists, Bernier acknowledged that the government had abandoned the status quo of 1968 in the park. In the next breath, however, he explained that the option of removing the logging companies was also politically and economically unacceptable. "The government has decided to maintain Algonquin Park in the context of the region of Ontario in which it lies," Bernier declared, "to preserve the 3,100 employment opportunities now provided and the economic base it now supports."[89] The option selected by the cabinet, but not detailed in Bernier's statement, would make 77 percent of the land base in the park available for commercial logging. Approximately 9 percent of Algonquin would be zoned primitive (up from 5 percent in the Provisional Master Plan of 1968), in three blocks in the central lakes section. In addition, fifty-three natural and historic zones would be removed from logging activities. According to the confidential economic impact studies, this zoning option would result in a loss of two hundred "direct" and an equal number of "indirect" jobs.[90] Although he chose not to disclose his data on the economic costs of the government's policies, Bernier did announce that his ministry would cancel all existing licences held by logging operators in the park, and establish a Crown agency – the Algonquin Forest Authority – to work out supply agreements with the companies. On the basis of the research on forest acoustics, the government also decided that the 2-mile (3.2-kilometre) sound-buffer zone along canoe routes could be reduced to 1.5 miles (2.4 kilometres).

With regard to the policy on leaseholders, Bernier explained that the government intended to modify the 1954 phase-out program by allowing the seven private youth camps to remain in the park. "These camps are operated primarily as educational experiences for young people and are world renowned for their accomplishments." Bernier promised that the government would emulate their example by establishing a publicly operated camp for the province's less advantaged children. In fact, within a year, the government, in cooperation with the Young Men's Christian Association (YMCA), created "The Algonquin Experience," a youth camp on Whitefish Lake, providing a camping vacation for some 200 children during the summer of 1974. In another departure from the advisory committee's report, the cabinet decided to permit the four lodges to remain in the park until 1996, when the last cottage leases were due to expire, since it was expected that by then private resort accommodation would be available outside the park's boundaries. This would avoid the risk of discriminating, the minister claimed, against the thousands of Ontarians who could not, or chose not to camp outdoors.

These revisions came only after a careful reassessment of the 1954 policy on leaseholders, a review occasioned by the minority report of the advisory committee, submitted by George D. Garland.[91] Garland had broken ranks with the rest of the Frost committee in order to draw attention to the plight of the leaseholders. Time was rapidly running out for them, since the first leases were scheduled to terminate in 1975. While Garland's arguments on behalf of the youth camps and lodges helped to generate sufficient public and political support to modify the policy laid down in 1954, his case on behalf of the 363 cottage leaseholders did not elicit much sympathy. He had argued that leasehold lakes provided park users with a much-needed "gradual transition into complete wilderness," since the cottagers regularly assisted novice canoeists in distress on the first lakes, away from access points. Without such aid, Garland argued, "Algonquin Park would be noted today for its tragedies." Rather than remove the cottagers, he had proposed that their numbers be expanded by providing another thousand cottage sites. Parks Division officials bristled at this suggestion. They viewed the difficulties of servicing the cottage communities as a costly management headache. Politicians were no less hostile to the idea. "The role of the leaseholders ... in providing safety for park visitors," commented René Brunelle, "appears to be the product of someone's overworked imagination. Canoe routes uninhabited by cottagers have no worse

[a] safety record than Canoe Lake. There are no leaseholders in Quetico or other similar canoeing areas but these are not noted today for tragedies of wilderness travel."[92] The cottage leases, the cabinet concluded, would be removed as the leases expired.

Apart from a few policy decisions like those on the children's camps and lodges, most of the recommendations of the Algonquin Park advisory committee were accepted by the minister in July 1973 and eventually embodied in the master plan of 1974. These policies included a number of attractive features: improved access to the perimeter of the park from ring roads and satellite parks; low-speed scenic roads; an expanded system of trails for hiking, cross-country skiing, snowshoeing, and possibly horseback riding; more canoe routes in the park and encouragement to use routes outside the park boundaries; a daily-visitor quota system at each access point into the interior; a can and bottle ban; the phasing out of snowmobiles, off-road vehicles and motorboats; and programs to manage fishing and bodies of water. Altogether, the minister accepted twenty-eight of the thirty-six recommendations made by the advisory committee, accepted two others with modifications, rejected two, and withheld judgment on three more, pending further study.

Predictably, the Algonquin Wildlands League assailed Bernier's policy statement. The government's decisions to continue commercial logging over most of the park, to reduce the sound buffer zones, to encourage additional automobile traffic in the park interior by building scenic roads, and its ominous silence on the specific size of the primitive zones, sent the league back on the warpath. The realization that Bernier had delayed his statement until after the legislature rose for the summer also angered the preservationist leaders and stiffened their resolve to carry on the fight. Accordingly, in a last-ditch attempt to prevent the inclusion of the offending policies in the master plan, the preservationists organized town hall meetings in Huntsville, Ottawa, and Toronto (the latter being aborted at the last minute by a fire in the St. Lawrence Hall). Their campaign was given a boost by the leaders of the two opposition parties, Robert Nixon and Stephen Lewis, who appeared at the meetings to announce their support for the removal of the logging companies from Algonquin Park.[93] When the legislature reassembled in October, the opposition leaders pointed to the chronic overcrowding in the province's parks and the shortage of outdoor recreational space in southern Ontario to justify their demand for a logging ban. Stephen Lewis also met with local politicians and workers in the Ottawa Valley to assuage their concerns. "I have written directly to the trade union locals involved," he informed the legislature, "and told them that in this choice the environment must come first and that we will find alternative employment."[94]

With the Liberals and the NDP suddenly demanding an orderly phasing out of commercial logging in Algonquin, the directors of the Wildlands League had to revise their position on the question, since they were still committed to their 1968 statement, which allowed for logging in the eastern half of the park. At their annual study weekend in October 1973, the preservationists jettisoned their earlier position and went on record "as being opposed to commercial natural resource extraction from any Ontario park."[95]

In June 1974, Stephen Lewis returned to the issue of logging in Algonquin. He claimed that a sufficient volume of hardwood existed in a fifty-mile (80-kilometre) radius of the park to satisfy industrial requirements and to allow for the removal of the timber operators.[96] Minister of Natural Resources Leo Bernier immediately ordered his forest research branch to review Lewis's claim. In November, Bernier reported back to the legislature that "I can reaffirm unequivocally that the 50-mile zone is not a feasible alternative source of supply for park-dependent mills."[97] According to ministry studies, the NDP's researchers had not taken sufficient account of economic considerations, such as the scattered distribution of the available Crown timber, the distance of the timber from the mills, and the high proportion of hardwood that grew on private lands and, therefore, could not be considered a guaranteed industrial supply. In spite of these arguments, neither opposition party retreated from its demand that a logging ban be imposed on Algonquin; but the government felt confident enough to proceed with the implementation of its previously announced policies.

On 22 October 1974, after six years of public debate and intensive study, Bernier finally unveiled the long-awaited *Algonquin Provincial Park Master Plan*. It was a beautifully produced document, 100 pages long, lavishly illustrated with coloured maps and pictures. William Calvert of the Parks Division prepared the document in concert with Leslie Frost and with guidance from a senior executive steering committee made up of Arthur Herridge and Walter Giles. Providing impressive detail, the plan fleshed out the government's policies for every aspect of park management. Since it contained no substantive changes from Bernier's policy announcement of 1973, the plan had an anticlimactic effect on anyone who had followed its evolution. Reactions were mixed and predictable. Dr. Vidar Nordin, dean of forestry at the University of Toronto, waxed poetic about the document and requested 100 copies to use "as a teaching aid in Multiple Land-Use Planning."[98] The Quetico Foundation also congratulated the Ministry of Natural Resources for the "efforts it is making to solve a most complex and difficult problem."[99] Embittered leaders of the Wildlands League considered the master plan "a disgrace." For them it was a symbolic defeat. On such fundamental matters as logging and the size of the area zoned as primitive, league spokesmen found little to distinguish it from the provisional document of 1968.[100] They dismissed the plan as yet another bundle of compromises that failed to give sufficient emphasis to the protection of natural values.

As prescribed in the master plan, Natural Resources Minister Bernier introduced legislation, in November 1974, to create the Algonquin Forest Authority (AFA). "The advantages of such a Crown corporation will be obvious," he explained. "First, it will facilitate a close control over logging operations in the park. Secondly, it will permit better utilization of timber resources, enabling more products to be obtained from fewer trees. Third, it would be much less disruptive than the 18 separate companies that now operate in the ... park. Fourth, it will allow the ministry to direct logging operations so that purely therapeutic logging can also be carried on."[101] The government appointed Vidar Nordin to chair the authority.

The completion of the Algonquin Park Master Plan put an end to the upsurge of preservation that had begun in 1968. Made wiser by their experience, preservationist organizations now turned their attention to lobbying for a "system" of Primitive parks, as outlined in *Wilderness Now*. In April 1973, at the annual meeting of the Federation of Ontario Naturalists, representatives of the Wildlands League, Canadian Nature Federation, FON, NPPAC, and the Sierra Club of Ontario created the Coalition for Wilderness. As its first task, the group drafted a comprehensive position paper for a provincial wilderness system. The coalition submitted its report, largely written by William D. Addison and J. David Bates, entitled "Wilderness in Ontario," to the government

Map 4: Zoning Plan for Algonquin Provincial Park, 1974, Adapted from Algonquin Provincial Park Master Plan (Ontario Ministry of Natural Resources, 1974)

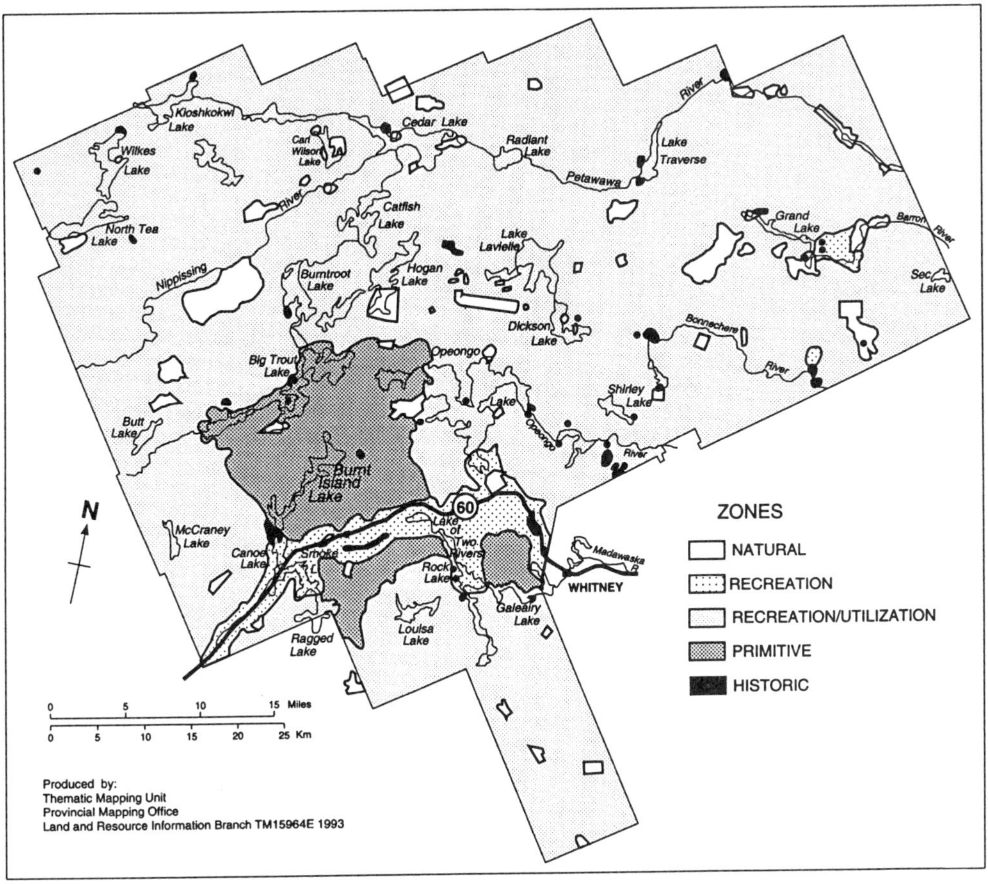

in January 1974 and published it in the *Ontario Naturalist* (1974). With this position paper, the preservationists were able to state in specific detail how much land they wanted set aside as wilderness parks, where, and why. They envisaged a system of fifteen parks, embracing a total area of 23,000 square miles (5,957,000 hectares), selected to represent all of the province's physiographic regions and forest zones. No park was to be smaller than 750 square miles (194,250 hectares).

Significantly, by 1973, the renamed Division of Parks, now headed by Executive Director James Keenan, had begun to march in step with the preservationists. "I believe ... that a wilderness policy is one of the more important issues that concerns this Ministry at this time," Keenan informed Leo Bernier in 1974. He explained that progress in establishing Primitive-class parks since 1967 had been "more the result of being shoved (Quetico, Killarney), than of leadership."[102] As early as 1972, Keenan had assigned two young planners, Cameron Clark and George Moroz, to undertake a review of the literature and produce a philosophical rationale for wilderness parks as a basis for policy formulation. They also examined questions such as the criteria for the selection of primitive areas, their projected use, user characteristics, area requirements, and the practical aspects of management. Keenan presented a status report of their work at the FON's annual meeting in 1973, the same meeting at which the Coalition for Wilderness was founded.[103] Subsequently, during the mid-1970s, parks division personnel benefited from the input of the Coalition for Wilderness in the development of a planning and management policy for a wilderness system in Ontario.

All of this indicated how profoundly preservationist thinking had influenced public policy and attitudes in the civil service. That influence went deeper than the highly publicized victories in the struggle to reclassify Quetico and Killarney and to create Pukaskwa National Park. It was also evident in the appointment in the parks division of a full-time biologist, Harold J. Gibbard, as a Nature Reserve supervisor. From 1969 to 1972, he worked with the Minister's Advisory Committee on Nature Reserves, made up of experts in biology, ecology, forestry, geology, and soil science, to produce a conceptual framework for a Nature Reserve systems plan and to identify specific areas worthy of designation as reserves.[104] Three new Wild River parks were also created in 1971, to appease recreationists clamouring for more readily accessible wilderness experiences: Mississagi Wild River Provincial Park, 193 kilometres in length, from Biscotasing on the CPR main line to Rocky Island Lake, north of Thessalon; exotic-sounding Chapleau-Nemegosenda Park, a 120-kilometre circular canoe route in the area between the town of Chapleau and Kapuskasing Lake, adjacent to the main line of the CPR; and Lady Evelyn Wild River in the legendary Temagami country.

Now that public participation in the master-planning process was institutionalized, the preservationists were confident that their views would always be taken into account by park planners and politicians. Another important medium through which preservationists, and indeed all segments of the public, could make their needs known became available in October 1974, with the appointment of the Provincial Parks Advisory Council. The council was given a broad mandate to monitor the implementation of provincial park master plans, beginning with the one for Algonquin, and to advise the government on a wide range of general parks policy issues. The MNR authorized the council, initially nineteen members strong and chaired by Dr. George Priddle, to hold public hearings throughout the province and to publish its reports annually. "The council is being established," explained Bernier, "because of the government's concern that changing recreational needs of the public ... be reflected in a meaningful way to ensure that both our management systems and our parks planning programs meet the needs of the people of Ontario."[105] Conservationist groups were soon impressed by the effective way in which the council both monitored the public pulse on outdoor recreation issues and proffered forceful and informed recommendations to the government. For instance, the council did not hesitate to register its displeasure, when the Ministry of Natural Resources was slow to implement the provisions of the Algonquin master plan.

The preservationists, of course, formed only one group among the many who had to be accommodated by those planning and managing provincial parks. There would be times when economic, social, and recreational circumstances would prevent organizations like the Wildlands League from realizing their aims. It had happened in Algonquin, and it happened again in the case of Lake Superior. By 1974, after considerable public consultation, the master-planning process for Lake Superior came to a halt when park and timber managers and forest industry officials failed to reach a consensus on zoning and logging issues.[106] As in Algonquin, many jobs in north-central Ontario depended on Lake Superior Park remaining open to the loggers. When the cabinet again faced what seemed to be a choice between employment and preservation, the wilderness movement suffered a fresh setback, and Lake Superior Provincial Park remained a Natural Environment–class park, in which commercial logging was permitted.

Even though they failed to reach their goal of having Algonquin and Lake Superior reclassified as Primitive parks and seeing the logging companies removed, the preservationists' impact was still considerable. Not only were strict controls placed over the timber companies in both parks, but forest management was also significantly reformed across all provincial parklands. In 1971, a chastened Timber Management Branch had reacted to the Wildlands League's pressure by implementing a new policy, no longer issuing timber licences in any other parks and operating them instead as Crown Management Units. Henceforth, if logging was deemed desirable, the bush operation would be carried out as a department project. Private companies would still undertake the cutting for the department, but each operation would have as its main purpose the management of the forest for its environmental values.[107] The branch even retained a consulting firm, Hough, Stansbury and Associates Limited, to develop a Forest Aesthetics Manual in order to establish guidelines for district officials to protect aesthetic and recreational values when supervising timber operations in provincial parks. Five years earlier, before the impact of the preservationists had been felt, such action would have been unthinkable.

The number of successes of the preservationist forces surprised many government officials at the time and left some shaking their heads in disbelief. The fact, however, that the Algonquin Wildlands League and its allies accomplished so much rested on their ability to attract the attention of the news media and, through the media, to convince the government that wilderness preservation enjoyed the support of a large constituency. The preservationists skilfully mobilized public opinion. They mastered the use of the press conference, public meetings, and radio and television appearances. Instead of the cooperative, behind-the-scenes approach favoured by the Quetico Foundation, the Wildlands League revelled in confrontation politics. Screaming about the "rape" of Algonquin or Quetico may not have been cricket, but it captured the attention of the media and the public.

As a pressure group, the Wildlands League would have been ineffective had not a large segment of the public sympathized with its cause. The generation of the late sixties, so quick to protest on behalf of rights for students, women, individuals, and animals, to demonstrate against the Vietnam War and racial segregation in the American South, and to denounce the effects on community stability of inner-city expressways and urban, high-rise development schemes, was predisposed to sympathize with the cause of wilderness protection. The many environmentally aware Ontarians, appalled by the extent of water and air pollution, were the most likely converts to preservationism. As a result, the battles for Algonquin and Quetico quickly became symbolic of environmentalism. The wilderness movement also benefited enormously from the talents of many imaginative and energetic people, drawn from all political camps, regions, social strata, and age groups.

Fortuitously for the preservationists, the timing of their campaign could not have been more politically opportune. When the Algonquin Wildlands League appeared in 1968, the Robarts government was suffering the consequences of promoting a number of needed, but relatively unpopular programs, like tax reform, regional government, and the mandatory reorganization of school boards on a county basis. The last thing the government wanted was another issue to complicate its life still further, so it was inclined to accommodate the environmentalists, especially when the opposition parties spoke on their behalf. Later, with the resignation of John Robarts in 1970 and the accession to power of William Davis in 1971, the window of political opportunity opened wider. In the months prior to the election of October 1971, as the new premier carefully undertook the metamorphosis from "bland Bill" to "decisive Davis," wilderness preservationists enjoyed dramatic gains with the decisions on Quetico, Killarney, and Pukaskwa. The breakthrough had been made.

Chapter 6

From the Politics of Special Funding to "Operation Restraint"

Apart from the challenge posed by the preservationist upsurge and the celebrated battles over wilderness after 1967, the Robarts and Davis governments grappled with another serious park-related problem in the same period – the intensifying demand for parkland and outdoor recreation opportunities in the heavily populated regions of southern Ontario. The Robarts administration addressed this issue by laying a foundation of planning studies for new parkland along the Niagara Escarpment, at Wasaga Beach, and near the major cities of south-central Ontario. However, as in the case of the wilderness battles, and in the hothouse atmosphere before the election of October 1971, it took a new premier, seeking to establish his own credentials on issues related to the environment and the quality of life, to persuade the provincial government to commit itself to underwriting these projects. The trouble with politically generated special funding, of course, is that the politicians can turn off the revenue flow as abruptly as they turn it on. This, indeed, occurred after the 1975 provincial election, when a chastened minority Davis government responded to a different mix of economic and political considerations in a period of economic stagnation and inflation, and brought the acquisition of parkland in southern Ontario to a virtual halt.

Outdoor Recreation: A Question of Equity

In March 1970, Stephen Lewis, the eloquent leader of the New Democratic Party, rose in the provincial legislature to remind the government of John Robarts of its failure to resolve the severe shortage of provincial park campgrounds, beaches, and day-use facilities in south-central Ontario. Citing ideas expressed in the early 1960s by the Conservation Council of Ontario, and more recently by recreation planner Norman Pearson, he noted that most provincial parks were too far removed from the so-called "Golden Horseshoe," the industrial and urban heartland of Ontario and home to approximately two-thirds of the province's 7.7 million residents. "In the urban regions between Oshawa and St. Catharines," Lewis argued, "18 per cent of Canada's population has 3,000 acres of public space when it requires 42,000." Why, he asked, when "we are in a state ... of acute emergency," were there only six provincial parks within a fifty-mile radius of Metropolitan Toronto?[1]

Lewis believed, as did many Ontarians, that the uneven geographical distribution of provincial parks and outdoor recreation opportunities was unacceptable. During the affluent sixties, a period of heightened interest in quality-of-life issues, Ontarians had redefined the concept of outdoor recreation and now viewed it as a social amenity, a necessary and enriching aspect of daily life. From this new perspective, the shortage of camping and day-use opportunities for outdoor recreation on provincial parkland in south-central and southwestern Ontario emerged as a question of equity in government services. For some, it was an issue serious enough to drive them to political protest. Angry residents in the Niagara Peninsula, organized as the Association for the Preservation of East Erie Lakefront, had been holding public demonstrations since 1966. Their anger boiled over into civil disobedience in 1968 when 100 people, led by the Reverend Robert Wright, blocked traffic and tore down part of a fence at the privately owned Sherkston Beach.[2] Furthermore, an equally exasperated Niagara Regional Development Council protested in its own fashion by publishing a booklet entitled *People Without Beaches* (1968), which documented the shocking lack of public access to the shorelines of Lakes Erie and Ontario. Wilderness preservationists also took part in the discussion, because they recognized the relevance of the issue to their cause. The shortage of Recreation-class provincial parks in south-central Ontario was forcing people to travel farther afield, thereby placing excessive user pressure on the larger northern parks.[3]

Attendance records reflected the increasingly heavy use of the provincial parks. In 1970, over 12 million people visited the system, an increase of 16 percent over the previous year and more than double the number recorded in 1960. Attendance finally peaked at 13,658,619 visitors in 1971, then gradually declined through that decade as the population aged, gas prices rose, effectively curtailing travel, and the economy deteriorated.[4] Overcrowding at provincial park campgrounds across southern Ontario in 1969 had reached what Parks Branch chief Peter Addison considered a "critical situation." Over 3,500 families had to be turned away from twenty-four southern parks during the August civic weekend in 1969, and these were only the people who disregarded the "full" sign at the highway entrances.[5] The situation worsened, as the number of campers using the provincial park system increased by 13 percent in 1970 (to approximately 1.5 million people), and by another 6 percent in 1971. Compounding the problem, the Parks Branch discontinued the practice of permitting overflow camping in 1970 because of unsanitary conditions and a deterioriating environment in the unserviced camping areas.

Without overflow camping, the families turned away at 89 parks in 1971 rose 33 percent and numbered 40,000. By the mid-1970s, planners estimated that in southern Ontario alone, there existed a deficit of over 3,000 campsites and approximately three million user days of day-use recreation.[6]

Opposition critics not only upbraided the Robarts government for its failure to provide sufficient parkland in southern regions; they also reproached the Conservatives for the class bias and social inequities they alleged were inherent in provincial park policy. Walter Pitman (NDP, Peterborough) observed that by locating parks in rural settings accessible only by automobile, the provincial park system "essentially served the well-to-do," the well educated, highly mobile segment of the population, while failing to meet the outdoor recreational needs of the less affluent, less educated, city-bound urbanites who relied on public transportation, or who could ill afford the costs of car camping.[7] A decade earlier, such comments might have been dismissed as socialist rhetoric, but in 1970 they were taken seriously by politicians of all parties, who had observed with shock the 1967 summer riots in some dozen cities across the United States, riots which left 83 people dead and 1,900 injured. American authorities who investigated the civil disorders learned that one of the serious complaints of those living in the affected areas was the lack of recreation programs. Some state and federal agencies had, indeed, already acted upon these findings. As a case in point, the state of New York reassessed its policy of creating Recreation-class parks in rural areas, accessible only by private automobile; subsequently, in 1968, Governor Nelson Rockefeller authorized the transformation of the west side of the Harlem River in New York City into Roberto Clemente State Park. That same year, the U.S. National Park Service also adopted a near-urban-park strategy and, in 1972, established Gateway National Recreation Area near New York City on Jamaica Bay and Golden Gate National Recreation Area in California. Over the next six years, Congress established four more such areas near major cities.[8]

Aware of this wider context, and sensitive to the NDP's stand on social and environmental issues, the members of the Ontario Parks Integration Board instructed the Parks Branch in 1971 to develop a planning model to identify those urban areas in southern Ontario most seriously underserviced in terms of outdoor recreation space and facilities, so that the province's limited land acquisition and development funds could be spent where they were most needed. Parks Branch planner, Ron Vrancart, subsequently devised the so-called OPIB recreation deficit model to measure the relative availability of day-use, camping, hunting, and fishing opportunities in provincially owned parkland in each of seven urban regions across southern Ontario. The study established statistically what knowledgeable observers had already suspected, namely that the Oakville and Windsor urban regions were the most severely deficient areas in terms of recreational opportunities offered in provincially owned parkland, followed by Ottawa, London, and Kitchener-Waterloo.[9]

By 1970, some politicians and parks administrators were beginning to think that the provincial government could no longer rigidly adhere to the traditional policy that municipalities and conservation authorities should assume responsibility for most day-use recreation within a one-and-a-half-hour drive of Toronto or other major cities in south-central and southwestern Ontario. Economic conditions seemed to be rendering this policy unworkable; for example, land acquisition and capital development costs for parks near major cities had become prohibitive for local and regional governments. Furthermore, municipalities bordering large cities were assuming the financial burden of providing recreational parkland that was primarily used by out-of-area residents. In the Region of York, for instance, 75 percent of the users of the region's park facilities lived in Metropolitan Toronto.[10] Under these circumstances, it seemed evident that the province would have to assume a more prominent role in providing outdoor recreational opportunities in municipalities contiguous to the cities. And conservationist groups had yet another argument to bring forward. They maintained that the government had a responsibility to preserve in the province's parks the unique and representative physical, biological, and cultural features of the south-central region – the Niagara Escarpment, the Great Lakes shoreline, and the Oak Ridges Moraine – and could not ignore that duty, simply because these areas lay close to the cities of the "Golden Horseshoe."

The pressure to provide provincial parks closer to major urban populations intensified after 1973, when the oil crisis brought about by the Organization of Petroleum Exporting Countries triggered a sharp rise in gasoline prices and raised the spectre of a shortage. Ontarians began to curtail their driving and to seek vacation and day-use recreation spots closer to home. Planners had already learned, from provincial marketing surveys of outdoor recreational demand conducted between 1967 and 1974, that 87 percent of all participation in outdoor recreation was of the day-use variety, and that most of it occurred within a one-and-a-half-hour drive from a person's residence. Participation rates in virtually all activities associated with outdoor recreation had increased since 1967, and survey respondents had indicated a desire and intention to pursue more outdoor recreation in the future. It was evident that participation would also increase when new opportunities were provided in an area lacking sufficient parkland such as south-central Ontario. With demographers forecasting that 90 percent of Ontario's population would be urban dwellers by 1986, and with the population of southern Ontario continuing to grow, the provincial government faced a big challenge simply to maintain its existing share of the outdoor recreation market. This was quite apart from the perceived necessity of relieving financially strapped municipal and regional authorities of some of the burden of near-urban outdoor recreation. In 1971, 24 percent of the existing opportunities for day-use outdoor recreation took place in provincially operated areas, 42 percent on areas operated by municipal or regional agencies, and 34 percent on privately owned land.[11]

Beginning in the late 1960s, the Robarts government initiated several courses of action to expand the number of provincial parks available to the urban residents of south-central and southwestern Ontario. In 1967, the premier committed his government to preserving the length of the Niagara Escarpment with its mosaic of cliffs, forests, and valleys as a recreation area, and commissioned Leonard Gertler to coordinate a wide-ranging evaluation of the escarpment. Gertler's *Niagara Escarpment Study, Conservation and Recreation Report* (1968), provided broad direction for subsequent parkland acquisition on the escarpment. It identified the prime lands worthy of preservation for recreational and environmental reasons, and recommended the creation of a park system along the escarpment. Gertler also urged outright public acquisition of 55,000 acres (22,258 hectares) of land, at a cost of some $18.5 million and the establishment of selective, regulatory public controls through easements on another 35,000 acres (14,164 hectares) at a cost of $14 million.

Parks Branch officials enthusiastically endorsed the report. They emphasized the "amazing" fact that 66 percent of the provincial population lived within eighty kilometres of the escarpment. "There is no doubt," wrote planner Russell Irvine, "that such a program would be expensive but if we are ... serious about planning for the needs of our future generations it is ... one that should go ahead with a priority second to none in the entire Province."[12] In fact, the Parks Branch had already begun acquiring property at many of the locations targeted by Gertler, including sites in the Short Hills area, at the forks of the Credit River near Caledon, along the Boyne River near Shelburne, and on the Bruce Peninsula.

Although the Robarts government did not commit itself to Gertler's four-year land acquisition and funding timetable, it did accept the basic principles of his report. In April 1970, the premier announced that his government intended to speed up its recreational land acquisition program on the escarpment. Subsequently, the Treasury Board approved a special budget of $750,000 for parkland purchases during 1970–71, a sum later increased to $1.6 million (40 percent of the Department of Lands and Forests' acquisition budget that year) for 1,226 hectares of recreational property.[13]

The government also attempted to resolve the problems that persisted at Wasaga Beach. The recreational importance of this park could scarcely be exaggerated; it accounted for 75 percent of the supply of provincial park beach opportunities within day-use range of the so-called Toronto-Centred Region. Nearly five million people, or 70 percent of the provincial population, lived within a two-hour drive of Wasaga. Not surprisingly, then, the Robarts government accelerated its land purchases in the late 1960s, spending a total of $3.2 million for off-beach property from 1963 to 1970 for the purpose of removing cars from the water's edge.[14] Meanwhile, planning for both the provincial park and the town of Wasaga Beach also moved forward. Although the 1967 report prepared by the Toronto consulting firm, Project Planning

Associates Ltd., was deemed to be overly ambitious and impractical, it did lay the foundation for future planning of a four-season "park community concept." Various government departments later launched a battery of planning and feasibility studies pertaining to traffic flow, bridge requirements, water and sewage facilities, and parking, all of which culminated in March 1971 with the publication of a progress report by the Department of Municipal Affairs. This document included a general plan for the town of Wasaga Beach, and committed the province to aid in the development of the town as a year-round park and recreation community by 1990.

Finally, the Robarts government began to address the outdoor recreation needs of south-central Ontario through a new program, entitled "Design for Development: The Toronto-Centred Region," unveiled in 1970 by the Regional Development Branch of the Department of Treasury, Economics and Inter-Governmental Affairs. "Design for Development" provided a basic planning concept for the orderly growth of the area within an arc extending 90 miles (144 kilometres) from Metropolitan Toronto. One of the policy recommendations for the region called for the maintenance of the Georgian Bay shoreline, Lake Simcoe, the Kawartha Lakes, and the Niagara Escarpment, for the sake of conservation and the recreational uses of the area's expanding population. And the OPIB, in order to play its part in the preparation of the Toronto-Centred Region concept, set an important precedent in 1969 by calling for the provision of seven near-urban parks along the Oak Ridges Moraine, which forms the height of land north of Lake Ontario and runs the length of the planning region.[15]

Ironically, instead of receiving verbal bouquets for these various efforts, the Robarts administration found itself showered with political brickbats. In April 1971, two weeks after William Davis replaced Robarts as premier, the Federation of Ontario Naturalists complained that the escarpment acquisition program had not been "proceeding at an adequate pace in view of the over-all need." Then, in early May, investigative reporters for the *London Free Press*, *Windsor Star*, and *Ottawa Citizen*, filed a series of stories about the escarpment, which painted a highly critical picture of the Robarts government's actions since Gertler's study. "Judging from the latest accounts of government inertia amid flourishing land speculation," editorialized the *Free Press*, "the escarpment may be in graver danger now than it was before the province proclaimed its interest in saving the magnificent bluff that runs from Niagara to the tip of the Bruce peninsula."[16]

The Liberal and NDP opposition parties also battered Premier Davis with charges that he, like his predecessor, was doing too little too late to save the escarpment from despoliation by developers. NDP Leader Stephen Lewis asserted that the government "is allowing the Niagara Escarpment to be sold, dismembered and denied to future public use ... we are alienating our finest recreational heritage in Southern Ontario through a perverse combination of neglect, indifference and special favours."[17] The reference to "special favours" added a sinister dimension to the political debate. Lewis and his Liberal counterpart, Robert Nixon, claimed that a 205-hectare property, purchased by the DLF in 1970 as part of the Forks of the Credit Provincial Park Reserve, had been acquired at a price double that paid for the same land a year earlier by Caledon Mountain Estates Ltd., a company with several prominent Conservative Party members on its board of directors. The opposition suspected that these directors might have been given confidential information prior to the public release of the Gertler Report in October 1969, information which would have enabled their company to buy the land rated by Gertler as a top priority for preservation by public acquisition. On 21 May, an angry and shaken Premier Davis responded to these charges by setting up a judicial enquiry, presided over by Chief Justice Colin E. Bennett.

The Wasaga Beach program also failed to win the Robarts government any praise. Despite the several million dollars spent on shoreline property acquisitions from 1963 to 1970, the blocks of land required for off-beach parking lots had not yet been consolidated when Robarts left office. Unfortunately, with the rise of Great Lakes' water levels after 1969, the width of the beach had been drastically reduced, resulting in extreme congestion and hazardous conditions for recreationists. In some places, there was barely space for two lanes of traffic; elsewhere, the road and one row of parked cars occupied all the available sand. Hope faded for an immediate solution to this situation when, in 1970, the DLF temporarily suspended land purchases at Wasaga because of financial constraints and the priority given to the Niagara Escarpment program in the property acquisition budget.[18] The residents and elected officials of Wasaga Beach became disgruntled when they saw no measurable returns to compensate for the loss of dozens of cottages and commercial establishments razed over the years to make room for the still-unfinished parking areas and recreational facilities.

Mounting complaints about the deteriorating conditions at Wasaga eventually caught the attention of the Toronto press. In June 1971, the *Globe and Mail* published an editorial that sharply criticized the province's record at the resort and claimed that the issue represented a test of Premier Davis's resolve to tackle difficult environmental issues. In the editor's opinion, the Wasaga issue was related on a philosophical plane to Davis's celebrated decision to halt construction of the Spadina Expressway, originally destined to run into the heart of Toronto. In justifying his Spadina decision, the premier had declared that "the future is for people ... [It] is not for profits, it is not for machines, it is not for systems and computers, it is not for technocrats – it is for people."[19] That being the case, insisted the *Globe and Mail*, it behooved Davis to translate his environmental credo into reality once again, this time by banishing cars from the Wasaga shoreline. "Now we have a Wasaga Expressway awaiting the Premier's attention."

Finally, toward the end of the Robarts regime, the proposal to build a chain of provincial parks along the Oak Ridges Moraine foundered. The timing of the proposal was poor. Despite favourable reactions to the OPIB's idea of creating provincial parks closer to Metropolitan Toronto, the Management Board of Cabinet chose not to fund the new initiative in 1970–71.

During the summer of 1971, then, as William Davis pondered the question of when to call his first general election as premier, he faced a host of provincial park issues left to him by the previous administration. Never before had so many park-related questions crowded the cabinet's agenda. Throughout that momentous pre-election period, the premier not only had to accommodate the preservationists in the battles over wilderness in Algonquin, Killarney, and Quetico, but also was compelled to grapple with the southern crisis in outdoor recreation.

The Davis Touch: Politics and Special Funding

The Wasaga Beach problem stood at the top of the cabinet's parks agenda during that summer. Stung by the criticism of the *Globe and Mail*, Davis rose to the challenge on 22 July by announcing that over the next six years, his government would allocate over $18 million to implement the official plan for the town of Wasaga Beach and expand the provincial park to rid the beach of the automobile. Such action, he promised, would create "what will be one of the finest year-round recreation centres on this continent." As the premier read his statement in the legislature, Stephen Lewis irreverently quipped: "Oh ho, the *Globe and Mail* wins again."

Davis then turned his attention to the Niagara Escarpment. On the morning of 13 September, he released the report of the judicial enquiry into the Caledon Mountain Estates affair.[20] Mr. Justice Bennett, having found no evidence of impropriety or wrongdoing, had exonerated the previous administration. Not accidentally, later that same day the premier called a general election for 21 October. Two weeks into the campaign, Davis answered the critics of the government's program for the Niagara Escarpment by announcing that over the next five years, his government would meet "the principal objectives and recommendations" of the Gertler report, and would make available the necessary funds (estimated at $30 million) for property and easement acquisition by dipping into the new land bank fund set aside in the previous provincial budget.[21]

Ten days after the escarpment announcement, Premier Davis declared his administration's intention to create Ontario's first near-urban-oriented provincial park at Bronte Creek, situated on the Oakville-Burlington town line, halfway between Hamilton and Toronto, along the Queen Elizabeth Way. This site had been considered for park purposes on previous occasions. As early as 1956, Ben Greenwood had inspected a small 32-hectare parcel of land, but rejected it because of its size and location. Three years later, the

Oakville-Trafalgar-Bronte Planning Board had recommended a 219-hectare site as a provincial park, but the proposal had been turned down by the OPIB because of high land costs, and because the site was deemed to be within the orbit of the Halton and Region Conservation Authority.[22]

Only after James W. Snow, MLA for Halton East and minister without portfolio in the first Davis cabinet, took an interest in the Bronte Creek site and approached the OPIB in the spring of 1971, did the idea of a near-urban park begin to move forward. On 27 July 1971, Snow gave the project the necessary political kick start in a persuasive presentation to the Ontario Parks Integration Board, emphasizing the area's potential for meeting the recreation objectives of the Toronto-Centred Region. After reevaluating the Bronte Creek site in August, Parks Branch planners recommended that some 809 hectares be acquired and developed as a provincial park.[23] Their proposal received the blessing of the OPIB and the Treasury Board in time for Premier Davis's pre-election announcement in September.

In his statement announcing the park, the premier emphasized that Bronte Creek would be "a dramatic departure from the established concept of provincial parks." For one thing, it would be "developed as a large recreational and educational park," designed to provide day-use recreation opportunities for the 1.5 million people who resided within a 40-kilometre radius in such urban communities as Hamilton, Burlington, Milton, Oakville, Mississauga, Port Credit, and Metropolitan Toronto. "This new park promises to bring a large number of city people closer to the pleasures and beauties of our natural environment," declared Davis. Bronte Creek would be operated on a year-round basis and be accessible by public transportation. It would also be the first provincial park to provide facilities designed with the needs of disabled people in mind. The visually impaired and persons with physical or developmental disabilities, who made up an estimated 7 percent of our population, explained the premier, "should find Bronte Creek Park unusually hospitable, with such special installations as nature trails with paved paths to accommodate wheelchairs, and hiking routes designed for maximum enjoyment by the blind." All in all, the Bronte Creek concept was a promising first response to opposition criticism about the geographical and class-based inequities of the provincial parks system.[24]

To its credit, the Davis government provided the special funding (that is, funding listed separately from the general budget for park acquisition), required to fill most of the park-related promises made during the 1971 election campaign. On the Niagara Escarpment, for instance, the Division of Parks alone spent over $13 million from 1972 to 1977 to acquire properties worthy of preservation for recreation and/or the protection of significant natural areas. This was the largest component of the $34 million total spent on parkland acquisition during this period.[25] While properties were being obtained, the government initiated the land-use planning required to conserve the

Children's farm, Bronte Creek Provincial Park. *Courtesy: Ministry of Natural Resources.*

Winter activities, Bronte Creek Provincial Park. *Courtesy: Ministry of Natural Resources.*

5,200-square-kilometre escarpment area. It proved to be an excruciatingly complicated and lengthy process, involving a maze of local planning issues, and requiring consultation with fifty-five municipalities and a host of interest groups and individuals. An interministerial task force, appointed in May 1972, began the process by holding public hearings, reviewing land acquisition priorities, and making recommendations on the possible implementation of the Gertler report. Acting on the basis of the task force's report, the government announced its escarpment policy in June 1973. The protection of recreation and natural resources would be achieved through a combination of property acquisition, purchase of easements, and land-use controls. Properties selected for public ownership would be chosen with three priorities in mind: their unique and historic features, their potential for offering near-urban recreational facilities, and whether they offered the best route for the Bruce Trail. That same month, the government adopted the Niagara Escarpment Planning and Development Act, legislation which established the Niagara Escarpment Commission (NEC) to prepare a master plan for the area. The purpose of the legislation was "to provide for the maintenance of the Niagara Escarpment and lands in its vicinity as a continuous natural environment, and to ensure [that] only such development occurs as is compatible with that natural environment." As it happened, the commission only published its proposed plan in November 1979, and followed it with another two years of review hearings and discussions with various municipalities. At last, in 1985, the Niagara Escarpment Plan, based on the recommendations of the NEC, the hearings officers, and the provincial secretary for resources development, received cabinet approval.[26]

Throughout this decade of planning, Parks Division personnel worked closely with NEC staff to ensure that the parks being created along the escarpment formed a compatible subsystem within the overall classification framework for provincial parks. The NEC applied the classification policy to all agencies owning and managing parklands on the escarpment, including municipalities, conservation authorities, the Niagara Parks Commission, Parks Canada, the St. Lawrence Seaway Authority, and the Ontario Heritage Foundation.

By the end of the Davis regime, a subsystem of provincial parks had already emerged in the planning region. When Leonard Gertler wrote his report in 1968, only three provincial parks could be found along the entire escarpment, the small Craigleith and Devil's Glen Recreational parks, inherited from the Department of Highways, and the more substantial Cyprus Lake Natural Environment Provincial Park at the tip of the Bruce Peninsula. Fifteen years later, an impressive chain of six Natural Environment, three Recreation, and seven Nature Reserve provincial parks had taken shape. All but one of the Natural Environment and Recreation parks were located directly on the Bruce Trail. Excluding Cyprus Lake and Fathom Five near Tobermory, all the new Natural Environment and Recreation parks were located within 120 kilometres of Toronto, making them all readily accessible to the urban residents of south-central Ontario. These new parks included the Forks of the Credit near Caledon, with its spectacular cataract and gorge and five distinct and significant ecological areas, containing over four hundred kinds of flowering plants; Mono Cliffs, located just north of Orangeville, a site rich in geological features typical of the escarpment, including the main scarp, two prominent outliers, crevice caves, a rolling upland plateau, cliff faces, and talus slopes; and the scenic Short Hills near St. Catharines, one of the few remaining areas between Hamilton and Niagara Falls that offered residents a relatively large natural environment, containing a headwaters area and a wonderful mix of Carolinian forest species, habitats, and open space for passive recreational opportunities.

The Federation of Ontario Naturalists acknowledged the significance of the government's accomplishment on the escarpment after most of the new parks were officially regulated in 1985. "These parks will preserve the Niagara Escarpment as an international treasure, both aesthetically and biologically," declared the FON. "The special geology, soils, forests, rare species, and pastoral landscapes all make the escarpment a key piece of Ontario's landscape legacy." FON members were especially gratified to see Nature Reserves established to protect representative and significant areas of the Bruce Peninsula – Smokey Head, White Bluff, Duncan Crevice Caves, Lion's Head, Bayview Escarpment, Little Cove, Cabot Head, noted for its spectacularly rugged and much photographed shoreline, and Hope Bay Forest, with its outstanding karst topography, eloquently described by one naturalist as a "jumbled stone surface lying atop ancient, collapsed caves, mantled with a 'cathedral' forest and lush mosses, lichens, and rare plants."[27]

Of all the escarpment parks created during this period, Fathom Five at Tobermory stands out as the most unique and innovative; it was Canada's first underwater park, embracing nearly 10,000 hectares of water space and a small land base on the mainland. The original advocates of the marine park in 1970 – Tom Lee, a future director of the Park Planning Branch (1972–75) and Interpretive Supervisor Gary Sealey – took advantage of the opportunity provided by the Gertler report and convinced the OPIB that it should authorize the project.[28] Their proposal for what was unquestionably one of the most intriguing and productive freshwater environments in Canada excited all who perused it. While most underwater parks elsewhere in the world were centred around a single resource, a reef or a series of shipwrecks, they explained how Fathom Five offered a variety of features. Nineteen shipwrecks had been located within the park's boundaries, a record which collectively evoked the history of Great Lakes sail and steam shipping. Biologically speaking, the park contains components of two distinct aquatic ecosystems – the deep, cold waters of Georgian Bay and the shallow, more temperate waters of Lake Huron – both merging to create an enormously rich and complex pattern of floral and faunal communities. Also, Fathom Five offers recreationists and researchers an opportunity to view some of the outstanding geological and

Map 5: Niagara Escarpment Parks System

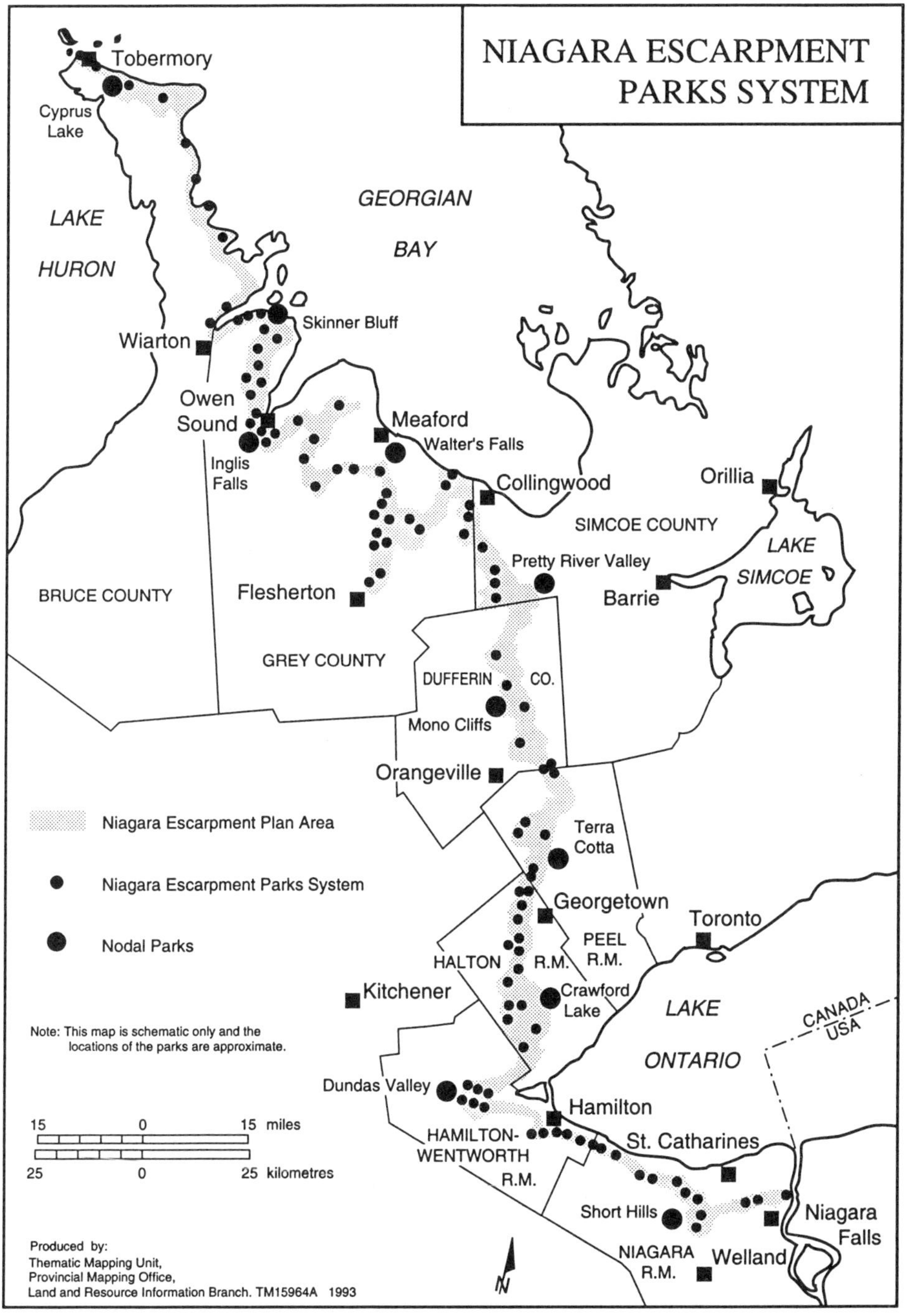

NIAGARA ESCARPMENT PARKS SYSTEM
Tobermory
Cyprus Lake
LAKE HURON
GEORGIAN BAY
Skinner Bluff
Wiarton
Owen Sound
Inglis Falls
Meaford
Walter's Falls
Collingwood
Orillia
SIMCOE COUNTY
LAKE SIMCOE
Pretty River Valley
Barrie
BRUCE COUNTY
Flesherton
GREY COUNTY
DUFFERIN CO.
Mono Cliffs
Orangeville
Niagara Escarpment Plan Area
Niagara Escarpment Parks System
Nodal Parks
Terra Cotta
Georgetown
Toronto
PEEL R.M.
HALTON R.M.
Kitchener
Crawford Lake
LAKE ONTARIO
CANADA
USA
Note: This map is schematic only and the locations of the parks are approximate.
Dundas Valley
Hamilton
15 0 15 miles
25 0 25 kilometres
HAMILTON-WENTWORTH R.M.
St. Catharines
Short Hills
Niagara Falls
NIAGARA R.M.
Welland
N
Produced by:
Thematic Mapping Unit,
Provincial Mapping Office,
Land and Resource Information Branch. TM15964A 1993

geomorphological features of southern Ontario. Fluctuating lake levels since glacial times have created raised boulder beaches, sea caves, and "flowerpots" on the shorelines, while beneath the surface, the absence of overburden allows for the viewing of dramatic glacial remnants such as erratics, *roches moutonnées*, tills, striae, and gougings. The creation of Fathom Five underwater park, and the release of its master plan in 1973, attracted international attention and elicited favourable comments from park agencies in North America, Europe, and Asia.[29]

After the election of October 1971, Premier Davis also made good on his Wasaga Beach pledge. By mid-1975, some $6.3 million had been spent on expanding the provincial park from just over 121 to 1,335 hectares in size.[30] Most significantly, in 1973, the back-land parking zones were finally consolidated, allowing for the removal of automobiles from the beach. The expanded park comprised two distinct sections, the beach and the dunes area, each to be developed independently, so as to form almost two parks under one name. Along the 142-hectare, 14-kilometre linear beach area, planners intended to provide a variety of water-oriented, day-use recreational activities, while in the 1,194-hectare dunes area, significant for its geomorphology, natural features, and cultural history, the master plan prescribed zoning and management policies to protect fragile areas.[31]

Once the park had been expanded and a draft master plan prepared (November 1975), the Division of Parks began to accelerate the development of the facility, especially in the beach area. This phase involved the construction of boardwalks, interpretive displays, children's creative playgrounds (an innovation for provincial parks), informal grass and sand court sports areas, amateur quality hard-surfaced courts for tennis and shuffleboard, open play spaces for field sports, artificial and natural skating rinks, change rooms and washroom facilities, and hiking and cross-country ski trails in the dunes area. This amount of recreational development drew a negative reaction from the members of the Federation of Ontario Naturalists. "We are prepared to accept the area currently being planned as a provincial park," conceded the FON, "*only* because we believe that it offers the sole hope for protecting any of the provincially significant, biological areas which occur at Wasaga Beach."[32] The Division of Parks justified the policy on the grounds that Wasaga Beach had to be treated differently, since it was the only park located entirely within the boundaries and built-up areas of a resort town. Provision had to be made to allow some community-oriented recreational opportunities, as well as the facilities to attract short- and long-term visitors. There the matter rested; the naturalists fretted over the concessions to the recreation-tourist imperatives, while the previously disenchanted local residents began to appreciate the benefits of having a provincial park in their midst.

The Davis government also swiftly fulfilled its 1971 pre-election promise to develop a near-urban provincial park at Bronte Creek. By 1975, the province had invested approximately $5.5 million to acquire some 809 hectares of ravine and previously cultivated tableland, and had spent another $2.4 million on the initial development of the park, including hydro-electric power, water and sewage services, grading, entrance roads, and parking facilities.[33] From the beginning, the government invited the public to play a role in the planning process. An advisory committee, appointed in January 1972, began its work by soliciting written submissions on policy, which were incorporated in a proposed policy planning report, released for public discussion in March 1972.[34] After conducting public hearings in Oakville and Burlington, the advisory committee submitted its final report to the consultant firm, Project Planning Associates Ltd., commissioned to prepare the provisional master plan for Bronte Creek. Completed in July, approved by the advisory committee in August, the master plan was adopted by the minister of natural resources in December. The following July, the Cabinet Committee on Resource Development endorsed in principle the construction of the essential features of the plan at an estimated cost of $10 million over five years, with completion to be phased in over a longer period. It was a remarkably rapid and successful planning exercise and a model of public participation. James Keenan described it in September 1973 as "perhaps our most complete achievement in master planning yet," and warmly acknowledged the role of division planner Norm Richards, a future director of the Parks and Recreational Areas Branch, who "personally spearheaded" the project.[35]

By the late 1970s, Bronte Creek boasted a unique atmosphere for a provincial park, one that balanced heavy day-use outdoor recreation, protection of the natural environment, and "living" agricultural history. The park had been developed to offer visitors a "threshold" experience, in which programmed recreation would provide young and old alike with an opportunity to expand their interest in natural and cultural environments. Interpretive trails allowed urbanites to learn about the natural history of the Bronte ravine, or the chance to observe the countryside and the changes it had undergone over the decades. Children's recreation was also built into the natural and cultural environments of the park. At the children's farm, for example, youngsters can amuse themselves in the barn's play loft (outfitted with swings, slides, and hay jumps) and experience a working farm environment first-hand. An adventure playground has also been constructed within a cherry orchard. Other recreation facilities in the park include a five-acre recreation complex that contains a 6,500-square-metre swimming pool, eight floodlit tennis courts, a multipurpose court for basketball, volleyball, and shuffleboard (converted into an artificial ice surface during the winter months), a toboggan hill, and bicycle and cross-country ski rental facilities.

In addition to this intensive recreational development, the Parks Division also made an unusual effort to protect and to utilize the late-nineteenth-century rural Ontario farm buildings in the park, and to interpret for visitors the agricultural traditions of the area. The Spruce Lane farmhouse, built in 1899, was meticulously renovated, then furnished as it would have appeared at the turn of the century. Even the farm outbuildings – cattle and horse barns, fowl houses, icehouse, and woodshed – were all painstakingly restored on the original foundations. Visitors now experience the everyday sights and sounds of an old-fashioned family farm with its horse-powered technology. With so much to offer the surrounding urban population, Bronte Creek quickly became popular, attracting 208,000 people in 1979 – making it the fourth most visited provincial park in the system that year.

The new departure in park development at Bronte Creek raised the question of whether the government would establish other near-urban parks elsewhere in the province. The answer came sooner than expected. In December 1971, a mere three months after the premier's announcement on Bronte Creek, the Ontario Parks Integration Board approved the creation of a provincial park on Pêche Island, located in the Detroit River, within the municipal boundaries of the city of Windsor. This decision came as a surprise for two reasons. First, it reversed the long-standing OPIB policy not to establish island parks because of the difficulties and expense of providing public access, water, and sewage facilities. Second, the OPIB had turned down Pêche Island as a provincial park location just seven months earlier, in May 1971. Although unwilling to establish a provincial park on the island, the Davis cabinet had bowed to local pressures in May and submitted a bid on the property, after it had been placed on the auction block by its American owners. On this occasion, the foreign-ownership issue prompted government action. Many Ontarians were anxious about the massive economic and cultural impact of American culture on their way of life, and it was an issue championed vigorously by the New Democratic Party. Sensitive to these trends, Provincial Treasurer Darcy McKeough, MLA for Kent West, favoured the idea and played no small role in persuading his cabinet colleagues to authorize the purchase of the property.[36] The province's offer of $424,000 for Pêche Island, an adjoining 40-hectare water lot, and a small area on the river-front mainland proved successful. As for the future disposition of the property, Lands and Forests Minister René Brunelle explained that it would be "retained in Canada to be developed at some future date by ... a municipal authority."[37]

All the same, by the end of the year, the government's thinking on the future development of Pêche Island had been reversed. In the excitement generated within the Parks Branch by the Bronte Creek project, planning supervisor Tom Lee reexamined the island as a possible site for a second near-urban provincial park. Together with Lake Erie District Naturalist Robert Mitton, and W.R. Jenkins, superintendent at Holiday Beach Provincial Park, Lee submitted a report extolling the island's virtues – its excellent beaches, safe water conditions, good fishing, wooded areas, numerous species of wildlife, high potential for picnicking, walking and bicycle trails, and outdoor recreational activities. Lee's enthusiasm was infectious. The report convinced the OPIB in December 1971 that it should reverse its previous decision and designate Pêche Island as a near-urban provincial park.[38]

Early in 1972, the OPIB also authorized the investigation of a third area, destined to become a near-urban park reserve – the scenic wooded valley and meadow land of the Kilworth-Komoka section of the Thames Valley, just west of London. As in the case of both the Bronte Creek and Pêche Island sites, this area had been proposed as a park as early as 1964, when the Central Middlesex Planning Board brought it to the attention of the DLF. The Parks Branch, however, had considered this property more suited to management by the Upper Thames Valley Conservation Authority.[39] Nearly a decade later, the government's thinking had changed in the face of demand for day-use outdoor recreation in the London region. Accordingly, the Davis cabinet agreed in December 1973 to establish a 526-hectare near-urban provincial park at Komoka. Minister of Natural Resources Leo Bernier outlined the reasons for the decision: "The park at Komoka will relate to the London area in much the same way as Bronte Creek Park will relate to the 'Golden Horseshoe ... In this era of restricted energy and gasoline supplies, we feel it is very important to bring parks to the people, instead of having them travel hundreds of miles."[40] Bernier expected the new park to reduce user pressure on Ipperwash and the Pinery, while setting a precedent as the first provincial park in southwestern Ontario not located on the Great Lakes shoreline.

Regrettably, the development of Komoka Provincial Park ran into trouble from the outset. Division and regional personnel had rushed to obtain government approval to create the park in a race against time to use up their land acquisition budget for 1973–74. In the haste, no one had thought to undertake a full property study of the site. The results were embarrassing. No sooner had Natural Resources Minister Bernier announced the park in January, than it came to light that a plan for a 20-hectare subdivision within the Komoka park reserve had been approved just a few weeks earlier, by local and provincial housing authorities. "This has created the obvious impression amongst the public," admitted James Keenan, "that the right hand does not know what the left hand is doing in the Government, and to the best of my knowledge we were not aware that this subdivision was being processed."[41] This administrative mix-up proved to be a portent of things to come.

During 1972–73, Division of Parks personnel also began to consider one of the Niagara Escarpment park reserves – Short Hills, near St. Catharines – for development as a near-urban provincial park. Following the successful experience with Bronte Creek, the government appointed an advisory committee in October 1973 to evaluate the reserve, hold public hearings, and to make policy recommendations for a ministry master-planning team.[42] Significantly, the type of near-urban park projected after the completion of this exercise contrasted sharply with the Bronte Creek model. Instead of being classified, developed, and managed as a Recreation park, Short Hills was to be designated a Natural Environment park, with more emphasis on the protection of outstanding natural features, such as the Niagara Escarpment and the Twelve Mile Creek cold water fishery. Like Bronte Creek, Short Hills would be oriented toward day-use activities on a year-round basis, but planners made no attempt to include such things as a recreation complex, children's farm, creative play areas, and the like. Such facilities would only be provided in areas around the perimeter of the park, if agreements could be negotiated with private and public landowners.[43]

By 1974, despite the noteworthy precedents at Bronte Creek, Pêche Island, Komoka, and Short Hills, the near-urban park concept was beginning to cause division planners many problems. No consensus existed as to how many of these parks were required, whether or not they should be designated a separate class of park, with distinct management policies, or as to the degree to which responsibility for their development would be shared with municipalities and conservation authorities. This situation prevailed, in part because the phenomenon of near-urban parks had not emerged out of any predetermined planning or policy framework. "The concern for near-urban recreation," explained James Keenan, "has been essentially a political matter."[44] Public and opposition pressure had prompted the Davis government to respond to individual near-urban park proposals on an ad hoc basis. Aware that a near-urban park program was evolving haphazardly, division personnel prepared a program initiative for cabinet approval in 1973. In the subsequent priority review of new programs by the six ministers grouped in the Resources Development Policy Field, no funds were allocated for the proposal. The following year, the Division of Parks presented for consideration a second, scaled-down version of the original submission. Briefly, the division wanted to concentrate its efforts in the Central Ontario Lakeshore Urbanization Complex (COLUC), an infelicitous bureaucratic name for the area contained within the boundaries of the new regional governments that had been created since the late 1960s in the Toronto-Centred Region. The Parks Division asked for no less than $22.4 million over five years for the acquisition of major sites in the COLUC area and another $24.4 million in development and operational funds. The division also requested another $4 million to develop the Komoka and Pêche Island park reserves.[45]

This program initiative turned out to be nothing more than a pipe dream. For one thing, it did not enjoy the support of influential senior managers within the Ministry of Natural Resources. The massive costs of Bronte Creek had disturbed people like William T. Foster, assistant deputy minister, southern Ontario, and Walter Giles, assistant deputy minister, lands and waters. They feared that a near-urban park program might drain limited financial resources from what they considered more important ministry activities. Foster's opposition was especially aggressive. He questioned the validity of the demand projections for outdoor recreation in provincial parks, and expressed the opinion that either municipal and regional governments or the conservation authorities would be able to provide near-urban parkland more efficiently and effectively than the Parks Division. Foster's thinking was later echoed by the Ontario Parks Association, a provincewide organization, representing seventy municipalities. This group argued that local governments should be given responsibility for near-urban parks through special legislation, and a provincial granting structure similar to the one provided under the Parks Assistance Act. To confuse the matter further, academics such as John Marsh, a geographer at Trent University, argued that the conservation authorities were "potentially the most suitable managing agency."[46] This debate dragged on unresolved through the 1970s. Lacking a consensus on the question of responsibility, the government was not inclined to favour any near-urban park program proposal.

Apart from the responsibility issue, the COLUC area proposal could not have been made at a less opportune time. The year before, Premier Davis had instructed all his ministers to curtail spending on existing programs and generally to avoid introducing new ones. The premier intended to keep "the growth ... of the public service during the next few years ... to an absolute minimum ... Any further expansion of the size of the government relative to the private sector," he believed, "could jeopardize our future economic survival and well-being in an increasingly competitive world."[47] For these reasons, then, the once-promising near-urban provincial parks strategy disappeared in 1974, lost in the clouds of constraint and agency confusion.

Nuclear Impact: Inverhuron and MacGregor Point

Although the Parks Division failed to obtain funds to develop near-urban parkland in southwestern Ontario in 1974, it did receive special funding from an unusual source to create a new thousand-hectare park at MacGregor Point, on Lake Huron in southern Bruce County. In this unique case, the Ontario Hydro-Electric Commission financed the purchase of the bulk of the privately owned lands required for the park at a cost of over $600,000 between 1974 and 1978. Ontario Hydro's involvement was due to an awkward situation that emerged in 1969, during the construction of a heavy-water plant on a site contiguous to Inverhuron Provincial Park. In November of that year, Parks Branch chief Peter Addison became alarmed when he read newspaper reports that Hydro had decided to relocate a planned nuclear generator farther away from the new heavy-water plant, "because of the danger to human life due to a possible escape of hydrogen sulphide gas." Understandably, Addison wondered about the safety of the overnight campers at Inverhuron, some 2,000 of whom crowded the park daily during the peak season. Discussions with the Radiation Protection Section of the Department of Health deepened his concern. Evidently "a real danger" did exist. Addison learned that a recent accident at the Glace Bay heavy-water plant in Nova Scotia had released thirty tons of hydrogen sulphide gas into the atmosphere. Fortunately, on that occasion the wind had blown the gas out to sea. "It is somewhat disturbing," Addison reported to Deputy Minister G.H.U. Bayly, "that this whole project was undertaken without notifying this department ... of the risks involved to patrons of our park ... [It is] conceivable that our park [will] have to be completely abandoned."[48] This was an unpleasant scenario, because Inverhuron was one of the region's outstanding Natural Environment parks, renowned for its recreational, archaeological, and earth and life science features.

Unfortunately, the Bruce Heavy Water Plant Safety Advisory Committee, set up under the auspices of the Atomic Energy Control Board of Canada, confirmed that the plant did indeed pose a threat to campers at Inverhuron. The campgrounds lay within the safety setback (Ontario Hydro used the euphemism "greenbelt"), required under the Atomic Energy Board's siting guidelines for heavy-water plant facilities. To resolve this situation, the Ministry of Natural Resources and Ontario Hydro negotiated an agreement in 1972, whereby title to Inverhuron was turned over to Hydro, and then leased back to the ministry for 999 years, to be maintained and operated as a day-use park only. In exchange, Ontario Hydro agreed to finance the purchase of private lands required for a new park at MacGregor Point, about twenty-five kilometres to the north of Inverhuron.[49]

The news of this arrangement occasioned an outcry from the NDP and from conservationist groups, who viewed the sale of Inverhuron as "an assault on the integrity" of the provincial park system. "This is not just a local issue," proclaimed the Algonquin Wildlands League, "it is a dangerous precedent that concerns all Ontario citizens, for parkland should be inviolate and *never* sold to industry, government-controlled or not."[50] The AWL deplored Ontario Hydro's failure, either to obtain prior "community consent" on the location of the heavy-water plant, or to invite public discussion on environmental and safety considerations. This was the dark side of the politics of special funding.

Federal-Provincial Agreements: ARDA and CORTS

In addition to the special-funding decisions made by the Davis government, two federal-provincial agreements shaped the priorities of Ontario's Division of Parks on parkland acquisition and development after 1967. The first of these intergovernmental relationships was worked out under the terms of the federal Agricultural and Rehabilitation (later Rural) Development Act (ARDA). Under this program, Ottawa provided financial assistance on a cost-sharing basis, to assist in underwriting the purchase and start-up costs on new provincial parks in economically depressed and declining rural areas. Governments now recognized that a major source of opportunities for alternative income and employment could be generated in depressed rural areas through the expansion of the tourist and outdoor recreation industry associated with provincial parks. Thus, in 1967, Ottawa agreed to provide half the funds required to purchase and develop five provincial parks in areas of rural Ontario deemed suitable for ARDA funding – Arrowhead in the Muskoka District, Carillon in Prescott County, Charleston Lake in Leeds County, Cyprus Lake at the tip of the Bruce Peninsula, and Silent Lake in Haliburton County. Subsequent agreements signed between 1967 and 1975 resulted in ARDA funding for Awenda, Bon Echo, Halfway Lake, McRae Point, and Murphy's Point provincial parks. By the end of the fiscal year 1972–73, Ontario's Division of Parks had received approximately $2.7 million in federal support.[51]

The second area of federal-provincial cooperation with potential for relieving outdoor recreational pressures in southern Ontario bore fruit in 1971 with the publication of *The Rideau–Trent–Severn: Yesterday, Today, Tomorrow*, the report of the Canada-Ontario Rideau-Trent-Severn (CORTS) Committee. Made up of representatives of fifteen federal and provincial departments and agencies, the committee had laboured for four years, in close consultation with local governments and the public, to examine the entire 680-kilometre Rideau-Trent-Severn waterway system between Ottawa and Georgian Bay. Through the program outlined in *Yesterday, Today, Tomorrow,* the committee hoped to provide along the waterway for a pollution-free environment, adequate undeveloped open space, optimum recreational development, the preservation and interpretation of significant historical and cultural resources, as well as adequate commercial and private development. The report identified sectors where deficiencies in the supply of outdoor recreation existed, and included recommendations for specific courses of action by various levels of government.

For Ontario's Division of Parks, the CORTS committee proposed a large and expensive program, involving the development of eleven extended-use parks on public lands already reserved for provincial park purposes along the waterway corridor, and the acquisition of new properties for both extended-use and day-use parks. In addition, the committee looked to the Parks Division to develop archaeological interpretation centres at Petroglyphs and Serpent Mounds parks, and systems of canoe routes, snowmobile, ski, walking, cycling, and horseback riding trails throughout the planning area. In February 1975, the federal and Ontario governments took the first step toward implementing the CORTS program and signed an agreement, accepting the broad objectives outlined in *Yesterday, Today, Tomorrow*, detailing the administrative arrangements and division of responsibilities required to proceed.[52]

In accordance with the agreement, the Division of Parks accelerated its activities along the waterway. In the Rideau sector, where substantial park reserves already existed, priority was given to development projects at Frontenac, Charleston Lake, Murphy's Point, Casey Point, Kilmarnock, and Mouth of the Tay. Land acquisitions along the Rideau were modest and undertaken primarily to expand existing parks and park reserves.[53] The major land acquisitions inspired by CORTS during the mid-1970s occurred along the Trent sector of the waterway, an area within the Toronto-Centred Region. Within the dual planning context of the CORTS–Toronto-Centred Region, the Parks Division obtained approval to proceed with the acquisition of park reserves at Indian Point on Balsam Lake, Boyd Island in Pigeon Lake near Bobcaygeon, Carthew Bay on Lake Simcoe, an extension to Lake on the Mountain Park in Prince Edward County, and the Quakenbush farm, the site of one of the most northerly Iroquois habitations known, dating back to sometime between 1400 and 1500 AD.[54]

A Trails System for Ontario: Opportunity Lost

For a brief time during the mid-1970s, it seemed as if the development of recreation trails would become another of the politically favoured elements deemed worthy of special funding within the Parks Division's program. Prior to 1967, the province's role in this area had been minimal, limited to creating hiking trails and canoe routes in provincial parks and on conservation authority lands. Outside the parks, as the great crush to get outdoors grew during the 1960s, voluntary trail organizations sprang into existence and began to plan and to develop recreation corridors on a self-help basis. The Bruce Trail Association, a leader in this work, laid out a hiking route along the entire length of the Niagara Escarpment, by successfully negotiating informal right-of-passage agreements with a host of private landowners. Completed in 1967, this remarkable achievement served as an inspiration for groups all over the province. Hiking enthusiasts began laying out the Ganaraska Trail from Port Hope to Collingwood, and the Rideau Trail from Kingston to Ottawa, while equestrians worked on the Great Pine Ridge Trail network, along the height of land from the Trent River to the Niagara Escarpment. On the local level throughout southern Ontario, snowmobilers, cross-country ski enthusiasts, hikers, bicyclists, trail bike, and four-wheel-drive vehicle owners developed dozens of smaller trails for their own enjoyment.

These volunteer projects, however, could not meet the burgeoning demand for trail-oriented recreation facilities. Recreation survey data gathered between 1967 and 1973 indicated that trail activities ranked among the most popular outdoor recreation pursuits, and that during these years participation rates in snowmobiling had increased roughly sevenfold, hiking fourfold, bicycling threefold, and canoeing twofold.[55] In the face of such demand, the trail clubs looked perforce to the provincial government for assistance, in the form of basic technical advice and the granting of rights of passage over Crown land when they developed trails for public use, and eventually for funding.

The province began to play a more active part after 1967. In that year the Parks Branch assumed responsibility for establishing, operating, and maintaining canoe routes and hiking trails on Crown land, a task previously undertaken by the Lands and Surveys Branch of the Department of Lands and

Forests. Programming canoe routes was tackled first, in view of the many requests for accurate and detailed information on paddling opportunities in areas other than provincial parks, but also because planners wanted to reduce congestion on the interior waterways in Algonquin and Quetico parks. Through the combined efforts of William Charlton and John Featherston in the management section at main office, assisted by district staff, the Parks Branch compiled detailed descriptions of approximately 17,700 kilometres of canoe routes throughout the northern part of the province. This research became the basis of the popular publication *Canoe Routes of Ontario* (1981).

Another dimension of trails programming also required immediate attention – the snowmobile phenomenon and the concomitant surge in demand for winter recreation trails, both in provincial parks and on Crown lands. With astonishing rapidity, Ontarians embraced the modern two-person snowmobile as a recreation vehicle. Introduced for commercial sale in 1959–60 by Bombardier Ltd. of Quebec (the company marketed a modest 225 of their Ski-Doo that winter), within a decade there were 113,000 registered snowmobiles in Ontario alone and, by 1973, 18 percent of the province's residents were snowmobiling. Two-thirds of the machines were bought by southern Ontarians, with ownership being equally distributed between urban and rural populations. Families who had previously gone into recreational hibernation during the winter months now waited eagerly for the first fall of snow. The snowmobile, noted one study, "made snow something to be eagerly anticipated by thousands who have traditionally considered it something to be shovelled, stuck in or cursed at."[56]

The sudden impact of the snowmobile boom at the end of the 1960s, quickly followed by the new interest in cross-country skiing, forced the Parks Branch to review its traditional winter programming in the provincial parks and on Crown land. Until 1968, the parks system had all but closed down for the winter months, with only a few exceptions. Beginning in 1960–61, for example, three parks were kept open during the winter to provide day-use sports activities, tobogganing and skating at Darlington and Kakabeka Falls, with skiing added to the mix at the Pinery. A fourth park, Kap-Kig-Iwan near Englehart, remained open for tobogganing in 1963–64. High operating deficits, low midweek use, the availability of alternative facilities, and an official policy against competing with the private sector kept the winter program from expanding further at that time.[57]

Recognizing the exploding popularity of recreational snowmobiling, Lands and Forests Minister René Brunelle announced an expansion of the winter program in provincial parks in February 1968. He officially acknowledged that snowmobiling was "a most acceptable form of healthful and enjoyable winter recreation," and would henceforth be "accommodated on certain parklands in a manner consistent with our park [master] plans and in areas ... designated for the purpose."[58] That same winter, the Parks Branch introduced

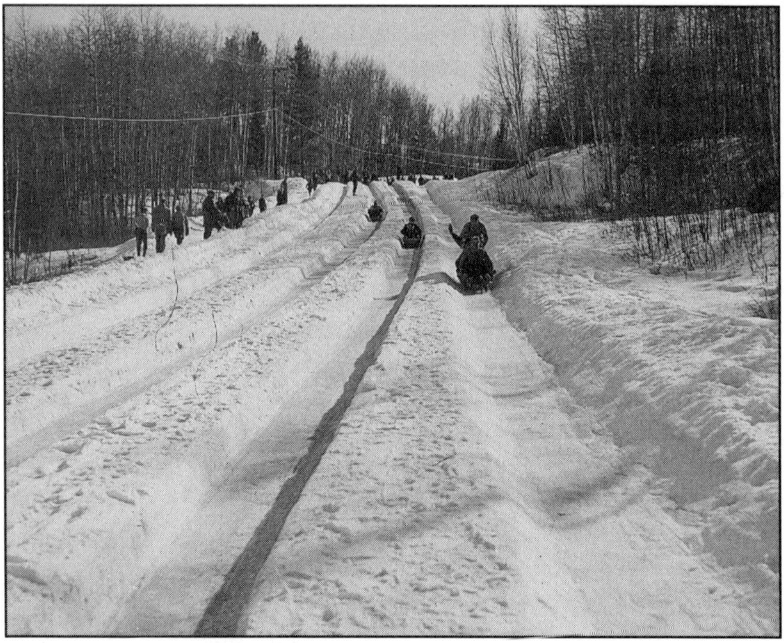

Sleigh riding, Kakabeka Falls Provincial Park, 1961.
Courtesy: Ministry of Natural Resources.

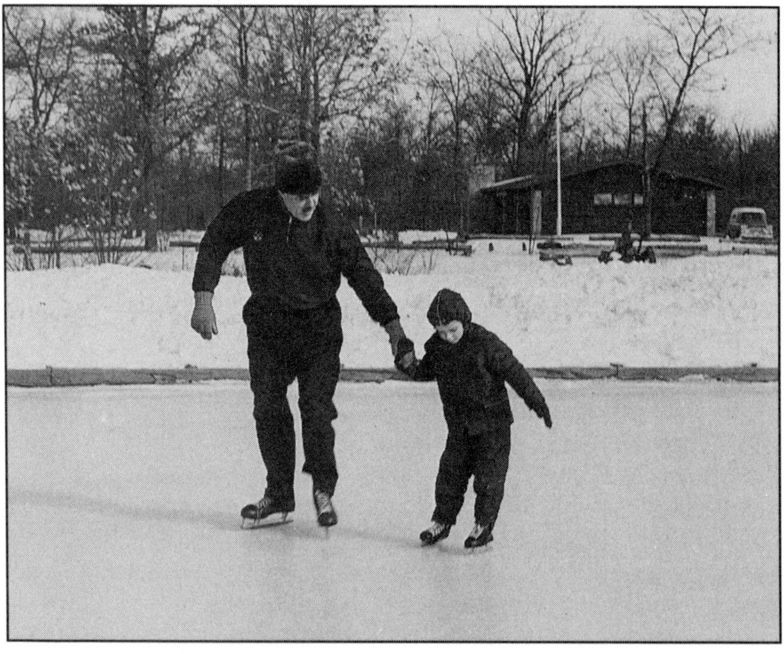

Premier John P. Robarts skating with son Timmy at Pinery Provincial Park, February 1963. *Courtesy: Ministry of Natural Resources.*

fully serviced winter camping in three provincial parks, Arrowhead, the Pinery, and Sibbald Point. Snowmobilers who lived in the cities of southern Ontario flocked in considerable numbers to those parks. As Management Section Supervisor William Charlton and his staff monitored their impact, restrictions had to be imposed to protect primitive, natural and historic zones, wildlife wintering areas, waterfowl habitats, and nature trails, but also to separate snowmobilers from cross-country skiers and other nonmechanized recreation seekers. At first, only eight provincial parks were entirely closed to the snow machines, but by 1971, the government had prohibited them in eleven provincial parks and five Nature Reserves, and had restricted snowmobile travel in fifteen other parks to designated and marked trails, when these were covered with a minimum of six inches of snow. Elsewhere, snowmobilers could use park roads (1,125 kilometres in total).[59]

Snowmobile usage across the provincial park system quickly reached troublesome proportions. In September 1970, Chief of Parks Peter Addison reported that "there is an urgent need for the designation and development of additional snowmobiling areas in southern and central Ontario to relieve the pressure from our park system."[60] Beginning in 1968, in fact, lands and forests field staff developed three trails (90 kilometres in total) on an experimental basis on Crown lands in the Coldwater and Parry Sound areas. The cost to the Parks Branch had not exceeded $10,000 a year. Addison now considered it time to augment the trails budget and pointed to the Minnesota example to support his case. That state, with approximately the same number of registered snowmobiles as Ontario, was already spending $190,000 a year to develop and maintain snowmobile facilities.

The government accepted the Parks Branch's arguments and subsequently expanded the number of winter trails on Crown lands, to supplement those available in provincial parks, as well as those maintained by clubs, winter resorts, and private landowners. By the winter of 1971–72, the management section was overseeing the operation of eleven snowmobile trails and two extensive areas of Crown land, which provided a total of 530 kilometres of marked trails. More significantly, the government inaugurated the Winter Trails Recreation Program in 1974, which provided grants to clubs and conservation authorities to assist in grooming and maintaining snowmobile trails, and the following year extended the program to include cross-country ski trail development. In the first four years of this scheme, the province granted $1.1 million to the clubs. By 1977–78, the annual budget for the program had reached $500,000, a figure sufficient to maintain 8,045 kilometres of trails.[61] On top of this, the Ministry of Natural Resources itself operated another 1,600 kilometres of snowmobile and cross-country ski trails on Crown lands outside provincial parks.

Snowmobilers were but one voice in the chorus crying out for more recreational opportunities on public lands in the 1970s. One of the refrains repeatedly heard in these years was the need for government to plan and to develop a network of provincial trails in a more comprehensive fashion, rather than continuing the sporadic and uncoordinated approach of the recent past. During the provincial election campaign of October 1971, the Conservation Council of Ontario and the Algonquin Wildlands League prodded the Davis government to expand its role in the planning and development of a trails system. "As the pressure increases," the CCO president, J.W.B. Sisam noted, "a wise amalgam of public and private effort will become necessary."[62] The conservationists also wanted legislation to provide mechanisms and guidelines for the establishment of a system of provincial trails, an interministerial council on trails, and a permanent citizens' advisory council.

In the Parks Branch, system planner Russell Irvine waxed enthusiastic about the proposal. Having specialized in recreational trails planning as a graduate student at the University of Illinois, he knew that trail opportunities were rapidly dwindling across the densely populated regions of North America. He also realized that the volunteer trail clubs were facing enormous difficulties as they tried to maintain the long inter-regional recreation corridors. On the Bruce Trail, for instance, landowners had begun to revoke the public's right of passage in response to the numbers of hikers and snowmobilers crossing their properties. Housing developers and quarry operators were also denying the public access to large and desirable sections of the escarpment. Lacking capital funds for land acquisition, the Bruce Trail Association was waging a losing battle to maintain optimum route alignments. To compound the problem, the thorny legal issue of liability for personal injuries sustained on trail rights of way was making many landowners reluctant to grant the right of passage to recreationists. Irvine also noted that the volunteer clubs could not resolve the intensifying conflicts between mechanized and non-mechanized recreation groups, since all were entitled to use the trails. Nor did the clubs possess the financial means to build facilities such as footbridges, shelters, and wells. Private entrepreneurs were not likely to come to the rescue; after all, recreation trail ventures promised little in the way of profits. All of these considerations led Irvine to recommend that the Parks Division launch a program to plan and develop a system of trails.[63]

In taking this position, Irvine and his colleagues drew their inspiration from the United States. In 1962, the Outdoor Recreation Resources Review Commission had raised the issue of trails planning by calling for greater efforts by all levels of government to build recreation into the environment and the landscape of everyday life, especially by means of walking and bicycle trails in near-urban areas. Federal authorities took no action on this recommendation until 1965, when U.S. President Lyndon B. Johnson used his "Natural Beauty Message" to invite state and local authorities and private interests to cooperate with his administration in developing a balanced national trails system. In April 1966, Secretary of the Interior Stewart Udall instructed the Bureau of Outdoor Recreation to undertake a nationwide inventory and assessment of existing facilities, and to make recommendations, both on appropriate roles for various levels of government, and on the necessary federal legislation that would be required to implement a national trails network. The bureau released its report, entitled *Trails for America*, in September 1966. It recommended that action be taken to create a national system plan to include National Scenic Trails, Park and Forest Trails, and Metropolitan Area Trails. Out of these proposals came the National Trail Systems Act, which received congressional approval in August 1968. Subsequently, at the state level, over a dozen governments adopted legislation which, among other things, included specific liability clauses, relieving landowners of responsibility toward recreationists traversing their property. These states also began to prepare system plans, and by 1973, a few had moved into the implementation stage. Meanwhile, across Canada, no province had yet begun the planning required to establish a comprehensive trails program.

A.B.R. "Bert" Lawrence, provincial secretary for resources development, was eager to rectify this situation. An early convert to the concept of a trails system, he emerged as the driving political force behind the programming of trails. The Davis cabinet, convinced by Lawrence that the province should assume a broader role in providing opportunities for recreational trails,[64] agreed to sponsor a symposium in Toronto, in June 1973, to discuss how the various provincial ministries might cooperate with local agencies and the volunteer groups to develop a provincewide network of such trails, and to identify the management and legislative obstacles involved. The keynote speaker, Bert Lawrence himself, promised to have "legislation in the hopper" by October. He was brimming over with enthusiasm, after having recently attended a United States trails conference with Tom Lee, director of the Parks Planning Branch. "In the Province of Ontario," Lawrence declared, "we have tremendous opportunities for moving more quickly and in a more rational and ... organized fashion than our cousins across the border ... We don't have the constitutional problems that they do ... and we can, if we wish, move very quickly and constructively in the field of trails."[65]

Lawrence's promise of rapid progress and legislation within four months proved to be illusory. His frustration grew as interministerial consultations took longer than expected, and Parks Division personnel, hamstrung by constraints and swamped with an enormous backlog of master-planning tasks, took a year to complete a program proposal for cabinet approval. On the basis of this submission, the government announced in November 1973 that a trails council, made up of representatives of all interest groups concerned with trail activities would be appointed to solicit public involvement and to assist in the development of policy and a trails system plan. Unfortunately, the program received a major setback when Bert Lawrence retired from politics in 1974. Without his influence and commitment, the government delayed appointing the trails council until 1 September 1975, just before a provincial general election. During its active two-year lifespan, however, the seventeen-person council conducted fifteen public meetings and received 352 written and verbal submissions before submitting a final published report to the minister of natural resources in November 1977. Expectations ran high that at last the province was on the verge of introducing and implementing a major new trails program.[66]

These high hopes went unfulfilled. To almost everyone's surprise, the trails council report had a minimal impact upon government policy and program development. From the bureaucrat's point of view, the report contained too many limitations; for example, MNR field staff questioned one-third of the ninety recommendations in the report on technical grounds. Parks Division planners were also troubled by the contradiction that the report contained between the council's user self-help philosophy, i.e., that the government should do only those things which the private sector, individuals, and clubs could not do for themselves, and the fact that "the overwhelming majority of recommendations require[d] government action." Finally, the report did not sit well with the politicians, particularly the minister of natural resources, Frank Miller. At a time when his ministry was labouring under the most severe constraints for decades and seeking ways to cut costs by delegating aspects of government programming to the private sector, the council's call for an increase from the existing $1.5 million in government funding for trails to $8 million a year was deemed unacceptable.[67]

Given the publicity generated by the trails council and the heightened expectations of trail users, the Parks Division expected a political uproar if the government summarily dismissed the report. To offset this possibility, the division drafted an "Ontario Trails Policy and Programme" (February 1979), which recommended a 25 percent increase. This would bring the existing annual trails budget to $2 million and be sufficient to expand the trails grant program to $800,000 a year, allowing for the creation of eight new staff positions in the field and two in Toronto. These administrators would stimulate club development, develop district and regional trails plans, and undertake the systems planning research that was required to answer questions such as what types of trails were required, and where, when, and at what cost. Initially, the program would be limited to developing recreational opportunities for canoeists, cross-country skiers, hikers, equestrians, and snowmobilers; the development of trails for fitness training, motorbikes, four-wheel-drive vehicles, and bicycles would be left to other provincial ministries or municipal authorities.

The proposal got no further than the desk of James Auld, the new minister of natural resources, who rejected it entirely for budgetary reasons. His decision put an end to over seven years of effort toward creating a comprehensive network of provincial trails. The one positive consequence of what, with the benefit of hindsight, seems like a long exercise in futility, was the resolution of the trails liability issue. Amendments to the Trespass to Property Act (1980) and a new Occupiers' Liability Act (1980) freed landowners who granted rights of passage across their property from the threat of legal action in the event of personal injury to trail users.[68] Apart from these legal reforms, the trail clubs had little to cheer about. Ontario still had no formal policy on trails and no system plan. Without program approval, funding soon dried up. Even the winter trails program, which was used to fund trail development and maintenance by snowmobile and cross-country ski clubs, was discontinued in 1982, but the anticipated hue and cry from the trail associations never materialized. This disappointed some parks personnel, who had counted on a sustained and aggressive political presence by their client groups to move trails programming forward. Sadly, with the dissolution of the Ontario Trails Council, the fragmented, geographically separated, and frequently competing trails clubs had lost the one organization that had the potential to represent their collective interests.

"Operation Restraint"

The demise of the near-urban initiative, followed by that of the trails program, reflected the harsh fiscal realities and the resurgence of conservative economic thinking that increasingly influenced Parks Division activities by the mid-1970s. In the first budget speech made by the Davis administration in April 1971, the influence of the so-called neoconservatism was already evident. The government talked of restoring "full employment growth" by expanding private-sector activity and investment, while maintaining "firm control over public spending in order to contain tax levels and the generation of inflationary pressures."[69] At first, the Parks Division was sheltered from the full impact of this policy, because political and social pressures compelled the government to commit new funds for parkland expansion along the Niagara Escarpment, at Wasaga Beach, at Bronte Creek, and elsewhere. Still, even during this relatively buoyant period of special funding, which lasted from 1972 to 1974, the division did get a foretaste of things to come. In 1973, for instance, park administrators were required to reduce their total budget request for the coming fiscal year to 88 percent of the printed estimates for 1973–74.[70] The following year, the efforts at constraint took a new turn, with demands for cuts in the current budget. At the same time, under the premier's general directive calling for a moratorium on growth in the public service, the Division of Parks was prevented from converting short-term contract positions, held year after year by dozens of highly skilled and committed professional people at main office and in the regions, into full-time posts. "How long can we continue to use (misuse?) contract employment to employ technical and professional staff to carry out the work demanded of us?" James Keenan enquired of Deputy Minister Walter MacNee in 1973. "Can we, or should we, invest hundreds of thousands of dollars in new parks when we can't get complement ... to build the parks? We have paid, and are paying, dearly in dollars, deteriorating park environments and visitor control problems because of poor park planning in the past. And yet we can't get staff to do the planning we know to be necessary. It doesn't make sense."[71]

As prosperity gave way to leaner and more inflationary times, and as the provincial deficit continued to mount, restraint became the order of the day throughout the Ministry of Natural Resources. This became particularly true after the Davis Conservatives emerged from the general election of 18 September 1975 with a minority government and the NDP as official opposition. Disillusioned Tories like defeated London candidate Gordon Walker attributed the electoral losses to what they considered the profligate, centralized, and interventionist policies of the Davis administration. Critics believed that many voters had reacted to the ham-handed way in which the government had forced regional governments on unwilling local communities, and to the extravagant schemes for futuristic public transportation systems with $1.3 billion price tags, or rural land-banking projects to create model towns at South Cayuga, near Hamilton, and at Townshend in eastern Ontario.[72] Walker, and those who shared his views, represented the Ontario manifestation of a general strengthening of the right in Western politics, a phenomenon soon to give rise to new stars in the political firmament like Britain's Margaret Thatcher, America's Ronald Reagan, and eventually, Canada's Brian Mulroney. "In Ontario, as elsewhere," explains economic historian Kenneth Rea, "there were expressions of disillusionment with government management of the economy, a growing sense that government spending was 'out of control' and that government intervention, instead of improving the performance of the system, was at least partly responsible for its perceived 'failures' to maintain full employment, stable price levels, a high rate of economic growth, and a 'fair' distribution of the fruits of economic effort."[73]

In the wake of the 1975 election, Premier Davis responded to these concerns by renewing his call for retrenchment and public-service efficiencies to battle inflationary pressures (Prime Minister Trudeau had introduced wage and price controls that year) and to encourage the expansion of the private sector. Subsequently, Provincial Treasurer Darcy McKeough introduced the highly publicized "Operation Restraint" and promised a balanced budget within five years. This was a pledge that Davis's minority government could not keep, given the pressures of brokerage politics. Ironically, during this period, when "Operation Restraint" curtailed established programming in many ministries, the province still continued to run up one record deficit after another. Government spending actually grew by 133 percent between 1975 and 1982, averaging approximately 16.6 percent annually, well above inflation rates.[74]

The Division of Parks did not benefit from these spiralling provincial expenditures; instead, it bore the brunt of "Operation Restraint." As the provincial deficit rose, the annual total budget for parks dropped from $29.1 million in 1974–75 to $28.4 million in 1977–78 – a 16 percent reduction, when inflation was taken into account. Parkland acquisition funding, which had reached a high point of $10.8 million in 1972–73, plummetted to $2.8 million in 1977–78. This dramatic decline in the property acquisition budget reflected the drying up of the special-funding accounts. In 1972–73, almost 70 percent ($7.3 million) had been targeted for the Niagara Escarpment, Bronte Creek, and Wasaga Beach. In 1975–76, the escarpment and Wasaga still commanded the bulk of the division's acquisition funding ($3 million from a $4.8 million total), but two years later, a mere $138,000 was spent on these projects.[75]

Under "Operation Restraint," land purchases at many locations came to a halt or were drastically reduced. At the Komoka site near London, for instance, only one-quarter of the 526 hectares required for the near-urban park had been acquired by 1978 and, by then, the government had declared that it did not intend to develop the park before the year 2000.[76] At the same time, capital expenditures in provincial parks across the system were slashed, from $9.6 million in 1974–75 to $4.2 million by 1977–78. Even projects in high-priority parks like Algonquin, Bronte, MacGregor Point, and Quetico were sharply curtailed, and the development of most facilities in the park reserves on the Niagara Escarpment did not go beyond the planning stage.[77] Much-needed campground expansion in the established and overcrowded southern parks also had to be postponed, as regional administrators committed their shrinking budgets to upgrading and completing the existing facilities. Finally, in 1978, provincial park user fees were substantially increased, both to keep up with inflation and to ensure that park revenues met a "fair proportion" (approximately 60 percent) of park operating and maintenance expenses.[78]

The impact of "Operation Restraint" evoked howls of frustration from regional park administrators, who found it extremely difficult to operate and maintain all of the established parks in their jurisdictions. As a case in point, T.W. Hueston, regional director in the eastern region, wondered how he was going to open the newly developed, ARDA-funded park at Murphy's Point within the budget assigned to him for 1976. "Although developed," he wrote to Parks Planning Branch Director Ronald Vrancart, "we are unable to operate, or, indeed, protect our present investment within a constrained budget."[79] Concerns such as these prompted both head office and regional administrators to recommend that for an interim period, at least, some small roadside provincial parks and campgrounds be closed, to release funds to maintain levels of service elsewhere in the system. Fearful of the political backlash in affected localities, the Davis cabinet turned thumbs down on the suggestion and ordered the Ministry of Natural Resources "to find the proposed savings elsewhere within its operations."[80]

Rather than close down the parks, the politicians preferred to pursue another line of policy – privatization – the neoconservative's way of delegating responsibility for governmental program delivery to the private sector, thereby at once lowering government expenditures, cutting the size of the public service, and encouraging private enterprise. The relevance of privatization to provincial parks was first brought to the government's attention by "The Report of the Special Programme Review" (1975) prepared by a committee chaired by Maxwell Henderson, a former auditor general of Canada. The report recommended that "new park facilities might be developed by privately operated camping organizations rather than the Province."[81] Coming as it did, at a time when many private campground operators were complaining about having to compete with heavily subsidized provincial parks, which did not have to balance revenues and expenditures, the Henderson report was doubly appealing to the minister of natural resources, Leo Bernier.

Parks Division personnel were not encouraged by the report. They had already canvassed agencies across Canada and in several American states about the history of private-sector involvement in public parks. The information on privatization obtained from these sources had been universally negative. American park agencies with a long tradition of private-sector activities reported that management conflicts between park administrators and the independent operators were serious, and that the United States Association of Park Concessionaires had become such a powerful lobby that it seriously interfered with the best management of the parks.[82] Armed with this knowledge, the division attempted to deflect the threatening impact of privatization. The division argued strongly against inviting the private sector to develop and operate campgrounds in new provincial parks, parks that had been established according to the criteria of the new classification system being drafted by the system planners. The political proponents of privatization, of course, still had to be accommodated. The division accordingly sought to appease the politicians by recommending that several small, established Recreation-class provincial parks, offering no more than overnight camping and containing no significant natural or cultural resources, be operated by the private sector as an experiment. On the basis of this proposal, the government proceeded in 1976 to put out two small parks for tender – Inwood, near Thunder Bay, and Sturgeon Bay, near Parry Sound – for a trial period. Entry and camping fees, as well as maintenance standards, were to conform with those in other provincial parks.

Conservationists of all shades, from the Ontario Federation of Anglers and Hunters to the Federation of Ontario Naturalists, vehemently denounced this new policy. They believed that any financial saving could only come "at the expense of great management problems" in the future.[83] Inevitably, the private operators would have to be granted long-term agreements or leases, for without such security, they would have no reason to care for the parks. Once provided with long-term contracts, the FON reasoned, the operators would become yet another vested interest, difficult for park administrators to control or dislodge, if circumstances warranted.

Most troublesome to the conservationists was the uncertainty as to how far the privatization of provincial parks and/or campgrounds in parks would be permitted to expand. Their worst fears seemed to be confirmed in December 1976, when Natural Resources Minister Leo Bernier stated, during a taped television interview in Sudbury, that the government's ultimate aim was "to phase out overnight camping in provincial parks" over the next twenty years.[84] This disclosure caused an immediate political brouhaha, and calls were made for the minister's resignation. Even the members of the Provincial Parks Advisory Council expressed indignation that Bernier had made what appeared to be a major policy decision on a subject that they had been studying for nearly a year, on his instructions. "We are being by-passed and ignored!" wrote the council chairman, George Priddle. "If that is the case we are wasting both our time and public funds."[85] Behind the scenes, Ron Vrancart wrote an urgent memorandum to Lloyd Eckel, who had recently replaced James Keenan as executive director of the Division of Parks. "I am concerned," explained Vrancart, "that the thoughts developing at senior levels in the Ministry on 'privatization' of camping are ... largely uninformed and subjectively based ... I would prefer to see the subject of 'privatization' of public camping developed within a policy on camping ... [and] within the overall Provincial Parks Policy that this Branch has been working on for several months."[86]

Vrancart and his staff believed that the private sector alone could not assume all responsibility for supplying camping opportunities, or for providing the estimated 3,740 campsites required in Ontario by 1991, at the locations where they were most needed. In their view, the growth and viability of private campgrounds in Ontario had not been curtailed by the growth of the provincial park system; on the contrary, from 1960 to 1974 the expansion of the private sector had outstripped that of the provincial parks. Compared to the capacity of the private sector, which had grown from 6,000 campsites in 1960 to roughly 83,000 in 1974 (a 1,383 percent increase), the provincial parks system had only expanded from 7,500 to 20,000 sites (a 267 percent increase). In 1974, the private sector provided 68 percent of the total number of campsites and the provincial park system only 23 percent.[87] As things stood, the private operators were not establishing campgrounds in locations that provided an equitable distribution of camping opportunities for Ontario residents, and there was little to indicate that they would do so, if the Division of Parks withdrew from campgrounds. Vrancart's planners also recognized that the intensively developed, facility-oriented private campgrounds provided an outdoor experience quite different from the one to be found in the provincial parks, with their large wooded sites and more natural settings.

Shaken by the barrage of criticism following his impromptu statement, Bernier acted swiftly to smother the political brush fire he had ignited. He retracted his statement, dismissing it as a regrettable slip of the tongue.[88] Apologies were also offered to the Provincial Parks Advisory Council, but the damage had been done. Those who opposed privatization believed that the minister had inadvertently let the cat out of the bag. They resolved to monitor the privatization experiment, as the government prepared to hand over the operation of more southern recreation parks to the private sector. The battle over privatization had yet to be joined.

Restraints, privatization, and relatively little growth in the provincial parks system became facts of life for Ontario's park administrators by 1978 and would remain so into the mid-1980s. There were, however, a few rays of sunshine in this gloomy picture. Hard times called forth creative responses from parks personnel, who began reviewing their modus operandi in a search for more efficient ways to achieve their objectives. They examined alternative methods for securing parkland,[89] and prepared to approach the Ontario Heritage Foundation (OHF) with suggestions of ways that that organization might help the parks program, by encouraging private citizens to donate natural heritage properties for nature reserves or to grant easements on land of natural value.[90] The division also began to explore ways of utilizing volunteers and cooperating societies. Some of these lines of enquiry would prove beneficial in the years ahead, but perhaps the most positive consequence of the grim financial climate was the decision by Parks Division personnel to put most emphasis on park policy and system planning. Since 1971, the division had been making progress toward defining the optimum park system for Ontario. After 1975, as we shall see, the push would be on to bring that important process to a successful conclusion.

Chapter 7

Creating the "Gospel Relating to Parks," 1967–1978

During the years when the politics of preservation and special funding stood at centre stage in the provincial parks story, the Parks Branch (reorganized as the Division of Parks in the Ministry of Natural Resources in 1972) underwent profound changes in both the quality and quantity of its personnel. The preservationist upsurge, in combination with the relentlessly expanding demand for outdoor recreational opportunities, accelerated these changes by greatly increasing the volume of work required of the branch, and by intensifying the conflicting demands on park administrators. After 1967, parks planning in Ontario became professionalized, as a steady stream of specialists from a wide spectrum of disciplines arrived on the scene to supplement the expertise of the foresters. By 1975, people with degrees in archaeology, biology, economics, geography, geology, history, historical architecture, landscape architecture, parks and recreation resource planning, sociology, and town planning could be found in the division's ranks.[1] Supported by a constantly expanding, multidisciplinary force of contract and seasonal personnel, both in the main and field offices, and with the benefit of comprehensive research data on provincial outdoor recreation, planning for the province's parks became an enormously enriched and complex process.

In June 1970, James Keenan, then supervisor of the Recreation Planning Section, had written: "We are at present too much preoccupied with reacting to externally proposed new park recommendations and not sufficiently geared to charting a well-reasoned and directed land acquisition development program. As a result, too much time is spent in unproductive processing of extraneous proposals. In brief, we don't have an action plan and we are paying the resultant price."[2] This state of affairs rapidly changed, once Keenan himself became chief of the Parks Branch in 1971, and executive director of the new Division of Parks the following year. He recruited the new generation of planners after 1967 and gave them both a sense of direction and the opportunity to realize their potential. Foremost among the new professionals stood Tom Lee, who became director of the Park Planning Branch in 1972. Considered by Keenan to be "the best parks person in Canada," and a "philosophical guru who could turn concepts into pragmatic plans,"[3] Lee played a central role in the evolution of the methodology of park master and system planning in Ontario. When Keenan left the Parks Division in August 1976 to assume new responsibilities within the MNR, both the provincial park master-planning and systems-planning programs were well established, and the division stood at the forefront of creative North American park agencies. The initiatives launched by Keenan culminated in 1978 with the adoption by the Davis government of an official parks policy, and the release of the *Ontario Provincial Parks Planning and Management Policies* manual, a document aptly described as "the gospel relating to parks."

Master-Planning Ontario's Parks in the 1970s

Nowhere was the trend toward professional and sophisticated research and planning methods more evident than in the work of master planning provincial parks. After the introduction of the 1967 classification and zoning policy, and in the heat of the struggles over Algonquin and Quetico, the process of master planning was radically redefined. Master plans evolved into comprehensive policy documents, containing an assessment and definition of the role and significance of each park within the classification framework, an explanation of the contributions each park would make to the objectives of the whole system, and the official policies for the protection, interpretation, use, development, and management of the park and its resources. Tom Lee, who joined the branch in 1967 after completing an M.Sc. in parks and recreation management at the University of Illinois, drafted the first of the modern master plans for Cyprus Lake in 1968; although never officially approved, it served as a prototype for his colleagues. During 1971, Lee, together with Mel Jackson, the superintendent of Pinery Provincial Park, and Robert Mitton, the district naturalist, prepared a master plan for the Pinery, the first actually to be approved in Ontario. Completed at a time when the park was suffering from all kinds of problems, the plan proposed an effective zoning system, the redesign of the campgrounds and day-use areas, and new operational policies to control rowdyism and the degradation of the environment. Thanks to the determination of Peter Addison and James Keenan, the plan was approved, funded, and implemented between 1971 and 1975.

By the mid-1970s, Ontario's Division of Parks had developed a sophisticated master planning program second to none in North America. When dealing with individual parks, planners now followed a carefully prescribed process. Before anything else, they sought to acquire a clear picture of the natural and cultural features in the park or reserve, of its potential users, and of any other factors relevant to the use of the resources. To obtain this background information, inventories of natural and cultural features had to be compiled and analyzed, and planning studies prepared by a variety of experts on the local and regional setting and the market area to be served. Once this phase was completed, it was the responsibility of an interdisciplinary team at the regional level to produce a "draft policy statement" to define the goals and objectives of the park, the land-use zones and management guidelines. Within the terms of this definition, the planning team then proposed "concept plan alternatives," outlining a number of possible courses of action for the protection, development, and use of the park. "Each alternative," explained Supervisor of Master Planning Norman Richards in 1976, "is evaluated according to the degree ... of resource protection; quality, quantity and type of visitor use opportunities; the effect on existing land uses, and ownership, and present socio-economic patterns in and surrounding the park area."[4]

Eventually one alternative, or possibly a combination of alternatives, was selected for further refinement as the basis of the "preliminary master plan," a document that was subjected to extensive government and public review and amendment before being adopted as the "official master plan." Once approved by the minister, the document was intended to have a twenty-year horizon, with provision for review at five-year intervals to take into account changing leisure needs, new survey data, political considerations, budget constraints, and the like. Public participation programs had also become mandatory features of master planning projects. Guidelines had been established to ensure that both individuals and groups became involved at an early stage, before policy decisions were made.

Regional and head office planners made rapid progress in preparing master plans for the 121 parks in the system. By the end of 1975, six parks had approved plans – the Pinery (1971), Bronte Creek (1972), Algonquin (1974), Mono Cliffs (1975), Frontenac (1975), and Ouimet Canyon (1975). Another twenty plans were awaiting final review and approval, and thirty-two others were in various stages of preparation. In short, master plans for approximately half of the existing parks were either complete or under way.

As master planning continued to evolve, such groups as the AWL, FON, and the National and Provincial Parks Association of Canada expressed concern that the documents had no official status and could be altered by political or administrative whim. To assuage this concern, the Davis government amended the Provincial Parks Act in 1976 to give legislative authority to the concept of a provincial park master plan. The act now defined "master plan" as "a program and policy, or any part thereof, prepared from time to time in respect of a provincial or a proposed provincial park and includes the maps, texts and other material describing such program and policy." These amendments also gave the minister of natural resources authority to prepare and approve master plans for existing or proposed parks, and to carry out periodic reviews of the documents.[5]

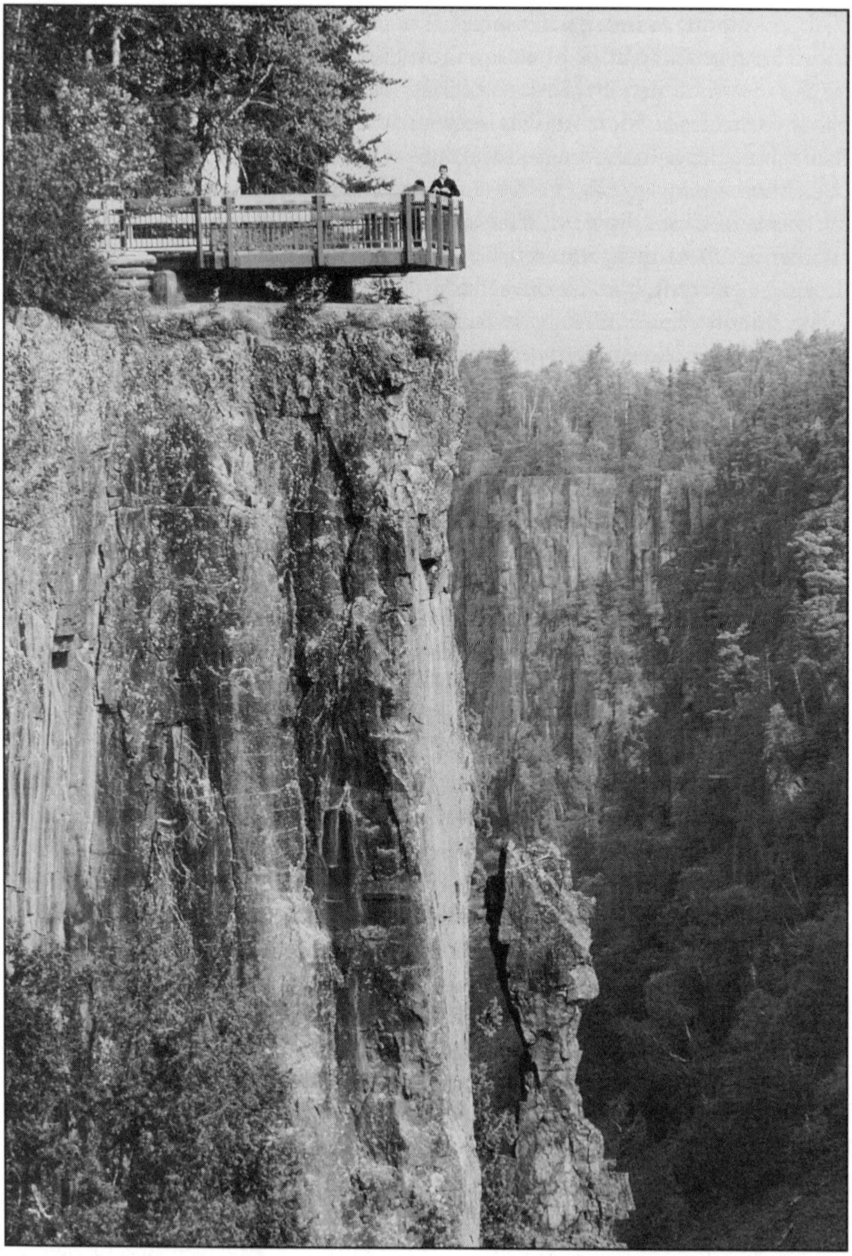

Ouimet Canyon Provincial Nature Reserve.
Courtesy: Ministry of Natural Resources.

The Demand for Policy Definition and System Planning

Not only did the landmark classification and zoning policy of 1967 serve as the foundation upon which the new master-planning process was built, but it also became the basis for conceptualizing the future "system" of provincial parks. It had, indeed, addressed the basic question of what kind of parks were required by Ontarians. Now planners had to determine how many of each class of provincial park Ontario needed, where these parks should be located, how they should be managed, and how the system would relate to other park agencies, as well as to the private sector. These questions, as we have seen, pointed to the same intractable problems which had stymied park planners since Ben Greenwood's time.

Major reforms of government structures and in the management systems governing the Ontario Public Service at last compelled parks administrators to come to grips with these long-standing issues. In 1969, the Robarts government introduced the Planning Programming Budgeting System (PPBS), which demanded that policy making and policy review be given priority in all departments.[6] The new system required all elements of the public service to define goals, establish clear priorities, and engage in multiyear planning and long-term forecasting. In the mid-1970s, the Davis government added another level of complexity by introducing a management-by-results system to complement PPBS, and charged the Management Board of the Cabinet to audit the performance, as well as the expenditures, of all ministries.

In April 1972, Premier Davis also implemented a wholesale reorganization of government structures, in an effort to improve the efficiency and effectiveness of the public service.[7] All the old departments were abolished and replaced by new ministries. The departments of Lands and Forests and Mines and Northern Affairs were amalgamated, along with the Conservation Authorities Branch (formerly with the Department of Energy and Resources Management), to form a new Ministry of Natural Resources. Furthermore, ministers with related or overlapping interests were grouped into policy fields, each headed by a senior cabinet minister, called a provincial secretary, whose task it was to coordinate the general policy direction of the group. The minister of natural resources became part of the Resources Development Field, along with the ministers of agriculture, environment, labour, industry and tourism, and transportation and communication. The MNR itself was made up of a number of divisions, including Lands, Forests, Fish and Wildlife, Parks, and Mines, each headed by an executive director (James Keenan in the case of Parks). Within the new Division of Parks, there were three branches – Planning, Management, and Historical Sites. The reorganization also aimed at decentralizing ministry functions; the eight regional offices of the MNR were accordingly expanded and given more responsibilities. Finally, in view of the increased opportunities for horizontal planning between cabinet ministers in the new Resources Development Field, the old Ontario Parks Integration Board was deemed redundant and was therefore dissolved.

All of these changes had profound implications for provincial park administrators. Lacking policy definition and parks system planning, the Division of Parks would surely languish in the new order of things. Under the new structures and management systems, every initiative proposed by the division would be rigorously scrutinized, first by competing elements within the MNR, and then, in turn, by the Resources Development Field, the Policy and Priority Board of cabinet (responsible for establishing general policy direction), and the Management Board (which decided if the province could afford the programs proposed).

To clear this formidable series of hurdles, the Parks Division required a clear, concise statement of policy. That statement had to define provincial parks and set goals and objectives for the system, so that the decision makers in the upper levels of government could evaluate the division's program performance and assess requests for additional funding, staff complement, or expansion. As matters then stood, too many aspects of provincial parks policy remained vague and ill-defined. This situation prevailed, in large part because parks policy had evolved implicitly and unsystematically, either simply following administrative precedent, politically inspired cabinet decisions on individual park proposals, or major new government initiatives, such as the Niagara Escarpment program. In the absence of comprehensive planning, the provincial parks system had developed serious problems. Parks were not distributed effectively enough, or in sufficient numbers, either to preserve significant and representative features of Ontario's natural and cultural heritage, or to provide day-use outdoor recreation and camping opportunities where they were most needed.

Even though convincing preservationist and recreational arguments could be made for the expansion of the provincial parks network, the division would not for long be allowed the luxury of building the parks system in an open-ended fashion, particularly as "constraints" became the government's catchword. And the battles over wilderness had revealed, without a clear policy statement to define the size, purpose, and objectives of the provincial parks system, it would be difficult to justify proposals for new Wilderness, Natural Environment, and Nature Reserve parks, in the face of competing arguments by timber and mining interests, urging alternative land uses for the same areas.

Another matter urgently requiring policy definition had arisen out of the near-urban parks initiatives at Bronte Creek, Short Hills, Pêche Island, and Komoka. The establishment of provincial parks or park reserves at these locations had, in fact, triggered a debate over the preferred division of responsibility for providing public parkland and outdoor recreation opportunities between the Division of Parks, the conservation authorities, and local or regional park agencies. Since the provincial government had altered the status quo by creating the new near-urban parks, it was incumbent upon the Division of Parks to make explicit the province's policy and intention of locating provincial parks near cities. Such a policy could then serve as a framework for liaison with local and regional agencies, and possibly motivate them to develop policies of their own, complementary to the role played by the province.

Pressure was also building on Parks Division planners to throw light on the relationship between provincial parks and the tourism objective of the MNR's Outdoor Recreation Program. Tourism considerations had become more prominent in government thinking in the late 1960s, when economists pointed to the widening gap in the province's tourism balance of payments, as a growing number of people travelled abroad. Ontario's Department of Tourism and Information reported in March 1970 that vacationing Canadians spent about $1.25 billion outside the country, some $200 million more than the Canadian travel industry earned from foreign visitors.[8] Economists predicted that the deficit could rapidly increase; after all, the airline industry was entering the era of the jumbo and stretched jet. As part of a strategy to address the impending crisis, the Ontario Department of Tourism and Information under J.A.C. Auld, recommended that the DLF accelerate provincial park development in ways conducive to the stimulation of tourism. Specifically, Auld recommended that new parks, both provincial and national, be located close to the urban centres of southern Ontario, that land and easements in scenic areas of the Niagara Escarpment be purchased, and that the DLF carry out the recommendations of the Canada-Ontario Rideau-Trent-Severn (CORTS) committee. Parks officials were bemused by this sudden concern for tourism. They had abstained for years from advertising in the United States, or elsewhere in Canada, because of excessive user pressure on the parks, especially on those in the southern regions. "Ontario is not meeting existing demands," noted the sceptical chief of parks, Peter Addison, "let alone making efforts to expand the tourist industry."[9]

All the same, the potential of the provincial parks system for tourism continued to intrigue the Robarts and Davis governments. The ARDA agreements further whetted the politicians' interest by informing them of the role parks could play in stimulating economic development through tourism in the depressed regions of the province. In May 1972, shortly after the creation of the MNR, Leo Bernier announced that the objectives of his new ministry's Outdoor Recreation Program were twofold: "first, to provide a wide variety of outdoor recreation experiences accessible to all citizens of Ontario; and secondly, to provide an optimum contribution from the tourist industry to the economy of this province and its regions."[10]

Parks Division personnel took advantage of this change in the political climate, and trotted out the argument about the "economic benefits of tourism" in support of proposals for new parks. Actually, the planners considered such economic considerations secondary to their main objectives of providing outdoor recreation opportunities and protecting the province's natural heritage. They frankly admitted that they had sought ARDA funding less for the sake of local and regional economies than "as a means of achieving other [recreation and protection] objectives for the parks system."[11] Park Planning Branch Director Ronald Vrancart acknowledged that "the commitment of park policy to economic objectives was not clear."[12] This situation now had to change. A deteriorating economy, together with the neoconservative push for privatization and cutbacks in government spending, would force division personnel to place more emphasis on the economic benefits generated by the parks system and to modify their thinking on the relationship between provincial parks and tourism.

It was not going to be easy to meet this enormous challenge, for in the late 1960s, park administrations across Canada were just beginning to come to terms with the complicated business of system and policy planning. A committee of the 1968 Federal-Provincial Parks Conference had tabled a report, recommending the basic principles of a coordinated approach on the subject, but the participants did not act upon the document until 1971, at which time a standing committee on system planning was established. The conference subsequently concentrated its efforts on promoting a common methodology across Canada, clarifying policies and defining basic concepts, and preparing guidelines and technical advice.[13] Throughout these years, the Ontarians, under James Keenan's direction, played a leading role in the work of the conference. As they developed a working concept of system planning for the parks, members drew heavily on the work being done by the U.S. National Parks Service on system and management policies for park classes, and on William J. Hart's book, *A Systems Approach to Park Planning* (1966).[14]

Reacting to the pressures brought to bear by the preservationist movement, by outdoor recreation enthusiasts in southern Ontario, and by the reforms in government structures and management systems, Parks Division planners began to chart the course that would place them ahead of other provincial agencies involved in developing methodologies of system planning. James Keenan established a systems planning unit in 1971 and appointed Russell Irvine as its head. In 1973, he was replaced as supervisor by Robert Mitton, who, along with Park Planning Branch directors Tom Lee (1972–75) and Ron Vrancart (1975–81) guided the policy document and manual of administrative policies through to completion.

As a starting point in the process of system planning, Russell Irvine undertook a thorough review of the American experience in parks development and determined to emulate the best of what the Americans had to offer. He also began to reassess the classification and zoning policy of 1967 in the light of five years of experience. His research revealed that no consensus yet existed among the MNR's field staff, academics, politicians, and elements of the public as to what was intended by the various classes and zones of parks. Even within the MNR, staff members at all levels of administration understood neither the classification scheme nor the role it should play with regard to park programs. Irvine realized that in order to rectify these problems, the division would have to produce a much more comprehensive and detailed policy and technical document than the one James Keenan himself had drafted in 1967. Among other things, the philosophy and rationale, as well as the goals, objectives, and management principles of the system had to be better defined. Targets had to be established, indicating how many parks of each class were required, where and why, and policies developed to guide the management of natural and cultural resources and to specify both permitted and nonconforming uses in each park class and zone. At least one new class of park – Historical – was needed, and some modifications would have to be made to others.

Fortunately, beginning in the late 1960s, the Ontario government had initiated research on supply and demand in outdoor recreation, research that was necessary before anyone could begin to address the unresolved questions about recreation needs and their relationship to parks. In 1967, the Federal-Provincial Parks Conference initiated the Canada Outdoor Recreation Demand Study (CORDS). This was a cooperative undertaking, in which Ontario completed an inventory of recreational facilities in 1968, and a user survey in 1969, at thirty-five provincial parks, forty recreational areas administered by conservation authorities, and seventeen municipal parks. Initial hopes that the CORDS data would enable each province to predict its needs for outdoor recreation facilities and space of all types were, however, not realized, in part because of problems with the statistical reliability of the information. Still, Ontario's planners benefited greatly from the pioneering work that had been undertaken. Much had been learned about conceptually defining the interrelationships of supply and demand in outdoor recreation, defining data needs, and carrying out strict quality controls in the collection of information. Moreover, the CORDS data proved useful in the early efforts to undertake multiyear planning under the PPBS system.

The program that benefited most from these lessons was the Tourism and Outdoor Recreation Planning Study (TORPS), an interdepartmental program of the Ontario government, initiated in November 1967 to be dovetailed with the CORDS project. Reflecting the Robarts government's insistence on greater horizontal linkages between government agencies, the TORPS committee involved five government departments, including the DLF. Using advanced mathematical models and computer technology, the TORPS group set about to create the most complete data base possible on outdoor recreation matters. After a pilot survey, the committee commissioned Market Facts of Canada Ltd. to conduct a provincewide study of leisure behaviour – the Outdoor Recreation Survey (ORS) – between 1 May 1973 and 30 April 1974. It involved interviewing over 10,000 households, selected from every social stratum, to collect information on the residents' participation in a wide range of recreational activities, their free-time preferences, constraints on their participation in recreation, weekend and vacation trip patterns, and the sociodemographic characteristics of participants in all activities.[15] Once tabulated and published during 1977–78, the data tapes were housed at York University's Atkinson College and the Leisure Studies Department of the University of Waterloo. This material represented "the most complete and accurate resident tourism and recreation data base of any province or state in North America."[16]

In addition to the survey of provincial demand, the TORPS committee launched the Ontario Recreation Supply Inventory in 1974, beginning with the area south of the French-Mattawa rivers. The committee sought to develop and to maintain a comprehensive inventory of public and privately operated recreational facilities and resources in Ontario, and to estimate the recreational opportunities provided by those facilities. Once gathered, these data on supply and demand were quickly put to use by planners, seeking to establish a more rational and equitable provision of camping and day-use opportunities in provincial parks in all regions, and by system planners, endeavouring to establish provincial and regional targets for each class of park. Regrettably, the TORPS committee failed to develop either an outdoor recreation policy or a master plan for the province. The task proved to be far more difficult than anyone had imagined; it was discovered that fifty-five different provincial and federal agencies in Ontario (exclusive of local agencies) were involved in aspects of recreation programming. Although unable to find their way through this jurisdictional quagmire, the TORPS committee performed an indispensable service by providing a wealth of recreation research data to park agencies, academics, and recreational planners alike.[17]

With these advances in leisure research, Park Planning Branch personnel began system planning in earnest. In 1973, they started the formidable task of preparing, for each class of park, administrative policy documents which would establish, among other things, the philosophical rationale for each class, its objectives and management guidelines, and targets for the number and distribution of the parks within that class. This proved to be a lengthy and complex process, only completed in 1978.

Toward a Provincial Nature Reserve System

Planning for the Nature Reserve system actually began as early as 1969, when, after several years of prodding by the Federation of Ontario Naturalists, the old Parks Branch created a Nature Reserves unit, headed by a full-time supervisor.[18] That same year, Lands and Forests Minister René Brunelle appointed a special Minister's Advisory Committee on Nature Reserves, made up of scientists from seven universities and several government agencies. The FON regarded both the appointment of qualified staff and the establishment of an advisory committee of experts as the prerequisites to the creation of a coordinated system of protected natural areas. In keeping with the recommendations of the naturalists, the minister asked his new advisory committee to come up with a plan that would tell him what should be included in a provincial Nature Reserve system, and to evaluate any proposals for Nature Reserves brought to its attention.[19]

Perhaps the most significant characteristic of the advisory committee was its considerable overlap in membership with the Ontario panel of the Conservation of Terrestrial Communities Section of the International Biological Programme (IBP-CT). The IBP-CT had been sponsored by the United Nations in 1963, to compile a worldwide inventory of significant natural areas and ecosystems, to determine to what extent these habitats were represented in protected natural areas, and to promote the appropriate protection of representative samples of habitats not yet set aside for preservation. The Canadian Council of Resource Ministers agreed to participate in the International Biological Programme in 1968, when the federal government offered to finance the research. Actual field work was conducted from 1970 to 1974. Four members of the Ontario panel of the IBP-CT sat on the Minister's Advisory Committee on Nature Reserves, including Dr. J. Bruce Falls (a co-chairman of the panel) and Dr. D.A. MacLulich, chairman of the advisory committee. Harold Gibbard, the new supervisor of Nature Reserves in the Parks Branch, served as secretary to the advisory committee and also sat on the IBP-CT panel.

The close linkage between the two groups from 1969 to 1972 (the period during which the advisory committee functioned) proved to be of mutual benefit and of no little consequence in advancing the cause of biological conservation in Ontario. Reflecting the IBP-CT's position, that Nature Reserve systems should be fully representative of natural environments, the advisory committee recommended that the classification policy of 1967 be changed to include the principle of "representation," rather than limiting the selection of Nature Reserves to "unique" features of the province's natural heritage.[20] Provincial park planners accepted this recommendation, and subsequently drafted a statement, which spoke of Nature Reserves as being "dedicated to the protection and preservation of representative and unique life and earth science features and ecosystems."[21]

Having established the principle of representation, the advisory committee grappled with the question of the classification framework to be adopted to organize the province's natural environments. Because of their expertise, the committee members decided to focus their attention exclusively on the life science aspect of the problem and to leave the earth science component to others. Eventually, the committee agreed that the Ontario Lands Classification framework was best suited to achieve representation of the full spectrum of biotic communities in Ontario. Designed by G. Angus Hills, a soil specialist with the Division of Research in the Department of Lands and Forests, and another co-chairman of the Ontario IBP-CT panel, the system divided the province into thirteen site regions, based on distinctions in climate, soil, land forms, and vegetation. The site regions were further broken down into sixty-five districts, each of which possessed distinctive physiographic and biotic conditions. As far as possible, the advisory committee recommended that both site regions and districts be represented in the Nature Reserve system and that, within each region and district, areas be chosen to represent the various ecosystems. The committee also recommended that one area, between 25 to 30 square miles (6,475 to 7,770 hectares) in size, representing a variety of landscapes, be set aside and preserved in each site district.[22] This was too ambitious a target in the estimation of park planners, who were having great difficulty in designating Primitive parks during this period. As a result, they set themselves the more modest goal of creating a large reserve in each site region.

Through its recommendations, the Advisory Committee on Nature Reserves provided the Parks Branch with the foundation of a theoretical framework for the classification of Ontario's ecosystems, and in so doing, took the first step toward determining what should be represented in a system of protected areas. To build upon this foundation, the new Division of Parks (1972) subsequently commissioned Dr. Paul Maycock, a plant ecologist at the University of Toronto, to create a more refined theoretical framework, one capable of classifying the hundreds of different terrestrial communities in Ontario. Maycock adapted Hills's site region boundaries and defined eight vegetation regions or "extensive latitudinal belts characterized by a broad uniformity of effective macroclimate and a corresponding uniformity of dominant forest types and other ecological patterns."[23] By using a series of matrices, one for each vegetation region, he partitioned each region into 150 theoretical habitats. Each habitat, or "site type," as he called it, was the result of different combinations of microclimate, soil texture, and moisture regime, producing a distinctive vegetation complex. Ideally, the life science component of the Nature Reserve system would include a full representation of each vegetative site type. As researchers began to apply Maycock's framework, they discovered that variation in habitat for individual site regions ranged from a low of thirty-one to a high of eighty-three site types.[24]

In addition to making contributions to theory, the Advisory Committee on Nature Reserves also served an important function by encouraging a working partnership between the Parks Branch and the Ontario panel of the IBP-CT in the task of taking inventory of the province's natural areas. Harold Gibbard instructed his field staff, who were conducting life science inventories in provincial parks for master-planning purposes, to adopt the survey method and check sheet used by the IBP-CT. Meanwhile, the IBP-CT's field workers focussed their efforts on areas outside the parks. The groups exchanged their findings. "This arrangement," reflected Thomas Beechey, "proved beneficial to both parties; the Ontario IBP-CT panel gained some comprehension of the landscapes and [biotic] communities ... protected in parks, while the Parks Branch obtained current, standardized information about significant areas beyond parks for consideration as Nature Reserves."[25] The IBP-CT surveys also confirmed what had been suspected, namely that to achieve adequate representation of Ontario's natural heritage within the parks system, considerable expansion would be necessary. Finally, when the IBP-CT panel completed its field work in 1974, it made the Division of Parks custodian of its data bank on natural areas in Ontario. In return, the division committed itself to add to the standardized inventory of natural areas worthy of protection.

The field work undertaken in partnership with the IBP-CT from 1969 to 1974 took place under less than ideal circumstances. Thanks to financial constraints, this important scientific research had to be undertaken entirely by limited-term park staff on annual contracts, or by qualified university students during the summer months. Throughout this period, Harold Gibbard remained the only permanent employee in the Nature Reserves unit (renamed the Environmental Planning Section in 1972). As late as 1974, no full-time environmental planners had been appointed to the regional offices of the MNR to coordinate and synthesize the research of the contract and seasonal field staff. Understandably, Gibbard frequently complained about the inordinate amount of work before him and the problems created by the lack of continuity, as some of his scientists took permanent positions elsewhere. Yet, despite these difficulties, the inventory process was considerably expanded after 1969, as division and regional planners recognized that environmental information was essential for both master planning in individual parks and in system building. The number of technical people in the field expanded from two in 1969 to twenty in 1974, with an additional three annual contract personnel at main office.[26] Biologist Thomas Beechey assumed most of the responsibility for advancing the life science component of the provincial Nature Reserve system, when Harold Gibbard left the public service in 1976, to pursue a career in environmental assessment in the private sector.

The collaboration between the IBP-CT, the Advisory Committee on Nature Reserves, and parks personnel had another significant result; it "solidified a scientific rationale for the establishment of Nature Reserves."[27] This proved to be an important development, given that there were many critics who considered the creation of a comprehensive system of natural areas a colossal waste of potentially valuable forest and mineral resources, and an extravagant amenity for just a few naturalists and scientists. After the IBP-CT experience, Parks Division personnel were capable of giving a powerful rejoinder to these narrowly utilitarian arguments. Planners built their case for the Nature Reserve program around the six major functions they believed it fulfilled. A system of Nature Reserves, they argued, would accomplish the following:

- Contain the original, natural genetic materials found in Ontario
- Represent the geological and natural processes which have shaped the Province
- Serve as benchmark areas against which to measure environmental conditions and change
- Make a positive contribution to scientific knowledge and to society through the application of this knowledge
- Provide for outdoor educational opportunities for individuals, groups, and institutions at all levels
- Perform a re-creative role for leisure time activities.[28]

What gave this rationale considerable impact was the knowledge that the Parks Division's efforts to create a Nature Reserve system were not extravagant or unique; other countries that had participated in the IBP-CT program had already recognized the need to preserve natural areas. "We can learn from the experience of other countries," Bruce Falls argued in 1967. "The British Nature Conservancy is a pioneer in this field. The United States is about to initiate an ecological survey. In Australia, in conjunction with the National Academy of Science and the universities, several of the states have set up systems of nature reserves."[29] Encouraged by the IBP-CT, Ontario's park planners took this advice to heart and looked for inspiration and guidance in the natural areas conservation programs of some of these countries.

The British program was considered by many to be the most advanced of its kind in the world and a model for other jurisdictions to follow. Since 1949, the British Nature Conservancy (replaced by the Natural Environment Research Council in 1965) had overseen the creation of a comprehensive reserve system across the British Isles. In addition to establishing publicly owned National Nature Reserves, by 1967 the conservancy had cooperated with private and public landowners to designate for protection over 2,000 "Sites of Special Scientific Interest." The planning, research, and management of this program was further advanced by the creation of the Nature Conservancy Council, a government agency, in 1973. Under its auspices, explained Thomas Beechey, "the programme incorporates sophisticated procedures for inventory, data collection and information storage concerning the distribution and abundance of species and plant communities as a basis to establish nature reserve acquisition and biological conservation priorities."[30] Within a few years, the council had also consolidated its biological data for all candidate Nature Reserve areas, in order to rank sites on the basis of their national and regional significance. Earth science features were also represented in the British program. By 1976, seven National Nature Reserves had been set aside, primarily for geological and geomorphological reasons, while many other reserves established for biological purposes also incorporated earth science features. Furthermore, over 1,600 areas of geological significance were being protected as Sites of Special Scientific Interest. During the 1970s, the Geology and Physiography Section of the Nature Conservancy Council began to evaluate the British landscape systematically in order to identify, rank, and protect additional sites.[31]

In North America, the Nature Conservancy of the United States was established in 1950 by members of the Ecological Society of America, concerned about the protection of natural areas in view of the quickening pace of urbanization, industrialization, and technological change. Subsequently, the conservancy promoted systematic planning for Nature Reserves and participated in every significant inventory of natural areas in the United States. A quarter-century after its founding, the conservancy reported that twenty-two of the fifty states were involved in programs to protect natural areas, thirteen of which included earth science components.

Planners in Ontario considered Wisconsin's Nature Reserve system exemplary. Beginning in 1941, Wisconsin had initiated a program to develop a system of natural areas to embrace all aspects of the state's native vegetation, including samples of woodland, marsh, bog, beach, and prairie. By 1974, the program's goal had been redefined and now called for the preservation of sufficient scientific and natural areas "to insure adequate representation of all biotic communities and unique natural features native to the region." Wisconsin also endeavoured to protect representative and significant examples of bedrock, soils, and land forms in over 140 scientific areas and state parks. The highlight of earth science conservation in Wisconsin was the Ice Age National Scientific Reserve and Trail, created by a cooperative federal-state effort, in conjunction with private organizations. The various sections of the reserve incorporated stratigraphic and topographic features representative of the period of Wisconsinian glaciation, while the 1,336-kilometre trail traversed a countryside that contained a wealth of glacial land forms, such as eskers, moraines, drumlins, and kettles.[32]

Canadian public and nongovernment agencies lagged behind their British and American counterparts until the 1970s. The Nature Conservancy of Canada (NCC) was only established in 1963, by a special task force of the Federation of Ontario Naturalists. Since that time, the NCC has promoted the protection of natural areas by purchasing lands outright, negotiating agreements, and by accepting gifts. Properties acquired are turned over to government agencies for administration and management. At the federal level, Parks Canada, too, only began to plan on a systematic basis in the late 1960s, about the same time as Ontario. Parks Canada planners eventually zoned the country into forty-eight natural regions, thirty-nine terrestrial and nine marine, according to physiographic and forest region criteria, and set as their goal the representation of each region in the national park system. This program of landscape protection was further supplemented in 1978 by the Landmark Policy, which aimed to preserve "exceptional natural sites of Canadian significance."[33] At the provincial level, British Columbia enacted a special Ecological Reserves Act in 1971, to provide for the creation of a system of reserves on Crown land. By 1976, Quebec and New Brunswick had followed suit.

During its brief tenure (1969–72), the Advisory Committee on Nature Reserves in Ontario restricted its efforts to the life science aspects of Nature Reserve planning and left the earth science component to parks personnel. The task of designing an all-encompassing classification framework, with which to identify and evaluate the representative and special units of the province's earth history, proved to be a major conceptual challenge for the young scientists assigned to the project. George Tracey, a geomorphologist, assumed this task in 1972. Before his tragic death, in a caving accident in 1974, he had adopted the International Geological Congress's chronostratigraphic classification system (the organization of rock strata in units with respect to their age or time of origin) as a primary planning framework, but had recognized that he would have to adapt to the conditions in Ontario a variety of classification schemes used to categorize rock strata, fossil assemblages, and land forms, and then fit them into the geological time scale.

Tracey's successor, Robert Davidson, explained the immensity of the classification problem in terms the nonspecialist could understand.

> The distinctive layers of strata of rock formed since the creation of the planet constitute earth history, as do the surface or geomorphological features (such as moraines, drumlins, eskers, beaches, river valleys) formed on top of the bedrock. In Ontario, geomorphological features derive from the recent or Quaternary glaciation of the last two million years. Strata are classified on both a lithostratigraphic basis (physical characteristics) and a biostratigraphic basis (fossil content). The earth history of the Quaternary period, as represented in rocks, soils, and organic materials below the surface and in surface formations, is classified on a geologic-climate basis which distinguishes periods of glacial advance and retreat.[34]

By the late 1970s, Davidson had worked out a tentative framework for the earth science component of the Nature Reserve system plan. In brief, his framework organized the rock formations, fossil assemblages, and land forms of Ontario according to the time, method, and location of their formation, into forty-two discrete, ancient and recent environmental themes, all of which he hoped would find representation in the Nature Reserve system.

The advances in theory made by the small Environmental Planning Section during the mid-1970s were matched by solid progress in the field. By the end of 1974, over one hundred Nature Reserves had been designated, most as zones within established parks and park reserves (sixty-three in Algonquin alone). Many other candidate reserve sites had been documented by IBP-CT field workers for possible inclusion in the emerging system, and the list was growing annually, as Parks Division field staff continued work on the standardized inventory. In 1976–77, the Niagara Escarpment Commission contracted with the division to undertake an extensive survey of the Niagara Escarpment planning area and to identify all the provincially, regionally, and locally significant earth and life science features. The commission later proposed that these sites be protected, either as Nature Reserves or zones within parks, or through agreements, easements, and land-use controls.

From 1969 to 1979, when planners concentrated on designing conceptual frameworks for identifying and evaluating potential Nature Reserves, only six such areas were officially regulated by the provisions of the Provincial Parks Act, making a total of twelve. The awe-inspiring Ouimet Canyon in the Thunder Bay District was one of these special cases. This spectacular geological formation – a deep, narrow crevasse between perpendicular rock walls – contained very unusual ecological conditions, including a number of plants possessing arctic-alpine affinities. The OPIB approved the canyon's establishment as a Nature Reserve, both for its tourism potential and the significant flora to be found on the site.[35] Two of the new reserves created in these years emerged from negotiations between the province, the Nature Conservancy of Canada, and local naturalist groups. Peter's Woods, a 34-hectare sample of original maple-beech forest, located north of Cobourg, was acquired in 1971 with the financial assistance of the Willow Beach Field Naturalists Club.[36] Similarly, with the help of a substantial $50,000 grant from the Nature Conservancy of Canada, the provincial government purchased the 70-hectare Ojibway Prairie Nature Reserve, located within Windsor city limits. The significance of this site, the last major remnant of undisturbed tall grass prairie in Canada and the Eastern United States, was recognized in 1969 by Paul Maycock and Angus Hills. They discovered on the site more than 25 percent of the specialized prairie-type plants known to grow in southern Ontario, as well as species thought to be extinct in the province. Excited by their findings, they resolved to save the property from the threat of impending industrial development by the Morton Chemical Company as a salt mine. Happily, at Maycock's behest, the company delayed its development plans, pending the decision to purchase the area as a Nature Reserve in 1973. "Its value and uniqueness from biological, ecological, conservation and educational viewpoints are such that as a single unit of its kind, it cannot be replaced," commented Natural Resources Minister Leo Bernier upon acquiring the property. "It thus assumes international importance."[37]

The acquisition of these few properties posed another set of problems for park administrators; Nature Reserves had to be managed carefully to ensure that fragile ecosystems were protected. However, the regional offices of the MNR, working under tight budgetary constraints in the mid-1970s, placed this matter low on their list of priorities. It took a crisis or an embarrassing revelation to jolt some regional officials into action. For instance, in 1974, the Parks Division in Toronto was shocked to learn that a pipeline had been installed across the Ojibway Prairie property. No information about this harmful project had been forwarded to the Parks Division at main office by district or regional administrators. "It is difficult to conceive how this could all happen so easily," wrote a distraught James Keenan. "The credibility and fundamental ability of this Ministry to be responsible for such an area is cast in grave doubt by ... events since the property was acquired."[38] The pipeline incident brought an instant response to the issue of managing the reserve. To create a set of management guidelines for the property, the Parks Division appointed a special task force of university scientists and struck an agreement with the city of Windsor to share the costs of a naturalist-planner for the reserve.[39] It is interesting to note that officials discovered that in order to keep the prairie fauna flourishing, prescribed burns would have to be conducted every few years, since periodic fires were a natural event in prairie environments. Thus the Ojibway Prairie pipeline episode at least served one useful purpose, by focussing the attention of administrators on the complex problem of how to manage Nature Reserves, once they were acquired. Planners developing the administrative policies for provincial parks recognized that they had to pay more attention to creating protective mechanisms for the management of the few Nature Reserves then in the system, and for the many more eventually to be added.

To Be or Not to Be? Historical Parks

When it came to system planning, historical planners made the most progress during the period from 1972 to 1974, a noteworthy development, considering that a class of Historical parks did not receive official recognition until 1972. Previously, the old Parks Branch's role in archaeological and historical site conservation and management had been largely limited to resources located within other classes of provincial parks. Many of these sites possessed considerable significance and were accorded a prominent place in park interpretation programs. These included the archaeological features at Serpent Mounds and Inverhuron; the prehistoric pictographs at Bon Echo and Agawa Bay in Lake Superior Provincial Park; the sections of the legendary route of the voyageurs located within Quetico Park and Samuel de Champlain Provincial Park (where staff constructed an authentic replica of a *canot de maître* in the late 1960s); the Pioneer Logging Exhibit in Algonquin; the Sibbald House in Sibbald Point Park, and the Museum of the Upper Lakes, constructed around the hull of the schooner *Nancy* at Wasaga Beach. To protect significant historical sites located on Crown land outside parks, the DLF used the vehicle of the Wilderness Areas Act in the absence of other cultural heritage legislation. Ten sites, including Fort Albany, Michipicoten fur-trade post, and Peterborough Petroglyphs were originally protected in this way.

Once a full-time historian joined the Interpretive Unit of the Parks Branch in 1967, and as the master-planning process evolved, planners gradually placed more emphasis on compiling inventories, appraising, managing, and interpreting cultural resources in all parks and reserves. "The theme that the Provincial Parks System wants the historical resource to support," explained Gary Sealey in 1969, "is that of 'man and the land.' We want to show man's historic relationship with nature in the Province of Ontario."[40] With a small research budget and the assistance of the Royal Ontario Museum and university archaeologists, the branch undertook studies in Algonquin, Carillon, Charlston Lake, the Dawson Trail in Quetico, Fitzroy, Inverhuron, La Cloche, the Mattawa, Methodist Point, Moose Factory, Serpent Mounds, and Sibbald Point.

In keeping with the DLF's traditional practices, the classification policy of 1967 defined a narrow role for the Parks Branch in the cultural resources field. The policy called for historical zones within all types of parks, but declined to create a separate class of Historical parks, in spite of recommendations contained in the classification frameworks issued by both the influential American Outdoor Recreation Resources Review Commission (1962) and the Federal-Provincial Parks Conference (1965). This decision can be attributed to the fact that the Ontario Department of Tourism and Information had preempted the role of "lead ministry" when it came to protecting, restoring, and interpreting historical sites. In 1964, that department had launched a program which, by 1971, included the reconstruction of the seventeenth-century Jesuit Mission of Sainte-Marie among the Hurons near Midland, the Penetang Naval and Military Establishment, and Fort William, the headquarters of the North West Company, located in Thunder Bay.

As it happened, the Parks Branch soon reconsidered its decision not to create a class of Historical parks. Too many significant archaeological and historical resources on Crown land remained unprotected, because they were located outside the boundaries of a provincial park and did not fall within the mandate of the Department of Tourism and Information. This problem came to light when the branch faced the question of how to preserve a resource such as the Peterborough Petroglyphs, first discovered near Stoney Lake in 1954. Researchers established that the site was one of the most important vestiges of Canada's pre-European cultural heritage. In terms of its size, variety, range, and time span, no other collection of petroglyphs in Canada rivalled this one. According to archaeologist Kenneth Kidd, the Peterborough Petroglyphs were nothing less than a North American equivalent of the palaeolithic art sites in Lascaux, France and Altamira, Spain.[41] Although deleted from a mining claim and fenced off in 1956, and later designated under the Wilderness Areas Act, the question of what to do with the site remained unanswered as late as 1969. James Keenan concluded that the situation at the Petroglyphs and elsewhere called for the creation of a class of Historical parks. Parks Chief Peter Addison agreed. "It is my own view," he wrote to Keenan in

December 1969, "that Ontario lags considerably in its attention to historical and related sites, and I should like to see the situation improved."[42]

Fortunately, their wish was soon realized. During 1970–71, the Parks Branch successfully pressed its case for an expanded role in the cultural resources field. Under the government reorganization of 1972, an Historical Sites Branch was created within the Parks Division of the MNR and given responsibility for historical research, planning, and interpretation, as well as the operation of Sainte-Marie among the Hurons, the Penetang Naval and Military Establishment, and Fort William (which was then only in the first stages of construction). At the same time, the government passed the Historical Parks Act (1972), authorizing the cabinet to set apart public lands for Historical parks. Responsibility for any parks created under this legislation rested with the Historical Sites Branch of the MNR.[43]

One of the first and most important initiatives taken by John Sloan, the first director of the branch, and Robert G. Bowes, his supervisor of research and planning, was to engage the services of an interdisciplinary team of professionals in archaeology, history, geography, and architecture to develop

The Peterborough Petroglyphs, Canada's most significant collection of Indian rock carvings, were discovered near Stoney Lake in 1954 and initially protected under the Wilderness Areas Act. Since 1989, the petroglyphs have been housed in an ingeniously designed, seven-sided, glass protective shelter. *Courtesy: Ministry of Natural Resources.*

an historical system plan. Completed in 1974, and published under the title of *A Topical Organization of Ontario History*, the plan provided the MNR with a tool with which to identify and protect unique and representative historical features of the province, and to plan, develop, and manage a comprehensive provincewide system of Historical parks and zones. This system would be developed around themes in Ontario's past, conducive to explanation in an outdoor recreational setting and which could be represented through a landscape. Using this thematic approach, the Historical Sites Branch anticipated presenting in "a tangible form the achievements and frustrations, technology, economy, social life, culture and thought," of the prehistoric aboriginal peoples and the more recent European occupants of the province. The fur trade, agriculture, lumbering, mining, and transportation were typical of the kind of history "oriented around activities and lifeways rooted in the landscape and physical environment," deemed suitable for representation in historical parks and zones. *A Topical Organization* identified 13 themes and divided these into 115 segments, which were then rated A, B, or C in terms of their "provincial historical significance."

To complement the systems plan, the planning team devised an historical resources evaluation scheme. An evaluation of a historical site would take into account themes already accommodated in provincial parks or in programs operated by other park agencies (national and regional) and give priority to those still in need of representation. An evaluation would also ascertain how well specific historical or cultural resources represented the various themes delineated in the system plan and how suitably the surrounding land base would serve the purposes of an Historical park. Already in 1974, the Historical Sites Branch had begun an inventory of historical resources, a data base supported by a rapidly expanding body of research reports (250 by 1976). All of these developments made the branch the envy of park agencies across Canada. Appropriately enough, in 1976, Petroglyphs Provincial Park became the first Historical park to be placed under regulations.

In view of these dramatic advances in historical system planning, no one anticipated the events that suddenly surfaced in 1975 to threaten the entire program. That year, the Davis government decided to relocate the Historical Sites Branch in the newly created Ministry of Culture and Recreation (MCR). In one stroke, the Parks Division lost its entire complement of archaeologists and historians. The reorganization took place over the objections of Natural Resources Minister Leo Bernier, who recognized that his ministry's capacity to achieve its objectives had been eroded, now that it literally had no one to undertake the research, planning, interpretation, and management of cultural resources.[44] Assurances by officials of the MCR that their Historical Planning and Research Branch (the old Historical Sites Branch) would continue to service the needs of the parks program did not assuage the concerns of personnel in the Parks Division. The Provincial Parks Advisory Council shared their anxiety and foresaw that serious problems of an administrative, financial, and operational kind would most certainly emerge, now that responsibility for Historical parks had been divided between two ministries.[45]

It was with such thoughts in mind that the Parks Division decided to delete Historical parks as a separate component of the provincial parks system and to hand over responsibility for developing this class of park to the Ministry of Culture and Recreation. The decision proved to be controversial and occasioned a spirited response from the Provincial Parks Advisory Council, the MCR, and the National and Provincial Parks Association of Canada.[46] The Parks Council argued that "a park system is the sum of its parts, it does not work if any one part is missing."[47] After further reflection, the division bowed to the pressure and reestablished Historical parks as a component of the classification scheme. System planners could only hope that the horizontal linkages between the two ministries would be sufficient to support the Historical parks program.

Alas, those critical intergovernmental linkages grew weaker with the passage of time. Once relocated in the MCR, the Historical Planning and Research Branch was given a much expanded mandate, which involved providing heritage conservation services to a growing list of provincial ministries and agencies, particularly the Ontario Heritage Foundation. As the responsibilities of the branch expanded, the level of service it was able to provide to the Parks Division declined. "We will not be conducting archaeological or historical inventories of specific Provincial Parks," branch director Robert Bowes informed the Parks Division in February 1977, an unexpected and nasty surprise for those responsible for the master planning of provincial parks.[48] Nor would the Heritage Planning and Research Branch provide assistance, as it had done previously, for interpretive programs in the parks. Given its other commitments, the branch could only "audit and comment upon work produced" by the Parks Division itself. Unfortunately, there were few archaeologists, historians, or cultural resource experts in the MNR to undertake that work. Historical system planning and research in the Parks Division had already been suspended, since there was no one left to speak forcefully for Historical parks and related programs or to compete aggressively for a reasonable share of the shrinking parks budget. At the same time, without direction from main office, historical system planning suffered at the regional level. Before its transfer to the MCR, the Historical Sites Branch had not had sufficient time to cultivate a sympathetic attitude for, or an adequate understanding of, the methodology underlying *A Topical Organization of Ontario History*.

Under these conditions, it was not long before serious problems began to appear in the planning process. For instance, the quality of the historical components of new master plans was uneven, since cultural-resource inventories in many parks and reserves had been carried out in a superficial manner. Moreover, regional master-planning teams often lacked expertise in cultural resources. Under questioning from the Parks Advisory Council in 1977, Robert Bowes observed: "At present we are reviewing five master plans in addition to Lake Superior: Carillon, Polar Bear, Quetico, Sandbanks and Short Hills. In none of these has the Systems Plan been fully utilized, and in certain cases (Quetico and Sandbanks, in particular), although significant heritage features are identified within the plans, no management of these features is proposed."[49] The Quetico master plan of that year disregarded the system plan altogether. No historical zones were delineated in the document, despite the fact that Quetico's history embraces themes of undisputed national and provincial significance. Regional and district personnel argued that because cultural features were located in wilderness zones, protection of those resources was assured. To this the Parks Advisory Council responded that "zoning serves an interpretive function as well as highlighting the need for particular management practices." By failing to delineate historical zones in the Quetico Master Plan, the opportunity had been forfeited to cultivate the public's appreciation and understanding of its heritage, the prerequisites for protection.[50]

Perhaps the most regrettable consequence of the removal of the Historical Sites Branch from the MNR was the destruction of important cultural resources that might conceivably have been saved, had the Parks Division possessed a vigilant and aggressive cultural-resource team. During the summer of 1978, for instance, the Turtle Club Lodge in Algonquin Park, a unique feature of historical and architectural significance in the province, was taken apart by private interests for reconstruction outside the park, even though the lodge had been designated an historic zone in the master plan and in two subsequent studies by the Historical Planning and Research Branch. The park's superintendent and interpretive staff made an understandable and pragmatic decision when they authorized the removal of the structure. With no funding to protect the historic building, either from the elements or vandals, they faced a choice of watching the lodge deteriorate beyond repair on its original site or having it reconstructed and preserved outside the park. They chose the latter option; but, much to their chagrin, the building was not reassembled and was left to rot in pieces at Camp Kandalore.[51] Similarly, Nominigan Lodge, another building of significance, which had been recommended for designation as an historical zone, was dismantled and trucked out of the park that same year, and suffered the same fate.

Within three years of losing the Historical Sites Branch in 1975, the future of Historical parks looked grim indeed. Lacking the personnel to update *A Topical Organization*, to undertake cultural resource inventories, or to advise field staff on cultural resource issues, the Parks Division was not inclined to establish many Historical parks or even to reclassify established parks like Serpent Mounds as historical. Lloyd Eckel, who replaced James Keenan as executive director of the Parks Division in 1976, reasoned that when the provincial parks policy was accepted by cabinet, perhaps the case could be made that the division must reacquire cultural-resource expertise in order to fulfil its mandate in the matter of Historical parks. Meanwhile, he instructed field personnel, confronted with the problem of managing and protecting significant cultural resources, to muddle through by using their "good judgment," and to rely on the preliminary administrative policies document issued for the Historical park class in 1975.[52]

From "Interpretive" to "Visitor" Services

The advent of historical, life and earth science systems planning, the development of a more sophisticated policy for the classification of provincial parks, and the demands being made by growing numbers of visitors in an expanding parks system wrought major changes in traditional interpretive programming. As the Parks Division responded to these developments, the original interpretive program, shaped by Alan Helmsley from 1955 to 1965, underwent a metamorphosis under Grant Tayler and Gary Sealey into the Visitor Services Section (1972), which, in addition to interpretation, assumed responsibility for a much broader array of activities in communications and public relations, recreation programs, and outdoor education services. In the mid-1970s, the Visitor Services Section, faced with the challenge of dovetailing its operations into the frameworks of system planning and park classification in a period of severe financial constraints, sought to rationalize its programming with a policy and a provincial strategy of its own.

When Alan Helmsley left the division in 1965, interpretive programs in nineteen parks were attracting 470,000 users a year, and the numbers were growing. Park visitors were demanding more from their experience than a campsite and a beach. Environmentally aware, better educated, and with more leisure time to enjoy, they wanted to see, learn, and do new things while in a park. To meet the pressure, Grant Tayler, who replaced Helmsley as interpretive supervisor, recognized that the parks program required professional staff in key district offices to advise in the planning and development of interpretive services. By 1969, in addition to the permanent positions at Algonquin and Rondeau, Tayler had obtained staff appointments at Fort Frances (Ferguson Wilson), Quetico (Shan Walshe), Sault Ste. Marie (Fred Cowell), Cochrane (Gerry O'Reilly), Lindsay (Jack Van der Meer), and Richmond Hill (Andy Harjula). During this period, interpretive programs were established in most of the Natural Environment parks in the province, places where previously only an evening of films had been offered to campers. By the time the Visitor Services Section was created in 1972, some 800,000 people a year were attending interpretive programs in 44 different parks. Four years later, visitor services programs in 69 parks attracted 1.5 million users.[53]

With the onset of the international oil crisis in 1973–74, many Ontario campers began to spend more time in one location, a trend which intensified the demand for a broader range of interpretive and recreational services.

Visitor services staff responded by introducing a wide variety of recreational programs. Meanwhile, school boards were turning to nearby parks as locations for outdoor educational activities, rather than acquiring expensive natural areas of their own. Gradually, then, visitor services grew not only in size, but also in purpose and method.

Traditional programs were also modified by the needs of park managers themselves. After 1967, the Interpretive Section was assigned the task of explaining to the public the significance of the provincial park classification and zoning system, and how it was designed to achieve a balance between recreation and preservation and to minimize user conflicts of all kinds. This assignment required an expanded communications and public relations effort, if prospective park users were to be directed to the class of park best suited to their needs. The introduction of the life and earth science and historical system plans also required a major retuning of visitor service programming, since the Visitor Services Section was expected not only to interpret and to publicize the distinctive and provincially significant natural and cultural features of each park, but to explain to the public the role each park in the system played in relation to the others.

In addition to meeting the needs of the system planners, the Visitor Services Section was called upon to develop programs that would encourage environmental conservation among park users. For instance, children's programs, designed to sensitize young people to the beauty of nature, to make them more aware of user impact on fragile landscapes, and to promote their sense of stewardship had been introduced in eight parks by 1972. The idea of using interpretation to stimulate respect and understanding for park environments was not new, but the concept assumed greater importance with the appearance of the environmental movement in the late 1960s, and with the persistence of serious management problems like overuse and rowdyism. Interpreters struck a more environmentally activist note and were encouraged to stress the ecological theme of "man and the land" in their presentations and publications. Special programs were also designed to deal with particular problems. Faced with the issue of the deteriorating canoe routes in the interior of Algonquin and Quetico, a special film was produced to promote proper behaviour in the wilderness. Similarly, to combat the litter problem in Algonquin, an automated slide show, encouraging wilderness trippers to pack out their unburnable garbage, was produced for mandatory viewing by all people requesting a camping permit for the interior. In 1971, Interpretive Supervisor Gary Sealey claimed that these initiatives had saved taxpayers some $50,000 in litter removal costs.[54]

The Visitor Service Section also attempted, albeit with limited results, to play a part in the ongoing battle against rowdyism, which had become a permanent management problem, as it had in other park jurisdictions across Canada and the United States. For park managers, rowdyism essentially boiled down to a serious conflict between "traditional" campers, whether families or single youths, and the so-called "party" campers, the people responsible for most of the unacceptable behaviour. Single young people comprised the latter group, were predominantly male between the ages of fourteen and twenty, came chiefly from major urban centres, and represented a mixed body of students, both employed and unemployed, who came to provincial parks for the sole purpose of enjoying a wingding.[55] A special study, undertaken at Sibbald Point in 1972, documented the behaviour typical of such "party" campers.

> Once inside the park, [they begin] cruising the campgrounds in search of similar groups, parties, eligible females and general excitement. Beer is consumed freely, both on and off campsites. In addition to cruising, they set up sound systems ... and begin using drugs as well as drinking. As the evening progresses, several campsites become a focal point for the night's activity. The results are a high noise level, frequent use of language which is offensive to family groups, racing of cars and motorcycles on campground roads, smashing of beer bottles, and malicious damage to picnic tables, signs, washrooms and trees.[56]

James Keenan investigated such behaviour himself in 1970. "I must confess," he reported after accompanying OPP officers on their rounds in Pinery Provincial Park during the August civic weekend, "that I wouldn't have believed the problems evident ... if I hadn't been there."[57] The following year, District Forester W.B.M. Clark followed Keenan's example and came away with similar impressions. "Pinery Park is a MESS," he wrote after the Dominion Day weekend, "and unless something is done ... we are going to end up with nothing more than a 'Woodstock'" [a reference to the August 1969 rock festival near Woodstock, N.Y., which attracted an estimated 400,000 young people].[58]

The problem of rowdyism was particularly acute in southern parks like the Pinery, located close to major cities, and in a few northern parks, also close to urban centres such as Sudbury, Thunder Bay, and Timmins. It followed a seasonal pattern, beginning at a fever pitch, as a rite of spring, usually on the Victoria Day weekend in May, with serious flare-ups likely to occur on any weekend of warm weather in May or June and the three long weekends in July and August.

In 1970, the phenomenon began to assume alarming proportions. The frequency of incidents seemed to be climbing, along with the number of serious misdemeanours, for which charges had to be laid. When park officials began to monitor statistically the extent of the problem, they found some 17,240 people had been involved in various occurrences of nuisance behaviour during 1972 and 1,284 charges laid. Three years later, the number of people involved in such incidents had jumped to 38,920, and 1,824 charges had been laid.[59] In some parks, events occasionally got out of hand; for example, one weekend in 1972, some 200 leather-clad motorcyclists descended upon the Pinery. They ignored regulations, rode their powerful machines through the fragile dunes, and defied park officials. Following this notorious incident, outraged politicians acted swiftly and placed a ban on motorcycles in the park. An even more serious situation occurred during the 1973 Victoria Day weekend, when thousands of young people congregated in unexpectedly high numbers at Sibbald Point. Seven park officials and two OPP constables found themselves facing a horde of 8,000 youths who "ran wild" in the park for part of the weekend. Eventually 1,200 individuals were evicted.[60] The following year, the phenomenon of "youth invasion" shifted to three other park locations.

"We do not know what causes rowdyism on a sociological basis," noted Operations Supervisor Warren Robertson in 1975.[61] Many theories had been put forward, but no serious research had yet been conducted on the subject by social scientists. "In general, we contend that we are not dealing with a phenomenon unique to provincial parks, rather ... it is simply an extension of urban social problems to park settings. It is perhaps no different than traditional teen-age hell-raising, except that parks have become a focal point, and the number of persons using parks has increased tremendously." The problem had been exacerbated, however, by the lowering of the drinking age in Ontario from twenty-one to eighteen in 1971, and the designation of a campsite as a legal place of residence for the consumption of alcohol.

To help to combat rowdyism, park personnel in main office and the field experimented with a variety of strategies. In 1970, for instance, they reduced vandalism in Outlet Provincial Park by making a special effort to familiarize all visitors with the park regulations, by emphasizing in their programs the fragility of the sand dunes and the need for cooperation of users to conserve them. The following year, at Serpent Mounds, rowdyism declined after the superintendent solicited the support of the residents of the nearby village of Keene. At the Pinery, planners enjoyed some success in reducing user conflicts by introducing a zoning system and redesigning the campgrounds and day-use areas. Pinery staff even experimented with a "Teen-Twenty Youth Programme," beginning in mid-July 1971 and provided special evening activities for young people, including campfire events, featuring rock and folk music. The district naturalist who monitored the initial activities noted that one-third of the group of about forty-five people were "obviously 'high' on something. A few individuals indicated to the staff that they had smoked hashish before coming."[62] To reduce complaints about noise from nearby campers, park officials tried segregating youth campers from the family groups. This practice raised ethical questions for some Park Division personnel. "Two immediate problems spring forth," explained Warren Robertson, "the possibility of discrimination and the contention that we may be condoning illegal activities by setting aside youth areas where ... law enforcement is relaxed."[63] The program for young adults at the Pinery proved to be a failure and was discontinued after 1972.

Even though some initiatives temporarily succeeded in reducing rowdyism at individual parks, the general problem persisted; indeed, within the system it expanded. After a review of the policies and experience of other park agencies in Canada and the United States, operations and visitor service staff concluded that the only way to reduce rowdyism to acceptable levels was a more rigorous program of law inforcement. Accordingly, the number of Ontario Provincial Police stationed in problem parks was increased and, in 1973, fifteen conservation officers were hired, specifically for law enforcement purposes, in ten provincial parks. At the same time, the division introduced a campground preregistration scheme in eleven parks to encourage family campers and to minimize the potential for spontaneous invasions by youths. In 1973, park superintendents and district supervisors attended week-long training courses at Humber College and the Dorset Ranger School on ways of controlling rowdyism. The following year, the OPP mounted a special course on law enforcement for seasonal personnel. When even these measures proved insufficient, the government took draconian action in 1978 and imposed an alcohol ban, from 1 May to 18 June, in eleven provincial parks where problems had been most frequent. The experiment resulted in dramatic reductions in nuisance behaviour; consequently, the policy was gradually expanded, and by 1981 included twenty-one parks.

Visitor services personnel faced many other problems during the decade from 1967 to 1978. On a more mundane level, as the number of parks offering interpretive programs increased, the division found it difficult to maintain high-quality programming in parks that lacked permanent naturalists and museum, library, or archival facilities. In 1972, there were only four full-time staff in the Visitor Services Section at main office, and nine permanent field coordinators at the district level, a number of people quite insufficient to select, train, supervise, and evaluate the hundreds of seasonal staff who mounted the interpretive programs in parks across the system. All too often, the university students, hired as seasonal naturalist-interpreters, possessed little knowledge of a park's features, yet were left to their own devices. Typically, they would arrive at their assigned park and be told by the superintendent to prepare an amphitheatre program – audio-visual slide shows on various aspects of the park's natural and cultural history, followed by a question period. Many students found themselves working under indifferent supervision and lacking basic resources, such as a library and slides. Not surprisingly, the quality of such programming varied enormously from one park to the next. Occasionally, word filtered through to main office about desperate and dispirited seasonal staff screening antiquated, United States Forest Service films of forest practices in the late 1940s, or American cartoon features on the use of firearms.[64]

Fortunately, such stories proved to be the exception, rather than the rule, and most seasonal naturalist-interpreters used films or prerecorded slide-show programs as they were intended to be used, as an adjunct to the live slide talk and question period format. By the early 1970s, moreover, there was little excuse to use outdated and imported material, since a steady stream of exceptionally high quality material was being put out by the Audio-Visual and Films Section of the Ministry of Natural Resources in Toronto. In 1973 and 1974, the section, headed by Lloyd Walton, submitted six entries to the extremely competitive United States Industrial Film Festival and received awards or citations of excellence for every one of them. Walton's *Logging in the Ottawa Valley* won the coveted Gold Camera Award at the festival in 1974. By 1987, Walton had received twenty international awards for his remarkable work.

Even where the quality of the live amphitheatre programs was acceptable, however, there was often a monotonous sameness in naturalist programs across the regions. This became a serious concern once the Parks Division embraced system planning. The seasonal employees would have to be encouraged to relate park resources to the provincially significant and representative natural and cultural themes delineated by the planners. "The problem with defining park themes persists," reported visitor services planner Wayne Yetman in 1975. "Some parks still labour under the delusion that 'interpreting the marsh' or talking about 'Ecology' represents a major provincial accomplishment."[65]

Recreational programming, which expanded dramatically in the early 1970s, also left much to be desired. Frequently, recreational activities in the parks had little apparent relationship to park values. There were notable exceptions. In some parks, visitor services staff created programs that emphasized skill development, including sessions on nature photography, canoe demonstrations, backpacking, and wilderness camping. In other parks, however, there seemed to be an inordinate emphasis on activities designed simply to entertain – sandcastle building contests, movies, or sports events like soccer, court, and baseball games.[66]

Given the increasing demand for all kinds of visitor services, and the problems with existing programming, Visitor Services Supervisor Russell Tilt assigned planner Wayne Yetman, in 1975, to review the entire visitor services operation. Yetman, a marathon runner, who represented Canada at the 1976 Montreal Olympics, concluded that many of the failings in the program stemmed from the lack of an approved visitor services policy and a systemwide strategy. In addition, he believed that unless the Parks Division established such a policy, there was little hope of obtaining the additional funding necessary to overcome the current staffing and programming deficiencies. With these realities in mind, he drafted what amounted to a visitor services system planning document, the "Provincial Park Visitor Services Policy Programme," which received division approval in 1975.[67]

Under the proposed policy, every provincial park would provide a basic public communications scheme that would include low-cost publications, modest displays and audio-visual presentations, self-guided walking trails, personal contact with park users by field staff, and appropriate press releases. The purpose of the basic program was to inform all users about the features and objectives of the provincial parks system, the regulations, facilities and activities in the park concerned, and nearby local attractions.

Beyond the basic level of service in each park, the policy called for the concentration of scarce funding and full-time staff in a few selected "nodal" parks in each region. In these parks, visitor services staff would provide interpretive programs designed to handle large numbers of people and a limited number of activities directed toward the development of recreational skills. In roughly one dozen such parks, the policy called for a "major" level of service, involving up to twenty permanent staff, operating on a year-round basis out of substantial museum, library, and research centres. A second group of some twenty-five "nodal" parks, with modest facilities and staffed by seasonal personnel, would provide interpretive services from May to September. In another limited number of provincial parks in each region, so-called "satellite" visitor service programs were to be developed by a few people who would travel from park to park on prearranged schedules to offer a variety of interpretive and recreational activities.

The visitor services policy of 1975 also sought to rationalize and coordinate the content of interpretive programs. Using the historical and earth and life science system plans, visitor services personnel were expected to inform users of "the story of the most significant stages or events in Ontario's natural and cultural history." For this reason, interpretive programs were best located in large Natural Environment parks, which contained the resources evocative of the provincially significant stories in each region. It was expected that thematic linkages would be forged between interpretive offerings in the different parks in each region and throughout the province.

Policy guidelines were also established to shape the content of recreational activities. Henceforth, organized programs would only be offered in parks where demand existed and where a public-sector alternative was not available. The philosophy and scope of organized recreational offerings in each park would be defined in the park's master plan. Recreational programming had to offer more than mere entertainment; each activity would be judged on the basis of its capacity to provide visitors with an experience that significantly contributed to their appreciation of the park and its resources. Essentially, this meant that encouragement would be given to recreational activities designed to introduce people to new outdoor recreation skills or to provide them with opportunities to sharpen existing skills. In all of this development, whether aimed at interpretation or recreation, the classification system would be a major determinant in the intent and scope of the visitor services offered in each park.

Once approved in December 1975, Yetman's policy resulted in a flurry of activity at the regional level, with the result that within two years, all but one of the eight regions had prepared appropriate visitor services plans.[68] Regrettably, the grandiose scheme, which envisioned both major and minor "nodal" parks, and satellite programs thematically interconnected across the regions, never materialized. It foundered, like so many other initiatives, on the shoals of fiscal constraint. Still, the exercise had not been entirely in vain. Yetman observed that seasonal personnel had begun to comprehend the role which their individual parks played in the system, and were communicating that understanding to the public. To a certain extent, then, these developments indicated that the Visitor Services Section was succeeding in dovetailing its operations with the system planning efforts of the Parks Division and, in the process, was becoming increasingly more professional.[69]

A Planning Triumph, 1975–78

In 1975, the system planning work of the Division of Parks entered a new phase with the release for discussion of six preliminary booklets on administrative policy, one for each class of park. The distribution of these documents marked the beginning of a three-year policy review process, which culminated in the cabinet's approval, in May 1978, of an official policy for provincial parks and the completion of the *Ontario Provincial Parks Planning and Management Policies* manual. The emphasis placed by division personnel on system planning during these years was unprecedented and, in part, a response to the massive cutbacks in parkland acquisition and development funding, which had resulted in a virtually static system of parks and outdoor recreation. As budgets grew smaller, and as new program proposals were shelved, system planning for the future became a logical, inexpensive alternative.

The administrative policy booklets of 1975 represented the product of four years' work by Robert Mitton's planning personnel to revise the landmark classification scheme of 1967. Cameron Clark and George Moroz had worked on the Wilderness and Natural Environment classes, Anthony Usher on the Waterways class, while Robert Beatty drafted the portions of the policy documents concerned with protection objectives. These planners addressed the weaknesses and deficiencies in the 1967 framework, and updated and broadened the management policies for each park class. The five classes established in 1967 – Recreation, Natural Environment, Nature Reserves, Primitive, and Wild River – had proved to be basically sound and, therefore, were continued with some modifications. The new Historical class was now officially added to the system. Two other park classes underwent name changes. Primitive parks became Wilderness parks, and the Wild River class was renamed and broadened into a Waterway parks class, since the term "Wild River" did not encompass the full range of water routes capable of providing quality recreational experiences. Waterway parks would, henceforth, include not only "wild" rivers for the wilderness canoeist, but also turbulent stretches of river for the white-water enthusiast, historically significant rivers, to allow users to identify with past river travellers, and easily accessible and developed watercourses for the pleasure boater.[70]

In the administrative policy booklets, planners presented an historical and a philosophical rationale for each park class, defined its objectives, specified the guidelines for resources and recreation management, identified permitted and nonconforming uses, and provided criteria for the selection and evaluation of future parks of each class. The documents also detailed the ways in which the various classes were interrelated, especially by means of zoning. There were now six types of park zone – Access, Development, Historical, Natural Environment, Nature Reserve, and Wilderness. Parks of a specific class would "combine zones in a particular way to provide protection and recreation opportunities distinctive to that class."[71]

The booklets also addressed the great unresolved question as to the ultimate size of the provincial parks system. In grappling with this problem, planners found Angus Hills's Ontario Land Classification framework, which divided the province into forest site regions and districts, to be one of their most useful planning tools. As we have seen, the biologists had first used Hills's site regions in combination with Paul Maycock's classification of vegetative habitats on site types to set a general target for the life science component of the Nature Reserve system. Briefly, their aim was to represent in Nature Reserve parks and zones all vegetative site types in each of Ontario's thirteen site regions. Since field researchers had not yet ascertained how many vegetative site types actually existed in Ontario, or how many of these were already represented in the provincial park system, division planners were still unable to calculate the number of Nature Reserves required to meet the life science target or to estimate the total land base involved.

Following the lead of the biologists, other park planners adopted Hills's site regions and districts as a framework for establishing targets for other classes of parks. Wilderness parks would be established on the basis of site regions. To meet the targets for the representation of both wilderness recreation and life and earth sciences, planners concluded that the mature park system required within each site region one Wilderness park, of at least 100,000 acres (40,470 hectares), and at least one Wilderness zone, of a minimum of 2,023 hectares, in a Natural Environment park. Planners arrived at the 100,000-acre minimum size for Wilderness parks by using recreation research data (definitive ecological data were not available), obtained from studies in Algonquin and Quetico parks. The average canoe trip in both places was of four days' duration, at a minimum of 8 to 10 miles (13 to 16 kilometres) per day. To arrive at the 100,000-acre figure, planners used these averages, assumed a hypothetical circular route, and added a one-mile (1.6-kilometre) buffer zone.[72]

When given the opportunity to review the administrative policy booklets, preservationist groups universally criticized the proposed minimum size for

Wilderness parks. The Coalition for Wilderness stuck to its position that such parks should cover 960,000 acres (388,507 hectares), to ensure both a quality wilderness experience and ecological integrity. The NPPAC and the Conservation Council of Ontario reworked the recreation research data used by the Parks Division and arrived at another figure. Using an *average* speed of 15 miles (24 kilometres) per day, rather than the *minimum* speed of 8 to 10 miles daily on a four-day canoe trip, and assuming a 5-mile (8-kilometre) buffer zone, both groups recommended a 400,000-acre (161,878-hectare) minimum park size.[73] Upon reviewing the issue, division planners subsequently decided that Wilderness parks representative of their site regions should average not less than 247,000 acres (100,000 hectares) in size, and set an absolute minimum size of 124,000 acres (50,182 hectares).[74] In 1975, full representation of Wilderness parks and zones had only been achieved in three site regions, and system planners recognized that in the two most southerly regions, the land base was simply not available to establish Wilderness parks. They hoped to compensate by establishing in northern Ontario parks substantially larger than the average size prescribed for the class. During 1974–75, Robert Beatty, in cooperation with regional and district staff, completed a project that sought to identify and evaluate wilderness systematically, so that potential Wilderness areas in each site region might be located.[75]

For Natural Environment and Waterway parks, planners decided to use a framework of site districts. In his land classification scheme, Angus Hills had subdivided the thirteen site regions into sixty-five districts, on the basis of land forms containing distinctive combinations of physiographic and biotic conditions. By carefully locating at least one Natural Environment park within each site district, it was intended that the system would embrace the full range of natural environments across the province, as well as incorporating the best examples of Ontario's recreational, historical, and natural features. Although the preliminary policy booklet remained silent on the question of size, it was later disclosed that these parks would cover areas of no less than 2,000 hectares. As of mid-1975, the provincial park system included thirty-six established Natural Environment parks, which represented twenty-six site districts. Park reserves that met the criteria for Natural Environment parks had already been set aside in another twenty site districts.[76]

Waterway parks would also be distributed geographically, on a site district basis. To represent the many diverse lakes and rivers in the province, planners set a target, aiming to locate Waterway parks up to 200 kilometres long and 2 kilometres wide within every site district. This target could also be met by rivers that were protected within parks of another class, particularly within Wilderness and Natural Environment parks. Since one watercourse could represent two or more site districts, planners estimated that between thirty and forty waterways would be required to create the basic system. In 1975, there were only five established Waterway parks, all having been placed under regulation as Wild River locations. However, within other park classes, several hundred kilometres of rivers met the criteria for designation as provincial waterways, including the Sand River in Lake Superior Park, the Petawawa River in Algonquin, and the Pickerel and Maligne rivers in Quetico. In addition, seven other significant watercourses had been set aside, in part or in whole, as provincial park reserves – the voyageurs' route in Quetico-Superior from Saganaga Lake to Lake Superior, the Madawaska, Missinaibi, Magnetawan, Berens-Dowling, and Lund and Telescope Lakes. Beginning in 1975–76, planners formulated the selection criteria required to identify candidate waterway parks, and launched field inventories to assess the suitability of all the province's rivers for inclusion in the system.[77]

In order to set the targets for Historical parks, the earth science component of the Nature Reserve system, and Recreation parks, conceptual approaches were required that were quite different from the relatively straightforward methodology provided by the site regions and districts of Angus Hills's Ontario Land Classification system. Historical parks and historical zones in other classes of parks would be established according to the framework outlined in *A Topical Approach to Ontario History*. Unfortunately, the total land base required to achieve the target of the Historical park class had not been estimated before the Historical Sites Branch was lost to the Ministry of Culture and Recreation in 1975. As for the earth science component of the Nature Reserve system, it would be built in order to represent all forty-two of the discrete ancient and recent environmental earth science themes identified in the Tracey-Davidson framework that organized Ontario's rock strata, fossil assemblages, and land forms according to the time, method, and location of their formation. Again, the Parks Division could not yet specify how much Crown land would be required to meet the earth science target, partly because representation would to some degree be achieved by establishing new Wilderness parks and zones in each site region, parks and zones yet to be created, and partly because inventories of candidate Nature Reserves had not yet been completed.

Establishing targets for Recreation parks called for analytical techniques different from those used for other classes of parks. Planners had to take into account actual demand for day-use outdoor recreation and camping opportunities, and then endeavour to provide basic and equitable levels of service in Recreation parks for the urbanized areas of Ontario. Using an approach developed by Ron Vrancart in the early 1970s, planners divided the southern portion of the province into twenty-five urban-centred population regions, demarcated six urban centres in northern Ontario, and then established travel time limits to define supply zones for each region and centre.[78] Data provided by the Ontario Recreation Survey were used to develop mathematical models for day-use and camping behaviour. The ORS had revealed that for swimming and picnicking, the two most popular day-use activities, 81 percent and

71 percent, respectively, of all participation took place on a single day's trip from home. Approximately 70 percent and 55 percent, respectively, of home-based participation in these two activities occurred within 30 miles (48 kilometres) of home. As little as 10 percent of swimming and 15 percent of picnicking from home base involved more than two hours of travel time in one direction. On the basis of such findings, planners decided that in order to assess the adequacy of supply in the southern urban population regions and the northern urban centres, a two-hour travel limit would be used to define day-use supply zones. Since the ORS had revealed that roughly two-thirds of all camping trips and 80 percent of all weekend excursions took place within 150 miles (241 kilometres) of respondents' homes, a three-hour travel limit would be used to define camping supply zones.[79]

In order to establish the basic levels of supply of day-use recreation and camping opportunities to be provided in provincial parks in each urban population region or centre, planners determined that the principle of equity would best be served by defining "basic supply" in terms of provincial mean averages for day-use recreation and camping in provincial parks for all of Ontario's population regions. The targets for Recreation parks were then described in the following terms: to provide to each population region a level of supply of day-use opportunities comprising 1.3 day visits per person per year (the 1976 mean supply per person for the population regions of the province) in provincial parks within a two-hour range, and to provide to each population region a level of supply of camping opportunities comprising 0.5 camper days per person per year (the 1976 mean supply per person for the population regions of the province) in provincial parks within a three-hour range.[80] Using these targets as a measure of the existing supply, nine of the twenty-five southern urban population regions and two of the six northern urban centres had a level of supply for day visits below the average for all population regions in Ontario. Similarly, for camping opportunities, six southern urban regions and two northern urban centres possessed a level of supply below the mean average for all population regions, yielding a total deficit of 3,740 campsites. The largest deficiencies of both day-use and camping opportunities were to be found in the Metropolitan Toronto and Western Lake Ontario population regions, the very areas which, demographers projected, would receive an increased proportion of population concentration between 1976 and 1991.

At this stage of planning, it was impossible to determine how the targets for Recreation parks would translate into numbers of new parks. Basic supply levels for day-use recreation and camping could be met by expanding facilities in established Recreation, Natural Environment, and to some extent Waterway parks, as well as by creating new parks of all three classes. The recreational facilities provided by the Niagara and St. Lawrence park commissions, and the St. Clair Parkway Commission, would also contribute to the achievement of basic supply levels in southern Ontario.

Finally, it was deemed necessary to set a third target for Recreation parks in northern Ontario, to take into account both tourists en route and destination campers, who travelled considerable distances to enjoy the natural and cultural resources within or near a park and remained for sojourns of three days or more. In 1975, the existing proportion of provincial park day-use and camping opportunities provided for travellers en route in the province was, on average, approximately 20 percent throughout the system. For want of better data, the planners set as their target the maintenance of the existing level of supply per person of camping opportunities, both for travellers and for destination campers in northern Ontario provincial parks.[81]

The six preliminary policy booklets were subjected both to a standard internal review by the MNR's program committees and field organization, and to an external review by various interest groups, the Provincial Parks Advisory Council, and academics. Within the ministry, the documents evoked surprisingly little reaction. Some observers attributed the lack of response to the fact that preliminary administrative policies posed a minimal threat, since documents of this kind implied no commitment to implement a program, and could easily and frequently be changed within the ministry organization.[82] In contrast, external reviewers, while expressing reservations and objections on a variety of points, were generally enthusiastic about the booklets. The chairman of the Sierra Club of Ontario regarded them "as an excellent basis for policy development," reflecting why "Ontario Parks are admired in all jurisdictions throughout the Continent, and are superior in most respects."[83] Likewise, the Conservation Council of Ontario considered them "an enormous step forward in governmental thinking on the role and importance of parks. For the first time the Province is proposing a carefully articulated policy which will clearly direct the planning and management of our Parks."[84] The NPPAC was no less laudatory, describing the booklets as "the best thought out and most important policy documents ever to have been produced by the Parks [Division]"; they could provide "consistent direction through the years and changing governments" for what the association considered "one of – if not *the* – best park systems in Canada."[85]

Buoyed by such positive comments, Robert Mitton and his system planners moved confidently to the next items on their agenda. Early in 1976, they revised the preliminary administrative policy booklets to incorporate the comments received during the review process and compiled them into one comprehensive document, the forerunner of the *Ontario Provincial Parks Planning and Management Policies* manual. Meanwhile, planners prepared an eighty-six-page document, entitled "A Provincial Parks Policy for Ontario: Preliminary Draft" (17 May 1976) and released it for internal ministry review before seeking cabinet endorsement. The document outlined both a goal and objectives for the provincial park system, explained the new classification scheme and the administrative principles to guide planning and management, established both program and park class targets,[86] and recommended priorities for the implementation of the policy. Within the MNR, the reaction to this document was much different from the one afforded the classification booklets. If approved by cabinet, the policy would imply commitment by the government to achieve the program and park class targets. With this in mind, the divisions of Fish and Wildlife, Forestry, Lands, and Mines scrutinized the document, and tried to assess its potential impact on their own activities. The result was an intense and sometimes unpleasant debate on what precisely would be recommended to cabinet.

In the divisions of Fish and Wildlife, Forestry, and Mines, a parks policy that prohibited most types of resource extraction in most classes of parks was bound to raise hackles. These divisions were the bastions of resource managers, dedicated to the concept of multiple use and the "wise-use" definition of conservation. Not surprisingly, then, they were greatly exercised upon reading in the opening pages that the word "conservation" would be used throughout the document to denote "preservation." "There is no 'preservation aspect of conservation.' They are absolutely incompatible," insisted R.M. Dixon, director of the forest management branch in the Division of Forests.[87] Notwithstanding the fact that the Parks Division could demonstrate its use of the word "conservation" was well-founded and internationally accepted by park agencies, the fuss over definitions brought to the surface the deep philosophical differences within the MNR and evoked howls of anger about the "unyielding preservationism" thought to pervade the draft parks policy.[88]

Much of the criticism aimed at the document arose from an understandable fear that if the Parks Division realized its program targets, so much Crown land might be closed to commercial logging, mining, hunting, and trapping that the other divisions would be unable to achieve their objectives. Anxiety levels rose, fueled by the recognition that the targets for Nature Reserve, Historical, and Recreation parks remained vague as to the projected size and number of parks required. Furthermore, the proposed geographical distribution of certain park classes did not sit well with some senior managers. "I have difficulty with the idea of uniformally stratifying a 'park system' across site regions," commented William T. Foster, assistant deputy minister, southern Ontario. "I fail to perceive the logic and am concerned at what this implies in terms of cost, both dollars and other uses."[89] He did not favour the idea of establishing large new Wilderness parks in each site region at the expense of commercial forestry and mining. "The concept that we need to designate Wilderness Parks for back-country travel is self-defeating," he added. "We should promote the use of our 200 million acres of public land for this purpose. Anyone who seeks wilderness in Killarney, Algonquin or Quetico would be very naive." R.M. Dixon, in a fit of hyperbole, took Foster's line of thinking to an extreme. "There is no convincing argument made for parks," he asserted, "most of the recreation and conservation is readily available outside park areas. All parks do is concentrate use, lead to overuse, abuse of water and vegetation."[90]

The Division of Mines challenged the draft parks policy on several points. Given the size and numbers of parks being proposed, G.A. Jewett, the executive director, guessed that "the cost to the people of Ontario in terms of waste of extractable resources will be high." While Jewett accepted the logic of locating Wilderness and Natural Environment parks on the basis of Hills's site regions and districts, in order to preserve outstanding examples of the biological environment, he was not convinced that Waterway parks should be set aside in each site district. He was most concerned, though, about the earth science component of the Nature Reserve system, particularly about the proposed representation of earth science features according to stratigraphy. On this question, Jewett was fundamentally opposed to the proposed policy: "To select nature reserves to preserve representative examples of every stratigraphic unit in the Precambrian, Paleozoic, and Mesozoic of Ontario would require enormous areas of land. To do so also would be pointless, for these stratigraphic units have survived many millions of years of erosion. Their removal or destruction by man is impossible. What should be preserved are outstanding examples of unique rock structures and geomorphological features representing geological processes rather than geological history. The whole concept is wrong and should be reconsidered."[91]

While geologists questioned the earth science framework, the director of the Wildlife Branch, D.R. Johnston, hammered away at the life science system plan. "We would find it very difficult," he argued, "to justify 60–150 Life Science Candidate Nature Reserves ... per site region," particularly since they would be closed to sports hunting and commercial trapping. In making this assessment, Johnston did not take into account the proposal that the majority of Nature Reserves would be set aside as zones within other park classes. A deep-seated divisional jealousy also surfaced in Johnston's commentary. "It can be argued," he claimed, "that Nature Reserves are outside of Parks' mandate. With regard to wildlife management, this Branch would prefer to establish and maintain such areas." Interestingly, at the end of Johnston's memorandum, one anonymous Parks Division scribe half-jokingly jotted: "typical, predictable reaction (innovators and prophets are rarely appreciated)."[92]

Despite the barrage of criticism from the competing divisions at main office, the draft parks policy found a broad base of support in the field, among regional and district staff. Even G.A. Jewett admitted in his memorandum that the policy, "on the basis of the information presented, could not be received with anything but favour by the government and the public." Regional and district personnel offered many constructive criticisms but generally gave the document the stamp of approval. R.A. Baxter, regional director in north-central Ontario, reported that his staff was "both favourable and enthusiastic," while regional supervisors and district managers in the northeast region regarded the policy as long overdue and "agree[d] in principle with its general intent."[93] Lewis Ringham, assistant deputy minister, northern Ontario, commented that the document was "probably the best policy proposal document to come out of the Division of Parks to date. It presents for the most part clear, concise and logical proposals."[94]

All nineteen members of the Provincial Parks Advisory Council endorsed the draft policy. Respected for the informed and independent positions they had taken on a variety of contentious issues, the council members rallied to the support of the Parks Division and unanimously passed a resolution that endorsed the policy, and recommended its release to the public without extensive revision. The resolution concluded by urging the minister of natural resources to "take immediate steps to obtain government approval of the proposed provincial parks policy and, thereafter, to implement [it] ... through the adoption of appropriate planning and management guidelines and the development of implementation strategies and programs."[95] The council had drafted this resolution for maximum effect, in close consultation with Parks Planning Branch Director Ronald Vrancart. Having devoted so much time to understanding and reviewing the earlier classification booklets and the policy, the council took a quasi-proprietary interest in the future of these documents. Vrancart and his staff greatly appreciated the council's assistance, especially since its advice seemed to be taken seriously in the minister's office.

Another welcome source of support for the draft policy document came from John Sloan, then general manager of the St. Lawrence Parks Commission. Sloan was emphatic that the parks operating under the jurisdiction of his commission should be seen as part of the provincial system. Accordingly, he informed the Parks Division that the commissioners wished to be recognized in the policy document as an agency reporting to the minister of natural resources, which served the goal and some of the objectives and targets contained in the policy. Most importantly, Sloan advised the division that the St. Lawrence parks commissioners would "strongly support the operation of the Commission under the provincial park general policy" – a powerful testimonial indeed.[96]

Once the appraisals of the draft policy had been received (by late October 1976), the system planners began to revise the document in the light of the many constructive criticisms, and also endeavoured to allay some of the concerns expressed by senior managers and the other ministry divisions. One of the objections raised most frequently was about the lack of information provided in the document on program delivery – the costs, timing, and staff needs associated with achieving the targets for each class of park. "Program aspects are intentionally not dealt with at this time," parks personnel explained, for the reason that before such matters could be properly addressed, the Division of Parks required broad policy direction.[97] After the cabinet had approved a provincial parks policy, they added, specific programs would be forthcoming to implement it. The worrisome matters of cost, timing, and staff needs could then be sorted out in standard fashion through new program submissions, presenting options so that the MNR, the Resources Development Policy Field, and eventually the cabinet might determine the level of services to be provided and the resources to be committed to the provincial parks system.

The Parks Division also tried to allay fears in the other divisions by emphasizing that park planning would, perforce, be fully integrated into the ministry's overall strategic land-use planning effort then under way. Each new park decision based on approved policy would have to be made within the larger context of land requirements for a spectrum of competing uses. The integration and coordination of proposed programs and targets for parks with other ministry programs would occur after policy approval, when the division directed its efforts toward the development of regional parks system plans. Park personnel were optimistic that as they developed regional plans, the controversial park targets would prove to be realistic. Preliminary strategic land-use planning work in the Algonquin Region already indicated "that all program targets can be met from the ... existing land base."[98] As for the fear in the other divisions that the total area required for Nature Reserve and Historical parks would be enormous, and a threat to many resource-consumptive programs, planners insisted that the area involved would be "very small relative to that required ... for Wilderness, Natural Environment, and Waterway Parks."[99]

Apart from going to considerable lengths to explain the differences between policy and program, the Parks Division endeavoured to accommodate the issues and concerns raised during the review by amending the draft policy. Among other things, its objectives were substantially revised. The initial draft listed five objectives for the provincial park system: Conservation, Recreation, Heritage Appreciation, Travel and Social Interaction, and Scientific Research. To begin with, "Conservation," as a parks system objective and activity, was dropped and replaced with the term "Preservation." The division wisely bowed to the pressure of those who insisted that "conservation," in the context of the MNR, denoted the "wise-use" definition. Ironically, the new term "Preservation" offended as many people as it pacified. For some like T.W. Hueston, regional director in eastern Ontario, this revision only served to fortify the impression that the provincial parks system seemed "much more concerned with preservation, single use and earth and life science features than [it was] with providing an enjoyable experience for the citizens of the province."[100] The renewed debate eventually resulted in another change; this time "Protection" was substituted for "Preservation."

The "Travel and Social Interaction" objective underwent more than a name change, being redefined as "Tourism." The original explanation had emphasized how the parks system, by including representation of Ontario's cultural and natural diversity, could attract travellers and enhance their appreciation and understanding "of the wealth of environments and lifeways of this complex province." However, the document said nothing about the economic benefits of tourism generated by provincial parks. Regional field staff in the north questioned this omission. "A system of parks can be a useful adjunct to the tourism economy in that it facilitates travel (and therefore spending) particularly in more remote areas of the Province," argued the district managers and regional supervisors in the northeastern region.[101] They believed that provincial parks had "a significant economic impact" and that this should be recognized explicitly. Planners in Toronto were not so certain. They had been reluctant to address the economic benefits of tourism, because recent research "showed very minor economic benefits accruing from parks studied across Canada."[102] This explanation did not sit well with the members of the Outdoor Recreation Programme Committee. They deemed it incongruous that the draft parks policy did not explicitly dovetail with one of the primary objectives of the MNR's general outdoor recreation program, that is, to provide an optimum contribution from the tourism industry to the economy of the province and its regions. Since it was obvious that the objective of "Travel and Social Interaction" implied tourism, the committee insisted that the Division of Parks assert this in a positive fashion in a redefined "Tourism" objective. Park planners did as they were instructed; still, they carefully avoided exaggerating economic benefits.[103]

As for the fifth objective, "Scientific Research," it was eliminated from the draft altogether. Various reviewers had commented that no mention had been made in the statement of goals about opportunities provided by provincial parks for scientific research into the ecology of natural areas. Why, then, they asked, was this role highlighted as a separate objective and a primary justification for the establishment of a provincial parks system?[104] The Division of Fish and Wildlife argued that the use of parks for scientific research was overstated, and that other means were available to provide such research opportunities.[105] Parks planners responded to these points, and resolved the problem, first by removing the objective of "Scientific Research" from the document and then by discussing the benefits of scientific research as part of the objectives of protection and heritage appreciation.

While most revisions to the draft policy required changes in organization and emphasis or the addition of explanatory paragraphs, there were fundamental objections to the policy raised by other MNR divisions. This became evident when the revised document went before the deputy minister's staff committee in March 1977. The committee strongly objected to those sections of the document prohibiting the commercial extraction of natural resources from provincial parks. They took umbrage at the description of Algonquin and Lake Superior – the only two parks in the system where commercial logging was condoned – as anomalous and nonconforming. "Unanimously," reported the executive director of the Parks Division, Lloyd Eckel, "the Committee feel that some measure of multiple use should be permitted as a matter of policy."[106]

The committee also took up an issue raised during the review by William T. Foster, assistant deputy minister, southern Ontario, who had argued that the parks policy-making process should be suspended until the government had developed a general outdoor recreation plan for the province.[107] The Division of Parks opposed this argument, maintaining that outdoor recreation agencies should each develop detailed policies at their own speed and within their own capabilities, out of which an overall plan would eventually be synthesized. "The development of comprehensive policies and plans in a field of endeavour as wide-ranging and fragmented as outdoor recreation is an almost impossible task," argued parks planners. "The 'grand design' is a romantic vision."[108] Faced with irreconcilable positions on this issue, the deputy minister's staff committee instructed the Parks Division to address the question once again. Interestingly, when asked for his opinion on the issue, R.J. Burgar, director of the Conservation Authorities Branch, thought the division was on the right track and that the draft policy would stimulate the other agencies to develop an overall policy framework. "The document," he wrote, "will indeed be a useful benchmark against which other agencies in recreation programming can relate during the preparation of their own program definitions, policies and priorities, and the flexible approach to target-setting will lend itself to a more co-ordinated approach to recreational planning in Ontario."[109]

Another item which the deputy minister's staff committee wanted reassessed was the question of near-urban parks. The committee had yet to be convinced that the provincial parks program should take an expanded role vis-à-vis the conservation authorities and municipal governments, by providing more day-use and camping opportunities in parks located closer to the cities. They feared that the draft policy called for "too high a commitment" in this area and cited the costs of acquiring and developing Bronte Creek as an example.[110] It seems to have escaped the committee's attention that the politicians, and not the Parks Division, had inspired the near-urban initiative in the first place.

The deputy minister's committee served a useful purpose by cutting through the minutiae and defining the basic issues still to be resolved within the MNR. It now remained for the politicians and their advisors to impose solutions at some future date. Meanwhile, the committee authorized the policy document to proceed to the next stage of the review process. It was subsequently circulated, with an appended memorandum outlining the three unresolved issues, to all ministries in the Resources Development Policy Field and other ministries with a relationship to provincial park programming, to give them an opportunity to comment before the formal submission reached the cabinet. This phase of the review went exceedingly well. "In general," the Division of Parks reported in September 1977, "support has been enthusiastic and discussions have been useful and gratifying. Where correspondence has not indicated a full meeting of minds, these concerns have for the most part been resolved in discussion."[111] Anticipating that the revised policy document would now be released for public review, the Division of Parks had copies printed for distribution. Unfortunately, senior ministry officials were not ready to agree. The professionally designed documents appeared "too official" for their liking, so approval to distribute the revised policy was not forthcoming. The booklets were placed in storage and later pulped.[112]

On 14 November 1977, Frank Miller, then minister of natural resources, and the members of his policy committee convened to discuss the parks policy. The potential for disaster at this meeting was high. It was conceivable that the minister would decide to halt proceedings pending the development, however improbable, of a general policy on outdoor recreation. Or, perhaps, he might assert the wise-use doctrine and throw open some classes of parks to commercial exploitation. As it happened, the Parks Division suffered only one serious setback during this encounter, emerging with its policy still otherwise intact. The committee required that the definition of a provincial park as "an area of land and water ... dedicated exclusively to public outdoor recreation and preservation" be amended, and that the word "exclusively" be removed. The minister would not tolerate its use when the MNR permitted commercial logging in Algonquin and Lake Superior parks, the two with the highest profile in the system.[113] This decision shocked Ronald Vrancart. "The definition of a park, without the word 'exclusively,'" he wrote, "would permit a policy under which new parks could be established in which commercial removal of resources could take place. Therefore, parks would not be preserved and protected landscapes representative of our cultural and natural heritage, but merely developed recreation spots among other land uses."[114] For Vrancart there was no alternative but to rewrite the definition, so as to remove any implication that parks might be open to commercial exploitation. Agreement was eventually reached on wording that described provincial parks as "areas of land and water managed for the benefit of present and future generations and dedicated to the people of Ontario and others who may use them for their healthful enjoyment and appreciation."

Happily, the two remaining issues were both resolved to the Parks Division's satisfaction. The minister's policy committee agreed "that it is sometimes impossible to delay formulation and implementation of individual policies until the overall policy approach is ready," and therefore instructed the division simply to acknowledge in its submission to cabinet "the need to mesh the ... Policy within the overall outdoor recreation system." Likewise, the committee required nothing more on the near-urban park issue than the inclusion of a statement in the submission of the government's "intention to take into account those other outdoor recreation opportunities already available or planned when planning provincial parks for any particular area."[115]

Once past the minister's office, the Parks Division prepared for the final steps of the policy-making journey. This involved reducing the large document into the mandatory format of about eight pages, for submission to the cabinet. At the beginning of the process, division planners had intended to include the program and park class targets in their final submission. This hope had, however, collapsed under the weight of the opposition expressed by personnel in the other MNR divisions, who viewed the targets as a Parks Division "land grab." Lloyd Eckel, Ron Vrancart, and Robert Mitton recognized that such perceptions existed, in part because the earth and life science frameworks for the Nature Reserve system had yet to be completed, and also because no one could determine how much land would be required for the scheme. Under the circumstances, it would have been foolhardy to have proceeded with such vague targets embedded in the cabinet proposal. The decision was accordingly made to incorporate all targets in the *Ontario Provincial Parks Planning and Management Policies* manual, along with other material contained in the original version of the park policy.

The cabinet submission itself was a remarkably terse document, considering that it had taken nearly three years of intensive planning to prepare. It included the following: a definition of provincial parks, the goal and objectives of the provincial park system, the principles to be used in managing the park system and the classes of parks, and the guidelines to be used as the basis for the preparation of program options to implement the policy.[116] Its text follows below:

Definition of Provincial Parks
Provincial Parks are areas of land and water managed for the benefit of present and future generations and dedicated to the people of Ontario and others who may use them for their healthful enjoyment and appreciation.

Goal of the Provincial Park System
To provide a variety of outdoor recreation opportunities, and to protect provincially significant natural, cultural, and recreational environments in a system of Provincial Parks.

Objectives of the Provincial Parks System

Protection	To protect provincially significant elements of the natural and cultural landscape of Ontario.
Recreation	To provide outdoor recreation opportunities ranging from high-intensity day-use to low-intensity wilderness experiences.
Heritage Appreciation	To provide opportunities for exploration and appreciation of the outdoor natural and cultural heritage of Ontario.

Tourism	To provide Ontario's residents and out-of-province visitors with opportunities to discover and experience the distinctive regions of the Province.

Principles to Be Used in Managing the Provincial Park System

Permanence	The Provincial Park system is dedicated for all time to the present and future generations of the people of Ontario for their healthful enjoyment and appreciation.
Distinctiveness	Provincial Parks provide a distinctive range of quality outdoor recreation experiences, many of which cannot be provided in other types of parks; for example, wilderness travel and appreciation.
Representation	Provincial Parks are established to secure for posterity representative features of Ontario's natural and cultural heritage. Wherever possible the best representations of our heritage will be included in the park system.
Variety	The Provincial Park system provides a wide variety of outdoor recreation opportunities and protected natural and cultural landscapes and features.
Accessibility	The benefits of the Provincial Park system will be distributed as widely as possible geographically and as equitably as possible socially so that they are accessible to all Ontario residents.
Coordination	The Provincial Park system will be managed in such a way as to be complementary to, rather than competitive with, the private sector and other public agencies.
System	Individual Provincial Parks contribute to the overall objectives of the Provincial Park system. All objectives may not be met in each park. The park system, rather than individual parks, provides the diversity of experiences and landscapes which are sought.
Classification	No individual park can be all things to all people. Park classification organizes Ontario's Provincial Parks into broad categories, each of which has particular purposes and characteristics as well as distinctive planning, management, and visitor services policies.

Zoning	Ontario's Provincial Parks are zoned on the basis of resource significance and recreational potential. Several types of zones ensure that users get the most out of individual parks. Planning and management policies appropriate to each zone type are applied consistently throughout the park system.

Park Classes

Wilderness Parks	Wilderness Parks are substantial areas where the forces of nature are permitted to function freely and where visitors travel by non-mechanized means and experience expansive solitude, challenge, and personal integration with nature.
Nature Reserves	Nature Reserves are areas selected to represent the distinctive natural habitats and land forms of the Province, and are protected for educational purposes and as gene pools for research to benefit present and future generations.
Historical Parks	Historical Parks are areas selected to represent the distinctive historical resources of the Province in open space settings and are protected for interpretive, educational, and research purposes.
Natural Environment Parks	Natural Environment Parks incorporate outstanding recreational landscapes with representative natural features and historical resources to provide high quality recreational and educational experiences.
Waterway Parks	Waterway Parks incorporate outstanding recreational water routes with representative natural features and historical resources to provide high quality recreational and educational experiences.
Recreation Parks	Recreation Parks are areas which support a wide variety of outdoor recreation opportunities for large numbers of people in attractive surroundings.

PROGRAMME PLANNING GUIDELINES

Recreation Objective

Day-Use	To ensure adequate day-use opportunities in Provincial Parks close to the Province's population centres.

Car Camping	To ensure adequate car camping in Provincial Parks in those areas of the Province which currently have inadequate opportunities.
Interior Camping	To ensure adequate interior camping opportunities within the Provincial Park system.

Tourism Objective

Day-Use and Short-Term Camping	To ensure an adequate level of day-use and short-term camping opportunities within Provincial Parks for Ontario's travellers.
Destination Camping	To ensure an adequate level of destination camping opportunities for Ontario residents and visitors.

Protection Objective

Earth Science Features	To protect a system of earth science features representative of Ontario's earth science history and diversity.
Life Science Features	To protect a system of life science features representative of Ontario's life science history and diversity.
Historical Resources	To protect a system of landscape related historical resources representative of Ontario's human history.

Heritage Appreciation Objective

Unstructured	To ensure adequate opportunities for unstructured individual exploration and appreciation of the outdoor natural and cultural heritage of Ontario.
Programmed	To ensure adequate opportunities for exploration and appreciation of the outdoor natural and cultural heritage of Ontario through the provision of a wide variety of interpretive and educational programs.

In April 1978, the submission breezed through the cabinet committee on resources development before presentation to the full Davis cabinet on 9 May. Without requiring any modifications, the government approved the submission as the basis of its policy for provincial parks and resolved to make the necessary changes to the Provincial Parks Act. Responding in a way that would have significance for the future, the cabinet took a keen interest in the "Tourism Objective," and instructed the MNR and the Ministry of Industry and Tourism to "work together to encourage tourism in the Provincial Park system."[117] Division personnel quickly produced a brochure to inform the public of the fact that, at long last, Ontario had a formal policy to guide the development of its parks system.

Later that year, in November, the companion manual *Ontario Provincial Parks Planning and Management Policies*, widely referred to as the "Blue Book," was distributed to the MNR's field offices, and made available for public scrutiny. "These policies," Ronald Vrancart explained to ministry personnel, "provide the basis upon which all decisions will be made relating to planning and management and until such time as formal changes are made in the policies they must be strictly adhered to."[118]

Conservationist groups were particularly enthusiastic about the manual, because it specified to an unprecedented degree the permitted and nonconforming uses for each park class and zone. The Federation of Ontario Naturalists, which had been asking for such a policy definition since the late 1950s, extended its "sincere congratulations" to the new minister of natural resources, James Auld, and his parks staff, "on the production of such a fine document."[119] The Conservation Council of Ontario concurred and gave the manual "their highest praise." These advocacy groups saw that the "Blue Book" set an agenda for the future. It would give them a common focus and a unity of purpose in the forthcoming struggle to implement the system plan.[120] The FON worried, however, that the "Blue Book" did not possess an official status, and urged that the Provincial Parks Act be amended to entrench it as a mandatory set of guidelines for planning and managing the park system. Deputy Minister Keith Reynolds thought this was unnecessary. "I note your concern about the status of these policies," he wrote to Mike Singleton, general manager of the FON, "and want to assure you they are, to use your words, the 'gospel relating to parks' ... Before their acceptance as Ministry policy they were the subject of careful review ... As a result ... their influence on action throughout the Ministry is assured."[121] This statement would be put to the test in the difficult years ahead.

The approved policy and its companion "Blue Book" constituted nothing short of a triumph for Ontario's Division of Parks. The production of these documents had required a remarkable planning effort, one of the most comprehensive and advanced endeavours of its kind undertaken in North America. The only other jurisdictions on the continent that had established similar policies describing in detail exactly what could or could not be done in each class of park were the U.S. National Parks Service and the State of California. In the whole of Canada, only Ontario possessed the planning and policy frameworks that would enable people to answer the questions that had plagued all park agency administrators for decades: How many parks of each class were required? Why? What levels of recreational services should be provided in the various classes of parks? What natural and cultural features should be preserved in provincial parks? Why? How much should be protected? Why? What activities should be permitted or prohibited in different park classes and zones? How should each park class and zone be managed? Daniel Brunton, a knowledgeable observer, who had served in both the Ontario and Alberta provincial park programs before becoming an environmental consultant and president of the Ottawa Field Naturalists' Club, recognized the significance of all this. "We have one of the best planned [parks] systems in the world," he wrote in *Seasons*, and "if we can find ways to have it implemented effectively, we may even have the best system in the world."[122] It is noteworthy, too, that other provinces paid Ontario the highest compliment by hiring the key members of the system planning team to develop their parks programs: Russell Irvine became general manager of parks and resorts in Prince Edward Island (1974), Tom Lee, director of parks in British Columbia (1975), and Robert Mitton, director of planning for Alberta's Kananaskis Country project (1978).

The approval of the official policy on parks, and the distribution of the "Blue Book," marked the end of one phase of the system planning process and the beginning of another. Ontario now had a firm idea of what the ideal network of provincial parks should look like. The conceptual and philosophical questions – what? why? where? – had for the most part been resolved. Now the Parks Division, in conjunction with regional personnel, had to flesh out the new policy by resolving the questions of how, when, and at what cost the program should and could be implemented. All the divisions within the MNR braced themselves for what lay ahead. System planners would now seek to fashion detailed regional plans, identifying the actual sites required to meet the program and park class targets set out in the "Blue Book." Whatever the regions proposed would have to be integrated with the MNR's Strategic Land Use Planning effort to accommodate the host of timber, mining, trapping, commercial, recreational, and environmental interests that were all seeking a share of Ontario's Crown land base. To make matters more difficult, this complicated task would have to be carried out after 1978, during years of economic and political upheaval. It would be a period of rising inflation, recession, and continued restraints, and would end with the collapse of the once seemingly invincible Tory dynasty.

Chapter 8

The Challenge of Constraints, 1978–1988

The years immediately following cabinet approval of the 1978 parks policy developed into one of the most difficult periods in the history of the modern provincial parks system. Unprecedented budgetary constraints, double-digit inflation, and recession played havoc with established programming and staff morale. The situation had grown so serious by 1981 that park advocacy groups began to fear that the system was teetering on the brink of disaster. As it happened, the Parks and Recreational Areas Branch (PB)[1] weathered the economic storms remarkably well, and in several important ways turned hard times to its advantage. Main office personnel, together with regional park coordinators and planners, responded to the constraints by introducing a range of efficiency measures, including programs for volunteers and cooperating associations. They also developed major new tourism and marketing strategies to reverse the decline in visitor numbers and to generate new revenues. And, keeping the objective of heritage protection firmly in view, the branch took what was, perhaps, its most important step; it struck a partnership with the Ontario Heritage Foundation and the National Heritage League to pursue alternative methods of protecting significant natural areas. In short, park officials succeeded during these years in making a virtue out of fiscal necessity.

Bleak Times

Budgetary constraints and inflation, above all other variables, conditioned most aspects of provincial park programming from the mid-1970s through the 1980s. Annual expenditures within the parks system (excluding land acquisition) rose only marginally from $30.3 million in 1976–77 to $33.5 million in 1981–82, but with annual inflation running between 7.5 percent (1976) and 12.5 percent (1981), the apparent increase in the budget actually represented a 30 percent decline in purchasing power. Some activities suffered more than others. For example, capital expenditures across the parks system declined 69 percent, from $9.6 million in the peak year of 1974–75 to $3 million in 1980–81. Taking inflation into account, these figures amounted to a staggering 82 percent decline in capital spending over the period. The costs of land acquisition showed greater variation, but the downward trend was the same. Spending on new parkland plummeted, from a high of $10.8 million in 1972–73 to $1.9 million in 1980–81. Even for the last-named period, most of the funding came from special accounts for the Niagara Escarpment ($741,000) and Wasaga Beach ($313,000), leaving a mere $888,000 for parkland elsewhere. Spending for land purchases bottomed out in 1983 and 1984, when the value of properties acquired for park purposes totalled only $55,440 and $342,856 respectively.[2]

As economic problems gripped North America – a second gasoline-price shock in 1979–80 combined with double-digit inflation to usher in the worst recession (1981–82) since World War I – parks officials had to accept the fact that they would be operating within severely constrained budgets for the foreseeable future. "It is our conclusion," wrote the assistant deputy minister for southern Ontario, William T. Foster, in February 1980, "that aside from the Niagara Escarpment area, there will be very little acquisition of land or development of recreation facilities in provincial parks over the next two decades."[3] This news came as a shock to park managers already reeling from the impact of five years of retrenchment. The quality and quantity of services rendered to the public had been declining in varying degrees from region to region, park to park. Operating seasons had been shortened, visitor services curtailed, winter activities suspended, capital projects and maintenance schedules shelved, and staff complements reduced, either through attrition in the ranks of permanent employees or reductions in the amount of seasonal help. For this diminished level of service, visitors paid higher entrance and camping fees, as well as new service charges for firewood and showers.

The situation at Sibbald Point, a Recreation-class park on Lake Simcoe, illustrates what was occurring throughout the system. In 1982 fifty-three employees struggled to complete the tasks undertaken by seventy-one people four years earlier. The visitor services section complement had been slashed from eight to three people. Winter programming, which had once included camping, ice-skating, cross-country skiing and snowmobile trails, no longer existed.

Similarly, in Algonquin Provincial Park, budget cutbacks meant that few of the proposals for development and new programs that had been embodied in the master plan of 1974 could be introduced. Constraints forced the superintendent to close the Canisbay campground in 1982 and to reduce drastically the level and frequency of maintenance on interior canoe routes. Visitor services programming also had to be curtailed, and the number of seasonal employees dwindled from twenty-three in 1978 to fourteen in 1983. By 1982, the park operating budget had been frozen for five years with no adjustments made for inflation – a 55 percent drop in spending power. "What other sector of government can show a reduction of even half that amount?" asked the Federation of Ontario Naturalists.[4]

In 1981, a special committee, appointed to develop efficiency strategies in view of the continuing constraints, assessed the detrimental impact of retrenchment. Operating expenditures across the provincial park system, the committee concluded, had been trimmed to the bone. "Recreation and heritage resources, both natural and cultural, are not being managed adequately given their provincial importance," the committee reported.[5] No more major savings could be achieved without further undermining the capability of the system to meet its objectives of protection, recreation, appreciation of the province's heritage, and tourism. The deteriorating physical plant and equipment, the reduction in services, and both higher and additional fees resulted in user dissatisfaction and contributed to the decline in the number of visitors to the parks. Morale among park staff was the lowest in memory. Overworked personnel were not being offered opportunities for training, professional and administrative employees had to assume tasks hitherto assigned to clerical and junior workers, and superintendents were being forced to rely on cheap labour provided by Junior Rangers and "Experience" program employees earning the minimum wage.

While no one in the Parks Branch quarreled with the necessity of observing the most stringent economy measures compatible with meeting the parks' policy objectives, everyone resented the fact that they were bearing an unreasonably large proportion of the ministry's efforts at restraint. Why, they asked in 1981, had the budget for branch activities increased only marginally (10 percent) since 1976–77, while the ministry's total spending had grown by 52 percent over the same period? Why had the Parks Branch's share of the ministry budget shrunk from 15.3 percent in 1974–75 to 9.2 percent in 1980–81?[6] To environmentalist groups, the reductions in the budgets for park programming seemed excessive, evidence, indeed, of an anti-park bias within the senior bureaucracy of the MNR – "persecution," one FON spokesperson called it.[7]

In Search of Efficiency Strategies

"The way in which constraint has been applied within this ministry has been devastating to the parks program ... and to staff morale," wrote the branch director, Ronald Vrancart, in 1979. "One of the qualifications to work in the parks ... these days is a thick skin (or head)."[8] Actually, those who remained with or joined the provincial parks program after 1979 were not so thick-skulled or dimwitted that they suffered the adversities of retrenchment with an oxlike placidity. With fiscal necessity serving as the mother of invention through the 1980s, parks personnel came up with a broad range of responses to counter the effects of constraints and inflation. At the annual meetings of the Federal-Provincial Parks Conference in 1982 and 1983, dedicated respectively to the related themes of "efficiency strategies" and "innovative management," branch director Norm Richards impressed his colleagues from across the country with details of how his staff had implemented twenty-three different efficiency measures since 1980 to minimize the effects of shrinking budgets.[9] He found a receptive audience. No park agency had been exempted from the constraints imposed during these years.

Many of the measures described by Richards involved relatively mundane operational decisions. Some were as simple as establishing self-service systems of registration and fee collection in many parks during the off-season or designing maintenance-free buildings. Other measures involved complex management procedures. For instance, during the mid-1980s, main office and field staff introduced a computerized system of asset inventory and management, developed capital maintenance standards to ensure the basic upkeep of aging park facilities, and implemented a policy on minimum operating standards to provide consistency of service across the system, and to establish a rational basis for making individual allocations from the park operating budget. The results of these efforts were, to be sure, sometimes mixed. For instance, savings realized by cutting gate and campground staff in favour of self-service systems were partly offset by the drop in revenues, when users failed to deposit their fees. The computerized asset-inventory and management system did not meet initial expectations. Nor did the minimum operating standards policy; the hope that the government, once it had agreed to the policy, would be committed to providing sufficient funds to maintain those standards, proved to be in vain.

Beyond these operational efforts that took place behind the scenes, parks personnel pursued efficiency strategies that touched the public more directly. One of these – privatization – even became a matter of political debate. When first introduced by the Davis government in 1976, many park officials had grave doubts about placing the management of provincial parks in the hands of private operators. Five years later, many of those fears had disappeared. The director himself extolled the virtues of the practice as a tool of cost-efficient management. By 1983, ten parks had been privatized, on the basis of either a lease or contract. In the first case, the lessee assumed all park operating costs and kept the entry and camping permit revenues. Depending on the cost-revenue balance of the park involved, the lessee then paid the government a fee or percentage of permit sales or received a subsidy from the province to cover predicted losses. In a contract agreement, the government took all revenues and paid the operator a set fee to run a park. Richards admitted that there had been a few problems at the outset, because of unsatisfactory operators or unrealistic contracts, but these had been largely rectified by instituting a careful selection process for qualified entrepreneurs, drafting sound agreements, assigning knowledgeable ministry employees as contract administrators, and undertaking regular audits. As time went by, more and more branch officials dropped the term "privatization" and used instead the less pejorative "whole-park contracting," a phrase deemed more appropriate, since the government, in entering agreements with private entrepreneurs to operate parks, did not divest itself of the responsibility of ensuring that "Blue Book" management guidelines were strictly observed.[10]

"The contracting of whole park operations has been successful," Richards insisted. "Operating costs have been reduced and a net savings to the Province realized."[11] Furthermore, user surveys indicated that the policy had been well received by the day-visitors and campers who frequented the privately operated parks. The surveys revealed no appreciable differences in visitor attitudes toward either contracted or publicly operated parks. Most visitors to contracted parks were either unaware that the area had been turned over to private operators or, if they knew, could not detect any significant changes in management, since the operator had to meet the same standards, offer the same services, and charge the same rates as all the other provincial parks.[12] Partly because of user satisfaction, and partly because the branch restricted whole-park contracting to small recreation parks, which contained no significant natural or cultural features, there was only token opposition to privatization from environmental groups. Encouraged by this state of affairs, senior managers within the MNR decided in 1983 to expand the policy. Over the next two years, another eight Recreation-class parks were contracted out, for an estimated net annual saving of over $300,000.[13] It is interesting to note that during these years the province of British Columbia began to contract out park operations in provincial parks that were accessible by road, a development which culminated in 1987 with that government's decision to privatize all campgrounds and day-use areas throughout the province's park system.

As the Ontario government pressed ahead with whole-park contracting, the Parks Branch, like government agencies everywhere, also began to rely heavily on business people to provide more services in parks, such as concessions for outfitting and camper supplies, convenience stores, equipment rentals, firewood sales, and laundry facilities. The incentive to expand this policy increased considerably in 1984, when the government allowed the branch to insert revenue-retention clauses in concession agreements, a provision that authorized the contractors to use a portion of their receipts for the development of capital facilities and renovation, rather than requiring them to turn over all revenues to the province's consolidated revenue fund. Operational efficiencies in provincial parks were also realized through the establishment of more service agreements with private contractors for grass cutting, garbage collection, building, and washroom or toilet maintenance. In 1984, there were 110 individual agreements for concessions and service contracts in 38 different parks. Three years later, the number had doubled; now there were 99 service contracts and 102 concessions.[14] In Algonquin, all of the offices at interior access points and even at the Rock Lake campground were gradually placed in the hands of private operators. The Algonquin experience revealed that service to the public actually improved in many cases. Contractors operating these offices stayed on site around the clock. All the same, the rapid expansion of private-sector involvement in the provincial parks after 1983, especially the growth of whole-park contracting, triggered alarms among unionized public employees as well as environmentalist groups. This concern blossomed into an effective political opposition to "privatization," both during and after the landmark provincial election of 1985.

Volunteers and Cooperating Associations

Fortunately, none of the other efficiency measures introduced in these years stirred up the same political fuss. In fact, initiatives such as the policies involving volunteers and cooperating associations had precisely the opposite effect, generating considerable public good will and satisfaction among park visitors. The practice of encouraging groups and individuals to volunteer their skills and enthusiasm to complement regular park programming had a long tradition in European and American park systems. The relatively newer Canadian park agencies, however, only began in the late 1970s to realize that volunteers could play a variety of useful roles, both in planning activities and park operations. In 1978, partly as an efficiency measure, Parks Canada established the first formal volunteer program in the country. Its success prompted some provinces, including Ontario, to do likewise.[15]

Modelled on the federal scheme, the Ontario program required that all volunteer projects be described and executed through promissory agreements, specifying the details of duties, out-of-pocket expenses, legal liability, accident insurance, the use of government equipment, and so on. Before commencing work, volunteers had to receive orientation to the provincial park system and the program area in which they would be involved. They also had to agree to serve under the supervision of a specific administrator. Considerable attention also had to be given to salaried employees, to assuage possible concerns that volunteers were a potential threat to their job security. The guidelines accordingly specified that volunteer activities were intended only to supplement the work assigned to career employees, and that union representatives were to be advised of all new agreements with volunteers. Park superintendents also had to be regularly reminded that the program would not reduce expenditures, since it cost money to train, supervise, equip, and cover the expenses of volunteers. The efficiency of the program lay in the fact that the supplemental work undertaken by volunteers could be done at a lower cost.

With these controls in place, the program was successfully tested during 1982–83, and approved the following year. By the summer of 1984, roughly 500 people had already contributed 9,500 days of service and had assisted in research projects, resource inventories, photographic reporting, canoe route maintenance and upgrading, serving as campground hosts and hostesses, and organizing and staging interpretive and special, visitor service events. "We have been able to accomplish more than would have been possible in normal circumstances with regular staff," reported Norm Richards.[16]

The Ontario Parks and Recreational Areas Branch also followed the lead of Parks Canada when it came to establishing cooperating associations. These were incorporated nonprofit charitable organizations, managed by elected boards of volunteer directors, which undertook activities related to the educational and interpretive objectives of the parks. In 1978, Parks Canada had commissioned Theodore Mosquin, a consultant in recreation and the environment, to determine whether or not the experience of the successful cooperating associations elsewhere – the National Trust for England and Wales, the National Trust for Scotland, the fifty-seven associations linked with the United States Parks Service, and L'Association des amis du Parc National de la Vanoise in France – could be transplanted to Canada. He concluded that such cooperating organizations would enormously benefit the national parks system by delivering certain interpretive and educational services to park users. The associations he had studied were especially adept at producing and making available through sales outlets a wide variety of park-related publications and products, including books, maps, guides, slides, posters, postcards, films, records, cassettes, videos, reproductions, replicas, and other kinds of souvenirs. In the United States, for example, the Eastern National Park and Monument Association operated 88 sales outlets with an inventory of 6,000 items. The few government-managed facilities in Canada's national parks paled by comparison. Mosquin also noted that the major cooperating associations in Britain and the United States regularly donated a portion of their earnings to support environmental projects, museum activities, library and research programs, and even land purchases.[17]

On the basis of Mosquin's report, Parks Canada established a policy for cooperating associations in 1980, a policy which was an immediate success. With financial support from Parks Canada, thirty-three different associations were established across Canada by 1984, in national parks, on historic sites, and along heritage canals. That year, these groups formed the National Affiliation of Cooperating Associations and resolved both to sponsor biennial workshops and issue regular newsletters, to inform members of new ideas, problems, and achievements.

With the benefit of Parks Canada's advice and experience, Ontario's parks officials determined to establish a cooperating association program of their own. They made this decision primarily as a way of dealing with the intolerable situation that had developed in Algonquin Park, where budget cuts had made it impossible for the visitor service staff to reprint its acclaimed series of booklets, trail guides, and the canoe route map. These popular publications had consistently generated a profit; unfortunately, government policy demanded that all earnings be deposited in the province's consolidated revenue fund, instead of being recycled into the park's publications program. As a way out of this dilemma, in June 1983, the Parks and Recreational Areas Branch encouraged the organization of the Friends of Algonquin Park. Under the terms of the first five-year agreement, signed between the Friends and the Crown, the branch turned over without cost to the association the entire remaining inventory of park publications, materials valued at over $50,000. In return, The Friends agreed to finance the revision and reprinting of the publications, and to use the profits from their sale to underwrite additional mutually agreed-upon educational and interpretive publications, products, and projects. The association could also raise funds through membership fees and by accepting donations.

From the outset, the association became a vital, even essential partner in the Algonquin visitor service program. It was extraordinarily successful, the brightest episode in what was otherwise a gloomy chapter of the park's history. The fee-paying membership of the Friends grew rapidly, from 487 in its first year, to 1,364 in 1987–88. The association opened a bookshop in the lobby of the park museum in 1984 and a second two years later – the Old Ranger Cabin Bookshop at the Pioneer Logging Exhibit. With the earnings from the shops, the Friends reprinted all the park publications, as required, and began to produce new titles, including booklets on the mushrooms, trees, and geology of Algonquin, two new trail guides, a children's activity book, a campers' cookbook, and an historical anthology of writings pertaining to the park. The association also developed its own line of products, ranging from nature postcards and slides, posters and hasty notes, to cassettes and videotapes. In 1988, the popular sales outlets offered an inventory of over 220 items and supplied materials on a wholesale basis, both to businesses outside the park and to the other cooperating associations in the parks system. By 1988, the operation reported revenues of $316,000 and required the services of a full-time general manager and seven part-time employees.[18]

Apart from its publications and sales outlets, the Friends of Algonquin Park generated sufficient funds during its first five years to contribute in numerous helpful ways to interpretive and educational programming. The association assumed the costs of materials required to replace the log seats at the Pog Lake Outdoor Theatre, contributed $2,000 to the cost of renovating displays at the museum, purchased two new films for the evening programs (*The Winter Camp* and *Peregrine Falcon*), paid the costs each year of mailing over 3,000 sets of *The Raven* (the park's educational newsletter), and shared with the Algonquin Forest Authority the expense of remaking the historical slide show at the Pioneer Logging Exhibit. In 1985, when budget cuts threatened to curtail conducted hikes, canoe outings, and special activities for camps and school groups, the Friends even paid for two seasonal naturalists, so that these programs could continue. Two years later, the association agreed to fund the salary of an archivist to organize and index the park archives. Several modest research grants were also awarded for studies of moose-deer relationships, wood turtles, and salamanders. Finally, in 1987, because of its status as a registered nonprofit group dedicated to heritage conservation, the association qualified for a grant from the Ministry of Citizenship and Culture for resource material equipment, a grant which covered 75 percent of the costs of a computer to process business matters and to permit desktop publishing.

The achievements of the Friends of Algonquin Park persuaded parks staff to encourage the formation of cooperative associations elsewhere in the system. In 1984, diving enthusiasts established a second association, The Friends of Fathom Five, which largely dedicated itself to researching and mapping the shipwrecks in the underwater park. Other cooperating associations were incorporated at Killarney, Quetico, Presqu'ile, Bon Echo, Petroglyphs, the Pinery, and Rondeau between 1986 and 1989.

Ad Hoc Funding and User Pay

The great advantage of bringing in volunteers and cooperating associations was that, unlike most efficiency strategies, these enhanced visitor services in provincial parks. So, too, did the branch's efforts to take advantage of every possible source of external funding from public agencies, at both the provincial and federal levels of government. In 1980, for instance, the MNR entered into a joint agreement with the Ontario ministries of Energy and Northern Affairs to fund alternative energy demonstration projects in ten parks. These projects contributed to much-needed facility upgrading, since they involved installing solar panels to provide hot water at comfort stations. The Ministry of Energy resumed this cooperative arrangement in 1984, and over the following two years, helped to fund the installation of solar-powered hot water equipment in nineteen parks and a wind-powered electrical generator in another.[19]

When the Davis government introduced the Accelerated Capital Works Program in the spring of 1984 to promote economic recovery, the Parks Branch seized the opportunity to submit proposals for a variety of projects. As a consequence, the provincial parks system obtained a $2.3-million allocation for capital works projects in six high-profile, intensively used parks. Similarly, in 1982–83, the branch tapped into the Canada-Ontario Special Employment Program to receive an $8-million allocation for 95 projects, including the renovation of park facilities, the rehabilitation of campsites, erosion control, boundary demarcation, and the removal of dead and dangerous trees. Some 1,200 people worked on these projects in parks across the province. This program continued to be a source of funds throughout the 1980s. By the spring of 1989, the federal government had contributed a total of $9.7 million, and the province $7.4 million, to underwrite the costs of 374 park improvement schemes, many of which otherwise would not have been completed.[20]

While ad hoc funding from outside sources provided relief to field personnel struggling to operate the provincial parks within constrained budgets, the amounts involved were insufficient to shield park users from having to assume a larger share of the costs of operating the system. Politicians and senior bureaucrats believed that the fee structures of provincial parks should be brought into line with those of private campgrounds. No one expected that the Parks and Recreational Areas Branch could eliminate its operating deficit (the mandate to protect natural and cultural resources made that impossible), but senior government officials did think that the parks program could improve upon the low, 40 percent annual cost-revenue ratio in park operations, recorded in the mid-1980s.

Accordingly, in 1985, the branch obtained approval for a new fee strategy, designed to increase the percentage of park operating costs recovered through fees to 55 percent.[21] Under the scheme, which was phased in over four years, the costs of daily and annual vehicle permits were doubled to $5 and $50 respectively, the fee for a prime campsite with electrical hookups rose from $8.75 to $13.25 per night, and the charge for interior camping permits doubled to $4 per night. In certain parks, a new winter trails fee of $5 was levied. As it happened, the gradual implementation of the new fee structure prevented both an angry reaction from traditional park users and a decline in visitor numbers, something that usually occurred when camping and day-use fees increased both abruptly and substantially.

The user-pay principle was also applied more rigorously to other areas of park programming. Under the new policy on winter trails established in 1983, the government phased out the traditional grants for trail maintenance and replaced them with a permit system, which gave individual clubs the right to charge for the use of trails on Crown land. The new policy reduced the government's financial commitment and placed the onus upon the clubs to control, maintain, and charge for recreational activities.[22]

The Parks Branch's effort to pass on the costs of providing and managing outdoor recreation opportunities on Crown land, and to promote private-sector initiatives, was even more widely applied through the Crown land recreation policy, introduced during the 1980s.[23] Recreation on public lands in northern Ontario had for many years been a growing headache for personnel in the Ministry of Natural Resources. They were bedevilled by conflicts between different kinds of recreationists, by declining populations of fish and wildlife species, and by complaints from local business interests about the meagre economic benefits being derived from American tourists using public land without cost. Responding to these concerns, the Parks and Recreational Areas Branch tested a new recreational areas policy in northwestern Ontario, beginning in 1983. Under the new plan, American recreationists were required to purchase a permit to camp overnight on Crown land. In certain heavily used localities, the ministry closed Crown land to nonresident campers to encourage the use of existing tourist facilities, private campgrounds, and provincial parks. Several popular Crown land sites were made available for lease or sale, to local entrepreneurs interested in providing new camping or tourist facilities. Nonresidents who wished to hunt or fish on Crown land were required to have a base of operation in the province with a licensed tourist outfitter. "The program will ... mean major changes for the 'pork-and-beaners,' the visitors with motorized homes and motorized boats who head for the back roads to do a little fishing," observed the Federation of Ontario Naturalists when the policy was announced. "And for the sake of the beleaguered wildlife of the north, perhaps that's not such a bad thing."[24]

The four-year pilot project to reshape Crown land recreation policy had many positive results. It generated revenues to offset land maintenance costs, it stimulated local tourist enterprises, it assuaged private-sector resentment about free camping on public land, it relieved pressure on overused campsites, and, by distributing anglers more widely, it reduced the overfishing of some waters. In 1987, the government applied the policy throughout northern Ontario.

A Tourism Strategy for the 1980s

Of all the revenue-generating initiatives pursued by the Parks and Recreational Areas Branch after 1978, the tourism strategy stands out as the most significant departure from traditional practices. The tourism thrust had its political origin in May 1978, when the Davis cabinet, during its meeting to approve the policy on provincial parks, instructed the ministries of Natural Resources and Industry and Tourism to explore jointly the ways in which tourism revenues might be enhanced and jobs created throughout the parks system. Although the cabinet's intervention accelerated the pace of events, Ontario's park officials, like many of their counterparts in the Federal-Provincial Parks Conference, would have embraced tourism and marketing concepts before long, in any case, as a way to reverse the decline in visitor numbers, to narrow the cost-revenue gap in park operations, and to strengthen their bargaining position at budget time by emphasizing the economic benefits of parks.

Responding to the cabinet directive, the two ministries quickly developed the outline of a tourism strategy. Consultants commissioned to assist in the process submitted reports to an interministerial steering committee within six months.[25] One of the consultants, Desmond Connor, a sociologist specializing in public participation, brought together sixty government officials and private-sector experts in six brainstorming workshops (two each in Toronto, Kingston, and Sault Ste. Marie), as well as collecting data through telephone interviews with representatives of fifteen provincial and state park systems and ten commercial theme parks in Ontario. Subsequently, in April 1979, the steering committee obtained cabinet approval to prepare implementation options for three sets of proposals: to improve the operational aspects of provincial parks so as to make them more appealing to tourists, to develop a marketing plan for the system, and to encourage new tourism-related investment in association with selected parks.[26] The latter two sets of proposals heralded the coming of substantial changes in traditional park management practices and thinking, advised Ken McCleary, the park official charged with overseeing the initiative. In October 1980, the cabinet approved the proposed plan of action, called "A Provincial Parks Tourism Strategy for the 1980s," and provided initial funding for its implementation. Future support for the program was made conditional on an increase in park attendance by at least 6 percent in 1981 – a target that the system succeeded in meeting. Meanwhile, Ron Vrancart reorganized the Parks and Recreational Areas Branch and established a new Marketing and Communications Section, which he placed under the supervision of Wayne Yetman.

As they developed their tourism and marketing schemes, Ontario's park managers recognized that potential pitfalls lay ahead. Other jurisdictions had learned the hard way that the promotion of and publicity for tourism, undertaken without considering the implications of a changing and expanded clientele, could lead to an excessive commercialization of recreation, undesirable user pressures, and even a weakening of government's commitment to the preservation of natural and cultural resources.[27] Some aspects of their initiative were also likely to elicit criticism from environmentalist groups, from traditional users, displaced by new visitors, and from established resort and commercial interests, concerned about unfair competition from government-encouraged private investment.

Despite all these potential problems, Parks and Recreational Areas Branch officials remained optimistic that they could find ways to maximize the economic benefits of activities designed to increase tourism in provincial parks without sacrificing the protectionist objectives of the system. They would rely heavily on the new parks policy and their manual – *Ontario Provincial Parks Planning and Management Policies* – the so-called "Blue Book." The latter document had already drawn some of the venom from the issue of tourism and the parks by outlining the kinds of activities that should be permitted in each class of park and zone. Branch planners also believed that fears of excessive user pressure following the promotion of tourism were unwarranted. The existing system could accommodate increased use, since many northern parks reported unused capacity throughout the summer, as did all parks in the spring and autumn. Furthermore, the strategy was intended to appeal to a limited segment of the market, namely, the "higher-income" vacationers. In this respect, the initiative reflected the conservative climate of the 1980s and contrasted sharply with the more egalitarian impulses of the late 1960s and early 1970s, when Ontario's politicians and bureaucrats had taken more interest in providing near-urban park opportunities for the less affluent, less mobile, and less advantaged groups in society.

The strategy unveiled in 1980 encompassed an integrated package of proposals; it included an economic impact study, market research surveys, a mass media advertising and promotion campaign, and a variety of operational improvements. Two research projects received priority from the outset. For one thing, the branch needed a better understanding of the economic benefits generated by the park system. In addition, as the first step in developing a marketing campaign, planners had to develop an up-to-date client profile and obtain more information on what both users and nonusers thought about provincial parks.

The task of assessing the system's economic benefits (that is, the sum total of the economic gains to all sectors of the economy associated with park-related expenditures) fell to Econometrics Research Ltd. Its reports were submitted in February and March 1981. They came as a revelation to many park officials and dispelled old notions that park-related benefits were modest. A conservative reading of the data indicated that in 1979, the total value of goods and services arising from park-related expenditures by visitors and government amounted to $230 million a year, and gave rise to 5,186 person-years of employment. The impact of these expenditures was diffused throughout the province's economy, with most benefits falling to transportation and trade, communications and services, food and beverages, and the manufacturing sector. Furthermore, the data indicated that many parks created economic activity and employment in less prosperous areas of the province, thereby enhancing the government's regional development objectives. Branch officials also learned that these benefits, which were substantial, were obtained at a notably low cost to the provincial treasury, since the government recovered, through taxes and revenues, 73 percent of the $24.4 million budgeted for the provincial park system in 1979.[28]

The Canadian Gallup Poll Ltd. carried out a survey to provide marketing information by means of home telephone interviews, conducted in late February and early March 1981. Some of its findings were sobering. For instance, a significant number of respondents indicated that their rate of use of provincial parks had been declining or had remained the same over the previous five years. A high proportion of middle-aged, middle-income earners avoided provincial parks, since they evoked an image of places for campers only. The survey suggested that this image problem could also be attributed to a widespread lack of knowledge about the changes made to the parks system since the late 1960s. Many had little or no idea of the number or types of parks now available. They understood neither the nature of nor the reasons for the classification system and policies associated with it, and were generally unaware of the attractions to be found in the parks, whether related to the province's culture or its natural heritage. All groups expressed a need for more information about what specific parks had to offer. The survey also supported a proposal that other consultants had recommended the year before: that the provision of alternative accommodation facilities, such as rustic rental cabins and family-oriented lodges, would appeal to potential users in every age category.[29]

Depressing though some of these findings were, they gave park administrators a better idea of the needs and wants of current and potential users in various age and income groups. Planner Don Hallman recognized the implications of the survey data and of the new marketing approach. Gone were the days, he observed, when park managers could take their user groups for granted and continue to develop facilities as they once had, blithely unaware of market needs and changes. "No longer can we assume that our traditional development and management approaches will serve [the public's] needs in the future."[30]

Once main office and field personnel had digested the survey data, they turned to the task of developing a marketing plan for the parks system. The cabinet had already agreed, the previous October, to fund a major advertising campaign. Since branch personnel had very little expertise in this area, they commissioned a professional advertising agency, Camp and Associates Ltd., to design and coordinate a multiyear media campaign that would cover Ontario and extend into neighbouring states and provinces. Subsequently, the agency fashioned a fresh image for provincial parks, as locations to enjoy high-quality recreation experiences, rather than as places to obtain camping accommodation at a low cost. Advertisements soon began to appear in newspapers, magazines, radio, and television, impressing on the public the idea that provincial parks provided visitors with unrivalled opportunities to discover the "incredible" natural and cultural history of Ontario. The advertisement campaign climaxed during 1985–86; that year, the branch's advertising budget came close to $1 million.[31]

To supplement the centralized advertising campaign, the Marketing and Communications Section (absorbed into the MNR's new Communications Services Branch in 1982) encouraged newspaper and magazine journalists to write more feature articles about the province's parks. Meanwhile, at the local level, superintendents and visitor services personnel were encouraged to take a more aggressive role in marketing their own parks. "In fact, many have become members of local tourism bureaus and Chambers of Commerce," noted Norm Richards in 1984.[32] What was initially optional for the field personnel became mandatory in 1986 with the establishment of a policy, requiring that a marketing strategy be prepared and implemented for each operating park, and that these be reviewed annually, as required.[33]

The Marketing and Communications Section also began to meet the public's need for more information about the parks system by issuing a stream of new booklets, information leaflets, and films. Most of these projects were more promotional in design and content than in the past. Beyond building an image, they helped to promote the provincial parks' mandate by informing the public about the variety and distinctiveness of each class of park and by highlighting a code of behaviour that would enhance the users' experience and reduce conflicts. As a major component of the early promotional campaign, the section produced an attractively designed traveller's guide, entitled *Ontario Provincial Parks, Yours to Discover* (1981), a project which cost approximately $300,000. At the same time, the branch produced *Provincial Nature Reserves in Ontario* (1981), the first booklet to describe in detail the special characteristics and significance of Nature Reserves, the need for them, and the methods for selecting and managing them. In the ongoing battle against rowdyism, the communications section also prepared a special leaflet and poster on the policies toward alcohol use in effect throughout the parks system.

Cinematographer Lloyd Walton contributed to the promotional campaign with three new films. *Natural Journey*, produced in cooperation with the Ministry of Industry and Tourism (MIT) to capture the essence of provincial parks, was translated into Dutch, French, German, and Japanese for distribution overseas. Another film, *Ontario by Canoe*, focussed on the natural and cultural resources and services available throughout the province's unrivalled waterway network and complemented the popular new book, *Canoe Routes of Ontario* (1981) published in cooperation with McClelland and Stewart Ltd. The volume provided thumbnail descriptions and maps of over 100 routes and 21 provincial canoe areas. A third film, *The Riverman*, featured the recreational and cultural opportunities available in Waterway parks, by following the adventures of two latter-day wilderness trippers, as they relived a fascinating phase of Ontario's history by retracing the route taken by an old river man. These and two dozen others were distributed to fifteen regional library systems across Ontario (960 branches in all), to the Ministry of Culture and Recreation's Audio-Visual Resource Centre in Toronto, and to TV Ontario.

Apart from paying attention to the promotional aspects of marketing provincial parks, branch personnel also invested considerable energy in improving park operations, so as to enhance both visitor satisfaction and tourism. To provide better travel counselling services, the Ministry of Industry and Tourism agreed to create special display sections for park brochures and booklets in information offices at the Eaton Centre in Toronto, at Queen's Park, and at travel centres elsewhere. Meanwhile, park superintendents and other front-line personnel attended the MIT's "We Treat You Royally" seminars, to learn the importance of hospitality skills and techniques in tourism promotion.[34] Thereafter, visitor satisfaction became a recurring theme in professional development sessions for parks personnel. In 1987, for instance, the annual park managers' meeting in Dorset, attended by 150 people, mainly superintendents, was devoted entirely to the topic of "Excellence in Customer Service." New training materials under the title "Visitors First" were also produced.

One of the major successes in the effort to improve park operations began in 1978, with the introduction of a campsite reservation system in twelve parks. Two years later, with the advent of the tourism campaign, the branch expanded the number of parks participating in the scheme from sixteen to seventy-seven. The service proved to be enormously popular with park users and travellers, who appreciated the convenience of an assured campsite. By 1985, over 75,000 applications were processed by the 76 parks then accepting reservations. That same summer, the scheme became even more convenient, when the government permitted the use of credit cards for the payment of camping fees and the purchase of annual vehicle permits. Travellers welcomed the innovation, because it created a guaranteed reservation service, similar to those of commercial establishments. Eventually, parks staff refined the scheme and required prepayment by those using credit cards, thereby eliminating the problem of no-shows, and increasing campsite revenues. Finally, following the successful testing of a computerized service at Killbear in 1985, the reliability of the system was again enhanced. Four years later, computerized reservation services were operating in a total of fifteen parks.

The quality and number of facilities available to users of provincial parks became another primary concern for those seeking to market the system. In this area, however, park staff found themselves caught in a vicious circle. They knew from market surveys that both current and potential users wanted upgraded facilities. Yet the fiscal reality of the 1980s was resulting in reduced maintenance and capital works schedules and an aging, deteriorating physical plant. Each year, main office and field personnel did their best to cope with this problem by cobbling together operating budgets with infusions of funds from outside sources.

Under these circumstances, the development of new park facilities within normal operating and capital budgets was limited. Special funding from another ministry was required to launch most of the major new capital projects during these years. Beginning in 1980, the Ontario Ministry of Northern Affairs (MNA), reconstituted as the Ministry of Northern Development and Mines (MND&M) in 1985, agreed to share the costs of major projects in six parks, located in the area between Fort Frances on the west and North Bay on the east. Northern Affairs chose to fund these schemes, because they were all intended to highlight the special natural and cultural features of each park, in order to attract more visitors and to contribute to local economies. At Kakabeka Falls, for instance, the MNA provided over $300,000 to develop a large new parking area, to produce historical display panels, and to construct viewing platforms at the edge of the cataract and along the river gorge. Following the completion of these improvements in 1982, the number of visitors to the park averaged 300,000 a year from 1982 to 1986, a turnout which rivalled the attendance at Old Fort William. Impressed by these results, the MND&M agreed in 1986 to share the costs of constructing a new visitor centre at Kakabeka Falls.[35]

In Quetico, the continuing joint efforts of the MNR and MND&M resulted in the construction, in 1985–86, of an award-winning visitor pavilion. The

Quetico Foundation also funded the establishment of the John B. Ridley Research Library in the pavilion and the salary of a librarian. Elsewhere during the period from 1982 to 1986, the two ministries shared the costs of improved road access, trails, viewing platforms, pedestrian bridges, and interpretive display panels at the Agawa Pictograph site in Lake Superior Park, at Potholes Provincial Park Nature Reserve, and Chutes Park. They also funded the expansion of two historical attractions, the open-air logging museum at Wakami Lake and the reconstructed, turn-of-the-century pine-logging camp at Marten River. The latter project, completed in 1986, provided the location for the film *The Winter Camp*, produced by the MNR and funded by the MND&M.

In southern Ontario, the most substantial and important new development occurred at Petroglyphs Provincial Park on the Trent-Severn corridor. With financial assistance from the province's Board of Industrial Leadership and Development program, and the advice of scientists at the Canadian Conservation Institute in Ottawa, an ingeniously designed, seven-sided glass protective shelter was erected over Canada's most significant collection of Indian rock carvings. Construction took place during 1984–85 at a cost of approximately $800,000. In 1987, nearby Serpent Mounds on Rice Lake also obtained a long-awaited visitor centre.

The effectiveness of the multifaceted tourism strategy could not be precisely measured, since many variables influenced the number of people visiting the parks. Still, initial results indicated that the tourism initiatives had helped to reverse the decline in the number of users since the mid-1970s. Initially, the results were gratifying. "Our parks visitation has increased by 6% in 1981, by 5.1% in 1982 and by 9.5% in 1983," reported Norm Richards. "Furthermore, the number of telephone inquiries about provincial parks in … travel information offices has increased substantially, by 39% in 1981, by 34% in 1982 and by 22% in 1983."[36] Ironically, over the next several years, when the advertising campaign was at its peak, visitor numbers dropped slightly and stabilized between 7.3 million and 7.5 million users a year – a reflection of the general stagnation in tourism across Ontario during the period. But numbers began to rise again in 1987, when 8 million were recorded.

Measured in terms of user satisfaction, the systemwide effort to improve park operations as part of the tourism strategy paid dividends and probably helped to offset the negative effects of constrained budgets. Individual park surveys conducted during the mid-1980s indicated high visitor-satisfaction levels, despite the introduction of so many efficiency measures. In 1987, the Provincial Parks Advisory Council confirmed these earlier findings during a study to assess how effectively the system was meeting the needs of visitors, particularly families. "The Ontario Provincial Parks continue to be, from the users' standpoint, an excellent system," the council concluded. When asked to give an indication of their overall level of satisfaction with the parks, most

The original Quetico Provincial Park nature museum in 1957.
Courtesy: Ministry of Natural Resources.

The new visitor pavilion at Quetico Provincial Park, 1986. *Courtesy: Ministry of Natural Resources.*

respondents had indicated that they were either satisfied (89.5 percent) or very satisfied (6.4 percent) with the existing state of affairs.[37]

Notwithstanding these signs that their strategy had succeeded, parks officials could not rest on their laurels. In 1988, for instance, the Provincial Parks Council deplored the lack of coordination between the MNR, other ministries and municipalities, when it came to marketing provincial parks at the local and regional levels. Furthermore, during its travels across Ontario, the council discovered that "Provincial parks are Ontario's best kept secret." To overcome this problem, the council asserted, it would be necessary to do more "advertising to heighten awareness of park opportunities and events." This touched a sore point with the personnel of the Parks and Recreational Areas Branch, whose advertising budget had just been slashed in the most recent round of constraints. In 1988, only two years after the government authorized the expenditure of nearly $1 million for television and print advertising, the budget had been reduced to $150,000. Whatever gains had been made were in danger of being lost. "To be effective," warned one marketing consultant, "advertising must be conducted as a continuous process."[38]

Despite the uncertainties surrounding funding, the branch began to lay the groundwork for a new strategy that would chart the course of the parks system through the 1990s and into the next century. In May 1988, a Toronto management consulting firm, Laventhol and Horwath, completed the most ambitious marketing research study ever commissioned by the branch to ascertain the characteristics of current and potential markets for Ontario's park system. The report did not paint a rosy picture; indeed, it suggested that the marketing of provincial parks would become an increasingly complex, difficult, yet essential business. The consultants argued that changing demographic and socioeconomic trends indicated that park managers faced a struggle merely to retain their existing market share. Competition was likely to increase as more investors offered a wider choice of consumer services. To complicate matters further, park managers would have to respond appropriately to major trends, including factors such as changes in family structure, household size and composition, an aging population, and decreased leisure time within the family, as women entered and remained in the work force in greater numbers. These trends were combining to create a more diverse and fragmented market for provincial parks, a situation which would require planners to introduce new developments and initiatives in communications to address the unique needs and wants of each market segment.[39]

According to the Laventhol and Horwath study, family camping would remain the mainstay of provincial park use, though the market had stabilized and would not likely expand. It followed that the greatest potential for growth in park visitation lay in day-use activities. The consultants recommended this might be achieved by expanding facilities in southern parks, or by marketing the province's parks to tourists while they vacationed in northern Ontario.

Determining the socioeconomic groups to be targeted in the new marketing strategy would call for some difficult decisions and not a little soul-searching. The consultants and branch personnel concerned with cost-revenue considerations wanted to attract market segments with potential, particularly those in the middle to upper income brackets, who were to be found among the middle-aged, well-educated, family-oriented residents of southern Ontario. The Provincial Parks Council, on the other hand, regretted the purely economic objectives that had been pursued by the first tourism strategy and urged the minister of natural resources to encourage the use of provincial parks by special populations – the disabled, single-parent families, people in institutions, and low-income groups – by including them in future marketing plans.[40] It was a commendable recommendation, which evoked memories of the social equity objectives behind the near-urban park concept of the early 1970s.

Another difficult marketing challenge identified by the consultants involved the problem of retaining the support of the mainstay, family camper group, while making adjustments to attract other primary targets. Little would be gained by introducing changes for potential users, if the family campers were alienated in the process. The survey data indicated that campers opposed intrusive developments such as resorts and lodges; they favoured instead service-oriented developments – interpretive centres, recreation programs, more equipment-rental facilities, improved food services, and provision for rustic, backwoods shelters or rental cabins. Family campers, however, made up less than half of the outdoor vacation group that the consultants had identified as a market segment with high potential for increasing the numbers of visitors to the parks. The noncamper segment of the outdoor vacationists preferred accommodation in cottages or modestly priced, family-oriented lodges. One way of meeting the needs of both groups, the consultants suggested, was to designate a few parks as locations for commercial lodge development.

In fact, the Parks and Recreational Areas Branch had been moving gradually in this direction throughout the decade. One of the original three sets of proposals in "A Provincial Parks Tourism Strategy for the 1980s" had been to encourage tourism-related commercial investment in association with selected parks. To that end, between 1983 and 1986, the government had commissioned four market feasibility studies for Algonquin, Lake Superior, Sibley (now Sleeping Giant), and Sandbanks parks, to ascertain whether commercially viable business opportunities existed in each location. The first and most promising study, funded by the Ministry of Industry and Tourism, focussed on the historic Lakeshore Lodge in Sandbanks Provincial Park, closed in 1970 after a century of operation. Three government ministries were interested in reopening the lodge as a means of preserving an outstanding heritage building, while creating a quality tourist attraction and resort complex. The study concluded that a restored Lakeshore Lodge would indeed be "a financially viable proposition," if developed to serve the requirements of families during the summer and the senior citizens' bus-tour market in the spring and fall.[41] Subsequently, the Ministry of Industry and Tourism prepared and distributed an investment booklet for the project and advertised in the *Financial Post* and the local media. The effort almost came to fruition in 1985 with the signing of a development agreement with local business interests. Regrettably, because of delays occasioned by the election held that year and the concomitant political uncertainties, the agreement lapsed.

Elsewhere, by the end of the 1980s, the effort to encourage tourism-related investment had not evolved beyond the stage of feasibility reports and planning. At Lake Superior, consultants determined that a lodge facility would not be a profitable venture, although, in time, modest cabin-type accommodation might be economically feasible.[42] The report on tourism development at Sibley concluded that lodge accommodation would be successful, provided that the government created the necessary climate for investment by developing the park's natural attractions and building the essential infrastructure. Eventually, many of the recommendations, calling for a host of new private and public developments, were embodied in the park management plan, unveiled in Thunder Bay by Natural Resources Minister Vincent Kerrio in November 1988. Kerrio announced that Sibley would henceforth be known as Sleeping Giant Provincial Park, and anticipated that it would soon play a role as a regional tourist attraction. The new management plan made provision for a lodge and seminar centre, serviced by hydro and telephone lines, improved highway access, equestrian trails and stables, a marina, and a store.[43]

At Algonquin, the development study of 1986, commissioned by the Ministry of Natural Resources, took on special importance, since the park would be celebrating its centennial in 1993.[44] Specifically, the government wanted to know what type of tourism services and new accommodation facilities should be encouraged, both within and adjacent to the park, to stimulate economic growth in the surrounding region. These were urgent questions because, as a tourist resource, Algonquin had been in serious decline for more than a decade. Constrained budgets had prevented park staff from implementing the improvements in facilities and programming, necessary to keep Algonquin abreast of the trends in the tourist industry. Between 1975 and 1985, the annual number of visitors to Algonquin had declined by 23 percent. Campsite permits were 33 percent lower in 1985 than they had been a decade earlier, while July-August campsite occupancy rates had dropped from 90 percent to 60 percent over the decade. Algonquin, in short, had not maintained its competitive edge in the marketplace of tourism and outdoor recreation. To regain that edge, the consultants argued, Algonquin would do well to follow the lead of those parks across North America that had successfully maintained or increased their market share by offering new programmed activities and interpretive services, and by providing updated facilities, including different types of roofed accommodation. Although Algonquin offered

Sleeping Giant Provincial Park (formerly Sibley). *Courtesy: Ministry of Natural Resources.*

high-quality lodge accommodation, no provision had been made for the large middle section of the market, which included family vacationers and senior citizens on coach tours.

On the basis of the recommendations contained in the study, regional planners sought funding for a comprehensive program of park renewal. Beyond a massive upgrading of existing facilities, the proposal called for the construction of a new visitor centre and restaurant, a four-season, family-oriented lodge, and a wilderness skill development centre along the Highway 60 corridor. For the interior, the plan anticipated major programming changes, including the introduction of themed canoe routes, rustic, ranger-type cabins along one canoe route, and paddle-in destination campsites. "A failure to proceed," regional personnel warned, "will result in a continuing deterioration of a significant provincial heritage and a further decline in park visitation."[45] Subsequently, the Algonquin proposals were placed at the centre of a larger provincial capital renewal plan, submitted to cabinet in 1987 by the Parks and Recreational Areas Branch. Recognizing the need to revitalize the provincial parks system for its centennial in 1993, the Peterson government announced that it intended to commit about $11 million annually over five years for the proposed scheme.

Top priority in the revitalization scheme went to Algonquin's visitor centre and restaurant complex. By virtue of the fact that a proposal for a new visitor centre had been included in the park's master plan since 1974, the ministry was able to proceed immediately with the project. Construction of the access road began in February 1989, and work on the centre and a new logging museum started in June 1990. As for the lodge, skill centre, backwoods cabins, and so forth, the implementation of these projects could only proceed pending public acceptance during the management plan review process in 1989.

How the public would respond to the inclusion of tourism-related developments in park management plans was by no means clear. Environmental groups expressed alarm over the Sleeping Giant plan in November 1988 and denounced the new "booster mentality" within the MNR. The FON opposed all attempts to locate lodges in provincial parks, and vowed to fight every effort to do so on a park-by-park basis. "From Woodland Caribou in the west to Bon Echo in the east," the FON declared in the spring of 1989, "the MNR has repeatedly shown its determination to force private commercial tourist developments into the parks of Ontario. The implication is clear: high-impact, high-intensity tourism is the newest major threat to our parks."[46]

The controversy over the development of tourism in provincial parks reflected the substantial changes that had taken place in provincial park management attitudes and practices since 1978. Previously, the term "marketing" was seldom used by park officials. There was no perceived need for paid advertising campaigns to increase the numbers of visitors to the parks. No policies existed that required an overall provincial marketing strategy or customized marketing plans for individual parks. No one called for publicly funded feasibility studies as a first step to encouraging private investors to develop lodges and other tourism-related commercial endeavours in parks. Planners, whose attitudes had been shaped by three decades of seemingly insatiable demands for parkland and outdoor recreation opportunities, still took visitors for granted and paid scant attention to market changes and needs. Had any one of them suggested that parks were "products," to be "packaged" and "promoted," it would have been viewed as sacrilege by most of their colleagues.

Attitudes changed after 1978, as main office and field personnel endeavoured to cope with constraints and declining numbers of visitors. Circumstances forced parks staff to accept the fact that they would have to make major management adjustments, simply to retain the system's share of the outdoor recreation market. As hard times took their toll, the advantages of marketing provincial parks became evident. By the mid-1980s, marketing jargon had become commonplace within the branch, and it was a rare administrator, indeed, who could not rattle off in catechetical fashion the six "Ps" of marketing. "We must carefully analyze our target markets or PEOPLE to identify their needs, revamp our PRODUCT (the parks) to meet those needs, and PRICE the product so that it is within their expectations," declared the 1986 policy on marketing strategies. "We must PLACE or distribute facilities and services where needed as well as distribute use throughout the parks, we must also develop PACKAGES which match customer needs, and finally PROMOTE the product to the potential customer."[47] In the light of continuing fiscal tribulations and compelling demographic, social, and economic trends, the application of marketing methods to the provincial parks had become an essential management practice.

New Directions for Natural Heritage Protection

Just as years of belt tightening modified the attitudes and practices of provincial park officials toward tourism and the marketing of provincial parks, so, too, did budgetary pressures bring major changes in the way they pursued the preservation of natural areas. As we have seen, up to 1978, planners and specialists had concentrated on meeting protection objectives by building a comprehensive system of Nature Reserve and Wilderness parks and zones across Ontario. To that end, they had conceptualized complex planning frameworks, so as to represent fully the province's natural earth and life science heritage in the parks, and in 1977 had obtained special funding from the Management Board of Cabinet to complete the area identification studies that were required to locate and document the province's significant ecological areas and sites of interest in earth science.[48] As field research teams submitted their inventory reports from 1977 to 1981, registries of significant natural areas were developed for each administrative region of the MNR. Gradually, an accurate picture of what was already protected in Ontario emerged, and also of what was known, but not yet included, within the parks system.

Midway through the inventory stage, questions of cost and the availability of significant natural sites began to dominate the thinking of branch personnel. It became apparent that achieving the objective of protection was a much larger and complex undertaking than originally anticipated, and that the goal of including a comprehensive representation of Ontario's natural heritage features in the parks system greatly exceeded the branch's financial grasp. With the exception of the Niagara Escarpment, where the Davis administration committed itself in 1984 to spending $25 million over ten years for the acquisition of significant natural areas, the cabinet was adamant about curbing parkland purchases. This presented branch personnel with a dilemma. "We have a good rationale and sound information," wrote the director, Ron Vrancart, in 1978, "to initiate the acquisition of provincially significant lands under private ownership that contribute substantially to our nature reserves ... Ironically, at the same time that we are prepared to move with confidence, we are powerless to acquire any of these lands."[49]

In deference to budgetary realities, park planners began to advocate a new approach to natural areas protection. David Boggs, manager of the planning section in 1980, acknowledged that "if we are ... to achieve the objective of setting aside for posterity a network of significant natural areas, it is going to require the co-ordinated efforts of like-minded government agencies, organizations, interest groups and indeed individuals."[50] A common-sense strategy of implementation called for a marriage of public and private efforts at preservation, the pooling of expertise and resources, and a much heavier emphasis on the concept of conservation as private stewardship. To advance these ideas and to promote interagency discussion of the new approach, the branch hosted the Nature Conservation Day seminar on 26 March 1980.

As planners reviewed their options under the weight of constraints, they concluded that the Ontario Heritage Foundation, an established government agency, directed by a board of private citizens, could play a central role in developing alternative methods of protecting the province's natural heritage. The trick was to persuade the foundation to move into the natural heritage field. Since receiving its charter in 1968, the OHF had focussed almost exclusively on activities directed toward cultural resources, which fell under the Ministry of Culture and Recreation's mandate: conserving buildings of architectural and historical significance, licensing and financing archaeological digs, serving as an official recipient of gifts to the province of works of art and museum artifacts, and funding historical publications. The foundation's statutory responsibilities, however, went beyond the field of cultural resources and included natural heritage activities under the MNR's mandate. According to the Ontario Heritage Foundation Act (1967), the OHF was empowered to receive, acquire, preserve, support and contribute to the acquisition, holding and management of property of "historical, architectural, recreational, aesthetic or scenic interest." In fact, the foundation had already played a modest role in the protection of natural areas by receiving gifts of natural heritage properties to the province (ten by 1982), which had, for management purposes, been placed in the custody of either a conservation authority or the Ministry of Natural Resources.[51]

Above all else, it was the foundation's function as a "trust" that intrigued parks personnel. A gift of property to the OHF resulted in generous tax exemptions for the donor (potentially to the full extent of his or her taxable income), a powerful incentive, indeed, to make gifts of land. Park officials looked forward to striking a partnership with the foundation and using this tax-exemption mechanism to encourage individuals and corporations to donate significant natural properties to the province for designation as Nature Reserves.

The Parks and Recreational Areas Branch also wanted to benefit from the OHF's expertise in the acquisition of conservation easements on privately owned property or buildings of architectural, historical, or archaeological significance for the province. Conservation easements were legally binding agreements, arranged with the consent of property owners to secure the protection of properties from unsympathetic alterations in perpetuity. An obvious cost-effective alternative to fee simple land acquisition, easements had not yet been employed to protect significant natural areas. Parks officials wanted to rectify that omission through an alliance with the OHF. They had discovered that, from a legal perspective, the foundation was best situated to expand the use of easements to preserve natural areas, since these were signed by the foundation under the authority of the Ontario Heritage Act and did not suffer from the weaknesses of previous common-law agreements. An OHF easement could be "enforced against the donor, or any future owner, regardless of the nature of the obligations posed by the easement or whether the body holding the easement owns adjoining lands."[52] Although none of the sixty-five conservation easements held by the foundation in 1982 protected natural areas, park officials recognized that there was nothing to prevent the OHF from employing this option to protect sites of biological and geological significance. Other jurisdictions in the United States already did so. For example, the state of Maine had negotiated over 180 agreements with private landowners to protect some 14,000 acres (5,666 hectares) of Atlantic coastline.

With these ideas in mind, Ron Vrancart and planner Robert Beatty appeared before the foundation's directors in January 1977 and endeavoured to convince them that they should expand their activities into the natural heritage field.[53] The directors, however, decided against such action, in fear of overextending the limited resources at the foundation's command.[54] Vrancart's response to this setback was to propose the establishment, under the auspices of the MNR, of an Ontario Outdoor Recreation Foundation, to duplicate, in the field of outdoor recreation and natural heritage, the work of the OHF in the area of cultural resources.[55] His proposal bore fruit, but in an unexpected way. It prompted senior management, both in the ministries of Natural Resources and Culture and Recreation, to reconsider the Ontario Heritage Foundation's roles and responsibilities. After intensive interministerial consultation, it was decided that a second foundation was unnecessary, and that the OHF should broaden the scope of its activities to include the protection of natural heritage.

The process was greatly facilitated by the naming of former provincial treasurer John White as chairman of the OHF in 1980 and the appointment to the foundation, at White's insistence, of G.H.U. "Terk" Bayly, a former deputy minister of the Department of Lands and Forests and the recently retired secretary to the Management Board. Both individuals brought an unprecedented level of political influence to the foundation and to the movement to preserve natural areas. Bayly was the first natural heritage specialist to sit on the OHF's board of directors and the ideal person to spearhead the foundation's efforts in this new field.

In consultation with park officials, White and Bayly agreed that the foundation must first concentrate on forging lasting connections between the many public and private agencies involved in the conservation of natural areas. Accordingly, the OHF teamed up with the Parks and Recreational Areas

Branch and the Nature Conservancy of Canada to sponsor a conference, "Toward Natural Heritage Protection in Ontario," at The Old Mill in Toronto on 23 November 1982. The conference was a carefully orchestrated event, attended by Ontario's leading environmental activists, executive officers of prominent private conservation groups, representatives of government agencies, and politicians, including no fewer than five cabinet ministers. In his keynote address, John White unveiled the agenda of the OHF and Parks and Recreational Areas Branch for promoting cooperation among all the organizations represented, so that "we can attain strength to reach goals that would lie beyond the reach of our separate efforts."[56] The conference, he added, represented "an attempt to sharpen our focus and direct our efforts to the protection of land of special value – of ecological and scientific value." The OHF offered to play a major role in this effort by providing the linkage between the various private-sector groups and government ministries. Moreover, White declared, the foundation would also encourage donations of significant natural properties and initiate a new easement program for natural areas. The current political and economic climate in Ontario, he insisted, demanded an unprecedented level of cooperation between public and private agencies. Different groups must identify the properties worthy of preservation; others must approach landowners and put them in touch with the OHF, which could negotiate conservation agreements. Still others might sign the agreement or take the agreement on assignment and assume responsibility for monitoring an easement.

White supported his case for a new era of interagency cooperation by informing the participants of the "creative teamwork" behind the recent effort to save Great Manitou Island in Lake Nipissing from development. The island was the site of one of Ontario's largest colonies of heron and osprey. It also possessed significant geological features, as well as considerable historical interest as a stopover and boat refuge for the fur trade voyageurs of the old Montreal-based North West Company. In the autumn of 1980, the Parks and Recreational Areas Branch learned that unless Great Manitou could be acquired immediately, it would be subdivided for cottage development. Parks personnel urgently wanted to acquire the property, but could not obtain the $300,000 for the purchase from current budgets. In desperation, they contacted the Nature Conservancy of Canada to explore alternative funding arrangements. Early in 1981, the conservancy bought the property on the understanding that the province would repurchase the island at full cost within two years. Shortly after, however, the conservancy approached a private donor, a descendant of one of the founders of the North West Company who, in a gesture of extraordinary generosity, made a donation of $310,000 to the Ontario Heritage Foundation. Serving as the link between the donor, the conservancy, and the MNR, the foundation reimbursed the Nature Conservancy of Canada, assumed title to the property, and then placed Great Manitou

Island in the custody of the Ministry of Natural Resources for management as a Nature Reserve.

Those in attendance at the conference were impressed by this precedent and applauded the OHF's declaration of intent to encourage cooperation between the disparate public and private conservation agencies. "A new actor has arrived on the natural heritage scene in Ontario," observed the Federation of Ontario Naturalists, "and is a welcome presence indeed."[57] Several weeks later, in mid-December 1982, the foundation organized a smaller follow-up meeting, at which time delegates representing fifteen organizations resolved to form a loose coalition called the Natural Heritage League, under Terk Bayly's "expert leadership."[58] The purpose of the league was to make it easier to protect the province's natural heritage by serving as a coordinating body for all public and private agencies concerned with the identification, protection, and management of natural areas. Within five years, the coalition would embrace twenty-eight member groups.

To help launch the league, the MNR assumed the salary costs of seconding a Parks and Recreational Areas Branch planner, William B. Sargant, to the Ministry of Citizenship and Culture for two years, to serve as a liaison between the two ministries, the Ontario Heritage Foundation, and the Natural Heritage League. At the same time, the MNR agreed to transfer $225,000 to the OHF over three years, to create a small revolving fund for land purchases. Patterned after a similar fund administered by the National Trust in Britain, it was intended to provide short-term bridge financing for flexible property acquisition by members of the Natural Heritage League. The fund would permit an agency to borrow money at low interest for one year, before arranging a repayment schedule at current interest rates. Conservationists quickly put the fund to good use, hailing it as one of "the innovative methods we must develop to protect lands immediately." The Federation of Ontario Naturalists, for example, "bought time" by using the fund to save the Stone Road Alvar site on Pelee Island, home to over 100 rare plants and the endangered blue racer snake.[59]

From the perspective of the Parks and Recreational Areas Branch, the conference "Toward Natural Heritage Protection in Ontario" and the subsequent formation of the Natural Heritage League established the prerequisites for the successful launching of a new program to protect what were to be known as Areas of Natural and Scientific Interest (ANSI). The inspiration for this initiative also came from the British Nature Conservancy, which had for over two decades successfully developed a system of Sites of Special Scientific Interest. In Britain, whenever the conservancy decided that a formal nature reserve was not feasible or necessary to protect an important natural area, it endeavoured to designate a Site of Special Scientific Interest, to provide a less rigid but acceptable level of protection, through various kinds of arrangements with private and public landowners.

The decision to adapt this model to Ontario was made during 1981–82 as the MNR's provincewide Strategic Land Use Planning (SLUP) process entered its final stages. At this time, park planners realized that more natural areas had been identified than could possibly be formally absorbed into the provincial parks system. The International Biological Program alone had located some 600 sites of international significance and worthy of preservation. In southern Ontario, the majority of areas were privately owned, and the cost of purchasing them lay beyond the financial means of the MNR's acquisition budget. A different situation existed across the north, where the resource industries, fearful of losing access to timber and mineral wealth on Crown land, lobbied successfully during 1982–83 to reduce the number of candidate Nature Reserves listed in the regional parks system plans from 151 to 74. For these reasons, and for want of alternatives to formal Nature Reserves, the Parks and Recreational Areas Branch faced losing over 550 provincially significant areas that were essential if they were to meet the parks system's protection objective.

To avoid such an unpalatable outcome, specialists Thomas Beechey and Robert Davidson conceived the ANSI program to embrace both the candidate Nature Reserves discarded during the Strategic Land Use Planning process and the many other significant sites contained in the branch inventories. Because all of these areas had been selected according to the same criteria used to select provincial parks, a system of ANSIs would form a program that would parallel and be mutually supportive of the Nature Reserve system. The ANSI concept would be acceptable to the timber and mineral interests because resource extraction could be permitted in ANSIs located on Crown land. Protection would be harmonized with industrial needs through zoning and management prescriptions. In southern Ontario, the ANSI program overcame budgetary obstacles, because sites would largely be protected through cooperation with landowners, typically involving methods other than acquisition, such as conservation easements, leases, and informal private agreements.[60]

The logistics involved in mounting the ANSI program, heavily dependent, as it was, on the cultivation of the private stewardship concept of conservation, made even the most optimistic environmentalists blanch. Parks Branch officials recognized that the task exceeded their capabilities and acknowledged that the scheme could only succeed with the active participation of a coalition comprising government agencies, nonprofit conservation groups, private corporations, and individuals interested in the preservation of natural areas.[61] It was with the idea of creating such a coalition that the branch helped to sponsor the conference "Toward Natural Areas Protection." Such was the genesis of the Natural Heritage League.

As it happened, the success of the league exceeded all expectations. Reflecting upon the "remarkable number of action-oriented projects," with which it was involved during its first five years, Stewart Hilts of the FON credited the league with creating "a spirit of innovation and cooperation ... to bring about a period of very rapid progress in the natural heritage field in Ontario."[62]

Member organizations quickly developed priority-action lists of provincially significant unprotected natural areas, and began approaching and soliciting property owners for their cooperation in conserving the threatened habitats and geological features located on their land.

Through its program of contacting landowners, the league pioneered the use of natural heritage easements. In 1984, the Ontario Paper Company signed the province's first natural conservation easement with the Ontario Heritage Foundation, for 300 acres of land contiguous to the Misery Bay Nature Reserve on Manitoulin Island. The company retained ownership, but transferred use of the land to the OHF so that the area might serve as a protective buffer for the distinctive botanical and ecological features at Misery Bay.[63] A second natural heritage easement was negotiated in 1988 for the Workman's Creek site, a significant, Ordivician bedrock-type section and invertebrate fossil locality near Meaford. As the first conservation easement in Ontario signed by a private citizen, and the first in Canada negotiated to protect a significant geological feature, the Workman's Creek agreement set a double precedent of no little importance in the history of conservation in Canada.[64]

In addition to generating the first natural heritage easements, the league's user-contact program resulted in some substantial gifts of cash and property to the Ontario Heritage Foundation. Through the joint efforts of the Nature Conservancy of Canada and the foundation, and a private donation of $350,000, the 325-hectare Fleetwood Creek ANSI near Peterborough – an upland forest that includes an important headwaters and IBP-CT site – was acquired in 1983.[65] The Kawartha Conservation Authority assumed responsibility for management of the property through an agreement with the OHF. The following year, Art Ellis, president of Artell Developments Ltd. of St. Catharines, donated twenty-four hectares of Carolinian forest in the Jordan valley to the Ontario Heritage Foundation, which, in turn, assigned the property to the Niagara Peninsula Conservation Authority for management.[66]

By 1987, the participating organizations in the Natural Heritage League had raised over a million dollars for various acquisition projects. The most impressive of the cooperative initiatives was the one named Carolinian Canada, conceived by the World Wildlife Fund and other league members to protect the last remaining significant habitats, flora, and fauna of areas in the deciduous forest or Carolinian zone of southwestern Ontario. In 1984, World Wildlife Canada and the Nature Conservancy of Canada launched a two-year study to identify all remaining Carolinian sites. This research culminated in the selection of thirty-six threatened areas (twenty-six already possessed ANSI designation) that scientists deemed essential for the retention of representative and unique Carolinian habitats and species. The identification study had cost approximately $400,000, obtained through a grant from the Richard Ivey Foundation of London and with matching government funds, made available to the Ontario Heritage Foundation during Ontario's Bicentennial Year.[67]

After the site identification program had been completed, three member groups of the Natural Heritage League – the World Wildlife Fund, the Nature Conservancy of Canada, and Wildlife Habitat Canada – raised $1.8 million in private-sector funding by 1987 to mount the protection program for the thirty-six Carolinian sites on the action list. At the annual meeting of the Federation of Ontario Naturalists in May 1987, a conference dedicated to Carolinian Canada, Natural Resources Minister Vincent Kerrio announced that the ministries of Natural Resources and Citizenship and Culture (MCC) would match the privately donated funds over a three-year period. A formal agreement, spelling out the roles and responsibilities of each ministry in the project, was signed on 1 June 1987.[68] It specified that "private stewardship is the preferred approach for securing Carolinian areas." In exercising control of the funds, the government, through the OHF, intended to reserve acquisition "as a technique of last resort," to be employed after all private stewardship options had been exhausted. To encourage landowners to participate, the Natural Heritage League agreed to expand its efforts to negotiate stewardship agreements with property owners and to issue Natural Heritage Stewardship Awards to those who voluntarily protected Carolinian sites.

By the spring of 1989, through the league's private stewardship drive operated by the University of Guelph, voluntary agreements had been successfully negotiated with 277 private landowners to protect approximately 3,845 hectares of property or 40 percent of the targeted Carolinian sites in southwestern Ontario. Over 90 percent of the landowners contacted had reacted positively, and half of these had expressed interest in qualifying for a stewardship award. All in all, the project was a remarkable cooperative effort, one viewed as "a template for dealing with other initiatives affecting natural and scientific areas, wetlands and endangered and critical species in the future."[69] In fact, because of its success, the MNR and MCC agreed to extend the private stewardship program to the Niagara Escarpment, under the auspices of the Ontario Heritage Foundation.

Obtaining private and public funding and support for Carolinian Canada was only one of several major successes registered by the Natural Heritage League during the late 1980s. In his 1987 address to the FON, Natural Resources Minister Kerrio unveiled the new ANSI implementation strategy and promised another $2.5 million over five years to carry it out. The strategy depended heavily upon the private stewardship approach and the use of nonacquisition techniques to protect most sites. The implementation strategy also provided guidelines, prescribing concepts and principles for management. Once a protection agreement had been struck with an owner, the MNR intended to prepare a management plan for the site to guide protection and to provide for compatible land use. Each plan would identify core, buffer, resource management, and access zones, and include prescriptions for land use to preserve significant natural features.[70]

The ANSI program received another boost in 1988, thanks to the efforts of the Nature Conservancy of Canada. To commemorate its twenty-fifth anniversary, the conservancy made the largest land purchase in its history by acquiring 40 percent (1,538 hectares) of the Alfred Bog for $725,000. Located midway between Ottawa and Montreal, the bog is the largest wetland in southeastern Ontario. For its part, the MNR contributed 25 percent of the purchase price. Other contributors included the vendor, Cobi Foods Ltd. ($100,000), Wildlife Habitat Canada, the FON, Vankleek Hill Nature Society, Ottawa Field Naturalists, Ottawa Duck Club, and the Laidlaw Foundation. The Ontario Heritage Foundation assisted the conservancy by providing a low-interest loan of $100,000, in addition to grants totalling $80,000.[71]

The provincial government's willingness to provide funding for Carolinian Canada and the ANSI program reflected the heightened sensitivity to environmental issues at Queen's Park after June 1985, when the minority Liberal government, headed by David Peterson, replaced the short-lived administration of Frank Miller, thus ending forty-two years of Tory rule. Environmental issues were prominent in the Liberal-NDP accord, entitled "An Agenda for Reform: Proposals for Minority Government," which guaranteed the first Peterson government a two-year life span.

The upheaval in Ontario politics set the stage for the Natural Heritage League's crowning achievement in June 1988 – the passage of the Conservation Lands Act[72] – which provided legal definitions for ANSIs, wetlands, and other conservation lands, and established a scheme for a provincial property-tax rebate for landowners willing to protect significant natural areas. The Natural Heritage League had begun lobbying for such an act in November 1984, at the behest of a group headed by the Federation of Ontario Naturalists. League members expected a long fight over the issue, since previous administrations had rejected earlier proposals for land-tax rebates. They were pleasantly surprised to discover that the Peterson government was more receptive to their arguments. In October 1986, the premier himself promised to introduce a bill "untaxing nature." He honoured that pledge, following his smashing victory in the general election of September 1987.

Under the Conservation Lands Act, the province offers a 100 percent property-tax rebate to owners of provincially and regionally significant wetlands, ANSIs, designated natural areas within the Niagara Escarpment area, non-revenue-producing lands that are owned by conservation authorities, and other conservation lands owned by nonprofit organizations. To be eligible for the tax rebate, owners of conservation properties must agree to the long-term maintenance of the land in its natural state and refrain from undertaking any activities detrimental to conservation values. Those who fail to keep the agreement will be liable to repay all rebates allowed over the previous ten years, including interest. Responsibility for administering the program falls to the MNR's Parks and Recreational Areas Branch.[73]

The Conservation Lands Act stands out as potentially one of the most important pieces of legislation in the history of natural heritage protection in Ontario. By recognizing in a tangible way the "outstanding contribution which privately owned conservation and heritage lands make to Ontario culture," it provides a tremendous boost to the fledgling private stewardship movement. Furthermore, as the FON acknowledged, the act represents "a major reversal in the Ontario government's land-use philosophy. For the first time, the government has acknowledged the ecological value of natural areas that are not being farmed or logged. At one time these 'wild places' were dismissed as mere wasteland."[74]

The change in the provincial philosophy of land use was also evident in the announcement, made in May 1987 by Natural Resources Minister Kerrio, that the government intended to introduce an Ecological Reserves Act for Ontario, a commitment reiterated in the throne speech of 3 November 1987. By favouring such legislation, the province was falling into line with other jurisdictions across North America and Europe. For example, beginning with British Columbia in 1971, every province except Ontario had passed special ecological reserves acts in the wake of the IBP-CT program.[75] During this period, Ontario's park planners had followed a different path, by preserving ecological areas as Nature Reserves under the Provincial Parks Act. Many scientists, naturalists, educators, and environmental groups in Ontario, after observing the trend elsewhere, gradually concluded that in the absence of specific legislation, ecologically significant areas in the province did not enjoy the high level of recognition and protection that they enjoyed in other jurisdictions. In short, Ontario's Provincial Parks Act was not explicit enough to guide the selection, protection, and management of ecological reserves.[76] The Peterson government agreed and instructed the Parks and Recreational Areas Branch to review statutory precedents elsewhere before drafting an ecological reserves bill for Ontario.

By 1989, the branch had prepared draft legislation in the form of a "white paper" for public review and comment.[77] Three years later, the document had yet to be released. Under the proposed bill, all existing Nature Reserve parks and zones would no longer be regulated under the provisions of the Provincial Parks Act, but would be regulated by the new legislation to provide the core of a network of ecological reserves. The system would preserve representative ecological areas as permanent reference areas for scientific research, provincial baselines for environmental monitoring, and opportunities for public education. An Ecological Reserve Council, made up of provincial and local officials, scientists, and representatives of nongovernmental conservation groups, would be appointed to advise the minister of natural resources on all matters pertaining to the selection, establishment, stewardship and withdrawal of the reserves.

The introduction of an Ecological Reserves Act would serve as a fitting conclusion to a remarkable period in the struggle to preserve natural areas in Ontario. In the depressing climate of constraint that prevailed in the 1980s, one might have expected the efforts of the natural heritage agencies to have ground to a halt, but such was not the case. In fact, the movement to protect natural areas accelerated its rate of progress, fueled as it was by new ideas, energetic leadership, and unprecedented cooperation between public and private agencies. To its credit, the Parks and Recreational Areas Branch stood at the forefront of most of the successful new initiatives and programs that were introduced. Rather than succumbing either to fiscal adversity or to the pressures of the resource industries during the Strategic Land Use Planning exercise, parks personnel had rescued the endangered candidate Nature Reserve sites by conceiving the ANSI program and thereby creating a parallel system of protected areas outside the provincial parks system. Instead of falling victim to resignation and ennui when deprived of funding for land acquisition, branch officials responded aggressively by striking an alliance with the Ontario Heritage Foundation, by helping to create the Natural Heritage League, and by encouraging the concept of conservation thorough private stewardship. At the end of the decade, the future of efforts to preserve natural areas depended as much on the success of conservation easements, stewardship agreements, programs to contact property owners, and land tax rebates as it did on the expansion of an official system of Nature Reserves.

As they entered the 1990s, Parks and Recreational Areas Branch personnel faced an old problem, created by the successes of the 1980s. With the ANSI program in place, and with a much expanded Nature Reserve system after the completion of the Strategic Land Use Planning process, branch administrators were now responsible for managing hundreds of relatively small natural areas scattered across the province. In 1988, the Federation of Ontario Naturalists expressed doubts about the MNR's ability to protect Areas of Natural and Scientific Interest and pointed to the "desecration" of Scott Point on Lake Huron, south of Port Elgin, as proof of this assertion. "The ANSI program lacks teeth," they complained. "To give it teeth we need a government policy statement on ANSIs which municipalities would have to respect in their official plans ... Without [such a policy,] the designation of a natural area as an ANSI means very little."[78] Apart from the deficiencies in policy, the problem of constrained budgets continued to weaken the Parks and Recreational Areas Branch's ability to fulfil its protection mandate. For instance, the promise, made in 1987, of $2.5 million over five years for the ANSI implementation strategy fell by the wayside, when the second instalment was reduced, following another round of constraints. In 1992, the parks system possessed neither the staff nor the financial resources to manage satisfactorily the hundreds of sites for which it was now responsible. The management question, then, is destined to become the central concern of the 1990s, both for park officials and their environmentalist client groups.

It is a risky business for historians to analyze recent happenings, let alone prognosticate about the future. Students of the past rely upon the passage of time to winnow the clutter of information, to provide a perspective on people and events, and to allow for balance and proportion in their analysis. Quite frequently, what seems important up close pales into insignificance as the years pass. While recognizing that very little of a definitive nature can yet be written about the history of the parks program in the 1980s, one thing is certain. Despite the enormous toll taken by the triple combination of re-trenchment, inflation, and recession, branch and field personnel succeeded in doing far more than merely surviving the arduous eighties. The parks system actually emerged from the decade a much more efficient and effective organization. The variety of efficiency strategies, the programs for volunteers and cooperating associations, the tourism and marketing initiatives, and the new directions taken to protect natural heritage all attested to the fact that highly motivated, dedicated park officials had succeded in overcoming the constraints imposed on them.

Chapter 9

Strategic Land-Use Planning and Its Aftermath, 1978–1989

During the late 1970s, when budget constraints brought a halt to land acquisitions and severely curtailed most aspects of park operations, one might have predicted that the new provincial parks policy (1978) would have little chance of being implemented. Paradoxically, precisely the opposite occurred, and within a decade the number of parks in the system had doubled. Expansion on such a scale was an unmatched historic event, the result of the convergence during the early 1980s of two major planning processes – the regional parks system's planning effort (which, in fact, resulted in the identification of most of the areas required to meet the parks' policy objectives) and the ministry's broader Strategic Land Use Planning (SLUP) program, designed to sort out the future uses of Ontario's vast Crown land base.

Integrating parks planning into the SLUP program from 1980 to 1983 posed an enormously difficult challenge for the Ministry of Natural Resources. In 1981, regional planners proposed the establishment of 245 new parks, of various classes, in order to achieve the policy objectives formulated in 1978. When placed in the context of SLUP, these park proposals had to be assessed against the land and water requirements of other ministry programs, and against the needs of other users of Crown land resources. In every MNR district, especially those in northern Ontario, a host of industrial and commercial interests, sportsmen, and native peoples viewed the candidate parks as potential threats to their economic and social well-being. The result was a battle of epic proportions. When the smoke cleared in May 1983, the Davis government announced the creation of 155 new provincial parks, including five in the Wilderness category. For preservationists, however, this historic development was soured by Natural Resources Minister Alan Pope's effort to mollify park opponents by permitting in the new parks what had previously been considered "nonconforming" activities – commercial tourism, hunting, trapping, and mineral exploration. As it happened, the unexpected collapse of the Conservative dynasty in 1985 provided an occasion for the review of Pope's compromise. After considerable soul-searching, Vincent Kerrio, minister of natural resources in the new administration of David Peterson, announced a new Liberal parks policy in June 1988, which called for the removal of most nonconforming activities from the post-1983 parks, and the application of "Blue Book" management policies throughout the system.

SLUP and Regional Parks System Planning: The Cart before the Horse

In 1978, the task of translating the new policy on provincial parks into reality fell to the eight administrative regions of the Ministry of Natural Resources. Regional parks coordinators, planners, and specialists had to undertake comprehensive studies to determine the extent to which the existing park system fell short of meeting the class and program targets detailed in the "Blue Book." Once this task had been accomplished, they turned to inventory analysis and field investigations, in order to identify the most suitable landscapes for inclusion as candidates for provincial parks in the regional system plans. During the selection process, field personnel generally rejected as candidates those areas with a high potential for timber, mining, and water power, so as to minimize resource conflicts later on. In 1981, after three years of intensive research and analysis, the regional system plans began to take shape.

When preparing the plans, regional staff took into account local conditions and new information that called for modifications to the original, tentative park class targets contained in the "Blue Book." Southern Ontario, for example, was short of Crown land for provincial parks, and senior management was indicating that land acquisition budgets would be curtailed for another twenty years. Parks and Recreational Areas Branch staff accordingly abandoned the ideal of incorporating in the southern parks a full range of earth science features and life science sites. Instead, they sought to include "the best possible representation of remnant undisturbed landscapes and features," and to realize protection objectives through the ANSI program, private stewardship efforts, and the assistance of other public conservation agencies. The shortage of large tracts of suitable Crown land in the south also led regional planners to reduce the standard minimum area for Natural Environment parks from 2,000 to 600 hectares, and to conclude that Natural Environment park representation in some site districts would be achieved by other public agencies, such as the conservation authorities or Parks Canada. Similarly, since many rivers in southern Ontario flowed through private lands or public areas administered by other agencies, planners decided that Waterway class park representation should be rewritten, "to include the *provision of access* to provincially significant resources," rather than designating stretches of river as Waterway provincial parks.[1]

Across the northern regions, which contained extensive Crown land holdings, planners had more leeway to change park class targets without sacrificing the objectives of the program. As a case in point, Natural Environment parks were deemed to be unnecessary in some northern site districts, because recreation needs were thought to be low. In these districts, regional staff still anticipated meeting protection objectives and achieving the representation of natural areas by establishing large Nature Reserves or Wilderness parks. Likewise, the regional plans for the Far North did not include many site candidates for Waterway parks, since representation and protection could be adequately provided for in other park classes. In the MNR's northwestern region, planners also decided that two site regions could be represented by one Wilderness park, rather than two. Finally, recreation targets for day-use and some extended-use activities in the northeastern region were reduced, as a result of new studies, which indicated that future recreation demand for these services would not be as high as originally calculated.

In order to meet the schedule for having the regional plans ready for integration in 1981 into the Strategic Land Use Planning program, five of the eight regions submitted drafts that were incomplete, as far as the representation of Nature Reserves was concerned. Field inventories and data analysis of earth and life science sites had not yet been completed. The Parks and Recreational Areas Branch simply assumed, however, that the draft plans did not represent the ultimate extent of the future Nature Reserve system, and that as inventories and analyses continued, additional candidate parks would be recommended.

Of all park classes in the regional system plans, Historical parks remained by far the most poorly represented. Only four candidates were listed in the plans for northern Ontario and two in the southern regional documents. This deficiency could not be avoided. No region had been able to mount the systematic inventories and field analysis, because the MNR lacked cultural resources experts in its regional offices, a consequence of the loss of the Historical Sites Branch to the Ministry of Culture and Recreation in 1975. In the entire MNR there was only one permanent expert on parks and cultural resources – Gary Forma, appointed in April 1980. During his first two years in the post, Forma had endeavoured to cultivate sympathetic and informed attitudes toward cultural heritage planning and management among field managers by conducting seminars, and by preparing *Caring for History: A Handbook for Managing Cultural Resources in Ontario Provincial Parks* (1982). Notwithstanding the value of his work, it had little impact, either on regional system planning or on the SLUP process. As for the historical component of system planning, the branch proceeded on the assumption that most protection of the province's cultural heritage would occur through historical zones in other classes of parks. Only in rare cases would Historical park designation be recommended as a protection mechanism.

With the draft regional parks system plans more or less completed, MNR program coordinators faced the daunting task of integrating the proposals into the ministry's broader Strategic Land Use Planning effort. At this stage, requirements for provincial parks would be analyzed together with the land and water requirements of all other ministry programs. Strategic Land Use Planning had been launched in 1972, as an attempt to sort out conflicts over the disposition of the province's Crown land and natural resources. Through strategic planning, the MNR hoped to serve as an honest broker in making the long-range (twenty-year) land and resource allocations for approximately 1 million square kilometres of Crown land, or 87 percent of the provincial land base. In 1972, however, almost everyone had underestimated the complexity of the task and the time required to accomplish it. This was understandable enough; no other province had attempted such an exercise. The MNR's resource managers soon recognized that they did not know how to proceed, and had to develop expertise in comprehensive long-range planning, as well as in encouraging public participation. Among other things, they learned that planning could not be advanced until policies had been developed for major programs such as provincial parks (1978), mineral aggregates (1978), fisheries (1979), and moose management (1980). Until the early 1980s, ministry planners also lacked inventories of Crown land resources, without which it was impossible to set program targets. Beyond basic research and policy needs, methods had to be developed to resolve conflict over land use, a task complicated by the regional decentralization of MNR operations during the 1970s.

Parks personnel recognized that the SLUP program would inevitably climax in a bitter showdown over land allocation. Many new proposals for candidate parks, especially in northern Ontario, would not be given a smooth passage through the SLUP process. The forest products and mining industries were poised to take an uncompromising anti-park posture in defiant reaction to the "Blue Book," which dictated that most kinds of resource extraction would be prohibited in most classes of provincial parks. Within the MNR, opposition to the regional system plans by the Timber, Mining, and Fish and Wildlife branches appeared long before the plans were ready to run the SLUP gauntlet.[2]

Until 1981, the planning of provincial parks and of strategic land use evolved separately. Park personnel had contributed what information they could to the SLUP process, but their participation had been hampered by the lack of an approved park policy until 1978, and then by the lack of regional system plans specifying the Crown land requirements for the park program. In a perfect planning scenario, the provincial park and SLUP efforts would have been synchronized, so that the regional parks plans were completed first, and thus incorporated into the regional strategic planning documents. Alas, it was a classic case of the cart preceding the horse. The proposed strategic plans for northeastern and northwestern Ontario were, for example, released in March and June 1980 respectively, before the system plans for the regional parks had even been drafted.[3] The parks component of the SLUP-Northwest document was particularly weak, since the inventories for all classes of parks in the vast West Patricia area were still incomplete. The response of the advocacy groups was predictable. They charged that the MNR had stacked the SLUP process in favour of the resource industries, by proceeding with strategic planning before the plans for the regional parks system had been completed.

Of the two northern SLUP documents, the northwestern plan received the harshest criticism. The Algonquin Wildlands League considered it to be "grossly inadequate in terms of its technical competence, policy orientation and approval process." The document provided neither an adequate set of objectives nor strategies for achieving targets. "In distinct contrast to the sections on forestry," noted the league's brief, "where in our opinion there is very little by way of policy to support the unequivocal targets, the pages devoted to parks furnish appropriate details of the official systems planning policies but fail to conclude with a firm commitment to implement them in a specified manner."[4] Preservationists were especially alarmed by what the northern SLUP documents had to say (and failed to say) with respect to Wilderness parks. None of the six Candidate Wilderness Areas had been described in sufficient detail to explain their significance or the reasons for their selection. And why only six? the preservationists asked. What about alternative sites in each region? Why had nineteen potential locations, identified in the parks branch's wilderness identification study, been eliminated prematurely, without benefit of public discussion, and this in spite of the MNR's own land-use planning guidelines?

While the two northern SLUP documents generated the most heated debate, the southern strategic plan – *Coordinated Program Strategy for the Ministry of Natural Resources in Southern Ontario* (1981) – also came under fire. Because it did not include details of the proposed parks system or explain the need for additional parks to meet regional planning targets, it gave the impression that parks system planning had not been taken into account. In short, from the environmentalists' point of view, all the strategic plans were "weak, vague and sometimes inconsistent on the subject of parks and wilderness protection."[5] This was extremely disconcerting to the park advocacy groups because, following public review and revision, the three regional SLUP documents would provide the policy framework and land-use guidelines for more detailed plans and strategies, to be prepared in each of the MNR's forty-seven administrative districts. Without a strong commitment to parks in the regional documents, they asked, what chance did the parks program have at the district level of planning?

Ironically, the forestry and mining industries, as well as many sportsmen, commercial tourism operators, and aboriginal groups argued that provincial parks had been given too much, rather than too little, consideration in the SLUP documents. These interests were especially agitated about the six substantial tracts of Crown land identified as Candidate Wilderness parks by ministry planners.

Fuelling this round of the wilderness controversy was the realization by both preservationists and timber men that they were rapidly running out of time and resources. So little wild land remained in Ontario that preservationists saw the SLUP process as their last chance to create a system of Wilderness parks. Those areas not set apart at this juncture would probably be lost forever. The timber companies viewed matters from an altogether different angle. They were facing an impending shortage of marketable timber. As they contemplated the effects of the "regeneration gap," and this at a time when the economy was beginning to slide into recession, the timber men feared that large areas of productive forest would be locked up in Wilderness parks where logging was prohibited. The realization that two of the candidate parks – Ogoki-Albany, to the northwest of Lake Nipigon, and Lady Evelyn–Smoothwater, to the north of Lake Temagami – were located in areas where timber commitments had already been made caused them no little anxiety. Indeed, these two areas became major focal points in the battle over wilderness stimulated by SLUP.

In the case of Ogoki-Albany, one of Canada's last large virgin boreal forests and home to one of Ontario's southernmost woodland caribou herds, the MNR had granted cutting rights to Great Lakes Forest Products Ltd. in 1957. Assuming that it possessed an assured wood supply, the company expanded its milling facilities in Thunder Bay during the mid-1970s.[6] And when the SLUP-Northwest plan appeared in 1980, Great Lakes was seeking approval to construct a forest access road into Ogoki-Albany. Environmentalists, together with the Armstrong Wilderness Outfitters Association, argued vehemently that logging must not be permitted in the area. The extremely shallow soils and short northern growing seasons, argued Bruce Hyer, a biologist and president of Environment North, would prevent full forest regrowth for 200 years. Logging would be nothing less than catastrophic to natural and recreational values. But Great Lakes Forest Products Ltd. denied that there would be a reforestation problem.[7]

Three different companies held timber licences in over half of the Lady Evelyn–Smoothwater Candidate Wilderness Park. When the MNR released the SLUP-Northeast plan, one of the companies, William Milne and Sons Ltd. of Temagami, was in the middle of a $4 million expansion program, based in part on obtaining the timber from the volume agreement it held in the area of the proposed park. The company had already received $582,000 in federal support and another $240,000 in provincial subsidies for a modern sawmill suitable for processing all tree species, in order to avoid having to close down when the white pine supply ran out. If the candidate park at Lady Evelyn–Smoothwater went forward, argued the president of the company, J.F. McNutt, it would reduce the company's allowable cut by an estimated 20 percent and place "our project in serious jeopardy," together with 200 full-time jobs.[8]

If the trees weren't cut in the proposed Wilderness parks, announced Ken Greaves, president of the Ontario Forest Industries Association, it could "only spell economic disaster for every citizen" in the province.[9] Greaves claimed

Environmentalists and wilderness enthusiasts clashed with the forest industries over the future of the Lady Evelyn–Smoothwater Candidate Wilderness Park during the strategic land-use planning process between 1981 and 1983. *Courtesy: Ron Reid.*

that billions of dollars would be lost to the northern economy as jobs disappeared and mills closed, and this for the recreational pleasure of an urban southern elite! "The employment needs of society must come before recreation needs," insisted the Ontario Forest Industries Association.[10] In northwestern Ontario, Great Lakes Forest Products Ltd. funded an aggressive media campaign against the parks to spread the industry's message. "We do not agree ... that large tracts of forest land should be left unmanaged in so-called 'wilderness' reserves for single-purpose activities such as canoeing and backpack camping," declared one of the series of advertisements placed by the company in various northern Ontario newspapers. The ads featured "Henry, A Second Class Citizen," sitting disconsolately in his motorized, aluminum fishing boat. Poor Henry was presented as the quintessential "hard working" northerner, "who pays his taxes and wants to enjoy a few simple pleasures," such as fishing in remote lakes, but who was deprived of his pleasures because of the ban on outboard motors in Wilderness parks, introduced at the behest of the southern-based canoeing and backpacking fraternity. Yet another of the Great Lakes advertisements exhorted northerners to oppose the "over extension of park lands" because "forests are the basis of our livelihood. Our jobs and our future are at stake."[11]

"The facts speak differently," countered the preservationists. "Each year the industry ... removes an area equivalent to one wilderness park from future timber production through professional neglect." Provincial parks, either established or proposed, were not a primary cause of the timber shortage; rather, they were a scapegoat for an industry that had failed to establish "a sustainable and efficient level of timber cutting on productive sites." Established provincial parks embraced only 2.9 percent of the total productive forest land in Ontario, and 28.5 percent of that was classified as production forest (much of it in Algonquin and Lake Superior), while the proposed Wilderness parks "involve less than 2% of the productive forest base in Ontario, only a few years cutting at present rates." The future of the forest industry, argued the preservationists, lay in the implementation of serious reforestation programs, not in defeating the proposals for Wilderness Areas. "If the government ... accepts the argument that the road to industry salvation runs through parklands, then the 21st century will bring with it an industry without wood and a province without wild country."[12]

By way of response to the uproar over the northern SLUP documents, James Auld, minister of natural resources, instructed the Provincial Parks Council to investigate the controversy. After holding public hearings and entertaining briefs, the council unanimously supported the proposed Wilderness parks. "The S.L.U.P. process has now eliminated all but the minimal number of Candidate areas required to fulfill the Park Policy mandate and targets," wrote the council's chairman, George Priddle, in January 1981. If the Ogoki-Albany and Lady Evelyn sites were abandoned because of forest industry pressure, it would "result in a nearly total commitment of the [Crown-owned] Boreal Forest ... to extraction rather than preservation and recreation." The council urged Auld to take a firm stand and to declare that no park, park reserve, or Candidate Wilderness park would be abandoned for a five-year period. Furthermore, if the ministry wished to eliminate a Candidate Wilderness park after five years, the council recommended that such a decision should rest upon the findings of a formal environmental assessment.[13]

James Auld, a seasoned cabinet veteran, was too sharp a politician to tie the government's hands by accepting these recommendations. Still, his response indicated that both the arguments and the support brought to bear in favour of preserving the wilderness were being taken seriously. "I can assure you that the park reserves have my support," Auld informed the council. Before he made any final Crown land and resource allocations, however, he required more information. To start with, he wanted a cost-benefit study undertaken for the Lady Evelyn park proposal. As for Ogoki-Albany, MNR staff were still investigating the question of forest regeneration in the area and were looking for alternative timber supplies for Great Lakes Forest Products Ltd., in the event that a park was established.

Although most discussion generated in 1980 by the Strategic Land Use Plans for northern Ontario centred on the issue of logging versus wilderness, other questions complicated the controversy. Mining industry spokespeople

Map 6: Candidate Wilderness Parks, from *Report of the Task Force on Parks System Planning*, 1981

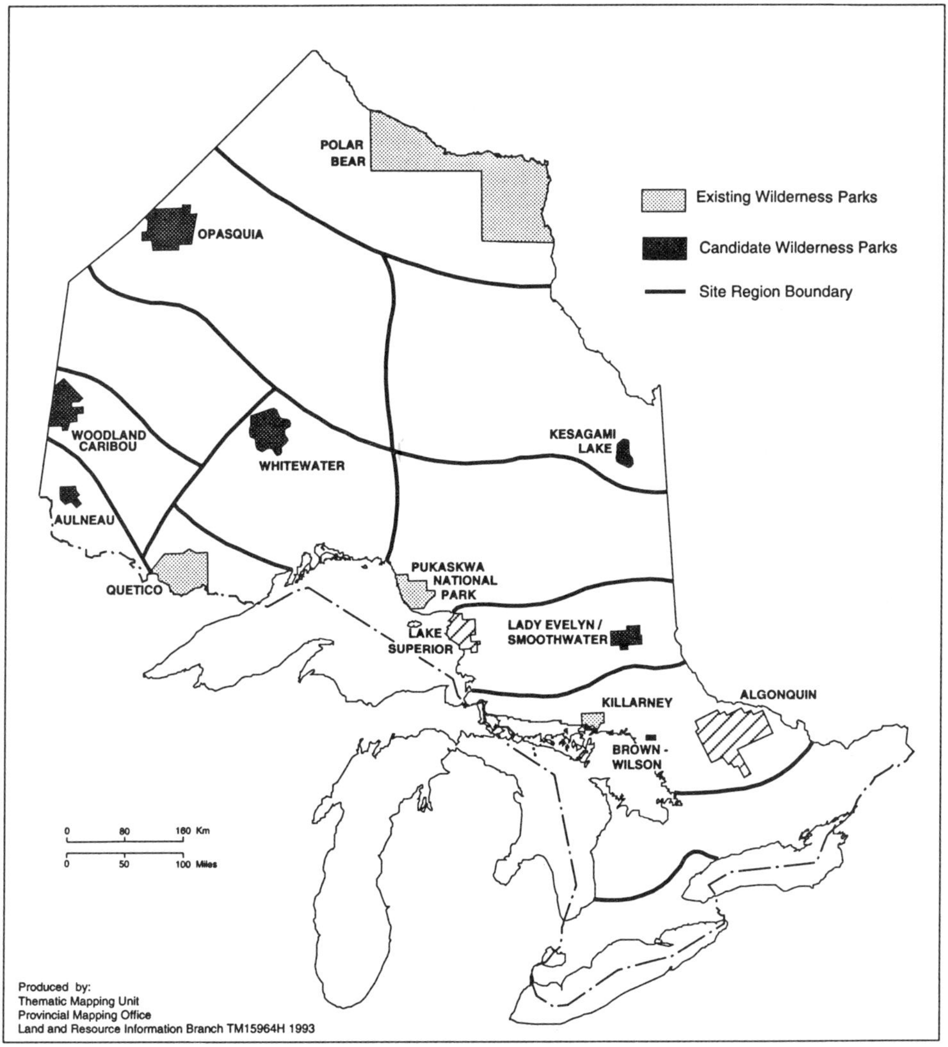

objected to the proposed parks as vehemently as did the foresters. "No further withdrawal of Crown Land for Provincial Parks or other reserves should even be contemplated," the miners argued, "as changing technology and new theories on mineral deposition along with changing demand for types of minerals not now in general use make it impossible to state with any real certainty where new deposits could occur."[14] Only if the MNR amended park policy to permit mineral exploration and extraction would the mining lobby be satisfied. Industry representatives insisted that the environmental impact of mining in parks would be minimal. "Exploration ... causes only minor temporary disturbance," they argued, and "Modern Mining is Clean."[15] Park officials and environmental groups were not persuaded by such arguments. Mines required access roads and work camps, features that could not be harmonized with the concept of a Wilderness park.

In addition to the forest and mining industries, the inclusion of the Candidate Wilderness parks in the strategic plans raised the ire of traditional users of these areas – sportsmen, trappers, commercial fishermen, and fly-in tourist operators – all of whom would be denied access if the parks were established. Many sportsmen favoured increased road access to remote northern lakes and resented the restrictions on mechanized access and hunting, as laid down in provincial park policy. "Principally, the [Ontario Federation of Anglers and Hunters] believes in the multiple-use concept as it applies to Crown land and parks in Ontario," declared its executive vice-president, Richard Morgan. "Putting in place regulations which prohibit the majority of uses and make a park the almost exclusive domain of one user group is, in our collective opinion, impractical and unfair." When it came to strategic land-use planning, the federation opposed any new park in which hunting would be prohibited.[16]

Tourist operators who owned fly-in outpost cabins or commercial lodges in the Candidate Wilderness parks, also joined the anti-park forces, since current park policy would require the removal of their businesses. They were joined by some local politicians, interested in promoting major resort projects. In northeastern Ontario, for example, the representatives of twenty-seven towns and townships, organized as the Temiskaming Municipal Association, opposed the Lady Evelyn proposal because they believed it would hinder the kind of investment in tourism they envisioned for their region.[17] Local businessmen-politicians realized that a park would end all hope that a large-scale four-season resort complex would be constructed at Maple Mountain. The subject of a comprehensive study by the Ministry of Industry and Tourism in the early 1970s, the Maple Mountain project had been placed in limbo because of the combined impact of a land claim by the aboriginal inhabitants at Temagami, the Teme-Augama Anishnabai (or Deep Water people), a determined resistance by the Alliance for the Lady Evelyn Wilderness, and the effect of inflation on cost estimates for the resort complex. Interestingly, Ministry of Industry and Tourism officials objected to the Wilderness park proposal, arguing that they still considered Maple Mountain as a prime site for resort development. "In our opinion," wrote the director of the Tourism Development Branch, "the classification of the entire area as a wilderness park would represent the least attractive alternative use of the area in terms of the region's economic and employment future."[18]

Not all northern tourist operators opposed the Candidate Wilderness parks; in fact, businessmen could be found on both sides of the controversy. Many recreational canoeing operators, who specialized in offering wilderness experiences, applauded the SLUP designations and welcomed the proposal to create provincial parks as a way of preserving the natural areas upon which their enterprises depended. In Temiskaming, one of the activists in the Alliance for the Lady Evelyn Wilderness was Trent University historian Bruce W. Hodgins, the director of the Wanapitei Wilderness Centre and youth camp, and a past president of the Ontario Recreational Canoeing Association. The role of the tourist interests in the wilderness controversy was even more complicated in the fight over Ogoki-Albany. Both the fly-in operators and lodge owners, who resisted the Candidate Wilderness park designation, and the outfitters, who favoured it, agreed on one thing: the area should not be logged. All were united in the Armstrong Wilderness Outfitters Association, the local group most vocal in its opposition to Great Lakes Forest Products Ltd. The association played an effective role in the battle against the company by appealing to the minister of the environment, Harry Parrott, to conduct an environmental assessment of the company's forest management plan for Ogoki-Albany and to impose a moratorium on road construction until the assessment had been completed.[19] Parrott would not act as requested; forest management activities were exempt from the Environmental Protection Act (1975), and Road Class Environmental Assessments did not apply to forest access roads. Nevertheless, he was concerned enough to bring his influence to bear upon his cabinet colleague, James Auld. "In my view," he wrote, "we must be careful that the Government is not pressured into making a commitment to developing roads into this area before a decision is made on the park and the facts are available on the acceptability of forest management in this area." Auld concurred and replied confidentially that he did not foresee a decision being made on the forest access road until after the public review of the strategic plan for northwestern Ontario.[20]

As the SLUP wilderness drama unfolded during 1980–81, most of the actors in the piece were veteran players, speaking well-rehearsed lines and engaging in a well-defined, almost ritualistic, political combat. What distinguished and also complicated this phase of the controversy, however, was the addition of a major new participant in the discussions – the First Nations of northern Ontario. During the upsurge in preservation in the late 1960s and early 1970s, the First Nations had remained largely in the background, while the preservationists struggled to have Algonquin, Killarney, Lake Superior, and Quetico reclassified as Primitive-class parks. Since the areas in question had already been designated as parkland, aboriginal groups were little affected. On the few occasions when new park decisions did impinge upon specific communities, the government endeavoured to modify policy to suit the aboriginal peoples. In creating Polar Bear Provincial Park in 1967, for example, Lands and Forests Minister René Brunelle had insisted that the "traditional hunting and trapping rights of the indigenous Indian population be ... guaranteed."[21] To that end, he met with the Attawapiskat First Nation to discuss the objectives of the park and provided background information in the Cree language. Since the band still lived off the land and had no alternative source of employment, the Department of Lands and Forests implemented what amounted to "a policy of discrimination in favour of the welfare of the local Indians as opposed to development by non-Indian tourist operators."[22] Only aboriginal peoples from the Ontario coastal communities on Hudson and James bays could qualify as guides in the park. The Polar Bear master plan also allowed for the continuation of their goose hunting camps within the park. Even the Federation of Ontario Naturalists, known for its firm opposition to hunting in provincial parks, bent its principles to accept these accommodations. The government showed the same flexibility after Quetico became a Primitive-class park, by permitting aboriginal guides belonging to the Lac la Croix First Nation to use motorboats in the western portion of the park, despite the general ban on outboard motors. Similarly, when the Winisk Wild River Park was established in 1969, the Ontario Parks Integration Board decided that the aboriginal community of Webequie would be allowed to provide guide services and tourist camps on the river.[23]

By the time that the strategic land-use plans for northern Ontario appeared in 1980, the First Nations were not as acquiescent about the establishment of new Wilderness and Waterway parks as they had been when Polar Bear and Winisk parks were created. During the 1970s, aboriginal peoples across Canada had become more militant and more determined than ever to work for self-determination, to rebuild their self-respect, and to break their dependency on white society. Their concept of "nationhood" rejected "white authority to allocate land ... or to restrict native use of wildlife."[24] For the Cree and Ojibway people of northern Ontario, who made up the Nishnawbe-Aski First Nation, the concept of a park was alien to their cultural tradition and their philosophy of being "one with the land." As Wally McKay, grand chief of the Grand Council Treaty Nine, explained, his people believed that "resource development and environmental preservation" should be achieved in equal balance "across our entire territory." McKay took issue with the very concept of a parks system, since it implied the "systematic resource exploitation of a large land mass and token preservation of a relatively much smaller wilderness tract. The proposed allocation of only 5–10% of land for parkland purposes throughout our homeland causes us to wonder, what is planned for the remaining 90% of our land mass?" Another problem with Wilderness parks, he argued, was that they would deprive his people of economic opportunities. "We strongly believe that the proposed Ogoki-Albany Wilderness Park will only hinder the Nishnawbe-Aski Nation, precisely because it destroys our peoples' resource development options, and therefore, our search for economic self-sufficiency." Accordingly, the Grand Council Treaty Nine formally opposed the creation of the park.[25]

The Teme-Augama Anishnabai also put a question mark against the future of the Lady Evelyn Candidate Wilderness Park. As early as 1973, to thwart the Maple Mountain project, the Teme-Augama Anishnabai had placed a legal caution on 10,000 square kilometres of Crown land (including the park area) and begun to press for the resolution of a land claim that had been pending for over a century. Band members argued that since neither they nor their ancestors had signed a formal agreement, surrendering their ancestral homeland to the Crown, the area in question remained in the constitutional category of "lands reserved for Indians" and fell under the band's ownership. The land caution of 1973 effectively froze most new development – the Maple Mountain project, cottages, mining – although the MNR permitted forest operations to continue while the case moved through the courts with glacierlike speed.

This, then, was the general setting, and these were the attitudes of the major participants, as the processes of SLUP and parks planning approached the critical point of integration. Everyone expected the parks issue to be a significant element of the discussions on strategic land-use planning, but no one anticipated how dominant that issue would become. By mid-1981, the main debate over SLUP had narrowed into a furious battle over wilderness, a battle which evoked memories of the preservationist struggles of a decade earlier.

Whither Now, Provincial Parks?

At the height of the controversy over SLUP and the wilderness, in the spring of 1981, the first of the draft plans for the regional parks system arrived at the Parks and Recreational Areas Branch in Toronto. The MNR was now in a position to begin integrating parks system and strategic planning across Ontario. To bring the two programs into phase, Deputy Minister William Foster struck a special four-person task force, headed by Richard M. Monzon, the deputy regional director for northwestern Ontario. Among its duties, the task force was instructed to compile, for internal review at the ministry, all proposed candidate parks listed in the regional system plans, to outline the extent to which both established and proposed candidate parks met the objectives of the cabinet-approved parks policy (1978), and to identify the conflicts associated with each candidate park. The task force submitted its report in September 1981. Six months later, in March 1982, the ministry released the document for public review.

The year between the appointment of the Monzon task force and the release of its report proved to be one of the most stormy periods on record in the relationship between park advocacy groups and the Ministry of Natural Resources. For a variety of reasons, leading environmentalists concluded that the MNR's "senior management" had become "increasingly anti-park and pro-resource extraction."[26] A bitter confrontation ensued, with some groups calling for the removal of the provincial parks system from the MNR. As it happened, in April 1981 a new minister of natural resources was appointed, Alan Pope, a thirty-five-year-old lawyer and the MLA for Timmins. Pope had, therefore, little opportunity to familiarize himself with planning issues, before he found himself rapidly slip-sliding into the quagmire of SLUP.

One of the issues heating up emotions in the spring of 1981 involved the matter of forest management agreements and their relationship to planning, both of a strategic nature and for provincial parks. Essentially, forest management agreements had been introduced by the Davis government to address the problem of reforestation in Ontario. MNR officials were greatly embarrassed at having to admit that twice as much forest was being logged as was being regenerated across Ontario; it was a state of affairs that made a mockery of Premier Davis's promise in 1977 to plant two trees for every one cut. The new agreements established long-term contractual arrangements between the Crown and the large forest companies, whereby the latter undertook to practise, with government subsidies, wise forest management, by constructing access roads, harvesting, and reforesting the territory. Theoretically, the agreements would provide the companies with a continuous supply of timber, while ensuring that forests were harvested and rejuvenated on the basis of a sustained yield. During the eighteen months prior to Pope's appointment as minister, five agreements had been signed with four companies, covering some 4.9 million hectares of Crown land. Ministry officials intended to sign agreements for another 15.5 million hectares over the next four years. Somewhat belatedly, precisely in the spring of 1981, park advocacy groups and the press began to raise questions about the timing of the forest management agreement program and the lack of public consultation. Did not the agreements preempt the SLUP process and the parks system planning? they asked. Why had there been no public participation prior to the signing of agreements that determined the future use of immense tracts of Crown land?

Some preservationists smelled a rat. Already in a state of agitation over the Candidate Wilderness parks controversy, they now jumped to the – erroneous – conclusion that there was a nefarious purpose behind the appointment of the Monzon task force, SLUP, and the signing of the forest management agreements. Could it be, asked Arlin Hackman, executive director of the Algonquin Wildlands League, that the Monzon task force had been established in order to slow down the SLUP process, so as to allow the MNR and the forest industry to negotiate the remaining agreements? If that were the case, it would give the industry "an advantage in staking its claim to the forests without having to hear from the environmentalists." The chairman of the

Provincial Parks Council, George Priddle, also believed this hypothesis.[27] No such plot existed. Indeed, the great irony here was that the Monzon task force had been appointed to speed up the synchronization of strategic and parks system planning, something the preservationists themselves had been insisting upon since the release of the SLUP regional plans.

All the same, by May 1981, many park advocates doubted that senior ministry officials wanted to implement the parks policy of 1978. The environmentalists knew that the assistant deputy minister for northern Ontario, George A. McCormack, a powerful administrator who was having a profound effect on SLUP, had recently instructed his district managers to give "mines, forestry, and hydraulic generation priority over potential parks" in strategic land-use planning.[28] Environmentalists' suspicions about a "resource-extraction bias" within the MNR deepened when the forest management plan for Algonquin Provincial Park received approval in the spring of that year. "The status quo has triumphed once again," declared the Algonquin Wildlands League. "Eighty percent of the park will be logged." It angered league members that the MNR would approve an extensive, permanent logging-road system in Algonquin, but refuse to enlarge the wilderness zone, as recommended by the Provincial Parks Council during the five-year review of the Algonquin master plan in 1979.[29] Arlin Hackman worried about what lay ahead. "This is a harbinger of things to come. We are at a very low point in parks policy."[30]

The environmentalists saw more evidence of an anti-park bias in the allocation of the MNR's annual budget. Government records indicated that the Parks and Recreational Areas Branch had borne an unreasonably large proportion of the ministry's constraint effort since the mid-1970s. The branch's share of the budget, had, for instance, shrunk from 15.3 percent in 1974 to 9.2 percent in 1981. "Right now," wrote one environmentalist, "there aren't sufficient funds to adequately run existing parks. Facilities are deteriorating, staff continues to be cut back, programs are eliminated, campgrounds are being closed ... The whole system is teetering on the brink."[31]

George Priddle had monitored all these developments with increasing trepidation. For years, he and the Parks Council had enthusiastically encouraged the implementation of the 1978 parks policy. Now he began to think that the plans to protect representative landscapes in a system of Wilderness and Nature Reserve parks might never be realized. An acrimonious meeting in January 1981, between the council and William Foster, the newly appointed deputy minister, confirmed Priddle's suspicions.[32]

Ironically, Deputy Minister Foster considered himself a parks proponent, albeit one who subscribed to an older school of thinking. His views had been formulated at the beginning of his exemplary career in the old Department of Lands and Forests, during the late 1940s and through the 1950s, when, as district forester in Fort Frances (1954–59), he had been responsible for Quetico. During that period, many foresters in the DLF had believed that provincial parks should be restricted to large and outstanding northern landscapes, areas such as Algonquin and Quetico, Sibley and Lake Superior. Like many of his colleagues, Foster had thought that such areas should be managed according to what were then considered progressive, multiple-use policies, as pioneered in Algonquin by Frank MacDougall. Those same foresters also thought that primary responsibility for providing recreational parkland in southern Ontario should be assigned either to the conservation authorities or the municipalities. In the early 1950s, as we have seen, the DLF almost succeeded in transferring responsibility for the southern parks to the Department of Municipal Affairs. When William Foster became assistant deputy minister for southern Ontario in 1972, and then deputy minister in 1981, he still held these ideas. Understandably, he did not harbour much enthusiasm for the complex park-policy framework being generated by "the bright, young and zealous" planners. Their approach to the development and management of the parks system, observed Foster, smacked of "urban academic elitism." He preferred the MNR to pursue a more "populist" approach, one that demanded fewer restrictions on permitted uses, especially in Wilderness and Nature Reserve parks, and that would not "sterilize large tracts of land."[33]

For George Priddle, a professor of environmental studies and an ardent exponent of system planning for parks, Foster's thinking had to be counteracted. Consequently, he threw himself into the task of organizing a conference, "Ontario Provincial Parks: Issues in the 80s," co-sponsored by the MNR, the Parks Council, and the Faculty of Environmental Studies of the University of Waterloo between 11 and 14 May 1981. The conference would be Priddle's swan song as chairman, since his tenure expired at the end of May. Beyond drawing media attention to the planning and management problems that he saw threatening the provincial parks system, he hoped the conference would build a consensus among environmentalists, academics, and public officials on the best strategy for advancing SLUP and the implementation of the parks policy of 1978.

The "Issues in the 80s" conference met the first of Priddle's expectations by providing a public forum for park advocates to document their grievances and to vent their frustrations.[34] Speaker after speaker complained of planning processes being "delayed, manipulated, 'laundered' behind the scenes" by senior bureaucrats thought to favour the pulp and paper industry, pilloried forest management agreements that compromised SLUP, and lamented the ability of pulp and paper companies to block the creation of new Wilderness parks. Other deficiencies they highlighted included excessive cutbacks in the parks branch's share of the MNR's budget, its failure to implement approved policies for Historical and Wilderness parks, and the weakness of the Provincial Parks Act. Priddle himself delivered a scathing analysis of "Parks and Land Use Planning in Northern Ontario." In summarizing the proceedings, Dr. George Francis, of the Man-Environment Studies Department at the University of Waterloo, observed that the papers suggested a problem in the MNR that "goes well beyond routine inefficiency."

In view of the events of the previous six months, it was predictable that many of the conference participants would delight in excoriating the MNR. However, by opting for confrontation, they wrecked any chance of producing a united front among the delegates. As a finale to the conference, the environmentalists introduced a motion, calling for a special parks trust and the removal of the provincial parks program from the Ministry of Natural Resources. Voting for such a motion, however, would have meant breaching professional ethics for the one-third of the 175 delegates who were public servants, many of them present or former MNR employees. Wayne Yetman, then acting director of the Parks Branch, bemoaned the fact that Priddle and others had publicly criticised the deputy minister and senior ministry officials. "It destroys the credibility of the conference," he argued,[35] urging the delegates to give the new minister, Alan Pope, time to address the issues they had raised, rather than passing a resolution calling for the removal of parks from the MNR. In deference to the delegates who held similar views, the environmentalists withdrew their controversial motion.

The "Issues in the 80s" conference fell short of the Park Council's objective of creating a common front among park supporters; still, it helped lay the foundation. Deputy Minister Foster himself inadvertently stimulated park advocates into united action. He accomplished this through his decision, in early August 1981, to suspend indefinitely, for reasons of constraint, what he had long considered an excessively ambitious master planning program for the provincial parks. The deputy minister's action took branch officials by surprise, especially the new director, Norm Richards, who, as supervisor of master planning during the 1970s, had been instrumental in developing Ontario's acclaimed master planning policies and procedures. Richards tried, in vain, to have the decision reversed, by reminding his superiors that the previous minister, James Auld, had committed the government to completing master plans for each of the 131 established provincial parks by 1983, a promise which Alan Pope himself had recently reiterated to representatives of the Sierra Club of Ontario. "Any change in this [policy] will not reflect well upon the Ministry," warned Richards, especially since only some thirty plans had been approved to date.[36]

When officials of the Algonquin Wildlands League learned of the suspension of park master planning, they immediately sought a meeting with Alan Pope. To their surprise, the minister himself had not been apprised of the situation.[37] The league representatives explained to Pope that, without master plans prepared in accordance with "Blue Book" management policies, provincial parks would be vulnerable to commercial exploitation. "Traditionally, master plans have been the mechanism for public involvement in park planning, as well as for ensuring that park policies are applied consistently," added the Federation of Ontario Naturalists. "Master plans have been the means of achieving a balance between competing demands in parks ... They have also been the primary means of ensuring the protection of sensitive resources through zoning and special management techniques."[38] By suspending master planning, protested the Algonquin Wildlands League, the one major opportunity for public participation in the entire planning process would be removed, thus ensuring that park planning became "dependent on special-interest lobbying and the whims of middle-management officials."[39]

Shocked by the vehemence of the environmentalists' response to this issue, Alan Pope promised that master planning would be resumed after December 1982, the completion date scheduled for the district land-use plans and for the termination of the SLUP program. Unfortunately, because the minister was still an unknown quantity, his announcement did little to assuage the environmentalists' fears. In fact, the suspension of master planning had shattered what little confidence many environmentalists still had in the capacity of the MNR to deal objectively with parks issues within the context of strategic land-use planning. For park advocates, the situation called for united action. Accordingly, in November, representatives of eleven national, provincial, and regional organizations convened in Toronto to work out a common position on all the outstanding park-related issues that threatened the future of the parks system, and subsequently communicated their concerns to Alan Pope.[40]

The fuss over master planning also revived the demand, first raised publicly at the "Issues in the 80s" conference, for the removal of the provincial parks program to another ministry, and the creation of an Ontario Parks Trust, to function on a provincial scale much as the Niagara and St. Lawrence parks commissions operated on a regional basis. These proposals were still topics of active discussion in February 1982, when Premier Davis restructured his cabinet and named Reuben Baetz to head a new Ministry of Tourism and Recreation. The cabinet shuffle provided another occasion for the preservationists to urge the premier to transfer provincial parks to the new ministry. George Priddle, now a director of the Algonquin Wildlands League, insisted that the proposal represented the "only chance for survival" for the parks system. "Moving parks into a new ministry," added Ron Reid, the FON's staff environmentalist, would rejuvenate the system "with new resources, new ideas and a new profile. It could also reduce the pressure on managers to allow incompatible uses, by removing recreation and protection areas from the multiple-use mindset of the Ministry of Natural Resources."[41]

In response to the environmentalists' proposals, the government appointed Robert Carman, secretary of the Management Board of Cabinet, to chair a senior-level committee, which would study the question of relocating the parks program. The committee eventually decided that the enviromentalists' demand was ill-advised. By late February 1982, the Monzon task force report had been reviewed internally by the MNR, and Alan Pope was poised to announce how he intended to integrate park planning and SLUP, and put them both on the fast track to completion. He was even prepared to announce that substantial numbers of new provincial parks would be placed under regulations during 1983. At this critical juncture, the removal of the parks program from the MNR, the ministry which controlled the Crown land base required for the new parks, might well have impeded these efforts. Interestingly, Deputy Minister Foster also argued persuasively for the retention of the parks program in his ministry. He explained to the committee that the parks system had become an integral component of the district and regional organization of the MNR. In another ministry, parks personnel would be divorced from the wealth of resource management expertise provided by MNR field staff.[42]

Although the environmentalists failed to effect the transfer of the parks program to another ministry, they believed that their efforts had not been in vain. "The whole parks issue had gained considerable momentum through this commotion," the FON reflected. "With parks back in his court, Minister of Natural Resources Alan Pope has to make some very definite decisions about the future of the Ontario provincial park system."[43] The environmentalists did not have to wait long. On 12 March 1982, Pope, now comfortable with his portfolio and possessed of a clear sense of direction, revealed how he intended to deal with SLUP and provincial parks.

The Strategic Land Use Planning program, he explained, would be accelerated and brought to a conclusion by the end of the year. The ambitious young minister intended to stake his political reputation on fulfilling this promise. In each administrative district of the MNR, staff were rushing to prepare drafts of district land-use plans, and strategies based on targets set out for each resource program in the revised regional SLUP documents. The previously criticized drafts of regional SLUP documents had now been substantially amended to include, among other things, all the proposed candidate provincial parks listed in the plans for the regional parks system and analyzed by the Monzon task force.

Pope emphasized that he was strongly committed to public consultation, especially at the local level. "It is the local residents who usually have the most thorough knowledge of their area," he argued, "and they who will be most often directly affected by the land-use decisions."[44] To measure public wants and needs, he explained, ministry staff would schedule open-house meetings in each district during a two-week period in June, at which time people could review the draft plans. Public discussion would be facilitated by the fact that the drafts would include more information about options and their implications than previously provided in the regional SLUP documents. Pope intended that the final plans for district land use would be completed by the end of the year. For the benefit of the park and environmentalist groups, the minister added that his schedule might permit district staff to resume park master planning even earlier than expected.

In addition to outlining the process for completing SLUP, Pope released the Monzon task force report, which identified the 245 candidate provincial parks to be included in the drafts of district land-use plans, and reviewed at the open houses. The report also painstakingly detailed the degree of conflict with other uses posed by each proposal for a candidate park. "The identification of these areas," the minister explained in the legislature, "will eventually mean significant expansion of our parks system." Indeed, he intended "to bring a significant number of the proposed parks under regulation in 1983."[45] He made it clear, however, that the decisions for or against retaining a candidate provincial park in the final district plans would depend to a considerable extent on the amount of public support, or opposition, registered during the open-house reviews.

For the candidate parks which survived the district reviews, Pope announced a new policy and set of guidelines for their interim use, prior to being regulated by the provisions of the Provincial Parks Act.[46] Some of the candidate park areas, he explained, "contain resources which are needed to meet existing resource production commitments. Immediate or total removal of access to these areas and resources could create significant economic hardship for local individuals, communities and industries." Pope believed that some of the larger areas could support activities such as logging and commercial tourism on a temporary basis. "Resource uses which are compatible with park values will be encouraged or permitted as interim uses. Uses which are incompatible with park values will be restricted or prohibited." Finally, the minister had another surprise for park advocates. He intended to give the whole subject of permitted uses in established and future parks another examination. Accordingly, he announced that the "Blue Book" manual of planning and management policies would be open for public review and comment during the district planning process.

"Are we winning or losing?" wondered the FON's Ron Reid, following Alan Pope's mixed bag of announcements on 12 March.[47] On the positive side, park advocates appreciated that the minister had extended the olive branch by promising that master planning would soon be resumed, and that a substantial number of new parks would be created in 1983. They were also pleased that the Monzon report at long last proposed to integrate parks system planning with SLUP, thereby ensuring that park objectives would receive full consideration in the district land-use plans. Earlier complaints that the MNR had appointed the task force as a ruse to delay strategic planning long enough to complete the negotiations for forest management agreements were set aside. The environmentalists now realized that Alan Pope's first priority was to complete the SLUP program as rapidly as possible. "The fact that he has held up the process for months to integrate parks planning ... is a hopeful sign indeed," admitted the FON's Ron Reid.

The fact that the minister of natural resources had elected to release the Monzon task force report also impressed the environmentalists, who had not expected to obtain a copy of what had been a confidential document. They soon appreciated that the report was the most important parks document since the completion of the manual *Ontario Provincial Parks Planning and Management Policies* in 1978. "I couldn't believe it," exclaimed long-time wilderness preservationist Bill Addison of Thunder Bay upon reading the report. He saw that the task force had not deleted any of the candidate parks contained in the regional systems plans; rather, it had simply compiled the proposals – a total of 7 Wilderness, 37 Waterway, 34 Natural Environment, 151 Nature Reserves, 10 Recreation, and 6 Historical parks – and subjected each of them to rigorous scrutiny, in order to establish the degree of conflict with other uses.[48] For Addison, the Monzon report raised the possibility that the provincial parks system, as defined in the "Blue Book," might well be completed, if the park advocacy groups generated enough public interest and pressure.

While park advocates welcomed the gains made on 12 March 1982, they still had many reservations about what the future held. The minister had taken away as much as he had offered. Ron Reid likened Pope's performance to a waltz, "where every step forward must be matched by a shuffle sideways, a little step back on the other foot, and occasionally a whirl."[49] Upon reflection, the park advocacy groups realized that their "starting position" in the forthcoming discussions of district land-use planning was "already a compromise and further compromises can be expected."[50] Even if every candidate park listed in the Monzon report survived the district reviews, the resulting system would still not meet all "Blue Book" targets, especially for recreation opportunities in the back country of northern Ontario, and for the protection and representation of earth and life science features and historical resources. More worrisome for the preservationists was the certainty that many candidate parks would be culled after the district open-house reviews. Parks and Recreational Areas Branch officials openly acknowledged that they might lose as many as 100 because of conflicts with timber, mining, and other resource users.

Pope's decision to introduce an interim use policy for candidate parks, prior to regulation under the Provincial Parks Act, greatly alarmed the preservationists. Mining exploration would be permitted in these areas, and the minister had candidly asserted that if prospectors located an economic deposit, he would withdraw the park reserve and allow mining development to proceed. The environmentalist groups were prepared to accept extended phase-out periods for certain nonconforming activities, such as commercial tourism and trapping in many candidate areas to minimize local disruption. But there were limits. They could not accept an interim use policy that allowed loggers to penetrate previously untouched wilderness areas in Ogoki-Albany, Woodland Caribou, or Lady Evelyn–Smoothwater.

Even more unsettling for the park advocacy groups than the new interim use policy was the minister's decision to review the "Blue Book" policy manual, the much acclaimed "gospel relating to parks." Clearly, Pope intended to amend the manual, but to what extent did he want to open new provincial parks to logging, mining, hunting, lodges, cottages, and motorboats? "We face the great danger of dilution – the watering-down of the ideal concept of parkland until nothing remains" to distinguish parks from "surrounding 'multiple-use' Crown land," warned Ron Reid.

Finally, park advocates did not think highly of the process of public consultation that Pope had laid out for the months ahead. How, they asked, could individuals and provincial conservation groups obtain a fair hearing, when they were expected to register their views on district land-use options at various open-house meetings in forty-six districts, scattered across the length and breadth of Ontario, during the same two-week period in June? "This is meaningful public input? Obviously it is not," they grumbled.[51]

The Chance of a Lifetime

Park advocates may have left Alan Pope's press conference on 12 March uncertain as to whether they were winning or losing the campaign for implementation of the 1978 policy, but they had no illusions about one thing. They had now entered what promised to be the most telling period in the history of Ontario's provincial parks. The number of candidate parks that would survive the district review process depended entirely on how effectively the advocacy groups and their supporters made their presence felt at the forthcoming district open houses. "We knew we had to move quickly, and the task would be enormous," reflected Nancy Patterson of the FON, "but we also knew this might turn out to be the chance of a lifetime."[52]

At Bill Addison's urging, representatives of eight park advocacy groups convened in late March at the offices of World Wildlife Fund Canada in Toronto to fashion a strategy for the district review process. The delegates decided that their best chance for success lay in organizing a committee of activists in each of the MNR's administrative districts. Local people would be in the best position to develop alliances amongst themselves, to generate public support for the candidate parks, to encourage attendance at the open-house meetings, to prepare written briefs, to organize petitions and letter-writing campaigns, and to arrange the media coverage necessary to excite the public imagination about what was at stake in SLUP. All the groups agreed to canvass their members for financial assistance to retain the staff support that would be necessary to launch and to coordinate the strategy of local action committees.

The members of the parks coalition faced a tough, uphill battle. Their combined membership amounted to only 20,000 people, and their financial resources were few. Only the FON and the Wildlands League could afford full-time staff, and even then, Arlin Hackman's position at the Wildlands League was never secure, since the organization operated on a meagre annual budget of under $50,000. Still, the parks coalition had strengths that no amount of money could buy. Individuals such as Addison, Hackman, and Ron Reid possessed exceptional organizational and public-relations skills, expertise in park matters, and a "fire in the belly" type of enthusiasm that would see them through adversity. The coalition also drew strength from the unity of purpose animating all its members. Since the unveiling of parks policy in 1978 and the advent of the "Blue Book," the advocacy groups possessed a common agenda for the first time, an agenda further clarified by the regional parks system plans and the Monzon report.

Bill Addison, the son of the former Parks Branch director, Peter Addison, and of Ottelyn Addison, author of the popular *Early Days in Algonquin Park* (1974), returned to Thunder Bay from the Toronto strategy meeting a man possessed. With a few hundred dollars of seed money from the Wildlands League (the name "Algonquin" had just been dropped, to reflect more accurately the organization's broadened focus), he and his allies in the northwest, including Dave Bates, Tom Miyata, and Marc Wermager, head of the Atikaki Coalition, undertook a telephone blitz to create a regional network of parks supporters. By month's end, they had created the Parks For Tomorrow group. "Its sole goal," they declared, "is to ensure solid public response to the SLUP process in general and support for parks in particular. It is a local organization responding to local issues! ... Our active representatives include trappers, loggers, foresters, teachers, secretaries, entrepreneurs, paper mill workers, tourist operators, carpenters – in fact, a good cross-section of society."[53] The rank-and-file supporters of Parks For Tomorrow were numbered in the hundreds rather than the thousands, and the local action committees sometimes depended on only a handful of volunteers. Still, they were highly motivated and would have a considerable influence. During the spring of 1982, with the assistance of a $2,000 grant from the Thunder Bay Field Naturalists Club, Addison and Bates set out on a marathon tour of the eleven districts of the MNR's northwestern and north-central regions. In every district, they assisted local activists in preparing well-reasoned briefs, each over 100 pages in length, in support of all the candidate parks under consideration.

Meanwhile, the Wildlands League endeavoured to coordinate the efforts of the scattered groups in the loose coalition. A special appeal for funds raised $7,300 which, when pooled with contributions from the other groups, allowed the coalition to hire Jeff Port as a provincial coordinator for the district review campaign. Through the network of personal contacts developed by the executive director, Arlin Hackman, and through its twenty-four-person board of directors, the league enjoyed close connections with the executive committees of most parks and environmental groups in Ontario.[54]

During the spring of 1982, the parks coalition, especially the Wildlands League and the Federation of Ontario Naturalists, went to extraordinary lengths to educate their members about the issues involved in the district land-use reviews and to exhort them to become involved at the local level. The Wildlands League, for instance, mailed out profile sheets on the Candidate Wilderness parks, provided descriptions and background information in *Wildland News* on other candidate-park "hot spots," and distributed to all its members a much expanded and illustrated edition of *Wilderness Now: A Statement of Principles and Policies of the Algonquin Wildlands League* (1972; 3rd ed. 1980). The league also convened meetings of its board of directors in Thunder Bay and other northern centres, to which representatives of local interest groups and agencies were invited. For its part, the FON solicited financial assistance from the Samuel and Saidye Bronfman Family Foundation, and the MNR, to publish a special issue of *Seasons* (Summer 1982) devoted entirely to Ontario's parks system. The biggest issue of the journal ever published, it was designed and written to make its readers "instant experts" on what the system was, what it contained, what was needed to complete it, and "to help build a political climate wherein completion of the system will become a reality."

The importance of disseminating such information was underlined as local activists began to form district action committees throughout the province. It became apparent that many people did not yet fully understand what was going on in land-use planning or what was at stake. This discovery prompted the parks coalition hurriedly to conduct a series of educational workshops across the province to prepare their supporters for the district open houses. Fortunately, the coalition got a welcome reprieve when the open-house meetings in southern Ontario were rescheduled from June to August.

The organizational effort made by the coalition of park and environmentalist groups paid dividends once the public review process began; indeed, the "remarkably high turnout" of park supporters at the 141 district open houses exceeded expectations. Altogether, some 10,000 people attended the meetings, the majority of whom expressed strong support, both for the proposed candidate parks and for maintaining the protectionist elements of the "Blue Book." Park advocates were particularly vocal in opposing commercial logging and the network of roads it would produce, if it were permitted in the proposed park areas. The MNR also received over 10,000 comment sheets, letters, and briefs on land-use issues, which according to the Wildlands League, "demonstrated to the Minister that public support for parks was strong and widespread."[55]

Opponents of the candidate provincial parks also made a strong showing at the meetings. Across northern Ontario, people connected with the timber companies argued vociferously that the proposed parks would seriously reduce the available timber supply and prevent the industry from meeting its future needs, especially for conifer wood. To get its message across to the public, Great Lakes Forest Products purchased television air time in Thunder Bay and financed a $50,000 film entitled *Evergreen*. Regrettably, the forest industry's public-relations campaign against Wilderness parks frightened many people into thinking that the parks issue boiled down to "a clear-cut choice between food on the table and a playground for rich southerners."[56] Such fears were unfounded, the park advocacy groups insisted, and used the preliminary results of the MNR's economic-impact studies for Ogoki-Albany and Lady Evelyn to bolster their case.

Leo Bernier, MLA for Kenora, former minister of natural resources and then minister of northern affairs, echoed the alarmist position of many of his constituents that more parkland would be "bad news" for the northern economy, and used his influence behind the scenes to attack the proposals for candidate parks. "I seriously question the need for the number of candidates ... identified so far," he wrote to Alan Pope. "While there is no question about the need to continue to set land aside for wilderness experiences, the amount of land currently being considered is in my view excessive and cannot be justified ... I would urge you therefore to seriously reassess the wilderness parks component of your plan and scale down the number of candidates."[57] A copy of this confidential memorandum reached the desk of the NDP's resources critic, Floyd Laughren, who immediately called for Bernier's resignation or dismissal.

Despite the successful turnout of park supporters at the district open houses, the review process still left many conservationists convinced that opportunities for public participation had been inadequate. They complained that a majority of the draft plans for district land-use had not been available for study prior to the meetings. "How were concerned citizens supposed to ask intelligent questions at the open houses if they didn't even have a chance to look at the plans?" asked Frank Mariotti, a biologist at Laurentian University. "The open houses in the North were a very feeble attempt at public involvement."[58] Even Alan Pope later admitted that the process had left a lot to be desired.

In September 1982, the combatants in the land-use struggle got the first measure of their success in influencing district decisions, when the MNR released for public comment a series of proposals for district land-use planning. The park advocacy groups did not like what these documents contained. "District officials have axed or deferred indefinitely approximately 20% of the candidates, 35% of these in northern Ontario," reported the Wildlands League. "Many that remain are mere shadows of the original proposals, having had their areas reduced drastically."[59] One of the six Candidate Wilderness parks – the Aulneau Peninsula on Lake of the Woods – had not survived the review, thanks to strong pressure by organized hunters, and the other Wilderness Areas had, indeed, been substantially reduced.

Alarm turned to anger when the pro-park groups completed their own *Progress Report on Parks System Planning in Northern Ontario* (September 1982), which provided an overview of all the draft plans for district land use in the north. The report concluded that not only did the proposed park system in the north fall short of "Blue Book" targets, but the "draft District Plans consistently demonstrate an anti-parks bias and a willingness to neglect parks policies in favour of other extractive resource policies." While the plans met, and often exceeded, the needs of timber and mining interests, the needs of the parks program had been "consistently neglected, or, in some cases, consciously sacrificed." According to Bill Addison, "the Ministry's preferred options [for the northwest SLUP region] sometimes decrease the amount of target achievement in parks by sixty percent in order to gain a two or three percent increase in forestry targets."[60]

In late August, representatives of the parks coalition met with Minister of Natural Resources Alan Pope to outline their concerns that the format of district open-house reviews had been inadequate and that provincial parks had received "second class treatment" in district planning. To offset what they considered the "anti-parks" trend in the draft district plans, the environmentalists urged the minister to make provision for public review of the revised documents, prior to approval by regional officials of the MNR in November. Alan Pope appeared receptive but remained noncommittal.

To keep the media spotlight on park issues and the pressure on the minister, the environmentalists resorted to tactics used successfully in the early 1970s – the staged media event and the carefully orchestrated "town hall" meeting. For media coverage, they came up with the idea of a "Portage for Parks." On 18 October, a drizzly Monday, some eighty plaid-shirted, latter-day voyageurs carried canoes across the grounds of the legislative buildings at Queen's Park in Toronto. They congregated at the doors of the Whitney Block, the location of the MNR's main offices, where they were welcomed by the Liberal and NDP resources critics, Julian Reed and Floyd Laughren. At a lighter moment during the proceedings, the protesters presented Reed with a spray can of "b.s. repellant," to protect him as he waded into the political arena on their behalf.[61]

The following day, the Sierra Club of Ontario, in cooperation with the Parks For Tomorrow group, organized a "town hall" meeting at the St. Lawrence Hall in Toronto, where Alan Pope agreed to be the keynote speaker. The event, which attracted some 400 people, evoked memories of a similar gathering twelve years earlier, when preservationists had gathered to "Save Quetico." Bruce Litteljohn, who had spoken at the 1970 meeting, was on hand again to act as narrator for his slide presentation, highlighting the unique qualities of the Candidate Wilderness parks. Other speakers reported on the status of parks in the three SLUP planning regions. Bill Addison added excitement by wielding an axe on a twenty-foot-high graphic, to demonstrate how he believed that parks policy had been sacrificed to the timber industries. Not to be outdone, Alan Pope gave park supporters good news by announcing that he intended to extend his deadline for completing the district land-use plans in order to take public participation one step further. He would personally chair a series of seven open forums during November and December "to hear all points of view" across the province.[62]

Pro- and anti-park forces again turned out in strength at the minister's forums; 800 people appeared in London, 700 in Thunder Bay, 600 in Toronto,

400 in both Ottawa and Kingston, 350 in Sault Ste. Marie, and 150 in Timmins. Measured in terms of attendance, letters, and briefs submitted, and the diversity of their arguments, park supporters came out on top. "Especially surprising," the FON reported, "was the support for parks creation in the north, where park advocates outnumbered opponents by a wide margin. In the south as well, the Minister could hardly help but be impressed by the depth of support for his plans."[63] Although outnumbered at these meetings, anti-park groups did not fail to make an impression. Sportsmen, opposed to new parks because of potential restrictions on hunting and motorboat fishing, were mustered to attend the meetings by the 50,000-strong Ontario Federation of Anglers and Hunters and its affiliated local groups. In Toronto, they subjected pro-park speakers to abusive heckling.

Evidently worried by the show of support for parks that was manifested at the forums, the OFAH counterattacked by striking an alliance with the professional associations of Ontario trappers, prospectors and developers, and Ontario's forest industries, to press the minister to impose a two-year moratorium on the establishment of any new park. "It's a major issue with us," asserted Rick Morgan of the OFAH. "We feel we need two years to give the government a chance to let people know what happens when you create a park."[64] Firmly committed to wrapping up land-use planning as soon as possible, Alan Pope was, however, not about to cave in to this eleventh-hour demand.

For a brief time in late December, park-related events in the United States sent shock waves through Ontario. On 30 December 1982, just after the ninety-seventh Congress had been dissolved, and with most politicians out of Washington, President Ronald Reagan's Secretary of the Interior, James Watt, conducted what the press dubbed a "midnight raid on wilderness." In a legally questionable manoeuvre, Watt released 660,000 acres (267,098 hectares) of public land from consideration for wilderness, thereby denying Congress the opportunity of deciding whether or not to preserve these areas. Since his appointment in 1981, Watt had become a symbol for the neoconservative reaction against environmentalism in the United States. He had aggressively pursued a policy of making more public lands and resources available for development. By mid-1983, he would succeed in reducing the public land under consideration for wilderness and protection by a total of 1.7 million acres (687,980 hectares).[65] In Ontario, the resource industries applauded this action, while the province's environmental and preservationist groups wondered to what extent these external events might influence their government's ultimate disposition of its Crown land.

Fortunately, Alan Pope was not a combative, neoconservative ideologue in the Watt mould who refused to let the facts interfere with his convictions. Pope was doing everything humanly possible to appear fair to all sides and to familiarize himself with the issues in every part of the province. During personal meetings with each district manager, ministry staff were amazed to discover that the minister's grasp of individual plans often exceeded that of the district managers themselves. Unlike the inflexible James Watt, Alan Pope was genuinely eager to find compromise positions between the pro- and anti-park coalitions. Accordingly, he called together representatives of twenty-seven different interest groups to meet with him personally in closed sessions on 26–27 January 1983 at the Guild Inn, Toronto.

At the beginning of the first day, the minister and his officials presented a list of unresolved issues that they were still pondering. Pope himself chaired an unstructured but lively round-table debate, all the while probing each speaker with "searching and controversial questions."[66] The entire second day of discussions focussed on the most contentious issue – the six Candidate Wilderness parks proposed in the district land-use plans. Throughout the morning, the delegates made no progress toward reaching a modus vivendi on the question. In an effort to move discussion forward, representatives of the environmentalists and the park groups, through their spokesperson Monte Hummel, revealed that they were prepared to compromise on the question of nonconforming activities in the new Wilderness parks. They would never condone forestry and mining in these areas, Hummel explained, but they were willing to consider limited sport hunting on a park-by-park basis, the continuation of some existing commercial tourism facilities, controlled mineral exploration, and hunting and trapping by the aborginal peoples.

Decisions as to whether to allow some or all of these activities in a given park, the environmentalists emphasized, would have to be made through the master planning process, and if approved, each activity permitted would have to be conducted in a way compatible with the classification of a Wilderness park. This meant, for example, that sport hunters would be restricted to travelling by nonmechanized means. Should tourist enterprises be permitted to continue, the operators must be prevented from expanding their existing facilities. The environmentalists opposed the transformation of "present outpost camps in parks into lodges which in turn would service an even broader network of outposts." Hummel also insisted that the tourist operators must not be given unrestricted access to all areas, either by motorboat or all-terrain vehicles. Any mineral exploration permitted in the new Wilderness parks must be undertaken by aerial geomagnetic surveys, or other methods that would have minimal impact on the environment. In the event that a commercially exploitable mineral deposit was found, the affected zone would have to be removed from the park and a comparable area added elsewhere.[67]

These were substantial concessions from dedicated preservationists, who considered any form of hunting, tourist establishment, or mining activity to be incompatible and inconsistent with the notion of a Wilderness park. As Hummel explained, the park advocates were challenging "the sport hunting organizations and … the tourist and mining industries to bring forward new proposals, to show us how their activities might be modified or carried out in … a way … respectful of a wilderness park." Alas, the representatives of sportsmen and industry at the Guild Inn failed to rise to the challenge and continued to argue that Wilderness parks were "unaffordable, undemocratic and unnecessary." Arlin Hackman bemoaned the fact that each "time discussion turned in the direction of sorting out conflicting uses in any of these areas, someone would haul it back to square one by demanding some justification for any new parks whatsoever."[68]

Despite their failure to reach agreement, park advocates left the meetings confident that they had scored well with the minister by being "better prepared and more reasonable in their presentations than other interest group representatives." Environmentalists also took comfort in the knowledge that ministry officials had confirmed that the proposed Wilderness parks would only "impact to a very minor degree (2–5%) on future timber supplies and access to potential mineral resource areas." Park supporters felt that they had reason to be optimistic as they waited to see how the government intended to reconcile the conflicting views on the future use of Ontario's Crown land. Pope informed those who attended the Guild Inn meetings that he would make up his mind on unresolved issues over the following weekend, then submit his decisions to cabinet, for approval by late spring.

On 2 June 1983, Alan Pope rose in the legislature to announce the outcome of the SLUP process. Interestingly, the minister now referred to the district land-use "plans" as "guidelines," a change made at the behest of the minister for northern affairs, Leo Bernier, who thought the less official-sounding title would be more palatable for many of his constituents. "In the guidelines," Pope explained, "we recommend 155 future provincial parks. These will include six wilderness parks, 35 natural environment parks, 25 waterway parks, 74 nature reserves, 12 recreational parks and three historical parks. Cabinet has already passed regulations to create the six wilderness parks immediately. Therefore, these parks already exist."[69] It was an extraordinary announcement: the government had created a wilderness system representative of most of the northern site regions, and had committed itself to more than doubling the number of provincial parks. Once in place, Ontario would possess a parks system second to none in North America. The new Wilderness park additions included a major extension to Killarney Provincial Park, south of Sudbury, and the establishment of Woodland Caribou and Opasquia parks, abutting the Manitoba border to the west and north respectively of Red Lake, Wabakimi (a much reduced version of Ogoki-Albany), Lady Evelyn in Temagami, and Kesagami at the southern tip of James Bay. Combined, these areas added some 1.2 million hectares to the parks system. Although there would be no Wilderness park for southern Ontario, Pope informed the legislature that as an alternative, negotiations were under way between the province and Ottawa for "the eventual establishment of a Bruce Peninsula National Park," which would encompass Cyprus Lake and Fathom Five provincial parks near Tobermory.

There was one more item of good news for park advocates. As a general policy, logging would be excluded from all but two of the new parks. Studies had revealed that the expanded system posed no threat to the future of the forest products industry. "In total, annual available wood supply will be reduced by only one per cent by the year 2000," an MNR press release explained.[70] This loss would be offset by an increase in timber utilization and through improved methods of forest protection. Pope acknowledged that throughout the public consultation process, one message had been come through loud and clear – most Ontarians viewed logging as an inappropriate activity in their provincial parks.

As the minister continued his statement, park advocates quickly learned that a heavy price had been exacted for the historic gains made that day. Ninety of the 245 candidate parks included in the Monzon task force's report had been discarded, most being casualties of trade-offs with other resource users. When the district land-use guidelines were published later that month, it also became evident that drastic cutbacks had been made in the size of many parks. Ogoki-Albany Candidate Wilderness Park, for instance, had been reduced by two-thirds, hence the name-change to Wabakimi Wilderness Provincial Park. "Overall the total area of the 155 new parks," reported the Wildlands League, "will be only about 40% of that contained in the original 245 candidate areas." Nature Reserves had been hit especially hard; their numbers dropped from 150 to 74, and the land base allocated to the reserves had been slashed by 93 percent, from 1.4 million to 97,100 hectares.[71] Environmentalists took consolation in the fact that the MNR intended to protect many outstanding natural features outside the parks system through the new ANSI programs and private stewardship.

Since the elimination of as many as one hundred candidate parks had been anticipated by most groups, this feature of Pope's announcement did not create much of a stir. What caused real consternation and burst the bubble of euphoria was the unwelcome news that the government had decided to set aside many of the protectionist features of the "Blue Book" in its proposals for managing the new parks. Henceforth, declared Pope, mining, hunting, trapping, and commercial tourism would be recognized as permitted uses in classes of parks where they had previously been prohibited. Mineral exploration, for example, would be allowed in 48 of the new parks, including the 6 Wilderness parks. In short, approximately 80 percent of the land base associated with the 155 new parks would be open to prospectors. Furthermore, sport hunting and trapping would be permitted in about half of the promised parks, including all the Wilderness, 14 Natural Environment, and 38 Nature Reserve parks. "Of the originally proposed parks [in the Monzon report], the Government has set aside 96.6 per cent of the land for hunting," reported Rick Morgan of the Ontario Federation of Anglers and Hunters.[72] Finally, existing commercial tourism operations would be permitted to continue in almost all the proposed park areas. Essentially, with the exception of logging, the range of permitted uses in the new parks reflected the manner in which Crown land was already being used.

Opposition members in the legislature – Julian Reed for the Liberals and Jack Stokes for the NDP – promptly assailed the government for modifying the "Blue Book" so as to allow mineral exploration, hunting, and commercial tourism in the new Wilderness parks. It was "misleading and dishonest," argued Reed, to classify an area as a Wilderness park and then allow activities within its boundaries which were nonconforming and incompatible with any accepted definition of wilderness.[73] In Thunder Bay, Bill Addison and Dave Bates of the Parks For Tomorrow group were "totally, utterly numbed" by Pope's decision on nonconforming uses. "Even a death in the family wouldn't have been worse," Addison recalled later.[74]

For Monte Hummel, the minister's decision smacked of betrayal. At the Guild Inn meetings in January, park advocates had been willing to consider compromises on some nonconforming activities in Wilderness parks. "The spirit of our position," Hummel explained, "was that hunting, tourism and mining exploration only be *considered* on a park by park basis, and only *permitted* if they were proposed to take place in such a way that is respectful of the status of a wilderness park." Pope had stepped well beyond these parameters by including nonconforming uses "in the regulations for every wilderness park, creating the impression ... that such activities *would* be permitted on the same terms as they had been practised in the past." Most exasperating of all for Hummel, the MNR's information kit, issued on 2 June, implied that the minister's decision enjoyed the support of the environmentalists, since it was ostensibly based on compromises they had proposed in January.[75] "In my view," concluded Hummel, "this was *not* a politically honest response to the spirit of the compromises offered at the Guild Inn."

Most park supporters experienced profoundly mixed emotions as they came to terms with the significance of the minister's decisions. Arlin Hackman, who had just left the Wildlands League to become staff environmentalist for the FON, was initially jubilant and proclaimed 2 June 1983 "the most important day in the history of the Ontario parks program." However, after reflecting upon the implications for the new parks of the changes in management policy, he became less enthusiastic and expressed "strong disappointment" with Pope's "less-than-visionary compromise that history will regard as no special achievement."[76] Such seemingly inconsistent reactions were understandable. After three years of hanging on tenterhooks over the outcome of the SLUP program, park activists had fallen short of their goal – the implementation of provincial park policy as laid down in 1978. Alan Pope had made history by providing the bulk of the land base required for an outstanding park system, but in their eyes, he had prevented proper management of the new parks by discarding the protectionist essence of the "Blue Book." Permission for nonconforming activities in Wilderness and Nature Reserve parks severely compromised the concept of a park system that was based on the principle of establishing distinct park classes and zones, so as to achieve a range of objectives and meet the needs of different groups of users.

Although it had been originally thought that SLUP would resolve user conflicts on public lands, the minister's decision on nonconforming uses guaranteed that the struggle between environmentalist groups and the other resource interests now permitted in the new parks would continue. This became apparent as the fall hunting season approached, when the FON sounded a clarion call for its members to resume the battle in defence of the concept of parks as wildlife sanctuaries. "It was the fierce and effective lobbying by organized hunters that led to Pope's compromise and the elimination of many potential parks," the FON reminded its members. "The hunters' campaign is continuing now as well, quietly, behind the scenes, to remove remaining prohibitions to hunting in existing parks."[77] True to form, the naturalists sought help from the media to inform a wider public of the shift in parks policy and to generate support for their cause. "Land plan hasn't stilled hunting-in-parks debate," declared a Toronto *Globe and Mail* headline on 1 July. "Hunters stalk our parks" warned the *Toronto Star* at the beginning of the hunting season. The FON informed all who would listen that a 1980 Gallup Poll had revealed that 86 percent of those surveyed opposed hunting in provincial parks. By permitting it to continue, the naturalists asked, was not the government discriminating against the 90 percent of the population who never engaged in sport hunting, and especially against women, who comprised but a small fraction of the hunting fraternity?[78]

These ritualistic outpourings of anger against hunting and other nonconforming uses served a valuable, cathartic purpose for the environmentalists and kept these issues before the public. Still, park activists recognized that the best opportunity to influence policy in the immediate future lay in the newly reactivated master or management planning program, as it was now called. That program provided for public consultation in the making of major decisions for each of the approximately 240 park areas requiring an approved management plan. The advocacy groups resolved to engage in a long, gruelling, park-by-park campaign to minimize the expansion of nonconforming activities.

In the meantime, they looked to the Environmental Assessment Act (1975) as a potential weapon in their struggle. The act called for a detailed statement of environmental impact for every project carried out by the government and allowed for hearings, if these were demanded by the public. Some environmentalists proposed to invoke the act every time the Parks and Recreational Areas Branch issued an interim management statement or sought approval for a permanent management plan. This prospect worried branch officials. For administrative reasons, they were seeking a blanket exemption from the Environmental Assessment Act, which covered both the establishment of parks and their interim management. Rather than meet the requirements of the act by conducting assessments on each park, the branch sought to obtain a "Class EA" document, which would lay down the principles and guidelines for planning all parks. However, the branch also needed the blanket exemption, in order to allow park planning and programming to continue, while officials developed the "Class EA" document. Under the act, the minister of the environment possessed an absolute discretion to reject formal calls for public hearings, if the government considered them frivolous, vexatious, or likely to cause undue delay.

The FON accepted the idea of exempting park establishments from environmental assessments and hearings, since the exercise would largely duplicate the recently completed review process on district land use. However, the federation insisted that all management planning decisions should be subject to approval under the Environmental Assessment Act. The minister "can't reasonably defend foreclosing the master planning process for each park by prescribing extractive uses – before specific park objectives and environmental sensitivities have been identified and publicly aired," the FON asserted.[79] The naturalists had a strong case; even the government's own Environmental Assessment Advisory Committee concurred with the federation's position. For eighteen months, however, as the government pondered the exemption question, none of the promised new parks could be formally established and placed under regulation. "Ministry officials have warned quite openly," Arlin Hackman informed the FON's membership, "that if we want to see any of these new parks established, we had better play along with Mr. Pope."[80] As it happened, such threats proved unnecessary. The cabinet granted Alan Pope his blanket exemption in late 1984.

The resolution of the environmental exemption question removed the barrier to the formal establishment of the provincial parks promised in June 1983. Beginning in mid-January 1985, the first batch of thirty-six parks was submitted to the provincial Regulations Committee. "Mr. Pope and his staff deserve our congratulations for following through on his excellent initiatives in creating new parks," the FON graciously acknowledged.[81] The naturalists were delighted that the first group of newly regulated parks included eleven on the Niagara Escarpment and three in the Carolinian zone. By the end of the year, 104 provincial parks, a number which included additions to established parks, had been regulated, thus boosting the system to a total of 220 parks, embracing 5.6 million hectares. "This is indeed a major legacy for our children," observed the naturalists.[82]

By this time, however, Alan Pope no longer held the Natural Resources portfolio. In February 1985, Frank Miller had replaced William Davis as premier of Ontario. Alan Pope was promoted, first to the Health portfolio, then made attorney general (May 1985), as reward for the major role he had played in Miller's successful bid for the leadership of the Conservative Party. For five months, Michael Harris served as minister of natural resources, until the Miller government unexpectedly lost its majority in the general election of 2 May and suffered defeat in the legislature six weeks later. On 26 June 1985, a minority Liberal Government, headed by David Peterson, assumed power under the terms of a special two-year accord negotiated with the NDP. As the winds of political change freshened, park and environmental groups looked to the new administration to put Ontario's provincial park management policies back in order, by resurrecting the protectionist features of the "Blue Book" and by reversing Pope's 1983 compromise on nonconforming uses.

A Liberal Approach

The first indication that the Liberals might bring a new approach to bear on provincial parks came in August 1985, when Vincent Kerrio, the new minister of natural resources, instructed the Parks Council to review the policy of whole-park contracting, or privatization, as it was commonly known. Privatization had surfaced as a minor issue in the general election, when, a week before voting day, the Ontario Public Service Employees Union had placed large advertisements, headlined "*Your* Provincial Parks ... FOR RENT!" in major urban daily newspapers. Union members protested the expansion of whole-park contracting – eighteen parks were in the hands of private operators by 1985 – and feared that the Miller government intended to "privatize" a dozen more. The practice was resulting in a loss of jobs as the operators replaced long-term, seasonal public employees, paid according to government wage scales, with part-time workers paid at minimum wage. "When parks are leased, workers lose jobs, students lose work experience, communities suffer," declared the newspaper advertisements. "Will commercial operators keep up the park environment, provide security, keep camping fees at affordable levels?"[83]

During the five public hearings conducted by the Parks Council during October and November 1985, the critics of privatization dominated the proceedings. With the exception of the occasional commercial operator, no one stepped forward to defend the policy of whole-park contracting. "Restore public lands to public hands," implored the Ontario Federation of Labour. The Ontario Public Service Employees Union submitted a petition supporting their cause, containing some 18,000 signatures, collected in various campgrounds during the previous summer. Park and environmental groups joined the antiprivatization chorus by arguing that the practice represented a false economy; leasing parks under short-term contracts would contribute to the long-term deterioration of capital assets and the natural environment.[84]

"Clearly," reported Parks Council Chairman Fred Gray in February 1986, "the public did not accept the contracting of whole parks for a substantial number of reasons." On the basis of the public hearings, he concluded that "the people consider the Provincial Parks a public trust to be administered by government." Consequently, the council recommended that whole-park contracting be terminated forthwith, and that any park currently contracted out be returned to the MNR for administration upon the termination of existing agreements. On 6 April 1986, the minister announced that he had accepted this recommendation, saying that he did so with some reluctance, since whole-park contracting saved the government an estimated $300,000 a year in operating expenses. Kerrio made it clear that in deferring to current public sentiment, he was not renouncing the policy in principle. "The Ministry shall continue to monitor public opinion concerning this practice," he said, "to determine its acceptability for possible application in the future."[85]

No sooner had this question been resolved than the Liberal government chose to review another park policy inherited from the Tories – the decision to phase out the cottage communities in both Algonquin and Rondeau parks. A policy that had seemed so straightforward in the beginning had become terribly complex by 1985. Under the original phase-out plan for Algonquin Park, cottagers whose leases came due after 2 July 1954 were entitled to renew their leases once. Some cottagers, however, were luckier than others. For instance, those whose leases expired just a few days before the cutoff date were entitled to renew them for twenty-one years and still be eligible for an additional twenty-one-year term. This meant a difference in eviction dates of as much as twenty-one years. When the first batch of cottagers faced eviction, beginning in 1975, the leaseholders' association rallied to their defence, claiming that the expiry process was unfair. In Algonquin, the leaseholders' outrage was fueled by the outcome of the park's master planning process in 1974. Although the cottagers received no relief under the plan, it allowed the private youth camps, operated under lease, to stay in the park in perpetuity, and permitted the commercial lodges to remain until 1996. Why, the cottagers wondered, had they been singled out when logging, private youth camps, and commercial lodges were all being allowed to stay?

Recognizing that the lease-expiry process had created inequities, the Davis cabinet had agreed in 1978 to modify the policy. Leaseholders in both Algonquin and Rondeau were given the choice of either maintaining their existing leases or opting for a new plan that would extend their right to stay in the park until the death of the lessee, that of his or her spouse, or until 1996, whichever came first. Under the new plan, the lessee could not transfer the lease interests, except to a surviving spouse, and would have to pay an annual rent equal to 10 percent of the market value of the land.[86] Unfortunately, this offer settled nothing; few leaseholders took advantage of what they considered a restrictive plan. Not surprisingly, as all the cottagers faced the termination of their leases, the clamour for an extension gained momentum. The Algonquin Park Residents' Association, for example, went so far as to engage the services of a consultant, Douglas Roseborough, the former director of the MNR's Wildlife Branch, to argue their case. Alan Pope resisted the pressure. He was comfortable in the knowledge that the ombudsman had ruled, in 1979, that the cottage owners had been treated fairly.[87]

With the advent of the Liberal regime in 1985, the cottagers immediately probed the new government's position on the issue. The Rondeau Park Leaseholders Association appealed to the Liberals' sense of fair play. They pointed out that since 1954, 140 cottagers (one-third of the original group) had been compensated at fair market value for their buildings, in return for surrendering their unexpired leases to the Crown. However, that option had been denied to leaseholders in recent years because of fiscal contraints. Did not fairness demand, asked the association, that the remaining cottagers receive compensation for their buildings or be allowed to stay in the park? Vincent Kerrio again turned to his advisory council and requested it to review the issue.

The Provincial Parks Council conducted three public hearings in Whitney, Chatham, and Toronto during March 1985. Some 900 people attended and submitted 63 formal briefs. A turning point in the review process came at the Toronto meeting, when the Wildlands League modified its previously inflexible position in favour of removing all private holdings in Algonquin Park, and came down on the side of the cottagers. "The League does not see the cottagers as anything close to the main problem with the Park," the brief read. There were far more serious matters to address, including the continuation of logging, the deterioration of interpretive programs and facilities under budget constraints, excessive development along the Highway 60 corridor, and the lack of a consistent policy on all private interests within the park. While the league's directors agreed with the current policy that no new cottage leases should be granted in Alonquin, Rondeau, or any other park, they recommended that the existing cottages be tolerated and that money be made available to acquire improvements at face value, should a cottager choose to turn over a lease to the Crown.[88] As a matter of principle, the FON parted company with the league on this issue. "Notwithstanding the existence of other inappropriate activities in parks," the naturalists reasoned, "the private cottages represent an anomaly on publicly owned provincial park lands, and should be removed according to the government's original schedule in a fair but uncompromising manner."[89]

Despite the FON's arguments, the Parks Council forwarded a recommendation to the minister that reflected the influence of the Wildlands League. The cottagers must eventually be removed, the council advised, but there was reason enough to offer them a final twenty-one-year lease extension until 2017. Kerrio accepted the recommendation and announced the revised policy on 1 August 1986.[90]

During the month of October, park and environmental groups were heartened by two more announcements from the Peterson government. Reversing a previous Conservative decision, the premier stated that he would introduce a bill "untaxing nature" – the future Conservation Lands Act (1988) – in order to encourage the private stewardship concept of conservation. Furthermore, on 3 October, Natural Resources Minister Kerrio and federal Environment

Map 7: Ontario's Provincial Parks System

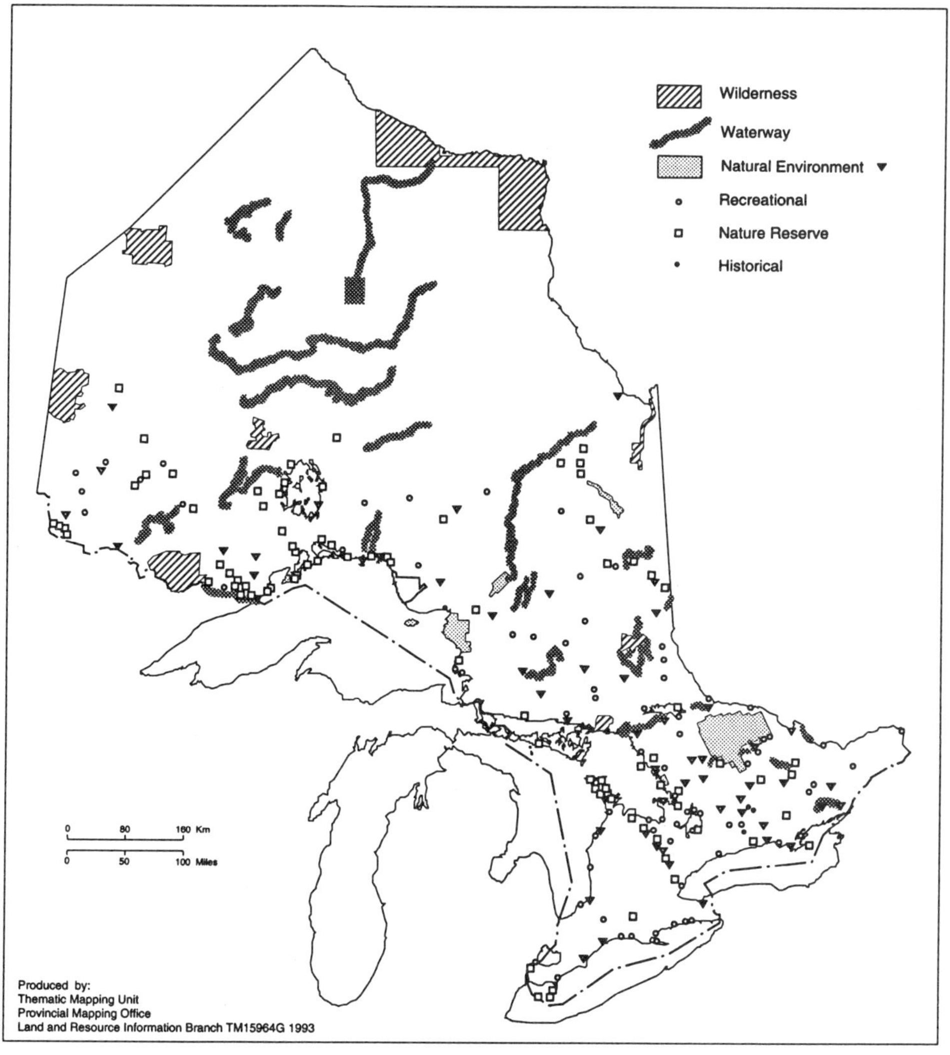

Minister Tom McMillan announced that they had reached an agreement in principle to create Bruce Peninsula National Park. The province of Ontario agreed to donate about half of the land (7,000 hectares) required for the park – an area that included Cyprus Lake and Fathom Five provincial parks, as well as the Cabot Head and Little Cove Nature Reserves – and $8.2 million in capital facilities and improvements. The federal government agreed to acquire the remainder of the land within ten years on a "willing seller, willing buyer" basis, at an estimated cost of $10 million. Despite vigorous opposition from organized sportsmen, who for years had stood in the way of an agreement, Kerrio and the Liberal cabinet accepted the fundamental tenet of national park policy that there would be no hunting in the new park. However, to appease the sportsmen, a 3,800-hectare hunting corridor had been excised from the proposed mainland park study area. The Ontario government also acceded to the wishes of the residents of Lindsay Township, who had rejected the national park proposal in a referendum held in 1985. No part of the township was included in the park. "Vincent Kerrio and the Ontario government have been very generous in this agreement," FON staff environmentalist Don Huff observed.[91]

Park advocacy groups welcomed the various Liberal initiatives undertaken in 1985–86, but these accomplishments were overshadowed by one great unresolved question. What did the Peterson government intend to do about the "nonconforming uses" permitted in the new parks promised by Alan Pope in 1983? Environmentalists would be satisfied with nothing less than a reversal of Conservative policy on this question; they wanted the government to return to the original "gospel relating to parks," as written in the "Blue Book" of 1978. When Vincent Kerrio first began to examine this issue, he did not anticipate the emotions it would generate or its potential for tarnishing the government's image as a champion of the environment. In fact, until September 1985, the minister proceeded under the misconception that Alan Pope's decision on permitted "nonconforming uses" had been made with the consent of the environmentalists who had attended the Guild Inn meeting of January 1983.[92] Even after being disabused of this notion, Kerrio was still not inclined to reverse Pope's compromise. As a former businessman in Niagara Falls, an angler and sport hunter, boating enthusiast and occasional canoeist, and a cottager in Temiskaming, the minister saw the question of "nonconforming uses" from every angle. From his vantage point, Alan Pope's provincial park policy of 1983 seemed reasonable.

In April 1986, Kerrio discovered that some of his colleagues in the Cabinet Committee on Regulations were of a different mind. This became evident when he asked the committee to place under regulation some of the approximately fifty remaining candidate parks promised in 1983 but still not formally established. As part of his submission, Kerrio also requested that the committee entrench the "nonconforming uses" in regulations, and include a proposal for a small-scale hydroelectric installation in one of the parks. His plans went awry when Gregory Sorbara, the minister of colleges and universities and chairman of the committee, questioned the proposal to pass regulations to allow the nonconforming activities, and insisted that it be set aside for a more detailed review. This action triggered an internal debate within the Peterson cabinet, a debate which lasted two years. That summer alone, the issue went before cabinet committee several times, on each occasion without being resolved. Gregory Sorbara, Jim Bradley, minister of the environment, and some officials in the premier's office, argued for the adoption of a more "Liberal approach" to provincial park management. Other ministers like Vincent Kerrio reminded them of the history of strategic land-use planning that lay behind the policy compromise of 1983, and emphasized the costs in lost jobs and revenues should mining, trapping, commercial tourism, and hunting be prohibited in the parks created after 1983. To complicate matters for the government, the public learned of the cabinet division at the very outset, when confidential documents were leaked to the FON. As early as 12 May 1986, the details of the schism were reported in the *Toronto Star*, by journalist David Israelson.

From that point on, park advocacy groups gave the government no rest on the issue of "nonconforming uses." The FON, for example, launched a publicity campaign against hunting in the parks. The highlight of the effort involved distributing a so-called "park-user survival device," a fluorescent orange triangular safety sticker, which read "DO NOT SHOOT. I am not a game species." The demand for the sticker was larger than expected, so that more had to be printed.[93]

Meanwhile, the release of the MNR's *Concept Plan Alternatives* (May 1986) for Woodland Caribou Provincial Wilderness Park, a preliminary step in the development of a management plan, also set off a storm of protest. The document proposed to accommodate a wide range of activities in the park; mechanized travel, hunting, trapping, fly-in tourist operations, outfitters located in the interior, 170 boat caches, and 27 private cottages. All of these uses were in keeping with the district land-use guidelines of 1983, but inconsistent with the 1978 "Blue Book." None of these activities should be allowed in a Wilderness park, insisted the preservationists. Since Woodland Caribou was the first of the five new Wilderness parks to be given a management plan, the decisions made here would set precedents for the others. Nothing less than the future of Ontario's wilderness system was at stake.[94] The publicity generated by the environmentalists had the desired effect. In late summer, the MNR announced the suspension of the management planning process for Woodland Caribou, pending the cabinet's decision on the "permitted nonconforming uses."

Shortly afterward, the embers of another controversy burst into flame. In November 1986, the world's largest alliance of conservation groups, the Swiss-based International Union for Conservation of Nature and Natural Resources

(IUCN) hearkened to the entreaties of the FON and placed Lady Evelyn–Smoothwater Provincial Park on a list of twenty-three protected areas in the world that were threatened with environmental disaster.[95] The IUCN's registry included a site in the then Soviet Union, threatened by the nuclear accident at Chernobyl in 1986, and a park in the Central African Republic, where rhinoceros and elephant herds were being decimated by poachers. According to the IUCN, Lady Evelyn fell into the same category because it was endangered by the impending logging activities that would result from the construction of a proposed extension of the Red Squirrel forest access road, which ran due west of Highway 11 into the area south of the park. The Red Squirrel Road Extension would link up with the existing Liskeard Lumber Road, which already bisected Lady Evelyn, and enable the Liskeard Lumber Company in Elk Lake to remove timber more economically from its limits to the south of the park. Finally, the extension would also connect with a proposed Pinetorch Corridor, which would run thirty-three kilometres farther west and north, in the area below the park. In the MNR's opinion, the Red Squirrel Road Extension was essential for the survival of two mills, William Milne and Sons Ltd. of Temagami and Liskeard Lumber of Elk Lake. Environmentalists were unconvinced. They argued that experience elsewhere in the world showed that the expansion of clear-cut logging activities, after the development of the road network, would have a disastrous impact upon the wildlife habitat and the prime scenic and recreational values of the Lady Evelyn wilderness. Apart from the deleterious effects of clear-cut logging, forest access roads would inevitably lead to an influx of hunters, motorboat users, and all-terrain vehicles. The environmentalists insisted that the way to protect Lady Evelyn was to designate the disputed area to the south of the park as a wilderness buffer zone, in which logging and mining would be prohibited.

Vincent Kerrio understandably took umbrage at the IUCN's listing of Lady Evelyn as an endangered natural area. He had not been informed that the park was being investigated, and only learned of the decision through a column in the *Toronto Star*. Surely, he commented, the provincial government deserved better, especially after it had responded to preservationist concerns the year before by voluntarily ordering an environmental assessment of the proposed Red Squirrel Road Extension – the first time a forest access road had been subject to an individual assessment. Kerrio believed the IUCN had been premature in placing Lady Evelyn on the registry of endangered natural areas, since the final environmental assessment had not yet been completed. Preservationists retorted that they had a reasonably good idea of what the MNR intended; after all, they had reviewed the contents of the draft environmental assessment, released in September 1986. The focus of that document, they noted, had been excessively limited. It assessed only the potential effects of building the twenty-metre-wide right of way and ignored the environmentally damaging impact of the clear-cut logging that would be undertaken following the completion of the road. Further, the draft had failed to address the significance of the distinctive landscape of Temagami and its biological features. The document concluded that "the benefits of proceeding with roads outweigh the disadvantages, and that impacts can be minimized to an acceptable level."[96] In the preservationists' opinion, the writing was on the wall for Lady Evelyn. Immediate action had to be taken to protect the endangered wilderness.

"By placing Lady Evelyn on this global registry," editorialized the FON, "the IUCN ... has helped to put matters in perspective for Ontarians. We look at the obliteration of the Amazon rain forest or the shooting of African rhinos and think, 'How can this be allowed to happen?' But suddenly the rest of the world is scrutinizing what's going on in our own backyard."[97] The IUCN's intervention transformed what had been a localized skirmish about logging versus wilderness into a provincial *cause célèbre*, which journalists soon described as symptomatic of "a much larger problem – poor management of the provincial park system."[98] Prominent Canadians, alerted to the danger facing the legendary Temagami country, quickly jumped into the fray with all the attendant media coverage they commanded. Authors Margaret Atwood, Pierre

Map 8: Temagami Area

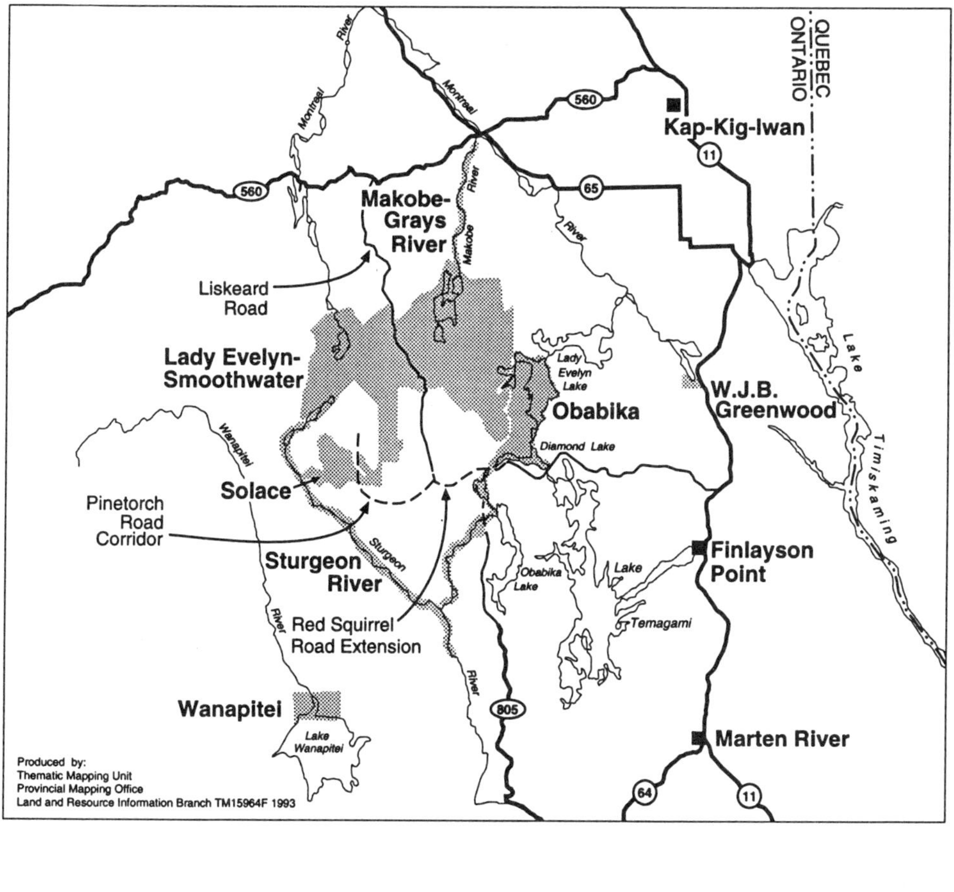

Berton, and Timothy Findley, wildlife artist Robert Bateman, and biologist David Suzuki among others formed the Save Temagami Committee, became patrons of a new Temagami Wilderness Society, and squared off against the MNR.

Throughout 1987, the preservationists prodded the government mercilessly. On 31 March, for instance, the FON's Don Huff timed a press conference and an appearance on the CTV network news to coincide with a cabinet meeting scheduled for the following day, at which time the politicians planned to discuss the merits of appointing special citizens' advisory committees, to help to resolve the issue of non-conforming activities in such parks as Lady Evelyn–Smoothwater and Woodland Caribou. Huff explained why resource extraction and sport hunting should be prohibited in Ontario's parks, and exhorted the government to establish the remaining 51 of the 155 parks announced in 1983, parks now being held in a state of suspension by the policy debate. The next day, investigative reporter Rosemary Speirs penned a less than flattering column in the *Toronto Star*, tracing the recent history of parks policy and the government's inability or unwillingness to resolve the current controversy.[99]

In July 1987, following the termination of the two-year accord between the Liberals and the NDP and with the government riding high in the opinion polls, Premier Peterson called an election for 10 September. This meant a further postponement of the decision on parks management policy. The environmentalists, however, resolved to put the Temagami issue before the voters. On 21 August, they got an opportunity to do so, when Natural Resources Minister Kerrio authorized William Milne and Sons Ltd. to begin logging a 637-hectare stand of old-growth forest, south of Lady Evelyn–Smoothwater Provincial Park. Unless the company quickly obtained new supplies of timber, Kerrio explained, it would be forced to close down and throw 180 people out of work. To minimize the environmental effects, however, the MNR rejected the company's application for an access road. The loggers would have to move their equipment into the forest by barge and take out the timber in booms via Lake Temagami. In addition, the company would also be required to leave 400-foot (122-metre) shoreline reserves along all waterways and suspend cutting during the summer tourist season.

The Save Temagami Committee denounced the minister for allowing logging in an old-growth forest they wanted preserved. "Now we are really in a stage where there is a war," declared Timothy Findley. "It's a war between [Kerrio's] department ... and the environment." Gary Potts, chief of the Teme-Augama Anishnabai, considered the logging decision "extremely contemptible," in view of the fact that his people were still in the process of challenging in the Ontario Supreme Court the province's jurisdiction over the Temagami wilderness. Vincent Kerrio was taken aback by the anger aroused by his announcement. In an effort to calm the aggrieved parties, he promised that the government would appoint a citizens' advisory committee to recommend long-term solutions for the disputed area.[100]

After the Liberals won their majority in the election of 10 September, the cabinet could not postpone its decision on provincial park management policy for long. But first, Natural Resources Minister Kerrio appointed the Temagami Area Working Group, a special advisory committee, to help the government to resolve the conflict over the future of the area around Lady Evelyn. The fifteen-person committee, made up of representatives of all the parties in the dispute, and chaired by John Daniel, president of Laurentian University, was appointed in December and given three months to submit its recommendations. Alas, on 5 March 1988, the committee broke up in disarray when Jack Craik, the president of the Ontario Federation of Anglers and Hunters, and six representatives of the forest and mining industries and local municipalities, refused to sign the final report.[101] Undeterred, Daniel submitted a set of recommendations that, he hoped, would protect the unique landscape, ecology, and recreational values of the Temagami wilderness without sacrificing forestry jobs. Among other things, he recommended that the Liskeard Lumber Road, which ran through the middle of Lady Evelyn, be phased out by reallocating existing timber licences in the area surrounding the park. Logging, added Daniel, should be continued in the disputed buffer zone, for the sake of the approximately 500 jobs generated by the forest industry in the region. This would necessitate the construction of the Red Squirrel Road Extension.[102]

Later that same month, the Environmental Assessment Branch of the Ministry of the Environment released its review of the MNR's Red Squirrel Road assessment document. The review concluded that despite the narrow focus of the study, it still met the requirements of the Environmental Assessment Act.[103] Preservationists were furious and flooded the office of the minister of the environment with a record 170 applications for a formal environmental hearing on the road extension. Their case seemed to be strengthened by the decision of the Toronto consulting firm, Del Can International Ltd., which conducted most of the MNR's Red Squirrel Road environmental assessment study, to remove its name from the final report, because it considered the scope of the study too narrow to comply with the law.[104]

All of these developments complicated an already complex situation for the Peterson government. As late as mid-April, the cabinet had yet to reach a consensus on either Temagami or the nonconforming-uses question. Environment Minister Jim Bradley favoured both holding an environmental hearing on the Red Squirrel Road Extension and revoking Alan Pope's 1983 decision on nonconforming uses. Vince Kerrio and David Ramsay, the minister of correctional services and MLA for Temiskaming, preferred that the cabinet adopt a more pragmatic position on both issues and emphasized the need to foster the economic development of small northern resource communities.[105]

In a noteworthy last-minute effort to provide a fresh perspective on the controversy, the Canadian Parks and Wilderness Society (CPAWS, previously the National and Provincial Parks Association of Canada) released a brief,

"The Temagami Crisis: A Critical Evaluation and Proposal for a Sustainable Future," in early May. The document was informed by the ideas of the much-heralded book *Our Common Future*, published in 1987 by the World Commission on Environment and Development, headed by the prime minister of Norway, Gro Harlem Brundtland. According to the CPAWS, the Ontario government needed to discard its traditional and limiting "economy versus environment attitude" when examining the Temagami issue, and embrace instead the "sustainable development" concept that lay at the heart of the Brundtland report. In the light of the report, the CPAWS brief explained, it was time to view the Temagami issue less as "a fight between wilderness advocates and loggers" than as a conflict resulting from "poor forestry practices, a lack of accurate information on timber supplies and wilderness areas, a lack of government accountability and inadequate attempts to diversify the local economy."[106] Present forestry practices and policy in Temagami, the brief went on, were designed "to sustain the forest industry, not the forests." Establish the area as a sustainable-development demonstration project, urged the society, with the goal of promoting "small-scale forestry, wilderness tourism, local processing of timber and other activities meant to diversify the local economy." The CPAWS also recommended the settlement of the Teme-Augama Anishnabai land claim before any major road construction or land-use decisions were made. Regrettably, this far-sighted brief came too late to influence the impending government policy statement on the Temagami question.

On Tuesday, 17 May 1988, Vincent Kerrio, along with Environment Minister Jim Bradley, convened a press conference to unveil the Liberal approach to managing Ontario's provincial parks system. The news was stunning; some observers likened it to a bombshell. As Kerrio spoke, it became clear that the Liberals had acceded to the demands of park and environmental advocates and were prepared to scrap Alan Pope's 1983 decision to allow "nonconforming" uses in the 155 new provincial parks. Henceforth, there would be no commercial logging, hunting, trapping, mining, or hydro-electric development permitted in Ontario's Wilderness and Nature Reserve parks and zones. "The government believes that the need to preserve a certain amount of 'pure' wilderness is too important to compromise," said Kerrio.[107] As for the other classes of parks, there would be no trapping, mining, or hydro development permitted in them, either, and logging would only be allowed in Algonquin and Lake Superior parks under stringent operating rules. All in all, this was one of the most significant statements of park policy ever made. It meant that the "Blue Book" had been resurrected, and for the first time, pre- and post-1983 parks would be managed as a unified system, according to the same set of policy prescriptions. To cap his announcement, Kerrio also promised that 53 new parks, all but two being the last of the 155 promised in 1983, would be placed under regulation within a year.

The Liberal policy on parks evoked a predictable range of responses. For park and environmental advocates, 17 May 1988 stood out as a red-letter day. "As citizens of Ontario we should feel elated that we now have a parks system of which we can be justly proud," declared the FON. The "new policy brings the Ontario parks system into line with an internationally accepted parks philosophy of non-exploitive uses. Bravo, Mr. Kerrio."[108] The Wildlands League also celebrated the victory. "Once again, Ontario has the foundation for an exemplary parks system. We can now move on to the incredible task of planning for the management of both the 'new' and pre-1983 parks."[109] In contrast to these accolades, conservationists who subscribed to the so-called multiple-use philosophy viewed 17 May 1988 as "Black Tuesday." John Power, a writer on the outdoors for the *Toronto Star*, condemned the government for reversing Conservative policy without full public discussion. "We've run the parks trail before," he wrote, "but in a democratic fashion. This time democracy has been usurped by autocracy."[110] Jack Craik, president of the Ontario Federation of Anglers and Hunters, agreed and pronounced the Peterson cabinet to be "anti-hunting, anti-trapping and ... biased against sports fishermen." In his "All Outdoors" column, the *Toronto Star*'s John Kerr deplored the fact that "yuppies," "tree-huggers and bunny-patters," all possessed of a "warped view of nature," had infected the thinking of the minister of natural resources. The Liberal policy shift, he lamented, "marks a move away from conservation ... toward total protectionism."[111]

Were the critics right? Did "total protectionism" prevail in the provincial parks system as of 17 May 1988? The facts suggest something else. Indeed, the hallmark of the new Liberal policy on parks was its balance and flexibility, not protectionist rigidity. Hunting and commercial tourism – activities considered exploitive by preservationists – were still to be allowed in selected Historical, Natural Environment, Recreation, and Waterway parks. Decisions on these uses would be made on a park by park basis, presumably after public consultation during the management planning process. Parks and Recreational Areas Branch officials revealed that under the new policy, 66 parks would still accommodate sport hunting. Status Indian peoples would also be allowed to continue their traditional activities, including trapping, hunting, and wild rice harvesting in all classes of parks located within their treaty areas. Flexibility was also built into the policy implementation schedule. In the interest of fairness, commercial fishing, wild rice harvesting, and trapping by non-Indians within park boundaries would be phased out in twenty-one years, or when a licensed operator, harvester, or trapper died, whichever came first.[112]

Even the policy for Wilderness parks could not be described as rigidly protectionist. In an extension of the tourism and marketing initiatives pursued by the Parks and Recreational Areas Branch since 1978, Kerrio had made a substantial alteration to policy, as defined in the "Blue Book," by deciding that existing tourism operations would be permitted to remain in Wilderness parks, and that some fly-in operations and the use of motorboats outside access areas would be accommodated within individual management plans. Status Indians located within treaty areas, who owned and operated hunt camps in Wilderness parks, would not be affected by the new policy, and their guests would be permitted to hunt under permit within park boundaries. Cottages on leased land in the Wilderness parks, and indeed in all classes of new parks, would be phased out after twenty-one years, beginning 1 January 1989. In short, then, the Liberal policy on "nonconforming uses" could have been considerably tighter. Rather than establishing the primacy of protectionism throughout the parks system, the Liberals had created a more effective and reasonable balance between the four policy objectives – heritage appreciation, protection, recreation, and tourism.

After announcing the new policy, Kerrio and Bradley turned their attention to the topic of Temagami. It became clear that the Temagami question had not been settled independently, without regard for the overall policy changes; it was part of a larger package of trade-offs and compromises. Kerrio led off by outlining a series of measures he hoped would return Lady Evelyn–Smoothwater "to its true wilderness status," while maintaining "the economic stability of the Temagami Region." Three new waterway parks – Obabika River, Solace Lakes, and Sturgeon River – would be established in the disputed buffer zone, adding some 26,670 hectares of parkland to the 72,400 hectares in Lady Evelyn. The Waterway parks created a circular canoe corridor, offering 225 kilometres of prime canoeing, which linked up with established routes within the Wilderness park. In addition, Kerrio also announced that the cabinet had decided to implement the key recommendations of the Temagami Area Working Group. The government intended to close, by 1994, the section of the Liskeard Lumber Road that bisected Lady Evelyn–Smoothwater Park. By that time, the timber licences issued to the Liskeard Lumber Company would have been reallocated in the area north of the park, thereby removing the need for the road. Kerrio also promised to appoint a citizens' advisory council, as recommended by the working group, to assist in the transformation of the Temagami district into a "model management area for recreational, forest, tourism and environmental resources."[113]

Once Kerrio had finished, Jim Bradley revealed what the cabinet had decided on the question of the controversial Red Squirrel Road Extension. "I have accepted the Ministry of Natural Resources' Environmental Assessment for the ... Extension," he announced, and "I have decided not to hold a hearing into this matter." In his estimation, a hearing would last more than a year, cause undue delay in road construction, and thereby jeopardize the local forest industry. To minimize the environmental impact of the extension, however, Bradley released a list of twenty-nine conditions his ministry had placed on road construction. "I believe this results in a fair and balanced policy serving the needs of Temagami," he concluded.[114]

Not everyone agreed. "The Temagami wilderness will be raped, and the credibility of the environmental assessment process has been seriously damaged," argued the FON.[115] Both the Temagami Wilderness Society and the Teme-Augama Anishnabai took swift action to delay the construction of the Red Squirrel Road Extension, the former by filing a lawsuit in June, challenging the minister of the environment's approval of the project, and the latter by blockading the right of way for the road, in an attempt to force a settlement of their 111-year-old land claim. In a conciliatory gesture to the Indians, the government agreed to hold off construction while it attempted to negotiate a settlement with the band out of court. As things turned out, with this decision, the Liberal compromise on Temagami began to unravel.

The delay in road construction caused great consternation in the town of Temagami, where it was believed the sawmill of William Milne and Sons Ltd. faced imminent closure because of insufficient timber supplies. Angry loggers, mill workers, and their families decided to stage a protest of their own, beginning on Friday, 2 September 1988, the start of the Labour Day weekend. Some 300 people blockaded the well-travelled Temagami Lake access road and prevented cottagers and lodge guests from reaching their destinations. As a publicity event, the blockade was enormously successful; the story was picked up by the provincial press and the major television networks, and included scenes of a phalanx of Ontario Provincial Police officers, many in riot gear, marching into the crowd of demonstrators and arresting fifty-one people.

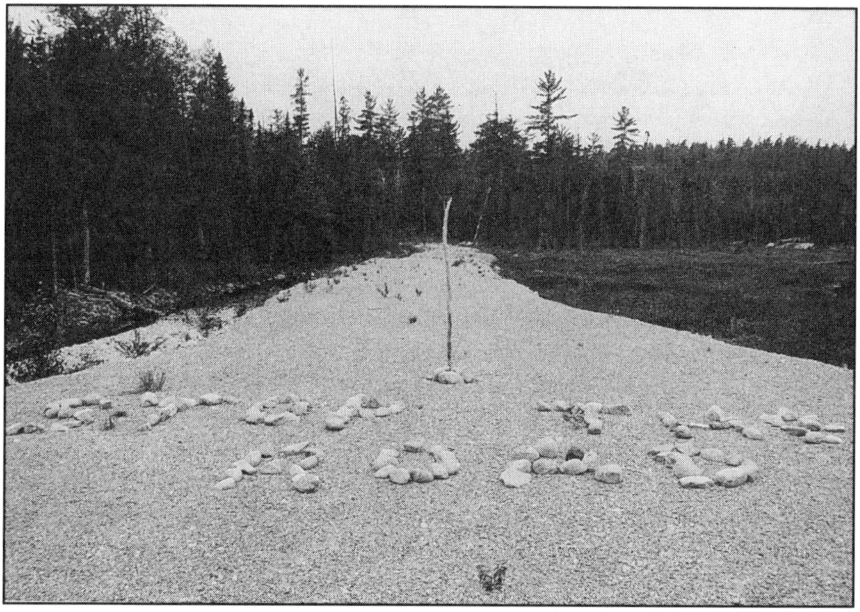

The controversial Red Squirrel Road Extension. *Courtesy: Ministry of Natural Resources.*

Temagami: old-growth pine.
Courtesy: Ministry of Natural Resources.

Later that fall, negotiations between the province and the Teme-Augama Anishnabai reached an impasse. During November, the government proposed a creative solution by offering to establish a forest stewardship council, made up of Indians, local non-Indian residents, and government officials, which would manage a 680-square-kilometre segment of the ancient Temagami pine forest. The Teme-Augama Anishnabai rejected the proposal, when the province insisted that the blockade of the Red Squirrel Road Extension be lifted, so that logging could begin immediately.

To make matters worse, just after the negotiations collapsed, the Bank of Nova Scotia called in a $5-million loan to William Milne and Sons Ltd. because of the uncertainty of timber supply. On 2 December, the company, the second-largest employer in the town, went into receivership. At this juncture, a frustrated Premier David Peterson called the Temagami question "the most difficult issue I have ever seen in politics." The following March, fate dealt the town of Temagami another devastating blow, when Dofasco Ltd., the town's largest and last major employer, announced that it intended to close its unprofitable iron-ore mine. The pressure on the government to promote new development in the economically depressed Temagami area intensified greatly.

By this time, the Ontario Court of Appeal had, in late February, unanimously dismissed the Teme-Augama Anishnabai land claim. Although the Indians announced that they would seek leave to take the case to the Supreme Court of Canada, the Ontario cabinet asked the courts to lift the Indian land-title caution of 1973, which had frozen new mining and other development in the region, though Attorney General Ian Scott reiterated his commitment to bringing about a negotiated settlement with the Teme-Augama Anishnabai. And in April 1989, the environmentalists also suffered a legal setback, when the Ontario Supreme Court upheld the government's decision to build the Red Squirrel Road Extension and the Pinetorch Corridor. According to the court, the government had acted properly in approving the roads, based on the MNR's assessment of their potential effects on the environment, and without a formal environmental hearing. Surveying and construction of the Red Squirrel Road Extension began forthwith.

It was a hollow victory for the government. The effort to balance wilderness protection and economic development in Temagami had left all parties disgruntled. Unemployed mill and mine workers blamed preservationists and the Indians for their plight and resented the fact that the government had pandered to these interests. The Teme-Augama Anishnabai were continuing their battle in the courts, while the preservationists resumed the fight to preserve the Temagami forest. Taking a cue from the international struggle during 1988–89 to save the Amazon rain forests, a struggle which saw celebrities and rock stars such as Sting and Bruce Cockburn rally to the cause, the Temagami Wilderness Society and Beaver Canoe Ltd. organized a benefit concert on 27 April at the University of Toronto's Convocation Hall. Entitled

"Temagami: The Last Wild Stand 2," it featured Canadian entertainers Gordon Lightfoot and Murray McLaughlan.

A month later, on 28 May, 600 environmentalists marched through downtown Toronto to Queen's Park, chanting "Save the trees. Cut down the industries," and "Save Temagami. Dump Peterson." The protesters were buoyed by recent opinion polls, which indicated that 64 percent of Canadians considered it more important to preserve forests than to guarantee jobs, and that only 37 percent of those surveyed saw forests as a resource primarily to be used for economic benefit.[116] None of these developments seemed to faze the Peterson government, which steadfastly held to its decision to complete the Red Squirrel Road. Accordingly, the Temagami Wilderness Society turned up the pressure in June by resolving to blockade the road right of way and to use passive resistance tactics. The blockade generated considerable publicity, particularly when NDP opposition leader Bob Rae joined the environmentalists in September and was arrested for his trouble. In late November, the Teme-Augama Anishnabai also resumed their blockade. Tiring of these tactics, the government obtained a permanent injunction from the Ontario Supreme Court to remove the protesters. Subsequently, construction of the Red Squirrel Road proceeded rapidly to completion.

Although the environmentalists had failed to stop road construction, the wilderness battle moved into another phase, one which focussed on the question of preserving "old growth" Temagami forests. The Ministry of Natural Resources discovered that it could not ignore the scientific findings of the Temagami Wilderness Society's Tall Pines Project, a forest research program launched in 1988 under the supervision of Dr. Peter Quinby. Based on Quinby's field work, the society had brought to the government's attention the importance of Temagami as the last significant old-growth pine ecosystem in North America. Old-growth forests, the society argued, were essential for soil stabilization, water purity, nutrient retention, wildlife habitat, and as a gene pool; but even more importantly, they possessed incalculable benefits for forest research and could well hold the key, both to forest regeneration and the long-term future of the forest industry.[117] The sudden concern about "old-growth" values caught the MNR by surprise. During the early 1980s, when the ministry selected the area for Lady Evelyn–Smoothwater Wilderness Park, the concept of old-growth forest had not even been part of the planners' vocabulary.[118] Only when Quinby and the Temagami Wilderness Society initiated the Tall Pines Project in 1988 did anyone attempt to identify the specific qualities of an old-growth forest in northeastern North America.

The findings of the Tall Pines Project and the society's strategy of focussing on the need to preserve "old-growth" values paid dividends. On 20 November 1989, two weeks before the completion of the Red Squirrel Road, the new minister of natural resources, Lyn McLeod, announced that the government intended to place a freeze on an environmentally sensitive 585-hectare area of

Temagami's Wakimika Triangle, pending further studies. Two months later, in January 1990, at a conference presented by the Faculty of Forestry at the University of Toronto, the minister revealed that her officials were currently preparing a new policy, designed to identify and protect tracts of Ontario's old-growth forest.[119]

In April 1990, the Teme-Augama Anishnabai also made gains, both for native self-government and the protection of the Temagami forests, by signing an historic agreement with the Ontario government for joint stewardship of some 40,000 hectares (four townships) in the region opened to logging by the completion of the Red Squirrel Road. Henceforth, the area covered by the agreement was to be administered by a stewardship council, made up of equal numbers of band representatives and government officials. The membership of the council effectively gave the band a veto over logging in the stewardship zone. As part of the agreement, the beleaguered William Milne and Sons mill in Temagami was to be closed and its assets purchased by the Ontario Development Corporation.[120]

It remains to be seen whether these initiatives of the Peterson government will achieve a modus vivendi between the disputants in Temagami. Initial reactions are not encouraging. The environmentalists continue to claim that too little is being protected, the timber interests challenge this assertion, while the Teme-Augama Anishnabai insist that the stewardship agreement is merely the first step toward a treaty of coexistence. With such conflicting values and so little middle ground, especially between loggers and the environmentalists, it appears that the battle over wilderness in Temagami is not yet close to playing itself out.[121]

Notwithstanding the persistence of the political storm over Temagami and Lady Evelyn–Smoothwater, the end of the 1980s brought to a conclusion a remarkable period of accomplishment for the provincial parks program. Since 1978, the theoretical frameworks contained in the cabinet-approved parks policy and the "Blue Book" had been largely implemented. Theory had been successfully translated into fact. Where there had been 128 provincial parks in 1978, the system in 1989 contained 261 parks, covering 6.3 million hectares or about 6 percent of the total land and water base of Ontario, an area larger than the province of Nova Scotia. The expanded system contained 83 Nature Reserve, 74 Recreation, 63 Natural Environment, 29 Waterway, 8 Wilderness, and 4 Historical parks. Where only three Wilderness parks existed in 1978, a full-blown wilderness system had been created, representative of the site regions of northern Ontario. The network of provincial Nature Reserves had grown, from a mere 13 in 1978 to 83 in 1988, and was complemented by a parallel system of Areas of Natural and Scientific Interest. Targets in earth and life science and historical protection, as set out in the "Blue Book," had still not been completely attained, but what had been accomplished was nothing short of exceptional. In May 1989, Parks and Recreational Areas Branch Director Norm Richards estimated that approximately 80 to

85 percent of planning targets for the parks system had been met.[122] Richards could take great satisfaction in the growth of the provincial parks program under his direction. As head of the branch since 1981, the longest tenure of any director, he had provided firm leadership behind the scenes through the entire SLUP process and the battle over nonconforming uses.

At various times throughout the 1980s, all of the main groups in the parks story – the bureaucracy, the advocacy groups, and the politicians – had an opportunity to take centre stage and play indispensable roles in the course of events. From 1981 to 1983, park and environmental groups responded brilliantly to the challenge posed by the SLUP process and mustered the public support required to convince Natural Resources Minister Alan Pope and the Davis cabinet to agree to the creation of 155 new parks. Pope's performance during these years was particularly noteworthy, especially his determination to bring SLUP to a rapid conclusion, to master the issues in the district land-use plans, and to give a fair hearing to all sides. His compromise on permitted "nonconforming uses" in the new parks may have been ill-advised, but his decision in June 1983 to double the size of the parks system stands out as the single most important event in the history of the parks program. Following Pope's exit from the limelight, the advocacy groups assiduously opposed the introduction of his compromise on "nonconforming uses" until 1988, when they succeeded in persuading the Peterson government to adopt a "Liberal approach" to parks policy. To his credit, Minister of Natural Resources Vincent Kerrio revised his own thinking and made the far-sighted decision to resurrect the "Blue Book" and rid the new parks of the most offensive of the "nonconforming uses."

During the 1980s, as the advocacy groups and the politicians struggled with the problems of strategic planning and nonconforming uses, and legitimately claimed most of the credit that came with the resolution of these issues, the park bureaucracy remained largely on the sidelines. Once the cabinet-approved parks policy of 1978 and the "Blue Book" were in place, and the regional parks system plans completed in 1981, the fate of the parks system was out of their hands. Few people realized, however, that these oft-maligned public servants were, in fact, the unsung heroes of the piece. Without the policy and planning documents that they produced between 1978 and 1981, the outcome of the SLUP process and the question of nonconforming uses would have been very different. Those documents provided a powerful, indeed irresistible, rationale for expansion, arguments which inspired the advocacy groups to extraordinary action and ultimately convinced the politicians that they should double the size of the provincial parks system and manage them according to "the gospel relating to parks."

Conclusion
A Century of Continuity and Change

Over the course of a century, Ontario's provincial parks system has undergone dramatic changes in terms of its size, form, and policy. This is especially true of the period from 1954 to 1989, when the original group of eight unclassified parks grew into a fully matured system of 261 parks, organized and managed according to a sophisticated framework of classification, zoning, and policy. The scope of this transformation notwithstanding, strands of continuous evolution span the decades from the establishment of the first parks to the present day. For instance, the basic rationale for creating provincial parks has not changed fundamentally. Current policy identifies protection, recreation, appreciation of the province's heritage, and tourism as the objectives of the system. To all intents and purposes, these are the same reasons evoked in the 1880s by those who sought to set aside Niagara Falls for public use, by Alexander Kirkwood in his pamphlet of 1886, calling for the establishment of "Algonkin Forest and Park," and by the Kent County–Chatham petitioners who requested that the Rondeau peninsula be reserved for park purposes in 1894.

Similarly, the cast of players in the story remains essentially the same today as in the late nineteenth century. The successors of the original "wise-use" conservationists, naturalists, recreationists, and commercial and industrial interests, who figured in the establishment and management of the first parks, still vie with one another to shape policy decisions to their liking. And throughout, government officials and politicians have endeavoured to serve as honest brokers in fashioning policies to accommodate all of the actors in the cast.

Continuity and change have been integrally connected through each phase in the development of the system. The elements of continuous evolution did not remain unaffected by the socioeconomic transformations spawned by an increasingly urban, industrial, and cosmopolitan province. As Ontario matured, so, too, did popular attitudes toward recreational values, the protection of natural areas, and the environment. When attitudes changed, other shifts occurred in the balance of political influence among the various groups of park users, which made it necessary for government officials to adjust policy accordingly.

Initially, the balance of influence in policy making was weighted heavily in favour of those who subscribed to utilitarian or "wise-use" conservationist ideas. This was to be expected; after all, the majority of those groups and interests responsible for the establishment of the first parks at Niagara, Algonquin, Rondeau, and Quetico understood conservation to mean efficient commodity management. Conservationists of this variety had no qualms about exploiting the forests, waterways, fish and wildlife, and recreational resources within Ontario's parks for "use and profit."

During the 1930s, however, the primacy of utilitarianism came under critical scrutiny by such groups as the Quetico-Superior Council and the Federation of Ontario Naturalists. Interestingly, the QSC did not reject traditional conservationism; rather, it insisted that recreational and aesthetic considerations be given priority over commercial and industrial activities in the Quetico. The FON, on the other hand, embraced the preservationist concept of conservation based on the emerging science of ecology. Among other things, the naturalists urged the government to give the protection of natural areas more emphasis, in part by establishing a system of nature sanctuaries or reserves for scientific, educational, and low-intensity recreational purposes. Frank MacDougall, first as superintendent of Algonquin Park (1931–41), and later as deputy minister of lands and forests, incorporated the proposals of both groups in his policy of multiple use, a policy which gave aesthetic and protectionist values a more prominent place vis-à-vis timber extraction in the management of Algonquin and Quetico parks.

After World War II, the balance in parks policy was upset again as rapid population growth, urbanization, a rising standard of living, increased leisure time, more personal mobility, American tourism, and a younger, more educated population, all combined to produce an explosion in outdoor recreation. In response to the great rush to get outdoors and to the massive demand for beaches, campgrounds, picnic sites, and access to natural areas, the recreation objective necessarily received most attention. In 1954, the Frost government responded by creating the Division of Parks within the DLF, and launched an unprecedented effort to develop, as rapidly as possible, a network of provincial parks, both around the shorelines of the southern Great Lakes and at regular intervals along the northern highways.

Even before the end of the 1950s, the primacy of recreation in policies of parks acquisition and management evoked a reaction from those who believed that the protection of natural areas was being given short shrift, in favour of recreational activities and resource extraction. In 1958, for instance, the FON issued its landmark publication, "Outline of a Basis for a Parks Policy in

Ontario," which called on the government to minimize the environmental impact of recreation through a zoning system for parks, by prohibiting sport hunting and commercial activities, and by discouraging the use of all forms of mechanical power. The federation also repeated its appeal for a system of Nature Reserves. The Quetico Foundation and the Conservation Council of Ontario also joined the debate by urging a massive expansion of the parks system, so that the objectives of recreation and protection could be more effectively balanced. As part of its response to these demands, the Frost government passed the Wilderness Areas Act (1959) to preserve areas of natural and historical significance. Although the new legislation made a breakthrough by recognizing the concept of Nature Reserves, and by providing a mechanism for protecting cultural resources on Crown land, it did not alter the status quo in the struggle between recreation, protection, and commercialism. The preservationist potential of the act was undermined by the clause that permitted "development and utilization" in any Wilderness Area over 640 acres (259 hectares).

Throughout the 1960s, the tension in park policy between the emphases on recreation, protection, and utilitarianism continued to grow. Government officials found themselves bedevilled by a host of problems: overcrowding, rowdyism, a deteriorating environment, and conflicts between canoeists and motorboat users, hunters and naturalists. Finally, toward the end of the decade, a major confrontation broke out between wilderness preservationists and loggers in Algonquin, Quetico, Killarney, and Lake Superior parks, a debate fuelled by the spread of the environmental movement. New-style pressure groups – the National and Provincial Parks Association of Canada, and the Algonquin Wildlands League – made the wilderness issue a test of the province's commitment to environmentalism. For the first time, these groups mobilized widespread public support on behalf of the protection of natural areas as the basis of parks policy. Ontarians who had experienced and enjoyed their parks and natural environments during the postwar explosion in outdoor recreation were ready converts to the environmentalists' message. People now valued parks and natural areas as a necessary component of their rising standard of living and a factor contributing to the quality of their lives. Part of this new way of thinking involved the changing public conception of Crown forests. Unlike traditional conservationists and most professional foresters, who viewed timbered lands as a tree farm, to be managed scientifically and in perpetuity, the environmentalists saw forests as an amenity to be enjoyed, as something that enhanced the quality of life.

Civil servants and politicians were, in their turn, sucked into the whirlpool of controversy at the centre of the parks issue. In 1967, however, in the light of the findings and recommendations of the American Outdoor Recreation Resources Review Commission (1958–62) and the annual Federal-Provincial Parks Conferences, Ontario amended its parks policy and adopted a system of classification and zoning. Conceptually, the policy of 1967 represented a giant step forward, a recognition of the fact that no one park could be all things to all people. Different classes of parks, each managed to achieve specific objectives, offered the best hope of resolving the imbalance between recreation and preservation, of controlling commercial interests, and of facilitating the rational planning of a balanced system. Three classes of parks in particular – Primitive (later Wilderness), Nature Reserve, and Wild River (later Waterway) – gave hope to environmentalists that the balance of parks policy was tilting toward preservation.

Implementing the 1967 policy on classification and zoning proved to be difficult. Northern resource industries and their supporters within government rejected proposals to create new Primitive, Nature Reserve, and Wild River parks, because they threatened to restrict timber and mineral extraction. The forest industry also resisted attempts to reclassify Algonquin, Quetico, Killarney, and Lake Superior as Primitive parks. The upshot was a remarkable crusade for wilderness in Ontario, lasting from 1968 to 1974, which resulted in the removal of commercial logging from all parks except Algonquin and Lake Superior, the reclassification of Quetico and Killarney as Primitive parks, and the establishment of both the first Nature Reserve and Wild River parks and the first large national park in Ontario at Pukaskwa. During these years, the preservationist pressure groups proved themselves indispensable to the cause, first by transmitting information and demands to and from the policy makers, then by galvanizing the necessary public support for programs of protection for natural areas. Thanks to their efforts, by 1974 the objectives of protection and heritage appreciation within the parks policy equation were being taken much more seriously by planners and politicians alike. Political scientist Paul Pross had such organizations in mind when he argued, in *Group Politics and Public Policy* (Toronto: Oxford University Press, 1986), that "the recent proliferation of pressure groups has enhanced Canadian democracy, not undermined it."

The problems and challenges of the 1960s and early 1970s greatly accelerated the trend toward increased professionalism in the Parks Division. Indeed, by 1973 the division possessed one of the best planning teams in North America and was poised to launch a planning effort of world-class quality. Within five years, the planners had obtained cabinet approval for a new parks policy and had developed the so-called "Blue Book," a policy manual that provided a rationale for each class of park, detailed how many of each type of park Ontario required, where and why, and specified the permitted and nonconforming activities for each class and zone. In these documents, the objectives of protection and heritage appreciation were given considerably more emphasis than in previous policy statements, particularly in the projected systems of Historical, Nature Reserve, Waterway, and Wilderness parks. Environmentalist groups lauded the "Blue Book" and referred to it as "the gospel relating to parks." In the years ahead, it would provide them with a much-needed unity of purpose and a common vision of the ideal parks system.

The 1980s will be remembered as the decade when Ontario doubled the size of its parks network and implemented much of what the system planners had mapped out earlier. It was also another decade of conflict, since the needs of the parks program had to be reconciled with the requirements of all other users of Crown land during the historic Strategic Land Use Planning exercise. Within this context, the parks question grew highly politicized, and the issue of the Candidate Wilderness Parks dominated the SLUP debate from 1980 to 1983. At the conclusion of the strategic planning process in 1983, Minister of Natural Resources Alan Pope announced that he would set aside the land base required to complete an outstanding parks system. Some 150 new parks would be created, and five Wilderness parks established immediately.

Unfortunately, in an effort to placate the alliance made up of the forest and mining industries, sport hunters, motorboat users, and trappers, Pope abandoned many of the protectionist elements of the "Blue Book" as it applied to the new parks. In a controversial trade-off, he allowed a host of so-called "nonconforming uses" – mineral exploration, commercial tourism, trapping, and sport hunting – into the post-1983 parks. His compromise tilted the policy balance back toward the traditional pattern of recreation and utilitarian uses.

Within a few years, however, the political climate in Ontario changed again, this time in favour of the environmentalists. With the collapse of the Tory dynasty in 1985 and the advent of the minority Liberal administration of David Peterson, the park advocacy groups launched another round of lobbying to restore the protectionist essence of the "Blue Book" in the parks created after 1983. In 1988, the Peterson government, now enjoying a majority, acceded to their compelling arguments and reversed Alan Pope's compromise on nonconforming uses. Sport hunters and resource industry spokespersons, who saw the gains made in 1983 swept away, complained bitterly about the "total protectionism" that now ruled the day in provincial parks policy.

The argument nonetheless flew in the face of the facts. The strategies of commercial tourism and marketing, the sport hunting that was permitted in some sixty parks, the hunt camps and trapping being carried on by aboriginal peoples, the logging in Algonquin and Lake Superior parks – all of these activities indicated that recreation and traditional "wise use" attitudes toward conservation still exercised a powerful influence in the now-mature parks system. The critics had misrepresented the meaning of the 1988 policy. It did not establish the dominance of preservation; rather, it simply placed protection and the appreciation of heritage on a more equal footing with recreation, tourism, and "use and profit" considerations.

In the aftermath of the historic events of the 1980s, asking what the future is for Ontario's provincial parks begs the question. If history teaches us anything, it is that the policy balance achieved in 1988 must be viewed as a temporary state of affairs. Indeed, as early as 1991 the policy was already being reworked in the light of changing economic, social, and political considerations. The savage recession of 1991-92, and worsening provincial deficits, gave rise to new budget constraints and more program cutbacks. Most significantly, the election in September 1990 of Ontario's first New Democratic Party government, under Premier Bob Rae, introduced a political catalyst for change that quickly modified a number of aspects of provincial park policy.

The NDP came to power determined to advance the cause of aboriginal rights and self-government, and committed to the principle that negotiation, rather than litigation, was the most appropriate way to settle the long-standing land claims of the aboriginal peoples. In keeping with these views, the government made a dramatic policy decision for Algonquin Provincial Park in January 1991. Minister of Natural Resources C.J. (Bud) Wildman issued an order, allowing members of the Golden Lake First Nation to hunt and fish, and to travel by motorized vehicle in the park, pending the settlement of the band's land claim to much of the Ottawa Valley, an expanse of territory that includes Algonquin Park.[1] For over a year, members of the Golden Lake First Nation had hunted openly in the park, testing what they believed to be their constitutional right to hunt for food in an area they claimed as their traditional lands. For Wildman, the issue was clear: "Were we going to settle this in court or were we going to negotiate a settlement that would be agreeable to both sides?"[2] The minister argued that had the question of aboriginal hunting and fishing rights in the area covered by the claim been settled in the courts, one possible outcome might have been unrestricted access to the park by the aboriginal peoples. In order to protect the park's wildlife, therefore, the province entered into a one-year renewable agreement with the Golden Lake band in October 1991. The agreement set harvest limits for deer and moose, delineated seasons and areas for hunting, and placed restrictions on off-road vehicle use in Algonquin Park. These actions were consistent with the historic Sparrow decision, reached by the Supreme Court of Canada in May 1990. The court had ruled that section 35 of the Constitution Act guaranteed aboriginal rights to hunt and fish in traditional territories, but added that, within limits, conservation could impinge on these rights.

The arrangements with the Golden Lake First Nation caused considerable controversy. Many park users, outfitters and lodge operators, environmentalists, and fish and game organizations expressed their opposition. While most of these interests acknowledged the need for a just settlement of the Golden Lake land claim, they took exception to the government's efforts to resolve the problem. The most persistent criticism came from the newly formed Ad Hoc Committee to Save Algonquin Park, whose members feared that the government might turn over the "administration and control of Algonquin Park" to the band. The Ad Hoc Committee undertook research to challenge the validity of the Golden Lake land claim, organized demonstrations and news conferences, and issued regular information bulletins.[3]

Meanwhile, in northwestern Ontario, the Lac la Croix First Nation began to press for redress of their historic grievances arising from the cancellation in 1915 of Reserve 24C, once located within Quetico Park, and from the effective extinguishment of their treaty rights, following upon the creation of Quetico Provincial Park. On 3 June 1991, Bud Wildman made what amounted to an historic and unprecedented act of atonement, by apologizing in the Ontario legislature for the treatment meted out to the Lac la Croix Ojibway, and promising that the government would provide immediate and long-term assistance to improve the economic and social conditions of the band.[4] Wildman also responded decisively to the band's request that the government amend the Quetico Management Plan, so as to allow mechanized boat and canoe access to additional waters in the Wilderness park, for the purpose of guiding, and to permit the operation and landing of aircraft on additional lakes. He announced an interim policy, granting the band members use of three additional lakes for a one-year period, while the Provincial Parks Council undertook a full public review of the proposal. Wildman made it clear that he was sympathetic to the Lac la Croix First Nation's position. The proposed amendment to the Quetico Management Plan, he explained, "is not to diminish Quetico's wilderness policy, but rather to move it forward in a fashion that recognizes the relationship between the Lac la Croix First Nation and the Quetico landscape."[5] Predictably, these actions on behalf of aboriginal peoples created controversy. Wilderness and environmental groups protested the opening of Quetico to motorboats and float planes, preferring instead other arrangements that would provide a sound economic base for the Lac la Croix people.[6]

The impact of these and other aboriginal land claims on the provincial parks system is difficult to predict.[7] One thing seems certain. Park administrators in the years ahead will be called upon to harmonize aboriginal rights with provincial parks policy. Almost certainly, this will require park officials to devise ways and means of involving aboriginal peoples more directly in the planning, management, and operation of some parks.

No one can predict what the challenges of the 1990s hold for Ontario's system of provincial parks. Some environmentalists fear that the protectionist objective will be weakened in the face of matters such as the aboriginal rights issue, the recession, deficits, program retrenchment, and new revenue-generating schemes for commercial tourism. More optimistic observers, on the other hand, hope that the strengthening public interest in environmentalism will result in more weight being placed on the protectionist objective. The Rae government, they note, is committed to environmental reform; indeed, the premier himself, when leader of the opposition, was arrested for his support of the Temagami Wilderness Society's blockade of the Red Squirrel Road Extension.

It is noteworthy that environmentalist groups have taken initiatives to ensure that the protectionist impulse prevails. On 6 September 1989, the World Wildlife Fund Canada and the Canadian Parks and Wilderness Society initiated a national campaign, entitled "Endangered Spaces," an initiative that included the publication of a book of the same title and the issuing of the Canadian Wilderness Charter. The objective of the campaign is to promote the preservation of Canada's natural diversity and to encourage all federal and provincial park agencies to complete their park systems by the year 2000. Among other things, the environmentalists called for the protection of 12 percent of Canada's lands and waters within a system of parks and protected areas by the end of this century. In December 1989, the federal minister of the environment, Lucien Bouchard, accepted the challenge issued by the WWF and the CPAWS, and agreed to complete the national park system by the proposed deadline.

In *Endangered Spaces: The Future for Canada's Wilderness* (Toronto: Key Porter, 1989), environmentalist Arlin Hackman acknowledged that Ontario stood out as a leader in establishing and managing Wilderness parks and protected areas. However, he also noted that the system remained unfinished. He therefore called upon Ontario to complete the implementation of its plan for the provincial park system by taking the following steps:

- Identifying new areas to meet unrepresented "Blue Book" targets
- Establishing buffers around both small Wilderness parks and Natural Environment parks in site regions where wilderness targets cannot be met
- Reviewing provincial park needs in northwestern Ontario by considering special management options for the Aulneau peninsula
- Strengthening the ANSI policy, program, and funding
- Completing the Carolinian Canada program and adopting it as a template for other regional and thematic studies such as wetlands on the Great Lakes
- Strengthening the Provincial Parks Act
- Introducing an Ecological Reserves Act.

The Rae government has responded positively to the challenge posed by the "Endangered Spaces" campaign. In cooperation with the WWF and the CPAWS, the Provincial Parks and Natural Heritage Policy Branch (renamed in 1990) began to fashion an overarching strategic plan for provincial parks and other protected areas, including ANSIs, conservation-area lands, ecological reserves, Natural Heritage League activities, and other related protection programs. Then, in January 1992, Minister of Natural Resources Bud Wildman officially endorsed the "Endangered Spaces" program and announced that the government was "committed to the protection of a representative sample of Ontario's natural history and diversity, including the full range of geological features, ecosystems and species," by the year 2000. "I am confident," he declared, "that this can be accomplished by adding another one to two per cent of Ontario's lands and waters to the parks and protected areas system."[8] To meet this commitment, Wildman explained, new Wilderness, Natural

Environment, Waterway, and Nature Reserve parks, as well as other protected natural areas, would have to be identified and established. In the short run, new parks and protected areas would be created in at least five site districts during 1993, the centennial year of the parks system. Unlike the park creation process of a century earlier, however, Ontario's First Nations would play a prominent role; this time, their treaty and aboriginal rights would be respected fully. "No decision respecting the acceptability of candidate sites will be made without full involvement and participation by aboriginal peoples," declared the minister, "and in consultation with the general public, including special interest groups."

These noteworthy developments on the parks front were clear indications of a fresh philosophical approach to resource management within the Ministry of Natural Resources. In a new corporate strategy document entitled "MNR: Direction '90s," – the government declared that "views about how we should use, or not use, our resources are changing," and that "changes and new directions are vital" in resource management. In keeping with conservation agencies across North America and elsewhere, the "Direction '90s" document embraced the concept of sustainable development as advanced by the Brundtland Commission (World Commission on Environment and Development).

In May 1991, the Rae government began to realize the promise of "Direction '90s" by unveiling a Sustainable Forestry program, described by Deputy Minister George Tough as "an important step toward a more integrated and holistic approach" to forest management.[9] The objective of the program, he explained, was "to lay the groundwork for managing Ontario's forest resources for current and future benefits without compromising the integrity of forest ecosystems." The program was made up of six initiatives including the development of a comprehensive forest policy, an enhanced program of silviculture, an old-growth conservation strategy, a strategy for private woodlands, and a forest audit. A year later, in May 1992, the province took another step toward protecting natural heritage areas by approving a major policy statement on wetlands, a statement which drew the applause of the Federation of Ontario Naturalists and the Canadian Environmental Law Association.[10]

Within the Ministry of Natural Resources' corporate strategy, then, provincial parks should serve as a protectionist cornerstone of the sustainable development edifice. In the light of this possibility, then, as well as that of recent policy statements on "endangered spaces," sustainable forestry, and wetlands, Ontarians have reason to be optimistic as they celebrate the centennial of their system of provincial parks and natural heritage areas.

Abbreviations

AFA	Algonquin Forest Authority
ANSI	Areas of Natural and Scientific Interest
APATAF	Algonquin Park Task Force
APEEL	Association for the Preservation of East Erie Lakefront
APM	Algonquin Park Museum
ARDA	Agricultural and Rural Development Act
AWL	Algonquin Wildlands League
BWCA	Boundary Waters Canoe Area
CBC	Canadian Broadcasting Corporation
CCO	Conservation Council of Ontario
CNR	Canadian National Railway
COGP	Committee on Government Productivity
COLUC	Central Ontario Lakeshore Urbanization Complex
CORDS	Canada Outdoor Recreation Demand Study
CORTS	Canada-Ontario Rideau-Trent-Severn Committee
CPAWS	Canadian Parks and Wilderness Society
CPR	Canadian Pacific Railway
DDT	dichloro-diphenyl-trichloroethane
DHO	Department of Highways of Ontario
DLF	Department of Lands and Forests
DLFM	Department of Lands, Forests and Mines
DMA	Department of Municipal Affairs
DPW	Department of Public Works
FON	Federation of Ontario Naturalists
FPPC	Federal and Provincial Parks Conference
IBP-CT	Conservation of Terrestrial Communities Section of the International Biological Programme
IUCN	International Union for Conservation of Nature and Natural Resources
LR	Land Records Branch, Whitney Block, Queen's Park, Toronto
MCC	Ministry of Citizenship and Culture
MCR	Ministry of Culture and Recreation
MIT	Ministry of Industry and Tourism
MLA	Member of the Legislative Assembly
MNA	Ministry of Northern Affairs
MND&M	Ministry of Northern Development and Mines
MNR	Ministry of Natural Resources
NCC	Nature Conservancy of Canada
NDP	New Democratic Party
NEC	Niagara Escarpment Commission
NPPAC	National and Provincial Parks Association of Canada
NRC	National Research Council of Canada
OA	Archives of Ontario

OFAH	Ontario Federation of Anglers and Hunters
OFIA	Ontario Forest Industries Association
OFL	Ontario Federation of Labour
OHF	Ontario Heritage Foundation
OPIB	Ontario Parks Integration Board
OPP	Ontario Provincial Police
ORRRC	Outdoor Recreation Resources Review Commission
ORS	Outdoor Recreation Survey
OSP	Ontario Sessional Papers
PB	Parks and Recreational Areas Branch (renamed Provincial Parks and Natural Heritage Policy Branch in 1990)
PDQ	Prevent Destruction of Quetico
PPAC	Provincial Parks Advisory Council
PPBS	Planning Programming Budgeting System
QPP	Quetico Provincial Park
QSC	Quetico-Superior Council
RCAF	Royal Canadian Air Force
ROM	Royal Ontario Museum
RPP	Rondeau Provincial Park Archives
SLUP	Strategic Land Use Planning
TORPS	Tourism and Outdoor Recreation Planning Study
WWF	World Wildlife Fund

A Note on Primary Sources

The major collection of documentary material pertaining to Ontario's provincial parks is to be found in the Archives of Ontario (OA), Record Group 1 (RG-1). Other essential sources at the Ontario Archives include the Niagara Parks Commission records, the Alexander Kirkwood papers, the Frank A. MacDougall papers, the E.C. Drury papers, and the G.H. Ferguson papers. Another extensive collection of park-specific documentary material dating back to 1893 is housed in the files of the Land Records Branch (LR), Whitney Block, Queen's Park. The current files of the Provincial Parks and Natural Heritage Policy Branch (PB), located in the MNR office in Peterborough since 1992, contain considerable historical material. Use has also been made of the archival collections in Algonquin, Quetico, Rondeau, and Lake Superior provincial parks, as well as in the Chatham District Office of the MNR (Daryl Smith files). The records of the Quetico-Superior Council (QSC), deposited with the Minnesota Historical Society at St. Paul, Minnesota, were invaluable to sort out the battles for wilderness over "the Quetico." For the many other primary sources used in the preparation of this book, the reader is invited to peruse the rich store of footnotes provided to assist the work of future researchers.

Notes

Chapter One

1 The standard studies on the Canadian conservation movement are George Altmeyer, "Three Ideas of Nature in Canada, 1893–1914," *Journal of Canadian Studies* 11, no. 3 (August 1976), 21–36; Robert Craig Brown, "The Doctrine of Usefulness: Natural Resources and National Park Policy in Canada, 1887–1914," in J.G. Nelson (ed.), *Canadian Parks in Perspective* (Montreal: Harvest House, 1970), 46–62; Janet Foster, *Working for Wildlife: The Beginning of Preservation in Canada* (Toronto and Buffalo: University of Toronto Press, 1978); R. Peter Gillis, "The Ottawa Lumber Barons and the Conservation Movement, 1880–1914," *Journal of Canadian Studies* 9, no. 1 (February 1974), 14–30, and "Rivers of Sawdust: The Battle Over Industrial Pollution in Canada, 1865–1903," ibid., 21, no. 1 (Spring 1986), 84–103; R.P. Gillis, B. Hodgins, and J. Benidickson, "The Ontario and Quebec Experiments in Forest Reserves, 1883–1930," *Journal of Forest History* 26, no. 1 (January 1982), 20–33; R. Peter Gillis and Thomas R. Roach, *Lost Initiatives: Canada's Forest Industries, Forest Policy and Forest Conservation*. Contributions in Economics and Economic History, no. 69 (New York: Greenwood Press, 1986); Bruce W. Hodgins and Jamie Benidickson, *The Temagami Experience: Recreation, Resources, and Aboriginal Rights in the Northern Ontario Wilderness* (Toronto and Buffalo: University of Toronto Press, 1989); Richard S. Lambert, with Paul Pross, *Renewing Nature's Wealth: A Centennial History of the Public Management of Lands, Forests and Wildlife in Ontario, 1763–1967* (Toronto: Ontario Department of Lands and Forests, 1967); H.V. Nelles, *The Politics of Development: Forests, Mines and Hydro-Electric Power in Ontario, 1849–1941* (Toronto: Macmillan, 1974).

2 For a more detailed analysis of and full documentation for the Niagara Parks story see Gerald Killan, "Mowat and a Park Policy for Niagara Falls 1873–1887," *Ontario History* 70, no. 2 (June 1978), 115–35. Reprinted in Geoffrey Wall and John S. Marsh (eds.), *Recreational Land Use: Perspectives on its Evolution in Canada*. Carleton Library Series no. 126 (Ottawa: Carleton University Press, 1982), 220–38. The most recent history of the Niagara Parks is George A. Seibel, *Ontario's Niagara Parks 100 Years: A History* (Niagara Falls: The Niagara Parks Commission, 1985).

3 Alfred Runte, "Beyond the Spectacular: The Niagara Falls Preservation Campaign," *New York Historical Society Quarterly* 57 (January 1973), 48.

4 Ontario Sessional Papers (OSP), no. 3, 1883, *Report of Delegation Appointed to Attend the American Forestry Congress Held in Montreal, Province of Quebec*, 110. Quotation by H.G. Joly. Refer to Gillis and Roach, *Lost Initiatives*, ch. 2 (see note 1 above) for the Montreal congress and its aftermath.

5 See Archives of Ontario (OA), RG–8, I–7–F–2, Petitions 1884–90, for the considerable lobbying undertaken by the sportsmen and trappers.

6 Royal Ontario Museum (ROM) Archives, Natural History Society of Toronto, Minute Book, 7 December 1885, 19 April 1886. See also *Transactions of the Canadian Institute* 4, ser. 3 (1887), 147.

7 OSP, no. 79, 1892, *Report of the Commissioners Appointed to Collect Information upon the Game and Fish of the Province of Ontario*, 189, 241.

8 Ibid., 198.

9 A.P. Pross, "The Development of a Forest Policy: A Study of the Ontario Department of Lands and Forests" (Ph.D. diss., University of Toronto, 1967), 60–63. Pross was the first historian to see that the idea of setting aside Algonquin Park as a wildlife sanctuary played a much more important role in the park's establishment than had been previously recognized.

10 OSP, no. 3, 1893, *Report of Committee Appointed to Attend the American Forestry Congress at Cincinnati, Ohio*, 21.

11 OSP, no. 4, 1885, *Forestry Report 1884*, 106–7, 116–19; ibid., no. 5, 1888, *Forestry Report 1886*, 68.

12 Alexander Kirkwood, *Algonkin Forest and Park, Ontario. Letter to the Honorable T.B. Pardee, M.P.P., Commissioner of Crown Lands for Ontario* (Toronto, 1886).

13 Altmeyer, "Three Ideas," 22, 31–34 (see note 1 above).

14 James Dickson, *Camping in the Muskoka Region* (Toronto, 1886), 26, 164.

15 OSP, no. 5, 1888, *Forestry Report 1886*, 70–71.

16 OSP, no. 7, 1888, *Report of the Canadian Institute 1886–87*, 1.

17 Gillis, "Ottawa Lumber Barons," 21 (see note 1 above).

18 The original report is no longer extant. Quotations from Audrey Saunders, *Algonquin Story*, reprinted with revised maps (Toronto: Ontario Department of Lands and Forests, 1963), 80–82.

19 *Annual Report of the Canadian Institute, Session 1888–89. Being Part of Appendix to the Report of the Minister of Education, Ontario, 1889* (Toronto, 1889), ix.

20 Toronto *Daily Mail*, 14 March 1888.

21 OA, Alexander Kirkwood papers, MU 1685, handwritten draft of "An Act respecting the Algonkin Forest and Park."

22 Newspaper Hansard, 4 May 1891.
23 *Transactions of the Canadian Institute* 3 (1891–92), 60.
24 Pross, "Forest Policy," 140 (see note 1 above).
25 Saunders, *Algonquin Story*, 83 (see note 18 above); Lambert and Pross, *Nature's Wealth*, 169–72 (see note 1 above).
26 Newspaper Hansard, Toronto *Globe*, 5 March 1892.
27 OSP, no. 62, 1893, *Recommendations of the Assistant Commissioner of Crown Lands*. Aubrey White, 21 June 1892, 3–5.
28 OSP, no. 31, 1893, *Report of the Royal Commission on Forest Reservation and National Park*, 9, 12–13, 23–26.
29 Quoted in Saunders, *Algonquin Story*, 98 (see note 18 above).
30 Lise C. Hansen, "Research Report: The Algonquins of Golden Lake Indian Band Land Claim," Ministry of Natural Resources (MNR), Office of Indian Resource Policy, 13 January 1986, 4.
31 Newspaper Hansard, 9 May 1893; James Dickson, "Ontario's Big Game," *Canadian Magazine* 4, no. 1 (November 1894), 11.
32 Kent County Council Minutes, 26 January 1894, Petitions, p. 439, "Petition to the Honourable Sir Oliver Mowat, Premier of Ontario, and the Members of the Executive Council to the Province of Ontario, 26 January 1894." I wish to thank Daryl C. Smith, Chatham District Office, MNR, for bringing this source to my attention. The same petition was sent to Prime Minister John Thompson. See also OA, RG–8, I–7–F–2, Petitions 1894, no. 23: "Petition of the Town Council of Chatham, Praying that Pointe Aux Pins may be set apart as a Public Park, 8 February 1894."
33 Chatham District Office, MNR, Daryl Smith historical files, copy of "Petition of the Warden and Council of the Corporation of the County of Kent to Lieutenant General in Council, 26 January 1867."
34 In *Historic "ROND EAU": A History of Rondeau Provincial Park* (Ontario MNR, n.d.), Prince and his friends are blamed for the destruction of wildlife at Pointe aux Pins. Considering that Prince was an ardent proponent of more stringent game laws and relinquished his lease in 1853, not 1863, as noted in *Historic "ROND EAU,"* it seems unlikely that he was responsible for the depletion.
35 OA, OSP, no. 21, 1885 (not printed). *Return ordered ... on the 29th of February 1884 shewing the name of the Care–taker ... in charge of the Crown Lands and Timber at Rondeau Point, the Salary ... paid to such officer, the Amount collected for Timber ... up to 31st of December 1883*. Confusion exists as to which level of government controlled Rondeau Point. Victor Lauriston, *Romantic Kent: More Than Three Centuries of History 1626–1952* (Chatham: Shepherd Printing Co., 1952), 260, argued that "in 1884 Pointe Aux Pins was more or less definitely designated a park, under joint federal and provincial control." In *Historic "ROND EAU,"* Lauriston's statement has been expanded into the idea that a dominion-provincial commission managed the park from 1884 to 1894: there is no evidence to support this assertion. The caretaker appointed by the province supervised the Crown lands after 1876, but had no authority over the 200-hectare block of federal ordnance land set aside in 1795.
36 Roy I. Wolfe, "The Summer Resorts of Ontario in the Nineteenth Century," *Ontario History* 54, no. 3 (September 1962), 149–61.
37 For the Weldon lease see OSP, no. 87, 1884.
38 Chatham *Daily Planet*, 27–28 March 1894.
39 Kent County Council petition, 26 January 1894; Chatham Town Council petition, 8 February 1894.
40 Chatham *Daily Planet*, 27 March 1894.
41 Newspaper Hansard, 23 March 1894.
42 OSP, no. 40, 1895. *Regulations Respecting Rondeau Provincial Park*.
43 Chatham *Daily Planet*, 27 March 1894.
44 Ibid., 27–28 March 1894, and Newspaper Hansard, 23 March 1894.
45 Bruce W. Hodgins and Jamie Benidickson, "Resource Management Conflict in the Temagami Forest, 1898–1914," *Historical Papers* (London, Ontario) 1978, 148–75.
46 Michael J. Piva, *The Condition of the Working Class in Toronto, 1900–1921*, Cahiers d'histoire no. 9 (Ottawa: University of Ottawa Press, 1979), 88–89, 171.
47 *Hamilton Spectator*, 27 June 1883; see also *Hamilton Beach in Retrospect. Report of the Hamilton Beach Alternate, Community and History Project* (Summer 1981), 16. For much of the research pertaining to Burlington Beach, I am indebted to Michele Root, a former student in my Ontario History seminar at King's College, the University of Western Ontario.
48 *Hamilton Weekly Times*, 24 August 1893; in Hamilton Public Library scrapbook, entitled "Victorian Hamilton," vol. 2, 65.
49 An Act Respecting Burlington Beach, *Statutes of Ontario*, 1907, c. 22.
50 Quoted in R. Newell Searle, *Saving Quetico-Superior: A Land Set Apart* (St. Paul: Minnesota Historical Society Press, 1977), 15.
51 Quetico-Superior Council (QSC) Records, Arthur Hawkes papers, P34, box 25, Draft manuscript of speech, n.d. (ca. 1927); Toronto *Globe*, 3–5 February 1909.
52 Hawkes papers (see note 51 above).
53 OA, RG–1, IA–7, box 12, file 27–0403–4, memorandum, Aubrey White to Frank Cochrane, 29 March 1909.
54 OSP, no. 52, 1912, *Final Report of the Ontario Game and Fisheries Commission 1909–1911*, 162, 177.

55 OSP, no. 13, 1913, *Sixth Annual Report of the Game and Fisheries Department of Ontario 1912*, 19.
56 *Statutes of Ontario*, 1913, c. 15; Newspaper Hansard, Toronto *Mail and Empire*, 26 March 1913.
57 Quoted in MNR, *Quetico Provincial Park: Lac La Croix Amendment Proposal (January 1992)*, 4.
58 "Grievance with Ontario," in *The Lac La Croix Story*, part of *Quetico Provincial Park Plan Amendment Proposal (January 1992)*, 7a–8a.
59 Land Records Branch (LR)–46338, B. Bowman to Peter Heenan, 21 April 1923.
60 Charles M. Johnston, *E.C. Drury: Agrarian Idealist*, Ontario Historical Studies Series (Toronto and Buffalo: University of Toronto Press, 1986), 20–22.
61 LR–30477, vol. 1, Joseph Cridland to B. Bowman, 19 July 1920.
62 *Port Rowan News*, 5 October 1937; see also LR–30477, vol. 1, E.C. Drury to Bowman, 12 November 1920.
63 LR–30477, vol. 1, H.H. Collier to F.E. Titus, 10 February 1921.
64 For complete documentation on Presqu'ile Park see LR–32180, vol. 1.
65 For complete documentation on Severn River Provincial Park, see LR–1416.
66 For complete documentation on Franklin Island Provincial Park, see LR–16089.
67 Peter Oliver, *G. Howard Ferguson: Ontario Tory*, Ontario Historical Studies Series (Toronto and Buffalo: University of Toronto Press, 1977), 202–23; Roy I. Wolfe, "The Changing Patterns of Tourism in Ontario," in *Profiles of a Province: Studies in the History of Ontario* (Toronto: Ontario Historical Society, 1967), 174–75.
68 OA, RG–3, box 37: E.C. Drury, General Correspondence 1923, Tourist commission file; W.G. Robertson to Drury, 22 January 1923; ibid., box 48: G.H. Ferguson, general correspondence 1923, tourist file; Robertson to Ferguson, 2 August 1923 and J.W. Regan to Ferguson, 10 December 1923; see also ibid., tourist industry file 1925, G. Philips to Ferguson, 13 February 1925.
69 *Annual Report*, Department of Lands and Forests (DLF), 1925, 1–2.
70 OA, RG–3, box 88: G.H. Ferguson papers, general correspondence 1926, DLF general file, Ferguson to C.H. Fullerton, deputy minister of northern development, 4 June 1926.
71 Ibid., box 92: G.H. Ferguson papers, general correspondence 1926, file on "Provincial Park," see also LR–62000, Allan Ferguson to Selby Draper, 7 June 1926.
72 LR–62000, Finlayson to Draper, 15 April 1932; see also Finlayson to Honourable Thomas G. Murphy, minister of the interior, 23 July 1931.
73 LR–90045, Finlayson to Honourable Charles McCrea, minister of mines, 14 July 1932.
74 D.F. Brunette, *Master Plan Background: Killarney Provincial Park*, 8 November 1974, 2.
75 For documentation on Finlayson Point, see LR–98902.
76 LR–62000, memorandum: Finlayson to cabinet, 26 May 1931.
77 Report of the Minister of Lands and Forests ... 1 November 1934 to 31 March, 1935, OSP, no. 3, 1936, 9–10; ibid., for fiscal year ending 31 March 1938, OSP, no. 3, 1939, 11; St. Thomas *Times-Journal*, 16 March 1936; LR–115420, file memo by Selby Draper, 19 November 1937; OA, RG–1, A–1–8, box 11, minister's file, Public Beaches, memo G.H. Ferguson to Kelso Roberts, 26 May 1965.
78 Report of the minister of lands and forests ... Year Ending 31 March 1938, OSP, NO. 3, 1939, 11–12; *London Free Press*, 19 September 1935.
79 Memo, Ferguson to Roberts (see note 77 above).
80 OA, MU, 1783, MacDougall papers, "Algonquin Park 1931–37," file, memo "Algonquin Park," n.d.
81 LR–110765, A.B. Conmee, president, Port Arthur Chamber of Commerce to Peter Heenan, 27 May 1936; LR–11217, vol. 1, W.A. Peach, Secretary, Port Arthur Liberal Association to Heenan, 13 June 1936.
82 LR–110765, W. Webster, secretary, Fort William Chamber of Commerce to Heenan, 13 January 1938; Petition, citizens of Port Arthur to Heenan, 24 October 1938; LR–22979, vol. 2, file memo, "Areas of Forest Reserves and Parks," 3 March 1947; W.F. Lothian, *A History of Canada's National Parks*, vol. 1 (Ottawa: Indian and Northern Affairs, Parks Canada, 1976), 76–91.
83 LR–110765, A.G. Pounsford, Provincial Paper Ltd. to Heenan, 27 August 1938.
84 See LR–110765.
85 LR–125864, N.O. Hipel to Mitchell F. Hepburn, 4 January 1943; "Summary of Comments of Ministers of Departments on Proposed ... Lake Superior Park," n.d.
86 Lake Superior Provincial Park Office, "Report on Lake Superior Provincial Park: DLF Investigative Survey, 1946" by H.N. Middleton; LR–125864, C.H.D. Clarke to W.J.K. Harkness, 27 January 1948.
87 See LR–168710 for White River Provincial Park and LR–169472 for Rainbow Falls.
88 LR–112317, W.C. Cain to R. Pifer, chairman, Fort William District Parks Committee, 14 April 1937; LR–126784, file memo by H.W. Crosbie, ca. December 1943.

Chapter Two

1 Algonquin Park Museum (APM), historical file, copy of T.W. Gibson, "The Algonquin National Park of Ontario," Bureau of Forestry, *Report* 1896, 123.

2 OSP, no. 22, 1894, "Mr. James Wilson's Report on Algonquin National Park for 1893," 16.
3 OSP, no. 72, 1914, memorandum by Aubrey White, 10 March 1914; see also Newspaper Hansard, 23 March 1900.
4 OSP, no. 22, 1894, Superintendent's Report, 7–8.
5 OSP, no. 5, 1896, Superintendent's Report, 65–66.
6 APM, historical file, copy of letter, Governor General Minto to Prime Minister Wilfrid Laurier, 1 May 1900; see also OSP, no. 30, 1905. *Report of Game and Fish Commission*, 10; OSP, no. 32, 1906, 6; and Toronto *Globe*, 20 March 1907.
7 OA, RG–1, IA–8, box 1: Bartlett Correspondence Book, Bartlett to T.W. Gibson, 5, 9, 23 May 1910.
8 Newspaper Hansard, Toronto *Mail and Empire*, 25 February 1911.
9 APM, historical file, copy of Aubrey White, "The Algonquin Park to be Preserved," 1 November 1910.
10 OSP, no. 72, 1914, memo by Aubrey White, 10 March 1914.
11 OSP, no. 3, 1916–17, Superintendent's Report, 93–94.
12 *A History of Pembroke Forest District* (DLF, 1967), 27.
13 OSP, no. 3, 1919–20, Superintendent's Report, 101.
14 LR–30351, Cain to Lyons, 16 June 1924; Cain to J.H. McDonald, 28 November 1924; and passim.
15 Peter Oliver, *G. Howard Ferguson: Ontario Tory*. Ontario Historical Studies Series (Toronto and Buffalo: University of Toronto Press, 1977), 214.
16 LR–67608, passim.
17 Ibid., excerpt of minutes of meetings between licenceholders and Premier Ferguson, and Lands and Forests Minister William Finlayson, 21–22 February 1927.
18 Toronto *Mail and Empire*, 24 March 1927; and LR–67608, J.S. Gillies to Finlayson, 31 March 1927.
19 OSP, no. 5, 1895, Superintendent's Report, 64; OSP, no. 3, 1905, Superintendent's Report, 126.
20 Chatham District Office, MNR, Daryl Smith historical file: "Survey of Forest Conditions and Administration of Rondeau Provincial Park, Kent County, Ontario. Reported on by R.S. Carman, April 1928," pt. 2, 41–42.
21 H.V. Nelles, *The Politics of Development: Forests, Mines and Hydro–Electric Power in Ontario, 1849–1941* (Toronto: Macmillan, 1974), 386.
22 LR–27213, A. Grigg to G.H. Ferguson, 20 August 1919; Grigg to Shevlin-Clarke Co., 20 August 1919; OA, RG–18, B-63. Timber Commission Proceedings 1920–22, vol. 6, 30 September 1920, 6127, 6146; Supreme Court of Ontario: Ruling Statement by J. Logie in the Crown vs. Shevlin-Clarke Co. Ltd., n.d.; *Report of the Timber Commission Appointed ... 9 March 1920, Province of Ontario* (Toronto: 1922), 6. In *The Politics of Development* (see note 21 above), Nelles claims that Shevlin–Clarke did not conduct the brush-burning experiments. In fact, they were carried out. For further documentation, see LR–27213.
23 Quetico Provincial Park (QPP), Cain-Jamieson correspondence, Cain to Shevlin-Clarke Co., Minneapolis, 19 July 1927; P.V. Eames, vice-president, Shevlin-Clarke, to Cain, 28 July 1927.
24 LR–90131, Mathieu to W. Finlayson, 16 February 1928.
25 OSP, no. 5, 1895, Superintendent's Report, 60.
26 OSP, no. 3, 1908, Superintendent's Report, 115.
27 Rondeau Provincial Park Archives (RPP), Isaac Gardiner papers, Gardiner to T.W. Gibson, 13 June 1896; OSP, no. 5, 1896, Algonquin Park Superintendent's Report, 66.
28 Daryl Smith, "The Pavilions and Rondeau – a Long History," 20 July 1973, Chatham District Office, MNR; OSP, no. 3, 1905, Superintendent's Report, 126; OSP, no. 3, 1907, Superintendent's Report, 134.
29 OSP, no. 3, 1909–10, Superintendent's Report, 100; OSP, no. 3, 1910–11, Superintendent's Report, 100.
30 RPP, Isaac Gardiner papers, Gardiner to T.W. Gibson, 18 April 1903; *Statutes of Ontario*, 1913, c. 15.
31 OSP, no. 5, 1895, Superintendent's Report, 65; OSP, no. 3, 1907, Superintendent's Report, 135.
32 OSP, no. 5, 1896, Superintendent's Report, 281.
33 OSP, no. 3, 1909, Superintendent's Report, 85; OSP, no. 3, 1911–12. Superintendent's Report, 75.
34 Daryl Smith, "The Life and Times of Isaac Gardiner," Chatham District Office, MNR.
35 OSP, no. 52, 1912, *Final Report of Game and Fisheries Commission*, 283.
36 OSP, no. 3, 1907, Superintendent's Report, 136.
37 OSP, no. 3, 1914–15, Superintendent's Report, 65.
38 OSP, no. 3, 1908, Superintendent's Report, 117.
39 OSP, no. 34, 1909–10, Superintendent's Report, 98; OSP, no. 3, 1910–11, Superintendent's Report, 99; OSP, no. 3, 1912–13, Superintendent's Report, 93.
40 *Annual Report*, Department of Lands, Forests and Mines (DLFM) 1918, 94.
41 OSP, no. 3, 1920–21, Superintendent's Report, 117.
42 Saunders, *Algonquin Story*, 114 (see chapter 1 above, note 18); OSP, no. 3, 1920–1, Superintendent's Report, 117.
43 OSP, no. 3, 1914–15, Superintendent's Report, 66.
44 OA, RG–1, IA–8, box 1: Bartlett Correspondence Book, Bartlett to Frank Cochrane, 19 October 1910; OSP, no. 3, 1911–12, Superintendent's Report, 73.
45 OSP, no. 3, 1912–13, Superintendent's Report, 92.

46 OSP, no. 3, 1913–14, Superintendent's Report, 87.
47 OSP, no. 3, 1919–20, Superintendent's Report, 99.
48 *Annual Report*, DLFM 1913, 92; ibid., 1922, 126.
49 OSP, no. 3, 1914–15, Superintendent's Report, 68.
50 OSP, no. 4, 1921–22, Superintendent's Report, 122.
51 QPP, A.J. McDonald papers, A. Moffat, Clerk, DLF, to McDonald, 13 October 1914; McDonald to T.W. Gibson, 10 November 1914; T.W. Gibson to McDonald, 16 November 1914. As in Algonquin Park, fur-bearing animals were harvested for revenue purposes in Quetico until 1920.
52 Oliver, *Howard Ferguson*, 157, 194–95 (see note 15 above).
53 Chatham District Office, MNR: Daryl Smith historical file, Cain to Goldworthy, 24 August 1923.
54 OSP, no. 3, 1921–22, Superintendent's Report, 129–30.
55 Data from LR–87383, passim.
56 OA, RG–1, IA–7, box 5, file 17–0109: R.S. Carman to W.C. Cain, 2 August 1929; Chatham District Office, MNR: Daryl Smith historical file, H–2–1, Superintendent's Report, 9 December 1931; OSP, no. 4, 1921–22, Superintendent's Report, 127.
57 Carman, "Survey" (see note 20 above).
58 Chatham District Office, MNR: Daryl Smith historical file, Superintendent's Report, 9 December 1931 and 1931–32. DLF *Report* 1931, 16.
59 Chatham District Office, MNR: Daryl Smith historical file, unidentified press clipping, 5 September 1933; and Superintendent's Report, 1931–32.
60 LR–22979, vol. 1, memo, Rondeau Finances, 18 May 1936. Revenues increased from $7,421 in 1926–27 to $14,546 in 1931–32; see also Superintendent's Report, 1931–32.
61 OSP, no. 3, 1921–22, Superintendent's Report, 134.
62 LR–19711, vol. 1, Ferguson to J.J. Grafton, 14 September 1917; memo, Cain to B. Bowman, 10 August 1922; and passim.
63 Ibid., J. Crooks, Chairman to J.A. Ellis, secretary, Unemployment Relief Fund, 17 October 1932.
64 OA, RG–3, box 88: G.H. Ferguson, General Correspondence 1926, DLF file, Ferguson to J.S. Martin, minister of agriculture, 8 September 1926.
65 LR–32180, vol. 1, Presqu'ile Park Commission: Report on Audit, 31 December 1926; G. Drewry to W.C. Cain, 10 April 1923.
66 LR–30477, vol. 5a, J.E. Biddle, secretary, Long Point Park Commission to leaseholders, 1 October 1941; see also LR–172517, copy of Loreen Mowers, "Growing up Prejudiced in Ontario," *Chatelaine*, ca. July 1965; Chatham District Office, MNR, see Daryl Smith, "Black Ontarians and Rondeau Park."
67 Searle, *Saving Quetico-Superior*, 34–41, 47–50 (see chapter 1 above, note 50); George Michael Warecki, "The Quetico-Superior Council and the Battle for Wilderness in Quetico Provincial Park, 1909–1960," M.A. thesis, University of Western Ontario, 1983, 41–44.
68 Roderick Nash, *Wilderness and the American Mind* (1967), revised edition (New Haven and London: Yale University Press, 1973), chs. 8–9; Donald N. Baldwin, *The Quiet Revolution: Grass Roots of Today's Wilderness Preservation Movement* (Boulder, Colo.: Pruett, 1972), ch. 3; Craig W. Allin, *The Politics of Wilderness Preservation*, Contributions in Political Science, no. 64 (Westport, Conn.: Greenwood Press, 1982), ch. 2.
69 LR–116062, vol. 1, Oberholtzer to Finlayson, 2 November 1927.
70 LR–116062, vol. 1, Oberholtzer to Finlayson, 16 February 1928.
71 QSC Records, William Finlayson file, P34, box 21, Finlayson to Oberholtzer, 9 November 1927; LR–116062, vol. 1, Finlayson to W.G. Dorr, 14 November 1927; J.A. Mathieu to Finlayson, 22 February 1927; Oberholtzer to Finlayson, 16 February 1928; Finlayson to Oberholtzer, 20 February 1928.
72 QSC Records, J.W. Dafoe papers, P34, box 16, Oberholtzer to Dafoe, 28 October 1929.
73 Ibid., *Toronto Star* papers, P34, box 55, Gregory Clark to Oberholtzer, 20 April 1929.
74 *Final Report of the International Joint Commission on the Rainy Lake Reference, Washington-Ottawa 1934* (Ottawa: J.O. Patenaude, 1934), 48–49.
75 See file LR–79218, September–October 1929.
76 *Toronto Daily Star*, 20 November 1930, OA, MU, 1788, F.A. MacDougall papers, memo, MacDougall to the Honourable H.R. Scott, 27 October 1947, "Analysis Algonquin Park Problem"; OA, MU, 1794, MacDougall papers, Algonquin Park reminiscences 1971–72.
77 *Toronto Telegram*, 6 December 1954; *Aski*, Summer 1975, passim; Lambert and Pross, *Nature's Wealth*, 354–57 (see chapter 1 above, note 1).
78 OA, MU, 1783, F.A. MacDougall papers, Algonquin Park file 1931–37, Finlayson to MacDougall, 25 March 1931; ibid., Annual Report for Algonquin Provincial Park for years ended 31 October 1931 and 31 October 1933.
79 OA, MU, 1783, MacDougall papers, Annual Report for Algonquin Provincial Park for year ended 31 October 1931; APM, historical file, "Confidential Report – Reorganization of Algonquin Park (1931)." All information in the following paragraphs is derived from these documents.
80 OA, MU, 1784, MacDougall papers, file,"Planning 1932–38," "Draft Plan for Algonquin Provincial Park (Proposed)," 30 September 1934.

81 Ibid., *Sanctuaries and the Preservation of Wild Life in Ontario* (Toronto: FON Publication 2, 1934).
82 OA, MU, 1783, MacDougall papers, Annual Reports for Algonquin Provincial Park for years ended 31 October 1932 and 31 October 1933.
83 Lambert and Pross, *Nature's Wealth*, 328–29 (see chapter 1 above, note 1).
84 Toronto *Evening Telegram*, 22 September 1933; OA, MU, 1794, MacDougall papers, Algonquin Park Reminiscences, 1971–2; and Annual Report for Algonquin Provincial Park for year ended 31 October 1933.
85 OA, MU, 1783, MacDougall papers, Annual Report for Algonquin Provincial Park for year ended 31 March 1936; see also APM, historical file, Algonquin Park *News Letter* 6, no. 1, 30 January 1937; and LR–119915, Annual Report for Algonquin Park for year ended 31 March 1939.
86 OA, RG–1, IA–7, box 39, file 27–1501–17, "Speech to Toronto Anglers Association," by F.A. MacDougall (1935); OA, MU, 1783, MacDougall papers, Annual Reports for Algonquin Provincial Park for years ended 31 March 1936 and 31 March 1937; OA, MU, 1784, MacDougall papers, file, "Planning 1932–38," "Draft Plan for Algonquin Provincial Park (Proposed)," 30 September 1934.
87 OA, MU, 1783, MacDougall papers, Annual Reports for Algonquin Provincial Park for years ended 31 October 1933 and 31 March 1935.
88 MacDougall, "Toronto Anglers" (see note 86 above).
89 See LR–79218, documentation for September 1934–January 1935 for modifications to the McRae licence; see LR–119915, Annual Report for Algonquin Provincial Park for list of shoreline reserves (year ended 31 March 1939); and copy of Algonquin Park *News Letter* 8, no. 3, 20 April 1939; OA, MU, 1784, MacDougall papers, file, "Planning 1932–38," memo, MacDougall to Cain, 23 November 1938 (personal).
90 LR–30351, vol. 2, MacDougall to Cain, 7 February 1939.
91 LR–79218, press clipping, Toronto *Globe and Mail*, 3 November 1938; and A.C. Hardy to the Honourable P. Heenan, 4 January 1939; Hamilton *Spectator*, 3 October 1938.
92 Quoted in Allin, *Wilderness Preservation*, 68 (see note 68 above).
93 LR–119915, Algonquin Park *News Letter* 8, no. 3, 20 April 1939.
94 LR–30351, vol. 2, "Notice to Timber Licencees Algonquin Provincial Park," 27 June 1939.
95 LR–119915, Algonquin Park *News Letter* 8, no. 6, 30 June 1939.
96 LR–122215, memoranda, MacDougall to Cain, 10 May and 26 June 1940.
97 OA, MU, 1783, MacDougall papers, Annual Report for Algonquin Park for year ended 31 October 1932; MacDougall, "Toronto Anglers" (see note 86 above).
98 Ibid., Annual Report for Algonquin Park for year ended 31 March 1936; LR–129915, vol. 1, Harkness to R.N. Johnston, chief, Division of Research, DLF, 15 February 1946.
99 LR–123615H, Algonquin Park *News Letter* 13, no. 2, 1 April 1944.
100 OA, MU, 1784, MacDougall papers, file, "Planning 1932–38," "Draft Plan for Algonquin Park," 30 September 1934; OA, MU, 1783, Annual Report for Algonquin Park for year ended 31 March 1937.
101 OA, MU, 1783, MacDougall papers, "Algonquin Park 1931–37" file, "Poaching in Algonquin Park."
102 MacDougall, "Toronto Anglers" (see note 86 above).
103 OA, MU, 1794, MacDougall papers, Algonquin Park Reminiscences 1971–72.
104 OA, RG–1, IA–7, box 37, file 27–1501–5. Copy of order-in-council, 27 June 1944. For full documentation, see LR–123615, vol. 3.
105 OA, RG–1, BA Technical Draft Circulars and Bulletins, b. 1 (1944–49), technical circular no. 44, 20 September 1944, and no. 75, 24 September 1945; LR–129915, vol. 1, Dymond to H.W. Crosbie, 2 November 1945.
106 APM, historical file, Audrey Saunders's notes on writing *Algonquin Story*, dated 9 March 1948 (see chapter 1 above, note 18).
107 QSC Records, C3207CC–In Re Quetico-Superior/Re Canada–25.G.6.3B, Kenneth Reid to Charles S. Kelly, 27 November 1941.
108 LR–116062, vol. 1, Kenneth Reid to the Honourable Mitchell Hepburn, 21 August 1941.
109 QPP, historical file, 1940s, W.D. Cram to J.M. Whalen, 15 October 1941.
110 Ibid., J.A. Mathieu to the Honourable N.O. Hipel, 29 January 1942; and Cram to MacDougall, 22 October 1941.
111 QSC Records, W.D. Cram papers, P34, box 16, Oberholtzer to Cram, 14 September 1942.
112 QSC Records, C3207CC–In Re Quetico-Superior/Re Canada-25.G.6.3B, Clifford Sifton to J.W. Dafoe, 25 November 1941, Kenneth Reid to Charles S. Kelly, 27 November 1941; ibid., Clifford Sifton papers, P34, box 53, Reid to Sifton, 12 January 1942.
113 LR–116062, vol. 1, Oberholtzer to MacDougall, 11 April 1942; QPP Archives, historical file, 1940s, J.M. Whalen to W.D. Cram, 29 April 1942.
114 LR–123616, Whalen to H.W. Crosbie, 13 June 1944.
115 QPP, historical file, 1940s, Lloyd Rawn to George Delahey, ca. March 1942.

Chapter Three

1 *Ontario Economic and Social Aspects Survey* (Toronto: Ontario Department of Economics, 1961), 70, 189; Freda Hawkins, *Canada and Immigra-*

tion: Public Policy and Public Concern (Montreal and London: McGill-Queen's University Press, 1972), 38, 64–66; K.E. Rea, *The Prosperous Years: The Economic History of Ontario, 1939–1975*. Ontario Historical Studies Series (Toronto and Buffalo: University of Toronto Press, 1985), 27.

2 Robert Bothwell, Ian Drummond, John English, *Canada Since 1945: Power, Politics, and Provincialism* (Toronto: University of Toronto Press, 1981), 10; *Ontario Survey* (1961), 80, 195 (see note 1 above).

3 *Ontario Survey* (1961), 30, 165, 172–74; Rea, *Prosperous Years*, 56, 63 (see note 1 above for notes on both titles).

4 *Outdoor Recreation For America. A Report to the President and to the Congress by the Outdoor Recreation Resources Review Commission* (Washington, D.C., January 1962), 29; Rea, *Prosperous Years*, 31–33 (see note 1 above).

5 Rea, *Prosperous Years*, 104–5 (see note 1 above).

6 APM, "Annual Report for Algonquin Park 1946."

7 LR–129915, vol. 2, Harold Bond to DLF, 11 September 1945.

8 Ibid., J.R. Dymond to MacDougall, 30 October 1947; OA, MU, 1788, MacDougall papers, memo to H.R. Scott, 27 October 1947, entitled "Analysis of Algonquin Park Problem."

9 APM, "Annual Report for Algonquin Provincial Park ... for year ended 31 March 1954"; Toronto *Globe and Mail*, 19 and 21 October 1953.

10 LR–129915, vol. 3, W.D. Cram to D.S. McKee, Chief Sanitary Inspector, Department of Health, 11 June 1952.

11 OA, RG–1, BA, Information Bulletins and Circulars, Circular no. 18, re "Anglers Using Aircraft to Algonquin Park 1948," 12 May 1949; LR–129915, vols. 2 and 3, passim; LR–123615, vol. 2, J.M. Taylor to F.A. MacDougall, 11 June 1943.

12 LR–129914, vol. 1, F.S. Newman to W.D. Cram, 11 August 1949.

13 LR–115420, vol. 1, J.F. Simmons to W.D. Cram, 11 February 1948 and 1 December 1949; see also Peterborough *Daily Examiner*, 7 June 1955 for the Kawarthas.

14 *Toronto Daily Star*, 6 December 1949; Legislative Assembly of Ontario, *Debates*, 13 March 1950.

15 LR–115420, W.D. Cram to H.R. Scott, 28 January 1952.

16 LR–115420, W.B. Greenwood to Clare E. Mapledoram, 4 October 1954; and passim; see also, OA, RG–1, IA–7, box 3, file 27–0106, "Summary of Developments Concerning Proposal re Pinery," ca. January 1952, submitted by the London Chamber of Commerce.

17 OA, MU, 1788, MacDougall Papers, memo to H.R. Scott, 6 September 1947; LR–129917, vol. 1, T.E. Mackey, chief, Division of Forest Protection, to W.D. Cram, 4 November 1948.

18 LR–129917, vol. 1, F.W. Beatty, T.E. Mackey, W.D. Cram to F.A. MacDougall, 19 May 1948; see also "Sketch of Preliminary Rondeau Park Facilities ... Shopping Centre, Restaurant, Post office," ca. March 1949.

19 Ibid., vol. 2, W.A. Orr, deputy minister, Department of Municipal Affairs to Andrew T. Ward, member of the Legislative Assembly (MLA), 11 June 1952.

20 Ibid., Charles Black, clerk, Township of Aldborough to F.A. MacDougall, 23 July 1952; J.J. Girling, secretary-treasurer, OFAH, to Premier Leslie M. Frost, 28 July 1952.

21 Ibid., F.W. Beatty, surveyor general to MacDougall, 4 and 19 November 1952.

22 LR–32180, vol. 4, passim. 1943–45.

23 LR–32180, vol. 4a, memo, H.L. Cummings to W.A. Orr, "Presqu'ile Park – Future Use and Development," 25 April 1950.

24 LR–30477, vol. 5a, H.L. Cummings to W.A. Orr, 29 April 1950.

25 LR–32180, vol. 4a, memo, "Creation of Provincial Recreational Areas," 13 January 1953.

26 Arthur Herbert Richardson, *Conservation by the People: The History of the Conservation Movement in Ontario to 1970* (Toronto: University of Toronto Press for the Conservation Authorities of Ontario, 1974), ch. 7.

27 OA, RG–1, BA, Information Bulletins and Circulars, Land and Recreation Circular no. 1, re "District Committee on Recreational Planning ...," 25 February 1953. Operations Circular no. 40, re "Annual Meeting – 1954 – Regional and District Foresters," 22 October 1953.

28 A.S. Bray, *National and State Parks in the Southern United States*; P. Addison, *Park Recreational Facilities in the Lake States and Central States*; W.B. Greenwood, *State Parks in New York and New Jersey*; F.S. Newman, *National and State Parks in Ohio and New York*; E.L. Ward, *Forest Recreation in Pennsylvania* (all titles published in the series Inspection of U.S. National and State Parks)(Toronto: DLF, 1964). All quotations in the following paragraphs are from these sources, unless otherwise indicated.

29 OA, RG–1, BA, Information Bulletins and Circulars, Lands and Recreation Circular no. 3, re Report of Committee on Recreational Planning, "Summary of the Minutes – District Foresters' Annual Conference, January – 1954," 5 March 1954.

30 LR–129917 vol. 3; see file memo by A.R.K. MacDonald, 26 January 1954 for ban on leases.

31 The Provincial Parks Act, 1954. *Statutes of Ontario* 1954, c. 75; see Legislative Assembly of Ontario, *Debates*, 9 March 1954, 421–24 and 15 March 1954, 538 for Challies's policy statements.

32 Legislative Assembly of Ontario, *Debates*, 15 March 1954, 541–42.

33 OA, RG–1, IA–7, box 39, file 27–1501–17,

"Algonquin Provincial Park," 16 June 1954 (approved by cabinet 17 June 1954); LR–129915, vol. 4, letter to leaseholders re new policy, 23 July 1954; OA, RG–1, BA, Draft Circulars Book no. 1 (1945–56), Lands Circular no. 24, re "Algonquin Provincial Park, Long-Term Plan of Restoration to its Natural State," 14 July 1954. For policy on camps and lodges see LR–129915, vol. 4, A.R.K. MacDonald to Eleanor Feely, 31 August 1954; OA, RG–1, IC, temporary box 1, accession no. 14195, OPIB records, Algonquin file 2, Clare Mapledoram to William Griesinger, 29 January 1957.

34 Toronto *Globe and Mail*, 15 July 1954.

35 OA, RG–1, BA, Draft Circulars Book no. 1 (1945–56), Park Circular no. 1, re "Policy on Quetico Provincial Park," 1 October 1954.

36 QPP, historical file, 1950s, clipping of *Steep Rock Echo*, n.d. (notation: "September 1954").

37 QPP, historical file, 1940s, Chester Wilson to DLF, 14 March 1944.

38 QPP, historical file, 1940s, Chester Wilson to W.G. Thompson, 27 April 1944.

39 LR–123616 H.W. Crosbie to F.E. Stewart, secretary, Fort Frances Chamber of Commerce, 1 June 1944; J.M. Whalen to Crosbie, 13 June 1944;

40 LR–116062, vol. 1, Crosbie to F.A. MacDougall, 26 July 1945; and Premier George A. Drew to Harold Scott, 13 April 1948.

41 LR–123616, Whalen to Crosbie, 16 September 1944.

42 QPP, historical file 1940s, memo, by W.D. Cram, "Re: Meeting – Minister's Office, 14th March, 1946."

43 LR–116062, Chester Wilson to H.W. Crosbie, 31 August 1946.

44 Ibid., Kenneth A. Reid to W.G. Thompson, 10 August 1946; Gov. Edward J. Thye to Premier George Drew, 21 October 1946, and passim.

45 QSC Records, C3207CC – In Re Quetico-Superior/Re Canada – 25.G.6.4F, "Report of Conferences in Toronto," by Sigurd Olson, 6 May 1948, and "Toronto Report–III" 7 May 1948.

46 QPP, historical file, 1940s, "Treaty for the Establishment of an International Peace Forest in the Quetico-Superior Area," draft 12–29–49.

47 LR–116062, "A Wilderness Conservation Clinic – A Plan to Establish an International Peace Memorial Forest in the Quetico-Superior Canoe Country," by H.C. Walker, to the premier and MLAs, and to the chairman and members of the Fish and Game Committee, 21 March 1950.

48 LR–116062, copy of Northwestern Ontario Associated Chambers of Commerce, 14th Annual Convention (26–27 September, 1949), "Quetico Park Resolution no. 6;" and memo, W.D. Cram to Keith Denis, chairman, zone 1, OFHA, 2 August 1951.

49 QSC Records, C3207CC – In Re Quetico-Superior/Re Canada – 25.G.6.4F, "Report to the Quetico-Superior Canadian Committee," by Don O'Hearn, executive secretary (September 1951).

50 OA, MU, 1788, MacDougall papers, memo to H.R. Scott, 12 May 1947, re W.B. Greenwood. Additional information on Greenwood from author's interview with A.R.K. MacDonald, 23 September 1984.

51 OA, RG–1, IA–7, box 22, file 27–1106, Greenwood to Mapledoram, 19 January 1955; LR–32180, vol. 5, F.A. MacDougall to Mapledoram, 22 February 1955.

52 OA, RG–1, IA–2, box 2, minutes of meeting on aircraft operation in parks, 5 January 1955; OA, RG–1, BA, Draft Circulars Book no. 1 (1945–56), Parks Circular no. 4, re "Air Travel, Algonquin and Quetico Provincial Parks," 22 April 1955.

53 For financial data see OA, RG–1, IB–1, accession no. #13103, schedule no. 203, temporary box 1, file 11–1, memo, "Provincial Parks 1957–1971."

54 OA, RG–1, IA–2, box 5, file 1–2, "Policy re Provincial Parks" (1954); ibid., IA–3, box 3, file 2–2–6, Minutes, Parks Supervisors' Conference, 8–10 October 1957; ibid., BA, Draft Circulars, Circular P.85, re "Responsibility for Establishment of Parks," 16 January 1959; PB, file (10–1), memo, "Long Term Planning as a Guide to Provincial Park Location and Development," 15 February 1961.

55 OA, RG–1, IA–7, box 40, file 27–150–1, Greenwood to J.W. Spooner, 24 September 1958.

56 For Bon Echo and Merrill Denison, see LR–107282.

57 For the Pinery, see OA, RG–1, IA-7, box 4, file 27–0106–1, and boxes 24–5, file 27–1205 for Sibbald Point.

58 OA, RG–1, IA–7, box 23, file 27–1107–1.

59 For Greenwood and MacDougall on Wasaga Beach, see PB, Operations, Special Parks Committee appointed by Treasury Board on 26 October 1955, Minutes 15 December 1955; and OPIB, Minutes (expanded version) 18 December 1956.

60 For conditions at Wasaga Beach prior to 1959, see LR–46004 and PB, WASBC file.

61 OA, RG–1, IB-3, box 3, file 25–14–31, Greenwood to J.W. Spooner, 22 February 1960.

62 For a compilation of park data see OA, RG–1, IB–1, accession no. 13103, schedule no. 203, temporary box 1, file 11–1, memo, "Provincial Parks 1957–1971." Data were also obtained from statistical reports published annually, beginning in 1957, by the Division of Parks. Interior user figures for Quetico grew from 16,309 in 1958 to 25,190 in 1961. Camper figures are based on the number of permits issued. The division kept no record of campers in partially developed, but operating, parks (twenty in 1956, fifteen in 1957), where no fee was collected. Not all operating parks were officially established; for example, only thirty-four of the fifty-seven operating parks in 1958 had been placed under regulation and

only fifty of seventy-seven in 1961.

63 For American camping patterns in 1960, see *Participation in Outdoor Recreation: Factors Affecting Demand Among American Adults*, ORRRC Study Report 20 (Washington, D.C., 1962), ch. 6.

64 Geoffrey Wall and R. Wallis, "Camping for Fun: A Brief History of Camping in North America," in Wall and Marsh, *Recreational Land Use*, 341–53 (see chapter 1 above, note 2).

65 *Statistical Report on Provincial Park Use 1956–57* (Ontario DLF, Division of Parks), 5; OA, RG–1, IB–1, accession no. 13103, schedule no. 203, temporary box 1, file 11–1, memo, "Provincial Parks 1957–1971." For American data, see *Public Expenditures for Outdoor Recreation*, ORRRC Study Report 25 (Washington, D.C., 1962), 100–9.

66 Information in this paragraph was culled from the annual reports of the DLF, 1957–61.

67 OPIB, Minutes (expanded version), 26 September 1956.

68 *Outdoor Recreation for America*, introduction and ch. 9 (see note 4 above).

69 OPIB, Minutes, "A Report to the Honourable Leslie M. Frost ... and Executive Council, Parks Committee (Treasury Board), 23 January 1956."

70 An Act to Establish the Ontario Parks Integration Board, *Statutes of Ontario*, 1955–56, c. 61; and Legislative Assembly of Ontario, *Debates*, 26 March 1956, 1531–32.

71 OPIB, Minutes (expanded version), 13 and 26 September 1956.

72 OPIB, Minutes, 20 August 1958.

73 PB, Operations, OPIB, advisory committee file, M.T. Gray to C.R. Tilt, 26 November 1958.

74 OA, MU, 1791, F.A. MacDougall papers, file notes, speeches, miscellanea (1960–66), memorandum, A.B. Wheatley to MacDougall, 6 November 1963; OA, RG–1, IB–1, box 1, file 11–1, "Provincial Park Needs to 1968," 20 April 1964.

75 OA, RG–1, IB–1, box 1, file 11–1, Premier John P. Robarts to J.W. Spooner, 24 May 1962; see also A.K. McDougall, *John P. Robarts: His Life and Government* (Toronto and Buffalo: University of Toronto Press, 1986), 89, 95.

76 Author's interviews with Alan R.K. MacDonald, 23 September 1984, and with C.R. Tilt, 5 June 1985.

77 OA, RG–1, IB–4, box 14, file 26–31, memo, "Land Acquisitions Programme," A. Kelso Roberts to Premier John P. Robarts, 4 March 1963. One instance in which property was acquired over the doubts of parks staff occurred in the case of Scugog Island, in the riding of Health Minister Matthew B. Dymond. Even though the Parks Branch believed the island had limited recreational potential, by 1967 some 165 hectares of property had been purchased as a park reserve; see OA, RG–1, IB–4, box 8, file 26–12–4 for Scugog Island, and ibid., A–1–8, box 5, minister's file, "Proposed Park Lake Scugog."

78 OA, RG–1, IA–3, box 1, file 2–1–7, file memo, "Public Lands on Great Lakes and Inland Waterways" (ca. 1966). For statistical data see ibid., IB–1, box 7, file 11–30, memo, W.G. Maslen to D.R. Wilson, 21 July 1967. Some 35.8 kilometres of Great Lakes shoreline acquisition involved expansions to Lake Superior and Sibley provincial parks, and the creation of Batchawana Bay Park, all on Lake Superior.

79 OPIB, Minutes, 26 January 1967.

80 OA, RG–1, IA–7, box 25, file 27–1208, A.R. MacDonald to A.B. Wheatley, 5 July 1962; also see PB, file 10–1208, file memo, "Wasaga Beach Provincial Park" (ca. 1965), file memo, 22 November 1965.

81 OA, RG–1, IA–7, box 26, file 27–1208, "Design Concept," Report of Project Planning Associates Ltd. for Wasaga Beach (1965); see also ibid., box 30, file 27–1208–6, "Assessment Consultant Report – Wasaga Beach Provincial Park," 7 October 1965; see also PB, file 10–1208 for Norman Pearson's comments (report dated 14 October 1964).

82 PB, WASBC file, memo, D.R. Wilson to A. Kelso Roberts, 16 May 1966; see also OA, RG–1, IA–7, box 31, file 27–1208–8, material for presentation to cabinet, ca. December 1967; and ibid., IC, temporary box 6, accession no. 14195, "Wasaga Park Commmunity Project Progress Report," Department of Municipal Affairs, Community Planning Branch, March 1971; ibid., OPIB, Wasaga file, "Initial Phase Program: Wasaga Beach Park – Community Concept," 10 July 1969.

83 Killarney Recreational Reserve Act, *Statutes of Ontario* 1962–63, c. 68.

84 See LR–170316 for documentation on Silver Peak and Killarney Provincial Park.

85 PB, D.F. Brunette, "Master Plan Background, Killarney Provincial Park," 8 November 1974, and "North Georgian Bay Recreational Reserve, Summary Report," 29 May 1971.

86 OA, RG–1, IA–7, box 8, file 27–0303 (Tidewater Provincial Park).

87 Ibid., IB–1, accession no. 13103, schedule no. 203, temporary box 1, file 11–1, see memo, "Provincial Parks 1957–1971," for statistical data. Ibid., IA–5, box 1, file 13–2–1, D.R. Wilson to Lloyd Brooks, 24 October 1966.

88 Legislative Assembly of Ontario, *Debates*, 15 May 1967, 3417.

89 OA, RG–1, IB–1, box 10, file 11–31, D.R. Wilson to A. Kelso Roberts, 8 August 1966.

90 Ibid., IA–2, box 5, file 1–2, Wilson to R.H. Hambly, 2 November 1966.

91 Ibid., IB–3, box 3, file 25–01–77, report to OPIB, 24 July 1967.

92 OPIB, Minutes 15 September 1959; see also OA, RG–1, IC, temporary box 6, accession no. 14195,

OPIB, Welland Co. file for documentation on public petitions. For Ellis Morningstar's role see ibid., A–1–8, box 6, minister's file, "Proposed Park Welland Canal Area 1963–67." Toronto *Globe and Mail*, 15 July 1963 and 18 July 1967; see also OA, RG–1, IB–1, box 7, file 11–30–1, memo, "Public Beaches on Lake Erie," P. Addison to R. Brunelle, 11 June 1970, for an overview of public protest 1962–70.

93 Legislative Assembly of Ontario, *Debates*, 28 February 1961, 1603.

94 OA, RG–1, A–1–8, box 6, minister's file, Proposed Park Welland Canal Area 1963–67, Morningstar to Kelso Roberts, 27 March 1963, 1 September 1965; ibid., IB–4, box 1, file 26–01–2, D.R. Wilson to Kelso Roberts, 17 February 1966, and E.J. Parker, Real Estate Branch, Department of Public Works (DPW), to C.R. Tilt, 13 September 1966, OPIB, Minutes, 23 November 1966, 24 August and 23 November 1967.

95 OA, RG–1, IB–3, box 5, file 27–07–0, Brunelle to Robarts, 7 February 1967.

96 Legislative Assembly of Ontario, *Debates*, 10 March 1967, 1279.

Chapter Four

1 LR–185215, file memo, "Summary of the Dealings by Cabinet and Parks Integration Board with Lease Matters (Algonquin and Rondeau Provincial Parks)," n.d.

2 LR–165517, Reynolds to Greenwood, 21 May 1959 (marked confidential).

3 OA, RG–1, IA–7, box 11, file 27–0403–1, W.T. Foster to Greenwood, 20 March 1956.

4 OA, RG–1, IA–2, box 2, file 1–1–2–4, Greenwood to Clare Mapledoram, 16 April 1956.

5 OA, RG–1, IA–7, box 37, file 27–1501–5, Frost to Mapledoram, 29 March 1956; see also ibid., box 39, file 27–1501–16, R.V. Scott to F.W. Beatty, 27 October 1959.

6 *Quetico Newsletter* 11, no. 2, 15 September 1956. All quotations from this source.

7 OA, RG–1, IA–3, box 6, file 2–3–7, A. Helmsley, "Interpretation in Provincial Parks," 21 September 1960; see also W.F. Lothian, *A History of Canada's National Parks*, vol. 4 (Ottawa: Parks Canada, 1981), ch. 11. For B.C., see R. Yorke Edwards, "What is Interpretation?" *Park News* 21, no. 1 (Spring 1985), 3–5.

8 Helmsley, "Interpretation" 2 (see note 7 above); see also *Annual Report of Provincial Parks Interpretive Programmes 1959*, passim.

9 Helmsley, "Interpretation" 4 (see note 7 above). The first two of the park publications were *The Reptiles of Algonquin Park*, Museum Bulletin no. 1 (DLF 1962), *Game Fish and Fishing in Algonquin Provincial Park*, Museum Bulletin no. 2 (DLF 1955, revised 1958, 1965).

10 *Interpretive Programmes 1959*, passim (see note 9 above).

11 OA, RG–1, IA–3, box 3, file 2–2–6, Minutes of Park Supervisors' Conference, 15–16 October 1958.

12 *Interpretive Programmes 1959*, 42 (see note 9 above).

13 OA, RG–1, BA, Draft Circulars (1956–57), Circular P. 10–1, re "Park Planning," 21 November 1956.

14 PB, Operations, Provincial Parks General File, Greenwood to OPIB, 25 September 1956.

15 PB, file 10–1, Inspection Reports by A.R.K. MacDonald, 19 July 1961.

16 OA, RG–1, IA–7, box 39, file 27–1501–15, "Material for News Release," by J.W. Giles, Timber Management Supervisor, 2 August 1957.

17 For newspaper clippings, see APM, historical files: *Hamilton Spectator*, 10 October 1957, *Ottawa Citizen*, 3 October 1957, Toronto *Globe and Mail*, 25 October 1957.

18 OA, RG–1, IA–7, box 37, file 27–1501–6, F.A. MacDougall to J.W. Spooner, 20 March 1959, and J.S. Yoerger to MacDougall, 28 April 1958.

19 Ibid., see undated newspaper clippings (ca. May 1958), for letters to the editor from the Conservation Council of Ontario and the Quetico Foundation.

20 Ibid., Gavin Henderson to Premier Leslie Frost, 26 May 1958.

21 OA, RG–1, IA–7, box 34, file 27–1501, "Plan For Development of Algonquin Park 1958–69."

22 Ibid., box 37, file 27–1501–6, "District Algonquin Park Plan," by A.R. MacDonald, 12 January 1959.

23 PB, policy box, copy of J.B. Ridley, Chairman, Quetico Foundation, "Brief to the Select Committee ... to Study the Administrative and Executive Problems of the Government of Ontario, 6 June 1961."

24 Aldo Leopold, *A Sand County Almanac. With Essays on Conservation from Round River* (New York: Ballantine Books, 1970), 262.

25 All quotations in the following paragraphs are from the Federation of Ontario Naturalists' "Outline of a Basis for a Parks Policy for Ontario," December 1958.

26 OPIB, Minutes, 22 October, 19 November 1958; PB, Operations, OPIB: Premier's Office file, Charles Daley to Frost, 5 January 1959.

27 PB, Operations, OPIB: Premier's Office file, minutes of meeting, 17 February 1959.

28 For the 1959 policy statement, see Legislative Assembly of Ontario, *Debates*, 24 March 1959, 1572–5. For the Park Assistance Act see OA, RG–1, BA, Draft Bulletins, Information Bulletin P. 8–15, re Municipal Parks, 23 December 1960.

29 *Statutes of Ontario*, 1959, c. 107; Legislative Assembly of Ontario, *Debates*, 10 February 1959, 277.

30 See OA, RG–1, IB–3, box 19, file 25–36 for copies of the Conservation Council of Ontario (CCO)

and FON briefs, dated 16 March 1959.

31 See LR–167441, passim, for documentation on the original reserves.

32 See *Provincial Nature Reserves in Ontario* (MNR: Parks and Recreation Areas Branch, 1981) for Matawatchan, Montreal River, Porphyry Island, and Cavern Lake. Four other wilderness areas created after 1961 became provincial parks: Gibson River, Waubaushene Beaches, Ouimet Canyon, and East Sister Island.

33 For Cape Henrietta-Maria Wilderness Area, see LR–167441, E.L. Ward to D.F. Robinson, 6 October 1965.

34 See OA, RG–1, IB–3, box 19, file 25–36–1, passim, for Ward's important role in the Pukaskwa story, especially memo, E.L. Ward to J.S. Yoerger, 23 February 1961, for the original rationale.

35 Legislative Assembly of Ontario, *Debates*, 29 March 1960, 1904, and 6 December 1960, 235–6.

36 OA, RG–1, IA–2, box 2, file 1–1–2–2, Greenwood to E.L. Ward, 11 March 1960. One of the major frustrations faced by parks personnel in the 1960s lay in their inability to strengthen the Provincial Parks Act to govern and control fishing and other wildlife activities. All of the regulations pertaining to the control of fishing, trapping, and hunting were in the Fish and Wildlife Act. The Fish and Wildlife Branch resisted efforts of the Park Branch to change this situation (communication received by author from Grant Tayler, 5 December 1988).

37 OA, RG–1, IA–2, box 5, file 1–2, "Provincial Parks Philosophy, Policies and Plans, 1961," 1961.

38 *Quetico Newsletter* 11, no. 1, 27 March 1956, and no. 2, 15 September 1956. The foundation amended its letters patent in 1958 to widen its role beyond Quetico Provincial Park.

39 OA, RG–1, IA–7, box 9, file 27–0403, Greenwood to Mapledoram, 30 June 1955.

40 OA, RG–1, IA–7, box 12, file 27–0403–4, Arthur W. Greeley to Clare Mapledoram, 19 March 1957; and LR–161516, "Analysis of letter dated March 19th, 1957 to ... Mapledoram ... from ... Greeley," n.d.

41 PB, Quetico-Superior Advisory Committee file, copy of Legislative Assembly of Ontario, *Debates*, 12 April 1960.

42 QPP, Charles Kelly to Shirley Peruniak, assistant park naturalist, 18 August 1982, and Searle, *Saving Quetico-Superior* (see chapter 1 above, note 50), 214. The advisory committee worked effectively for seventeen years until disbanded by President Jimmy Carter in 1977. Since then, field staff of the DLF and the Boundary Waters Canoe Area (BWCA) have coordinated management policies.

43 Author's interview with Ronald Vrancart, 13 October 1976. Vrancart and James Keenan (who wrote the classification policy announced in March 1967) first saw the 1959 document in September 1976!

44 LR–164940, D.W.R. McKinley, assistant director, National Research Council of Canada (NCR) to F.A. MacDougall, 18 September 1958.

45 Ibid., Patrick A. Hardy to J.W. Spooner, 25 November and 17 December 1959.

46 *Outdoor Recreation for America* (see chapter 3 above, note 4). Its appendix C contains an annotated list of the study reports.

47 OA, RG–1, IA–6, box 1, file 14–3, Gavin Henderson to J.W. Spooner, 24 May 1961.

48 Ibid., FON brief to the Select Committee ... to Examine ... the Administrative and Executive Problems of the Government of Ontario," 13 June 1961.

49 Ibid., CCO brief to the Select Committee ... etc., 13 June 1961.

50 Toronto *Globe and Mail*, 14 and 15 June 1961.

51 OA, RG–1, IA–6, box 1, file 14–2, CCO brief, "The Need for an Outdoor Recreational Survey for Ontario," with covering letter from D.N. Kendall to Premier John P. Robarts, 5 April 1963.

52 OA, RG–1, IA–7, box 17, file 27–0702, Addison to A.B. Wheatley, 6 February 1964.

53 OA, RG–1, IA–7, box 4, file 27–0106–20, brief to Master Planning Committee, Pinery Provincial Park, from Professor John Sparling, 1967.

54 OA, RG–1, IA–2, box 3, file 1–1–2–8, Wheatley to MacDougall, 20 August 1963.

55 OA, RG–1, IA–4, box 1, file 8–2–16–2, G.E. Tayler to D.R. Wilson, 17 November 1965.

56 OA, RG–1, IA–2, box 5, file 1–1–7, memo, "Provincial Police in Provincial Parks," by C.R. Tilt, 1965; and OA, RG–1, BA, Draft Circulars, Circular P. 2–8 re "Ontario Provincial Police Assistance in Provincial Parks," 23 November 1966.

57 OA, RG–1, IA–2, box 3, file 1–1–7 PA, Addison to G.H. Bayly, 2 June 1967.

58 Ibid., M.J. Jackson, superintendent, Pinery Provincial Park, to district forester, Aylmer, 26 May 1967; and "Police Report for Pinery Park 1967."

59 Forestry Study Unit, *Multiple Use of Forest and Related Lands 1966* (Ontario DLF).

60 PB, Operations, premier's office file, copy of John Ridley, Chairman of the Quetico Foundation, to J.M. McClinton, president of the Northern Ontario Associated Chambers of Commerce, 9 December 1960.

61 Ibid., McClinton to Premier Leslie Frost, 11 November 1960.

62 OA, RG–1, IA–2, box 2, file 1–1–2–4, quoted in J.S. Yoerger to A.B. Wheatley, 25 April 1961.

63 Ibid., Wheatley to Yoerger, 28 April 1961.

64 OA, RG–1, IA–7, box 15, file 27–0403–5, memo, "Meeting ... November 13th, 1961," dated 27 November 1961.

65 Legislative Assembly of Ontario, *Debates*, 17 December 1962, 372.

66 OA, RG–1, IA–2, box 2, file 1–1–2–4, unsigned

file memo, dated 1965.

67 OA, RG–1, IB–1, box 1, file 11–1, D.R. Wilson to G.H.U. Bayly, 14 October 1966.

68 OA, RG–1, IA–7, box 42, file 27–1702, memo, "Elliot Lake: Summary of Information," by C.R. Tilt, 4 August 1966; see also OPIB, Minutes, 29 June 1960; and OA, RG–1, IC, temporary box 3, accession no. 14195, OPIB Mississagi file, passim.

69 OA, RG–1, IA–7, box 42, file 27–1702, Department of Mines brief to OPIB, "Proposed Mississagi Provincial Park, 26 Oct. 1966."

70 OA, RG–1, IB–3, box 19, file 25–36–1, memo, "Meeting with D. Douglass, Dep. Min. of Mines," 15 November 1966, by J.W. Keenan.

71 OA, RG–1, IA–7, box 43, file 27–1703, Douglass to Bayly, 10 February 1967.

72 See Ian Radforth, *Bush Workers and Bosses: Logging in Northern Ontario, 1900–1980* (Toronto, Buffalo, London: University of Toronto Press, 1987), chs. 9–10.

73 OA, RG–1, IA–4, box 1, file 8–1, A.R.K. MacDonald to W.B. Greenwood, 2 March 1960, and passim.

74 Ibid., copy of Circular T. 10–2, 7 March 1961.

75 Legislative Assembly of Ontario, *Debates*, 25 February 1963, 1033–37.

76 Ontario MNR Library, *Jim Mathieu Lumber Ltd.: Unauthorized Cutting, 1962*.

77 QPP, historical file, 1960s, L. Ringham to F.A. MacDougall, 23 March 1965.

78 OA, RG–1, IA–7, box 15, file 27–0403–7, Helmsley to M.B. Morison, Chief, Timber Branch, 6 April 1965; see also Helmsley to T.W. Hueston, 6 April 1965.

79 APM, historical files, "Timber Management in Algonquin Provincial Park," n.a., n.d., background report for Algonquin Park Master Plan (1974).

80 OA, RG–1, IA–7, box 40, file 27–1501–20, "Opinion on the Forest Management of Algonquin Provincial Park," by W.L. Plonski, October 1962.

81 Ibid., "Recreation and Timber Management, Algonquin P.P.," by A.F. Helmsley, 22 November 1962; Helmsley to A.B. Wheatley, 3 December 1963; "Comments on the Plonski Report ...," by Bruce Litteljohn, n.d. Communication to author from Grant Tayler, 5 December 1988.

82 OA, RG–1, IA–7, box 36, file 27–1501–4, memo by T.W. Hueston, 9 December 1963.

83 Ibid., T.W. Hueston to M.B. Morison, 21 December 1966, and D.R. Wilson to G.H.U. Bayly, 20 April 1967.

84 George B. Priddle, "Recreational Use and 'Wilderness' Perception of the Algonquin Park Interior," M.A. thesis, Clark University, 1964, 10; see also Robert C. Lucas, "Wilderness Perceptions and Use: The Example of the Boundary Waters Canoe Area," *Natural Resources Journal*, January 1964; "Wilderness-User Concepts," *Naturalist* (Winter 1964); *Recreational Use of the Quetico-Superior Area*, U.S. Forest Service Research Paper LS–8, April 1964; *The Recreational Capacity of the Quetico-Superior Area*, U.S. Forest Service Research Paper LS–15, September 1964.

85 OA, RG–1, IA–7, box 35, file 27–1501, Minutes of Meeting between Pembroke District Forest Industry and DLF, 16 November 1967; and PB, *A Study of Visitor Attitudes Towards Quetico P. P.*, Conducted for Parks Branch, DLF, by Gordon Lusty Research Ltd., 15 March 1968.

86 OA, RG–1, IB–2, box 6, file 18–7, D.R. Wilson to F.E. Sider, 3 March 1966.

87 *Visitor Attitudes* sec. 22 (see note 85 above).

88 Priddle, "Algonquin Park Interior," 30, 22–33 (see note 84 above).

89 Lucas, *Quetico-Superior*, 2, 26 (see note 84 above).

90 Ibid., 27.

91 Bruce M. Litteljohn, *Quetico-Superior Country: Wilderness Highway to Wilderness Recreation* (Quetico Foundation; reprinted from *Canadian Geographical Journal*, August and September 1965), 28.

92 OA, RG–1, IA–2, box 1, file 1–1–1, memo, "Restrictions Algonquin and Quetico Parks."

93 OA, RG–1, IA–2, box 3, file 1–1–2–10, "Regulations Concerning the Leaving of Boats Unattended in Provincial Parks," 23 February 1961, and file 1–1–2–9, G.H. Ferguson to A. Kelso Roberts, 12 April 1965.

94 OA, RG–1, BA, Draft Circulars, Circular P. 2–9, "Re Use of Water Skis, Surf-Boards and Water Sleds Algonquin P.P.," 30 April 1965.

95 OA, RG–1, IA–2, box 3, file 1–1–2–9, D.R. Wilson to G.H. Ferguson, 2 April 1965; OA, RG–1, IA–7, box 44, file 27–1903, G.H. Ferguson to René Brunelle, 14 March 1967.

96 OA, RG–1, IA–7, box 46, file 27–2107, News release re Sandbanks Provincial Park, 10 February 1964, passim.

97 D.H. Pimlott, J.A. Shannon, G.B. Kolenosky, *The Ecology of the Timber Wolf in Algonquin Provincial Park* (Ontario DLF, 1969).

98 Douglas H. Pimlott, "The Preservation of Natural Areas in Ontario," *Ontario Naturalist* 3, no. 2 (1965), 10.

99 OA, RG–1, IA–3, box 2, file 2–1–3, Pimlott to D.R. Wilson, 27 May 1965.

100 D.H. Pimlott, "Should We Be Proud of Ontario's Park System?" (Unpublished address to 1966 annual meeting in Kingston of the OFAH, copy in "Quetico – Let It Be," leader's kit.)

101 OA, RG–1, IA–3, box 2, file 2–1–3, Pimlott to Wilson, 27 May 1965.

102 Pimlott, "Natural Areas," 16 (see note 98 above).

103 Ibid., 10–11.

104 Ibid., 4.

105 OA, RG–1, IA–3, box 2, file 2–1–3, Pimlott to D.R. Wilson, 27 May 1965.

106 Fred Bodsworth, "Why Wilderness?" *Ontario Naturalist* 5, no. 4 (December 1967), 4–7.

107 See OA, RG–1, IB–3, box 19, file 25–36, T.W. Hueston to R.G. Code, 21 February 1966, re meeting with Falls et al. on 18 February 1966; see OA, RG–1, IA–6, box 1, file 14–1, "Practical Considerations for the Establishment of a System of Nature Reserves – a Memorandum for Discussion," by J. Bruce Falls, and his "Federation of Ontario Naturalists: Notes for Discussion of Ontario Nature Reserves," both dated 21 November 1966. Also see his "The Importance of Wilderness to Science," *Ontario Naturalist* 5, no. 4 (December 1967), 15–18.

108 OA, RG–1, IA–3, box 1, file 2–1–3, copy of speech by Gavin Henderson, 30 April 1965.

109 OA, RG–1, IA–6, box 2, file 14–17, "Should There Be an Algonquin Park Association?" by Douglas Pimlott, 5 September 1965. The quotation is from *Wilderness Now: A Statement of Principles and Policies of the Algonquin Wildlands League* (AWL) (Toronto: AWL, 1972), 25. For information on the role of parks staff in the formation of the AWL, I am indebted to a personal communication from Grant Tayler, 5 December 1988.

110 Samuel P. Hays, *Beauty, Health, and Permanence: Environmental Politics in the United States, 1955–1985* (Cambridge, Mass.: Cambridge University Press, 1987), ch. 1. The following paragraphs are based on Hays's interpretation. For the best Canadian study of the environmental movement, see David Israelson, *Silent Earth: The Politics of Our Survival* (Markham, Ont.: Viking, The Penguin Group, 1990).

111 William Ashworth, *The Late Great Lakes: An Environmental History* (New York: Alfred A. Knopf, 1986), ch. 12.

112 R.Y. Edwards, "The Preservation of Wilderness – Is Man a Part of Nature – or a Thing Apart?" *Canadian Audubon* (January–February 1967), 1.

113 Quoted in *Quetico Newsletter* 10, no. 3 (Winter 1964).

114 OA, RG–1, IA–3, box 4, file 2–3–4, Wheatley to G.H.U. Bayly, 7 December 1961.

115 PB, file 10–1, Parks Planning General, MacDonald to Wheatley, 16 June 1964.

116 OA, RG–1, IA–7, box 40, file 27–1501–20, Tilt to Wheatley, 29 September 1964.

117 OA, RG–1, IA–7, box 5, file 2–3–5, Press release, "Closer Federal-Provincial Co-operation in Parks Management," 21 November 1962, and ibid., file 2–3–5–1, "Proposed Basis for a Park Classification System," 17 July 1963.

118 A.K. McDougall, *John P. Robarts: His Life and Government*. Ontario Historical Studies Series (Toronto and Buffalo: University of Toronto Press, 1986), 272.

119 OA, RG–1, IB–1, box 8, file 11–30–2, "The Ontario Park User Survey – Methodology and Results," by J.W. Keenan, 15 September 1966; and memo, Keenan to P. Addison, "Analysis of Park User Survey," 2 June 1967; see also R.I. Wolfe, *A Use-Classification of Parks by Analysis of Extremes: Final Report of a Recreational Travel Study*. DHO Report, no. RR134 (January 1969).

120 See the two reports provided by Gordon Lusty Survey Research Ltd. 1: *A Study of the Attitudes of Metro Toronto Campers Toward the Ontario Provincial Parks*, Project 901, 12 December 1966; 2: *A Study of Regional Ontario Attitudes Towards the Ontario Provincial Parks*, Project 516, 29 December 1967.

121 OA, RG–1, IA–6, box 1, file 14–3, "Ontario Federation of Anglers and Hunters, Provincial Park Committee, Report 1964," by Jack O'Dette, chairman, 10 January 1965; OA, RG–1, IB–1, box 1, file 11–1, A.P. Frame, president, NPPAC, to A. Kelso Roberts, 16 June 1966; OA, RG–1, IA–2, box 5, file 1–2, K. Acheson to D.R. Wilson, 16 December 1966, re "Resolutions: Annual Meeting of the Progressive Conservative Association of Ontario."

122 Legislative Assembly of Ontario, *Debates*, 16 March 1967, 1447. All quotations from this source, unless otherwise noted.

123 *Classification of Provincial Parks in Ontario 1967* (Parks Branch, DLF), 3; see also OA, RG–1, IB–1, box 1, file 11–1, Gavin Henderson, executive director NPPAC, to D.R. Wilson, 8 September 1966.

124 See OA, RG–1, IA–5, box 2, file 13–3, D.R. Wilson to A. Kelso Roberts, 14 March 1966, for Parks Branch analysis of the American bill.

125 OA, RG–1, IB–1, box 1, file 11–1–1, Frame to Premier John P. Robarts, 20 June 1967.

126 OA, RG–1, IA–6, file 14–1, Dr. Martin Edwards, president, FON, to Robarts, 26 June 1968.

127 OA, RG–1, A–1–8, box 9, minister's file, FON, Woodford to Robarts, 24 April 1968.

128 OA, RG–1, IA–7, box 8, file 27–0304, Frame to Robarts, 18 June 1968.

129 See OPIB, Minutes 21 March, and 11 April 1968, for the first reserves. For the advisory committee idea, see OA, RG–1, IB–3, box 18, file 25–33, J. Bruce Falls to Brunelle, 26 February 1968.

Chapter Five

1 OA, RG–1, IA–3, box 2, file 2–1–8, submission to the Standing Committee ... on Natural Resources and Tourism by C. Abbott Conway, 13 March 1968.

2 OA, RG–1, IA–6, box 2, file 14–17, statement delivered at press conference, Royal York Hotel, 10 July 1968.

3 *Wildland News* 1, no. 1 (September 1968). For information on Walter Gray's role, I am indebted to a personal communication from Patrick Hardy (27 June 1988) and to George Warecki for a transcript of an interview with Gray (6 January 1989).

4 OA, RG–1, IA–6, box 1, file 14–0, Addison to Bayly, 12 July 1967. As a pressure group, the AWL fits the theoretical framework outlined in A. Paul Pross, *Group Politics and Public Policy* (Toronto: Oxford, 1986).
5 OA, RG–1, IA–3, box 1, file 2–1–4–1, opening remarks by G.H.U. Bayly to the first Parks Certificate Course, 21 October 1968.
6 Toronto *Globe and Mail*, 26 July 1968 and *Toronto Daily Star*, 27 July 1968.
7 See *Wildland News* 1, no. 1 (September 1968).
8 OPIB, Minutes, 17 October 1968.
9 OA, RG–1, IA–7, box 40, file 27–1501–20, Keenan to Addison, 9 September 1968.
10 Ibid., Tayler to Addison, 9 September 1968.
11 PB, Operations, Algonquin file, a copy of the "Provisional Master Plan – Algonquin Provincial Park" (DLF 1968). Unless otherwise noted, copies of the briefs presented to the hearings cited below can be found in this file; see also "Algonquin Provincial Park, Public Hearings on the Provisional Master Plan. Summary of Briefs," report by George Moroz, 1 June 1969.
12 Toronto *Globe and Mail*, 12 November 1968.
13 OA, RG–1, IA–7, box 40, file 27–1501–20, regional director, Maple to G.H.U. Bayly, 10 October 1968.
14 PB, Operations, Algonquin File, "The Algonquin Provincial Park Master Plan – Where Do We Go From Here?" by J.W. Keenan, 6 December 1968.
15 *Toronto Daily Star*, 2 December 1968.
16 Toronto *Globe and Mail*, 30 November 1968.
17 OA, RG–1, IA–7, accession no. 12598, schedule no. 188, temporary box 7, file 27–1501–20 for many of these letters.
18 PB, Operations, Algonquin Park Task Force (APATAF) file, "Confidential. Report of the Meeting of the Algonquin Park Task Force," 17 February 1969.
19 Ibid., memo re "Active Committees – Algonquin Park Task Force," 30 December 1968.
20 Ibid., "Confidential. Report of Meetings of APATAF," 12, 26 May, 9, 23 June 1969, and 12 February 1970; see also "Algonquin Provincial Park. Economic Impact Study" (November 1969).
21 OA, RG–1, IA–7, accession no. 14604, schedule no. 188, temporary box 15, file 27–1501–20, "Algonquin Park Wilderness Use and Perception Study of Interior Users and Canoe Network Analysis."
22 OA, RG–1, IA–4, box 1, file 8–1 (1970), "Interim Progress Report, Forest Acoustics" (Project FM–93) by D.V. Myles. Forest Management Institute, Canadian Forestry Service, Ottawa 1970.
23 Legislative Assembly of Ontario, *Debates*, 29 April 1969, 3681–83.
24 OA, RG–1, A–1–8, box 21, Killarney file, statement by C. Abbott Conway ... Press Conference, Queen's Park, 24 June 1969.
25 Toronto *Globe and Mail*, 16 April 1969.
26 *Toronto Telegram*, 18 April 1969.
27 See *Toronto Star*, 2 August 1969; Toronto *Globe and Mail*, 4 August 1969; *Toronto Telegram*, 30 August 1969.
28 OA, RG–1, IA–3, box 7, file 2–1–11, "Excerpts from letters received by Mayor William Kutschke, Pembroke."
29 *Special Report 1969 OFIA Press Tour of Algonquin Provincial Park* (Toronto: OFIA, 1969).
30 A.K. McDougall, *John P. Robarts: His Life and Government*. Ontario Historical Studies Series (Toronto, Buffalo, London: University of Toronto Press, 1986), 274.
31 OA, RG–1, A–1–8, box 21, Killarney file, statement by C. Abbott Conway ... Press Conference, Queen's Park, 24 June 1969.
32 All quotations from *Wildland News* 2, no. 6 (July 1969).
33 OA, RG–1, IB–2, box 2, file 11–1–2, Addison to Bayly, 2 October 1969.
34 QPP, *Master Plan, Quetico Provincial Park* (March 1969), by J. Ferguson Wilson.
35 OA, RG–1, A–1–8, box 113, minister's J.A. Mathieu Ltd. file, A.J. Herridge to Brunelle, 7 July 1969.
36 OA, RG–1, A–1–8, box 114, minister's Ontario-Minnesota Pulp and Paper – Boise-Cascade file, Brunelle to Randall, 9 October 1969.
37 *Quetico Newsletter – Special Supplement* 15, no. 3 (Winter 1969–70).
38 *Quetico Newsletter* 14, no. 3 (Winter 1968–69).
39 OA, RG–1, IA–7, accession no. 12598, schedule no. 188, temporary box 5, file 27–0403–3, Walter Gray, director, AWL to John B. Ridley, chairman, Quetico Foundation, 21 January 1969 and Ridley to Gray, 28 January 1969.
40 Legislative Assembly of Ontario, *Debates*, 30 October 1969, 7759–60.
41 Ibid., 31 October 1969, 7872, 7875.
42 OA, RG–1, IA–7, accession no. 12598, schedule no. 188, temporary box 5, file 27–0403, Herridge to Bayly, 12 November 1969.
43 Ibid., Addison to Bayly, 13 November 1969.
44 See OA, RG–1, A–1–8, boxes 50, 51, 84, minister's Parks file, 1970.
45 OA, RG–1, IA–7, box 11, file 27–0403, "Regulations covering logging operations in Quetico," in Herridge to Bayly, 14 April 1970.
46 OPIB, Minutes, 7 May 1970.
47 OA, RG–1, IA–7, box 15, file 27–0403–10. See "Quetico Advisory Committee," 17 November 1970 for biographical sketches of members.
48 OA, RG–1, IA–7, box 38, file 27–1501–10, press release by C. Abbott Conway, president, AWL, 7 April 1970.
49 *Wilderness Now. A Statement of Principles and Policies of the Algonquin Wildlands League*, 1st ed. (May 1972), 30–31; 3rd rev. ed. 1980.
50 Bruce M. Litteljohn and Douglas H. Pimlott, (eds.) *Why Wilderness: A Report on Mismanage-*

ment in Lake Superior Provincial Park (Toronto: New Press, 1971), 49–51. See also note 93 below.

51 OA, RG–1, IA–7, box 47, file 27–2203, memo re Lake Superior Report by AWL, J.R. Oatway to G.H.U. Bayly, 28 July 1970.

52 OA, RG–1, A–1–8, box 39, minister's Lake Superior Provincial Park file, Conway to Brunelle, 6 July 1970. The final report is contained in *Why Wilderness* (see note 50 above), 45–75. The quotations which follow can be found in both the final report and OA, RG–1, IA–7, box 47, file 27–2203, "Preliminary Report on Lake Superior Provincial Park" (AWL, 1970).

53 In *Why Wilderness* (see note 50 above), the league hardened the position taken in the preliminary report by calling for a moratorium on logging pending study by an independent organization on the future of the park.

54 The league erred in claiming that there were eleven patents and sixty-one claims; see OA, RG–1, IA–7, box 47, file 27–2203, memo re Lake Superior Report by AWL, Oatway to Bayly, 28 July 1970.

55 Ibid., memo to P. Addison, 13 July 1970.

56 Ibid., Brunelle to Conway, 13 August 1970.

57 OA, RG–1, A–1–8, box 28, minister's advisory committee on Quetico Park file, Conway to Premier John P. Robarts, 15 September 1970; see also press release, AWL, 17 September 1970.

58 Paul Grescoe, "This Beauty Must Be Preserved," *Canadian Magazine*, 19 September 1970.

59 OA, RG–1, IA–3, box 7, file 2–1–2, Henderson to Brunelle, 6 October 1970; OA, RG–1, IA–7, box 10, file 27–0403, statements by Henderson, excerpted from "Weekday" interview with Barbara Frum. Brunelle consented to an interview with Frum on 20 October 1970; see transcript in OA, RG–1, A–1–8, box 28, minister's advisory committee on Quetico Park file.

60 *Thunder Bay News Chronicle*, 8 October 1970.

61 Legislative Assembly of Ontario, *Debates*, 6 October 1970, 4670; 7 October 1970, 4732–33; 14 October 1970, 4966; see also OA, RG–1, IA–7, box 11, file 27–0403, transcript of CBC's "Provincial Affairs," 28 October 1970.

62 OA, RG–1, IA–7, box 15, file 27–0403–10, Brunelle to S.G. Hancock, chairman, Quetico Advisory Committee, 28 October 1970, and comments re management of resources of Quetico Provincial Park, by Peter Addison, chief, Parks Branch, 26 October 1970.

63 OA, RG–1, IA–7, box 10, file 27–0403, transcript of PDQ meeting, St. Lawrence Centre, 3 November 1970. All quotations from this source.

64 Legislative Assembly of Ontario, *Debates*, 5 November 1970, 6025–26. For transcripts of the CKEY radio discussions see OA, RG–1, IA–7, box 10, file 27–0403. The information on the number of letters received is contained in ibid., box 15, file 27–0403–10, Addison to S.G. Hancock, 17 November 1970.

65 OA, RG–1, IA–7, box 15, file 27–0403–10, Brunelle to Hancock, 12 November 1970.

66 Legislative Assembly of Ontario, *Debates*, 13 November 1970, 6502–3.

67 OA, RG–1, IA–7, box 10, file 27–0403, Ontario Federation of Labour (OFL), "Statement on Environment, Conservation and Pollution Control," December 1970.

68 OA, RG–1, IA–7, box 16, file 27–0403–20, Keenan to Bayly, 27 November 1970.

69 The transcripts of the hearings are contained in *Public Hearings by and Briefs to the Quetico Provincial Park Advisory Committee* (1971), vol. 1. The written briefs submitted to the advisory committee are contained in volume 2.

70 OA, RG–1, A–1–8, box 66, minister's advisory committee on Quetico Provincial Park file, Hancock to Brunelle, 11 May 1971.

71 Ibid., box 90, minister's Quetico file, Brunelle to Bayly, 30 March 1971.

72 Toronto *Globe and Mail*, 8 May 1971.

73 OA, RG–1, A–1–8, box 66, minister's advisory committee on Quetico Provincial Park file, Hancock to Brunelle, 11 May 1971.

74 OA, RG–1, IA–7, accession no. 14604, schedule no. 188, temporary box 13, press release by Gavin Henderson, executive director, NPPAC, 13 May 1971.

75 *Algonquin Provincial Park Advisory Committee Report. Government Policy*, 14.

76 *Toronto Telegram*, 15 May 1971. For Howard's critical assessment of his experience on the advisory committee, see Richard B. Howard, "Algonquin: A Park Perspective," *Ontario Naturalist* 14, no. 2 (June 1974), 13–17.

77 *Toronto Telegram*, 15 May 1971.

78 OA, RG–1, IA–7, accession no. 14604, schedule no. 188, temporary box 20, file 27–1501–10, press release by Gavin Henderson, executive director, NPPAC, 14 May 1971.

79 Ibid., file 27–1501–20, "Terms of Reference for a Study of the Socio-economic Implications of Proposed Policy for Algonquin Park," 7 September 1971.

80 Claire Hoy, *Bill Davis* (Toronto: Methuen, 1985), 89.

81 OA, RG–1, IA–5, box 1, file 13–2–3, Patrick Hardy, managing director, Canadian Audubon Society, to Kelso Roberts, 28 November 1962; and Roberts to Hardy, 14 December 1962; see this file for full documentation.

82 OA, RG–1, A–1–8, box 4, minister's National Parks file, A. Kelso Roberts to John P. Robarts, 31 May 1965.

83 Legislative Assembly of Ontario, *Debates*, 21 March 1966, 1745. Here Roberts states that he did not favour national parks; ibid., 15 May 1967, 3427, for Brunelle on the same subject.

84 OA, RG–1, A–1–8, box 80, minister's National Parks file, Remarks by Jean Chretien, signing ceremony creating Pukaskwa National Park, 13 July 1971.

85 PB, policy box, "Proposed Policy on National Parks in Ontario" (a discussion paper for the Outdoor Recreation Program Sub-Committee, 14 December 1974) by J.W. Keenan; and "Summary of Comments on the Proposed Policy on National Parks in Ontario" by G.M. Moroz, 30 January 1973.

86 See, for example, OA, RG–1, A–1–8, box 9, minister's Sandbanks file, statement by Gavin Henderson, executive director, NPPAC, 2 October 1971.

87 *Report of the Quetico Provincial Park Advisory Committee* (26 May 1972), sec. 6.1; and Legislative Assembly of Ontario, *Debates*, 21 June 1973, 3613.

88 PB, Policy Field submission, submission to Resources Development Policy Field Committee re policy and management framework for Algonquin Provincial Park, 26 March 1973.

89 *Algonquin Provincial Park Advisory Committee Report. Government Policy*, Statement by Leo Bernier, 17 July 1973, 4–8.

90 Policy Field (see note 88 above). The two other options considered and rejected were based on making 70 percent and 60 percent of the park available to logging, with direct job losses of 650 and 875 respectively.

91 *Algonquin Provincial Park Advisory Committee Report. Government Policy*, "Minority Report," by G.D. Garland, 17–18; see also *Algonquin Park: A Park for People*, Recommended to the Honourable René Brunelle, minister of lands and forests by the Algonquin Park Leaseholders Association, December 1969.

92 OA, RG–1, IA–7, accession no. 14604, schedule no. 188, temporary box 15, file 27–1501, Brunelle to A.A. Wishart, minister, Financial and Commercial Affairs, 15 June 1971; see LR–185215, T.W. Hueston to J.W. Keenan, 15 September 1972, for the problems created by leaseholders for park administrators; and A.B.R. Lawrence, provincial secretary for resources development, to Premier W.G. Davis, 26 October 1973.

93 *Wilderness Now* (see note 50 above), 3rd rev. ed. (1980), 30.

94 Legislative Assembly of Ontario, *Debates*, 12 October 1973, 4230. For R.F. Nixon, see 4224–27.

95 *Wildland News* 7, no. 3 (November 1974), 7.

96 Legislative Assembly of Ontario, *Debates*, 24 June 1974, 3561.

97 Ibid., 21 November 1974, 5523.

98 OA, RG–1, IB, accession no. 14300, schedule no. 1098, temporary box 8, file 27–1501, J.W. Lockwood, executive director, Division of Forests to D. Helliwell, Division of Parks, 14 November 1974.

99 *Quetico Newsletter* 20, no. 2 (Fall 1974).

100 Bruce Litteljohn, "Algonquin Park: Call It What It Is, or Make It What You Call It," *Ontario Naturalist* 16, no. 1 (February 1976), 16–19; Patrick Hardy, "The Disgrace of Algonquin Park," *The Living Wilderness* (October–December 1978), 42–43.

101 Legislative Assembly of Ontario, *Debates*, 25 November 1974, 5663. Initially, the AFA was little more than a glorified logging company. Not until 1983 did it assume responsibility for forest management. Subsequently, the MNR's role became one of auditing the timber management done by the authority.

102 OA, RG–1, IB, accession no. 14300, schedule no. 1096, temporary box 1, file 11–1–1, Keenan to Bernier, 9 April 1974.

103 OA, RG–1, IB–1, accession no. 13103, schedule no. 203, temporary box 1, file 11–1–1, "Part 1: A Philosophical Overview," 23 January 1973, by G. Moroz; OA, RG–1, IB–3, accession no. 13103, schedule no. 200, temporary box 5, file 25–37, "Primitive and Wild River Parks in Ontario," FON Annual Meeting Workshop on Parks, 27 April 1973 by J.W. Keenan.

104 See OA, RG–1, IB–3, box 18, file 25–33 for the Advisory Committee on Nature Reserves.

105 Statement [in the Legislature] by the Honourable Leo Bernier, minister of natural resources concerning Ontario provincial parks, 22 October 1974.

106 PPAC files (author's copy), "The Planning and Policy-Making Process for Lake Superior Provincial Park," 30 November 1976.

107 OA, RG–1, IA–4, box 3, file 8–1, memo, A.J. Herridge, executive director, Resource Products Division to regional directors/district foresters, etc., 29 July 1971.

Chapter Six

1 Legislative Assembly of Ontario, *Debates*, 19 March 1970, 915; see also Norman Pearson, "Recreational Planning in a Developing Region," address to OFAH, 20 February 1970.

2 Port Colborne *Evening Tribune*, 29 July 1968.

3 OA, RG–1, IB–2, box 3, file 18–4, P. Hardy to Premier W. Davis, 3 November 1971; ibid., IB–4, accession no. 13103, schedule no. 201, temporary box 7, file 26–12–15, P. Hardy to Leo Bernier, 6 December 1973.

4 *Ontario Provincial Parks Statistics 1985* (MNR 1986), Statistical Comparison 1965–1985, 5. The decline in visitor numbers after 1971 can also be explained in part by short-term dislocations, specifically, increases in entrance fees in 1972 and 1978, and cool, wet weather conditions, such as occurred in northern Ontario in 1973. For a perceptive analysis of declining visitation, see John S. Marsh, "Ontario Provincial Parks: Visitation,

Activities and Attitudes," *Environments* 14, no. 1, 1982, 11–17.

5 OA, RG–1, IA–2, box 8, file 1–2–7, Addison to G.H.U. Bayly, 19 August 1969.

6 OA, RG–1, IB–1, accession no. 13103, schedule no. 203, temporary box 1, file 11–3, "Parks and Recreation Areas: Present System Inadequate to Provide for Public Needs," 1972.

7 Legislative Assembly of Ontario, *Debates*, 11 May 1971, 1476–77.

8 John G. Mitchell, "The Re-Greening of Urban America," *Audubon* 80, no. 2 (March 1978), 29–52.

9 R.J. Vrancart, "Towards an Outdoor Recreation Policy for Ontario: Phase 1 – Recreation Supplied on Provincially Operated Facilities," Division of Parks, Ontario MNR, Toronto, 1972.

10 OA, RG–1, IB–1, accession no. 13103, schedule no. 203, temporary box 6, file 11–32–1, memo, J.W. Keenan to A.J. Herridge, "Near Urban Outdoor Recreation," 6 September 1974.

11 Ibid; see also OA, RG–1, IB, accession no. 14300, schedule no. 1096, temporary box 2, file 11–1–2, submission to Cabinet Committee on Resources Development re Near Urban Outdoor Recreation, 30 September 1974.

12 OA, RG–1, IB–1, box 8, file 11–30–3, Irvine to Keenan, 4 March 1969.

13 OA, RG–1, IB–2, box 5, file 18–5, press release, DLF, re Niagara Escarpment land acquired for recreation, 15 April 1971.

14 PB, file (WASBC), "Wasaga Beach Acquisition History Summary, Beach and Backlands (1963–75)," and "Outline of Plans for Wasaga Beach (1963–1974)."

15 See note 11 above.

16 *London Free Press*, 15 May 1971; see also Jonathan Manthorpe, *The Power and the Tories: Ontario Politics – 1943 to the Present* (Toronto: Macmillan, 1974), 142–43. Ironically, Gertler reviewed the government's land acquisition record in May 1971 and was far less pessimistic than the press and the opposition; see OA, RG–1, IB–2, box 5, file 18–5, draft of L.O. Gertler, "The Niagara Escarpment Study: Implementation of a Resources Strategy," a paper presented to the Canadian Association of Geographers, 28 May 1971.

17 Legislative Assembly of Ontario, *Debates*, 13 May 1971, 1541, 1545–49.

18 PB, file (WASBC), René Brunelle to Peter Addison, 14 August 1970.

19 Toronto *Globe and Mail*, 29 June 1971.

20 OA, RG–1, IB–2, box 5, file 18–5, statement by William Davis ... 13 September 1971.

21 Toronto *Globe and Mail*, 29 September 1971.

22 OA, RG–1, IC, temporary box 1, accession no. 14195, OPIB Bronte Creek file, C.R. Tilt to D.W. Brown, secretary, Oakville–Trafalgar–Bronte Planning Board, 10 June 1960.

23 Ibid., "Bronte Creek Park Proposal," by R.J. Irvine, 13 August 1971.

24 Ibid., "Statement by the Hon. William Davis ... Announcing Development of Bronte Creek Provincial Park," 8 October 1971.

25 PB, file MO–1–M, minister's briefing notes, 13 December 1976.

26 *The Proposed Plan for the Niagara Escarpment* (Niagara Escarpment Commission, November 1979); *The Niagara Escarpment Plan*. 3 vols. (Provincial Secretariat for Resources Development, July 1984).

27 Ron Reid, "Earthwatch," *Seasons* 25, no. 2 (Summer 1985), 6.

28 OA, RG–1, IB–3, box 5, file 25–07–0, memo, Lee and Sealey, "Fathom Five Provincial Park: A Proposal," June 1970; see also OPIB, Minutes, 12 May 1971.

29 OA, RG–1, IB–4, accession no. 13103, schedule no. 201, temporary box 5, file 26–07–10, memo, T. Lee, "Fathom Five Underwater Park," 20 November 1973; see also PB, file MO–2 (II), for the international correspondence.

30 PB, MNR annual land acquisition summary sheets (1971–75).

31 Wasaga Beach Provincial Park Master Plan Draft Copy (November 1975).

32 OA, RG–1, IB, accession no. 14300, schedule no. 1098, temporary box 8, file 27–1208–20, FON submission on Wasaga Beach P. P. Preliminary Master Plan, 16 January 1975.

33 PB, Policy Field Submissions file, submission to Cabinet Committee on Resources Development, 29 June 1973.

34 *Bronte Creek Provincial Park Policy Recommendations Report*, prepared by Bronte Creek Provincial Park Advisory Committee for minister of lands and forests, Province of Ontario (March 1972).

35 OA, RG–1, AA–2, box 14, deputy minister's files, "Parks and Recreation Administration," J.W. Keenan to director, Personnel Branch, 7 September 1973.

36 For McKeough's role see OA, RG–1, IB–4, accession no. 13103, schedule no. 201, temporary box 1, file 26–01–75, Walter Q. MacNee to Leo Bernier, 6 March 1972.

37 OA, RG–1, IB–4, box 1, file 26–01–04, "Notes for Mr. Brunelle's Speech, Windsor, 21 June 1971," signed P. Addison, 14 June 1971.

38 OA, RG–1, IB–4, box 2, file 25–01–7, "The Peach [sic] Island Report. Potential for Outdoor Recreation," 9 August 1971; see also OA, RG–1, IC, temporary box 6, accession no. 14195, OPIB, Pêche Island file, report to OPIB, 17 December 1971.

39 OA, RG–1, IB–3, box 3, file 25–01–31, "A Proposal for the Establishment of a Wilderness Park Straddling the Thames River Between the Kilworth and Komoka Bridges, Delaware and Lobo Townships, Middlesex County, Ontario."

Prepared for the Central Middlesex Planning Board, June 1964 by Associate Professor Osmund Langtvet, Department of Geography, University of Western Ontario.

40 OA, RG–1, IB–3, accession no. 13103, schedule no. 200, temporary box 4, file 25–01–0, statement by Bernier, London, Ont., 14 January 1974.

41 OA, RG–1, IB–4, accession no. 13103, schedule no. 201, temporary box 8, file 23–31, Keenan to T. Lee, 29 January 1974.

42 *Short Hills Provincial Park Policy Recommendations Report*, Short Hills Provincial Park Advisory Committee (July 1974).

43 *Short Hills Provincial Park Master Plan* (Ontario MNR 1977); see also Clark W. Thomson, "Short Hills Provincial Park – An Evaluation," *Park News* 13 (November 1977), 31–36.

44 OA, RG–1, IB–1, accession no. 13103, schedule no. 203, temporary box 6, file 11–32–1, Keenan to A.J. Herridge, 6 September 1974.

45 Submission to Cabinet Committee on Resources Development, re Near Urban Outdoor Recreation, 30 September 1974.

46 OA, RG–1, IB–1, accession no. 13103, schedule no. 203, temporary box 6, file 11–32–1, W.T. Foster to A.J. Herridge, August 1974, J.W. Giles to Herridge, 12 August 1974; see also PB, file MO–2 (I), submission by the Ontario Parks Association Concerning "Near Urban Parks" ... June 1976; file MO–3–L, John Marsh to R.J. Vrancart, 10 May 1978.

47 PB, Multi-Year Plan file, Premier William G. Davis to Leo Bernier, 19 June 1973.

48 OA, RG–1, IA–7, box 17, file 27–0702, P. Addison to G.H.U. Bayly, 27 November 1969.

49 OA, RG–1, AA–2, box 14, deputy minister's files, Parks Division (1973) file, memo, "Inverhuron Park – Chronological Summary." See Legislative Assembly of Ontario, *Debates*, 7 June 1973, 2785.

50 Toronto *Globe and Mail*, 25 June 1973. For NDP criticism, see Legislative Assembly of Ontario, *Debates*, 30 October 1973, S–2274.

51 OPIB, Minutes 20 June 1967; see also OA, RG–1, IA–2, box 4, file 1–1–5, news release, Department of Forestry and Rural Development, Ottawa, 27 October 1967.

52 PB, Operations, CORTS file, cabinet submission, "The Canada-Ontario Rideau-Trent-Severn Study (CORTS)," draft 25 April 1974; see also PB, file MO–3–CL, copy of *CORTS Canada-Ontario Rideau-Trent-Severn Interim Land Use Guidelines* (Peterborough: CORTS Agreement Board, December 1977).

53 OA, RG–1, IB–4, box 14, file 26–21–4, Report to OPIB, 5 December 1967; see also OPIB, Minutes, 18 December 1967.

54 PB, file 11–1, cabinet submission, "Provincial Park Land Acquisition Proposals for Southern Ontario," 25 October 1973 (approved 6 December 1973).

55 OA, RG–1, IB–2, accession no. 13103, schedule no. 202, temporary box 1, file 18–4, "Proposed Policy on Recreation Trails in Ontario," 16 February 1973.

56 R.W. Butler, "The Development of Snowmobiles in Canada," in Geoffrey Wall and John S. Marsh (eds.), *Recreational Land Use: Perspectives on its Evolution in Canada*, Carleton Library Series no. 126 (Ottawa: Carleton University Press, 1982), 365–90.

57 OA, RG–1, IA–2, box 5, file 1–2, D.R. Wilson to K. Acheson, 19 December 1966.

58 OA, RG–1, IA–2, box 8, file 1–2–5, copy of press release "Snowmobiles in Provincial Parks," 9 February 1968.

59 DLF *Newsletter* 24, no. 37 (1971). By 1977, the MNR had prohibited snowmobiles in eighteen provincial parks and all Nature Reserves, but permitted use of them on the roads in seventy-six parks, and on designated areas or marked trails in sixteen others.

60 OA, RG–1, IA–2, box 8, file 1–2–5, P. Addison to R. Brunelle, 17 September 1970.

61 Annual Report, MNR 1977.

62 OA, RG–1, IB–2, box 3, file 18–4, J.W.B. Sisam to Premier W. Davis, 7 October 1971; and P. Hardy to Davis, 3 November 1971.

63 OA, RG–1, IB–2, accession no. 13103, schedule no. 202, temporary box 1, file 18–4, R.J. Irvine, "Proposed Policy on Recreation Trails in Ontario," 16 February 1973.

64 PB, Policy Field Submission file, "Submission to Cabinet Committee on Resources Development, Ontario Trails Programme," 18 June 1974.

65 "First Ontario Trails Symposium Proceedings, Queen's Park, 27 June 1973," 7.

66 *Ontario Trails Council Final Report* (Ontario: MNR, 1977).

67 PB, file MO–8 (general), draft cabinet submission, "Ontario Trails Policy and Program: A New Proposal," 6 February 1979.

68 *Property Protection and Outdoor Opportunities: A Guide to The Occupiers' Liability Act, 1980 and The Trespass to Property Act, 1980* (Queen's Printer: Ministry of the Attorney General, n.d.).

69 Rea, *Prosperous Years*, 235 (see chapter 3 above, note 1).

70 PB, Multi-Year Plan file, J.W. Keenan to A.J. Herridge, 25 June 1973.

71 OA, RG–1, AA–2, box 14, deputy minister's files, "Parks, Division of," file 1973, Keenan to Walter Q. MacNee, 19 February 1973 (confidential).

72 Hoy, *Bill Davis*, 210–13 (see chapter 5 above, note 80); Rosemary Speirs, *Out of the Blue: The Fall of the Tory Dynasty in Ontario* (Toronto: Macmillan, 1986), 7.

73 Rea, *Prosperous Years*, 234 (see chapter 3 above, note 1).

74 Hoy, *Bill Davis*, 211–12 (see chapter 5 above, note 80).

75 Data compiled from Ontario Public Accounts and PB records by Syd Girling (Girling to author, 10 February 1981).

76 *London Free Press*, 16 July 1988.

77 PB, file MO–1 (II), "Implementation Plan, Recreation Areas Activity, $4.4 million Cut in Park Capital Budget for 1977–78," 15 December 1976.

78 The Ontario Provincial Parks Council, *Second Annual Report* (Toronto: MNR, 1976), 5–6. In 1975–76, park users contributed only 40 percent of park operating and maintenance costs.

79 PB, file MO–3–CL, T.W. Hueston to R.J. Vrancart, 19 July 1976.

80 PB, Cabinet Minutes file, M. Mogford to A.J. Herridge, 27 April 1976.

81 PB, file MO–3–L, Federal and Provincial Parks Conference (FPPC), W. Robertson, "Privatization Experiences in Ontario Provincial Parks: A Paper Presented to the Federal-Provincial Parks Conference in Victoria, B.C.," September 1978.

82 Ibid., Appendix I, "Reprivatization of Public Services," January 1976.

83 PB, file SAND–2, FON submission on Sandbanks P. P. Preliminary Master Plan, 1977. The bulk of this submission pertained to the privatization of campgrounds.

84 Toronto *Globe and Mail*, 9 and 10 December 1976.

85 Author's PPAC records, copy of telegram to Bernier, 10 December 1976; see also Toronto *Globe and Mail*, 15 December 1976.

86 PB, file MO–O, Vrancart to Eckel, 14 December 1976.

87 PB, file MO–3–P (Parks Policy), handwritten memo, "Why can't the 3740 additional campsites needed by 1991 be provided by the private sector?" 14 November 1977.

88 Legislative Assembly of Ontario, *Debates*, 9 December 1976, 5505–6.

89 "Alternative Methods for Securing Parkland," A Report Prepared by the Division of Parks ... August, 1977, Appendix 1 of *Role of the Federal and Provincial Parks*. Proceedings of 16th Federal-Provincial Parks Conference ... 3–7 October 1977 (St. John's, Newfoundland: Department of Tourism, 1978); see also PB, file MO–2, "Private Donations for Provincial Parks. Draft Policy Proposal 28 October 1977."

90 PB, file MO–3 (I), Leo Bernier to A.B.R. Lawrence, chairman, Ontario Heritage Foundation (OHF), 2 July 1976; see also *Preserving Ontario's Natural Heritage: Background Information*, prepared for board members, Ontario Heritage Foundation by Ontario MNR, Division of Parks, Parks Planning Branch, January 1977.

Chapter Seven

1 The first of the new recruits arrived at head office in 1967. They included Tom E. Lee and Russell J. Irvine, both of whom possessed M.Sc.s in Parks and Recreation Management from the University of Illinois. They share the distinction of being the first professionally trained parks planners in the DLF. Between 1967 and 1974 historians Gary Sealey, Robert Bowes, and Brian Wolsley joined the branch, as well as landscape architects Ismet Olcay and Garrett Pittinger, biologists Harold Gibbard and Thomas Beechey, geomorphologist George Tracey, geologist Robert Davidson, economist Richard Kirsch, and parks and recreation resource planners Norman Richards, William Sargant, and Ronald Vrancart. Richards had a B.A. in Geography (University of Toronto) and a M.Sc. in Parks and Recreation Resources (Michigan State). Sargant's degrees were in Sociology (B.A., Guelph) and Recreation Resource Development (M.Sc., Guelph). Vrancart held a B.A. in Geography (University of Western Ontario) and a M.Phil. in Town Planning from the University of London, England. The first Ph.D. to join the Division, Don Hallman, was a geographer who specialized in statistical modelling and system planning. In contrast to the period before 1967, foresters were now in the minority. They included Jim Keenan, John Bell, and Robert Mitton, all planners, and George Ashenden and Robert Hambly in the management section.

2 OA, RG–1, IB–1, box 8, file 11–30–3, Keenan to D.H. Hanlan, 23 June 1970.

3 Communication to author from J. Keenan, 20 February 1989.

4 PB, file MO–2, "Progress Report – Master Planning Ontario Provincial Parks," Norm R. Richards, 2 July 1976. As we have seen, during the 1970s, for parks which posed special problems (such as Algonquin, Quetico, Bronte, and Rondeau), advisory committees were also added to the process. To assist the division in handling the backlog in master planning, consulting firms were also occasionally engaged. In 1972, for instance, consultants were hired to draft provisional master plans for Bronte Creek, Credit Forks, Duclos Point, Fathom Five, and Pêche Island.

5 *Statutes of Ontario*, 1976, c. 371; see also Legislative Assembly of Ontario, *Debates*, 8 June 1976, 3284. The amendments to the act did not satisfy environmentalists, who argued that master plans still lacked sufficient legal standing. The plans could be changed by bureaucratic or political decree without public review or legislative debate; see David Estrin and John Swaigen, *Environment on Trial* (Toronto: Canadian Environmental Law Association and the Macmillan Co., 1974), and John Swaigen, "Does Ontario Need a New Provincial Parks Act?" *Environments* 14, no. 1 (1982), 57–59.

6 *Effective Management through PPBS* (Treasury

Board of the Province of Ontario, Toronto, October 1969).

7 Premier Davis took this step on the advice of the Committee on Government Productivity (COGP), appointed in December 1969 by Premier Robarts. The committee concluded that insufficient horizontal coordination and planning existed between departments with related or overlapping responsibilities.

8 OA, RG–1, IB–1, box 6, file 11–30, "The Growing Gap in the Tourist Balance of Payments and Possibilities for Control," included in J.A.C. Auld to René Brunelle, 11 August 1970.

9 Ibid., P. Addison to G.H.U. Bayly, 11 September 1970.

10 Legislative Assembly of Ontario, *Debates,* 4 May 1972, 2012.

11 PB, policy box, D. Hallman, "Evolution of Provincial Parks Policy in Ontario," October 1976.

12 R. Vrancart and G. Moroz, "Establishing Investment Priorities Park Systems Planning in Ontario: A Case Study," presented to Federal-Provincial Parks Conference, Victoria, B.C., 26 September 1978.

13 "Report of the Park Systems Planning Committee," in *Tourism and Parks,* 12th Federal-Provincial Parks Conference, Ottawa, 17–21 September 1973 (Ottawa: Parks Canada), 66–85.

14 W.J. Hart, *A Systems Approach to Parks Planning.* Supplemental Paper, no. 4, International Union for the Conservation of Nature and Natural Resources, Morges, Switzerland, 1966. For Hart's influence, see OA, RG–1, IB–1, accession no. 13103, schedule no. 203, temporary box 1, file 11–1, R.J. Irvine, "The Concept of a Parks System," 7 April 1972; and OA, RG–1, IB–4, accession no. 13103, schedule no. 201, temporary box 8, file 26–31, R.L. Mitton, "Guidelines for Recommending Lands for Acquisition for the Provincial Parks System," 19 November 1973.

15 D.M. Simkin, "Brief Progress Report on Ontario Tourism and Outdoor Recreation Plan Study, June 1974," *Recreation Review* 4, no. 1 (September 1974), 43; PB, file MO–1, Dan Ross, "TORPS – Where We Are and a Peek at Where We Want to Go," May 1977.

16 PB, file MO–1, "Ontario Recreation Survey Progress Report," no. 2: May–October 1973, TORPS Committee, Queen's Park, Toronto, September 1974, 2.

17 Robert Douglas Irvine, "Planning Provincial Park Systems in Ontario: An Overview" (M.Sc., Cornell, 1975), 78; see also PB, file MO–3–POL, R.L. Mitton to R.J. Vrancart, 30 May 1977, for a discussion of the failure of TORPS to produce an overall policy for outdoor recreation in Ontario.

18 For the FON's role, see OA, RG–1, IB–3, box 18, file 25–33 (60–1–10), "Practical Considerations for the Establishment of a System of Nature Reserves – A Memorandum for Discussion," by J. Bruce Falls, Parks and Reserves Committee, FON, 21 November 1966; and file memo, re "Wilderness Areas Committee," 6 September 1967.

19 OA, RG–1, IB–3, box 18, file 25–33, "Minister's Speech to the Advisory Committee on Nature Reserves," 7 March 1969.

20 OA, RG–1, IB–3, box 18, file 25–33, "A Submission to the Minister of Lands and Forests from the Advisory Committee on Nature Reserves," 15 December 1969.

21 PB, file 10–1, "Nature Reserves – Goal Statement," n.d. (ca. 1973).

22 OA, RG–1, IB–3, box 18, file 25–33, "The Status of the Nature Reserves Programme," 29 October 1970.

23 T.J. Beechey, "A Framework for the Conservation of Ontario's Biological Heritage," draft for discussion May 1980, 172.

24 Administrative Policies of the Ontario Provincial Parks System in Ontario, preliminary draft (Division of Parks, MNR, 1975), 21–23.

25 Beechey, "Framework," 19 (see note 23 above).

26 PB, Multi-Year Plan file, memo, H.J. Gibbard to T.E. Lee, 7 May 1974.

27 Beechey, "Framework," 20 (see note 23 above).

28 Administrative Policies, Nature Reserves, preliminary draft 1975, 11.

29 J. Bruce Falls, "The Importance of Wilderness to Science," *Ontario Naturalist* 5, no. 4 (December 1967), 18.

30 Beechey, "Framework," 257 (see note 23 above).

31 R.J. Davidson, "Earth Science Framework," working copy, second draft, 1981, 7.

32 Ibid., 8, and Beechey, "Framework," 260 (see note 23 above). These two sources provide the best overview of the nature reserve programs in other jurisdictions up to 1980.

33 Davidson, "Earth Science," 10 (see chapter 7 above, note 31). For the Nature Conservancy of Canada, see A.K. Stuart "Remarks," in *Towards Natural Heritage Protection in Ontario: Conference Proceedings, November 23, 1982* (OHF, 1983), 17–21.

34 "A Provincial Parks Policy for Ontario: Preliminary Draft," Systems Planning Section, Park Planning Branch, 17 May 1976, 39.

35 For documentation on Ouimet Canyon, see LR–186279.

36 OA, RG–1, IB–4, box 7, file 26–11–6, P. Addison to Willow Beach Field Naturalists, Cobourg, 28 April 1971.

37 For documentation on Ojibway Prairie, see OA, RG–1, IB–4, box 3, file 26–01–8, Maycock to Gibbard, 16 April 1970; and MNR press release, 26 October 1973.

38 OA, RG–1, IB–4, box 3, file 26–01–8, Keenan to W.H. Charlton, regional director, 27 November 1974.

39 OA, RG–1, IB, accession no. 14300, schedule no. 1098, temporary box 16, file WINDP–5, "Summary of Windsor Prairie Task Force Meeting," Windsor, 20–21 January 1975; T.E. Lee to Nature Conservancy of Canada, 27 May 1975; copy of SE.054 form, Planning and Management Agreement with City of Windsor, June 1975.

40 OA, RG–1, IB–1, box 6, file 11–30, "History: Inventory, Appraising and Developing a Park Resource," by Gary Sealey, n.d. (ca. 1969).

41 OA, RG–1, IB–4, box 7, file 26–11–9, Kenneth Kidd to J.W. Keenan, 15 September 1971; see this file for documentation on Petroglyphs Provincial Park.

42 OA, RG–1, IB–1, box 2, file 11–1–1, Addison to Keenan, 8 December 1969; and Keenan to Addison, 5 December 1969.

43 *Statutes of Ontario,* 1972, c. 6. Most provisions of the Provincial Parks Act applied to Historical parks.

44 PB, file MO–1, "Historical Resources and The Provincial Parks and Recreation Areas System: Transfer of Historical Sites Branch to Ministry of Culture and Recreation," A. Usher, 10 January 1975.

45 Gerald Killan, "History in Ontario's Provincial Parks: A System in Crisis?" *Environments* 14, no. 1, 1982, 1; see also Ontario Provincial Parks Council, *First Annual Report 1975*, 19.

46 Parks Council, *Report 1975*; 19. OA, RG–1, IB, accession no. 14300, schedule no. 1096, temporary box 10, file MO–3–POL, Stephen Otto, executive coordinator, Heritage Conservation Division, MCR, to James Keenan, 25 June 1975; author's Parks Council records, NPPAC, "Brief Presented to the Provincial Parks (Advisory) Council, ... Regarding Proposed Provincial Parks Classification and Atikaki Wilderness Park Proposal," 20 October 1975.

47 Quote from Tom Lee's presentation on the new classification system to the Parks Council, 6 March 1975.

48 PB, file MO–1, Bowes to R.H. Hambly, 9 February 1977.

49 Letter to author from R.G. Bowes, 15 November 1977.

50 Parks Council, *Third Annual Report 1977*, 9.

51 Ed McKenna, *A Systematic Approach to the History of the Forest Industry in Algonquin Park, 1835–1913; with an Evaluation of Algonquin Park's Historical Resources and an assessment of Algonquin Park's historical zone system* (Toronto: Ontario Ministry of Culture and Recreation, Historical Planning and Research Branch, 1976); Ray Thompson, *Varieties of History in Algonquin Park: A Proposal for the Creation of Historical Zones in Algonquin Park* (Toronto: Ontario Ministry of Culture and Recreation, Historical Planning and Research Branch, 1977).

52 PB, file MO–3–COS, Eckel to H. Mattson, 9 May 1977.

53 *Ontario Provincial Parks. Statistics 1985* (Ontario: Ministry of Natural Resources, 1986). All data are from this source.

54 Gary Sealey, "Interpretation: (What is it?)" March, 1971 (mimeographed instruction sheets distributed to seasonal staff in 1971).

55 OA, RG–1, IB, accession no. 14300, schedule no. 1096, temporary box 9, file MO–1, "Rowdyism and Violence in Provincial Parks," 1975.

56 PPAC records, Warren Robertson, "Rowdyism in Ontario Provincial Parks," a discussion paper presented to the FPPC Central Region at Toronto, Ontario, 11 September 1974.

57 OA, RG–1, IA–7, box 3, file 27–0106, Keenan to Peter Addison, 7 August 1970.

58 OA, RG–1, IA–7, accession no. 14604, schedule no. 188, temporary box 13, file 27–0106, Clark to R.D. Carman, regional director, 7 July 1971.

59 "Rowdyism and Violence," 1975 (see note 55 above).

60 OA, RG–1, IA–2, box 14, "Parks Management Branch" file, R.C. Hambly, "Report on Rowdyism in Provincial Parks – 1973," 21 June 1973.

61 "Rowdyism and Violence," 1975 (see note 55 above). For a literature review, see P. White, G. Wall, and G. Priddle, "Anti-Social Behaviour in Ontario Provincial Parks," *Recreation Research Review* 6, no. 2 (May 1978), 13–23.

62 OA, RG–1, IA–7, accession no. 14604, schedule no. 188, temporary box 13, file 27–0106–4, R.L. Mitton, report on "Teen-Twenty Youth Program – Pinery Park," 19 July 1971.

63 Robertson, "Rowdyism" (see note 56 above).

64 OA, RG–1, A–1–8, box 85, minister's file, "Parks," W.E. Thomson to René Brunelle, 10 August 1971.

65 PB, file MO–2, "Annual Report Provincial Park Visitor Services Programme 1975–76."

66 PB, file MO–2, Wayne Yetman, "Recreation Programmes in Provincial Parks – A Discussion Paper," 1978.

67 PB, file MO–2, Provincial Park Visitor Services Policy Programme, Interim Policy, 1976.

68 PB, file MO–2, "Annual Report Provincial Park Visitor Services Programme 1976–1977."

69 The 1975 policy formed the basis of a revised Visitor Services Policy issued 1 May 1987, entitled "Parks and Recreational Areas. VISITOR SERVICES: Planning and Programming Guidelines." The components of the visitor services program are now information, interpretation, and outdoor recreation. Currently there are five levels of service offered in parks throughout the system – Basic, Self-use, Recreational, Seasonal Activity, and Major Activity. In 1987, there were fourteen parks offering major activities and twenty-six parks providing seasonal activities, most of which were Natural Environment parks.

70 *Provincial Waterways in Ontario: Recreational Rivers, Wild Rivers, Historic Rivers,* Administrative

Policies of the Ontario Provincial Parks System (Division of Parks, Ministry of Natural Resources, 1975). This original preliminary administrative policy booklet proposed three distinct types of Provincial Waterways: Recreational Rivers, Wild Rivers, and Historic Rivers. The revised booklet (8 April 1976) called for one type of water-related park, a Provincial Waterway Park, with zoning to serve as the basis for differentiating between and managing specific recreational, historic, and scenic resources within this park class.

71 The classification scheme of 1967 had provided for five zones: Primitive, Natural, Historic, Multiple Use, and Recreation. The Multiple Use zone was dropped, since it applied only to zones in Algonquin and Lake Superior parks. The more accurate term, "Recreation utilization zone" was used in the master plans for those parks. Two new zones – natural environment and access – were added in the classification booklets. Primitive, natural, historic, and recreation zones were renamed wilderness, nature reserve, historical, and development zones respectively.

72 *Wilderness Areas in Ontario,* Administrative Policies of the Ontario Provincial Parks System (Division of Parks, MNR, 1975), 34–35.

73 CCO, "Presentation on the Proposed Parks Classification System from the Conservation Council of Ontario to the Provincial Parks Council and the Ministry of Natural Resources," 22 July 1975; NPPAC, "Brief Presented to the Provincial Parks (Advisory) Council ... Regarding Proposed Provincial Park Classification and Atikaki Wilderness Park Proposal," 20 October 1975.

74 *A Provincial Parks Policy for Ontario. Preliminary Draft* (Systems Planning Section, Park Planning Branch, 17 May 1976), 46.

75 *Wilderness Identification and Evaluation Project. Summary Report*, Park Planning Branch, 1978.

76 *Policy Draft* (1976), 47 (see note 74 above).

77 Ibid., 50, 52; see also PB, file MO–3–REL, copy of "Waterway Planning," paper delivered to Water-Based Recreation Conference, 11 November 1978, n.a.

78 PB, Ron Vrancart, "Towards an Outdoor Recreation Policy for Ontario – Phase 1 (1972)," report prepared for the OPIB.

79 *Recreation Parks in Ontario,* Administrative Policies of the Ontario Provincial Parks System (Division of Parks, MNR, 1975, 16–17.

80 *Policy Draft* (1976), 57, 61 (see note 74 above). In the original administrative policy booklet for Recreation Parks, the levels of supply figures were calculated by using the mean averages for southern population regions only, and included supply data provided by conservation authorities, park commissions, and access points. Thus the mean supply figures were higher (2.22 for day visits and 1.18 for camper days).

81 *Recreation Parks* 1975, 34 (see note 79 above).

82 Vrancart and Moroz, "Investment Priorities," 83 (see note 12 above).

83 OA, RG–1, IB, accession no. 14300, schedule no. 1096, temporary box 10, file MO–3–POL, L.R.L. Symmes, chairman, Sierra Club of Ontario, to Leo Bernier, 20 October 1975.

84 CCO, "Presentation to the Provincial Parks Council," 22 July 1975.

85 NPPAC, "Brief to Provincial Parks Council," 20 October 1975.

86 The *Policy Draft* of 1976 (see note 74 above) distinguished between targets for park classes and those for programs. Both sets were complementary, defining together what was to be achieved, and specifying the types and numbers of parks required to create the optimum system. Program targets, set for each of the five objectives established in the document (Conservation, Recreation, Heritage Appreciation, Travel and Social Interaction, Scientific Research) defined the composition of the parks system overall: 1) the natural and cultural resources to be protected as defined by the earth and life science frameworks and the historical systems plan; 2) the number of opportunities to be provided for day-use, camping, and back-country recreation; 3) the emphasis to be given to interpreting park resources; and 4) the contribution to be made to tourism and scientific research. Park class targets complemented those set for programs by indicating the preferred way in which the provincial parks system would develop. Division planners acknowledged that the park class targets were tentative and would have to be revised, perhaps because of a lack of suitable or available resources, because of future decisions by regional planners to attain program targets through some other combination of parks and zones, or because the required type of park was already provided by another agency.

87 PB, file MO–3–POL, R.M. Dixon to J.W. Lockwood, executive director, Division of Forests, 28 June 1976.

88 Ibid., D.R. Johnston, director, Wildlife Branch to K.K. Irizawa, executive director, Division of Fish and Wildlife, 28 September 1976.

89 Ibid., W.T. Foster to Lloyd Eckel, 2 November 1976.

90 Ibid., Dixon to Lockwood, 28 June 1976.

91 Ibid., G.A. Jewett to A.J. Herridge, 30 July 1976.

92 Ibid., Johnston to Irizawa, 28 September 1976.

93 Ibid., R.A. Baxter to L. Ringham, 16 September 1976, and J.H. Lever to J.M. Hughes, regional director, northeastern region, 24 August 1976.

94 Ibid., L. Ringham to J.W. Keenan, 21 June 1976.

95 The Ontario Provincial Parks Council, *Second Annual Report* (1976), 9.

96 PB, file MO–3–POL, R.L. Mitton to R.J. Vrancart and L.H. Eckel, 14 October 1976, and J.R. Sloan to Vrancart, 27 October 1976.

97 Ibid., "A Summary of the Ontario Government's Review of the Proposed Provincial Park Policy," n.a., n.d.
98 Ibid., L.H. Eckel to L. Ringham, 1 March 1977.
99 Ibid., R.J. Vrancart to W.K. Fullerton, 1 March 1977.
100 Ibid., T.W. Hueston to J.K. Reynolds, deputy minister, 17 November 1977.
101 Ibid., J.H. Lever to J.M. Hughes, 24 August 1976.
102 Ibid., Minutes, Outdoor Recreation Program Sub-Committee, Special Meeting, 30 September 1976.
103 Ibid., "Submission to Cabinet Committee on Resource Development: A Provincial Parks Policy for Ontario," 21 January 1977.
104 Ibid., J.H. Lever to J.M. Hughes, 24 August 1976.
105 Ibid., Johnston to Irizawa, 28 September 1976.
106 Ibid., file memo by L. Eckel, 14 March 1977.
107 Ibid., Foster to Eckel, 2 November 1976.
108 Vrancart and Moroz, "Investment Priorities," 78 (see note 12 above).
109 PB, file MO–3–P (Parks Policy), R.J. Burgar to L.H. Eckel, 12 December 1977.
110 PB, file MO–3–POL, file memo by L. Eckel, 14 March 1977.
111 PB, file MO–3–P (Parks Policy), "Provincial Parks Policy Status Review as of September 14, 1977." See also "A Summary of the Ontario Government's Review of the Proposed Provincial Park Policy," n.a., n.d.
112 For a copy of the ill-fated *Ontario Provincial Parks: A Proposed Policy* (MNR, Division of Parks, March 1977), see PB, file MO–3–P (Parks Policy).
113 Ibid., M. Mogford, secretary to the minister's policy committee to L.H. Eckel, 28 November 1977.
114 Ibid., R.J. Vrancart to L.H. Eckel, 12 December 1977.
115 Ibid., Mogford to Eckel, 28 November 1977.
116 Ibid., cabinet submission, "Provincial Parks Policy," 22 March 1978.
117 Ibid., A.J. Herridge to L.H. Eckel, 18 May 1978, memo re "Cabinet Minute no. 2–28/78 – 19 May 1978. Agenda Item: Provincial Parks Policy."
118 Ibid., Vrancart to D.A. Fawcett, regional director, north-central region, 8 June 1979.
119 Ibid., Peter A. Peach, president, FON to James Auld, 19 January 1979.
120 Ibid., CCO, "Brief to the Ontario Ministry of Natural Resources Respecting the Ontario Provincial Parks Planning and Management Policies," 30 May 1979.
121 Ibid., J.K. Reynolds to Mike Singleton, 8 January 1979.
122 Daniel F. Brunton, "A Plan for Parkland," *Seasons* 22, no. 2 (Summer 1982), 53.

Chapter Eight

1 Following a major reorganization of the MNR in 1977–78, the Parks Division became the Provincial Parks Branch. The following year, when the branch assumed responsibility for developing a recreation policy for Crown lands, it was once more named the Parks and Recreational Areas Branch (July 1979).
2 PB, file MO–0 (1981–82) Policy Constraints Committee, Progress Report 1, "An Initial List of Management Strategies for Managing Provincial Parks and Recreational Areas With Reduced Budgets" (n.d., ca. fall 1981); see the report's appendix 6.2 for expenditure data. Inflation calculations are made by using constant 1971 dollar figures, standardized according to the Consumer Price Index from *Ontario Statistics 1980*, 370. Land acquisition spending figures were obtained from annual land acquisition summary sheets (1974–88).
3 PPAC, author's copy of W.T. Foster to L.H. Eckel, 6 February 1980.
4 Ron Reid, "Groundswell," *Seasons* 22, no. 2 (Summer 1982), 70; see also PB, file MO–0 (1981–82), Warren Robertson to Norm R. Richards, 22 June 1982, re Algonquin Provincial Park.
5 Policy Constraints Committee (see note 2 above).
6 Ibid., appendix 6.2; see especially copy of W.D. Yetman, acting director, to M. Fordyce, director, Policy Coordination Secretariat, 13 May 1981.
7 Ron Reid, "Ontario Parks: The Challenge of the Eighties," *Seasons* 20, no. 2 (Summer 1980), 17.
8 PB, file M–10–G, Vrancart to Eckel, 7 February 1979.
9 PB, director's FPPC files, Norm Richards, "State of the Nation Report, Ontario," 1982–83, 1983–84.
10 Ibid., 1982–83.
11 Ibid., 1984–85.
12 Elizabeth Ann Tuck, "Privatization of Ontario Provincial Parks: Park User Awareness," master's thesis, University of Western Ontario, 1985.
13 PB, director's FPPC files, copy of paper delivered by Ken McCleary to FPPC board of directors' meeting, Quebec City, 22 August 1988.
14 Ibid.
15 *Parks Canada Volunteer Program Guidelines* (Community and Cooperative Activities, National Parks Branch, May, 1978; revised January, 1979); "Ontario Provincial Parks Volunteer Program Guidelines," draft no. 1; Ken Vogan, Operations Section (February 1981).
16 "State of the Nation,"1983–84 (see note 9 above).
17 Theodore Mosquin, "The Idea of Cooperating Associations for Canada's National Heritage Areas," *Park News* 15, no. 1 (Spring 1979), 26–30.
18 Information on the Friends has been compiled from the annual newsletters. At the end of the 1987 season, the Friends of Algonquin reported revenues of $282,844, expenditures of $233,473, a balance of $123,784 and an inventory of $111,809.

19 "State of the Nation," 1980–81, 1984–85, 1985–86 (see note 9 above).
20 Ibid., 1982–83, and Special Employment Program file, Approved Projects Reports (1982–83) – (1989–90).
21 PB, Operations, file 4–6–1, "Ontario Provincial Parks Fee Proposal 1986–1989," 28 June 1985.
22 "State of the Nation," 1982–83 (see note 9 above).
23 For the evolution of policy see PB, file MO–3–REP (1979–83).
24 Ron Reid, "Earthwatch," *Seasons* 23, no. 1 (Spring 1983), 5.
25 PB, file MO–3–REL, Desmond M. Connor, "Tourism and Parks: Increasing the Contribution of Provincial Parks to Tourism," 29 November 1978; Balmer, Crapo and Associates Inc., "Enhancing Tourism in Ontario By Means of Changes in Ontario Parks: A Discussion Paper," 30 November 1978. For a scathing critique of the Balmer, Crapo report, see J.A. Van der Meer to R.J. Vrancart, 28 December 1978.
26 Ibid., cabinet submission, "Provincial Parks and Tourism: Proposals for Future Action," 9 April 1979.
27 Bruce Downie and Bob Peart (eds.), *Parks and Tourism: Progress or Prostitution?* (Victoria: NPPAC, British Columbia Chapter, 1982).
28 Econometrics Research Ltd., "The Economic Impact of Provincial Park Expenditures in Ontario" (February 1981); and "The Regional Economic Impact of Provincial Park Expenditures in Ontario" (May 1981). Data quoted in text from "Economic Impact of Provincial Parks in Ontario: A Summary Report," PB, MNR, n.d. The branch interpreted the data more liberally in PB, file MO–3–RSR, "Extracts from the Economic Impact of Provincial Park Expenditures in Ontario 1979" (n.a., n.d.).
29 "Gallup Opinion Poll for Provincial Parks February 1981. Summary of Results," Planning Section, PB, MNR, July 1981.
30 PB, file MO–3–RSR, D. Hallman, "Future Trends – Travel and Leisure," 17 March 1980.
31 See *Ontario Provincial Parks Marketing Research Study, Final Report*, Laventhol & Horwath Management Consultants (May 1988), 4–8.
32 "State of the Nation," 1983–84 (see note 9 above).
33 PB, Operations Section, "Marketing Strategies for Provincial Parks," Policy PM 6.05, 1 September 1986.
34 For the planning behind hospitality training, see PB, file MO–O, "Hospitality Sub Committee of the Parks Policy Committee, Report," April 1979.
35 The MNR–MND&M projects have been examined in detail in Tommi Lloyd, "Getting There," *Landmarks* 4, no. 2 (April 1986), 6–13.
36 "State of the Nation," 1983–84 (see note 9 above); see also Ontario Provincial Parks Statistics 1987 (MNR, 1988).
37 The Ontario Provincial Parks Council, *Annual Report 1987/88* (Toronto: Queen's Printer, 1988), 29, 46.
38 *Research Study*, 8–14 (see note 37 above).
39 Ibid., Section 3 – "Trends Analysis."
40 Parks Council 87/88, 17 (see note 37 above).
41 "Lakeshore Lodge Development Concept and Feasibility Study, Sandbanks Provincial Park, Prince Edward County," prepared by Marshall Macklin Monaghan Ltd., February 1983.
42 "Lake Superior Provincial Park, Final Report, Concept Plan for Future Development," the DPA Group Inc. in association with Kreslin Engineering and Planning Ltd., 1986.
43 "Executive Summary, Tourism Development Study, Sibley Provincial Park," n.a., n.d.
44 "Algonquin Park Marketing and Tourism Development Study: Executive Summary," Laventhol & Horwath with Hough, Stansbury & Associates Ltd., October 1986.
45 MNR, "A Proposal to Renew Algonquin Provincial Park for its 100th Anniversary" (1987).
46 "Earthwatch," *Seasons* 29, no. 1 (Spring 1989), 8, 12.
47 "Marketing Strategies for Provincial Parks," Policy PM 6.05, 1 September 1986.
48 For details on the inventory process, see: T.J. Beechey, "Information Collection, Storage and Retrieval for Ecological Areas in Provincial Parks and Areas of Natural and Scientific Interest: Statement of Evidence," PB, MNR, 2 June 1988; T.J. Beechey and D. Powell, "Catalogue of Open File Ecological Reports: A serial listing of ecological studies for provincial parks, areas of natural and scientific interest and other natural areas," PB, MNR, 1988; R.J. Davidson, "A Strategy for the Conservation of Ontario's Earth Science Heritage," PB, MNR, 28 June 1988; T.J. Beechey and R.J. Davidson, "Protection of Provincially Significant Wildlife Areas: The Nature Reserve System," in Suzanne Barrett and John Riley (eds.), *Protection of Natural Areas in Ontario*, York University, Faculty of Environmental Studies, Working Paper no. 3 (November 1980).
49 PB, file MO–3–COR, memo, R.J. Vrancart to L.H. Eckel, 11 May 1979.
50 G.D. Boggs, "Planning for the Protection of Natural Diversity," in *Nature Conservation Day Seminar Proceedings 26 March, 1980*, PB, MNR (March 1981), 14.
51 John White, "Keynote Address," *Toward Natural Heritage Protection in Ontario Conference Proceedings November 23, 1982* (OHF, MCR, 1983), 3.
52 Ibid., 6.
53 PB, file MO–3, "Ontario Heritage Foundation Presentation," 26 January 1977.
54 PB, file MO–1, Larry T. Ryan, executive secretary, OHF, to R.J. Vrancart, 31 January 1978.
55 PB, file MO–1, R.J. Vrancart, "Outdoor Recreation Foundation Proposal," 7 December 1977.
56 White, "Keynote Address," 2–13 (see note 51

above). Much of what was said in this address had been anticipated by R.J. Davidson and T.J. Beechey in "An Agenda for a Natural Heritage Conservation Strategy," presented to the conference "Ontario Provincial Parks: Issues in the 80's," University of Waterloo, May 1981 and published in *Environments* 14, no. 1, 1982, 77–84.

57 Reid, "Earthwatch '93," *Seasons* 23, no. 1 (Spring 1983), 5.

58 Stewart G. Hilts, "Ontario's Natural Heritage League: A Model for Inter-Agency Cooperation in Landscape Planning," in Michael R. Moss (ed.), *Landscape Ecology and Management*, Proceedings of the First Symposium of the Canadian Society for Landscape Ecology and Management: University of Guelph, May, 1987 (Montreal: Polyscience Publications Inc., 1988), 231–36.

59 "Stone Road Alvar," *Seasons* 25, no. 2 (Summer 1985), 43; see also the feature article in the same issue on "Stone Road Alvar," 24–27.

60 Norm R. Richards, "A Discussion Paper on Areas of Natural and Scientific Interest," in *Toward Natural Heritage*, 52–65 (see note 51 above).

61 See R.J. Davidson and T.J. Beechey, "Areas of Natural and Scientific Interest: A Proposed Policy," (January 1982), PB, MNR, 9.

62 Hilts, "Natural Heritage ," 233 (see note 58 above).

63 "Ontario's First Natural Heritage Easement Signed," *Wildland News* 16, no. 2 (April 1984), 8.

64 Davidson, "Strategy for the Conservation of Ontario's Earth Science Heritage," 11.

65 "State of the Nation," 1983–84 (see note 9 above).

66 "Jordan Valley," *Seasons* 25, no. 2 (Summer 1985), 43.

67 "Private Stewardship Thrust of Carolinian Canada Projects," in *National Heritage Forum News* 2, no. 1 (January 1988), 2. The FON devoted an issue of *Seasons* (25, no. 2 [Summer 1985]) to the theme of Carolinian Canada.

68 "Carolinian Canada Land Protection and Stewardship Programme. Memorandum of Understanding Between the Minister of Natural Resources and the Minister of Citizenship and Culture," 1 June 1987.

69 T.J. Beechey, "Protecting Ontario's Ecological Diversity," presentation to 15th Annual Natural Areas Conference, State University of New York, Syracuse, N.Y., 6–9 June 1988.

70 *Implementation Strategy: Areas of Natural and Scientific Interest* (MNR 1988).

71 Ron Reid, "Alfred Bog: The Price of Preservation," *Seasons* 28, no. 3 (Autumn 1988), 20–25.

72 *Statutes of Ontario*, "An Act to Promote the Conservation of Certain Land," 1988 C. 41. For the origins of the act, see Marion Strebig, "Earthwatch," *Seasons* 28, no. 1 (Spring 1988), 7–8.

73 MNR, *Fact Sheet*, "The Conservation Land Tax Reduction Program," October 1988.

74 Strebig, "Earthwatch '88," (see note 72 above). For another noteworthy expression of the Peterson government's new philosophy of land use, readers might investigate the wetlands program administered by the Wildlife Branch of the MNR; see "Policy Statement: Wetlands. A Proposed Policy Statement of the Government of Ontario Issued for Public Review," (MNR, MMA, 1989); and "Wetlands Planning Policy Statement: Implementation Guidelines," MNR, November 1988. This draft policy, under public review in 1989, proposed to provide an added measure of protection for wetlands by requiring municipalities and planning authorities to have regard for provincially significant wetland areas. The previous "Guidelines for Wetlands Management in Ontario," of 24 September 1984 only requested this of local governments. The Peterson government also provided significant funding for the wetlands program. In September 1986, the MNR signed separate three-year agreements, with Ducks Unlimited and Wildlife Habitat Canada to provide a total of $1 million a year (50 percent from Wildlife Habitat Canada, 25 percent from Ducks Unlimited, and 25 percent from the province) to secure the most valuable remaining wetlands in Ontario. Another agreement between Ducks Unlimited Canada and the MNR calls for a combined expenditure of $19.3 million over five years (1989–94) directed at waterfowl habitat, rehabilitation, creation, protection, and management. It should be noted that PB and Wildlife Branch programs overlap in this area, since provincial parks and ANSIs include choice examples of the province's various wetland types.

75 P.M. Taschereau, *The Status of Ecological Reserves in Canada* (The Canadian Council on Ecological Areas and The Institute for Resource and Environmental Studies, Dalhousie University, April 1985).

76 PB, file Eco Reserves Act, "Submission to Policy Committee re Ecological Reserves Act," 4 October 1988.

77 PB, file Eco Reserves Act, draft, "An Act to Establish, Protect and Manage Ecological Reserves in Ontario," and "Summary of Legislation" (in other jurisdictions).

78 Susan Montonen and Don Huff, "Earthwatch," *Seasons* 27, no. 3 (Autumn 1987), 6; Marion Strebig and Ian Kirkham, "Earthwatch," *Seasons* 28, no. 3 (Autumn 1988), 6.

Chapter Nine

1 MNR, *Report of the Task Force on Parks Systems Planning*, vol. 1 (September 1981), 26–27.

2 PB, file MO-3-P (SLUP), L.H. Eckel to R.J. Vrancart, 25 September 1979.

3 *Strategic Land Use Plan: Northwestern Ontario* (Toronto: MNR, 1980); *Proposed Strategic Land*

Use Plan: Northeastern Ontario (Toronto: MNR, 1980).

4 Arlin Hackman, "A Response to the Strategic Land Use Plan For Northwestern Ontario," *Park News* 17, no. 1 (Spring 1981), 26–7.

5 Arlin Hackman, "Strategic Land Use Planning and the Future of Wilderness in Ontario," *Park News* 16, no. 4 (Winter 1980), 36.

6 PB, file NC–3, M.R. McKay, vice-president, Great Lakes Forest Products Ltd., to A.H. Peacock, executive director, Forest Resources Group, MNR, 16 June 1980.

7 Ibid., Armstrong Wilderness Outfitters Association to MNR, 20 May 1980; and copy of "The Ogoki-Albany: A Primer," prepared by Ron Reid of the FON (1980); see also Ron Reid, "Ogoki-Albany: A Classic Case of Wilderness," *Seasons* 21, no. 2 (Summer 1981), 21–5.

8 PB, file NE–3, J.F. McNutt to W.G. Cleaveley, regional director, Northern Region, 1 May 1980.

9 Quoted in Toronto *Globe and Mail*, 4 March 1981; see also *Wildland News* 14, no. 5 (November 1982), 7, in which Greaves is quoted as saying that the potential loss to the economy of establishing provincial parks in Northwestern Ontario would amount to $24 billion. An environmental economist for the Wildlands League demonstrated that this estimate was grossly exaggerated.

10 PB, file MO–3–P, R.B. Loughlan, manager, OFIA to J.K. Reynolds, deputy minister, MNR, 22 September 1976, with appended OFIA brief, "Response to the Background Information and Approach To Policy for the Strategic Land Use Plan for Northeastern Ontario," 21 September 1978.

11 PB, file MO–3–CON, C.J. Carter, president, Great Lakes Forest Products Ltd. to R.A. Baxter, regional director, north-central region, 1 December 1988. Copies of the advertisements are appended.

12 Arlin Hackman, "Shaping a Future for Ontario Parks: The Protagonists," *Seasons* 22, no. 2 (Summer 1982), 28; see also PB, June 1981, "Forest Area Classifications in Provincial Parks: Total Acreages," (PB, June 1981).

13 PB, file NC–3, Priddle to Auld, 22 January 1981, and Auld to Priddle, 4 March 1981.

14 Quoted in Hackman, "Shaping a Future," 29 (see note 12 above).

15 J.W. Griffith, general manager, Prospectors and Developers Association, "Forum: Mining Industry," *Seasons* 22, no. 2 (Summer 1982), 38–39.

16 R.G. Morgan, "Forum: Hunting and Fishing," ibid., 39–40.

17 *The North Bay Nugget*, 30 January 1981.

18 PB, file NE–3, R.L. Brock to R.B. McGee, district manager, Temagami, 3 September 1981. For the background of the Maple Mountain project, see Hodgins and Benidickson, *The Temagami Experience:*, ch. 12 (see chapter 1 above, note 1).

19 PB, file NC–3, W. Ferring, Sr., president, Armstrong Wilderness Outfitters Association to Parrott, 15 February 1980.

20 Ibid., Parrott to Auld, 3 July 1980; Auld to Parrott, 23 August 1980.

21 OA, RG–1, IA–5, box 1, file 13–2–3, Brunelle to J.K. Reynolds, 19 October 1967.

22 OA, RG–1, IC, temporary box 4, accession no. 14195, OPIB Polar Bear file, Report to OPIB, 8 March 1971.

23 OA, RG–1, IB–3, box 7, file 25–08, P. Addison to Neil Campbell, 2 April 1969.

24 Ron Reid, "The Native Question," *Seasons* 22, no. 4 (Winter 1982), 46.

25 Wally McKay, "Forum: Native People," *Seasons* 22, no. 2 (Summer 1982), 40–41.

26 *Wildland News* 13, no. 1 (June 1981), 7.

27 Robert Matas, "Ontario stalls public participation in forest planning, naturalist says," Toronto *Globe and Mail*, 7 May 1981.

28 PB, file MO–3–L, Lorne Almack, president, FON to Alan Pope, 26 May 1981.

29 *Wildland News* 13, no. 1 (June 1981), 9.

30 Toronto *Globe and Mail*, 13 May 1981.

31 Daniel F. Brunton, "A Plan for Parkland," *Seasons* 22, no. 2 (Summer 1982), 53.

32 George B. Priddle, "Parks and Land Use Planning in Northern Ontario," *Environments* 14, no. 1 (1982), 49.

33 Author's interviews, with William Foster, 11 April 1989, and with George Moroz, 31 January 1989.

34 For the conference proceedings, see the special issue of *Environments* 14, no. 1 (1982).

35 Toronto *Globe and Mail*, 15 May 1981.

36 PB, file MO–2, Richards to Lloyd Eckel, 11 September 1981.

37 PB, file MO–2, Arlin Hackman to Pope, 4 September 1981.

38 Ron Reid, "Earthwatch," *Seasons* 21, no. 4 (Winter 1981), 6.

39 Toronto *Globe and Mail*, 16 November 1981.

40 Representatives of the following groups signed a letter of protest to Alan Pope on 5 November 1981: the AWL, Canadian Environmental Law Association, Canadian Nature Federation, Canoe Ontario, CCO, Environment North, Lady Evelyn Alliance, NPPAC, Sierra Club of Ontario, and the Wilderness Canoe Association. The AWL circulated a copy of the letter to all its members.

41 Ron Reid, "Ontario Parks: Last Chance for Survival?" Toronto *Globe and Mail*, 26 February 1982.

42 Author's interview with Norm Richards, 15 March 1989.

43 Nancy Patterson, "Earthwatch," *Seasons* 22, no. 2 (Summer 1982), 6.

44 "Background Information on Land Use Planning and Park System Planning in Ontario," March 1982, 4–6.

45 Copy of "Statement to the Legislature by the Honourable Alan W. Pope, Minister of Natural Resources, Friday, March 12, 1982," appended to MNR *Newsrelease*, 12 March 1982.
46 "Background Information ... Appendix: Policy and Implementation Guidelines for Interim Uses in Candidate Parks." (See note 44 above.)
47 Ron Reid, "Wilderness Waltz," *Seasons* 22, no. 2 (Summer 1982), 23.
48 MNR, *Report* (1981), 2 vols. 1: text; 2: appendices (see note 1 above). Interview with W.D. Addison and J.D. Bates, 20 September 1986, conducted by George Warecki.
49 Reid, "Wilderness Waltz," 22 (see note 47 above).
50 "Now or Never for Ontario's Wildlands," *Wildland News* 14, no. 1 (April 1982), 5.
51 Reid, "Wilderness Waltz," 24 (see note 47 above).
52 Quoted in Jeff Port, "Gambling With Our Resources," *Park News* 18, no. 3 (Fall 1982), 24.
53 "'Parks For Tomorrow' – Who Are We?" Quoted on the first page of each of the eleven Parks For Tomorrow reports, submitted to the MNR in response to the draft plans for district land use issued for the Northwest and North Central MNR regions in 1982. Additional information on the Parks For Tomorrow group was obtained from the Warecki interview with W.D. Addison and J.D. Bates, 20 September 1986 (see note 48 above).
54 For biographical profiles of the directors and a summary of the league's efforts during the spring and summer of 1982, see *Wildland News* 14, nos. 3–4 (September 1982), passim.
55 "Annual Meeting: President's Report 1983," *Wildland News* 15, no. 3 (June 1983), 10.
56 *Wildland News* 14, no. 1 (April 1982), 11, and "Hot Spots," ibid., 8–11 for the forest industry campaign against parks; see also ibid., Vol. 14, no. 2 (June 1982), 10 and Vol. 14, nos. 3–4 (September 1982), 15.
57 Quoted in *Wildland News* 15, no. 2 (March 1983), 6.
58 Quoted in Port, "Gambling," (see note 52 above).
59 *Wildland News* 14, nos. 3–4 (September 1982), 20.
60 Quotations from ibid., 21–22.
61 "Portage for Parks," ibid., Vol. 14, no. 5, 4.
62 "Pope Meets the People," ibid., 5.
63 "Minister's Forums Draw Crowds," *Seasons* 23, no. 1 (Spring 1983), 8.
64 Burt Dowsett, "Sportsmen Buck Parks," *London Free Press*, 15 December 1982.
65 Jonathan Lash, Katherine Gillman, and David Sheridan, *A Season of Spoils: The Reagan Administration's Attack on the Environment*, (New York: Pantheon, 1984), 235–39; see also Michael Posner, "Good Lands on the Hit List," *Maclean's*, 10 January 1983, 17.
66 For reports of the meeting see *Park News* 19, no. 1 (Spring 1983), 27 and *Wildland News* 15, no. 2 (March 1983), 4–5.
67 Canadian Parks and Wilderness Society (CPAWS) Office, Toronto, vertical file, SLUP (Ont.) folder, Monte Hummel to the Honourable Vince Kerrio, 17 September 1985. In this letter, Hummel provides a detailed account of the park advocates' position at the Guild Inn meetings.
68 "Pope's Roundtable Talks Lead in Circles," *Wildland News* 15, no. 2 (March 1983), 5.
69 Information Kit: Land Use Guidelines, "Statement to the Legislature by the Honourable Alan Pope, Minister of Natural Resources, Thursday, June 2, 1983."
70 Ibid., MNR, *Newsrelease*, 2 June 1983, "Natural Resources Minister Announces Resource Land Use Guidelines."
71 *Wildland News* 15, no. 3 (June 1983), 4; and "The Canadian Assembly: Part 2," *Park News* 21, no. 4 (Winter 1985/86), 20.
72 Ron Truman, "Land Plan Hasn't Stilled Hunting-In-Park Debate," Toronto *Globe and Mail*, 1 July 1983.
73 Toronto *Globe and Mail*, 3 June 1983.
74 Warecki interview with W.D. Addison and J.D. Bates, 20 September 1986 (see note 48 above).
75 CPAWS 1985 (see note 67 above); see also MNR, *Backgrounder: Land Use Guidelines* (June 1983), 9.
76 Toronto *Globe and Mail*, 3 June and 1 July 1983; Arlin Hackman, "New Parks for Ontario," *Seasons* 23, no. 3 (Autumn 1983), 46.
77 Arlin Hackman, "Earthwatch," *Seasons* 23, no. 4 (Winter 1983), 6.
78 Ibid.
79 Arlin Hackman, "Earthwatch," *Seasons* 24, no. 4 (Winter 1984), 4.
80 Ibid.
81 *Seasons*. 25, no. 1 (Spring 1985), 6.
82 Ibid., no. 2 (Summer 1985), 6.
83 See, for example, *Toronto Star*, *Globe and Mail*, and *London Free Press*, 27 April 1985. The ads were run again on 18 May 1985.
84 Mary Gellatly, "Parks, Privatization and Promises, Promises," *Wildland News* 17, no. 4 (November 1985), 6–7; and Jennifer Young, "Parks Council to Make Recommendations to Minister," ibid., 8–9; see also Ron Reid, "Ontario Parks on the Auction Block," *Seasons* 25, no. 1 (Spring 1985), 6.
85 *Provincial Parks Council Report on Contracting in Provincial Parks*, 6 February 1986, with appended copy of Kerrio to Gray, 5 April 1986.
86 PB, file MO–6, MNR, *Newsrelease*, "New Plan for Algonquin and Rondeau Park Cottagers," 18 August 1978.
87 Don Huff, "Earthwatch," *Seasons* 26, no. 4 (Winter 1986), 4; see also "Rondeau Cottage Owners Treated Fairly, Says Pope," *London Free Press*, 24 October 1984.
88 *Wildland News* 18, no. 2 (Spring 1986), 9.

89 Suzanne Barrett and Don Huff, "Earthwatch," *Seasons* 26, no. 2 (Summer 1986), 8.

90 MNR, *Newsrelease*, "Ministry of Natural Resources Extends Cottage Leases in Rondeau and Algonquin Provincial Parks"; appended Fact Sheet, "Leasing of Cottage Lots in Algonquin and Rondeau Provincial Parks," both 1 August 1986.

91 Don Huff, "Earthwatch," *Seasons* 26, no. 4 (Winter 1986), 4. The formal agreement for Bruce Peninsula National Park was signed on 20 July 1987.

92 CPAWS 1985 (see note 67 above); see also excerpts of Ron Reid to Kerrio, n.d., in Don Huff, "Earthwatch," *Seasons* 25, no. 4 (Winter 1985), 8.

93 The sticker was distributed with *Seasons* 26, no. 2 (Summer 1986).

94 Jennifer Young, "A New Wilderness Policy for Ontario? Woodland Caribou: Update," *Wildland News* 18, no. 2 (Spring 1986), 10–12; Daniel Brunton, "Woodland Caribou," *Seasons* 26, no. 23 (Autumn 1986), 36.

95 David Israelson, "Wilderness Area Put on World List as Threatened Site," *Toronto Star*, 27 November 1986.

96 Huff, "Earthwatch," *Seasons* 27, no. 1 (Spring 1987), 4–5; Julian A. Dunster, "Roads to Nowhere: Incremental Access and the Shrinking Wilderness," *Alternatives*, Vol. 15, no. 3 (September/October 1988), 22–29.

97 Huff, "Earthwatch," 5 (see note 96 above).

98 David Israelson, "'War' Waged over Future of Ontario's Wilderness," *Toronto Star*, 10 July 1987.

99 Rosemary Speirs, "Cabinet Wrestles with Provincial Parks," *Toronto Star*, 1 April 1987.

100 John Temple, "Logging Approved in Virgin Forest," *Toronto Star*, 22 August 1987.

101 John Temple, "Wilderness Committee Breaks up in Disarray," *Toronto Star*, 6 March 1988; Hodgins and Benidickson, *Temagami Experience*, 284–85 (see chapter 1 above, note 1).

102 Temagami Area Working Group, *Final Report* (Toronto: MNR, March 1988).

103 Review of the Environmental Assessment for Primary Access Roads in the Latchford Crown Forest Management Unit [Red Squirrel Road Extension/Pinetorch Corridor] (Toronto: Ontario Ministry of the Environment, 1980); Environmental Assessment Branch, EA file no. NR–NE–02.

104 Christine McLaren, "Temagami Logging Roads Given Go-Ahead," Toronto *Globe and Mail*, 13 April 1989.

105 Christine McLaren, "Wilderness Use to Test Cabinet," ibid., 7 April 1989.

106 "Temagami Axed," *Wildland News* 20, nos. 1–2 (Winter–Spring 1988), 7.

107 MNR, *Newsrelease*, "Ontario Announces New Parks and More Protection for Wilderness and Nature Reserves," 17 May 1988.

108 Strebig, "Earthwatch," 4 (see chapter 8 above, note 72.

109 "Liberal Government Reaffirms 'Blue Book' Policies!" *Wildland News* 20, nos. 1–2 (Winter–Spring 1988), 4–6.

110 John Power, "Trapping, Hunting Ban a Blow to Democracy," *Toronto Star*, 21 May 1988.

111 John Kerr, "Crisis in Our Parks," *Toronto Star*, 25 May 1988.

112 MNR, "Staff Briefing Notes: New Provincial Parks Policy," Tuesday, 17 May 1988; see also *Fact Sheet*, "New Provincial Parks and New Protection Policy," May 1988, and *Fact Sheet*, "Provincial Parks Policy Implementation," December 1988.

113 MNR, *Newsrelease*, "Natural Resources Ministry Announces Decision on *Temagami Land Use*, 17 May 1988; MNR "Speaking Notes for the Honourable Vincent Kerrio ... Regarding the Temagami Area Land Use Decision 17 May 1988, 12:30 p.m." Both these documents were contained in an information kit distributed on 17 May.

114 "Statement by Jim Bradley, Minister of the Environment Regarding Ministry of Natural Resources' Environmental Assessment for Primary Access Roads," 17 May 1988.

115 Marion Strebig, "A Short History of the Temagami Campaign," *Seasons* 28, no. 2 (Summer 1988), 21; Hap Day, "'Deep Water Country': The Battle to Save Temagami from Logging Is a Fight for the Very Spirit of Wilderness," ibid., 15–21.

116 Lisa Shimko, "Save Temagami, Liberals Urged," Toronto *Globe and Mail*, 29 May 1989; Christine McLaren, "Canadians Want Logging Changed, Poll Finds," ibid., 19 May 1989.

117 "Save Temagami Trees, Scientist Says," ibid., 15 February 1989; "Old Growth as a Weapon," *Insider's Dispatch: News of the Temagami Wilderness Society* 4, no. 1 (September 1989); Brad Cundiff, "New Ideas about Old Growth," *Seasons* 29, no. 4 (Winter, 1989), 31 35; three reports prepared by Peter A. Quinby for the Temagami Wilderness Society: "The Ecological Values of Old-Growth Forest with Specific Reference to White and Red Pine Forest Ecosystems in the Temagami Area of Ontario: A Literature Review" (October 1988); "A Survey of Old-Growth White and Red Pine Forest in the Shelburne Township Area, Temagami Region, Ontario" (January 1989); "Self-Replacement in Old-Growth White Pine Forests of Temagami, Ontario" (January 1990).

118 Author's interview with Cameron Clark, 3 October 1989.

119 David Israelson, "Ontario Moves to Protect Oldest Forests from Logging," *Toronto Star*, 21 January 1990.

120 MNR, *Newsrelease*, "Province and Teme-Augama

Anishnabai Sign Historic Stewardship Agreement," 23 April 1990.

121 Gene Allen, "Ontario Gives Natives Veto over Logging in Temagami to Save Ancient Pine Tracts," Toronto *Globe and Mail*, 24 April 1990; Craig McInnes, "Not Quite Out of the Woods Yet," ibid., 28 April 1990; "Premier Peterson, Temagami Has *Not* Been Saved!" (Broadsheet distributed by Temagami Wilderness Society, 4 July 1990).

112 Norm Richards, "A Provincial Perspective on Parks and Protected Areas," paper delivered to Heritage Conservation and Sustainable Development Conference, Ottawa, 14 May 1989. For a careful analysis of the extent to which class and program targets had been met, see PB, Planning and Development Section, "Protecting Ontario's Natural Diversity Through Provincial Parks and Areas of Natural and Scientific Interest," draft for discussion, 12 June 1989.

Chapter Ten

1 PB, memo re "Enforcement Direction on Activities of Golden Lake Indians in Algonquin Park," from A.J. Stewart, regional director, Algonquin Region, to R.M. Christie, assistant deputy minister, southern Ontario, 18 January 1991.

2 Quoted in Brad Cundiff, "Bargaining Away Algonquin," *Seasons* 32, no. 1 (Spring 1992), 16.

3 Ad Hoc Committee to Save Algonquin Park, Information Bulletins 1–4: 1. Peter N. Ward, "Major Flaws in the Golden Lake Land Claim to Algonquin Park," 15 June 1991; 2. Blair Dawson, "Superb Algonquin Park Fisheries in Danger," 15 September 1991; 3. Scott Hayden, "Proposal by Golden Lake Band to Take Over Algonquin Park for Their Economic Independence is Financially Unsound," 12 July 1992; 4. Roderick I. MacKay, "More Historic Research Indicates that the Golden Lake Claim to Algonquin Park is Invalid," 28 September 1992.

4 Richard Mackie, "Ontario Apologizes to Indians," Toronto *Globe and Mail*, 4 June 1991.

5 "An invitation from the Minister of Natural Resources," *Quetico Provincial Park Lac La Croix Amendment Proposal January 1992.*

6 Robert Reguly, "Rallying to keep the wilderness wild," Toronto *Globe and Mail*,18 May 1992.

7 A large portion of Killarney Wilderness park is being claimed by the Wikwemikong First Nation; see "The Boundaries of the Point Grondine Reservation under the Lake Huron Treaty of 1850," issued by the Wikwemikong First Nation, July 1992.

8 MNR, *Newsrelease*, "Minister Announces Commitment to Protect Endangered Spaces," 23 January 1992.

9 Memorandum to all MNR staff, "Sustainable Forestry," issued by George Tough, deputy minister, 1 October 1991; see also "New Program for Sustainable Forestry," *Branching Out* 1, no. 1 (January 1992), 1.

10 *Wetlands*, a Statement of Ontario Government Policy, Issued under the Authority of Section 3 of the Planning Act 1983, approved by the Lieutenant Governor in Council, Order in Council no. 1448/92, 14 May 1992; see also "Earthwatch," *Seasons* 32, no. 3 (Autumn 1992), 7.

A Select Bibliography for the General Reader

Addison, Ottelyn. *Early Days in Algonquin Park*. Toronto: McGraw-Hill Ryerson, 1974.

Ashworth, William. *The Late Great Lakes: An Environmental History*. New York: Alfred A. Knopf, 1986.

Bella, Leslie. *Parks for Profit*. Montreal: Harvest House, 1986.

Bray, Matt, and Ashley Thomson, eds. *Temagami: A Debate on Wilderness*. Toronto and Oxford: Dundurn Press, 1990.

Dunlap, Thomas R. *Saving America's Wildlife: Ecology and the American Mind, 1850–1990*. Princeton: Princeton University Press, 1988.

Foster, Janet. *Working for Wildlife: The Beginning of Preservation in Canada*. Toronto, Buffalo and London: University of Toronto Press, 1978.

Fox, Stephen. *John Muir and His Legacy: The American Conservation Movement*. Boston and Toronto: Little, Brown and Co., 1981.

Gillis, R. Peter, and Thomas R. Roach. *Lost Initiatives: Canada's Forest Industries, Forest Policy and Forest Conservation*. Contributions in Economics and Economic History, no. 69. New York: Greenwood Press, 1986.

Hays, Samuel P. *Beauty, Health and Permanence: Environmental Politics in the United States, 1955–1985*. Cambridge, Mass.: Cambridge University Press, 1987.

Hilts, Stewart, Malcolm Kirk, and Ron Reid. *Islands of Green: Natural Heritage Protection in Ontario*. Toronto: Ontario Heritage Foundation, 1986.

Hodgins, Bruce W., and Jamie Benidickson. *The Temagami Experience: Recreation, Resources, and Aboriginal Rights in the Northern Ontario Wilderness*. Toronto, Buffalo and London: University of Toronto Press, 1989.

Hodgins, Bruce W., and Margaret Hobbs, eds. *Nastawgan: The Canadian North by Canoe and Snowshoe*. Toronto: Betelgeuse Books, 1985.

Hummel, Monte, ed. *Endangered Spaces: The Future for Canada's Wilderness*. Toronto: Key Porter Books, 1989.

Israelson, David. *Silent Earth: The Politics of Our Survival*. Markham, Ont.: Viking, The Penguin Group, 1990.

Lambert, Richard S., with Paul Pross. *Renewing Nature's Wealth: A Centennial History of the Public Management of Lands, Forests, and Wildlife in Ontario, 1783–1967*. Toronto: Ontario Department of Lands and Forests, Hunter Rose Co., 1967.

Litteljohn, Bruce, and Lori Labatt, eds. *Islands of Hope: Ontario's Parks and Wilderness*. Toronto: Firefly Press with the Wildlands League, 1992.

Litteljohn, Bruce, and Jon Pearce, eds. *Marked by the Wild: An Anthology of Literature Shaped by the Canadian Wilderness*. Toronto: McClelland & Stewart, 1984.

Nash, Roderick. *Wilderness and the American Mind*. 3rd rev. ed. New Haven and London: Yale University Press, 1982.

Nelles, H.V. *The Politics of Development: Forest, Mines and Hydro-Electric Power in Ontario, 1849–1941*. Toronto: Macmillan, 1974.

Radforth, Ian. *Bush Workers and Bosses: Logging in Northern Ontario, 1900–1980*. Toronto, Buffalo and London: University of Toronto Press, 1987.

Saunders, Audrey. *Algonquin Story*. Reprinted with revised maps. Toronto: Ontario Department of Lands and Forests, 1963.

Searle, R. Newell. *Saving Quetico-Superior: A Land Set Apart*. St. Paul: Minnesota Historical Society Press, 1977.

Seibel, George A. *Ontario's Niagara Parks 100 Years: A History*. Niagara Falls: Niagara Parks Commission, 1985.

Terrie, Philip G. *Forever Wild: Environmental Aesthetics and the Adirondack Forest Preserve*. Philadelphia: Temple University Press, 1985.

Theberge, John B., ed. *Legacy: The Natural History of Ontario*. Toronto: McClelland & Stewart, 1989.

Wall, Geoffrey, and John S. Marsh, eds. *Recreational Land Use: Perspectives on Its Evolution in Canada*. Carleton Library Series, no. 126. Ottawa: Carleton University Press, 1982.

Wilderness Now. A Statement of Principles and Policies of the Algonquin Wildlands League, 3rd rev. ed. Toronto: Algonquin Wildlands League, 1980.

INDEX